WATERSIDE ESCAPES

In the Northeast

Great Getaways by
Lake, River & Sea

By Nancy and Richard Woodworth

Wood Pond Press
West Hartford, Conn.

Prices and hours, especially in restaurants and lodging establishments, change seasonally and with business conditions. Prices quoted are for peak season as this edition went to press. They are offered as relative guides, rather than as absolutes.

Lodging rates are for double occupancy and include breakfast, unless specified to the contrary, except for motels. EP (European Plan) means no meals. MAP (Modified American Plan) means breakfast and dinner.

Places are assumed to be open year-round, unless otherwise specified. But schedules vary. Readers should call ahead to avoid disappointment.

The authors value their reputation for credibility and have personally visited the places recommended in this book. No fees are charged for inclusion.

Readers' comments and suggestions are welcomed.

Cover Photo: St. Andrews Harbor and Maine coast, from waterside terrace at the Treadwell Inn in St. Andrews By-the-Sea, N.B.
Cover Photo by Richard Woodworth.

Published in the United States of America.
All rights reserved.
Fifth Edition.

Contents

About the Authors

Nancy Woodworth grew up in Montreal, a city on the St. Lawrence River. She spent summers in St. Andrews-by-the-Sea, N.B., and at a girls' camp and a cottage with her family on Lake Memphremagog, Que. During her college years at McGill University, she waitressed at summer resorts on Quebec's Gaspe Peninsula, in the Muskoka Lakes region of Ontario and at Jasper Park Lodge on Lac Beauvert in the Alberta Rockies. She worked in London, England, and for a Greek ship owner in Montreal prior to her marriage to an American newspaper editor. She since has lived in Geneva, N.Y., in the Finger Lakes area; in Rochester, N.Y., near Lake Ontario and the Barge Canal, and in West Hartford, Conn., where her family's home is near the lake that gives Wood Pond Press its name. She is the co-author with her husband, Richard Woodworth, of *Getaways for Gourmets in the Northeast, Best Restaurants of New England, New England's Best* and three editions of *Inn Spots and Special Places,* for New England, the Mid-Atlantic region and the Southeast. She is an Aquarius.

Richard Woodworth has lived near the water most of his life. He grew up in suburban Syracuse, N.Y., where a nearby creek and a swimming hole were favorite haunts. He attended a summer camp on Lake Champlain, vacationed with his family in the Thousand Islands and first saw the ocean at a young age in Narragansett, R.I., where he liked the surf better than the lobster. After graduation from Middlebury College, he was a reporter for daily newspapers near Chautauqua and Seneca lakes and Lake Ontario in upstate New York before moving to Connecticut to become editor of the West Hartford News. Since then, he and his family spent vacations near the ocean here and abroad. He is publisher of Wood Pond Press and with his wife has collaborated on numerous editions of seven travel guidebooks. Some of his off-hours are spent at the ocean – in summer in St. Andrews, N.B., and in winter in New Smyrna Beach, Fla. He is an Aquarius.

To Our Readers

Everyone wants to be near the water. A cottage or a room close to the shore. A meal on a deck or a balcony. A cooling dip at the beach. Perhaps a boat ride, with the breeze in your face. Or a cruise out to sea to look for whales.

Whatever your preference, you'll find it in this book. Water lovers from way back, we guide you to the best waterside destinations and activities in the Northeast. Watch the wild ponies swimming in Chincoteague, Va. Sail with the yachtsmen along the Chesapeake Bay. Raft in tubes down the Delaware River in Bucks County, Pa. Revive the Victorian era at the Jersey Shore. Find the quiet side of Lake George and climb mountains with a water view in Lake Placid. Explore the Thousand Islands. Hike through glens and gorges in the Finger Lakes region. Venture beyond Niagara Falls to charming Niagara-on-the-Lake, Ont.

Check out the Connecticut River and shoreline. Live the good life in Newport, R.I., and Nantucket Island, Mass. Stray off the beaten path in Falmouth and Woods Hole on Cape Cod, and stretch your horizons in Provincetown. Join the artists and fishermen in Rockport and Gloucester. Relive seacoast history in Portsmouth, N.H., and the summers of yesterday in Wolfeboro on Lake Winnipesaukee. Get away from it all in the Champlain Islands of Vermont.

Relax on the beaches of Ogunquit and Kennebunkport in Maine. Learn why lobster is king in Boothbay Harbor. See where the mountains meet the sea in Camden. Detour down Deer Isle to Stonington on your way to Acadia National Park on Mount Desert Island. Experience for yourself why the Roosevelts so loved Campobello Island, N.B. Succumb to the allure of St. Andrews By-the-Sea and Mahone Bay in the Maritime Provinces. Scale the heights of the Cabot Trail on Cape Breton Island in Nova Scotia.

These are destinations that will draw you. In each location, we recommend a variety of lodging options, from motels and inns to campsites and cottages. For meals, we guide you to good restaurants, relaxing bistros and rustic lobster pounds. For outings and activities, we offer favorite sightseeing excursions, hikes and nature walks, boat cruises, attractions and shops. We have sought out the novel as well as the indigenous, and share personal insights and experiences. In every possible instance, the water is the angle, as journalists would say.

So come along as we reveal our finds, some well known and some barely known at all. Add your own discoveries to create the ultimate waterside escape.

Nancy and Richard Woodworth

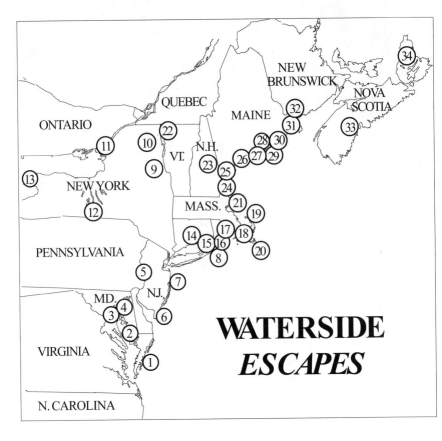

WATERSIDE ESCAPES

Wild ponies graze near Chincoteague National Wildlife Preserve.

Chincoteague Island, Va.

The Indians called it "the beautiful land across the water." Old-time residents say theirs is a tranquil, loving community. And visitors employ superlatives in describing this scenic, fascinating place that considers itself Virginia's only resort island.

Chincoteague, a diminutive strip that's home for an active fishing community, is the postmark for its larger barrier-island neighbor, Assateague Island, a 37-mile ribbon of sand that stretches northward across the Maryland state line before petering out just south of crowded Ocean City. It is the longest stretch of accessible, undeveloped land along the northern East Coast.

Think of Chincoteague and you'll likely think of oysters and the wild ponies made famous by Marguerite Henry's book, *Misty of Chincoteague.*

Chincoteague oysters – pronounced "arsters" by the natives – are gathered to this day by watermen of the old school. Crabbing and clamming are other leading pursuits in what remains an active fishing community.

Wild ponies roam the Chincoteague National Wildlife Preserve, swimming the Assateague Channel during the annual Pony Penning Days that draw thousands of spectators in late July.

But there's more, much more, to raise Chincoteague's permanent population of 4,300 to 20,000 or more on summer weekends.

"Most people come here for the nature," reports a Chamber of Commerce official. The Chincoteague National Wildlife Preserve, a prime Atlantic flyway habitat, harbors more than 300 species of birds. They're among the most exotic we've seen this side of the famed J.N. "Ding" Darling National Wildlife Preserve on Florida's Sanibel Island. Sika deer, whitetail deer, river otters and the occasional dolphin vie with the ponies for visitors' attention. Hiking and biking trails, nature programs, safaris and channel cruises beckon those partial to birding and wildlife.

Backed by fragile, shifting, manmade dunes, the beach is one of the East's most prized. With access to its 37 miles of sand limited by available parking facilities, it's also one of the few where you can find your own isolated plot on the busiest holiday weekend for swimming, surfing or surf fishing.

"This is Cape Cod the way it used to be," said a local innkeeper, a much-traveled Boston native who will always be a "come-here," as off-islanders are called. "It's the most New Englandish Southern place there is." Chincoteague, for most visitors pretty much a two-street town, is home to artists and craftsmen known for fine carved decoys. It has no high-rises and little honky-tonk. The only jarring notes are the mile of billboards rising one after the other from the marshes along the causeway entrance to the island (a never-ending source of consternation among the come-heres) and, at the entrance to the refuge, a McDonald's, the first corporate come-here.

Otherwise relatively unspoiled and not yet yuppified, Chincoteague coexists with the space age. Rockets are launched periodically by the National Aeronautics and Space Administration from its Goddard Space Flight Center on Wallops Island, just across Chincoteague Bay. The NASA Visitor Center here stands in high-tech contrast to the U.S. Fish and Wildlife Service's visitor center a dozen or so miles away on Assateague.

That's part of the appeal of Chincoteague to families, who take over its motels and campgrounds in summer to enjoy the beach plus wildlife and space-age diversions. Older folks prefer the quieter pace of spring and fall, which lingers past Thanksgiving.

Getting There

Chincoteague is an island in Chincoteague Bay, just inland from the Atlantic Ocean on the south side of the Maryland-Virginia state line. The wildlife refuge is at the southern end of Assateague Island, a barrier beach stretching south from Ocean City, Md. Chincoteague is reached by Route 175 off U.S. Route 13, which runs from Wilmington, Del., to Norfolk, Va., and is crossed by U.S. Route 50 via the Chesapeake Bay Bridge out of Annapolis, Md.

Where to Stay

Although the peak season is summer, the tourist season here runs from March to December. Accommodations vary widely. Most are motels and campgrounds, with a sprinkling of B&Bs and many rentals of summer houses, whose owners from Washington and Baltimore use them in spring and fall.

On or Near the Water

Cedar Gables Seaside Inn, 6095 Hopkins Lane, Box 1006, Chincoteague 23336.

One of the more luxurious, waterside B&Bs anywhere is this contemporary house looking out across Little Oyster Bay to Assateague Island. Fred Greenway built the waterside home of one's dreams in 1990 and converted it to B&B use in 1997. He and wife Claudia offer guests four spacious bedrooms, a screened-in Florida room with a swimming pool and hot tub, a porch for gourmet breakfasts and outside decks everywhere. There's even an observation tower with a table and two chairs, an architectural fillip that sets the house apart from its distant neighbors and yields the best view on the island. The tower goes with the Captain's Quarters, a hideaway that occupies the entire third floor and includes a kingsize brass bed, a loveseat facing a corner gas fireplace and TV/VCR, and a bathroom with whirlpool tub.

Except for the tower, similar attributes characterize the other rooms. The Oriental Suite is stunning in yellow striped wallpaper with blue and red accents and original art purchased by the Greenways when they lived in the Orient. Every room has one or more water-view decks along the rear of the house. Individual tables on a screened porch are the setting for breakfast. The day of our visit it involved fresh fruit, homemade granola, muffins and eggs benedict. There's a boat dock, and the Greenways rent canoes and kayaks.

(757) 336-6860 or (888) 491-2944. Fax (757) 336-1291. www.cedargable.com. Four rooms with private baths. Doubles, $165 to $190.

Island Motor Inn Resort, 4391 Main St., Chincoteague 23336.

Among the larger establishments, the area's best waterfront setting and positioning are offered by this newish motel, whose 60 comfortable units on three stories are about the only ones to face the water head-on. A bit off the tourist path, the site is quiet and nicely landscaped, with 600 feet of waterfront boardwalk. You can sit on the balcony off your room, enjoy the antics of shore birds and look west across the Intracoastal Waterway, which laps at lawn's edge beneath you, and beyond an island onto Chincoteague Bay. (The view is fine from every room, though rates rise by the floor.) Each room includes a vanity dressing area and a mini-refrigerator off the bathroom. A lighted swimming pool is in front, and there's an observation platform with deck chairs and a hammock at the side. A later wing holds the lobby and twelve deluxe units with kingsize beds. A two-story addition houses an indoor pool, hot tub and exercise facility. The Island Café offers food and room service.

(757) 336-3141. Fax (757) 336-1483. www.islandmotorinn.com. Sixty rooms with private baths. Doubles, $105 to $175.

Refuge Inn, 7058 Maddox Blvd., Box 378, Chincoteague 23336.

The closest accommodations to the wildlife refuge are in this weathered wood structure nestled in the loblolly pines. The complex on six acres is complete with an observation deck overlooking lighthouse and marsh, individual balconies and patios, a nicely landscaped swimming pool (half covered, so it can be enclosed for use in winter) and jacuzzi, laundry room, sauna, picnic tables and hibachi grills. Of the 72 rooms off an interior hallway on two floors, the fifteen considered deluxe come with attractive sitting areas. Many have been upgraded, most in a country style, with bleached pine furniture and appropriate touches like geese on the shower curtains and egrets on the lamps. Room 207, for instance, is done in nautical motif, with a blue and white striped sofa and a wall border of sailboats. Its balcony is shaded by a big pine tree. Beds are queensize and, given the shade from the pines, rooms appear pleasantly dark and cool, even in summer. The latest additions are two suites to end all suites. We were upgraded into one with a full-length screened veranda off a huge cathedral-ceilinged living/dining room, a balcony off the master bedroom, a skylit bathroom with jacuzzi, a full kitchen and a loft bedroom – at $250, quite a bargain for a large family or two couples traveling together. The motor inn is run very personally by sisters Jane Stewart and Donna Leonard. Art Leonard, a decoy carver,

displays his private collection of decoys in the Rookery, a good gift shop off the lobby. Bikes are available for rent from a bicycle shop out front. Youngsters enjoy the ponies grazing in the adjacent pasture.

(757) 336-5511 or (888) 257-0039. Fax (757) 336-6134. www.refugeinn.com. Seventy rooms and two suites with private baths. Doubles, $110 to $130. Suites, $220 and $250.

Comfort Suites, 4195 Main St., Chincoteague 23336.

Locals wonder not only how this motel chain got in to Chincoteague in 1999 but managed to snag one of the prime waterfront locations. They concede, however, that the developer did a nice job of blending the new place in. Accommodations on three stories face Chincoteague Channel, and one side looks across a duck pond. Each has a small deck or balcony off the sitting area and the kingsize or two queen beds that characterize the chain's suites. Some with direct bay views have jacuzzi baths. Amenities include an indoor pool, fitness center and a deluxe continental breakfast. Out back are a small lawn, a sundeck off the indoor pool, an outdoor pool and a boardwalk along the water.

(757) 336-3700 or (800) 228-5150. Fax (757) 336-5452. Eighty-seven rooms and suites with private baths. Doubles, $149.95 to $179.95.

Hampton Inn & Suites, 4179 Main St., Chincoteague 23336.

The Comfort having gotten a national chain's foot in the door, this one-upped its neighbor in 2002 and soon won a Conrad Hilton award as the second-best Hampton Inn & Suites in the country. Guest rooms with the latest motel amenities come in a variety of configurations. All have waterfront or water views with private balconies. Some king suites have whirlpool tubs beside the bed in the room; beyond is a sitting area overlooking the Channel. Some studio suites with two queen beds have wet bars. All have microwave, refrigerator and coffeemaker. Guests enjoy an indoor pool with spa tub, plus an exercise room. Continental breakfast is offered in a spacious waterfront lounge and adjacent veranda.

(757) 336-1616. Fax (757) 336-1617. www.hamptoninnchincoteague.com. Fifty-nine rooms and suites. Doubles, $149 to $209.

Payton Place, 2569 Main St., Chincoteague 23336.

John and Elaine Lang, who had vacationed here for 30 years, retired and moved from Baltimore to operate this hybrid establishment that combines rental suites with a B&B. They occupy the upstairs of the large waterfront structure in a quiet residential area, and offer three ground-floor suites with private porches and entrances. The venture gets its B&B credentials from the danish pastries, muffins and orange juice set out in the office from 8 to 11 each morning. The extra touch might seem superfluous, given the 800-square-foot "suites" with queen bed, sofabed, TV, refrigerator, microwave and coffeemaker. Occupants of the waterside end unit "feel like they're on a boat that doesn't move," Elaine says. She has a mural of egrets on the shared deck, as well as a 350-foot-long pier into a channel bed "loaded with clams." She also offers a gazebo, a gas grill and picnic tables.

(757) 336-3572 or (800) 237-5856. Three suites with private baths. Doubles, $125 to $140. Closed November-March.

Waterside Motor Inn, 3761 Main St., Box 347, Chincoteague 23336.

This three-story affair sits sideways to the water, so the view of Chincoteague's notable sunsets from the balconies of most rooms is across land. The best view is from the heated waterside pool at the rear, directly beside Chincoteague Channel, or from the fishing and crabbing pier stretching 220 feet into in the channel. An "adult solar health spa" offers a large jacuzzi with a view of the sunset. Standard rooms have two beds (one queensize and one double), two chairs flanking a round table, a refrigerator and a dressing area with vanity. Deluxe rooms include sofabeds and queen or king beds. The promotion stresses "No pets of any kind!" and, for those into such things, the "only glass elevator on the island." There's a tennis court, too.

(757) 336-3434 or (877) 870-3434. Fax (757) 336-1878. www.watersidemotorinn.com. Forty-five rooms. Doubles, $104 to $165.

Driftwood Lodge, 7105 Maddox Blvd., Box 575, Chincoteague 23336.
Billed as the closest accommodations to the beach, this good-looking motor inn is near the entrance to the National Wildlife Refuge. The front of the establishment has a view of McDonald's restaurant, but the rear looks out across the marshlands and the Assateague Channel. You can see all the way down the channel from the third-floor end unit. The recently refurbished rooms are spacious and cheery, each with two queensize or one kingsize bed, mini-refrigerator, coffeemaker, full bath and dressing area with vanity. Each has a private patio or balcony. There's a small pool with a deck and gazebo out front. Owners Scott and Lisa Chesson have taken over from her parents, who opened the establishment in the mid-1970s. They recently added a two-bedroom suite and offer a complimentary "breakfast bar."

(757) 336-6557 or (800) 553-6117. Fax (757) 336-6558. www.driftwoodmotorlodge.com. Fifty-three rooms. Doubles, $109 to $120. Suite, $198.

Assateague Inn, 6570 Coaches Lane, Box 1038, Chincoteague 23336.
Twenty-one efficiency suites make this quirky hideaway a favorite of families. They enjoy balconies as well as picnic tables on a deck built over a marsh. Beside the marsh is a small saltwater creek, one of the serpentine waterways that slice through the island's salt marshes and loblolly pine forests and are locally called "guts." Each suite has a queensize sofabed or two loveseat sleepers, a sturdy wood dining table that takes up nearly half the living room, a kitchenette, and a bedroom with a queensize bed. An apartment is available (three-night minimum), as are six standard motel rooms, four of them in the back and lacking a water view. An indoor hot tub in a freestanding spa building accommodates eight people, and there's an outdoor pool.

(757) 336-3738. Fax (757) 336-1179. Six rooms and 21 efficiency suites with private baths. Doubles, $102. Suites, $135.

Inn at Poplar Corner, 4248 Main St., Box 905, Chincoteague 23336.
A guest at their former Watson House provided the name for this B&B in a contest. Owners David and JoAnne Snead and their daughter and son-in-law, Jacque and Tom Derrickson, thought the choice appropriate for the inn, which they built from scratch at the corner of Main and Poplar streets. Quite luxurious, it evokes the Victorian period with its five ornate gables and an interior full of fine antiques. Guest rooms have queen or kingsize beds and private baths with marble-top sinks and jacuzzis. Three rooms yield good water views and the Main View on the second floor includes a private balcony. A common area on the third floor is available to all for watching the sunsets across Chincoteague Bay. Fancy food is a feature here, and guests praise the fare in the room diaries and the common restaurant review book. One or the other of the owner couples prepares an elaborate breakfast, served at a twelve-foot walnut table in the dining room or on the wraparound veranda. Breakfast the day of our visit included bran muffins, onion cheese bread, eggs Colorado with salsa and potatoes au gratin. Besides their B&B, the Sneads and

Derricksons also rent a two-bedroom townhouse and a three-bedroom cottage, both with jacuzzis, by the weekend or week.

(757) 336-6115 or (877) 336-6111. Fax (757) 336-5776. www.poplarcorner.com. Four rooms with private baths. Doubles, $139 to $179. Closed December-March.

The Watson House, 4240 Main St., Box 905, Chincoteague 23336.

What once was considered the ugliest house in Chincoteague is now a Cinderella, thanks to the restoration efforts of former owners David and JoAnne Snead and now maintained by Bob and Carole Mabin. The Mabins gave up corporate life in suburban Philadelphia in 2004 to purchase the 1898 residence that had been renovated into a paragon of Victorian elegance and comfort. Guest rooms in the front of the house catch glimpses of the water across the street. The Bayview and Sun rooms are billed as deluxe with queen beds and sitting areas. Breakfast consists of two hot dishes, presented buffet style following recipes from the former owners. Carole might put out a sausage-apple dish and blueberry-stuffed french toast one day and an oven-baked omelet the next. The meal is taken in the dining room or at individual tables on the wraparound front veranda. Afternoon teatime, which stretches from mid-afternoon into early evening, might yield homemade cookies and addictive caramel brownies.

(757) 336-1564 or (800) 336-6787. www.watsonhouse.com. Five rooms with private baths. Doubles, $119 to $139.

Miss Molly's Inn, 4141 Main St., Chincoteague 23336.

This Victorian bed and breakfast is famous as the place where Marguerite Henry stayed while writing Misty of Chincoteague. British-born restaurateur Lin Mazza and her Boston-bred husband Sam, who ran hotels here and abroad, took over the B&B in 2004 and enhanced an enterprise that already had a British/Victorian flair with gourmet accents. A portrait of Miss Molly, daughter of the home's original owner and with whom Marguerite Henry stayed, is at the foot of the stairs (Miss Molly lived in the house until she was 84). Bedrooms, all nicely done with antiques in the Victorian style, are on the second and third floors. By far the largest is the front-corner Marguerite Henry Room with a kingsize bed (the rest hold double beds except for one with twins). Porches and decks are all over, and from the second-floor deck in back you can see the water. Water also can be glimpsed from the large screened back porch with a gazebo effect in the corner. This is the setting for elaborate breakfasts prepared by Lin, who had a gourmet shop and restaurant in Britain and with her husband has been in the hospitality business for 30 years. She uses local blueberries in her fruit compote, bakes her own breads and picks figs from a tree in back to make fig jam. The main course might be stuffed french toast with cream cheese and marmalade one day, and a smoked salmon and asparagus quiche with a puff pastry basket of fruits and cream the next.

(757) 336-6686 or (800) 221-5620. Fax: (757) 336-0600. www.missmollys-inn.com. Five rooms with private baths and two with shared bath. Doubles, $99 to $165.

Channel Bass Inn, 6228 Church St., Chincoteague 23336.

After 25 years as a restaurant and inn of great expense and renown (not all of it favorable), this old-timer was acquired by the owners of the rather more down-to-earth Miss Molly's Inn. Erudite chimney sweep David Wiedenheft and his British-born wife Barbara lowered the rates, added carpeting and renovated several of the guest rooms, half of which they conceded were greatly in need of work. In 2004, after running two inns for ten years, they sold Miss Molly's to concentrate on the Channel Bass. Rooms here are elegantly furnished with reproduction pieces, luxurious bedding, comforters and imposing artworks. Most have king or queen beds and sitting areas, and one suite adds a sitting room. Three on the third floor yield views of Chincoteague Bay. The Wiedenhefts turned the dining room into a tearoom, where afternoon tea service is available for guests and the public four days a week. Barbara, a baker of note, bakes 400 scones for the purpose every few days. She also serves an elaborate breakfast, perhaps her specialty, eggs on a croissant with green onions, red peppers, cheese, dill and Louisiana hot sauce, teamed with cinnamon kuchen and nut bread and a warm fruit compote with granola. Guests gather in a pleasant parlor on the main floor or in colorful gardens alongside and in back.

(757) 336-6148 or (800) 249-0818. Fax (757) 336-6599. www.channelbassinn.com. Five rooms and one suite with private baths. Doubles, $129 to $195.

CAMPING. Camping is one of Chincoteague's attractions, especially for families. **Tom's Cove Park,** 8128 Beebe Road, (757) 336-6498, is Virginia's largest campground. When full, its population outnumbers the 3,500 fulltime residents of Chincoteague. It offers waterfront facilities, a view of Assateague Island, a saltwater swimming hole and pine-shaded sites – very close together, as is the area's norm. **Maddox Family Campground,** 6742 Maddox Blvd., (757) 336-3111, touts itself as closest to the beach and has a pool and a mini golf course. **Pine Grove Campground,** 5283 Deep Hole Road, (757) 336-5200, is secluded on 37 wooded acres and boasts six ponds favored by waterfowl. There is no camping on the Virginia end of Assateague Island, but the National Park Service has two campgrounds and seven backcountry campsites in the **Assateague Island National Seashore** in Maryland. Also in Maryland, **Assateague State Park** offers a campground with bathhouses.

Seeing and Doing

Chincoteague National Wildlife Refuge.
Established in 1943 as a wintering area for migratory waterfowl, the 14,000-acre refuge occupies the Virginia end of Assateague Island and is maintained by the U.S. Fish and Wildlife Service. Some 1.4 million visitors a year make it the nation's third most popular wildlife refuge. More than 300 species of birds have been identified on the refuge. Whitetail deer and the small Sika deer, an oriental elk released here in 1923, also populate the pine forests of the island's interior. The most popular inhabitants undoubtedly are the wild ponies, the only wild herds still grazing east of the Rockies.

The Chincoteague Refuge Visitor Center provides information, brochures and interpretive activities, including guided walks and auditorium programs. Beyond is the renovated Tom's Cove Visitor Center operated by the National Park Service, with "Please Touch" aquarium exhibits and a fascinating display in glass jars of varieties of sand from Key West to Utah.

Driving the main refuge road, past Swan Cove and Tom's Cove, to the Tom's Cove Visitor Center provides a good overview. On visits in early December and in May, we saw herons, egrets, cormorants, mute swans and untold geese, plus whitetail deer and wild ponies coming and going. Local guide Donna Leonard pointed out things we might otherwise have missed, including a baby snapping turtle, endangered Delmarva Peninsula fox squirrels and Sika deer. The best place to see the ponies is around Tom's Cove, especially from the 1.6-mile-long Woodland Trail. A 3.2-mile Wildlife Loop around Snow Goose Pond is reserved for walkers and bikers until 3 p.m. daily, when it opens for vehicles. During the ten days of Waterfowl Week at

Thanksgiving, visitors can drive up Assateague Island on the 7.5-mile Service Road for a better look at migratory waterfowl.

(757) 336-6122. Open daily, 5 a.m. to 10 p.m., May-September; 6 a.m. to 8 p.m. in April and October and 6 to 6 rest of year. Admission, $10 per car.

THE BEACHES. Fragile manmade dunes shield the glorious sands of Assateague, producing some of the East Coast's nicest and most remote beaches. Folks generally park near the Tom's Cove Visitor Center and hike to their favorite spot along the horseshoe-shaped, five-mile long Tom's Cove Hook beach or the ten-mile unsupervised Wild Beach to the north. Certain sections are designated for surfing and surf fishing (no saltwater license required). Beach capacity is limited by parking. When lots are filled, one car is allowed in when another leaves. On weekends, officials recommend arriving before 10 or after 2 or bicycling. "Biking not only helps you avoid parking problems, but also helps alleviate them," the park brochure notes.

WILDLIFE TOURS AND EXPEDITIONS. Assateague Island Wildlife Tours, (757) 336-6155, offers a narrated, fifteen-mile wildlife safari in an enclosed tram along National Wildlife Refuge service roads not otherwise open to the public at 10, 1 and 4 daily in summer (adults, $12). The 90-minute tours depart from the refuge parking lot.

Run by a former park ranger, **Assateague Explorer,** (866) 766-9794, schedules 90-minute "pony express" tours and two-hour "circle island" sightseeing cruises several times daily (adults, $30 to $40) from the Assateague Channel Marina, East Side Road.

Captain Barry's Back Bay Cruises, Landmark Plaza, (757) 336-6508, offers half-day and two-hour sea-life adventure tours during the day, a birding tour at 7 a.m. and champagne sunset cruises at 6:30 p.m. With a personality as colorful as his purple and yellow pontoon boat, Barry Frishman is an easygoing guide who lets people go crabbing, swim or even dance on his various expeditions.

Oyster Bay Outfitters, 6332 Maddox Blvd., (757) 336-0070 or (888) 732-7108, gives guided sea kayak excursions at sunrise, sunset and in between. Participants paddle along the shoreline and coves of Chincoteague Island, viewing oyster and clam beds, wild ponies and myriad birds. Kayaks are also available for rent.

THE PONIES. Their origin is debatable (legend has it that their ancestors swam ashore from a Spanish ship that was breaking up in a heavy storm), but the wild ponies inhabiting Assateague and Chincoteague date to the 17th century. To prevent overgrazing on the refuge, the herds are limited to 150 in Maryland and another 150 in Virginia. The latter are maintained by the Chincoteague Volunteer Fire Company, which sponsors an annual two-week carnival that culminates in the famous roundup and swim called Pony Penning on the last Wednesday and Thursday in July. Firemen turn into cowboys as they round up the horses to swim across Assateague Channel to Memorial Park in Chincoteague, where some are sold (average price about $2,000) at auction. On Friday, the rest swim back to Assateague. Upwards of 50,000 visitors turn out to watch. At other times, the ponies are best viewed from the Woodland Trail in the wildlife refuge, the beach road beside Tom's Cove, the wildlife safari, and in the Refuge Inn's corral behind McDonald's restaurant, the last commercial enterprise before crossing the bridge to Assateague.

BICYCLING. Biking, as the refuge brochure puts it, is a good way to get around Chincoteague and Assateague, and bicycle lanes are being added along shoulders of some roads. A bike path leads from the town to the refuge visitor center, circles

Wildlife Drive, and continues to the Tom's Cove Visitor Center. The Woodland Trail is also open for biking. Bike rentals average $3 an hour from the Bike Depot & Beach Outfitters at the Refuge Inn.

BOATING. Chincoteague Bay and Assateague Channel are shallow, so sailing is discouraged. Bottom fishing is good. Several small motels cater to fishermen and rent boats. Clamming and crabbing are popular in the shallow waters, guts and marshes. Skiffs and scows powered by outboards are available at boat-rental establishments.

Oyster & Maritime Museum, 7125 Maddox Blvd.

Oysters, their predators and the equipment used by watermen to catch them are the dominant theme in this museum portraying the history of Chincoteague. A good audio-visual diorama details the oyster industry, and you're told it's not true that you should eat oysters only during "r" months. Oyster shells from across the world and shell byproducts (like buttons) are shown. Among "oddities" are shells found implanted on an inner tube, a pipe, a fuse and a chisel. Also on display are the postcard collection of a New Church woman and famous newspaper front pages ("Snow in Miami," from the Miami Herald). We were fascinated by the press clippings of the 1962 winter storm that flooded Chincoteague. A newer wing reflects marine life, local culture and history. Exhibits of wildlife art and carvings, marine specimens and the original Fresnel lens from the Assateague Lighthouse are highlights.

(757) 336-6117. Open daily, 10 to 5, Memorial Day to Labor Day; weekends rest of year. Closed December-February. Adults $3, children $1.

NASA Visitor Center, Wallops Island.

Since 1945, the National Aeronautics and Space Administration has launched 12,000-plus rocket research vehicles and nineteen earth satellites from its Wallops Island Flight Facility. In keeping with the area, the small visitor center is rustic and low-key, lacking the glitz of the Kennedy Space Center in Florida. A few model rockets are poised among picnic tables outside. Inside, you'll find a collection of spacecraft and flight articles, exhibits on the space flight program, movies and video presentations. A moon rock sample from the Apollo 17 mission and the practice suit of Apollo 9 astronaut Russell Schweickart are highlights from the manned space era. Also part of Wallops Island is the National Oceanic and Atmospheric Agency's weather satellite tracking station.

(757) 824-1344. Open 10 to 4, daily in summer, Thursday-Monday rest of year. Free.

Refuge Waterfowl Museum, 7059 Maddox Blvd., (757) 336-5800. Many aspects of waterfowling are depicted in this structure, which looks a bit like a retail establishment. On display are decoys, boats, traps, weapons, art and carvings by local carvers and watermen. Open daily, 10 to 5. Adults $2.50, children $1.

Chincoteague Veterans Memorial Park, East Side Drive. Called the best-kept secret on the island is this small town park with a playground, boat launch, sports facilities, tennis courts, picnic tables and a cross in memory of deceased watermen. The cross was built from the mast of an old ship. The park is at its busiest during Pony Penning Days, when the ponies arrive here after swimming across Assateague Channel.

Sunset Watching. As in the few other East Coast ocean areas where you can see the sun setting over the water, sunset watching is something of a local tradition. For an unobstructed view, regulars head "down the marsh" along South Main Street to Captain Bob's parking lot, where the boat trailers are gone by sunset and the vista is unimpeded. Nearby, you might spot yellow-crowned night herons nesting in the trees.

SHOPPING. Hand-carved decoys are the area's leading sales item. Delbert "Cigar" Daisey is the resident carver at the Refuge Waterfowl Museum. The Chincoteague Decoy Carvers Association numbers about 25 active members. Their works are on sale at their homes and in many shops.

Two of our favorite shops are almost across the street from each other on Maddox Boulevard. At **Island Arts** at 6196 Maddox, artist Nancy Richards West displays her fine paintings of nature, carvings by Russell Fish, photographs by Julie West (her sister-in-law and co-owner), hand-painted clothing, handsome pottery and the fantastic wall sculptures of George Wazenegger. Nancy Hogan Armour sells her paintings at **Island Gallery & Gifts,** 6219 Maddox. We like her depictions of the wild ponies, as well as those of herons and other birds.

You'll find Pony Tails taffy in many stores on Chincoteague. Watch it being made at the **Pony Tails** shop at 7011 Maddox Blvd. The peanut-butter version is especially good. You'll also find a zillion bathing suits and T-shirts here, as well as many Christian books and tracts. One of the largest gift shops is **The Brant** at 6472 Maddox Blvd., with something for everyone and an entire second floor devoted to wicker baskets. **The Rookery** at the Refuge Motor Inn includes quite a collection of decoys among its display of crafts and gifts, from banners to bird baths. **White's Copperworks** at 6373 Maddox offers unusual things, from copper hammers to weathervanes.

The **Main Street Shop & Coffeehouse,** which anchors the main intersection of Main Street and Maddox Boulevard, dispenses the best lattes around. Elsewhere along Main Street, shops come and go. About the biggest establishment is the **Island Roxy** theater, one of the last of the big-screen cinemas. It shows first-run movies and, during Pony Penning Week, free reruns of the classic "Misty of Chincoteague." A good new specialty-food shop is **Wine, Cheese & More. Diana's** offers women's fashions. Across the street is **Crazy Lady** clothing. The **Osprey Nest Art Gallery,** 4096 Main St., features the works of owner Kevin McBride, including his posters done annually for Pony Penning Days. Decoys, baskets by local weavers, handsome cards and much more are available. We fell for the incredible teapots fashioned by Carol Meyers at the **Main Street Pottery,** 3891 Main, but demurred when we saw the $250 price tags. The wares, many by local potters, in her display room are upstaged only by the water view from her rear studio, which, she agrees, is "to die for."

Where to Eat ──────────────── ⌒⌒⌒

A.J.'s on the Creek, 6585 Maddox Blvd.

"Chincoteague oysters and clams are naturally salty – we don't salt them, nature does," advised the menu here. April, Lisa and A.J. Stillson also specify that they sauté and grill their seafood, and surround their patrons in mahogany, lace and candlelight. A heron statue in bulrushes beside a globe in the corner watched as we lunched on the assorted fried veggie platter, enough for four at $9, and scampi spaghetti with a good side salad dressed with artichoke vinaigrette, mushrooms and strips of salami ($8). Garlic is not used sparingly here in dishes like shrimp scampi. Dinner entrées range from mussels marinara over linguini to loin lamb chops and veal oscar. Oysters Rockefeller, seafood-smothered flounder, crab imperial and veal dishes are house specialties. At a recent visit, we liked the night's special, grilled tuna, better than the seafood lasagna, which turned out to be rather like spaghetti. White tablecloths, black chairs and booths, and a vaguely Italianate decor dignify the main dining room. Outside is a large screened porch for dining beside the water – in this case, Eel Creek.

(757) 336-5888. Entrées, $15 to $29. Lunch daily, 11 to 4:30; dinner, 4:30 to 9 or 10.

The Village Restaurant, 6576 Maddox Blvd.

Some tables get a view of Eel Creek at this restaurant, a favorite of many locals. The Connors family used to own a seafood restaurant; here, he's in the kitchen and she's out front. Dining is by candlelight in two rooms, and there's a mellow lounge where we paused for an after-dinner drink upon finding other places too noisy or closed. The menu is a bit more inspired than others of its ilk, from fried oysters to seafood platter, from seafood-stuffed tomatoes to veal with crab imperial. You also can get beef liver with sautéed onions, fried chicken or filet mignon. The soft-shell crabs, crab cakes and blackened snapper are highly regarded. Chicken or grilled steak salad, fettuccine and Cantonese stir-fry are available under light fare.

(757) 336-5120. Entrées, $9.95 to $22.50. Dinner nightly, 5 to 9.

Etta's Channel Side Restaurant, 7452 East Side Drive.

White lights outline this long gray house overlooking Assateague Channel and the Assateague Lighthouse. There are picnic tables on a large side deck. Inside, votive candles flicker on glass-topped pink tables flanked by walls of pine paneling and pinkish print wallpaper. Etta and Mac MacDowell specialize in seafood platters, but you can also get a crab-cake sandwich, baked ham sandwich or fried chicken. For dessert, try the turtle cheesecake, made with candy turtles. Breakfast-type items are among the offerings for weekend brunch/lunch.

(757) 336-5644. Entrées, $7.95 to $16.95. Open Monday-Thursday 4 to 9, Friday and Saturday 11:30 to 9:30, Sunday noon to 9. Closed January-March.

Capt. Fish's Steaming Wharf and Deck Bar, 3855 Main St.

Mike and Linda McGee and family, who own and operate the Chincoteague Island Brand oyster packing business nearby, diversified with this place at water's edge. And it's quite a place – a covered and semi-enclosed pavilion, with potted palm trees for decor, and an open bar where we lunched on bar stools that could topple tipsy occupants into the drink. There was a $1,000 prize offered for karaoke on Thursday nights, for good measure. The raw bar offers succulent Chincoteague oysters, steamed or on the half shell, steamed blue crabs, snow crab legs and a steamed seafood platter. Otherwise, look for platters – oysters, scallops, shrimp, flounder, crab cakes, clam strips or seafood (one of each) – served with hushpuppies, corn on the cob and french fries. Other platters yield swordfish, tuna, salmon, codfish and drum. Appetizers include crabmeat cocktail, garden salad and seafood boats (baked potato skins stuffed with scallops, shrimp and crabmeat and doused with cheese sauce and sour cream). We liked the single-fried oyster sandwich (the "single" turned out not to mean one oyster but fried individually, one at a time).

(757) 336-5528. Entrées, $12.95 to $26.95. Lunch and dinner daily, 11 to 10. Earlier closing in off-season and closed two weeks in January.

Steamers, 6251 Maddox Blvd.

With brown-paper-covered tables and the ubiquitous crab-cracking mallet, the bright and basic, all-you-can-eat crab restaurant is wildly popular. Those who order the all-you-can-eat specials start with salad and clam or corn chowder. Next come fried clam strips, popcorn shrimp, hushpuppies, sweet potato biscuits, fried chicken and corn on the cob. You wonder how people have room left for the steamed crabs and shrimp that follow. But "we dump the crabs on the table, give you a mallet and a knife and you go at it," says the owner. Steamers also has other seafood offerings, from flounder to broiled scallops to soft-shell crab stuffed with crab imperial, which sounds to us like overkill. Non-seafood eaters are appeased by veggie lasagna, fried chicken, barbecued pork ribs or delmonico steak. Most people adjourn for dessert next door to the Island Creamery, owned by the former owner of Steamers. Order a root-beer float, milk shake or banana split. Or how about the Round Up? It's five scoops of ice cream, three toppings, nuts, whipped cream and a cherry ($4.95). Entices the menu: "Eat this alone and your picture goes on our bulletin board." Homemade ice cream and frozen yogurt in belgian waffle cones come in untold varieties, old South pecan, strawberry cheesecake and key lime and watermelon sherbets among them.

(757) 336-5478. Entrées, $13.95 to $21.95. Dinner nightly, 5 to 9, May to mid-October. Creamery open daily, 10 to 10.

Bill's Seafood Restaurant, 4040 Main St.

For local character, this old-timer is the place. Watermen and NASA base workers start their day here at 5 a.m.; businessmen end theirs with a coffee klatch about 4 p.m. In between, owners Kevin Krone and Steve Potts, who also own Sugarbakers Bakery & Café (see below), offer an enormous menu in what was described as upscaled surroundings – although who would guess? Theirs is a mixed bag of local favorites, from ham steak, baby beef liver and southern fried chicken to shrimp and scallop brochettes, seafood norfolk, veal chesapeake and filet mignon. Vegetables are true to the southern tradition of coleslaw, string beans, applesauce, mashed potatoes and such, accompanied by caesar, garden or tropical shrimp salad. Meals are served at booths and pine tables. There's a full service bar, and Bill's does a land-office takeout business. For many repeat vacationers, this is the first (and sometimes only) restaurant stop in Chincoteague.

(757) 336-5831. Entrées, $9.95 to $24.95. Open daily, 5 a.m. to 9 p.m.

Sugarbakers Bakery & Café, 4095 Main St.

The baked goods here are highly regarded, as are the espressos and gourmet coffees. Ditto for the soups, sandwiches and salads offered in the little storefront's café addition. Stop in for low-fat muffins in the morning or for cappuccino in the evening.

(757) 336-3712. Open daily in summer, 7 a.m. to 9 p.m.; fewer days in off-season.

FOR MORE INFORMATION: Chincoteague Chamber of Commerce, 6733 Maddox Blvd. at the Rotary, Box 258, Chincoteague, Va. 23336. (757) 336-6161. www.chincoteague.com.

Landmark lighthouse attracts visitors to Chesapeake Bay Maritime Museum.

St. Michaels/Oxford, Md.

You're sitting on your inn's veranda on a late summer evening. Gone are the crowds of sailors who make St. Michaels the second busiest transient harbor along the Chesapeake Bay. Yet to come are the hunters who flock to this area every fall.

Egrets and ospreys can be seen and ducks heard; Canada geese are all around. Tall southern pines sway in the breeze. The foliage tends to magnolia, holly and boxwood trees. The homes are pillared and porched. You detect a drawl in the natives' speech.

There's an unmistakable Southern air about St. Michaels and Oxford, its neighbor some distance away across the Tred Avon River, as well as about remote Tilghman Island between the Choptank River and the Chesapeake Bay.

This is Tidewater territory. It's also below the Mason-Dixon Line, noted the woman who checked us in at the Harbourtowne Resort. "People think that with my accent I'm from Virginia, but no, I was born and raised on the Eastern Shore."

Both St. Michaels and Oxford date back to the 1600s and played key roles in the developing nation and its boat building interests before yielding their importance to Washington and Baltimore. For years they languished, cherished by the watermen who make their livelihood from the bay but undiscovered by tourists and bypassed by the masses headed for Ocean City's beaches.

The opening of the Bay Bridge out of Annapolis in 1954 forever altered the Eastern Shore's lifestyle. It wasn't until James Michener penned *Chesapeake* in the area that this choice piece of waterside real estate really took off, however.

St. Michaels claims an array of new inns, B&Bs, restaurants, shops and, of course, more than enough yachtsmen, sportsmen and visitors to patronize them. It appears rather self-consciously precious, and getting ever more so. Quieter Oxford and Tilghman Island remain little changed, and their residents and devotees hope to keep them that way.

The focus of western Talbot County – which has an incredible 602 miles of shoreline, longest in the continental United States – is St. Michaels, its landlocked harbor located half way up the Miles River from the Eastern Bay toward Easton, the historic county seat. Hidden beneath the clapboards of modernized houses are logs or bricks dating to the 18th century. When the British bombarded this strategically important town from the Miles River one night in 1813, townspeople blacked out the lamps and hung lanterns in the treetops to confuse the invaders. The ploy worked and the British overshot. Only the now-famous Cannonball House was hit, and St. Michaels earned a place in history as the town that fooled the British. Today, visitors tour one of America's earliest seaports, enjoy the Chesapeake Bay Maritime Museum and share the harbor with the 20,000 boats that put into St. Michaels annually.

The wildlife that lures hunters and the waters that attract mariners will appeal to you, too. So will the abundance of Eastern Shore crabs and oysters as well as the Tidewater's unhurried lifestyle.

Getting There

St. Michaels is located on the east side of the Chesapeake Bay, about 40 miles due east of Washington, D.C. Main approaches are U.S. Route 50 via the Chesapeake Bay Bridge out of Annapolis, Routes 13 and 301 from Wilmington, Del., and Routes 13 and 50 from Norfolk, Va. From Route 50 near Easton, take the St. Michaels bypass to Route 33, which leads to St. Michaels and Tilghman Island, which is connected to the mainland by a small bridge at Knapps Narrows. Take Route 333 from Easton to Oxford. To get from St. Michaels to Oxford, use the Bellevue-Oxford ferry.

Where to Stay ⎯⎯⎯⎯⎯⎯⎯⎯⎯⎯ _ᏬᏬᏬ_

Because of its location and its wealth of fish and game, the tourist season is longer in St. Michaels than in more northerly areas (November and December, for instance, are peak periods). Most lodging facilities are open year-round.

Small and Choice

Black Walnut Point Bed & Breakfast Inn, Black Walnut Road, Box 308, Tilghman Island 21671.

We found the ultimate waterside escape at this B&B, which has a 57-acre monopoly on paradise at the end of Tilghman Island. Water (the wide Choptank River on the east and south and the Chesapeake Bay on the west) surrounds the landscaped grounds and wildlife preserve on three sides. The point is so secluded it's not surprising to learn that this once was the summer retreat for the Soviet embassy. The state acquired the property and ultimately leased it to Tom and Brenda Ward to run as a B&B. In the charming main house, part of which dates to before the Civil War, they offer four guest rooms. The Bay Room, with a queen bed and a twin, has a beamed ceiling and windows on three sides. Overlooking the pool is the refurbished Tilghman Room, with a king bed and a twin. We like to stay in any of the three cottages with fireplaces at water's edge, rebuilt and updated after

Hurricane Isabel hit the area in 2003. Each is a cocoon of knotty pine with a spacious bedroom, a comfortable living room with a futon and TV open to a well-equipped kitchen, an ample screened porch, and birds twittering and waves lapping at the rocky shore outside – just like the summer cottage of one's dreams. The main house has a living room with TV/VCR, games and grand piano, a summery sun porch with rattan furniture, a chandeliered dining room, a back porch with rockers facing the bay and a room off the kitchen where guests help themselves to lemonade, iced tea, soft drinks or wine from the refrigerator. Morning brings a continental-plus breakfast with choice of juice, fresh fruit, cereal and homemade muffins. Outside are a jacuzzi beside a delightful freeform swimming pool, roses blooming around it, and a lighted tennis court, a swing and rope hammocks – once you stretch out in a hammock by the bay, you won't want to get up. The place has a casual, laid-back feeling that's perfect for a getaway beside the water.

(410) 886-2452. Fax (410) 886-2053. www.blackwalnutpoint.com. Four rooms and three cottages with private baths. Doubles, $120 to $175. Cottages, $225. Closed weekdays in winter.

The Lazyjack Inn, 5907 Tilghman Island Road, Tilghman Island 21671.

Sailing enthusiasts Mike and Carol Richards from Reston, Va., had just set sail southward for two years when they happened upon Tilghman Island and, as Mike tells it, "liked it so much we decided to stay." They found a 160-year-old house backing up to Dogwood Harbor, which he restored to take in B&B guests and use as a base for a new charter boat business. (Damaged by Hurricane Isabel, the foundation was raised five feet and the place rebuilt in 2004.) All four accommodations come with modern baths, interesting decorative touches and heirloom quilts. A Victorian settee and a chair with ottoman face the water in the spacious, high-ceilinged Nellie Byrd Suite, which offers a kingsize brass bed, a built-in vanity in the bureau, a double jacuzzi tub and a shower with three sides of glass. Another good water view is afforded from the East Room, with exposed beam ceiling, heart of pine floors and Waterfall series furniture bearing shell hardware. Like the Nellie Byrd, the Garden Suite contains a jacuzzi tub and one of the inn's three in-room fireplaces. Mike, whose background is in residential construction, enclosed the big side porch to serve as a breakfast room. That and the rear deck with water view are the sites for the morning repast, which included a fresh fruit cup in a phyllo flower and baked stuffed french toast with cottage cheese and apricot glaze at our visit. Folded crab omelets, banana rum cake and sticky buns are other specialties. Sherry and chocolates are put out when the beds are turned down. Mike takes guests onto the Chesapeake Bay on the Lady Patty, his 45-foot ketch.

(410) 886-2215 or (800) 690-5080. Fax (410) 886-2635. www.lazyjackinn.com. Two rooms and two suites with private baths. Doubles, $139 to $189. Suites, $199 to $259.

Chesapeake Wood Duck Inn, Gibsontown Road, Box 202, Tilghman Island 21671.

A prime waterfront location along Dogwood Harbor and gourmet breakfasts commend this stylish B&B in a restored boarding house built in 1890. Owners Kimberly and Jeffrey Bushey offer six small, cheerful bedrooms and a cottage, all but one with water views. Five rooms have queensize beds and two have doubles. A guest favorite is the Dogwood, smartly decorated in Laura Ashley style with windows on three sides. Another is the cozy Chesapeake Cottage next door, its sitting room enhanced with a TV and stereo and its private deck enjoying a water view. The main-floor common rooms are embellished with artworks by impressionist artist Maureen Bannon, Kim's mother – "we are her gallery," says Jeff. A former chef with the Hyatt hotel chain, Jeff better enjoys "cooking for eight rather than 350." That accounts for his four-course dinners ($55 per person) available for the first eight guests to reserve on Saturday nights, featuring what's fresh and regional. He also does elaborate breakfasts, featuring treats like smoked salmon hash, a trio of crêpes, Tilghman Island egg puff or a crab, corn and spinach pie. It's taken in the formal dining room or, more likely, in the sun room or screened porch overlooking a deep back lawn and gazebo.

(410) 886-2070 or (800) 956-2070. Fax (410) 667-7156. www.woodduckinn.com. Six rooms and one cottage with private baths. Doubles, $159 to $189. Cottage, $229.

Wades Point Inn on the Bay, Wades Point Road, Box 7, St. Michaels 21633.

Very Southern looking, this imposing white brick plantation-style home at the end of a long lane is surrounded by uncommonly attractive grounds and backs up to the Chesapeake Bay about five miles west of St. Michaels on the way to Tilghman Island. The original house was built in 1819 by Baltimore shipwright Thomas Kemp. A summer wing was added in 1890 and it has operated as a guesthouse in the old Bay tradition ever since. "We've been updating it but want it to stay comfy and homey," said innkeeper Betsy Feiler. The newer Mildred T. Kemp Building has twelve hotel-style rooms, each with one or two queen beds and four with kitchenette facilities to encourage families. All but two have waterfront balconies that you may never want to leave. Each is furnished individually with down comforters, plush carpeting and interesting window treatments, with Bibles on the nightstands, and TVs noticeably absent. The main house has eleven guest rooms, all now with private baths. Separate baths (with showers) were added lately in the Victorian summer wing, whose high-ceilinged rooms open off a long corridor and are barely big enough to hold a double bed but yield water views through tall windows. Larger bedrooms and baths are located on the second floor of the main house and in the third-floor attic. Two of the latter rooms have clawfoot tubs from which you can watch the sun set, if you're so inclined. The country farmhouse out front sleeps up to fourteen in five more bedrooms, three with private baths. Inn guests enter a reception area in the original summer kitchen. The main parlor is comfortably furnished with sofas, a piano and more books than a Southern gentleman could possibly have read. Beyond is the large Bay Room, a sensational space with columns and arches, a fireplace, white wicker furniture, bleached floors topped with colorful patterned rugs and windows on all sides onto the water. Here is where guests linger over an expanded continental breakfast of fruit salad, cereal, muffins, french rolls and sometimes eggs contributed by chickens raised on the inn's 80-acre organic farm. A rear porch looks onto the bay, where Betsy says guests catch the biggest crabs off the dock (she'll boil them for you). There's great fishing, and you'll marvel at the deer and birds along the inn's mile-long nature trail. That is, if you leave the hammocks or Adirondack chairs spread out on the shady lawns facing the Eastern Bay and Kent Island.

(410) 745-2500 or (888) 923-3466. Fax (410) 745-3443. www.wadespoint.com. Twenty-six rooms with private baths. Doubles, $140 to $240. Closed January and February.

Bay Cottage, 24640 Yacht Club Road, St. Michaels 21663.

A long tree-lined drive ends at a large gray house on a tranquil point stretching to a quiet harbor cove, one of the prime waterfront properties in St. Michaels. It was built in the early 1900s by a man who ran the area's largest hunting and fishing guide business and was a leading benefactor of the Chesapeake Bay Maritime Museum nearby. Retirees Bob and Jackie Fletcher share their home with overnight guests in five air-conditioned bedrooms, furnished in the manner of an early Chesapeake cottage – that is to say, rustic and masculine. Bedrooms have queensize beds, private baths and original pine floors. Each is a corner room with a water view.

The best views are offered from the deck of the newest accommodation, the second floor of a cottage along the shore. Guests enjoy a common living room with a stone fireplace, pine-paneled walls and homey furnishings. The enclosed sun porch is the favorite inside space for its wide water views. On good days, Jackie serves her full breakfast here, featuring eggs flavored with herbs from her garden. The grounds are surrounded by 500 feet of shoreline from which guests enjoy the water birds, fish or crab from the pier, launch a kayak or just savor the scene along Long Haul Creek, where James Michener wrote *Chesapeake.* A pleasant swimming pool by the shore is a bonus.

(410) 745-9369 or (888) 558-8008. Fax (410) 745-4177. www.baycottage.com. Five rooms and one cottage with private baths. Doubles, $145 to $195. Cottage, $295. Closed mid-December to mid-April.

Hambleton Inn, 202 Cherry St., Box 1007, St. Michaels 21663.

Young owners have upgraded and revitalized this established B&B in an 1860 house that occupies a prime harborfront site in the heart of St. Michaels. Steve and Kimberly Furman added a handsome dining room in which they offer a continental breakfast at a table for ten beside a fireplace. The Furmans also refurbished and lightened up the decor in five guest rooms, each of which has at least a partial water view. A bedroom in the original living room has a fireplace, kingsize poster bed, plump chair, sage green walls and fancy window treatments characteristic of the rest of the house. Another king-bedded room, this with a crown canopy, is handsome in mauve colors, with upholstered chairs and fine furniture on a refinished floor. Queen poster beds are in two second-floor rooms, one with windows on three sides. The old Crow's Nest on the third floor, where tall guests are warned not to bump their heads on the ceiling, is pretty in pale yellow. The newest accommodation is a two-bedroom suite fashioned from the former owner's quarters. The second-floor front porch serves as the common room at this B&B. Outfitted in wicker, Kimberly says it's "the best spot in the house." It certainly offers a great view of the harbor goings-on. The Furmans installed a new dock in the harbor, landscaped the entrance and grounds, and provide bicycles for guests.

(410) 745-3350 or (866) 745-3350. Fax (410) 745-5709. www.hambletoninn.com. Five rooms and one suite with private baths. Doubles, $225 to $245. Suite, $295 for two, $490 for four.

Victoriana Inn, 205 Cherry St., Box 449, St. Michaels 21663.

A former private residence built in 1883 and facing the harbor, this elegant gem was opened as a B&B in 1988 by a perfectionist who was into Victoriana. Later owners Charles and Maria McDonald of Alexandria, Va., refurbished, added a mini-suite and finished an attractive water-view deck. They offer a mix of period and traditional furniture in six guest rooms. The new junior suite off one side of the main floor has a queensize pencil-post bed, sitting area with loveseat, full bath and the only in-room TV. Sliding glass doors open onto a private cedar deck facing the harbor. In the center of the main floor are a fireplaced parlor and a dining room. On the other side of the same floor are two guest rooms, each with a fireplace and one with a canopy bed and water view. Two larger rooms upstairs also face the water. A small sunroom overlooking the lawn and waterfront contains a TV/VCR. A front porch looks onto lovely flower gardens, one of the biggest magnolia trees we ever saw, a little fish pond and, of course, the boats in the harbor. Lounge chairs are scattered about, and the setting is quite idyllic. The full breakfast might include fresh fruit and juice, cereals and perhaps pancakes, french toast or eggs benedict.

(410) 745-3368 or (888) 316-1282. www.victorianainn.com. Seven rooms with private baths. Doubles, $159 to $319.

Combsberry, 4837 Evergreen Road, Oxford 21654.

If you're to the manor born, especially one by the water, here's one for you. The inn's brochure or website cannot possibly convey the totality in all its glory. Drive down a one-third-mile-long driveway lined with trees and daylilies and enter another world. Set among arching willows and sixteen mature magnolia trees on ten acres along the banks of Brigham's Cove is an 18th-century Georgian manor house, flanked by a caretaker's cottage and a carriage house. The property was saved in 1996 by Dr. Mahmood Shariff, a Cambridge cardiologist, and his wife Ann. She and resident innkeeper Cathy Magrogan transformed the complex into a sumptuous B&B. In the brick manor dating to 1730, fireplaced common rooms unfold from one end of the house to the other. A spacious living room done in sprightly floral chintz leads into a Queen Anne-style dining room. A cozy library is paneled in green. The awesome kitchen opens onto a breakfast room with tiled floor and curving, floor-to-ceiling windows onto lawns and water. Upstairs are two guest rooms and two suites, including the majestic Magnolia Suite with a kingsize canopy bed, working fireplace and a bathroom the size of many a bedroom, equipped with a double jacuzzi, double vanity and enormous walk-in shower. Off the bedroom is a private waterfront balcony, overlooking some of the sixteen towering magnolias in full bloom at our visit. All Combsberry guest quarters enjoy water views, five have fireplaces and four have jacuzzis. Two cottage suites with jacuzzis share a living room and dining area in a newly built carriage house. The joint common room here has french doors onto an arched brick veranda overlooking the water and is often used for executive retreats. Those seeking the ultimate in privacy opt for the Oxford Cottage, with a plush living room, efficiency kitchen and jacuzzi bath on the main floor and a queen brass bed upstairs. French doors open onto a brick terrace enclosed in a white picket fence. Lawns dotted with Adirondack chairs lead to water's edge, where there's a dock with a couple of canoes. As innkeeper Cathy pointed out salient features, she paused to haul up a crab trap. The contents would go into the next morning's crabmeat omelets, the finale to a breakfast including fresh fruit cup and home-baked breads.

(410) 226-5353. Fax (410) 228-1453. www.combsberryinn.com. Two rooms, two suites and three cottages with private baths. Doubles, $250. Suites, $295 and $395. Cottages, $350.

Larger Inns and Resorts

The Inn at Perry Cabin, 308 Watkins Lane, St. Michaels 21663.

Run by Orient-Express Hotels, this is a country-house hotel like no other inn on the Mid-Atlantic coast. With an idyllic waterfront location, beautiful grounds, sumptuous accommodations and a first-class restaurant (see Where to Eat), it's luxury to the max. Many millions have been spent in several expansions and refurbishings of what started as a cabin for Commodore Oliver Perry ("we have met the enemy and they are ours") after the War of 1812. A 2003 expansion that doubled the inn's size added 40 guest rooms and suites, a spa and a heated outdoor pool and enlarged the kitchen to serve an expanded restaurant renamed Sherwood Landing. A refined nautical look reflects its new logo, the skipjack, a St. Michaels icon. Most rooms have views of Fogg Cove, and those on the first floor have doors to the gardens. On the second floor, some have balconies. A couple of two-story suites have living rooms on one floor, bedrooms on the next and jacuzzi bathtubs. They share a balcony overlooking the river and harbor. American and English antiques dignify the newest studio rooms and suites. Most have king beds in ostrich leather sleigh style with Frette linens, fireplaces, a balcony or terrace overlooking the river or harbor and Italian marble baths with heated floors. Minibars, pop-up televisions with DVD players and dual phone lines are standard. Evening turndown produces fresh towels, a refilled ice bucket and a couple of oatmeal-raisin cookies. On the main floor, three plush living rooms are filled with lovely antiques and spectacular flower arrangements. French doors lead to a brick terrace, where comfortable chairs invite sitting and looking at the water. Houseguests may take tea here or in the living rooms – a proper British one with little sweets and scones upon which to spread lemon curd and whipped cream. Breakfast is extra. Served in the dining room, ours was an unusual chargrilled "salmon ham" with scrambled eggs and scallions and a classic English mixed grill, from grilled tomato to kidneys to blood pudding, with a poached egg in the middle.

(410) 745-2200 or (800) 722-2949. Fax (410) 745-3348. www.perrycabin.com. Fifty-five rooms and 26 suites with private baths. Rates, EP. Doubles, $345 to $500. Suites, $625.

St. Michaels Harbour Inn, Marina & Spa, 101 North Harbor Road, St. Michaels 21663.

Redecorated and refurbished from top to bottom by new owner Bob Pascal, this L-shaped, three-story contemporary structure commands a prime location at the head of the busy St. Michaels harbor. Lodging consists primarily of two-room suites facing the water. Each has a living room with a sofabed, desk, television and kitchenette with a sink and refrigerator, and a bedroom with one or two queensize beds and a large bathroom with double vanities and thick towels. French doors lead from each room onto a private terrace or balcony with good-looking chairs and a table overlooking the harbor. Smaller quarters on the third floor have rooms with one queen bed, a refrigerator and a private balcony. During the recent refurbishing, bathrooms were updated throughout. Several now have double jacuzzi tubs with separate showers. Four suites on the third floor got expanded balconies. The pleasant **Harbour Lights** restaurant serves three meals a day (see Dining Spots). Lighter fare is available in **Pascal's Tavern** and its new poolside grill. At breakfast, we enjoyed a stack of apple-pecan pancakes while watching the harbor activity. A small outdoor pool beside the harbor is flanked by a jacuzzi and a bar for beverages and snacks. Overnight docking slips are available for 60 boats. There's a Ship's Store, and an aqua center offers canoes and aquabikes for adventuring around the harbor. A full-service spa was added on the third floor in 2004.

(410) 745-9001 or (800) 332-8994. Fax (410) 745-9150. www.harbourinn.com. Eight rooms and 38 suites with private baths. Doubles, $189 to $525.

Harbourtowne Golf Resort & Conference Center, Route 33, Box 126, St. Michaels 21663.

The first new lodging facility in St. Michaels in the 1980s, this was patterned after a similar development at Hilton Head. Hence the resort-like resemblance with an eighteen-hole, Pete Dye-designed golf course, Olympic-size pool, tennis courts, conference facilities and posh homes all around. Situated a couple of miles west of town and a mile off the main road through the luxury 573-acre planned community known as Martingham, this is smack up against the rocky Miles River shore on a peninsula with water on three sides. A major upgrading program in the 1990s produced 35 new guest accommodations, six of them suites with fireplaces and 24 with wood-burning stoves, in two new wings right beside the water. We stayed in one of the second-floor rooms of the original 48-unit complex. They are nicely secluded in several cedar buildings, have brick walls up to vaulted ceilings, spacious dressing areas and private balconies overlooking a tree-lined inlet and lagoon populated by flocks of birds. Some of the villas in five buildings on the point are right on the shore, the most coveted having water on three sides. The large **Bayside**

Restaurant in the main conference center has water views and a big outdoor deck right beside the river. The dinner menu appeals to the golf and conference clientele the inn attracts. A continental breakfast buffet is included in the rates.

(410) 745-9066 or (800) 446-9066. Fax (410) 745-9124. www.harbourtowne.com. One hundred five rooms and six suites with private baths. Doubles, $189.99 to $229.99. Suites, $259.99.

The Oaks, 329 Acorn Lane, Box 187, Royal Oak 21662.

The former Pasadena Inn gave way to this handsome pale yellow and green structure on seventeen waterfront acres along Oak Creek. Paul Milne and Candace Chiaruttini, who own the acclaimed 208 Talbot restaurant in St. Michaels, gutted the 1748 manor house but retained the antebellum facade. Fifteen guest rooms with king or queen beds open off a maze of hallways. Eleven have jacuzzi tubs, eight have gas fireplaces and some contain TVs. Twelve yield water views and all are furnished, in Candace's words, with "antiques that came with the place." The premier accommodation is a large waterfront room on the third floor with a king bed, a double jacuzzi at the edge of the room, a two-person shower in the bathroom and a private balcony overlooking the water. A new waterside cottage comes with a fireplace and double jacuzzi. The pastry chef for 208 Talbot provides the baked goods for a breakfast buffet that includes a hot entrée. It's served in a large dining room with the original center fireplace in the middle. The vast main floor holds banquet space, a common room with TV in the original section and a screened side porch furnished in wicker and overlooking a watery scene. More seating is on decks all around overlooking grounds where shuffleboard, horseshoes, badminton, a putting green and a swimming pool are available. Canoes and bicycles are complimentary for guests.

(410) 745-5053. www.the-oaks.com. Fifteen rooms with private baths. Doubles, $140 to $300. Cottage, $375.

Robert Morris Inn, 314 North Morris St., Box 70, Oxford 21654.

Built prior to 1710, the home of the important Robert Morris family has been expanded several times since it housed Robert Morris Jr., who was to become a close friend of George Washington and financier of the Revolution. Painted butterscotch yellow with gingerbread trim, it remains a study in Colonial architecture and the fame of its dining room and tavern (see Where to Eat) extends far beyond the Eastern Shore. Best of all, for those who seek a Southern experience beside the water, is **Sandaway Lodge,** the inn's refurbished riverfront mansion. It has a small den with TV and seven spacious rooms lavishly furnished with antiques, including kingsize canopy and pencil-post beds, large baths and rocking chairs on screened porches facing the Tred Avon River. Surrounded by shady lawns leading to the wide river, Sandaway offers several riverfront cottages, a small beach and a view of the Tred Avon Yacht Club. Sixteen rooms in the 18th-century, mansard-roofed main inn are more historic but well appointed and all now have private baths. One of the nicest, Room 1 with a river view, has a four-poster bed, a sofa and upholstered chair near a non-working fireplace of English bricks, and hooked rugs over the sloping, wide-board floor. The handmade nails, hand-hewn oak pegs and original Georgia white pine flooring are typical of the Colonial detail throughout the inn. Innkeeper Jay Gibson says the inn caters to couples who like a restrained, historic atmosphere.

(410) 226-5111 or (888) 823-4012. Fax (410) 226-5744. www.robertmorrisinn.com. Thirty-five rooms with private baths. Rates, EP. Doubles, $130 to $350. Closed December-March.

The Tilghman Island Inn, 21384 Coopertown Road, Box B, Tilghman Island 21671.

The view of the wildfowl marsh and bay is the primary lure of this modern resort with motel units, restaurant, lounge and marina – an "inn" more in name than in reality. Yet it's good for those who want creature comforts and a waterfront location, this one where Knapps Narrows joins the Choptank River and the Chesapeake Bay. Owners Jack Redmon and David McCallum have renovated most of the twenty rooms, half of which face the water. Most have kingsize beds and three have two doubles. Some are available as suites with efficiency kitchen areas, and a couple of fireplaces were added in 2001. Caribbean-style rattan furnishings and a piano bar characterize the Narrows Lounge. The dining room (see Where to Eat) looks onto the marshes and inlet; an open umbrellaed deck overlooks the bay. Also part of the ongoing renovations are a clubhouse by the outdoor pool and an airy lobby. Guests are served a continental breakfast in the morning.

(410) 886-2141 or (800) 866-2141. www.tilghmanislandinn.com. Twenty rooms with private baths. Doubles, $150 to $300.

The Inn at Knapp's Narrows Marina, Box 277, Tilghman Island, MD 21671.
Erected in 2001 in the midst of a marina, this three-story motel and conference center has twenty rooms, each with private deck or balcony looking onto a working boatyard. All have queen beds except for five with two doubles. Decor is spare and beachy – rooms are all white except for the carpeting and furnished in wicker. The third-floor end unit 307 offers the best view of the Narrows and the bay. Overnight guests enjoy the marina's 60-foot pool and cabana. Continental breakfast is included. The marina's Bay Hundred restaurant serves lunch and dinner.

(410) 886-2720 or (800) 322-5181. www.knappsnarrowsmarina.com. Twenty rooms with private baths. Doubles, $120 to $160. Suite, $275.

Seeing and Doing ———————— *♪♪♪*

On or Near the Water

Chesapeake Bay Maritime Museum, Navy Point, St. Michaels.
Founded in 1965 and built on mounds of crushed oyster shells, this expanding museum is the town's major tourist attraction. The nation's most complete collection of Chesapeake Bay watercraft, artifacts and visual art is on display, detailing life in a typical waterman's village of the 19th century. Already, the museum harbors the largest floating fleet of historic Chesapeake Bay boats in existence. Among the more than 80 vessels are a skipjack, log-bottom bugeye, oyster boat and crab dredger. They're maintained in a working boat yard and a traditional boat shop, where you get to see craftsmen at work and view a small display of primitive boat-building tools.

A focal point is the 1879 Hooper Strait Lighthouse, one of only three cottage-type lighthouses remaining on the bay. Its move to St. Michaels was the impetus that inspired the museum. You learn what a lightkeeper's life was like and pass some interesting exhibits of fog signals, lamps and lenses as you climb to the top level for a bird's-eye view of the St. Michaels harbor. Waterman's Wharf has an interactive crabber's shanty where you can pull up a crab trap and tend a soft-shell crab shedding tank. You can climb aboard a Chesapeake oyster dredge boat and learn that more oysters have been harvested form the Chesapeake than any other place. The Waterfowling Building contains an extensive collection of decoys, guns and mounted waterfowl, all so important in this area. The 18th-century corn crib houses gunning boats now outlawed for use on the bay. The Bay History Building traces the area's geological and social history. The Steamboat Building traces the use of the bay as a highway and the change from sailing to propelled vessels.

Among other sights are the Small Boat Exhibit Shed, a Potomac River bell tower, and a Tolchester Beach bandstand where concerts are still staged in summer. Quite a sight is the landmark at the museum's relocated entrance – a sign identifies it as the drawbridge that "once connected Tilghman Island to the rest of the world." Exit via the museum store. It's exceptionally good, containing many books, cookbooks for sailors, decoys, needlepoint coasters and Chesapeake Challenge, an intriguing game.

(410) 745-2916. www.cbmm.org. Museum open daily in summer, 9 to 6; spring and fall, 9 to 5; winter, 9 to 4. Adults $9, children $4.

Patriot Cruise, Navy Point, St. Michaels.

The best way to see and savor this part of the Eastern Shore – most of its meandering shoreline is very private and far from view – is by boat. Capt. Carl Thornton pilots the area's largest excursion boat, offering a leisurely 80-minute cruise up the Miles River. The 65-foot, two-deck boat with bar carries 200 passengers. The captain advised beforehand that he points out "birds, houses, duck blinds, whatever I see." We saw the Mystic Clipper in the distance, various kinds of bulkheading to prevent shore erosion, several osprey nests on channel markers, the ruins of St. John's Chapel, and some mighty impressive plantations and contemporary homes. We learned that the Miles River is not really a river but a brackish tidal estuary of the bay, and that James Michener wrote *Chesapeake* in a rented house along the river. The river was originally called the St. Michaels, the captain said, but the Quakers dropped the "Saint" and local dialect turned Michaels into Miles. Our only regret was that the boat didn't go closer to the sights the guide or the taped narration were pointing out on the eleven-mile round trip.

(410) 745-3100. Cruises daily at 11, 12:30, 2:30 and 4, April-October. Adults $14, children $8.

Dockside Express Cruises and Tours, (410) 886-2643 or (888) 312-7847, schedules a variety of tours aboard the 49-passenger Express Royale from the Maritime Museum dock. Ninety-minute narrated ecology cruises to observe wildlife, touch sea creatures and watch watermen at work leave daily at 10 a.m. and 2 p.m.; adults $20, children $10. Also available are a champagne sunset cruise and a variety of land tours.

Chesapeake Skipjack Sailing Tours, (410) 745-6080, features oyster-dredging on two-hour sails aboard the 32-passenger Skipjack H.M. Krentz, Capt. Ed Farley, a waterman for more than twenty years, pilots one of the last remaining skipjacks, leaving from the Crab Claw Restaurant.

Outboard runabouts, sailboats and bicycles are available for rent or charter at **St. Michaels Town Dock Marina,** 305 Mulberry St., (410) 745-2400. Two-hour sails on a 36-foot catamaran are offered from this marina by the **Lucky Dog Catamaran Co.,** (410) 745-6203.

Dogwood Harbor on Tilghman Island – home of the skipjacks that make up the last commercial fishing sailing fleet in North America – is a center for **sailing outings**. Capt. Mike Richards of the Lazyjack Inn, (800) 690-5080, offers three tours to lighthouses around the bay aboard the **M/V Sharps Island** and features $40 champagne sunset cruises on the **Lady Patty,** his 45-foot classic ketch built in 1935. Also on Tilghman, Capt. Wade H. Murphy Jr. offers two-hour sails aboard the **Skipjack Rebecca T. Ruark,** (410) 886-2176. **Selina II,** a 26-foot catboat, offers two-hour sails and sunset cruises for up to six passengers from the Bridge Restaurant, (410) 726-9400. It's piloted by Iris Clarke, granddaughter of the original owners.

Kayak rentals and tours are offered by **Chesapeake Water Sports & Outfitters,** 7857 Tilghman Island Road, Sherwood, (410) 886-2083. Kayakers usually spot herons, egrets, terns, ospreys and more as they paddle the flats around Tilghman Island.

Oxford-Bellevue Ferry, Route 329, Royal Oak.

America's oldest privately owned ferry (established 1683) crosses the Tred Avon River between Oxford and Bellevue. It's the shortest way to get from St. Michaels to Oxford and the scenery conveys a feeling of the Thames and Great Britain, to which this area was so closely allied. The main ferry holds nine cars. A smaller, older one is pressed into service weekends and in summer.

(410) 745-9023. Continuous crossings every 25 minutes, June-August, Monday-Friday 7 a.m. to 9 p.m., weekends 9 to 9; off-season, daily service stops at sunset. Closed December-February. Car and driver $6, passengers $1.

Jean Ellen duPont Shehan Audubon Sanctuary, 23000 Wells Point Road, Bozman.

The former farm and fox hunting grounds for the duPont family are now a wildlife sanctuary and an environmental education center. The sanctuary on a 950-acre peninsula is bordered by three creeks and has more than eight miles of shoreline. Visitors can explore the shoreline, forests, wetlands, ponds and 200 acres of warm-season grass meadows. The sanctuary is open to the public on selected days and during special events for biking, hiking, canoeing, kayaking, horseback riding, mule wagon rides and bird walks. More than 160 species of birds are found here during the year.

(410) 745-9283. www.audubonmddc.org/JEDSAS. Open to the public on selected days – most Mondays from 9 to 4 and some summer Sundays from noon to 4 – and during special events.

Other Attractions

St. Michaels Walking Tour. The town and the St. Michaels Business Association provide a self-guided walking tour with map. It covers the meandering waterfront, including the footbridge from Cherry Street to Navy Point (one wishes there were more footbridges to get from point to point), the Talbot Street business section and St. Mary's Square. The last is an unusual town green laid out away from the main street and apt to be missed unless you seek it out. The map identifies seven historic houses and sites. You'll likely discover equally interesting things along the way.

St. Mary's Square Museum, On the Green, St. Michaels, (410) 745-9561. One of the town's oldest Colonial houses was moved to this site, restored and furnished. It is joined to the 1860 Teetotum Building, so named because it resembles an old-fashioned top. The display areas of local memorabilia and history are open May-October weekends from 10 to 4, other times by reservation. Free.

Oxford. The Strand at Oxford's north side, facing Bellevue across the Tred Avon River, is the only real beach we saw in this area. Few people swim in the Chesapeake or its estuaries because of sea nettles that sting everything but the palms and feet. Once Maryland's principal port, Oxford is a lovely, tree-lined town in which the presence of water on all sides is felt more than in St. Michaels. Never in one small area have we seen so many sailboats, yachts and marinas. Besides marinas and restaurants, there are a few shops, several historic buildings, the Oxford Customs House and the small Oxford Museum, open Friday-Sunday from 2 to 5.

BIKING. The flat, meandering country is good bicycling terrain. Favorite day trips by bike or car are across the old Tred Avon River ferry to Oxford, which has an ever-so-British yet southern feeling, or out to a different world on Tilghman Island, where much of the Eastern Shore's famed seafood is caught and the watermen are ubiquitous. Another scenic byway is Route 579 to Bozman and Neavitt. Bicycles are available at **St. Michaels Town Dock Marina,** (410) 745-2400, and the **Oxford Mews Bike Boutique,** 105 South Morris St., Oxford, (410) 820-8222.

SHOPPING. Most of the area's shopping is found along narrow Talbot Street in St. Michaels, and much of it has to do with the area's position as a sailing and waterfowl center. One of the most stylish shops is the **Chesapeake Trading Company,** which started dispensing coffee, cold drinks and books and now, in expanded quarters, also showcases fine apparel, hats, jewelry, clocks, frames and coffee mugs with the carved heads of loons as handles, along with books and an espresso bar. Lately, owner Linda Boatner added a sophisticated home accessories and furnishings shop in a former art gallery out back. **Bags Aloft** includes wind socks along with all kinds of bags, from laundry to lunch. At the **Blue Swan,** we liked the nautical Christmas ornaments. Resort-type clothes are found at **Shaw Bay Classics** and **Chesapeake Bay Outfitters,** while the **Broken Rudder** carries sportswear with a Chesapeake accent. **Sailor of St. Michaels** offers sportswear and accessories of interest to sailing types. Women's sportswear joins tableware, garden accessories and kitchen items at **Sign O' the Whale. Keepers-Orvis** appeals to the fly fisherman and carries clothing, equipment and decoys. **Wood That Works** stocks interesting handcrafted wooden items. A resident decoy carver works at **The Calico Gallery,** which has a large selection of local art posters. **Galerie Francaise** specializes in vintage posters. **The Mind's Eye Craft Collection** stocks unusual American crafts (check out the painted stools) from more than 250 leading artisans. Local artisans show at **Artiste Locale,** where we liked the mobiles of stained glass.

On Tilghman Island, we admired the Tilghman Island tote bags at an eclectic store called **So Neat Card & Gift Shop**. It's an adjunct to the **So Neat Café & Bakery,** where you can get continental breakfast and good sandwiches. Open on weekends only is the **Book Bank,** a nautical bookstore in an old red brick bank on Tilghman Island. The owners, who also run Crawfords Nautical Books in Arlington and have a summer home on Tilghman, take a busman's holiday here and display more than 12,000 "watery books" of all types.

Where to Eat _____ _Ʌↄↄↄↄↄↄↄↄↄↄↄↄↄↄↄↄↄↄↄↄↄↄↄↄ_

On or Near the Water

Sherwood Landing, Watkins Lane, St. Michaels.

A more stylish waterfront restaurant than this at the Inn at Perry Cabin would be hard to imagine. The serene, peak-ceilinged dining room in two sections bears a sleek, nautical look. Expansive windows and french doors in one section look out onto a terrace and treed lawns leading to Fogg Cove. Chef Mark Salter offers a contemporary à la carte menu, and a tasting menu is available for the entire table at $85 each. Three kinds of complimentary canapés – one with boursin cheese and another of salmon – whetted our taste buds for treats to come. So did the signature crab spring roll with pink grapefruit, avocado and toasted almonds. Proper fish service was provided for the main courses. One of us enjoyed fillet of grouper with a pineapple and mint quinoa cake, mango chutney and pappadams. The other sampled John Dory with wild rice, shiitake mushrooms and bok choy. Presentation was in the architectural style, beautiful but small portions. A selection of four sorbets (mango, pineapple, apricot and espresso, topped with chocolate curls in a silver bowl) was a refreshing ending to a memorable meal. High-rollers enjoy à la carte luncheon fare at hefty prices – the angus burger with blue cheese and coleslaw is among the cheapest items at $15.50.

(410) 745-2200. Entrées, $32 to $38. Lunch daily, 11:30 to 2 or 2:30. Dinner nightly, from 5:30.

Town Dock Restaurant, 125 Mulberry St., St. Michaels.

The waterfront setting at this huge establishment is one of the town's best. The food measures up since it was purchased by Michael Rork, formerly executive chef at Baltimore's posh Harbor Court Hotel. The restaurant tiptoes down in tiers via a two-level, glass-enclosed patio and a two-level outside deck beside the harbor. We were impressed with a summer lunch on the outside deck. Cups of crab bisque and saffron bouillabaisse preceded the main events, crab monterey and a fried oyster sandwich with brabant potatoes and homemade coleslaw. All proved exceptional, bursting with assertive tastes. The two big chocolate-covered strawberries that came with the bill made dessert redundant. Daily specials supplement the extensive dinner menu. Typical are grilled salmon topped with roasted leeks and peppers, soft-shell crabs with a tomato-herb cream sauce and grilled duck breast with dried cherries and currants. These are standouts on a seafood-oriented menu ranging from fried shrimp and oysters to lump crab cakes and bouillabaisse.

(410) 745-5577 or (800) 884-0103. www.town-dock.com. Entrées, $18.95 to $26.95. Lunch daily, 11:30 to 4. Dinner, 4 to 9. Closed Tuesday and Wednesday, November-March.

The Bridge Restaurant, 6136 Tilghman Island Road, Tilghman Island.

Taking its name from the adjacent drawbridge over Knapps Narrows (said to be the busiest in the world), this attractive restaurant on two levels has some great water views, especially from the expanded outside deck and from four tables in the upstairs crow's nest with glass on all sides. The Bridge has had a merry-go-round of owners, names and themes, but new chef-owner David Clarke seems to have found a niche. His fare roams the world, from Maryland crab cakes, crab imperial and deep-fried oysters to a seafood dish from Thailand, chicken marsala, duck à l'orange, wiener schnitzel, steak au poivre and New Zealand rack of lamb. The fish of the day is offered in California, South Carolina or cajun styles, and the vegetarian entrée is from Sri Lanka. We liked the deep-fried oyster dinner, served with garlic fries and coleslaw, and the flounder stuffed with crab imperial. You could start with cream of crab soup, escargots bourguignonne or oysters rockefeller. Finish as we did with alexander crème brûlée topped with ice cream, bananas foster or the specialty key lime cheesecake. There's some interesting cooking going on, nicely served up in unpretentious surroundings.

(410) 886-2330. www.bridge-restaurant.com. Entrées, $14 to $24.50. Lunch daily, noon to 3 or 3:30. Dinner, 5 to 10.

The Tilghman Island Inn, Coopertown Road, Tilghman Island.

A watery setting and new American cuisine draw folks to this convivial establishment, where an outdoor deck beckons in warm weather and a pianist plays for singalongs in the lounge on weekends. Innkeepers Jack Redmon, the host, and David McCallum, the chef, offer a pleasant, white-linened Gallery dining room done up in rose and green, with works by local artists on the bleached barnwood walls. There's a good view of boats and, around the corner and beyond the jaunty outdoor deck and patio bar, a glimpse of the Chesapeake Bay. At one dinner, we started with zesty blackeyed pea cakes served with salsa and a crab bisque so thick that a spoon could stand vertical in it. The crab imperial and the grilled soft-shell crabs were excellent. Another time we were smitten by the roasted salmon with wilted greens and the oysters Choptank, teamed with julienned ham and spinach in puff pastry. Gourmet magazine has featured the oysters Choptank as well as other recipes from David's repertoire. Homemade ginger-pear ice cream and cantaloupe sorbet were refreshing endings. We couldn't resist joining in a few songs at the piano bar before departing.

(410) 886-2141 or (800) 866-2141. Entrées, $19 to $32.50. Lunch daily except Wednesday in season, noon to 4; dinner nightly except Wednesday, 6 to 9 or 10. Sunday, brunch noon to 4, dinner 6 to 9. Closed Tuesday in winter and month of January.

Harbour Lights, 101 North Harbor Road, St. Michaels.

A commanding water view is offered from the contemporary dining room on the second floor of the St. Michaels Harbour Inn and Marina. The nicely angled room is decked out in cream tablecloths and blond wood chairs. Part is beneath billowing fabric and part beneath a pressed tin ceiling, but both areas command a good view across the harbor. Typical entrées are cashew-crusted red snapper topped with a roasted corn salsa, diver scallops with celeriac puree and honey-lacquered duck with a tart cranberry relish. Baked prosciutto-wrapped quail, pepper-seared tuna carpaccio and a garlicky cheese and artichoke crab dip with focaccia are favorite starters. Desserts include strawberry tartlets with crème anglaise and bourbon pecan pie. A good wine list offers many by the glass as well as pre-selected small samplings called flights, or you can create your own flights. Also available are specialty martinis, microbrews and espresso. Lighter fare is available from morning to night in **Pascal's Tavern** and its new poolside grill.

(410) 745-5102. Entrées, $18.95 to $31.95. Lunch daily, noon to 4. Dinner, 5:30 to 10. Closed Monday and Tuesday in winter.

The Crab Claw, Navy Point, St. Michaels.

The first tourist attraction in St. Michaels, this self-styled "tradition" has been operated very successfully since 1965 by Bill and Sylvia Jones, whose daughter Tracy says "we feel responsible for the development of St. Michaels." Certainly they are responsible for feeding hundreds of diners at all hours (except at 9:30 one slow September weeknight when we tried to get in and were told the kitchen had just closed). The knotty pine main room looking onto the harbor has open windows to let in the breeze, a vaulted ceiling crossed by a mishmash of beams, large tables where you sit family style, a bare floor and mallets for cracking crabs. There's more dining in a back room, and in summer you can eat by the water at picnic tables and a raw bar, watching the staff steam crabs and shuck oysters. The menu is all seafood, except for hamburgers and fried chicken. The placemat tells you how to tackle your crab. Fried hard blue crab is the house specialty, but crab also is served in soup, cocktail, salad, quiche, backfin crab cake, soft crab sandwich, crab dip, imperial and even a crab dog. There are platters from crab cakes and soft-shell crabs to mixed seafood. The seafood is fresh and priced right, and the atmosphere casual and fun.

(410) 745-2900. Entrées, $14.95 to $24.95. Open daily, 11 to 10 (most of the time). Closed mid-December to March. No credit cards.

St. Michaels Crab & Steak House, 305 Mulberry St., St. Michaels.

There's a dark and pubby interior, but the picnic tables on the dock offer water-lovers the seats of choice at this casual restaurant at the St. Michaels Marina. The building dates to the 1830s when it was one of the town's earliest oyster shucking sheds. Today its waterfront dining room and tavern dispense a touristy menu of the usual suspects, from a crab benedict sandwich to steamed crabs to oysters imperial. You'll likely find soft-shell crabs, fried oysters, chicken Maryland (with crab imperial), fried flounder and baby back ribs. Chef-owner Eric Rosen added the strip steaks, porterhouse and filet mignon that helps the place live up to the other half of its name.

(410) 745-3737. www.st.michaelscrabhouse.com. Entrées, $12.95 to $24.95. Lunch and dinner from 11:30, daily in summer, Friday-Monday in winter.

The Masthead at Pier Street, 104 West Pier St., Oxford.

Ruined in the 2003 hurricane, the old restaurant at the Pier Street Marina was rebuilt and reopened in 2004 as The Masthead, successor to a departed restaurant of that name on Mill Street. The owners are Wendy Palmer and Gretchen Gordon, who continued to run Latitude 38 (see below) in the meantime. Their newest hit offers 85 seats inside and out, right on the concrete bulkhead beside the wide Tred Avon River. Beautiful sunsets and spectacular views vie for top billing with "the best crab cakes in the world – James Michener never had one of ours," a reference to the late author's oft-quoted praise for another local restaurant's version. Besides the crab cakes, steamed crabs and sautéed soft-shell crabs are the specialty, as they were at the original Masthead. Look also for grilled rockfish, blackened yellowfin tuna, shellfish stew and slow-roasted prime rib. Start with cream of crab soup, corn and crab fritters with a zesty mango-chipotle sauce or crispy fried calamari with a sweet and spicy Thai dipping sauce. Finish with the signature Masthead derby pie or a chocolate-chip cookie ice cream sandwich.

(410) 226-5171. www.themastheadatpierstreet.com. Entrees, $18 to $27. Lunch daily, from 11:30. Dinner nightly, from 5. Closed in winter.

Other Choices

208 Talbot, 208 North Talbot St., St. Michaels.

From a culinary standpoint, this has been the area's hottest, best regarded restaurant since it opened in 1990. Culinary Institute-trained chef Paul Milne and partner Candace Chiaruttini present what she calls casual gourmet dining. A delightful lounge with a marble bar leads into a serene main dining room and three smaller rooms. The contemporary menu changes frequently to incorporate the freshest ingredients and newest ideas. Dinner is prix-fixe four courses on Saturdays and à la carte the rest of the week. Among dinner entrées might be pan-seared rockfish with wild mushrooms, crispy soft-shell crabs with green tomato butter, grilled ribeye steak with homemade worcestershire sauce and a signature New Zealand rack of lamb with roasted garlic and rosemary sauce. Start with a napoleon of smoked salmon with crispy wontons and wasabi sauce, fried Ipswich clams with oven-dried tomatoes and a brandy-tarragon mayonnaise or baked oysters with prosciutto, pistachio nuts and champagne cream sauce. Candace makes the delectable desserts, perhaps apple spice cake with warm caramel sauce, lemon tart and assorted ice creams.

(410) 745-3838. www.208talbot.com. Entrées, $27 to $30. Prix-fixe Saturday, $55. Dinner, Wednesday-Sunday 5 to 9 or 10.

Bistro St. Michaels, 403 South Talbot St., St. Michaels.

Chef David Stein and his father, a Washington, D.C., lawyer, converted a 125-year-old clapboard house into this urbane restaurant. The ambiance is authentic French bistro on the main floor with a zinc bar, banquettes and marble-top tables, and a semi-enclosed porch alongside with a new seafood raw bar. Upstairs is a more formal dining room with lace-curtained windows and close-together white-clothed tables. The dinner menu is short but sweet. On a chilly autumn evening, one of us made a satisfying dinner of three starters: a zippy borscht, a fancy salad of greens tossed with cheddar, honeyed walnuts, apples and bacon, and grilled butterflied shrimp satays with a sweet chili-orange vinaigrette. The main courses included broiled halibut with a tapenade crust, a choucroute garni, grilled entrecôte with bourbon-cherry sauce and pomme frites, and grilled venison rib chops with cumberland sauce. We were well satisfied with the sautéed red snapper, scallops and shrimp in a fennel, tomato and roasted pepper broth served over orecchiette. David's wife Indra prepares the desserts, including crème brûlée, chocolate mousse with strawberries and streusel-topped apple pie with whipped cream and vanilla sauce.

(410) 745-9111. www.bistrostmichaels.com. Entrées, $24 to $28. Dinner, Thursday-Monday from 5:30.

Latitude 38, 26342 Oxford Road, Oxford.

This highly rated bistro is lovingly run by the owners of The Masthead, a popular restaurant first located on Mill Street, where we had enjoyed a couple of good meals. Relocating here and later reopening The Masthead at Pier Street (see above), Wendy Palmer and Gretchen Gordon oversee two cheery dining rooms with burnt red cane chairs at butcher-block tables, white and green wainscoted walls, fresh flowers, and floral murals here and there. They enlarged the lounge area, which has a large square bar in the middle, and added a bar menu. A rear brick courtyard terrace is popular for outdoor dining in the summer. Executive chef Doug Kirby's fare is ever-changing, with starters like cream of crab soup, a spring roll of shrimp and lobster with julienned vegetables, and alligator fritters on a spicy black bean puree. Served with house or caesar salad, typical main courses are wasabi-encrusted tuna steak on a pool of avocado cream with a cucumber-kiwi salsa, grouper en papilotte with truffle oil and sherry, and pecan-rubbed rack of lamb with a robust dijon demi-glace. Desserts include seasonal pies, espresso mocha cheesecake and white chocolate mousse. Sunday brunch, a local tradition, brings choices from crab benedict to Mediterranean frittata.

(410) 226-5303. www.latitude38.org. Entrées, $20.95 to $25.95. Lunch, Tuesday-Saturday 11:30 to 2:30. Dinner, Tuesday-Sunday 5 to 9:30 or 10. Sunday brunch 11 to 3.

Robert Morris Inn, Morris Street at the Strand, Oxford.

No dining reservations are accepted at this landmark inn with a large and atmospheric restaurant, which advertises to this day that James Michener rated its crab cakes the highest of any restaurant on the Eastern Shore. Lunch in the Tavern is an experience straight from the 18th century, the staff in Colonial costumes amid walls of brick, floors of Vermont slate and the Morris coat of arms above the fireplace. Many like to start with a hot buttered rum or the 1710, a mixture of amber rum and fruit juices in a Colonial glass that you get to keep. A basket of corn muffins (ours happened to crumble all over the table) preceded the crab soup, a house specialty chock full of vegetables, and a paltry dish of three mushrooms stuffed with crab imperial. More filling was a delicious and pure oyster stew. You can order anything from a crab cake sandwich platter to prime rib on the extensive lunch menu, or mix and match appetizers as we did. The dinner menu is even more extensive – from assorted juices to prime rib supreme topped with crabmeat, a combination we wouldn't care to order. As you'd expect, crab is the specialty, although so are fried oysters and baked seafood "au gratin" cakes. Desserts run from cheesecake to assorted parfaits. The formal, carpeted and chandeliered dining room has well-spaced tables, stenciled chairs and impressive murals.

(410) 226-5111. Entrées, $18 to $36. Breakfast, 8 to 10. Lunch, noon to 3. Dinner, 5:30 to 8:30. Closed December-March.

FOR MORE INFORMATION: Talbot County Office of Tourism/Welcome Center, 11 South Harrison St., Easton 21601. (410) 770-8000. www.tourtalbot.org.

St. Michaels Business Association, Box 1221, St. Michaels 21663. (410) 745-0411 or (800) 808-7622. www.stmichaelsmd.org.

Oxford Business Association, Box 544, Oxford 21654. (410) 226-5730. www.portofoxford.com.

Downtown skyline is backdrop for water activity in Baltimore Harbor.

Baltimore Harbor, Md.

"Harbor of History," it's called by the operators of excursion boats that ply thousands of visitors daily along the Baltimore waterfront in a variety of craft. They might also call it a harbor of fun. Baltimore's transformed harbor has an abundance of both.

For history, consider that the guardian of the harbor, old Fort McHenry, is where Baltimore turned back the British in the War of 1812. The course of American history might have been altered, had the city not withstood the challenge, And Francis Scott Key's "Star Spangled Banner," written as he watched the bombardment by dawn's early light, might not have become the national anthem. The past lives on across the harbor from Fort McHenry in Fells Point, still a working urban seaport community.

Baltimore's harbor area is making history today. Little more two decades ago, it was a wasteland of rotting piers, factories, warehouses and railroad yards, and the city in general was the butt of jokes around the country. Today, the restored Inner Harbor – the horseshoe-shaped land area around which the Patapsco River flows from downtown out toward the Chesapeake Bay – is alive with new buildings, boats and people in a rejuvenation that has had Baltimore starring on the covers of national magazines.

The early focus was hometown developer James W. Rouse's Harborplace, the twin pavilions of shops and restaurants that opened in 1980. That sparked the renewal of both harborfront and downtown in a joint public-private revitalization effort considered the best in the nation. On either side of Harborplace are the Maryland Science Center, the National Aquarium, the Power Plant entertainment center, the Pier 6 Concert Pavilion and new visitor attractions.

Twenty-five years later, Baltimore's second renaissance is spreading around the harbor. It's centered around Inner Harbor East and, across the harbor, at Locust Point. Pedestrian skywalks and promenades link the harbor with a dozen new and renovated hotels, a vast convention center, the Oriole Park at Camden Yards baseball and the M&T Bank football stadiums and an incredible number of museums, including Port Discovery and the American Visionary Art Museum.

No wonder Baltimore Harbor now attracts more visitors each year than Disney World.

They come to be near the water, of course, and to enjoy a bit of history, in the past and in the making. They also come to have fun.

Rarely do you find so many things to see and do – most of them fun-oriented – in such a compact area by the water.

Getting There

Baltimore is a major transportation center well served by airlines and trains. Interstate 95 passes under the harbor via the Fort McHenry Tunnel. Also serving the city are Interstate 83 from the north and Interstate 70 from the west. Well-marked exits lead to downtown, where unusually good (and numerous) signs steer you to the Inner Harbor and other points of interest.

Where to Stay

For a city that had only a few hotels 25 years ago, Baltimore now has an abundance. More than 5,000 hotel rooms have been added around the Inner Harbor. You can get around to Inner Harbor attractions by walking the promenades and pedestrian skywalk system, taking a water taxi (see below) or the seasonal Baltimore trolley.

Hotels

Baltimore Marriott Waterfront Hotel, 700 Aliceanna St., Baltimore 21202.

This new 32-story hotel – billed as the only one fully on the waterfront, which must mean the closest – is part of a $500 million redevelopment of a once-gritty industrial area called Inner Harbor East. It now links the downtown Inner Harbor area with two gentrifying waterfront neighborhoods, Fells Point and Canton. Guests arrive under a porte-cochere about 60 feet from the edge of the water and enter a vaulted lobby. The outside of the glass and gray building is undistinguished from an architectural standpoint, but the elegant, neoclassical interior is something else. All 750 rooms have water views, through extra-tall windows. Rooms come with kingsize or two double beds covered with comforters or duvets and dust ruffles. The ultimate are penthouse luxury suites with views in all directions. Amenities include an indoor pool and exercise facility. The hotel's main-floor restaurant, **Grille 700,** has an angular display kitchen running the length of the room and features wood-fired Chesapeake Bay specialties. Its side glimpses of the water are surpassed by the head-on views of **Kozmo's,** a clubby waterfront lounge with water on two sides and an umbrellaed patio for outside dining. In the hotel's adjacent parking garage are two restaurants under separate ownership, **Fleming's Prime Steakhouse and Wine Bar** and **Roy's,** featuring Hawaiian fusion cuisine.

(410) 385-3000. Fax (410) 385-0330. Seven hundred twenty-eight rooms and 22 suites. Doubles, $274 to $319. Suites, $350 to $2,000.

Pier 5 Hotel, 711 Eastern Ave., Baltimore 21202.

Appealing looking in red brick with a peaked roof, this low-rise boutique hotel is surrounded by water on three sides. It's a bit removed from the Inner Harbor action, though linked to it by water taxi, and the action is edging this way. Part of the local Harbor Magic lodging group, the Pier 5 has decided assets: easy access to the water from the landscaped grounds, outdoor seating areas by the water, a trademark Chesapeake Bay lighthouse at the end of the pier and three good restaurants. The tiled, three-story atrium lobby is quite stunning. Custom European-designed guest rooms and suites with oversize bathrooms come with one king or two queen beds. Each room is equipped with two telephones (including two lines) and a safe. The

Presidential Suite has a wraparound harbor view, whirlpool tub and complete entertainment center. About one-third of the rooms overlook the water but, alas, only a few on the second floor have balconies for really enjoying the view. Rooms on the third floor compensate with cathedral ceilings. The glass-walled waterfront restaurant at the rear of the hotel is run by the **McCormick & Schmick's** seafood chain based in the Pacific Northwest (see Where to Eat). The front corners of the hotel hold the all-day **Peacock Café,** an offshoot of a Georgetown establishment, and the dinner-only **EurAsian Harbor,** a pan-Asian bistro.

(410) 539-2000 or (866) 583-4162. Fax (410) 783-1469. www.thepier5.com. Sixty-five rooms and suites. Doubles, $169 to $349.

Harbor Court Hotel, 550 Light St., Baltimore 21202.

Opulent, personalized, an exclusive retreat – all characterize this elegant, European-style hotel that debuted in 1986 as Baltimore's version of the Ritz. The Harbor Court's understated six-story brick facade fronts onto the Inner Harbor opposite the Maryland Science Center, beneath a towering condominium complex of which it is a part. About half the guest rooms, including 25 suites and "staterooms," yield harbor views. Each is a study in luxury with custom-designed furnishings and such amenities as oversized desks, bathrooms with large tubs and television sets, separate makeup areas and bathrobes for guests. The eighth-story penthouse suite contains two bedrooms, a wood-burning fireplace, grand piano, wet bar and whirlpool tub, and rents for up to $1,500 a night. Meals are served with a harbor view in the cheery, aptly named **Brighton's Café** or the sumptuous **Hampton's,** considered by some the city's best dining room (see Where to Eat). Guests work out in a large rooftop health club with an indoor pool. They gather around the busy concierge in the library off the lobby, full of rare books from across the world, or in the **Explorer's Lounge,** colorful with hand-painted African scenes and exotic objets d'art.

(410) 234-0550 or (800) 824-0076. Fax (410) 659-5925. www.harborcourt.com. One hundred seventy-three rooms and 22 suites. Doubles, $215 to $385. Suites, $410 to $800.

Hyatt Regency Baltimore, 300 Light St., Baltimore 21202.

Opened in 1981 shortly after Harborplace, which is just across the street, the glitzy Hyatt with its trademark six-story atrium and outdoor glass elevators was the forerunner of the city's hotel boom. Located fully in the thick of things, the hotel offers an action-packed view – if you're lucky enough to snag one of the booked-far-in-advance harbor-view rooms. Each is spacious and furnished in typical Hyatt style. The outdoor swimming pool and three tennis courts atop a roof over the fifth floor are surprisingly popular, given all the attractions around and on the harbor. The lobby is a beehive of activity (especially on the Friday when we arrived to a noisy happy hour with orchestra and a multitude of partakers). Hotel guests get to admire the harbor every time they go up or down the glass elevators; transients have to be satisfied with the view from the fifteenth-floor restaurant and lounge, **Pisces,** where every table in a two-level dining room looks onto the harbor.

(410) 528-1234 or (800) 532-1496. Fax (410) 685-3362. www.baltimore.hyatt.com. Four hundred sixty-one rooms and 25 suites. Doubles, $139 to $279.

Renaissance Harborplace Hotel, 202 East Pratt St., Baltimore 21202.

The most central location to Baltimore's waterfront venues is claimed by this deluxe hotel that opened in 1988. All the action is just across the street, which may explain its appeal to the surprising number of young families the weekend we were there. The hotel has 622 rooms and suites on floors 6 to 12 above the Gallery at Harborplace. Most in demand are those (about one-fourth) facing the harbor head-on. Our room, a seemingly endless trek from the elevators, compensated with a fabulous harbor view. It came with a kingsize bed, a table desk with two side chairs and an oversize club chair and ottoman facing the entertainment center, whose TV's audio was piped into the bathroom. The hotel has an indoor pool and a health club with whirlpool and sauna. It offers direct access to the 75 high-style Gallery shops and restaurants, as well as its own fifth-floor lounge and restaurant – appropriately called **Windows.** The lounge is blessed with a harbor view, while most of the gray and cream-colored dining room settles for a look at Light Street from several levels. Prime rib is the signature item on the dinner menu.

(410) 547-1200 or (800) 535-1201. Fax (410) 539-5780. Five hundred eighty-six rooms and 36 suites. Doubles, $219 to $259.

Brookshire Suites, 120 East Lombard St., Baltimore 21202.

Part of the local Harbor Magic group, this renovated fourteen-story hotel fashioned from a parking garage is especially good for families or those who, like us, want room to spread out. Although close to the harbor, do not expect a view – the view from ours, and most others, was blocked by buildings across the street. But the suite was spacious, containing a comfy living room, a kitchenette with coffee supplied, an ample bedroom with kingsize bed, a marble bathroom, two telephones, two TVs, and a complimentary morning paper. Business people like the exercise room. A breakfast buffet is offered in the rooftop Cloud Club with a harbor view.

(410) 625-1300 or (866) 583-4162. Fax (410) 625-0912. www.brookshiresuites.com. Twenty-seven rooms and 70 suites. Doubles, $149 to $199.

Inns and B&Bs

Admiral Fell Inn, 888 South Broadway, Baltimore 21231.

Across the street from the working harbor, this is one of the earliest and nicest city inns we've seen. It's located a bit off most tourists' path in historic Fells Point, and was in the vanguard as a charter member of Historic Hotels of America, a program of the National Trust for Historic Preservation. The first three buildings were carefully restored in 1985 into a 38-room inn. An expansion a decade later more than doubled its size. The inn now flows seamlessly into five more buildings and includes a rooftop ballroom, meeting center and balcony with 360-degree views of the harbor and city. The brick exterior of the complex gives little indication of its past dating to 1790 as, variously, a seamen's hostel, the home of a Baltimore mayor, a vinegar bottling plant, a dance hall and a house of ill repute. Inside, all is quite elegant, from the fireplaced drawing room where you check in to the comfortable library to the **Admiral's Lounge & Raw Bar.** Fourteen guest rooms and suites yield views of the harbor, and a few have jacuzzi tubs. A two-story suite features a fireplace and a jacuzzi. Most rooms have rice-carved or pencil-point canopied beds, Federal period antiques or reproductions, and TVs hidden in armoires. Each room is different in size and shape, and you'll be struck by the various color schemes as well as the winding corridors through which you reach them. Those in the front rooms facing Broadway may be kept awake into the wee hours, as we were, by nighttime revelers; the inn's location puts it in the thick of the action on summer weekends. Continental breakfast is complimentary. Guests enjoy shuttle transportation around the Inner Harbor. The inn lately became part of the local Harbor Magic group, which also owns the Pier 5 Hotel and Brookshire Suites. After being closed for several years, the inn's stone-walled restaurant reopened in late 2004 as **True,** "a pure dining experience." Stressing natural ingredients from area purveyors, its opening menu offered a dozen regional American dinner items ranging from Chesapeake Bay rock fish topped with raspberry-chipotle glaze to Amish farm-raised duck breast and confit over lentils.

(410) 522-7377 or (866) 583-4162. Fax (410) 522-0707. www.admiralfell.com. Eighty rooms and suites with private baths. Doubles, $199 to $249.
Entrées, $19 to $32. Dinner, Tuesday-Saturday 5 to 10.

The Inn at Henderson's Wharf, 1000 Fell St., Baltimore 21231.

Part of a six-story brick condominium complex and a marina on a wharf, this nicely secluded B&B inn could not be closer to the water. At least that's true of those rooms that face the harbor at eye-level – more than half face a city street or what the advertising touts as an English country garden courtyard. The inn occupies the point of land that gave Fells Point its name. All rooms are on the ground floor and have large windows screened by shuttered blinds from view of passersby on the boardwalk promenade, the inner courtyard or the street. Those we saw contained two queensize featherbeds with Cuddledown pillows from Maine, Bose radios, plasma TV, a desk and an armchair. The hotel-style lobby appeared rather austere, showing vestiges of the restored building's heritage as a late 19th-century tobacco warehouse (cargoes were shipped from Southern plantations by rail down Fell Street, stored here and then loaded onto ships for export overseas). The upper floors of the gated National Register landmark building have been converted into luxury residences. A complimentary breakfast includes seasonal fruit, French pastries, yogurts and cheeses. A water shuttle takes guests to the Inner Harbor.

(410) 522-7777 or (800) 522-2088. Fax (410) 522-7087. www.hendersonswharf.com. Thirty-eight rooms with private baths. Doubles, $149 to $259.

Celie's Waterfront Bed & Breakfast, 1714 Thames St., Baltimore 21231.

Here is one smashing B&B, taking full advantage of its Fells Point location but well hidden from public view. Only a small sign and a locked gate mark the entry to a long, mysterious-looking corridor that appears European and leads into the spacious home acquired in 2003 by Kevin and Nancy Kupec, who live around the corner. Newly built from the ground up by Celie Ives for an opening on Valentine's Day in 1990, the romantic and luxurious place is long and narrow in the Baltimore rowhouse tradition. It offers seven guest rooms on three floors, a rear brick terrace and garden oasis, a private courtyard and an atrium, balconies, and a fourth-floor rooftop deck with seating all around for enjoying the view of the harbor and city. All rooms have updated baths (four with whirlpool tubs), telephones, satellite TV and king or queensize beds. Two have fireplaces and balconies. They are lavishly furnished and bear such touches as interesting art, terrycloth robes and duvet comforters. Two new suites with kitchens sleep four to six. A hearty continental breakfast is put out in the morning in the downstairs dining room. Guests can enjoy it there or take it to their rooms, balcony, rear garden or rooftop deck.

(410) 522-2323 or (800) 432-0184. www.celieswaterfront.com. Seven rooms and two suites with private baths. Doubles, $129 to $349.

Scarborough Fair B&B, 1 East Montgomery St., Baltimore 21230.

Two blocks from the Inner Harbor, this Georgian-style brick building dating to

1801 is at the entrance to historic Federal Hill, on a corner facing both busy Charles and residential Montgomery streets. Its gabled and dormered roof and bricks laid in Flemish bond indicate that it is one of the oldest structures in the neighborhood. Ashley and Ellen Scarborough offer six air-conditioned guest rooms, each decorated simply but stylishly to the period. Five have queen beds and one has twins. Four rooms have working fireplaces and two have double whirlpool tubs. The private baths for two of the rooms are across the hall. The Scarboroughs offer sweets and complimentary beverages in the afternoon. A hearty breakfast is served in a cheerful blue and yellow dining room. Free parking and a location convenient for walking are among the assets.

(410) 837-0010. www.scarborough-fair.com. Six rooms with private baths. Doubles, $149 to $189.

Seeing and Doing

Baltimore's Inner Harbor is "a masterpiece of planning and execution," in the words of the American Institute of Architects, which honored it as "one of the supreme achievements of large-scale design and development in U.S. history." That development continued with a second renaissance early in the 21st century. One definitely senses that this is a happening place, exciting for young and old.

Here is one urban destination where you can abandon your car for the duration of your visit. Follow the emerging, 7.5-mile Waterfront Promenade, nicely landscaped and with benches for resting. And, as the sign says, "discover great neighborhoods, old and new architecture, galleries, food and drink, marine life, parks, museums, shops and other shoreline attractions." Or take one of the ubiquitous water taxis that make getting around the harbor easy – and great fun.

On the Harbor

The Inner Harbor is a continuing and colorful pageant of excursion boats, shuttles, sailboats, yachts and paddleboats, many available for hire. The choices are legion:

Ed Kane's Water Taxis, 1615 Thames St.
One of the easiest, most enjoyable ways to get around the Inner Harbor is by water taxi, in this case open pontoon boats run by Harbor Boating Inc. They're used both for sightseeing and shuttle service between Harborplace, the Maryland Science Center, the National Aquarium, Pier 5, Little Italy, Fells Point, the Canton Waterfront Park, Fort McHenry, Locust Point and Federal Hill. Now with fourteen blue and white vessels of different sizes, local celebrity Ed Kane's 30-year-old enterprise gives access to more than 35 attractions from fifteen landings. Included in the ticket price, good for unlimited trips all day, is the seasonal downtown trolley. There's also a "frequent floater" annual pass for $45.

(410) 563-3901 or (800) 658-8947. www.thewatertaxi.com. Taxis run roughly every fifteen to twenty minutes, daily May to Labor Day, 10 a.m. to 11 p.m., Friday and Saturday to midnight, Sunday to 9; April and September-October, weekdays 10 to 8, weekends to midnight; November-March, daily 11 to 6, weather permitting. Unlimited use all day: adults $6, children $3.

Seaport Taxis, National Historic Seaport, Pier 5.
The collective of attractions known as the National Historic Seaport operates the newer Seaport Taxis, green and beige covered pontoon boats serving sixteen stops around the harbor. Their landing points are close to but different from those of the

more established water taxis, so the visitor interested in a specific stop should first check each service's map.

(410) 675-2900. Taxis run daily, May-August 10 a.m. to 10 p.m., Friday and Saturday to midnight, Sunday 10 to 9; rest of year, Monday-Thursday 11 to 8, Friday 11 to 10, Saturday 10 to 10, Sunday 10 to 6. Unlimited use all day: adults $6, children under 10, $3.

Harbor Cruises, 301 Light St.

Since 1981, this outfit has been running excursions around the Inner Harbor, starting with lunch and dinner cruises on the Bay Lady and the Lady Baltimore and, most recently, offering sightseeing cruises. The new, 250-passenger **Prince Charming** boat gives 60-minute narrated tours of the harbor. The trips are informative and, on a hot day, refreshingly cooling. You see the old Procter & Gamble plant where Ivory Soap bars were produced (now undergoing conversion into a high-tech business center), a freighter "offloading" into the Domino sugar plant, the six-sided island Fort Carroll and the Francis Scott Key Bridge. Beyond is the Dundalk Marine Terminal, where the Queen Elizabeth II sometimes docks and giant cranes lift massive tractor-trailer boxes in two minutes. You pass Fells Point, Federal Hill and Fort McHenry, countless marinas where slips may be priced at $15,000 and up, condo developments and the towering HarborView Condominiums and Apartments, home of major-league athletes and team owners. There's lots of activity and we never knew an industrial-city port could be so fascinating.

The Bay Lady and the **Lady Baltimore,** 500-passenger showboats, offer meal cruises year-round on two enclosed decks and an open-air top deck. Most popular are the dinner cruises, where you enjoy a buffet dinner, live bands and a musical revue, and everyone usually comes back singing and dancing, according to participants.

(410) 727-3113 or (800) 695-2628. Four sightseeing trips daily, 11:30, 1, 2:30 and 4, April-October; adults $10, children $6. Lunch cruises, Monday-Saturday noon to 2, $30. Sunday champagne brunch cruise, noon to 3, $39.95. Dinner cruises, Monday-Saturday 7 to 10, Sunday 5 to 8, $46.50 to $65. Moonlight party cruises with dancing and cash bar are offered summer weekends from 11:30 to 2 a.m., $27.

Baltimore Ride the Ducks, Light Street south of Harborplace.

World War II amphibious vehicles that transported troops and supplies from ship to shore now transport whistle-quacking sightseers on 80-minute fun tours on land and water around the Inner Harbor. Most of the expedition is by land, but from a hidden landing near Fells Point what resembles a tank on wheels plummets into the water and becomes a boat for a short cruise around the harbor. Passengers quack on yellow duckbill-shaped noisemakers at passersby, laugh (mostly) at the captain's jokes and thoroughly enjoy an up-close look at Baltimore's major attractions. The ride provides a good orientation for first-time visitors.

(410) 727-3825. www.baltimoreducks.com. Trips depart frequently on demand, daily April-October. Adults $24, children $14.

Paddle Boats, opposite Pratt Street Pavilion, Harborplace. Many of those colorful little boats that one sees bobbing around the inner harbor are pedaled by their occupants, and they say it's hard work. But they're obviously popular, with waiting lines on busy weekends for the 80 available boats. Half-hour rentals are $7 for one, $8 for two passengers and $10 for four.

Trident Electric Boat Rentals, opposite Pratt Street Pavilion. Lazier types enjoy the electric-powered two-seaters, which rent for $12 per half hour ($18 for three-seaters), plus $1.50 for every five minutes overtime. Posted rules are strict; most important is one that says, "Never go left of the aquarium," out into the busy river. The larger vessels have a difficult enough time dodging all the boats.

Clipper City, Light Street near Maryland Science Center, (410) 539-6277. Baltimore's Tall Ship, billed as the largest in America licensed to carry passengers, gives two-hour sailing excursions from mid-April to mid-October. The two-hour sails depart Monday-Friday at 2 and 6, Saturday at noon and 3, and Sunday at noon, 3 and 6; adults $12, children $4. Three-hour party sails with live Caribbean bands depart Friday and Saturday at 8 (adults, $20). A three-hour sail and champagne brunch is offered Sunday at 11 (adults, $30).

Skipjack Minnie V, Harborplace Amphitheater, (410) 685-9062. The 24-passenger skipjack, part of America's last fleet of oyster boats on Chesapeake Bay, catches oysters in the winter and harbor sightseers in summer. Ninety-minute narrated tours around the harbor focus on the history of skipjacks and oystering. Tours May-September, Saturday, Sunday and holidays at 10:30, 1, 3 and 5. Adults $16, children $4.

Around the Harbor

Harborplace, Pratt & Light Streets. The James Rouse-designed marketplace put the Inner Harbor on the map when it opened in 1980. Patterned after Rouse's Faneuil Hall Marketplace in Boston and precursor of his South Street Seaport in New York, this in one way is better than the others since it takes full advantage of its waterside location – especially its restaurants, many with outdoor cafés. Harborplace consists of two glass-enclosed, two-story pavilions linked by a promenade along the harbor and a four-story Gallery across Pratt Street. Most of the 55 restaurants and specialty eating places, gourmet markets and the mammoth Food Hall are located in the Light Street Pavilion. The Pratt Street Pavilion is a mix of eateries and retail shops, where you shouldn't be surprised to find the California Pizza Kitchen across from the Yankee Candle Co. The predictable upscale national clothing stores are located in the Gallery. Outside on an amphitheater between the two pavilions, free performances are given day and night by a variety of entertainers, from jugglers and mimes to Scottish bagpipers and brass bands. A sensational magician and trickster with a witty sense of humor entranced young and old at one visit. Another noontime when we were there, hari krishnas chanted on the grass as a Fuji film blimp floated overhead. Harborplace is at the heart of the harbor and is linked by overhead pedestrian skywalks and promenades with hotels, tourist attractions and the baseball and football stadiums, so it's busy much of the time. Shops are open daily 10 to 9, Sunday 11 to 7. Most restaurants are open daily until 10, midnight or later. A handful of small eateries open at 8 for breakfast, but most open with the shops.

The Power Plant, located just to the east at 601 East Pratt St., claims to be the country's pre-eminent entertainment complex, with waterside dining decks along Pier 4. Featured are the **Hard Rock Café** and the first-ever **ESPN Zone.** When the ESPN sports network and Disney scouted locations for their prototype, they sought a vibrant sports city on the cusp of major growth. Baltimore qualified, and the resulting Zone is equal parts restaurant, sports bar and interactive game room. A recent attraction is a multi-media, multi-sensory cross between theater and amusement park ride called **Passport Voyages.** The four-dimensional theater transports riders through history on Time Elevator America and below the seas on an Oceanarium submarine. For some, the Power Plant's most interesting feature is the soaring **Barnes & Noble** bookstore, fitted in and around the infrastructure of the plant that once powered Baltimore's trolley system. Its upstairs café and coffee shop opens onto an outdoor balcony overlooking the water.

Across Pratt Street is **Power Plant Live!** It's billed as Baltimore's one-stop restaurant and entertainment district.

National Aquarium in Baltimore, Piers 3 and 4, 501 East Pratt St.

The crown jewel of the Inner Harbor is the colorful and architecturally striking National Aquarium in Baltimore, described by Time magazine at its opening as the most advanced and most attractive in the world. Although Congress did not contribute to the city-funded project, it did designate it a national aquarium before the first phase was finished in 1981. Such is its appeal, both to generalists and specialists, that every morning people queue up in lines for entry every fifteen minutes. We visited late on a Friday afternoon, entered immediately and had the place fairly much to ourselves, which is the best way to see it.

The aquarium's main seven-level structure is so big that you don't walk around it, you walk around in it. Its two large tanks are rings, and you move via escalators and moving sidewalks through the hole in the middle of the rings as fish swim in circles around you. Start at Wings in the Water, where dozens of stingrays glide around among sea turtles and small sharks in a circular tank beneath the skeleton of a giant humpback whale. As the recorded glug-glug, squeak and grunt sounds of surf, sea creatures and birds are heard, you wend your way upward through an unusually enlightening mix of descriptions and live displays: the Tidal Marsh, where two fast-moving crabs prance in front of a sign, "No Crabbing or Fishing;" an informative eight-minute slide show called "The Bay at Risk," after which you may want to join the effort to save the Chesapeake; the playful puffins on the North Atlantic sea cliffs, imported from Iceland, and the busy Pacific Reef, populated by colorful fish that you'll try to identify from their pictures above the tank. Next comes a 57-foot stretch of riverbank in the Amazon River Forest. When it's not curled up in a coil, a 16-foot-long green anaconda snake may steal the show as it forages for food amid oblivious piranhas and dwarf caimans, turtles and fish.

The open tropical rain forest at the top, enclosed in the 64-foot pyramid of glass that is the structure's most striking architectural feature, provides a jungle refuge for free-roaming birds, reptiles and amphibians. You're apt to come face to face with a friendly parrot in a ficus tree or be joined by a golden ringed trumpeter hopping onto your platform. On the way back down past the 335,000-gallon Atlantic Coral Reef that's among the nation's largest, you'll enjoy a circular parade of fish swimming both ways. One turned and seemed to wink at us, as spotted eagle ray, silver tarpon and shark teams played follow the leader. You may even see a scuba diver floating amid the fish, handing out dinner. You finish nose-to-nose with sharks at the bottom. All told, the 115,000-square-foot building holds more than 10,500 marine and freshwater creatures representing more than 560 species.

An enclosed skywalk leads to the aquarium's 94,000-square-foot **Marine Mammal Pavilion** in a companion building on Pier 4, connected to the existing building by an enclosed skywalk. Visitors examine the life and lore of marine mammals through inter-active exhibits, videos, graphics and innovative technology found nowhere else on the East Coast. Dolphins perform daily in the pavilion's 1,300-seat amphitheater, which surrounds a 1.2-million-gallon pool.

A major expansion in 2005 produced a shimmering crystal pavilion featuring rare Australian fish and wildlife and transformed the existing Pier 3 plaza into a natural waterfront park.

(410) 576-3800. www.aqua.org. Entry times: July-August, 9 to 6 Sunday-Thursday, to 8 Friday and Saturday; March-June and September-October, daily 9 to 5, Friday to 8; November-February, daily 10 to 5, Friday to 8. Building open for 90 minutes after last ticket sale. Adults $17.50, children $9.50.

Maryland Science Center, 601 Light St.

The first major attraction at the Inner Harbor, the science center with three floors of live exhibits and hands-on displays has been growing in stature and doubled in size in 2004. Go on a Saturday morning and you'll think all the kids age 10 and under in Baltimore (and their parents) are there, playing games with computers, learning about energy, gawking at dinosaurs, watching gerbils and the like. The National Visitors' Center for the Hubble Space Telescope allows visitors to see farther into the depths of space than ever before. The hands-on exhibit explores distant galaxies as well as our own solar system. The five-story, 400-seat **IMAX Theater** shows a couple of changing films daily on its 50-by-75-foot screen. Hundreds of images and special effects mix with 8,500 stars in a variety of shows in the acclaimed **Davis Planetarium**. All the planetarium shows are original, created at the center and distributed world wide to other facilities. The latest expansion produced a new gallery for permanent exhibits and a soaring Dinosaur Hall revealing a dozen full-size dinosaurs from above and below, plus hands-on fossil exhibits. There are films and demonstrations throughout the day, and the Science Store is great fun for kids.

(410) 685-5225. www.mdsci.org. Open daily Memorial Day to Labor Day, Sunday-Wednesday 10 to 6, Thursday-Saturday 10 to 8; rest of year, Tuesday-Friday 10 to 5, Saturday 10 to 6, Sunday 11 to 5. Adults $14, children $9.50.

Port Discovery, 35 Market Place.

The old Baltimore Fishmarket building has been transformed into the nation's third largest children's museum, the only one designed by Walt Disney Imagineering. Billed as the "Kid-Powered Museum," this has 80,000 square feet of hands-on exhibit space where every kid who's not at the Science Center now hangs out. Youngsters are in their element in the three-story fun house, which their elders may find dizzying. The centerpiece is a three-story high rope maze called Kidworks, through which one crawls and climbs and swings his way to the top. The oddball Miss Perceptions Mystery House is filled with sensory illusions and strange mysteries. The Adventure Expeditions area transports one back to ancient Egypt; you may come face-to-face with slithery cobras and see a mummy or two on your way to the pharaoh's hidden tomb. Imaginations run wild in the R&D Dreamlab, and the MPT Studioworks is a realistic TV studio. The Hi-Flyer, a helium-filled tethered balloon holding 25 passengers in its gondola, soars 450 feet above the museum seasonally. The museum's target age group is 6 to 12. They may be the ones who can best figure out how to work the bar-coded wristbands that you're given at the ticket desk for entry. We could neither find our way nor work the automated gates to get in – and once inside we had a hard time getting out.

(410) 727-8120. www.portdiscovery.org. Open Memorial Day to Labor Day, daily 10 to 5, Sunday noon to 5; rest of year, Tuesday-Friday 9:30 to 4:30, same weekend hours. Adults $11, children $8.50.

American Visionary Art Museum, 800 Key Hwy., Inner Harbor.

This compelling new museum on the waterfront at the foot of Federal Hill celebrates uncelebrated artists – the amateur and the self-taught – from around the country. Seven galleries on three floors hold the whimsical and poignant works of farmers, housewives, retirees, the disabled, the homeless – all inspired by a creative vision within. The theme is set by the towering 55-foot Whirligig sculpture by farmer/mechanic Vollis Simpson in the outdoor plaza linking the original building with the 2004 expansion into the Jim Rouse Visionary Center at the foot of Federal Hill. We're always moved by the exhibits, which change annually. The inaugural Tree of Life exhibition showed 400 remarkable works created from wood and tree products.

Who could not be uplifted by the 2004 exhibits combining Golden Blessings of Old Age and Out of the Mouths of Babes? Best of all was the year-long "Treasures of the Soul – Who is Rich?" exhibition, which featured handmade clothing, furniture, machinery and artwork created by 50 self-taught artists in the depths of isolation and despair. Illustrative were "The Button Lady," a dress covered with tens of thousands of buttons, and another artist's ten intricate cocoons of yarn and fiber up to nine feet tall. The director said it showed the outsider artists' ultimate art of creative self-reliance and their "ability to make something wondrous out of nothing." That exemplifies what this visionary museum is all about.

(410) 244-1900. www.avam.org. Open Tuesday-Sunday 10 to 6. Adults $9, children $6.

National Historic Seaport of Baltimore, Pier 5.

This collective is the sum of its parts, established in 1998 to promote some of the maritime attractions that ring the harbor. The natural, deep-water harbor has attracted ships from around the world since the 1600s, and the city grew up around it. Today, visitors can retrace history on the decks of ships and on the cobbled streets of waterfront neighborhoods like Fells Point, Canton, Federal Hill and Locust Point. The rich heritage exists side by side with an active, modern port. Ocean-going ships come and go, handling cargo from across the world and unloading raw sugar cane for refining at the landmark Domino Sugar plant, whose over-the-top neon sign facing the harbor is the largest on the East Coast (the dot on the "i" is six feet tall on a grid the size of a basketball court). East of the Inner Harbor, busy piers line the waterfront as far as the eye can see. Stunning tall ships and military vessels dock in the harbor under Sail Baltimore's visiting ships program and most welcome visitors for tours. The Seaport day pass includes discounted admission to member attractions like the restored USS Constellation, the historic ships and lighthouse of the Baltimore Maritime Museum, and transportation around the waterfront on the Seaport Taxi.

(410) 783-1490. www.natlthistoricseaport.org. Day pass: adults $15.50, children $8.50.

USS Constellation, Pier 1, 301 East Pratt St., Inner Harbor.

The first commissioned ship of the U.S. Navy, the frigate Constellation was launched from Baltimore in 1797. Its successor, the last-all sail ship built by the Navy in 1864, returned to the city in 1955, where the last Civil War ship afloat – lately restored for $7.5 million and still a work in progress – ended up occupying a starring position at a specially designed pier in the Inner Harbor. Before boarding you receive a hand-held electronic device that provides a personalized audio tour. Go down the old, steep stairs of the 179-foot sailing sloop to three decks below, where you'll marvel at the cannons on the gun deck, peer at the barrels in the cargo hold and view the preserved food served to the sailors, most of whom slept communally in hammocks. "Mind your head," warns a sign on the stairway to the officers' quarters, where you stoop to look into tiny bunkrooms with berths, a chair and a bureau and see period uniforms. The captain's quarters, with a dinner table ready for twenty, is relatively elegant by contrast. You see the carpet that explains the origin of the saying "to be called on the carpet." This vessel sure looks, smells and feels old. Its cannon goes off at noon to cheers in a shot heard 'round the harbor.

(410) 539-1797. www.constellation.org. Open daily, 10 to 5:30 April-October (later in summer), 10 to 4 rest of year. Adults $7.50, children $3.50.

Baltimore Maritime Museum, Piers 3 and 5.

The submarine U.S.S. Torsk, the U.S. Coast Guard cutter Taney and the Lightship Chesapeake, a floating navigational lighthouse, are open for self-guided tours at the end of the pier in what is loosely called the Baltimore Maritime Museum (there being no museum as such). Instead you board the football-field-length World War II sub, known as the Galloping Ghost of the Japanese Coast, and get an idea of what dungeon life beneath the sea was like. The vigilant sub patrolled the Pacific, torpedoing the last Japanese warships and even a train during the war. The Taney is the last ship afloat to have survived the attack on Pearl Harbor. Nearby is the Lightship 116, which served 40 years anchored in coastal waters, mostly off the mouth of the Chesapeake Bay, its beacon lantern atop the mainmast a welcome sight to ships' captains negotiating difficult waters. At the end of Pier 5 you can climb into the squat red Seven-Foot Knoll Lighthouse, built in 1856 and the oldest "screwpile" lighthouse in Maryland. It marked the entrance to Baltimore's harbor for 133 years before being moved to the Inner Harbor behind the Pier 5 Hotel.

(410) 396-3853. www.baltomaritimemuseum.org. Open daily, 10 to 5 or later, depending on attraction and season; January-March, Friday-Sunday 10:30 to 5. Adults $7, children $3.

Frederick Douglass/Isaac Myers Maritime Park, Chase's Wharf, Fells Point.

The first African American-owned shipyard in the country was started by Frederick Douglass, a Renaissance man if ever there was one, and Isaac Myers with fourteen fellow African Americans. The park, scheduled for opening in 2005 along the waterfront promenade between Inner Harbor East and Fells Point, commemorates Baltimore's African-American maritime heritage. It includes a working shipyard/ marine railway and a deep-water pier, monuments to Douglass and Myers, exhibits detailing African-American shipbuilding history and the restored "Sugar House," the oldest remaining industrial building on the waterfront.

Nearby at Pratt and President streets is the new **Reginald F. Lewis Museum of Maryland African-American History and Culture,** the East Coast's largest museum chronicling the history of African Americans.

Fells Point Maritime Museum, 1724 Thames St., Fells Point.

The old trolley barn for horse-drawn trolleys became the home for this new museum in 2003. It tells the story of the Fells Point seaport neighborhood – a story that played a larger role nationally and internationally than is generally recognized, according to museum manager Meghan McGinnes. From the 1730s to the mid-19th century, Fells Point was Baltimore's "original harbor" and its twelve shipyards and the tradesmen that served them drove the city's maritime commerce and international politics. The waterfront neighborhood produced the world-famous Baltimore clipper schooners, the world's fastest as they carried cargoes both legal and contraband. You see ship models, shipbuilder tools, weapons and photos. A joint venture of the Maryland Historical Society and the Society for the Preservation of Federal Hill and Fells Point, the museum is of most interest to historians and those curious about the intricacies of shipbuilding and Fells Point.

(410) 732-0278. www.mdhs.org. Open Thursday-Monday 10 to 5. Adults $4, children free.

Baltimore Museum of Industry, 1415 Key Hwy., Locust Point.

A huge gear sculpture stands outside this waterfront museum and the 1906 steam tugboat Baltimore is moored at the pier nearby. Housed in an 1865 oyster cannery, the museum traces the industrial and maritime history of one of the busiest seaports in America. The location is at Locust Point, second only to New York's Ellis Island in the number of immigrants who arrived during the Industrial Revolution and entered the American work force. Exhibits include re-creations of a garment loft, print shop, metalworking shop and an early dock and dockmaster's shed. Port-related exhibits include shipping, warehousing, sailcloth manufacturing, and import and export services. You can walk through an 1886 bank and the 1910 Bunting Pharmacy, where Noxema was invented. The Maryland Milestone Wall points out local innovations that impacted the world, from the first disposable bottle cap to the first typesetter. Hands-on activities make this "the museum that works." Visitors get to operate several machines, work in a cannery, make toy trucks on an assembly line and board the mayor's official steam tugboat, a common sight on the harbor for more than half a century.

(410) 717-4808. www.thebmi.org. Open Monday-Saturday 10 to 4. Adults $10, children $5.

Fort McHenry National Monument and Historic Shrine, foot of East Fort Avenue. "There are 79 million acres of National Park System," says a sign at the Visitor Center entrance. "Welcome to 43 of them." Although small, it's powerful, this star-shaped citadel at the entrance to the harbor where Baltimore held off the British in 1814, and even the most cynical cannot help but be moved. Local poet-lawyer Francis Scott Key was inspired to write "The Star Spangled Banner" after watching the historic bombardment from a ship on the river. Visitors are usually inspired to join in song with the recorded U.S. Naval Academy Choir as the window curtains part, revealing the unfurled flag at the end of an informative fifteen-minute movie in the Visitor Center. A park ranger then leads a 25-minute tour through the fort, which was restored to its pre-Civil War appearance after serving as the world's largest hospital for returning veterans following World War I. Outside is a pleasant waterside park, with benches and picnic tables scattered here and there.

(410) 962-4290. Open daily June-Labor Day, 8 to 7:45; rest of year, 8 to 4:45. Adults $5. Grounds open free.

Harbor Neighborhoods

Little Italy. Out Pratt Street and Eastern Avenue just east of Pier 6 is Little Italy, one of the more famous of Baltimore's neighborhoods and the heart of its older restaurant district. The four corners at Fawn and South High streets bulge with leading Italian restaurants and sidewalk cafés.

Fells Point. Just southeast of Little Italy is the original Baltimore harborfront, now considered unique in America as a surviving Colonial working seaport community. Listed on the National Register of Historic Places, it was established in 1730 by shipbuilder John Fell, and streets such as Ann, Bond and Aliceanna were named for members of his family. Fells Point shelters 350 restored structures from the 18th century. Many of its tree-lined streets are cobblestoned and some of its residents still are working seamen. It's being somewhat gentrified with inns, restaurants and antiques shops, but maintains a mixed character. In the middle of the main street is the Broadway Market, one of six municipal offspring of the downtown Lexington Market, the nation's oldest. Brown's Wharf is a restored complex of shops and restaurants between Thames Street and the waterfront. Savor the past in some of the seamen's bars, the old houses along Ann and Bond streets, and the commercial establishments along South Broadway and Thames Street. Although longtime residents would balk, Fells Point could be the Georgetown of Baltimore someday, if developers and restorationists have their way.

Federal Hill. Already a Georgetown of sorts is this nationally designated landmark area just south of the Inner Harbor and the original site of Baltimore's pioneering "dollar-housing" homestead program. For a mere dollar bill, the city sold rundown houses in the 1970s to purchasers who pledged sweat equity. Some of the results can be seen on Federal Hill, where 19th-century red-brick rowhouses have been transformed into places of charm (and are selling for more than the asking price the day they are listed). Note the numerous rooftop decks added lately so residents can see the harbor. The heart of the community is the Cross Street Market, another of the municipal markets and full of local color. Here we enjoyed a stand-up lunch of a dozen raw oysters and fried oyster sandwiches. You can walk the quiet residential streets above the Inner Harbor and rest at the top of Federal Hill Park, named for the place where Baltimoreans celebrated the ratification of the U.S. Constitution. The hill, the highest in Baltimore, grants a panoramic view of the downtown skyline, harbor and the industrial port beyond.

Canton. To the east of Fells Point is this old Baltimore blue-collar neighborhood along the Outer Harbor, also a National Register historic district and rapidly being gentrified, especially by young professionals. It's now called "Baltimore's Gold Coast." Rowhouses are being restored and the new Patapsco River waterfront park has a Korean War Memorial. The old American Can Company factory at 2400 Boston St. has been restored into an Emerging Technology Center with offices, restaurants and shops.

Locust Point. The last waterfront area for development is the south side of the Outer Harbor near Fort McHenry. Like Canton a working-class neighborhood home to generations of longshoremen and laborers, it was undergoing change with the restoration of the former Procter & Gamble soap factory. Five buildings named Ivory, Joy and such on the fifteen-acre site along the waterfront were filling up with high-tech businesses in a $63-million development known as Tide Point. It's part of the city's "Digital Harbor" vision to make Baltimore's waterfront a hub of high-tech enterprises along with tourist attractions.

Where to Eat _____ _↶↶↶_

Hampton's, Harbor Court Hotel, 550 Light St., Inner Harbor.

Restaurant reviewers swoon over this small, sumptuous hotel dining room, one going so far as to write that he had his most memorable meal in ten years of travels here. Overlooking the Inner Harbor, the dining room styled after an English country house is a high-ceilinged beauty of upholstered chairs and swagged draperies in luscious coral colors. The new American fare is pricey but worth it for entrées and accompaniments like potato-crusted grouper with grilled grouper cheeks with lobster-champagne sabayon and Meyer lemon relish, flambé of Maine lobster in Oban scotch, ostrich wrapped in house-cured pancetta with smoked salsify and grilled fig polenta, and roasted lamb loin and lamb chop with truffle port glace, braised barley, haricots vert and jerusalem artichokes. Baltimore's ubiquitous crabmeat might turn up as accents on the five-course prix-fixe menu ($65) that might include Maryland crab caesar salad, grilled dover sole and cervena venison medallions. The pastries on the dessert table, among them a white chocolate and cherry terrine with morello cherry coulis, live up to their billing. So does the exotic Sunday brunch.

(410) 234-0550. Entrées. $34 to $52. Dinner, Tuesday-Sunday 5:30 to 10. Sunday brunch, 10:30 to 2. Jackets required.

Charleston, 1000 Lancaster St., Inner Harbor East.

Ensconced in a prime corner of the new Sylvan Learning Center building near Pier 7, this widely acclaimed restaurant offers a harbor and skyline view from its elegant lounge and its small sidewalk terrace. Chef Cindy Wolf and her husband, manager/sommelier Tony Foreman, opened this after making their debut locally with the Savannah restaurant in the Admiral Fell Inn. Cindy got her restaurant start in Charleston and features modern American cuisine with a Southern accent. Her menu changes daily, but always includes such Low Country favorites as she-crab soup, a fried green tomato "sandwich" with lobster and lump crab hash, cornmeal-crusted oysters with lemon-cayenne mayonnaise and her signature heads-on Gulf shrimp with andouille sausage and tasso ham served over creamy stone-milled grits. Those are just for starters. Main-course presentations change more readily: the night we were there the possibilities included grilled yellowfin tuna with niçoise and picholine olive beurre blanc, roasted duck breast with a tropical fruit compote and grilled jugtown bacon-wrapped beef tenderloin with chimichurri. Desserts were a crunchy chocolate napoleon with praline tuile and berry coulis, Mother Wolf's cheese pie with caramel sauce, and a trio of homemade ice creams and sorbets. Few can resist the tableside presentation of the chef's artisan cheeses to accompany one of Tony's rare wines. His 600 selections are stocked in floor-to-ceiling cabinetry in the Wine Library, one of several serene dining areas separated by trellises, palm fronds and etched-glass dividers. The setting is beautiful, and the service consistently the best in town.

(410) 332-7373. www.charlestonrestaurant.com. Entrées, $32 to $36. Dinner, Monday-Saturday from 5:30.

McCormick & Schmick's, 711 Eastern Ave., Pier 5.

Voted "best view restaurant" by Baltimore magazine readers, this 500-seat offshoot of an Oregon-based seafood restaurant group has much else to commend it: A wraparound dining room with two tiers affords every table a view of the water, and rich wood paneling and stained-glass chandeliers, fine nautical art, and a separate mahogany bar/lounge, add a decided aura of elegance and class. Not to mention the freshest of fish, flown in twice daily from around the world. We think there's no better place in town for a suave lunch or dinner outside by the harbor. A couple of large terraces are edged with potted hibiscus trees for the purpose. The relocated Seven-Foot Knoll Lighthouse that long guarded the entrance to the harbor is almost at tableside and water taxis dock and depart beside. One of us made a memorable lunch of the oyster sampler and spicy seafood potstickers with sweet and sour cashew sauce. The other was well satisfied with a rare yellowfin tuna niçoise salad. The all-day menu, printed daily, is daunting in size and scope. It offers more than a hundred options, from Key West snapper, Idaho trout and tilapia from Costa Rica to Puget Sound manila clams, South Carolina blue crab and Alaskan halibut. They're available as appetizers, pastas, light fare, combination appetizer platters and regular dinners. So you can order a crab melt on sourdough, Georges Bank fish and chips, Bodega Bay salmon roasted on a cedar plank with Oregon berry sauce or lobster thermidor. There's something for everyone, and a variety of settings in which to enjoy.

(410) 234-1300. Entrées, $10.95 to $25.90. Lunch and dinner daily, 11:30 to 11.

Joy America Café, 800 Key Highway, Federal Hill.

Overlooking the harbor from the top of the whimsical American Visionary Arts Museum beside Federal Hill Park, Joy America Café celebrates the tastes and traditions of New World cuisine. Great harbor views are offered at white-clothed tables beside large, half-moon windows in the mod, arty dining room. Even better are the vistas from the circular outdoor balcony behind the kitchen. Billed as an organic gourmet restaurant, it features Latin American and Caribbean dishes. Servers prepare guacamole at your table for slathering on house-made chips. You might start with black bean or fish soup, four kinds of chalupas, tuna and shrimp seviche, salt cod fritters or wild boar chili. Main dishes range from plantain-wrapped rockfish with lime beurre blanc to wood fire-grilled ribeye steak with chimichurri salsa. The Caribbean bouillabaisse with white wine-chile broth and the whole bronzini grilled over mesquite with lime drizzle are highly recommended. Ginger-lime cheesecake is a dessert favorite. A fried oyster sandwich with key lime aioli and a grilled salmon burrito appealed at our lunchtime visit.

(410) 244-6500. Entrées, $22 to $26. Lunch, Tuesday-Saturday 11:30 to 3. Dinner, Tuesday-Sunday 5:30 to 10. Sunday brunch, 11:30 to 4.

Kali's Court, 1606 Thames St., Fells Point.

Mediterranean seafood and chops are the specialty of this winner facing the water. Alas, only a few tables on the brick courtyard terrace get a view – and they were all taken when we stopped by for lunch, expecting to order an oyster po' boy in a brick-oven pita and a grilled seafood kabob with saffron rice. The two-story interior is dark and rich in brick and mahogany wrapping around an atrium, but not the place to be if you yearn to be outside on a pleasant day. Kali's could pass for an elegant Greek taverna, which is as its owners planned. A basket of colorful vegetables on an old stove at the entry sets the stage for the freshest of fare. The day's seafood catch – obtained from New York's Fulton Fish Market – runs a spectrum from New Zealand red snapper to Florida pompano to whole Mediterranean royal daurade. Crab soup with orzo, a trio of tuna presentations and grilled sushi-grade octopus topped with balsamic vinegar and extra-virgin olive oil are typical starters. The brick oven bakes specialties like monkfish medallions wrapped in applewood bacon and Australian swordfish with tomatoes and herbs. Or you could order broiled lump crab cakes, grilled arctic char with cucumber-dill cream sauce, Gulf shrimp stuffed with lump crab, or Colorado rack of lamb in a cabernet and port reduction. Lately, Kali's expanded into an adjoining warehouse and opened the less formal **Kali's Court Mezze,** an angular bar and a two-story ramble of small dining rooms. It offers a wonderfully tempting choice of Mediterranean small plates. Amazingly, the same tiny kitchen serves 200 diners in both restaurants.

(410) 276-4700. www.kaliscourt.com. Entrées, $18.95 to $31.95. Lunch daily, 11:30 to 2:30. Dinner from 5:30.

Pierpoint, 1822 Aliceanna St., Fells Point.

Nancy Longo, one of our favorite Baltimore chefs and a seafood cookbook author, runs this delightful bistro with two partners. Early on, the Baltimore Sun reviewer said of Pierpoint: "it might do for Maryland cuisine what Chez Panisse did for California's." The sleek boxcar-size space seats 58 at tables of gray marble, with black lacquered chairs, small votive candles flickering in etched glass and arrangements of fresh flowers all around. From her small open kitchen, Nancy turns out a short but tantalizing menu of what she calls "Maryland-terranean cuisine" from a repertoire of 600 items. For dinner, we started with the specialty bruschetta, fabulous thick bread laden with garlic and parmesan, and overheard great things about the fresh tuna tapenade, the potato and herb tart, and the warm Eastern Shore rabbit sausage with wilted greens and cider vinaigrette. Super main courses were the Maryland-style cioppino simmered in rich crab stock and the soft-shell crabs served with homemade red and green tomato salsa. We found Nancy's favorite smoked crab cakes wonderful, but remain partial to the unsmoked (she will serve them either way). Crisp matchstick potatoes, an interesting slaw of brussels sprouts, snap peas and tiny new potatoes accompanied the various dishes. A sensational raspberry sorbet with chocolate chips and a heavenly blueberry tart, topped off with good decaf cappuccino, ended as fine a meal as we've had in Maryland. Why the restaurant's name? It's located two blocks from the pier and three blocks from

Fells Point, so Pierpoint was a natural, says Nancy. Her unpretentious restaurant is a natural for those into exciting cuisine.

(410) 675-2080. Dinner, $19 to $25. Lunch, Tuesday-Friday 11:30 to 2. Dinner. Tuesday-Saturday 5 to 9:30 or 10. Sunday, brunch 10:30 to 1:30, dinner 4 to 9.

The Rusty Scupper, 402 Key Highway, Federal Hill.

The Rusty Scupper chain always seems to have a corner on waterfront views, and this one at the Inner Harbor Marina is no exception. It was among the first to settle on the Inner Harbor and is superbly situated right at water's edge at the foot of Federal Hill. Big windows take in the view of all the harbor action from the inside dining areas, but the only outside dining is on a deck upstairs. The lengthy menu is typically Rusty Scupper, embracing everything from chargrilled swordfish and salmon, rosemary chicken and filet mignon to coconut fried-shrimp and pastas. The pan-seared rockfish and the shrimp stuffed with crab imperial are standouts. Lunch and happy hour on the outdoor deck are popular; it's a busy singles spot at night, when there's live piano music. The Sunday champagne brunch buffet claims everything from carved roast beef and ham to mussels marinara, eggs florentine and cheese grits.

(410) 727-3678. Entrées, $14.95 to $28.95. Lunch, 11:30 to 2. Dinner nightly, 5 to 10 or 11. Sunday jazz brunch, 11 to 2.

Victor's Café, 801 Lancaster St., Pier 7.

This place at the Inner Harbor East Marina looks like a ship, when viewed form the water. From the large curving deck at water's edge and from the curving dining room with big portholes as windows, you get arguably the best head-on view of the Inner Harbor in all of Baltimore. If the setting surpasses the food, who cares? Certainly not the younger set who favored the place the weekend afternoon we stopped by. The extensive menu offers something for everyone and the prices are right. There are good and hefty sandwiches, pizzas and pasta dishes, as well as appetizers and salads – how about Cantonese chicken or caesar with barbecued salmon? Dinner entrées could be sesame orange roughy, raspberry salmon, chicken with crabmeat, tequila barbecued pork and shrimp, veal piccata and angus strip steak. Breakfast burritos, eggs florentine and garlic mashed potato omelets are among the choices at weekend brunch, when the mimosas and bloody marys are too cheap to pass up.

(410) 244-1722. www.victoritaliancafe.com. Entrées, $14.95 to $24.95. Lunch daily, 11 to 4. Dinner nightly, 4 to 10 or 11. Weekend brunch, 11 to 2.

Bo Brooks Restaurant & Crab House, 2701 Boston St.. Canton.

This old-timer up and moved from northeast Baltimore to Lighthouse Point, where it occupies a prime waterfront site. The interior has windows on three sides onto Baltimore Marine Center. It's modern but plain, the better for dealing with the crab-cracking debris that comes with the territory. Outside is the Crab Cove Deck, a floating pier that's right on the water and handles the bulk of the crowd – up to 200 people at a time. The deck wrapping around the restaurant proved a surprisingly quiet and peaceful setting for a waterside lunch, in contrast to the hubbub of the Inner Harbor. Here, the lanyards clanged and, but for all the crab eaters, you felt you were at some posh yacht club. The tomato-based Maryland crab soup was spicy, but stronger on vegetables than crab. The "national award-winning" crab puff more than compensated – a tasty mix of crabmeat, gorgonzola and spinach wrapped in puff pastry and topped with sherry cream sauce. Also good was a fried oyster sandwich with coleslaw. There's more to Bo's than crab. A Taste of the Bay appetizer sampler yields fried calamari, clams casino and crab quesadillas. And at dinner you can order broiled bay scallops, pecan-encrusted salmon, pan-seared chicken or espresso-rubbed strip steak.

(410) 558-0202. www.bobrooks.com. Entrées, $14 to $30. Lunch and dinner daily, 11:30 to 9 or 10, weekends from noon. Closed Monday in winter.

Phillips Harborplace, 301 Light St., Harborplace.

The largest and most crowded restaurant of many at Harborplace is this offshoot of the Ocean City seafood establishment that began as a beachfront takeout in 1957. Dominating the Light Street Pavilion, Phillips Harborplace is actually three concepts under one roof, seating a total of 870. The main dining room offers indoor and outdoor seating. Particularly appealing is its sidewalk café looking onto the water and the National Aquarium. The enormous menu typical of its genre offers oysters on the half shell, cream of crab soup, shrimp salad and crab cake sandwiches. Seafood entrées range from Idaho rainbow trout amandine and seared sesame ahi tuna with seaweed salad to flounder stuffed with crab imperial and twin lobster tails. Service is fast (those waterfront seats are coveted); at night you can wait for a table at the piano bar. If you can't wait, head for **Phillips Express and Seafood Market,** which serves crab cake sandwiches, soups and salads to go. There's also an all-you-can-eat **Phillips Seafood Festival Buffet** dining area.

(410) 685-6600 or (800) 782-2722. Entrées, $14.99 to $36.99. Open daily, 11 to 9 or 10.

Little Havana, 1325 Key Hwy., Inner Harbor South.

It's not much to look at, and the outdoor patio is like something you might expect of a rural crab house along the Chesapeake Bay. But this Cuban-inspired restaurant and cantina is popular with locals who know of its off-the-beaten-path location down a side street in an industrial section between Federal Hill and Locust Point. They like the cavernous interior, where tables flank a lively tropical-themed bar, and especially the funky harborside patio, one of the few on the south side of the harbor. Without cover or umbrellas, it appeared too sunny and hot on a bright September weekend, but there were plenty of takers for the $11.95 brunch. No wonder, given the unlimited mimosas and bloody marys. There were a dozen enticing breakfast treats, from Cuban-style fried eggs over rice and a crab omelet to Cuban scrambled eggs with onions, peppers, peas and cheddar cheese. The Cuban pork and ham sandwich and the citrus-marinated grilled chicken and jack cheese sandwich also appealed. More Cuban specialties are offered at night, when this place really swings. The black bean soup, crab cakes with habañero rémoulade, paella, spice-rubbed chicken, Cuban beef stew, oxtail pie and plantain-crusted mahi mahi are favorites. With its lease expiring in 2005, the restaurant was planning to move nearby to 1000 Key Hwy.

(410) 837-9903. www.littlehavanas.com. Entrées, $12.95 to $19.95. Lunch or brunch, Friday-Sunday 11 or 11:30 to 3. Dinner nightly, 4 to 10 or 11.

Bay Café, 2809 Boston St., Canton.

You want water, boats, sunshine, a sandy beach with a tiki bar for cocktails, a young crowd, action? Get them all at this hot spot facing Fort McHenry. The Saturday afternoon we were there the patio was closed for a private party with a calypso band, and the inside was standing-room only, though there seemed to be a few seats in the upstairs dining room with its soaring ceiling. Could the attraction be the food? It's a mixed bag of raw bar, finger appetizers, sandwiches, burgers, pizzas, a signature shrimp salad and a handful of dinner entrées ranging from a soft crab platter to filet mignon, served by a staff clad in fluorescent Caribbean shirts

The draw is more likely the large lounge, the jaunty patio and the views – of water and people.

(410) 522-3377. Entrées, $16.95 to $27.95. Open daily, 11 to 10 or 11.

John Steven, Ltd., 1800 Thames St., Fells Point.

From the entry, this corner establishment across from the harbor appears to be mainly bar, packed with people enjoying pints of honey-colored beer and steamed shrimp. Venture beyond and you'll find a small dining room in the rear, more dining in a house next door and a hidden garden courtyard that's quite pleasant for outdoor dining. Known for the best steamed shrimp in Baltimore, the place actually offers quite a range, including a sushi bar that was the city's first. The with-it dinner menu varies from fish and chips to pan-seared halibut, seafood cassoulet and crab cakes. Grilled tuna with pineapple and roasted jalapeño salsa, cajun crawfish pie and steak au poivre were other options when we were there. A light-fare menu adds things like chicken quesadilla, a safari burger (made of ostrich meat) and a muffuletta sandwich. About twenty beers, including several local brews, are on tap.

(410) 327-5561. Entrées, $15.50 to $21.95. Open daily, 11 to 11 or midnight.

Fells Point, incidentally, is a trove of varied food and drink emporiums. **Bonaparte Breads & Café,** 903 South Ann St., is not so much a café as a bakery and patisserie. The sign advertised a French breakfast for $7 and French sandwiches for $4, but most folks were lined up to buy the wonderful breads and remarkable dessert pastries, to eat here or to go. One storefront away is **Kawasaki Café,** a Japanese sushi bar for lunch and dinner on the waterfront. Nearby at 1720 Thames St. is **The Daily Grind Coffee House,** which advertises "Drink where the stars do," a reference to the players in the TV show "Homicide" filmed here. You can sip coffee and sample baked goods in several quirky rooms. **Black Olive** at 814 South Bond St. is a best-of-Baltimore award-winner known for whole grilled fish and delightful Greek specialties. **Peter's Inn** at 504 South Ann St., a hole-in-the-wall biker's bar without bar food, serves some of the most serious, imaginative fare in the city. The same can be said for **Henninger's Tavern** at 1812 Bank St. Breakfast is the main deal at **Blue Moon Café and Coffee House,** 1621 Aliceanna, a rowhouse where the specialty is french toast along with crab benedict. **Louisiana** at 1708 Aliceanna offers French cuisine with a Creole twist. "Eat Bertha's Mussels," say the ubiquitous bumper stickers for **Bertha's,** and everyone seems to at the dark and kooky place at 734 South Broadway with a mix of brick, tile and wood floors and a zillion wine bottles overhead.

Federal Hill, diagonally across the harbor from Fells Point, provides more dining options. **Corks,** an 1849 rowhouse at 1026 South Charles St., reflects the owners' passion for food and wine. Next door at 1024 is **Bandaloops,** serving "casual gourmet food" in a skylit atrium and other dining rooms on two floors. **Vespa** at 1117-21 South Charles is a little Italian wine bar and bistro as trendy as the scooter for which it is named. **Regi's** at 1002 South Light St. is a charming neighborhood bistro carved out of adjacent 19th-century townhouses. Regional Mexican cuisine and 90 varieties of tequila are dispensed with flair at **Blue Agave,** installed in the former lobby of the historic McHenry Theater at 1032 Light St. Chef-owner Michael Marx was looking to open **Rub,** an authentic Texas barbecue, in 2005 at Locust Point.

FOR MORE INFORMATION: Baltimore Area Convention & Visitors Association, 100 Light St., 12th Floor, Baltimore, Md. 21202. (410) 659-7300 or (877) 255-8466. www.baltimore.org. Its new, state-of-the-art Baltimore Visitor Center is located at 401 Light St., just south of Harborplace.

Bayard House Restaurant terrace faces C&D Canal in Chesapeake City.

Upper Eastern Shore, Md.

There was a time when steamships used to deliver boatloads of summertime escapees from Baltimore and Washington to the Eastern Shore across the Chesapeake Bay. They'd spend the day on the beach at Betterton or at the amusement park at Tolchester before returning home to the steamy Western Shore.

The steamship era and their passengers have come and gone, as have the resort hotels and amusement centers that catered to them. The opening of the Bay Bridge from Annapolis to the Eastern Shore made Ocean City and Rehoboth, Chincoteague and St. Michaels more accessible to the hordes. It left Maryland's Upper Eastern Shore – that section along the Chesapeake Bay's east shore from the Bay Bridge north toward Elkton – very much off the beaten path. That, today, is its special charm.

The waterfront sections of Kent and Cecil counties remain much as they were in the 18th and 19th centuries. One can scarcely imagine so large a remote and undeveloped area so close to a sprawling megalopolis – a scant 25 miles from Baltimore, as the gull flies.

This is a gently rolling land of farms, of soybean crops and of cornfields as high as the proverbial elephant's eye. They're interspersed along the bay between inlets and rivers with names like Bohemia and Sassafras. It is also a watery area of marinas and boaters, working watermen and recreational fishermen.

Historic Chestertown is the area's best-known town. But more water-oriented are two small towns at either end of the territory this chapter covers. Each is quite different from the other.

On the southern end facing the Chesapeake is Rock Hall, an early port and fishing town. Today it claims as many boat slips for visiting yachtsmen as it does residents. State-of-the-art marinas co-exist with watermen carrying on a fishing tradition of many years. They give Rock Hall a distinctive, old/new mix that's unique on such a scale along the bay.

On the northern end is Chesapeake City, a colorful town of 700 souls along the banks of the Chesapeake & Delaware Canal. More than 16,000 vessels of all descriptions pass the town's shores annually, making the canal the third busiest in the world.

Between the canal and the tranquil, nettle-free waters of the upper bay, this area is a mecca for water activities. For those otherwise inclined, there are wildlife refuges, hunting grounds, bicycle routes and antiques shops. And there are always surprises, like the nun from the Sisters of St. Basil convent who was sitting out by the road in full regalia selling jars of preserved fruit as we drove down the road into north Chesapeake City. The area's off-the-beaten-path location is likely to keep it quiet and unspoiled for years to come.

Getting There

The Upper Eastern Shore section covered here lies along the eastern bank of the Chesapeake Bay from Kent Narrows north of the Bay Bridge out of Annapolis to the northern reaches of Maryland near the Delaware state line. Other than by boat, it is best reached by car. Maryland Route 213 is the main through road, roughly paralleling U.S. 301 to the west. The Route 213 bridge over the Chesapeake & Delaware Canal passes above Chesapeake City. To reach Rock Hall, take Maryland Route 20 off Route 213 from Chestertown.

Airplane, rail and bus service is provided into Philadelphia, Wilmington, Baltimore and Washington. There is no public transportation into this area.

Where to Stay

Rock Hall and Area

Great Oak Manor, 10568 Cliff Road, Chestertown 21620.
Prolific apple trees were shedding their bounty along the path as we arrived at this stately, red brick Georgian manor house grandly situated on twelve acres overlooking the Chesapeake Bay. The tasty apples were a harbinger of treats to come at this watery dream of a B&B, as tended by new owners Cassandra and John Fedas from Annapolis. The 25-room mansion, built in 1938 by an heir to the W.R. Grace shipping fortune, has twelve guest rooms and suites, regal public rooms and a tree-shaded expanse of lawn that takes eighteen hours to mow. The bay is on view from four bedrooms with large windows on the second floor and three more with smaller windows on the third. Bedrooms vary in size and decor, but all are plush in an understated way. Each comes with a full tiled bath, kingsize bed with feather topper and a sitting area with comfortable chairs, TV and telephone. Five have working fireplaces. The manor offers plenty of common space in which to relax: a

formal living room called the Music Room, a library with shelves of books, a dark and cozy TV room with ship's models reflecting the owners' sailing interests, and a side porch full of wicker and wisteria stenciling. The Fedases added a lovely conservatory with a small pool in 2004; it serves as a site for conferences and weddings. In back are a pleasant terrace and the vast lawn leading to a bluff above the bay, where benches, a screened gazebo and a deck with rocking chairs await. The vista takes in Poole's Island across the main bay channel and at night, you can see the lighted sky above Baltimore 25 miles away. From bluff's edge, a path and a service road descend to a sand beach, where swimmers find no evidence of the sea nettles that discourage bay swimming farther south. Guests also have access to golf, tennis and a swimming pool at the Great Oak yacht club next door. A full breakfast is served at individual tables amid much silver and china in the dining room. The buffet holds fresh fruit, many cereals and granola, delectable muffins and, at our latest visit, eggs strata. We took ours on trays to the back terrace and felt like we were in paradise.

(410) 778-5943 or (800) 504-3098. Fax (410) 810-2517. www.greatoak.com. Twelve rooms with private baths. Doubles, $160 to $285.

Swan Haven Bed & Breakfast, 20950 Rock Hall Ave., Rock Hall 21661.

Situated next to the Waterman's Museum, this renovated three-story Victorian house started with four bedrooms and, under owners Diane and Harry Oliver, has been greatly expanded and upscaled. A large new addition to the south takes full advantage of the waterside location. Its main floor includes a dining room and a great room opening onto a huge deck and a pier on the Haven inlet. Upstairs are three deluxe bedrooms, all with kingsize beds and sliding doors onto a deck with great water views. Two here have whirlpool tubs and the third a rainforest shower for two. Also prized in the original house is the Cygnet Room with a kingsize bed, a whirlpool tub for two and an antique wooden glider chair in the room, plus a screened porch facing the Haven. The side Heron Room with cathedral ceiling and kingsize iron bed comes with a private balcony overlooking Swan Creek and the marinas. Other rooms convey a distinctly older feel, but all have central air conditioning and TVs. Two on the second floor, each with a queensize bed, open onto an old-fashioned front porch. Two more are up steep stairs in the attic. Diane puts out a continental breakfast in the dining room. The couple also run **Swan Haven Rentals** on the property, offering small sailboats, dinghies, kayaks, canoes and bicycles.

(410) 639-2527. Fax (410) 639-2254. www.swanhaven.com. Ten rooms with private baths. Doubles, $98 to $148.

Moonlight Bay Inn, 6002 Lawton Ave., Rock Hall 21661.

Situated on a residential street, this B&B sports a wicker-filled wraparound porch, a screened gazebo and garden chairs scattered about the large lawn. All are sited to take advantage of one of the more appealing water settings anywhere. As the sun sets over little Swan Island, yellow lights outline docks in the foreground, white lights twinkle on the Bay Bridge in the distance and the glow of Baltimore to the west lights up the evening sky. It's an idyllic backdrop for a restored mid-19th-century farmhouse in which ex-Long Islanders Bob and Dorothy Santangelo unite their goals, he for a marina and she for a B&B. They started with five handsome bedrooms, one of them the upstairs Harvest Moon in which we stayed. It was comfortable with a kingsize bed and windows onto the water and, Dorothy advised, we could lie in bed and "watch the boats pass outside." We'd happily stay in any of the five rooms in the newer West Wing, a two-story structure at bay's edge. Each has a kingsize bed (one can be separated into twins), whirlpool tub and a private balcony with a wooden chair and lounge overlooking the water. Four balconies face the bay head-on. Moon Struck, upstairs in the rear, has a side balcony with views of both bay and an inlet known as the Haven. Each room has caring touches, from a clock radio and decanter of sherry to a guest diary and a framed wall hanging called "Inn Reminders," in which the usual guest instructions are rendered in poetry. Each building has a guest parlor. Dorothy serves a full breakfast in a dining room and enclosed atrium porch overlooking a showy English garden. Ours included a fruit cup with bananas and strawberries, two kinds of muffins and belgian waffles. English tea is served in the late afternoon.

(410) 639-2660. Fax (410) 639-7739. Ten rooms with private baths. Doubles, $125 to $165.

The Inn at Mitchell House, 8796 Maryland Pkwy., Chestertown 21620.
A long driveway leads to this lovely old manor house in the Tolchester section near the Chesapeake Bay. The ten-acre property beside Stoneybrook Pond was part of a 1,000-acre working plantation. The manor, built in 1743 and expanded in 1825, is still fit for the landed gentry. Jim and Tracy Stone share the expansive house with guests in six rooms. Theirs is very much a family home, with lots of heirlooms and mementos from both sides of the family in two large parlors. Artworks from Jim's grandmother, who started painting oils at age 60, enhance the Joseph Mitchell Room, the largest bedroom with a queensize canopy bed, a fireplace and a sitting area with sofabed. The large Ringgold Room has a queensize bed, a sofabed and a fireplace. On their way to other bedrooms, guests pass a refrigerator stocked with complimentary sodas and beer and a hallway decorated with flapper dresses and hats that belonged to Jim's great aunt. A sumptuous country breakfast (often french toast or omelets) is served in the high-ceilinged dining room. Outside, guests enjoy a spacious screened porch overlooking the pond, which you can traverse by means of two bridges. Jim put in the raised herb and flower garden, terraced gardens and a fishpond beside the old smokehouse.

(410) 778-6500. www.innatmitchellhouse.com. Six rooms with private baths. Doubles, $100 to $140.

The Inn at Osprey Point, Route 20, Rock Hall 21661.
Philadelphia Main Line investors who like to sail built this yacht club, marina, inn, restaurant and bar from scratch along a section of Swan Creek known as the Haven, an inlet from the nearby Chesapeake Bay. The place looks and feels new, although it was scrupulously designed with a Williamsburg look and actually patterned after the Coke-Garrett House, the mayor's house in Williamsburg, Va. Situated on a rather barren landscape that strikes arriving visitors as mainly sailing masts and parking areas, the endeavor has a split personality. Overnight guests "register" at a second-story office that also serves the marina or, after hours, in the main-floor restaurant. The seven guest quarters are on the second and third floors above the restaurant. All equipped with modern baths and TVs, they are true to the Williamsburg look, from paint colors to wide-plank floors, and feature "showcase furnishings and gallery art throughout," according to the slick inn brochure. The rooms we saw seemed rather spartan and not the kind in which you'd likely curl up with a book for the evening. The two-room Escapade suite with a jacuzzi in the marble bathroom and the Bolero room with a gas fireplace and queen poster bed have the best water views, but the jacuzzi room "can be noisy due to the restaurant" below, the inn literature advises. A third-floor landing area, described as a common room, holds

two wing chairs and some reading materials. A complimentary continental breakfast is offered in the restaurant's Hunt Room. In addition to the restaurant, an asset for guests here is the marina's large, club-like swimming pool and deck area with bathhouse adjacent to the inn.

(410) 639-2194. www.ospreypoint.com. Six rooms and one suite with private baths. Doubles, $130 to $180. Suite, $200.

Huntingfield Manor, 4928 Eastern Neck Road, Rock Hall 21661.

This 1950s farm estate, a former hunting lodge turned into a B&B, is flanked by two creeks that flow into the Chesapeake Bay. Set equidistant from the road and the bay on 70 rural acres, the pillared house is on the flight path for Canada geese and is surrounded by grain and cornfields ("part of its charm," says owner George Starken, a retired missile engineer who assists his wife Bernadine, the innkeeper). Free-ranging peacocks roam the grounds, which back up to an inlet from the bay beyond the woods. The "telescope house" is 136 feet long and one room wide, with 61 windows and three staircases serving separate sections of the house. Much of the main floor is devoted to a dining room, a reading room and the long and comfy Red Room with TV and fireplace. Beyond is a big, three-sided screened porch. Five bedrooms with updated baths are located in separate sections of the house, recently rebuilt following a fire and looking brighter and more cheery than when we first visited. The New Yarmouth Room is billed as the New England room, with twin beds joined as a king between a vaulted ceiling. Other rooms also have twins joined as kingsize, but beds can be readily split for the bicycle and hunting groups that are frequent visitors. Rooms are outfitted functionally but simply. An efficiency cottage offers a fireplace and TV. Breakfast is continental, with a selection of fruits, cereals and three kinds of baked goods, from white or dark breads to sweet sticky rolls.

(410) 639-7779. Fax (410) 639-2924. www.huntingfield.com. Five rooms and one cottage with private baths. Doubles, $125 to $165. Cottage, $200.

North Point Motel, 5639 Walnut St., Box 298, Rock Hall 21661.

This recently renovated establishment bills itself as the only motel with a view of the bay. As it happens, it's also one of the area's few motels. Five motel units on the second floor above the North Point Marina office and store share a great watery prospect from a common balcony with a head-on view of the Chesapeake. Owners Joe and Lori Campbell invested heavily in their renovations and furnishings. The nicely furnished rooms have two double beds, a table and two chairs, a refrigerator and sink, nautical prints on the walls, carpeting and sliding glass doors onto the balcony. Two larger rooms also contain a sofabed. There's a pool at water's edge.

(410) 639-2907. Five rooms with private baths. Doubles, $70 to $90.

Mariners Motel, 5681 South Hawthorne Ave., Rock Hall 21661.

Only five of the twelve rooms at this 30-year-old motel look onto the water and marina. The rest face what a tour book calls "open grassy grounds" across from the harbor and, but for a covered picnic gazebo with gas grill, could be anywhere. Rooms are basic: two double beds, telephone, TV, refrigerator and tiled bath. Volleyball and horseshoes facilities and a swing set are popular with families. Guests have access to a pool at the Rock Hall Landing Marina. The motel is part of an enterprise called Rock Hall Landing Lodging, which also offers waterfront condominiums of two and three bedrooms overlooking the marina ($195 a night).

(410) 639-2291. Twelve rooms with private baths. Doubles, $70 to $80.

Chesapeake City

Ship Watch Inn, 401 First St., Chesapeake City 21915.

From the street, lovely window boxes and gardens enhance the facade of this handsome gray structure with green and maroon trim. Venture beyond and you'll be struck by the three levels of decks and balconies on the water side. Built as a residence in 1920 and later converted to apartments, it was renovated in 1996 into an appealing B&B right at the edge of the Chesapeake & Delaware Canal. A turn-of-the-century map hanging in the lobby denotes the site now occupied by the inn as owned by "Capt. Firman Layman, proprietor of the Bayard House. First-class accommodations for Man and Beast." The proprietor's descendant, Thomas Layman Vaughan, and his wife Linda continue the innkeeping tradition, although they are quick to point out that beasts are no longer allowed. The B&B has ten rooms, all with french doors onto decks yielding breezy vistas of the canal. New in 2004 was an addition with two master suites that have king beds, oversize whirlpool tubs, DVD players, mini-refrigerators, sitting areas and private decks with the best views of the water. All rooms come with TVs, telephones and binoculars for watching the passing boats. Four others have whirlpool tubs. There's also a canal-side hot tub for all guests. Two rooms have double beds, though the rooms we saw had king or queen beds and armoires. The beige tapestry fabric spread on the bed in Room 7 was nicely color-coordinated with two club chairs and an oriental rug. A mural of the Lord Baltimore steamer enhances a wall of the dining room, where tables look onto the canal. A full breakfast is served here or on the guests' deck. The entrée might be crab benedict or belgian waffles. Guests also have access to a small parlor, but obviously the prime attraction is having their own waterside deck.

(410) 885-5300 or (877) 335-5300. www.shipwatchinn.com. Eight rooms and two suites with private baths. Doubles, $115 to $190. Suites, $195 to $245.

Inn at the Canal, 104 Bohemia Ave., Chesapeake City 21915.

The rear porch full of wicker and rockers faces the Back Creek Basin and, beyond, the busy Chesapeake & Delaware Canal. The porch is a great vantage point for watching not only the canal action but also the summer Sunday band concerts in the bandshell at Pell Gardens next door. "We make Sunday evenings special," says Mary Ioppolo, innkeeper with her husband Al. Hosts and guests gather on the porch with wine and hors d'oeuvres to enjoy the music. The elegant gabled Victorian, once occupied by the owners of tugboats that traveled the canal, has ornate twelve-foot-high ceilings on the main floor. The dining room with four tables set for breakfast is classical in style, Mary says, while the guest parlor across the hall is more Egyptian in feeling. The couple's antiques are showcased throughout the house (they also run an antiques shop called Inntiques beneath the inn in stone-walled quarters reached through a lovely courtyard). Up a stairway lined with a collection of door stops are seven guest accommodations, all with TVs and telephones and four with queensize beds. Three yield water views. We liked one way back in the house with a four-poster bed, two wing chairs and an original European soaking tub. A third-floor suite includes a bedroom with kingsize half-canopy bed and fireplace, a wet bar with a stocked refrigerator, sitting room with TV/DVD and day bed, and a new water-view balcony. From her kitchen bearing quite a collection of old cooking and baking implements on the fireplace wall, Mary prepares a hearty breakfast. Typical fare might be ham and cheese pie or stuffed french toast with raspberry sauce.

(410) 885-5995. www.innatthecanal.com. Six rooms and one suite with private baths. Doubles, $90 to $145. Suite, $165 to $225.

The Blue Max Inn, 300 Bohemia Ave., Chesapeake City 21915.

There's no water view except from a new suite in winter, but two great wicker-filled wraparound verandas, one up and one down, greet guests at this blue-shuttered Georgian Federal facing the quiet end of the main street. Wayne and Wendy Mercer offer elegant common rooms and eight spacious guest rooms with king or queen beds, TVs and telephones, period furnishings and a teddy bear here and a doll there. Plush pillows and puffy comforters and window shams are the norm. "Decorating is my thing," says Wendy, "restrained only by my credit-card limit!" Vintage aircraft prints are featured in the Blue Max room. The Hunter and Randall rooms open onto a private veranda in front. A second-floor suite has a queensize bed, private balcony and whirlpool bath. Another whirlpool bath is enjoyed by guests in the main-floor Lindsay Room. The rear of the main floor holds a new suite with king canopy bed, fireplace, DVD/VCR, and double whirlpool tub. The house, built in 1854 by sawmill owner William Lindsay, once was owned by author Jack Hunter, who wrote the book for which the inn was named. Breakfast at our visit was caramel-pecan french toast with ginger-peach sauce, preceded by a fruit course of peaches and kiwi and accompanied by music from a player piano. Southwest frittata was planned the next day. The meal is taken in the fireplaced dining room or in a side sunroom beside a rock garden, fishpond, fountain and waterfall. A gazebo is in back.

(410) 885-278 or (877) 725-8362. Fax (410) 885-2809. www.bluemaxinn.com. Seven rooms and two suites with private baths. Doubles, $100 to $155. Suites, $170 to $225.

Seeing and Doing ⎯⎯⎯⎯⎯⎯⎯⎯⎯⎯⎯ ♫♫♫

For many visitors, inland Chestertown is the major draw to the Upper Eastern Shore area, but its Chester River waterfront is overshadowed by its historic and commercial attractions, including inns, restaurants and shops. The area covered in this chapter focuses on two less well known, very different small towns with more of a watery presence.

Rock Hall dates to 1707 as an early port town on the turnpike from New York and Philadelphia to Annapolis and Washington (Presidents Washington, Madison and Jefferson crossed the bay here). Today it's at once a simple waterman's community of working fishermen and a busy yachting center favored by sailors from Philadelphia and Wilmington, for whom it's more readily accessible than for those from Baltimore or Washington on the other side of the bay. A bronze waterman's statue at harbor's edge welcomes visitors who see it, but the dozen marinas are much more evident. There's also a new observation pier over the marsh at Blue Heron Park, near the end of Route 20. The Rock Hall Trolley shuttles visitors around town and into Chestertown in season. The town and its 1,500 residents are dispersed across a wide, mile-long promontory between Rock Hall Harbor off the bay and the Haven, a sheltered inlet from Swan Creek. Other than yachts and shops, there are few signs of sophistication or affluence.

Chesapeake City is a tight little canal town on two sides of the wide Chesapeake & Delaware Canal, a time warp beneath a soaring highway bridge. The main, south side is a toy land of colorful, pint-size Victorian structures squeezed together like dollhouses. This unique, truly quaint community is made for walking. Historic plaques mark many houses, some of which have been converted into shops and B&Bs. Plying the canal are cargo vessels and container ships of all sizes, tankers, barges with their tugboats and countless recreational craft. Visitors may observe the "changing of the pilots" ritual here as Delaware Bay pilots transfer their charges to Chesapeake Bay pilots, and vice versa, while the vessels continue without stopping. Beside the waterfront is Pell Gardens, a park and amphitheater with a bandshell (summer concerts on Sunday evenings from 6 to 8). A waterfront promenade from the Bayard House restaurant winds around Pell Gardens and the anchorage basin to the Canal Museum.

Between the two focal points of Rock Hall and Chesapeake City is a sleepy, Tidewater-like expanse of rolling farmlands, thoroughbred horse farms, river basins and the odd hamlet in which antiques shops seem to be the chief draw. This is good bicycling country, with relatively low-trafficked roads and wide shoulders. More urbane diversions are close at hand in suave Chestertown, the historic Kent County seat just inland along the Chester River.

SHOPPING. At Rock Hall's main corner, **The Shops at Oyster Court** started in 1996 as a homey bookstore and gathering spot called the America's Cup Café. Its owner bought up old fishing shacks and outbuildings to move to the property and lease to artisans and craftspeople. The result is a charming alleyway lined with colorful enterprises that tend to come and go. Oyster Court also includes a small museum called Tolchester Beach Revisited. It traces the rise and fall of the nearby amusement park, which opened in 1877 and expanded over 85 years to become the most popular family playground along the mid-Atlantic seaboard. Also related to Oyster Court is the fledgling Mainstay Performing Arts Center, which occasionally stages live concerts. Beside the alley is **Bay Leaf Gourmet,** a good little deli and coffeehouse where you can pick up soups, salads and quiches at prices from yesteryear. Adjacent is the **Reuben Rodney Gallery,** a co-op showing local artists. Around the corner is **Fishbone,** an antiques and collectibles shop.

Rock Hall's revitalized Main Street includes **Smilin' Jakes** for tropical island attire and **Tallulah's on Main,** a gallery and gift shop with eclectic wares from travel vests to art glass salt and pepper shakers to Fabergé eggs. Everyone stops at **Durding's Store,** an old corner drugstore built in the 1860s and restored to the period. It's the *real* thing, from the pressed-tin ceiling and hanging brass lamps to the wooden booths, swiveling counter stools and the timeworn pine floor. Ice cream sodas made with real vanilla beans are served at the original marble soda fountain amidst a selection of cards, gifts and sundries. Owners Mary Sue and Art Willis save most of their Chesapeake memorabilia as well as clothing and fine furnishings for home and yacht for **The Cat's Paw** at 21144 Green Lane. It's an exceptional gift shop at their Sailing Emporium, which has to be about the best landscaped marina you'll ever see, complete with planters, rose garden, picnic benches and pavilion. Clothing of interest to boaters and nice gifts also are carried at **The Ditty Bag,** the marine store at Haven Harbour Marina.

Colorful Chesapeake City offers colorful shopping, too, along Bohemia Avenue and George Street and their cross streets. Start at **Canal Artworks** and **The Victorian Lady** specialty shop in a restored 1915 Sears, Roebuck house at the foot of Bohemia. The restored **Back Creek General Store** has gourmet foods, crafts and collectibles. Nearby are **Canal Lock Antiques,** and **The Vintage Traveler.** The corner of Third and Bohemia is home to **Black Swan Antiques** and **Almost History,** a good primitive furniture, gift and garden accessory shop. Make the circuit around to George Street to visit **Neil's Artwork** for marine art and seascapes by the artist-owner. A good place to finish is **Canal Creamery,** an ice cream parlor with picnic tables by the water. Ducks quacked merrily as we paused for frozen yogurt.

On the Water

BOATING. Although this is an exceptionally busy yachting area, no public cruises are advertised. Charter boats for fishing and sightseeing are based in various marinas in Rock Hall and environs, and visitors are advised to contact the captains directly. **Swan Haven Rentals** at Swan Haven B&B in Rock Hall rents small boats for sailing, fishing and crabbing. None of the marinas seems to rent small boats, but charter service is offered at Haven Harbour and the Sailing Emporium in Rock Hall.

You can sail aboard **The Kathryn,** a 43-foot ketch captained by Bruce and Kathy Meeks, both AT&T retirees. Two-hour trips leave Rock Hall Harbor by reservation, (410) 639-9902, Friday-Sunday at 1:30; $30 per person. Evening sunset cruises also are scheduled. .

Chester River Kayak Adventures, 5758 Main St., Rock Hall, (410) 639-2001, offers seven guided tours and kayak rentals. Half-day, full-day and sunset paddles are scheduled.

CRABBING. Crabbing is a serious activity hereabouts, and one that novices (known locally as "chicken neckers") find relaxing and sometimes addictive. All you'll need is a spool of cotton line, lead weights, bait, a dip net and a pail or cooler to hold your catch. Although almost any inlet or cove will do, the favorite area for netting the blue crab seems to be in the waters and tidal mud flats around Eastern Neck Island, where you can rent a boat and equipment or drop your line from the roadway bridge. First-timers who team up with Rock Hall watermen like Bob Gibson, who offers morning crabbing charters in July and August, may catch up to six dozen (the daily limit for sport crabbers) in five or six hours. He also leads charter fishing expeditions on his new **Daddy's Girl II,** (410) 778-9424. Capt. T. Wayne Fletcher also leads crabbing and charter fishing expeditions for up to 30 people on the new 42-foot boat **Miss Carolyn II,** (410) 810-2941.

SWIMMING. The upper reaches of the bay are about the only areas where people swim, since sea nettles make life unpleasant for human interlopers in the lower bay in July and August. The cooler waters here are generally nettle-free except in the hottest summers. We spotted youngsters swimming at the Rock Hall town beach off Beach Road in early June, while their elders picnicked inside a couple of gazebos. The best public beach is at Betterton, a once thriving resort town that has seen better days. A few trees shade the sandy beach. High on a bluff above the beach is a picnic pavilion with a fine bay view.

Sights to See

Waterman's Museum, 20880 Rock Hall Ave., Rock Hall.

This small museum, nicely renovated from an abandoned house, was opened in 1993 by the owner of Haven Harbour Marina to preserve the history and lore of the watermen of Rock Hall. Exhibits on oystering, eeling and crabbing, plus fishing gear, local photographs and carvings, are nicely mounted in glass-front crates in three display rooms. "If it's been used on the water, we've probably got it," advised curator Richard Burton, former marina manager who came out of retirement to oversee the well financed local venture. One of the more interesting exhibits involves a replica of a waterman's shanty, a cramped room on the scow of a boat, in which a realistic-looking waterman (actually a female mannequin) is asleep in the bunk, with pup beside. Another details the decline of the local oyster industry. A pier was designed to accommodate several workboats, including a skipjack, for visitors to board. *(410) 778-6697. Open daily, 10 to 5. Free.*

C&D Canal Museum, 2nd Street and Bethel Road, Chesapeake City.

A glimpse of the Chesapeake & Delaware Canal's early days is gleaned from this small museum in the original pump house, which holds the early waterwheel and steam engines that pumped water to the canal locks. You'll marvel at the three-story high cypress waterwheel, which raised water from the Back Creek anchorage basin and dumped 20,000 gallons a minute into the locks. The steam engines are the oldest of their type still on their original foundations in America. A fifteen-minute video tells the story of the canal, first envisioned in 1661 by a Dutch mapmaker who proposed a shortcut across the narrow strip of land separating the Delaware River and Chesapeake Bay. The thirteen-mile-long canal, which finally opened in 1829, cut by nearly 300 miles the roundabout trip between the busy shipping ports of Philadelphia and Baltimore. Forty percent of all ship traffic calling on Baltimore now uses the waterway, the nation's busiest. Not your typical canal, this looks more like a river. It's 400 feet wide and 35 feet deep. The Army Corps of Engineers oversees all canal operations from a two-story white clapboard house on a point overlooking the canal on the east side of the anchorage basin in south Chesapeake City. In the ivy-covered stone pump house, a National Historic Landmark, are interactive videos, maps, documents, paintings and artifacts that portray the story of America's only major commercial waterway still in use from the early 19th century. A television monitor shows live locations of ships as they travel through the canal.

(401) 885-5621. Open Monday-Saturday 8 to 4. Free.

Eastern Neck National Wildlife Refuge, 1730 Eastern Neck Road, Rock Hall.

This remote, 2,285-acre island refuge at the confluence of the Chester River and the Chesapeake Bay covers all of Eastern Neck, an island promontory at the southern tip of the area. One of the first settled areas in the New World, it's surprisingly deserted today. The brackish tidal marshes, croplands and forests provide feeding and resting places for migratory and wintering waterfowl. It's also a refuge for the endangered Delmarva fox squirrel and the threatened southern bald eagle. The fall and spring are the best times to view the 32 species of migratory birds. Nearly six miles of roads and trails are open to visitors most of the year. Walk along a boardwalk across the marshes out to the observation platform alongside Calfpasture Cove. Egrets, herons and osprey are supposed to be in their element here, but the only wildlife we encountered one summer morning were a couple of humans atop the platform. More interesting at our particular visit were all the boaters crabbing in the Eastern Neck Narrows at the entrance to the refuge.

(410) 639-7056. Open daily, dawn to dusk. Free.

Chesapeake Farms Wildlife Habitat, 7319 Remington Drive (off Route 20), Chestertown.

A driving tour leads through the 3,300-acre wildlife management demonstration area formerly known as Remington Farms, operated by the du Pont company in conjunction with Remington, the arms manufacturer. An informative brochure points out wildlife management practices being applied here. The self-guided tour takes one past ponds, swamps, woods and fields and involves fifteen marked – and some unmarked – stops for wildlife and plants. The first stop is the main rest area, where up to 10,000 ducks, geese and other waterfowl may be observed at a busy time. The leisurely driving tour is the closest thing we've found so far north to the famed J.N. "Ding" Darling National Wildlife Preserve on Florida's Sanibel Island, although the finds are neither so prolific nor so exotic. The quantity and variety of waterfowl you'll see depends on the season and the time of day. The habitat tour can take an hour or more, depending on stops.

(410) 778-8400. Open daily, dawn to dusk, from February to Oct. 10, when it's closed to the public for hunting season. Free.

Where to Eat

The Inn at Osprey Point, 20786 Rock Hall Ave., Rock Hall.

The handsome restaurant at this waterside inn is known for good food and pleasant ambiance. White linens cover the well-spaced tables in the L-shaped dining room, which wraps around a small, historic-looking bar. A formal Colonial Williamsburg look is conveyed by french doors and tall, many-paned windows, a large fireplace, and white walls with Williamsburg blue trim. Window tables along the front catch a glimpse of the harbor through all the boats in the marina. The short dinner menu bears a contemporary touch. Among starters, people rave about the sherried cream of crab soup. The braised calamari with spinach and tomato-basil ravioli was another winner. Typical main courses are sautéed cobia with grilled papaya and orange-vanilla vinaigrette, grilled pork tenderloin with mushroom demiglace, and pan-seared duck breast with toasted pecan chutney. The wine list is strong on boutique California wineries.

(410) 639-2194. Entrées, $20.75 to $26. Dinner, Thursday-Monday 5 to 8 or 9, Sunday 3 to 7.

P.E. Pruitt's, 20895 Bayside Avenue, Rock Hall.

This large and popular restaurant and raw bar has a screened porch and large outdoor deck overlooking the harbor, and fishing boats and sunset cruises leave right from its dock. The inside has linen-covered tables in a simple, vaguely nautical decor. The kitchen crew knows what it's doing with New Orleans-style seafood dishes that give a distinctive flavor to the fare. House specialties are Louisiana alligator toulouse, jambalaya, coconut creole shrimp, blackened catfish creole and salmon wellington, although you also can order the locally ubiquitous lump crab cakes and crab imperial or a roast turkey dinner. Start with turtle soup, seafood gumbo or oyster stew. The oyster lovers among us are also well served by six versions of oyster appetizers available year-round. Others range from crab balls and steamed spiced shrimp to gator bits, catfish fingers and, different for the area, tuna sashimi with teriyaki ginger glaze, wasabi and seaweed salad. Much of the same is available at lunch, when you also can get five versions of po-boy sandwiches.

(410) 639-7454. www.pepruitts.com. Entrées, $11.99 to $25.99. Lunch daily, noon to 4. Dinner nightly, 4 to 9. Sunday, brunch 10 to 1, dinner noon to 9.

Waterman's Crab House Restaurant, Sharp Street Wharf, Rock Hall.

The choice harborfront location is the draw for this old-timer, which sprawls across a pier beside the Rock Hall harbor and was nicely rebuilt and expanded following a hurricane in 2003. You can see lots of marina activity from the sturdy, six-sided picnic tables shaded by jaunty umbrellas on the pier, from another section with picnic tables and a 40-foot bar under a vast tent, and from interior dining rooms made more stylish in shades of beige and brown. A handsome bar and lounge emerged in 2004 in space occupied by the former gift shop. On a sunny summer day, we were quite happy with a cold beer and a frozen tequila sunrise. We were not so happy with the fried oyster sandwich, a travesty of four small oysters on a hamburger bun, and the "shrimpy caesar salad," a timid affair that lived up to its name in terms of size. Since our first visit, the menu has taken on a colorful new appearance, if not a new culinary style, and the food is said to be much improved. Steamed crabs, shrimp and oysters continue to be featured in various guises, along with the specialty broiled rockfish, pastas, baby back ribs, fried or barbecued chicken and, surprise, prime rib and hand-cut steaks. Cheesecake and ice cream sundaes are popular desserts.

(410) 639-2261. Entrées, $11.99 to $22.99. Open daily, 11:30 to 9 or 10:30.

Bay Wolf, Rock Hall Avenue, Rock Hall.

A sidewalk patio is a welcome addition to this locally acclaimed restaurant, housed in a former funeral home and notable for church-like stained-glass windows. Owners Larry and Hildegard Sunkler (he of the Schaefer's Canal House family from Chesapeake City) mix a heavy dose of Austrian fare with an Eastern Shore accent in three pleasant dining rooms. They bill their bar as "the most convivial – and certainly the longest – in town." The menu covers a range from fried oysters, shrimp scampi and crab imperial to wiener schnitzel, schweinsbraten and veal scandia. The mixed grill combines filet mignon, chicken breast and a pork chop, served with french fries. Starters vary from french onion soup au gratin to fried calamari and chicken wings. Desserts run from apple strudel to black forest cake. Some of the same items are available on the lunch menu.

(410) 639-2000. Entrées, $16.95 to $20.95. Open daily, noon to 9.

Harbor House Restaurant, 23145 Buck Neck Road, Chestertown.

The dining room and enclosed porch on a hillside overlooking the Worton Creek Marina offer water views and – a novel touch – dishes named for the diner. The latter happens to anyone who makes a dinner reservation before 4 p.m. The computer prints out the night's menu listing, say, crab Buckley, Povey rockfish, Roberts broiled salmon and Vogel chicken. It's a fun gimmick, as is the lineup of photos of 25 lighthouses behind the bar. Identify them correctly and win dinner for two. Bob Jester, the creative chef-owner whose son does the cooking, draws a sophisticated crowd not necessarily with the gimmicks, but also with the dark and intimate dining room, the lovely view from the porch and the consistently excellent, always changing fare. The crab imperial is the best around, but we ordered the Woodworth crab cakes – how could you not, when they're named for you? – pure lump crab, garnished with a spicy cajun crawfish. Also good were the oyster sampler appetizer, the house salad with raspberry vinaigrette dressing and the basket of breads (banana nut, cranberry-nut and corn). Snapper soup and oysters topped with garlic and cheese are signature starters. Homemade desserts could be apple crisp, grasshopper ice cream and apricot sorbet.

(410) 778-0669. Entrées, $20 to $28. Dinner, Tuesday-Sunday 5 to 8:30 or 9.

The Bayard House Restaurant, 11 Bohemia Ave., Chesapeake City.

Appealing water views and innovative food make this the Upper Shore's No. 1 culinary destination. It occupies the oldest building in Chesapeake City at the foot of the main street, right up against the C&D canal. On two levels, the restaurant has an enclosed main-floor porch, all windows bordered by puffy curtains beside the water, and a couple of appropriately historic inner dining rooms. Almost a mirror image in terms of layout is the walkout basement, with another enclosed waterfront porch. Also on the lower level is the Hole in the Wall Bar Lounge (so named because one wall sported a hole through which drinks were served for consumption outside). Adjacent is a beguiling canal-side patio, perfect for dining al fresco at umbrellaed tables surrounded by attractive landscaping and flowers. The chef's menu is equal to the setting. For lunch, you might sample pecan chicken salad with fried oysters, salmon fettuccine alfredo, Chesapeake crab quesadilla with green chile salsa or sautéed Idaho trout with roasted red bell pepper coulis. Dinner could start with the crab quesadilla, brie in puff pastry, grilled portobello mushrooms or a bowl of crab soup, regularly voted the state's best in the annual Maryland Seafood Festivals. Main courses range from blackened yellowfin tuna with chile hollandaise sauce and spiced anaheim chile peppers stuffed with lobster and crabmeat to sautéed duck breast with apple-raisin compote and tournedos Baltimore (one topped with a crab cake and the other with a lobster cake and served with two sauces). Finish with baked alaska or key lime pie.

(410) 885-5040 or (877) 582-4049. www.bayardhouse.com. Entrées, $21 to $30. Lunch daily, 11:30 to 3. Dinner nightly, 5 to 9 or 10.

Chesapeake Inn, 605 Second St., Chesapeake City.

The owners of **The Tap Room,** a bare-bones crab establishment at Bohemia Avenue and Second Street, branched out with this fine-dining restaurant elevated on pilings in the anchorage basin on the waterfront near Pell Gardens. Here they offer a 200-seat dining room, a 250-seat open deck, a 60-seat bi-level veranda and a new tiki bar at one end. The layout is such that more than half the tables in the long, vast, white-clothed dining room have water views. Marble floors, white columns and rich wood accents add elegance. Pizzas, pastas, sandwiches and salads are available on the deck, day and night. The dining room menu is offered on the veranda as well as inside. Crab is the specialty on the extensive menu. Expect appetizers like crab bisque, crab en croûte, bruschetta with crab claws, stuffed mushrooms with crab imperial, baked oysters topped with crab imperial and shrimp chesapeake, stuffed with – yes – crab imperial. The crab treats continue with main-course specialties like crab ravioli and veal "della casa," topped with crabmeat and mozzarella cheese. There are sautéed crab cakes, chicken and crab cake creole, veal oscar and filet neptune (topped with crab imperial). Even the mixed grill combines a lamb chop, filet mignon and chicken topped with crab imperial. A 65-slip marina is available outside for those who arrive by boat.

(410) 885-2040. www.chesapeakeinn.com. Entrées, $19 to $32. Lunch daily, 11 to 3, Sunday noon to 3. Dinner nightly, 3 to 10.

Schaefer's New Canal House, 208 Bank St., North Chesapeake City.

This huge and venerable establishment is a restaurant plus a large banquet facility, a marina and a gift shop – just across the canal from the southern section of Chesapeake City. Two veteran Philadelphia restaurateurs have enhanced the food and entertainment situation. They added an Italian accent to the traditional seafood menu strong on – what else? – crab. Appetizers run from portobello pasquale to oysters rockefeller. For main courses, expect the likes of fried shrimp amandine, cioppino, crab imperial, chicken dijonnaise, veal chesapeake, prime rib and filet mignon. The main, upper-level restaurant offers a huge expanse of windows onto the water. Barstools and tables face the water in the adjacent bar/lounge. Outside along the canal is a terrace where big bands entertain. A pianist plays for the gala $17.95 Sunday brunch.

(410) 885-2200. Entrées, $16 to $27. Lunch daily, 11 to 4. Dinner nightly, 4 to 10.

FOR MORE INFORMATION: Kent County Tourism Office, 400 High St., Chestertown, Md. 21620, (410) 778-0416. www.kentcountry.com. Rock Hall Office of Tourism, (410) 778-09416. www.rockhallmd.com. Historic Chesapeake City Merchants Association, (410) 885-2415. www.chesapeakecity.com.

Delaware River and Milford, N.J., are seen from balcony at Bridgeton House B&B.

Delaware River/Bucks County, Pa.-N.J.

When William Penn came upon Bucks County back in 1682, it so reminded him of Great Britain that he named it after Buckingham, the shire in which he was born.

The resemblance still is clear: A rolling countryside dropping down to the wide Delaware River, just as England's does along the Thames River west of London. Crossroads pubs, stone houses and quaint hamlets that would look at home in the Cotswolds. Narrow, winding roads eliciting rural charms at every turn. Even the place names are similar: Solebury, Warminster, Chalfont, Wycombe. Such is the influence of the area's English Quaker settlers.

Although the area straddling the Delaware River became a stagecoach stop on the old York turnpike linking New York and Philadelphia, it retained its rural heritage and, to this day, remains a surprisingly unspoiled refuge amid the sprawling megalopolis.

The tranquil, idyllic setting of river and hills attracted a colony of painters known as the New Hope Artists early in the 20th century. Since then it has lured countless visitors, most of them to New Hope, a chic but quaint town whose mystique far exceeds its size (about 1,500 residents). Lately, the New Jersey river towns of Lambertville, Frenchtown and Milford have attracted tourists as well.

The arts colony, antiquing and the Bucks County Playhouse are prime attractions. So are several concentrations of small inns and good restaurants.

In the midst of this varied milieu is the Delaware River, narrow and deserted as it cuts beneath hillsides and cliffs of strange-colored layers of rock at Upper Black Eddy, majestic and lazing at New Hope and Lambertville, mysterious and historic at Washington Crossing. Towpaths and canals flank the river on both sides. Islands occasionally part the river in the middle.

River Road (Pennsylvania Route 32) undulates along the west bank through sharp turns and the odd hamlet and past hillsides strewn with rhododendron for a slow 30 miles from Washington Crossing northward to Upper Black Eddy. On the east bank, New Jersey's Route 29 speeds motorists along the same distance through rural terrain interrupted by an occasional town.

The river, the canals and the towpaths lure people for all kinds of rest and recreation – canoeing, rafting, fishing and swimming in the water; bicycling, jogging, strolling and dining alongside.

Getting There

This area along the Delaware River in Pennsylvania's Bucks County and New Jersey's Hunterdon County lies about 30 miles north of Philadelphia and 60 miles southwest of New York City. Interstates 95 and 78 plus the Pennsylvania and New Jersey turnpikes are nearby. U.S. Route 202 is the main approach to New Hope and Lambertville.

Where to Stay ⎯⎯⎯⎯⎯⎯⎯⎯⎯⎯⎯⎯⎯ _♫♫♫_

Travelers have paused for rest and sustenance at inns and B&Bs along the river since Colonial days. Today, the numerous but generally small lodging places are booked far in advance, particularly in summer and on weekends. You won't find any large chain motels except for a Best Western near New Hope. Many inns require two-night stays on weekends (three nights for holiday weekends).

Larger Inns

The Inn at Lambertville Station, 11 Bridge St., Lambertville, N.J. 08530.

Following his success with the restored Lambertville Station restaurant (see Where to Eat), local developer Dan Whitaker built this architecturally impressive, three-story luxury inn on riverfront land that had long been an eyesore at the western entrance to Lambertville. You check in at a counter resembling the ticket office of an old train station, perhaps tarry for tea or a drink from the honor bar in the towering lobby (higher than it is wide) and then get your bags up the elevator to your room. Prized antiques are in the 45 guest rooms, each named for a major city and decorated to match. Ours was the corner New York Suite, high in the trees above a rushing waterfall that lulled us to sleep. There were chocolates at bedside,

the bathroom had a whirlpool tub, and around the L-shaped room were heavy mahogany furniture, leather chairs facing the fireplace and TV, handsome draperies, ornate mirrors and fine art. A light continental breakfast with carrot-nut muffins arrived at our door with a newspaper the next morning. Other rooms that we saw were equally impressive, all individually decorated by an antiques dealer. Though no rooms face the river directly, occupants on the south side beside the woods hear the sounds of Swan Creek spilling down from the canal. Those on the north side view the lights of Lambertville and New Hope glimmering on the river. The large Riverside Room, which does face the river with windows on three sides, is used for the Sunday champagne brunch ($21.95 for quite a spread).

(609) 397-4400 or (800) 524-1091. Fax (609) 397-9744. www.lambertvillestation.com. Thirty-seven rooms and eight suites with private baths. Doubles, $120 to $205. Suites, $165 to $285.

1740 House, 3690 River Road, Lumberville, Pa. 18933.

This inn's serenity, its quiet location in a quaint hamlet beside the Delaware and its unusual motel-style privacy appeal to repeat visitors who tend to book the same river-view rooms year after year. Opened in 1967, the 1740 House was built to look old, each room in two wings opening from a front corridor and extending to patios or balconies perched out back at canal's edge. Following the death of the founding owner, a team of investors brought the idiosyncratic place into the 21st century: new kingsize and twin beds, new furnishings, new decor and – abhorrent to the original owner – television sets in armoires, telephones and data ports. Six deluxe rooms were given gas fireplaces and minibars, and two others were enlarged into suites. A number of bathrooms were updated. A cozy barroom was added, opening onto a canopied patio beside the pool. The prices were hiked, of course, and now credit cards are accepted. Each room is different with poster beds, toile wall coverings and folk art, but all have glass doors opening onto brick patios or balconies. You can laze in a tiny swimming pool or paddle the canal beneath your room in the inn's canoe, except there's never been enough water when we've been there. Complimentary mountain bikes are available for exploring the towpath. A continental breakfast is put out buffet-style in a cheery, flagstone-floored garden dining room, where if it's busy you'll share tables. In the afternoon, the staff puts out quite a spread of cakes and cookies along with tea and lemonade.

(215) 297-5661. Fax (215) 297-5243. www.1740house.com. Twenty-one rooms and two suites with private baths. Doubles, $150 to $195. Suites, $195 to $325.

Centre Bridge Inn, 2998 North River Road, New Hope, Pa. 18938.

Wonderfully situated beside the Delaware across from the pleasant New Jersey village of Stockton, this striking white structure with red shutters built in Colonial Williamsburg style has a large restaurant-tavern downstairs and nine guest rooms on the first and second floors. Fires destroyed inns that had occupied the site since 1705, so this is of early 1960s vintage and some of it looks barely changed since. Overnight guests enter an enormous formal vestibule, with a fireplaced parlor on the river side. Ahead are the three most desirable quarters. Room 9 has a queensize four-poster bed, TV, two plush chairs on thick carpeting, cedar-lined bath and private river-view terrace – "our nicest room," according to our guide. A suite offers a kingsize bed, TV, sitting and dressing areas and a river view. A two-room suite in front has a queen brass bed and sitting room with sofa, loveseat and TV. Upstairs are seven more rooms, five with king or queen beds (two with canopied doubles) and all outfitted lately with TV. All are notable for Schumacher wall coverings and a well-worn feeling. A luxury riverside suite was being readied for occupancy in 2006. A continental breakfast is served in the suites, the parlor or outside on a terrace off the main floor, which enjoys one of the nicest views of the river anywhere.

(215) 862-2048. Fax (215) 862-3244. www.centrebridgeinn.com. Eight rooms and two suites with private baths. Doubles, $135 to $180. Suites, $225.

EverMay-on-the-Delaware, River Road, Box 60, Erwinna, Pa. 18920.

A three-story, gold and tan Victorian mansion set back on a broad lawn facing the river, EverMay is the inn and gourmet-dinner venture of antiques dealers William and Danielle Moffly. Guest rooms are located upstairs in the manor house (six with river views) as well as in a nearby carriage house, cottage and barn. All with air conditioning and telephones, they are furnished with collectibles and antiques from the Victorian era. Ours in the Carriage House seemed a bit austere, despite the presence of fresh flowers and a large bowl of fresh fruit. Some inn rooms retain the original fireplaces. Walnut beds, oriental rugs, marble-topped dressers, fancy quilts and lacy pillows are among the furnishings. Two newly remodeled rooms in the barn come with king beds, Vermont castings fireplaces and whirlpool tubs. Downstairs in the mansion's double front parlor, where afternoon tea is served at 4, a fire often burns in the fireplace and decanters of sherry are at the ready. A continental breakfast is served in the conservatory dining room at the rear; we liked the incredibly flaky croissants and a delicious compote of fresh fruit. Prix-fixe dinners of six courses for $68 are served Friday and Saturday at 7:30 and four-course dinners for $45 Sunday from 5 to 7:30. We remember an extraordinary fall dinner of lamb noisettes and poached Norwegian salmon, beautifully presented with exotic accompaniments.

(610) 294-9100. Fax (610) 294-8249. www.evermay.com. Seventeen rooms and one suite with private baths. Doubles, $145 to $275.

Small Inns and B&Bs

Bridgeton House, 1525 River Road, Box 167, Upper Black Eddy, Pa. 18972.

This onetime wreck of an apartment house built in 1836 was transformed with sweat and love by Bea and Charles Briggs into a comfortable B&B with a glorious location beside the river. Although smack up against the road, the inn opens to the rear for a water orientation. Lovely stenciling, fresh or dried flowers, a decanter of sherry and potpourri grace the dining room. A rear parlor and upstairs balconies look onto a landscaped courtyard beside the canal. Most of the guest quarters overlook the water. Each is exceptionally fashioned by Charles, a master carpenter and renovator, and interestingly decorated by Bea. Some have four-posters and chaise lounges. All have private baths, country antiques, colorful sheets, fresh flowers and intriguing touches. Our main-floor room had a private porch with rockers and lovely stenciling. The dramatic penthouse suite is billed as Bucks County's ultimate, with its twelve-foot cathedral ceiling, a kingsize bed, black and white marble fireplace, marble bathtub, backgammon table, black leather chairs, a stereo-TV center and a full-length deck. It shares top billing with the new Boat House, a riverside cottage with cathedral-ceilinged living room, mini-kitchen, kingsize bed, double whirlpool tub, TV/VCR and terrace beside the river. A full breakfast brings freshly baked breads or muffins and a hot dish like cheddar cheese omelet or scrambled eggs.

(610) 982-5856 or (888) 982-2007. Fax (610) 982-5080. www.bridgetonhouse.com. Ten rooms, one penthouse and one cottage with private baths. Doubles, $139 to $229. Penthouse and cottage, $299 to $399.

Chestnut Hill on the Delaware, 63 Church St., Milford, N.J. 08848.

The river lazes past this 1860 Victorian house, considered the grandest in town, and a great place to view it is from the long lineup of rockers on the veranda just a shady front yard away. Linda and Rob Castagna offer six guest rooms, two of which can be joined as a suite called Teddy's Place on third floor. All come with featherbeds and discreetly hidden TVs. The premier guest room in the house is the new Summer Morning, light and airy with kingsize bed, sitting area by the window overlooking the river, electric fireplace and bath with double whirlpool tub and rainforest shower. The second-floor Rose Garden room also has a whirlpool tub and a beautiful river view, but most guests prefer to watch the river from the drawing room, the living room or that neat veranda. Apothecary wall units in the formal drawing room in the Eastlake tradition contain books, gifts and potpourri. Here also are iron mannequins modeling Victorian outfits that Linda found in trunks belonging to the first owners when she and Rob bought the house in 1982. Guests are served a country breakfast at a long, lace-covered table in the dining room – perhaps German apple pancakes "or whatever I'm in the mood to do," says Linda. Those seeking seclusion opt for the Country Cottage by the River, a self-contained suite next door with living room, fireplaced queen bedroom, stocked kitchen and wraparound veranda. The best river view is from the similarly outfitted Paradise Suite, available with one or two bedrooms on the cottage's second floor. Guests in either can relax by the cottage fountain, reminiscent of a European courtyard, or nap in the hammock to the sounds of trickling water. Everyone gets to enjoy the spectacular riverside gardens.

(908) 995-9761 or (888) 333-2242. Fax (908)995-0608. www.chestnuthillnj.com. Five rooms and two cottage suites with private baths. Doubles, $100 to $250. Suites, $200 to $350. No credit cards.

Golden Pheasant Inn, 763 River Road, Erwinna, Pa. 18920.

As in the country auberges of his native France, well-known local chef Michel Faure from Grenoble and his family live upstairs over their restaurant. They have renovated and redecorated six guest rooms to offer "a taste of France on the banks of the Delaware," according to wife Barbara. All have river or canal views, and four have fireplaces. Rooms we saw had queen canopy beds and were nicely appointed with colorful fabrics and window treatments. Each has a telephone and a CD clock radio that emits romantic music for guests upon arrival. The prime accommodation is called a cottage suite. In addition to a whirlpool tub and fireplace, it has a kingsize poster bed, living area with a dining table and a kitchenette. Guests enjoy a rear patio and terraces beside the canal. A continental breakfast is offered in the morning.

(610) 294-9595 or (800) 830-4474. Fax (610) 294-9882. www.goldenpheasant.com. Five rooms and one suite with private baths. Doubles, $95 to $175. Suite, $225.

Pineapple Hill, 1324 River Road, New Hope, Pa. 18938.

This 18th-century Bucks County farmhouse is one of the few places in which to stay along the river on the near south side of New Hope. The B&B started with three suites clustered in separate areas on the second and third floors and since has added five rooms and an apartment suite. All rooms have queen or kingsize beds, gas fireplaces, cable TV and telephones. Suites have separate living rooms, and one adds a full kitchen. The Buckland Room, attractive in white and blue, has Battenburg pillows and a private balcony. Decor is homey but smart with country accents. A full buffet breakfast is offered at individual tables in a large common room with fireplace. The serving table holds fruits, pineapple bread and a hot entrée, perhaps a zucchini, onion and ham quiche or french toast stuffed with cream cheese and strawberry jam. Out back are gardens and a tiled swimming pool enclosed in the ruins of a stone barn. Beyond is the towpath by the canal.

(215) 862-1790. www.pineapplehill.com. Five rooms and four suites with private baths. Doubles, $116 to $195. Suites, $138 to $279.

Seeing and Doing ⌒⌒⌒

Many are the attractions and varied the appeal of the Delaware River and the narrow canals on both sides. Built in the 1830s, the Delaware Division Canal was used for floating coal and limestone from Easton through New Hope south to

Bristol. During its 60-mile course, barges dropped 165 feet through 25 locks and under 106 bridges. New Hope was the only point on the canal where four barges could pass at once, and after 1854, barges shuttled across the Delaware River to Lambertville and the Delaware & Raritan Canal, and then to Princeton, Newark and New York. The last shipments of coal and manufactured goods were floated down the canal about 1930. These days, there is seldom enough water in the canal for the traditional canoeing except in the immediate New Hope area. Pennsylvania's Delaware Division Canal has become the Theodore Roosevelt State Park and a National Historic Landmark. Most of New Jersey's Raritan canal also is a state park.

On or Near the Water

Walk the Towpath. We thoroughly enjoy walking the canal towpaths along the river, particularly the Pennsylvania portion between Lumberville and Phillips Mill and particularly in spring when all the daffodils are abloom. Start in Lumberville at the footbridge to Bull's Island, a New Jersey state park. The Black Bass Hotel's friendly ducks may greet you, the gardens and back yards of English-type manor houses are sure to intrigue, and everywhere are wildflowers, singing birds, joggers, picnickers and other strollers. A footbridge leads to the Cuttalossa Inn, where the outdoor terrace beside a millstream and waterfall appeals for lunch or a drink. You can stop at the Centre Bridge Inn for a drink, or cross the highway bridge to Stockton, N.J., to pick up a picnic lunch at the market and a bottle of wine at the incredibly well-stocked Phillips wine store. Just down river is Phillips Mill, an ever-so-British looking cluster of stone houses hugging the River Road, and the colorful grounds of **Lenteboden,** the business and residence of the bulb specialist whose gardens full of daffodils, tulips and hyacinths herald the arrival of spring. Like almost everything else along the towpath, they're free and open for the exploring. A word of caution: the towpath walk is lulling and may take the better part of a day. Unless you have a car meeting you at the end, you'll have to walk back or hitch a ride, as we did (and it took almost an hour before anyone stopped).

Bucks County River Country, 2 Walters Lane (Route 32), Point Pleasant, Pa.

The river is so popular for canoeing, kayaking, rafting and tubing that owner Tom McBrien has turned his original tubing enterprise into the East's largest water recreation facility. Tubing remains the biggest operation, with up to 3,500 people a day renting bright orange, yellow, blue or green inner tubes for floats of three to six miles ($20 per person weekends, $18 weekdays). Canoeists and kayakers are transported up to Tinicum or Upper Black Eddy for trips down river of six to thirteen miles ($25 to $35 per person). Rafts and two-person "snuggle tubes" also are available. McBrien says there's nothing like floating or paddling down the Delaware (which he calls "the Eden of the East"), watching fish leaping and osprey feeding, and pausing for a swim in the warm, clear waters. He recommends a stop at the "Famous River Hot Dog Man," whose **Island Café** on Adventure Island provides lunches and snacks in the middle of the river, four miles above Point Pleasant. Greg Crance's endeavor has been written up in the National Enquirer. It's accessible only by water, but you can't miss the sign, the music or the goings-on.

(215) 297-5000. www.rivercountry.net. Open daily, 9 to 6, Memorial Day to Labor Day, weekends in spring and fall. Parking fee, $5.

Boat Rides. Gen. George Washington advised: "Be sure to take the ferry by Coryell's as it is the swiftest, surest route." Today's **Coryell's Ferry** rides aren't the swiftest, but they are among the surest ways for the public to see the New Hope section of the river. Capt. Robert Gerenser, whose name is attached to much activity and enterprise in New Hope, gives scenic half-hour excursions with an informative narrative on a ferry boat from 22 South Main St., New Hope, (215) 862-2050. Rides leave roughly every 45 minutes from 10 to 5:30, May-September; adults $8, children $5. Excursions on a 37-foot pontoon boat are offered daily May-October from noon to 7 by **Wells Ferry Boat Rides,** 14 East Ferry St., New Hope, (215) 862-5965; adults $7, children $4.

New Hope Canal Boat Co., 149 South Main St., New Hope, Pa.

Mule-drawn canal boats revive the past for hundreds of visitors daily on the old Delaware Canal. The boats have been hauling tourists since 1931 when the canal's commercial usage ended. Co-owners Paul Raywood and Lee Urbani, canal aficionados both, lease the operation from the state. They have four mules, "two boys and two girls." Working in pairs, the mules draw the boats about 1.5 miles up the canal past Colonial homes, artists' workshops, hidden alleys, gardens and countryside to the Route 202 bridge and back. A musician-historian in period costume relates canal lore and strums folk songs during the one-hour excursion. The enterprise conducts happy-hour cruises Fridays and Saturdays at 6:30. At the boat landing, the restored 19th-century canal locktender's house is open with exhibits.

(215) 862-0758. www.canalboats.com. Four trips daily at noon, 1:30, 3 and 4:30, May-October, also Friday-Sunday 12:30 and 3 in April. Adults $10, children $8. Parking $5.

FISHING. Considered one of the best fishing rivers in the East, the Delaware is known to harbor more than 30 species, including trout, bass, muskies and pike. Whenever we visit in the spring, the shad seem to be running and the fishermen are out in force, in boats or in hip boots just offshore in the Lumberville-Bull's Island launch areas.

Covered Bridges. Thirteen of 36 covered bridges built in Bucks County remain standing, crossing creeks and canals. A self-guided driving tour gives locations and details for each.

Delaware Raritan Canal State Park, Route 29 north, Stockton, N.J., (609) 397-2949. For nearly a century, the old D&R Canal was one of America's busiest. A 22-mile-long navigable feeder canal stretching from above Stockton at Raven Rock south through Lambertville to Trenton brought water from the Delaware River to the main canal, which ran from Bordentown to New Brunswick. The canal and its adjacent towpath by the Delaware River are now part of New Jersey's longest park. The towpath is a favorite of joggers and hikers. North of Stockton are the Bulls Island Recreation Area at Raven Rock and a pedestrian bridge crossing to Lumberville, Pa. At the edge of town are the 18th-century **Prallsville Mills,** included on the National Register of Historic Places and part of the D&R Canal State Park. Local citizens formed the Delaware River Mill Society to restore and interpret the mill site, which includes a four-story gristmill now used for periodic arts and crafts exhibits, lectures and concerts. Original mill machinery is on display.

Washington Crossing Historic Park, 1112 River Road (Route 32), Washington Crossing, Pa.

History was made here in 1776 when George Washington and 2,400 troops crossed the Delaware on Christmas night to attack the British in Trenton. Now the Pennsylvania side has a large, 500-acre state park in two sections.

The northern Thompson Mill section is two miles south of New Hope. It features **Bowman's Tower,** a 110-foot-high stone observation point with an elevator (admission included in the park's six-building ticket). From the top of the site where sentries watched enemy troop movements, you get a panoramic view of river and valley. Around the tower is the noted 100-acre **Bowman's Hill Wildflower Preserve,** with 26 acres of trails and habitat areas plus a headquarters building with gift shop and displays. Across River Road are the 1702 **Thompson-Neely House,** requisitioned in 1776 as a battle headquarters and now a museum, plus a gristmill and picnic areas.

Four miles south is the park's McConkey Ferry section and visitor center. Here a 25-minute film tells the story of how George Washington and his half-frozen troops regrouped at this location from encampments stretching from New Hope to Yardley to cross the river and capture Trenton. The film ends rather abruptly, we thought. Then you can take a walking tour and enter four historic buildings. Included are the **McConkey Ferry Inn,** where Washington is believed to have eaten dinner the night before the Battle of Trenton, the 1816 **Taylor House,** the **Hibbs House** and the **Durham Boat House,** where replicas of iron ore boats such as those used by Washington's troops are stored. One area of this park has a picturesque lagoon populated by incredible numbers of Canada geese and other birds, surrounded by picnic facilities.

The biggest event of the year is the annual reenactment of Washington's crossing of the Delaware at 1 p.m. on Dec. 25. The dress rehearsal about two weeks earlier offers a quieter preview.

(215) 493-4076. Park and buildings open Tuesday-Saturday 9 to 5, Sunday noon to 5. Admission, $1 per vehicle. Building and guided tour ticket, adults $4, children $2.

Washington Crossing State Park, 355 Washington Crossing-Pennington Road, Titusville, N.J.

Across the Delaware River at Washington's crossing point is this 841-acre New Jersey state park. It includes a visitor center with exhibits and videos, an overlook area, nature trails, an open-air theater for the annual Summer Festival of Music and Drama, the George Washington Memorial Arboretum and a couple of house museums. The restored **Johnson Ferry House,** commandeered by Washington to use as a transient headquarters, is furnished to the period. A wooden pedestrian bridge adjacent to the ferry house crosses the street along the Delaware River and offers an overlook of the crossing site. It leads to the **Nelson House** at the landing spot, which served as a ferryman's residence and traveler's tavern. It features period furnishings and old photographs of the canal and railroad transportation.

(609) 737-0623. Park open Wednesday-Sunday 9 to 4, free. Parking fee $5 on weekends from Memorial Day to Labor Day.

Around the Towns

Walk New Hope. A compact village, New Hope is made for walking. That's fortunate, because in summer things get really congested. Outlying lots charge for parking, and it's best to leave your car. The small information center in the 1839 jail-town hall at South Main and Mechanic streets logged a staggering 6,577 visitors one August before it was inexplicably downscaled into an overly commercial, not very helpful resource. A short New Hope walking tour guides you to the East Ferry Street landing and mill complex, the hub of early village life (now including Martine's restaurant, Farley's New Delaware Bookshop and the Bucks County Playhouse), the historic Logan Inn and the old houses of West Ferry Street (they're among the town's 243 properties included in 1985 on the National Register of Historic Places). The 1784 **Parry Mansion Museum** has eleven rooms open for tours, late April to early December, Saturday and Sunday 1 to 5; adults $5, children $1. Stroll along the

Delaware Canal park and gardens, through the alleys filled with art galleries, and along the streets lined with more shops than we can possibly enumerate. Take our word: if it's for sale, someone in New Hope or environs carries it.

Cross the Delaware River bridge from New Hope to **Lambertville,** an up-and-coming riverside town of interesting shops (it's now considered the antiques capital of New Jersey) and restaurants. Lambertville's nationally recognized Shad Festival, staged annually the last full weekend in April, draws thousands to celebrate arts and crafts as well as the Delaware River and shad.

For the ultimate rural small-town experience, walk through tiny **Lumberville** and savor the past, including the historic Black Bass Hotel and the **Lumberville Store,** which dates to 1770 and encompasses the post office, an art gallery, groceries and sandwiches, books and bicycle rentals.

Wine Bars and Pubs. A favorite pastime of many is stopping at a wine bar, something of an early local phenomenon. Full of nautical items, the intimate, vine-covered **Boat House** bar at the Porkyard in Lambertville is nearest the water. The **Swan Hotel** at 43 South Main St. is a large and urbane bar with much atmosphere as well as food service. Nearby is the **Inn of the Hawke,** 74 South Union St., an English pub and restaurant with British ales on draught. Another popular spot for English pub food and a pint of bitter is the **Ship Inn** in Milford, the site of New Jersey's first brew pub. It dispenses home brews and more than 50 British favorites.

New Hope & Ivyland Railroad, 32 West Bridge St., New Hope, Pa., (215) 862-2332. The 1891 New Hope train station with its witch-hat peak has been restored as part of a museum that includes a 1906 wooden baggage car and the Freight House Gift Shop. The steam locomotive and vintage 1920s Reading Railroad passenger coaches take passengers on a nine-mile, 50-minute round trip up Solebury Mountain to Lahaska and back. Trips are scheduled daily (at least hourly 11 to 4 or 5 in peak season) from the New Hope Station. Adults $10, children $7.

Horse-drawn carriage rides around New Hope and Lambertville are offered daily, March-November, by **Bucks County Carriages,** 2586 North River Road, New Hope, Pa., (215) 862-3582. Horseback rides are available at the enterprise's West End Farm, as are trail rides along the canal. Horse-drawn carriage rides also are offered by **Stockton Carriage Tours,** 94 Worman Road, Stockton, N.J., (609) 397-9066. Rides are scheduled Sundays 1 to 4 at Prallsville Mill and by appointment.

Bucks County Playhouse, 70 South Main St., New Hope, Pa., (215) 862-2041. The old town mill that backs up to the river ceased operating in 1938. It was purchased by local citizens who turned it into a summer stock theater, which debuted in 1939 with Edward Everett Horton in "Springtime for Henry." The 457-seat theater runs an ambitious 30-week schedule from May to late December, generally Wednesday-Sunday with one or two shows daily. Tickets, $22 to $24.

Where to Eat

Dining is a big deal along the Delaware, and the choices are legion. Some restaurants are not licensed for liquor, but allow guests to bring their own.

Up the River

The Inn at Phillips Mill, North River Road, New Hope, Pa.

For charm and good food, this quaint gray stone building right next to a bend in the River Road is tops. Looking as if it had been transported from the British

Cotswolds, the 1750 structure has a copper pig above the entrance – a symbol of the stone barn's origin as a gristmill that stood next to the village piggery. Architect Brooks Kaufman and his innkeeper wife Joyce transformed it into a country French restaurant, plus a cozy inn with five cheerily decorated guest accommodations ($80 to $90) upstairs. The dining setting could not be more romantic: candles augmenting light from the fireplace in low-ceilinged rooms with dark beams, and arrangements of flowers all around. In season, the rear dining room opens onto a garden courtyard. The chef's terrine and escargots with garlic butter are favored appetizers. We've never tasted such a tender filet mignon with such a delectable béarnaise sauce or such perfect sweetbreads in a light brown sauce as on our first visit. On another occasion, we liked the sautéed calves liver in a cider vinegar and the veal medallions with roasted shallots in cognac sauce. The pastry chef's desserts are triumphs, among them a lemon ice cream meringue pie, about six inches high and wonderfully refreshing, and a vanilla mousse with big chips of chocolate and chocolate fudge sauce.

(215) 862-9919. Entrées, $17.50 to $26. Dinner nightly, 5:30 to 9:30 or 10. BYOB. No credit cards.

Black Bass Hotel, 3774 River Road, Lumberville, Pa.

The river view from the rear dining rooms, full of historic memorabilia and atmosphere, is surpassed perhaps only by that from the ground-level riverside terrace. That the food has improved under new ownership is a bonus, and the Sunday brunch is considered one of the best around. Though we recall a memorable dinner some years ago, we like the Black Bass best for lunch, when you can feast on the riverside scenery outside the long rear dining porch or up close on the terrace. Many favor the Charleston Meeting Street crab, a fixture on both the lunch and dinner menus. The New Orleans onion soup, thick with onions and cheese, came in a proper crock. The crisp greens in the house salad were laden with croutons and a nifty dressing of homemade mayonnaise, horseradish, dijon mustard and spices. Famished after a lengthy walk along the towpath, one of us devoured seven of the nut and date mini-muffins that came in a basket. The with-it dinner menu ranges from potato-crusted tilapia with smoked salmon beurre blanc to coffee-lacquered duck with ginger-pear chutney. Desserts here are excellent: perhaps banana-walnut bread pudding with rum sabayon or a macadamia nut tartlet topped with white chocolate mousse. Upstairs are seven bedrooms sharing two baths ($80) and two suites ($150 to $175).

(215) 297-5770. www.blackbasshotel.com. Entrées, $25.95 to $39.95. Lunch, Monday-Saturday 11:30 to 3. Dinner, 5:30 to 9:30. Sunday, brunch 11 to 2:30, dinner 4:30 to 8:30.

The Frenchtown Inn, 7 Bridge St., Frenchtown, N.J.

Chef-owner Andrew Tomko's food is inventive, the service flawless yet friendly, and the setting comfortable in this acclaimed restaurant with a handsome grill room on the side. Arriving for a Friday lunch without reservations, we found the front dining room with its planked ceiling and brick walls full. So we were seated in the more austere columned dining room in the rear, outfitted with pink and green wallpaper, crisp white linens and Villeroy & Boch china. Everything on the menu looked great; we can vouch for an unusual and airy black bean soup, the selection of smooth pâtés and terrines, the corned beef sandwich on brown bread and a sensational salad of duck and smoked pheasant with a warm cider vinaigrette, loaded with meat and mixed greens like radicchio and arugula. A layered pear-raspberry tart with whipped cream was a perfect dessert. A later visit produced a memorable (and reasonably priced) dinner in the white-linened Grill Room, where singles were eating at the bar. A special salad of baby lettuces and goat cheese, an appetizer of crispy rock shrimp with wasabi and mustard oils, and two small, exotic pastas were enough for two to share. With a raspberry sorbet for dessert and a $15 bottle of Preston fumé blanc, we were well satisfied for less than $50. That was barely half what you'd expect to pay for one of the remarkable dinners in the more formal dining venues just across the hall, where main courses range from rare yellowfin tuna with a ginger-soy sauce to the signature filet of beef wrapped in puff pastry and surrounded by white truffle mousse. The food comes from the same expert kitchen, but the grill represents unusual value for the area.

(908) 996-3300. Entrées, $21 to $28; Grill, $9.75 to $17.95. Lunch, Tuesday-Saturday noon to 2. Dinner, Tuesday-Friday 6 to 9, Saturday 5:30 to 9:30. Sunday, brunch noon to 2:15, dinner 5 to 8.

Golden Pheasant Inn, 763 River Road, Erwinna, Pa.

The glamorous, plant-filled solarium in this 1857 fieldstone inn that originally served bargemen along the canal was the setting for one of our more memorable meals, so we're glad that the rest of the restaurant has been fixed up as well. French chef Michel Faure and his wife Barbara, owners in residence since 1986, restored the two dark inner Victorian dining rooms to an elegant country French look of the 1850s, showcasing an extensive Quimper collection from Brittany. We'd still choose the solarium, where you can see the canal and the gardens and trees illuminated at night, to enjoy some of Michel's dinner creations of country French classics. Dinner begins with a complimentary amuse-bouche, in our case melba toast with a cream cheese spread enlivened with spicy olives and roasted peppers. Start perhaps with the renowned lobster bisque, pheasant pâté with peach chutney or smoked trout. Continue with such main dishes as the poached Atlantic salmon with champagne shrimp sauce that one reviewer called the best he'd ever had, sautéed scallops with a lobster and white wine sauce, veal medallions with morel demi-glace, roasted duck with a raspberry-rum sauce, filet mignon béarnaise or grilled lamb chops with a roasted shallot-mint sauce. Worthy endings include cappuccino cheesecake, crème caramel and, a specialty, Belgian white chocolate mousse with a raspberry coulis.

(610) 294-9595 or (800) 830-4474. www.goldenpheasant.com. Entrées, $20 to $28. Dinner, Wednesday-Saturday 5:30 to 9. Sunday, brunch 11 to 3, dinner 3 to 8.

Centre Bridge Inn, 2998 North River Road, New Hope, Pa.

The lower-level tavern/dining room with beamed ceilings, stucco walls and huge open fireplaces could not be more attractive, nor the glass-enclosed porch overlooking the river more inviting. Outside by the river overlooking the bridge to Stockton is a brick patio with white wrought-iron furniture and a circle of granite tables around a fountain. Here is the ultimate riverside setting in the country, although some think the food doesn't measure up to the surroundings. The short menu gives contemporary twists to the traditionally continental fare. Appetizers could be coconut shrimp with raspberry sauce or a trio of pheasant, venison and buffalo sausages with assorted mustards. Main courses range from pistachio-crusted salmon with spiced rum and lime butter to grilled strip steak with green peppercorn sauce. Cappuccino and international coffees are available, and we recall a happy evening sipping after-dinner drinks at the bar as a pianist entertained.

(215) 862-2048. Entrées, $22 to $38. Dinner, Wednesday-Saturday 5 to 9, Sunday 2 to 10.

Cuttalossa Inn, 3487 River Road, Lumberville, Pa.

Another place where the surroundings may upstage the food is the venerable Cuttalossa. The setting is tough to beat. Inside the 1758 stone landmark are three history-filled dining rooms. Outside is a vast, sylvan and beautifully landscaped, multi-level terrace beside a millstream and waterfall, where we'd gladly tarry for an al fresco meal. Co-owner Marilyn MacMaster, something of a showperson, travels the world to find new recipes, perhaps Thai shrimp with coconut plum sauce, broiled red snapper Brazilian and even tofu florentine served over pasta. Otherwise, the dinner menu mixes traditional continental and American: the specialty crab imperial, blackened swordfish, grilled tuna with mango salsa, "berry, berry chicken" on a bed of spinach and prosciutto, pork porterhouse teriyaki with peach glaze, veal oscar and rack of lamb with a mint julep sauce. Entrées come with a house salad. You might start with shrimp cocktail, venison rack or ostrich filet with blue cheese and pomegranate sauce. Finish with homemade strawberry cheesecake, key lime pie or rum-walnut pie. Cross a little bridge for a drink in the outdoor bar, ensconced in the stone ruins of an old lumber mill and illuminated at night by twinkling white lights. With the woods, gardens and stone buildings lit and the roar of the falls in the background, the setting is quite magical.

(215) 297-5082. www.cuttalossainn.com. Entrées, $22.95 to $42.95. Lunch, Monday-Saturday 11 to 2. Dinner, Monday-Saturday from 5:30. Closed in January.

Atrio Café, 515 Bridge St., Stockton, N.J.

Chef-owner Ricky Franco, a native of Brazil who cooked in New York at the Plaza and the Waldorf-Astoria hotels, is one of the trio that opened this appealing café named for their partnership, "a trio." The decor in hunter green and burgundy is simple. The eclectic cuisine with a Brazilian "flare," as they advertise, is quite sophisticated. Appealing main courses range from pan-seared salmon with peppercorn sauce on a chickpea cake to roasted rack of lamb topped with a cannellini bean, mushroom and wine demi-glace. The ravioli might be topped with a shrimp, tasso ham and chickpea sauce. The monkfish could be sprinkled with black pepper, splashed with mustard-curry sauce and served over watercress drizzled with a roasted shallot dressing. Start with lump crab cakes with a sweet onion salsa or a salad of pepper-crusted scallops and grilled portobellos with watercress and shaved parmesan. Finish with key lime pie or a tart of poached pear with ginger-mascarpone cream.

(609) 397-0042. Entrées, $16.95 to $22.95. Lunch, Thursday-Saturday 11:30 to 3. Dinner, Tuesday-Saturday from 5. Sunday, brunch 10:30 to 3, dinner 4 to 8. BYOB.

The Bridge Café, 8 Bridge St., Frenchtown, N.J.

Casual country fare is available in this little train station converted to a bakery and deli-café. There are a handful of tables inside and many more on a large enclosed patio beside the river. You could lunch on a charbroiled chicken club sandwich on a fresh café roll, a Middle Eastern sampler plate or double grilled spinach cakes paired with feta and lentils. These also are available for weekend dinners, when chef-owners Ken and Lisa Miller might offer grilled Atlantic salmon with tomato concasse and chicken saltimbocca. Get scones for English tea, or a cup of cappuccino. Everything from salads to pies is available for takeout.

(201) 996-6040. www.bridgecafe.net. Entrées, $7.50 to $8.95 at lunch, $10.95 to $14.95 at dinner. Lunch, daily 11 to 3. Dinner, Friday-Saturday 6 to 9, May-October. BYOB. No credit cards.

In Town, On or Near the River

The Landing, 22 North Main St., New Hope, Pa.

The only restaurant with a river view in the heart of New Hope, this establishment is tucked back off the main street in a small house with windows onto the water. The two interior dining rooms on either side of a bar are intimate and cozy for fireside dining on cool days. In good weather the crowd heads for the expansive riverside terrace – billed as the most coveted in Bucks County. The dining patio is brightened with colorful planters and umbrellas, dignified at night by tablecloths and made practical by an enclosed bar at one side. If there's obviously a gardener at work around the exterior, there's an equally talented chef in the kitchen, for The Landing has been known for New Hope's best and most consistent food for more than 25 years. The changing menu arrived in a picture frame the night we ate here. Entrées range from peppercorn-crusted yellowfin tuna with curried carrot broth and Moroccan-crusted soft-shell crabs with curry turmeric sauce to grilled pork tenderloin with cider-ginger gravy and mustard-crusted loin of lamb with sweet tomato-thyme jus. Expect starters like pork and shrimp spring rolls with mandarin-sesame dipping sauce and P.E.I. mussels steamed in Corona beer with chorizo, corn, chipotle and cilantro. Dessert could be an extra-rich dark chocolate mousse terrine with a mandarin orange coulis or a custard cake of summer berries.

(215) 862-5711. Entrées, $22.95 to $32.95. Lunch daily, 11 to 2:30, to 4 in summer. Dinner nightly, from 5.

Hamilton's Grill Room, 8½ Coryell St., Lambertville, N.J.

White-linened tables on a covered patio beside the canal and around the courtyard fountain are the summer venues of choice at this Mediterranean grill hidden at the end of an alley in the Porkyard complex. Inside, patrons dine at tables rather close together in the grill room, in the Bishop's Room beneath angels and clouds surrounding a huge gilt mirror on the ceiling and in an airy rear gallery. Former Broadway set designer Jim Hamilton installed an open grill beside the entrance and built the wood-fired pizza oven himself. Our convivial dinner began with grilled shrimp with anchovy sauce and a crab cake with wilted greens and sweet red pepper sauce. We enjoyed an exceptional grilled duck on bitter greens with pancetta and honey glaze as well as the signature grilled ribeye au poivre with leek aioli and pommes frites. The oversize plates were filled with fanned razor-thin sliced potatoes and grilled zucchini and green and red peppers. The signature grappa torta and the grand marnier cheesecake were fine desserts. Two biscotti came with the bill. While the main grill is BYOB, Hamilton's serves its regular menu at the **Boat House** bar annex across the courtyard on weekends for folks who want full liquor service.

(609) 397-4343. Entrées, $18 to $30. Dinner nightly, 6 to 10, Sunday 5 to 9. BYOB.

Lambertville Station, 11 Bridge St., Lambertville, N.J.

The once-abandoned 2½-story train station is now a stylish Victorian restaurant and lounge that fairly oozes atmosphere. Diners on several levels of the glass-enclosed Platform Room can watch geese glide by on the Delaware & Raritan Canal and tiny lights reflecting off the water. With good-size drinks, our party of four sampled the unusual appetizer of alligator strips, which we dipped into a mustard and green peppercorn sauce. The carpaccio of buffalo also was very good. Among entrées, the jambalaya was spicy, the boneless roast duck was properly crispy and had a raspberry sauce, the seafood fettuccine was more than ample and the veal medallions with jumbo shrimp in garlic butter were excellent. The honey-mustard dressing on the house spinach salad was super, and we relished lime-almond cheesecake and key lime mousse pie for dessert. The Sunset on the Delaware special, served weekdays from 4 to 6:30, is considered one of the best bargains around: soup or salad, entrée and dessert for $12.95. A Victorian lounge is on the mezzanine, and a dance club on the lower level.

(609) 397-8300. Entrées, $14.95 to $25.95. Lunch, Monday-Saturday 11:30 to 3. Dinner nightly, 4 to 10 or 11. Sunday brunch, 10:30 to 3.

Lilly's on the Canal, 2 Canal St., Lambertville, N.J.

This is the successor to the late Fish House, restaurant/theater designer Jim Hamilton's short-lived marquee attraction in a restored brick warehouse beside the canal. The showy gourmet seafood restaurant gave way in 2003 to a populist restaurant trying to be all things to all people. Caterer Lilly Salvatore offers a lively blend of restaurant, diner, soda fountain and sideshow on two floors around an open kitchen. From the wraparound mezzanine, patrons watch the young cooks implementing an eclectic menu from plain to fancy. Both grilled tortilla chips with salsa and grilled baby lamb chops with pita bread and crème fraîche might be among the starters, while entrées range from penne à la vodka to filet mignon. Desserts also are haute (crème brûlée) or homey (ice cream sundaes and root beer float). A cubano sandwich and salad niçoise are featured on a casual dinner menu. Such sandwiches and salads make this a particularly good bet for lunch (the warmed salad topped with poached eggs, bacon bits and goat cheese might make a late breakfast). Tables on both levels wrap around the open square pit, where the food preparation takes place in full view. The show may be upstaged by a fanciful 50-foot-long mural depicting an underwater wedding on one wall and the waterfall cascading down another wall.

(609) 397-6242. Entrées, $14 to $25. Lunch, Monday and Wednesday-Saturday 11 to 3. Dinner, Monday and Wednesday-Saturday 5 to 9 or 10, Sunday noon to 4.

Odette's, 274 South River Road, New Hope, Pa.

For some, this is the ultimate Bucks County dining experience: big, lavish and theatrical. The enclosed screened porch, the glassed-in room facing it and another room above afford gorgeous views of the river in this, a former boatmen's tavern dating to 1794. Live music from a piano bar, beautiful flowers, and formal table settings and service contribute to a perfect atmosphere in which to see and be seen. Three hundred people can be seated in the various dining rooms or in the lounge. The Barbone family, successors to founding restaurateur Odette Myrtil Logan, a Parisian stage and screen star, continue her weekend cabaret tradition. The menu varies seasonally. You might start with a duck confit and Chinese vegetable napoleon or grilled tiger shrimp served with tropical fruit salsa and fried plantains. Main courses could be ginger-crusted ahi tuna with a lobster-truffle vinaigrette, pork tenderloin with guava rum sauce, muscovy duck breast with creamy foie gras butter on wilted frisée and gorgonzola-topped filet mignon with zinfandel demi-glace. Chocolate fudge cake and fruit tortes are among mainstays on the dessert tray. The $20.95 Sunday buffet brunch is a tradition.

(215) 862-2432. Entrées, $20 to $29. www.odettes.com. Lunch, Monday-Saturday 11:30 to 3. Dinner, 5 to 9 or 9:30. Sunday, brunch 10:30 to 1:30, dinner 4 to 9.

FOR MORE INFORMATION: New Hope Information Center, 1 Mechanic St., Box 633, New Hope, PA 18938, (215) 862-5880. www.newhopepa.com.

Lambertville Area Chamber of Commerce, 239 North Union St., Lambertville, NJ 08530, (609) 397-0055. www.lambertville.org.

Bucks County Conference & Visitors Bureau, 152 Swamp Road, Doylestown, PA 18901, (215) 345-4552 or (800) 836-2825. www.buckscountycvb.org.

Ornate Victorian landmarks face oceanfront in Cape May.

Cape May, N.J.

Cape May, America's oldest seaside resort, is an oasis of exuberant Victoriana not far from the Mason-Dixon line.

Near the end of a peninsula between the Atlantic Ocean and the Delaware Bay, where South Jersey fades away, this late bloomer has been reborn into a remarkably diverse charmer that is the closest thing to a Key West up north. Some of the similarities are unmistakable: a salubrious ocean setting with water on three sides, showy Victorian architecture, a spate of period bed-and-breakfast inns, outstanding restaurants and, by Northern standards, something of a Southern air.

Time had forgotten Cape May since the late 1800s when it was the playground for presidents and personages from Ulysses S. Grant and William Harrison to Bret Harte and Henry Ford. Fires, new transportation modes and changing lifestyles took their toll. Atlantic City and other more accessible resorts left Cape May languishing as a country town out of the mainstream.

Not until 1970 when a group of citizens banded together to save the landmark Emlen Physick House from demolition did Cape May's fortunes turn. Along came the U.S. Bicentennial spurring an interest in history and, as a local tour guide tells it, "ours was still standing all around us." Having declined the honor a few years earlier, Cape May in 1976 was designated a National Historic Landmark city, one of only five in the nation, and its future would be forever altered – and preserved.

The Mid-Atlantic Center for the Arts, founded to save the Physick Estate, has left its imprint on the entire community. Two of its founding officers restored neighboring landmarks into museum-quality guesthouses, launching a B&B style that was a model throughout Cape May and elsewhere.

Some 670 Victorian structures from the late 1800s, the largest concentration anywhere, have been preserved. They range from gingerbread cottages to ornate showplaces, from slivers of guesthouses to block-long hotels. And everywhere there are front verandas – seemingly all of them in use from late afternoon to sunset or later. So immersed is Cape May in its past that it celebrates an entire Victorian Week (now nearly two weeks) in mid-October and a spring Tulip Festival, not to mention a Dickens Christmas Extravaganza, Victorian house and inn tours, lighthouse and fisherman's wharf tours and more.

The Cape May area is one of America's best birding spots, and in season the bird-watchers outnumber beachcombers, fishermen, souvenir shoppers, restaurant-goers and even Victorianophiles.

Such is the annual crush of tourists that one local newspaper wag suggested a spring Festival of Lawns. With tongue firmly in cheek, he wanted to celebrate the last view of grass before it disappeared beneath the influx.

Getting There

Cape May, at the southern terminus of the Garden State Parkway, is about 90 miles southeast of Philadelphia. From the Delmarva peninsula, it can be reached by ferry from Lewes, Del. New Jersey Transit buses serve the area from Philadelphia and New York. Air and train service is available into Atlantic City, about 50 miles to the north.

Where to Stay ────────────────── *♫♫♫*

The city of 4,200 year-round residents plays host to half a million visitors annually. It offers more than 3,000 rooms, many of them in efficiency motels and rooming houses. A growing proportion is in B&Bs, of which there are more than 100. Most B&Bs require minimum stays of two or four nights and allow access only via the combination locks installed in the doors (many of these are museum-quality homes and curious passersby would be an intrusion). Breakfasts tend to be light in summer, more formal and filling the rest of the year. The Cape May ritual is for the innkeepers to serve afternoon tea or beverages as well as breakfast, many mingling with their guests all the while.

Locals call the oceanfront road both Beach Avenue and Beach Drive in about equal proportion, as noted in the addresses here. They're actually one and the same.

Bed and Breakfast

The Mainstay Inn, 635 Columbia Ave., Cape May 08204.

The Mainstay led the way, and is the most likely to be filled weeks, if not months, in advance. Tom and Sue Carroll began the B&B movement in Cape May in 1971 and when they sold the Mainstay in 2004 to David and Susan Macrae, the Carrolls were the senior B&B innkeepers in the United States. The fourteen-foot-high public rooms in the 1872 Italianate villa are furnished in Victoriana right down to the sheet music on the piano. Especially notable is the ceiling of the entrance hall, where a stunning combination of seventeen wallpapers makes a beautiful accent. The twelve accommodations in the inn and in the pleasant 1870 Cottage next door are named for famous visitors to Cape May. The Henry Ford room has

its own small porch and the Bret Harte room (with many of his books in a case) opens onto the entire second-floor veranda. Lace curtains, stenciling, tall walnut bedsteads with matching dressers, armoires and rockers comprise the museum-quality decor. Some bathrooms retain their original copper tubs. Climb a very steep ladder with a wavering rope for a railing to the tower on the third floor, where, with cushions on two sides and windows on all four, you get a good view of town and ocean across the rooftops. The inn and the cottage, both with wide verandas and rocking chairs, are separated by a brick walk and a handsome trickling fountain; the front gardens are brilliant with flowers. Across the street in the Officers' Quarters, a restored naval officers' building, are four modern two-bedroom suites with queensize beds, TVs and gas fireplaces. Each suite contains a spacious living room with a dining area, kitchenette and a marble bathroom with whirlpool tub and shower. Guests here have tea at the main inn; continental breakfast is delivered to their quarters. Sue Carroll's recipes for her breakfast and tea goodies were so sought after that she published eight editions of a small cookbook called Breakfast at Nine, Tea at Four. In summer, breakfast is continental-plus, served buffet-style on the veranda. Other seasons it is formal sit-down around the table for twelve in the dining room. Ham and apple pie, California egg puff and chicken-pecan quiche are among the offerings. "Young children generally find us tiresome," the inn's brochure advises sensibly. Except for the Officers' Quarters, the inn is, as the new owners say, "a total Victorian experience."

(609) 884-8690. www.mainstayinn.com. Twelve rooms and four suites with private baths. Doubles, $180 to $295. Officers' Quarters suites, $260 to $395. Officers' Quarters open year-round; inn closed January to mid-March.

The Queen Victoria, 102 Ocean St., Cape May 08204.

Toned-down Victoriana and creature comforts are offered by Doug and Anne Marie McMain, who purchased Cape May's largest B&B operation from its visionary founders in 2004. The inn began with twelve rooms in its original 1881 corner property. In 1989, the Victorian house and carriage house next door was turned into eleven luxury rooms and suites with queensize beds, sitting rooms or areas, whirlpool baths, fireplaces and television. Furnishings in both guest and public rooms are authentic in the post-Victorian Arts and Crafts style and not so haute Victorian as in other inns. Each house has a parlor, one in the original building with a piano and a fireplace and the new one with TV, games and jigsaw puzzles. Pantry areas are stocked with the makings for popcorn, tea, sherry and such. Baked eggs, cheese strata and a spinach or corn casserole might be offered with homemade breads for breakfast at a long table beneath a portrait of Queen Victoria in the dining room of the main house and in a dining room outfitted similarly in the newer addition. In 1995, an 1876 building across the street was converted into **The Queen's Hotel,** offering eleven rooms with baths featuring whirlpool tubs or glass-enclosed marble showers, TVs, telephones, in-room coffeemakers and more privacy.

(609) 884-8702. www.queenvictoria.com. Fifteen rooms and six suites with private baths. Doubles, $205 to $245. Suites, $265 to $475.

Rhythm of the Sea, 1123 Beach Ave., Cape May 08204.

The ocean is on full view from the wicker front porch of one of the few Cape May B&Bs that can boast a Beach Avenue address with the beach right across the street. The 1915 summer house, from which you can hear the roar of the surf, also appeals to those who perhaps tire of Victoriana. It is furnished simply in the Arts and Crafts style with Stickley furniture and Mission-style lanterns, wooden blinds and table linens. Seven large bedrooms come with queensize beds and TV/VCRs, and the painted walls are done in the rose, pumpkin and olive palettes of the period. Five rooms have ocean views and several have gas fireplaces. The new Library guest room, hidden behind bookshelves off the second-floor hallway, comes with a wicker settee and an ocean view from the bed. Innkeepers Wolfgang and Robyn Wendt converted the former owners' quarters in the main house into a two-bedroom suite with a sitting room. They recently added a carriage house suite with king bedroom, living room, kitchenette and ocean view. Wolfgang, a pastry chef who trained in his native Europe, shows off his baking talents during afternoon tea and cooks four-course dinners for inn guests by reservation, $65 per person. A full breakfast is offered at four tables in the huge dining room. The signature main course is eggs oscar.

(609) 884-7788 or (800) 498-6888. www.rhythmofthesea.com. Seven rooms and a three-room suite with private baths. Doubles, $205 to $295. Suites, $325 to $365.

Leith Hall, 22 Ocean St., Cape May 08204.
Ocean views are among the assets of this colorful Victorian B&B (moss green with accents of deep peach and mustard) lovingly run by preservationists Elan and Susan Zingman-Leith. The guest accommodations reflect the fun the couple has had working miracles with the wallpaper and paint techniques popular at the time. "We're trying to create an 'aesthetic movement' house," says Susan. The Iris Room off the parlor has rag-rolled walls and a dragonfly and butterfly pattern on the ceiling. The floors are stenciled with lily pads. The two-bedroom Audubon Suite has "everything anyone has ever asked for," in Elan's words: a queen brass bed in one room and two twins in the other, a gas fireplace, whirlpool tub and TV/VCR, not to mention a paneled Bradbury & Bradbury frieze of birds and flowers plus other bird-related accessories in the sitting room. Bedrooms on the second and third floors have views of the ocean (especially good on the third floor). Their beds have been positioned so you can lie in bed and see the water. Exotic touches include the white net draped from a ring over the bed in the checkerboard-stenciled Empire Room and silver and gold stars painted all over the ceiling in the Turkish Suite. The latter has an Arabian Nights feel, a queensize bed and a whirlpool tub. Elan, the cook, serves big breakfasts of perhaps scrambled eggs with cream cheese and dill, mixed berry pancakes or apple and cheese crêpes. At tea time you might find scones and crumpets, brownies or even chocolate mousse cake. In summer it's served outside on the big wraparound porch.

(609) 884-1934 or (877) 884-1400. www.leithhall.com. Five rooms and three suites with private baths. Doubles, $150 to $215. Suites, $250.

The Humphrey Hughes House, 29 Ocean St., Cape May 08204.
The scent and the feel of the sea are evident from the expansive wraparound veranda at this imposing shingled Colonial Revival house geared "for ladies and gentlemen on seaside holiday." Lorraine and Terry Schmidt call their B&B "perhaps the most spacious and gracious of them all." From the veranda you enter directly into the living room, which opens into a big parlor, complete with an Italian game table and an 1870 square grand piano. The parlor flows into a large fireplaced dining room, graced by silver pieces left by the Hughes family who built this in 1903 as a summer home. There's also a side wicker sun porch. All the air-conditioned guest quarters have TV and are furnished with Victorian antiques. Eight have queen beds, while the smallest has a double bed. An exception is the largest, the Doctors' Suite on the garden level. It has a kingsize bed and, the Schmidts emphasize, is decorated in wicker and traditional furniture rather than Victorian. Omelets, french toast,

pancakes and welsh rarebit are in the breakfast repertoire. Afternoon tea with cookies and cakes is taken on the veranda, full of rocking chairs and gliders.

(609) 884-4428 or (800) 582-3634. www.humphreyhugheshouse.com. Seven rooms and three suites with private baths. Doubles, $195 to $295. Suites, $235 to $350.

The Angel of the Sea, 5 Trenton Ave., Cape May 08204.

Rising a bit starkly in an area a half block from the ocean and away from the historic district, this gray and mauve B&B with colorful gardens in front bills itself as Cape May's most deluxe. It's one of the few that can justify a claim to a significant ocean view, although even that is now interrupted by substantial residences that have risen along Beach Avenue. The owners have garnered restoration awards and considerable publicity for their jaunty johnny-come-lately, which pays off in high occupancy rates but also gives guests in public areas and porches the feeling of being part of an active stage set, for better or worse. Guest rooms in two turreted Victorian buildings have all the amenities: baths with pedestal sinks and clawfoot tubs, antique queen or double and a few kingsize beds, ceiling fans, small TVs, reproduction furniture, and handcrafted wood-slat ceilings and wainscoting. Many possess interesting angles and niches. Some third-floor rooms have ocean views but lack the balconies that enhance some on the second floor; everyone gets to share the main-floor verandas. Staffers bake cookies and breads for tea at 4, offer wine and cheese at 5:30, and serve a full breakfast in a dining room with high-back, red velvet chairs at tables set for six. Breakfast the morning we were there included fresh fruit buffet, apple crisp, cinnamon-walnut pancakes, country vegetable frittata with bacon and toast, and blueberry-apple coffeecake. Family photographs lend a personal touch to the living room, the inn's only common room, where the inn's cookbook is much in evidence and for sale. Owners Lorie and Greg Whissell also run the Angel's next-door neighbor, the oceanfront Peter Shields Inn.

(609) 884-3369 or (800) 848-3369. www.angelofthesea.com. Twenty-seven rooms with private baths. Doubles, $175 to $315.

The Peter Shields Inn, 1301 Beach Drive, Cape May 08204.

A B&B for some time and recently a restaurant, this 1907 Georgian Revival mansion facing the ocean took on new life in 2000 when it was acquired by the owners of the Angel of the Sea, a two-building B&B complex directly behind it. Greg and Lorie Whissell bill it as "the perfect compliment to the Angel" with its restaurant, additional guest rooms and conference space. Above the busy restaurant are nine guest rooms, most upgraded to the standards of the Angel. The five premier rooms with ocean views have queen or king beds and working fireplaces. Four others have queen beds – one with a glimpse of the ocean, another with a freestanding stovepipe fireplace, and the smallest notable for Victorian charm. Besides the main-floor restaurant and cappuccino bar, the lower level holds an exercise facility convertible into a conference room. Breakfast involves a choice of two entrées, perhaps belgian waffles and ham and cheese omelets, or french toast and eggs benedict.

(609) 884-9090 or (800) 355-6565. www.petershieldsinn.com. Nine rooms with private baths. Doubles, $195 to $265.

Motels and Motor Inns

Sea Crest Inn, 101 Beach Ave., Cape May 08204.

Two new wings and a new fourth floor doubled the size of this good-looking motor inn, which tries to set itself apart from most beach motels in limiting the number of occupants and cars per unit. It advertises Cape May's newest luxury oceanfront suites – a total of 40 condo-style units with living room, fully equipped kitchen-dining area and separate bedroom. There are fifteen motel rooms as well. For ocean views, you can scarcely get closer than the six suites beside the street that face the water head-on; occupants take seats on the wide balconies and never seem to leave. Other suites open onto common walkway-balconies, which some find lacking in privacy, overlooking the pool, whirlpool and gazebo. A picnic area includes a sundeck with barbecue grills. Bed configurations range from two doubles to one or two queensize to one kingsize.

(609) 884-4561. Fax (609) 898-9675. www.seacrestinn.com. Fifty-five rooms and suites with private baths. Doubles, $145 to $219. Closed mid-November to mid-April.

Periwinkle Inn, 1039 Beach Ave., Box 220, Cape May 08204.
The former Stockholm Motor Inn has been nicely renovated into the Periwinkle, an oceanfront motor inn with 50 rooms and efficiencies. Half face a garden courtyard and an exceptionally attractive pool and lawn area, with a six-story high-rise looming on the far side. The ocean view from most is marginal, but we were satisfied with both the view and the surroundings from the private balcony off our spacious and spiffy room facing the ocean from the rear of the complex. The only thing it lacked was a telephone. Two bi-level units in front, with upstairs bedrooms and balconies, face the ocean head-on.

(609) 884-9200. www.periwinkleinn.com. Thirty-six rooms and fourteen suites. Doubles, $168 to $209; efficiencies and suites, $215 to $339. Closed mid-October to mid-April.

La Mer Beachfront Inn, 1317 Beach Ave., Cape May 08204.
This appealing, formerly low-key motor inn is coming up in the world – literally. What started as a two-story motel with a shingled roof gave way in 2005 to an all-new, four-story motor inn with 86 units. Some are standard motel rooms, some are efficiencies and some have separate sitting and bedroom areas with kingsize or two double beds. Since the new building was erected above ground-level parking, all rooms have head-on ocean views. That attribute was missing from the first-floor units in the original, screened by the pool or parking and the breakwater along the beach across the street. The new building joins a four-story "tower building" of recent vintage with side views of the ocean. The complex includes a pool, a children's playground, a miniature golf course, barbecue area, laundry facilities and an adjacent restaurant and lounge called **Water's Edge** (see Where to Eat).

(609) 884-9000 or (800) 644-5004. www.capemaylamer.com. One hundred fifteen rooms. Doubles, $140 to $241. Closed mid-November to mid-April.

Montreal Inn, 1025 Beach Ave., Cape May 08204.
Opened in 1966 with 27 units, this oceanfront motel has grown to four floors with 70 motel rooms and efficiency suites, plus a restaurant and lounge, a package store, large pool, sauna and mini-golf layout. Neither the Montreal nor the inn connection is clear, but the values are – especially in the off-season, when we got a fine room for $70. The only minus was the noise from a group of carousing fishermen in the next room. Another time the only availability was in a recently renovated and refurbished efficiency suite. Its rear bedroom had two double beds and the living room had a sofabed and a dining table for four, with french doors opening onto the patio and pool. The decor was muted and suave and the furnishings better than average. The only downside, again, was noisy neighbors next door.

(609) 884-7011 or (800) 525-7011. Fax (609) 884-4559. www.montreal-inn.com. Twenty rooms and fifty suites. Doubles, $125 to $200. Suites, $169 to $300. Closed after Thanksgiving to mid-March.

Hotels

The Virginia Hotel, 25 Jackson St., Box 557, Cape May 08204.

Built in 1879 as one of Cape May's first hotels, the Virginia reopened 110 years later as what owner Curtis Bashaw billed as a deluxe "boutique" hotel – one that local B&B innkeepers highly recommend for those who want contemporary amenities. Tiny white lights frame the handsome exterior year-round, and inside all is plush. Upstairs on the second and third floor are 24 guest rooms varying in size and shape. They are equipped with modern baths, telephones, and TV/VCRs hidden in built-in cabinets, and are furnished in a simple yet sophisticated manner with down comforters and a soft peach and gray color scheme. The wraparound balcony on the second floor gave our already expansive front premium room extra space. It was particularly pleasant the next morning for a continental breakfast – delivered to the room at precisely the time specified – of fresh orange juice, fruit, danish pastries and croissants. The main floor has a parlor, where a pianist plays during the dinner hour, a small lounge and an elegant restaurant called **The Ebbitt Room** (see Where to Eat).

(609) 884-5700 or (800) 732-4236. Fax (609) 884-1236. www.virginiahotel.com. Twenty-four rooms with private baths. Doubles, $195 to $425.

Congress Hall Hotel, 251 Beach Drive, Cape May 08204.

A seaside retreat for four presidents since 1816, one of the nation's most historic hotels reopened in 2002 after two years and $22 million worth of top-to-bottom renovations. Managing partner Curtis Bashaw and team updated the four-story hotel's infrastructure, but retained much of the original fabric and patina, recycling floors, baseboards, doors and knobs, porcelain tiles, plumbing and light fixtures where possible. The summery guest rooms retain a simple, minimalist look. The plaster walls are painted in pastels and simple valances and shades screen the windows, which open. Many baths feature pedestal sinks and deep soaking tubs. Some deluxe rooms offer larger baths with separate showers. Some have kingsize beds and private balconies with views across the colonnaded veranda and front lawn to the sea. Three meals a day are served in the inn's restaurant, **The Blue Pig Tavern.** Hotel facilities include a ballroom, fitness center and spa, outdoor pool and an arcade of retail shops.

(609) 884-8821 or (888) 944-1816. Fax (609) 884-6094. www.congresshall.com. One hundred four rooms and two suites. Rates, EP. Doubles, $250 to $405.

The Chalfonte, 301 Howard St., Cape May 08204.

Cape May's oldest continuously operating hotel (1876) is in some ways its most revered. It's off the beaten path, three short blocks from the ocean at the edge of the historic district, and we bumped into it quite by accident on a walking tour. Owners Judy Bartella and Anne LeDuc are refreshing both the public rooms and guest quarters continually. Although the rambling three-story hotel has 103 rooms, only 70 are rented. They're appointed simply in the endearing manner of an earlier era. Each has a new bed and a sink, but most bathrooms are shared and down the hall; twelve have private baths. The front porch is lined with rocking chairs, and a single TV and two telephones are available for guests' use inside. Four generations of the Dickerson family have been cooking Southern food served family style in the long, echoing Magnolia Room since 1876. The late Helen Dickerson, head chef for more than 40 years, was succeeded by her daughters, Dot Burton and Lucille Thompson. Helen's cookbook, *I Just Stop Stirrin' When the Tastin's Good,* typifies their style. The Virginia country breakfast ($8.50) includes spoonbread and biscuits. Four-course Southern dinners with a set menu and all the trimmings are $29.50 to the public in the Magnolia Room; the traditional jacket requirement has been dropped in favor of a more general "dress code." There's cabaret entertainment most nights in the Henry Sawyer Room off the King Edward Bar, and a classical music series, Concerts by Candlelight, has been offered since 1984. "This is really still like a large boarding house," Judy Bartella concedes, and guests keep returning for the experience.

(609) 884-8409 or (888) 411-1998. Fax (609) 884-4588. www.chalfonte.com. Twelve rooms with private baths and 58 rooms with shared hall baths. Doubles, $213 to $314, MAP. Breakfast daily, 8:30 to 10, Sunday to 10:30. Dinner, 6 to 9. Closed Columbus Day to Memorial Day.

Seeing and Doing ⎯⎯⎯⎯⎯⎯⎯⎯⎯⎯⎯ ⨏⨏⨏

Besides enjoying the beach, there's enough in Cape May and environs to keep one busy for days. No wonder the minimum-stay requirements don't bother most; many come for a week or more and return season after season. Incidentally, Cape May's season – from Memorial Day to mid-September – is extending every year as new events are staged and more B&Bs and restaurants stay open longer.

Cape May is best seen and appreciated by walking or bicycling along the beach and through the tree-lined historic district, which consists of a compact area generally east of Washington Street between Franklin and Congress streets. Columbia Avenue and Hughes Street and their cross streets are at the heart.

Touring Cape May

There are no Gray Line bus tours here – only old-fashioned trolley tours and walking tours sponsored by the Mid-Atlantic Center for the Arts (MAC), which seems to have a hand in just about everything that's good in town.

Guided Trolley Tours. Leaving regularly from the Washington Street Mall information booth at Ocean Street, these MAC tours take half an hour and cover the Historic East End (considered the best tour if you have time for only one), the Historic West End and the Historic Beachfront (viewing a century of oceanfront housing along Beach Drive). Our guide, a tenth-generation resident, told about the town's bad luck with hurricanes and fires and pointed out his house, "which cost more to paint this year than it did to buy in 1904." He explained that the Washington Inn was moved three times, showed how Victorian cottagers were trying to outdo each other (including his favorite house, now the Abbey B&B, where the original owner was not content to compete only with his neighbors but also with himself on every side), and pointed out the largest mansion in town, the George Allen House (lately restored into the Southern Mansion, an inn) and its prized outhouse, a two-seater with cupola. His comments made our subsequent wanderings much more informed. Sunset and romantic moonlight trolley tours are added nightly in summer. Tours daily from 10, early spring to late fall; adults $6, children $3.

Walking Tours. Following maps or instinct, you can explore on your own, but the guided walking tours offered by MAC are more informative and entertaining. Geared to those who like to see history close up and in detail, the 90-minute tours are led by knowledgeable residents, who share insights into Victorian traditions and customs. Tours leave from the Washington Street Mall information booth most afternoons in season at 1. Adults $10, children $5.

A self-guided, audio walking tour with a handheld narration unit details 96 historic buildings on 68 sites, available at the Visitor Center in the Emlen Physick Estate for $6 for two hours.

MAC offers four specialized tours in summer, whose schedules and specifics vary from year to year. The **Inns and Outs Tour** combines a walking tour of the historic district with an interior tour of two of Cape May's bed and breakfast inns; Thursdays at 11, adults $10. The **All Victorians Great and Small Walking Tour** begins with real-life Victorian landmarks on an East End walking tour and concludes with a step back into the world of tiny Victorian treasures at the Doll House and Miniature Museum of Cape May; Mondays and Tuesdays at 10.

More MAC Tours and Events. If it's worth touring or packaging, MAC is apt to tour or package it. Examples are gourmet and Sunday brunch walks, Christmas candlelight and lamplighter Christmas tours, Victorian fashion and vaudeville shows at the Cape May Convention Hall, Victorian Mystery Dinners and Victoria's Fling singalongs at the Chalfonte Hotel, Curator's Choice Tours at the Emlen Physick Estate, Steeped in History tea tours, a Dickens Christmas Extravaganza and Sherlock Holmes weekends. Special events include crafts and antiques shows at the Convention Center.

Emlen Physick Estate, 1048 Washington St.

The four-acre property where Cape May's restoration effort started is now a Victorian house museum and the headquarters of MAC, the group whose arts offerings funded its restoration. The eighteen-room house was designed by Philadelphia architect Frank Furness in 1879 for a young physician (an eminent surgeon's grandson, who never practiced and never married) and his mother. Many of the original furnishings have been retrieved and returned to the house. The family parlor has the original fireplace, sofabed and pipe organ. A crazy tureen in the corner of the formal parlor was a housewarming present. The upstairs library bears striking Japanese wallpaper, even on the ceiling. Tapestry curtains, porcelain lamp fixtures and chandeliers are all around. We liked best the owner's bachelor bedroom beside a sunken marble bathroom; right next door is Mother's bedroom, her fan collection framed over the fireplace. Don't miss the costume collection across the hall. The tours take 45 minutes or longer, our informant advised, if you get "a long-winded tour guide." The restored **Carriage House Gallery** has changing art exhibitions. It also offers **The Twinings Tearoom**, where tea luncheons and afternoon tea are available daily amidst restored horse stables and outside on a canopied patio. *(609) 884-5404 or (800) 275-4278. Tours daily, 10 to 3, times vary. Adults $8, children $4.*

Cape May Firemen's Museum, 643 Washington St. In Cape May you're not surprised to stumble across another museum, this one operated by the Cape May Volunteer Fire Company in front of the fire department headquarters at Washington and Franklin streets. The small establishment houses a 1929 Hale pumper, badges, alarm boxes and other memorabilia pertaining to fires in a city in which fires have played an important role. Open daily; free.

SHOPPING. Shopping is big business in Cape May, although much of it is of the souvenir variety. The city's Washington Street Mall – one of the nation's first to be closed to traffic in 1971 – is filled with pedestrians, particularly on inclement days. The small City Center Mall even has an atrium and an escalator. Newer is the quirky little Carpenter's Square Mall off Carpenter's Lane.

The Whale's Tale is a nifty ramble of rooms containing everything from regional books and specimen shells to imported toys and an extraordinary collection of cards. **McDowell's Gallery of Gifts** is literally that, its walls between marble floors and high ceilings brightened by colorful kites and wind sockets. There's an interesting assortment of jewelry, glass, crafts, wood products and games. A special shop for the birders and nature lovers who visit Cape May is **For the Birds.** Tins are available for fill-your-own candies at **Fralinger's** original saltwater taffy emporium, housed in an elegant vintage Victorian interior. **Swede Things in America** offers just what it says, mainly small items but some furniture. The **Cape May Linen Outlet** has good bargains, especially in placemats. **Down by the Sea** specializes in lighthouse arts and gifts.

On or Near the Water

BIRDING. Cape May lies on the heavily populated Atlantic Flyway and more than 400 species of birds, plus the entire migration of monarch butterflies along the East Coast, head south through Cape May Point. Spring and fall are the peak migration seasons, but many species stay year-round. Off Sunset Boulevard south of town is the **Cape May Migratory Bird Refuge,** a 180-acre wildlife preserve and migratory bird refuge owned by the Nature Conservancy. A U-shaped trail across the meadow into the dunes, with grazing cattle at the side, is a mecca for birders. A more popular one is **Cape May Point State Park,** where a ramp and platform beside a pond provides a pleasant and cooling spot to watch for birds and listen to the surf beyond. A professional hawk counter and hawk banders can be seen at work, and a scoreboard is posted in the hawk-watch area charting the number of species counted the previous day and the year to date. The adjacent **Cape May Bird Observatory,** run by the New Jersey Audubon Society, conducts bird walks in the fall. Another bird-watching spot is **Higbee's Beach Wildlife Management Area,** 600 acres of dune forest along Delaware Bay. Just north of Cape May off Stone Harbor Boulevard is **The Wetlands Institute,** surrounded by a 6,000-acre salt marsh. Included are a self-guiding marsh trail, observation tower and boardwalk, plus a touch museum called Wetlandia, saltwater aquaria, a library and a gallery with changing art and crafts shows.

Cape May Point State Park. Located near the famed lighthouse in the quaint summer colony of Cape May Point, this 190-acre site is a favorite with birders, naturalists and those who like to walk the dunes, beaches and three miles of trails. Walk out to the World War II bunker built to guard Delaware Bay from enemy attack. Today it is an open "fortress" with benches and picnic tables above the surf. The beach here is unprotected and swimming is discouraged, although some sunbathers ventured into the water the late-September afternoon we visited. Nearby, St. Peter's-by-the-Sea, a tiny gray Episcopal chapel with fancy trim, crouches behind the dunes that line the beachfront.

Cape May Point Lighthouse, Cape May Point State Park. MAC has restored this 1859 landmark, which is open for tours. The hardy climb the 199 tower stairs to the Watch Room Gallery just below the lantern for a panoramic view of the area. A visitor center in the restored Oil House on the lighthouse grounds contains a photo mural showing the lighthouse view, a twelve-minute video detailing the structure and a museum shop. When MAC sponsors its twice-weekly "The Keeper Is On Duty" event (Wednesdays and Sundays at 1), actors playing roles as the lighthouse's last keepers greet visitors at the top with tales of their life and work. There are also Stairway to the Stars tours for star gazing on summer Tuesday and Thursday evenings at 8:45 (tickets, $12). Lighthouse open daily April-November, 9 to 8, and most weekends in winter; visitor center free. Climb to top, adults $5, children $1.

Sunset Beach, Cape May Point. At the end of Sunset Boulevard is a sheltered beach with free parking and a small hodgepodge of snack bars and souvenir stands.

Just offshore is the shell of the USS Atlantis, one of twelve concrete ships built during World War I and brought to the Point in 1926 to serve as a breakwater; it ran aground in a storm and has been trapped ever since. The beach often yields Cape May diamonds, stones of pure quartz that are found only here. They can be polished, cut and set to make attractive jewelry. We latched onto someone who seemed to know what he was doing and he showed us how to seek out the good stones from the bad. Otherwise, we'd never have guessed.

SWIMMING. The aforementioned beaches, including Higbee's, are more secluded than Cape May's strand, but the latter is where the action is. Daily beach passes are required ($4 a day; the beach is patrolled in season so no one gets on free). A boardwalk flanks the beach in Cape May and provides a view of the goings-on.

MAC TOURS. The ubiquitous Mid-Atlantic Center for the Arts sponsors a number of watery excursions, some of which change with the years (days and hours vary). Called **Harbor Safari,** one series has a marine biologist leading participants through beach and marsh habitats for 90 minutes around the Cape May Nature Center, 1600 Delaware Ave.; adults $6, children $2. Another is **Fisherman's Wharf Tours,** 45-minute guided tours of the Lobster House dock and fish packing plant, Tuesday and Thursday in summer at 11, $6 and $3. Special MAC boat excursions are noted below.

FISHING AND BOATING. Cape May claims to be the second largest commercial fishing port on the East Coast and to have possibly the largest clam beds in the world. More than 30 species of fish inhabit the waters of the Atlantic, the Delaware Bay and the inland waterways that separate the barrier resort islands from the mainland. Entered in Cape May's year-long fishing tournament are everything from winter flounder to mako sharks; the Canyons, said to be one of the world's great white marlin areas, are easily accessible. Boat rentals and charter boats are plentiful, and launching ramps are available along the Intracoastal Waterway and the bay. The center of fishing activity is Fisherman's Wharf, where the commercial fleet unloads beyond the Lobster House restaurant. Boating is concentrated on the inland waterway near the Cape May Bridge at the north end of town.

Cape May Whale Watcher, Miss Chris Marina, Second Avenue and Wilson Drive, (609) 884-5445 or (800) 786-5445. The largest whale-watch boat in New Jersey (290 seats) is the only one that guarantees a whale sighting. If you don't see a "marine mammal," says owner-captain Jeff Stewart, you get a free ticket for another trip. Three-hour whale watch tours leave daily at 1, March to December (adults $30, children $18). Two-hour dolphin watches are offered at 10 and 6:30 (adults $23, children $12). There are dinner cruises nightly at 6:30 and celestial star watch cruises Wednesday and Saturday at 9. Captain Jeff runs MAC's bi-weekly **lighthouse cruises.** Participants on the 60-mile afternoon lunch cruise get a look at six offshore lighthouses visible only from the water out in the Delaware Bay; adults, $65.

Cape May Whale Watch and Research Center, 1286 Wilson Drive, (609) 898-0055 or (888) 531-0055, offers whale- and dolphin-watching cruises aboard a 70-foot catamaran specially designed for non-obtrusive viewing. Three-hour cruises sighting whales, dolphins and birds are offered daily at 1 for $30, children $18. The cruises have "an 80 percent sighting rate on whales and 100 percent on dolphins," Capt. Ron Robbins advised. Three whales, two humpbacks and a finback, were spotted five to six miles offshore the day before our latest visit. Shorter dolphin-watching cruises are offered at 9:30 (continental breakfast) and 6:30 (pizza and hot dogs), both for $23 adults, $16 children.

Saltmarsh safari nature cruises are offered daily at 10, 1:30 and 6 by **Wildlife**

Unlimited Inc., (609) 884-3100, generally sailing from Miss Chris Marina at Second Avenue and Wilson Drive. Naturalists point out birds and marine life in what they call Cape May's "greatest wilderness," the Atlantic coastal back bays and marshes.

The 80-foot **Schooner Yankee** offers "a Tall Ship adventure" daily at 10 and 2 and a sunset cruise at 6 from the Ocean Highway Dock between Cape May and Wildwood, (609) 884-1919; adults $20 to $26.50 depending on trip, children $10 to $20. **Cape Island Sailing Cruise,** (609) 884-6333, offers leisurely afternoon or evening sails, viewing Cape May from the ocean and from the bay aboard the 26-foot Free Spirit. A 30-foot Catalina sailboat, the **Key of Sea,** (609) 884-1919, offers cruises for up to six passengers three times daily from Utsch's Marina, 1121 Route 109.

U.S. Coast Guard Base, Pennsylvania and Buffalo Avenues. The public may join families at the weekly Coast Guard recruit graduation ceremonies Friday at 11 a.m. at the Coast Guard Training Center, the only one in the United States. They're billed as a unique Cape May tradition. Bet you didn't know that all Coast Guard recruits from around the nation are indoctrinated at the Cape May boot camp in eight-week cycles, with a cycle graduating every Friday. Some of the graduates attend the U.S. Coast Guard Academy in New London, Conn., before going on to serve in the nation's maritime service. Visitors may view a Coast Guard film in the Ida Lewis Auditorium prior to the weekly ceremony.

Where to Eat ———————————— _♪♪♪_

The choice in Cape May is staggering and the prices fairly high. The tab may seem more reasonable at the many places that do not have liquor licenses but allow you to bring your own wine. Many restaurants are open seasonally, with reduced hours in the spring and fall. The focus here is on those near the ocean.

Water's Edge, Beach Drive and Pittsburgh Avenue.
This sleek, hotel-style dining room in a building in front of La Mer Motor Inn is outfitted with banquettes and booths dressed in white linens. An outdoor dining deck at the entry captures the feel of the ocean beyond. Chef Neil Elsohn and his wife Karen, who is hostess, offer some of the best and most inspired food in town. On one occasion, we enjoyed an appetizer of strudel with escargots, pignoli and an ethereal garlic cream sauce before digging into poached fillet of Norwegian salmon with lime and salmon caviar, and sautéed sea scallops with tomatillos, cilantro and grilled jicama. At another visit, we grazed happily through appetizers and salads, including scallop chowder, spicy pork and scallion empanadas with pineapple-ginger chutney, fusilli with grilled tuna, oriental vegetables and szechuan vinaigrette, and grilled chicken salad with toasted pecans, grilled red onions and mixed greens. Desserts could be lemon tart with berry coulis, banana-bread pudding with hot chocolate sauce and bittersweet chocolate-walnut pâté with espresso and vanilla sauces. In summer, a lounge menu is offered in the spacious bar. Salads and appetizers are available there anytime. The lunch and brunch menus contain some exotic choices as well.

(609) 884-1717. www.watersedgerestaurant.com. Entrées, $29 to $36. Breakfast in summer, 8 to 11:30. Lunch in summer, noon to 2. Dinner nightly from 5, mid-May to Columbus Day; Wednesday-Sunday in off-season and weekends in winter. Closed January to Valentine's Day.

Tisha's, 714 Beach Drive.
Cape May got what it needed – a good, beachy, oceanfront restaurant right on the water – with the arrival of this seasonal winner in the Solarium Building jutting out over the ocean beside Convention Hall. Pretty in pink and white, it seems to be

mostly windows beneath a high ceiling, with close-together tables and a few art and floral accents on the walls. There's patio dining outside as well. Such is the summery backdrop for some mighty fine fare, as prepared by chef-owner Paul Negro, whose fisherman-father often provides the day's catch and whose mother, Tisha, persuaded him to open a restaurant in nearby Wildwood before moving into the thick of the Cape May scene. Terrific bread and excellent salads preceded our main dishes, pork tenderloin with a dijon cream caper sauce and clams aglio over penne at one summer visit, grilled lamb chops with mint sauce and grilled duck with raspberry sauce at another. The menu changes every two weeks, but the choices – from smoked salmon parfait to cajun fried oysters, from profiteroles to strawberry fondue – never fail to impress.

(609) 884-9119. www.tishasfinedining.com. Entrées, $25 to $31. Dinner nightly, from 5. Closed Tuesday and Wednesday in off-season and November-March. BYOB.

Union Park Restaurant, 727 Beach Drive.

Award-winning local chef Christopher Hubert moved from the Ebbitt Room of the Virginia Hotel to take over the restored dining room of the 85-year-old beachfront Macomber Hotel. Here he is the chef-proprietor, occupying space leased from hotel owner Crystal Czworkowski, formerly a hotel general manager in Boston. The ambitious, now year-round venture consists of two dining rooms with fireplaces, cherry and mahogany furnishings, antique fixtures and silver service. The main room is a high-ceilinged, summery space appointed mostly in white and evocative of the Cape May of the 1930s. The cutting-edge menu usually begins with Chris's signature yellowfin tuna crusted with sesame seeds. Other possibilities include Chinese five-spiced Atlantic salmon, pan-roasted diver scallops with chinoise sauce, braised venison osso buco, and grilled beef tournedos with béarnaise sauce. Starters are exotic: perhaps lobster bisque with fine cognac and a lobster flan, seared lobster and water chestnut dumplings, pheasant and foie gras terrine with truffle sauce, and ragoût of buffalo sausage and fall mushrooms topped with rare cheese and truffle oil. This is fine dining at its finest.

(609) 884-8811. www.unionparkdining.com. Entrées, $26 to $34. Dinner from 5, nightly in summer, Wednesday-Monday in off-season, Friday-Saturday in winter. BYOB.

The Peter Shields Inn Restaurant, 1301 Beach Drive.

This Georgian Revival mansion owned by the adjacent Angel of the Sea B&B is the only restaurant in town where you can sit in front of a fireplace and see the ocean, we were advised. The water is on view from two large and elegant, high-ceilinged dining rooms, each graced with crystal chandeliers and Victorian wallpapers, as well as from the expansive West Sun Porch. It's the kind of place where one would not be surprised to walk into a fashion show, as we did, literally, one weekday afternoon when we stopped to peruse the menu. Dinner here is a special occasion for many, according to local innkeepers who recommend the place both for its food and its waterside setting. Executive chef Eric Hegyi's menu might start with crab served in three styles, seared sea scallops wrapped in salmon and beef carpaccio. Expect entrées like the signature lobster-crab cakes, rare ahi tuna glazed with tamarind and wasabi, sea scallops with jumbo prawns in cognac sauce, roasted veal with sautéed crab over risotto, and dijon-crusted rack of lamb. Finish with one of the changing desserts and coffee from the cappuccino bar.

(609) 884-9090 or (800) 355-6565. www.petershieldsinn.com. Entrees, $21 to $31. Dinner from 5:30, nightly in summer, Tuesday-Sunday rest of year. BYOB.

The Ebbitt Room, 25 Jackson St.

Named for the original owners of Cape May's first hotel, the sophisticated, candlelit dining room in the restored Virginia Hotel is an exceptionally pleasant setting for some of the best food in Cape May. Fine progressive American cuisine is served up by executive chef Andrew Carthy. His ever-changing dishes range from pancetta-crusted day boat halibut and cumin-crusted scallops with red pepper vinaigrette to spice-rubbed duck breast with garlic-caramel sauce and pine nut-crusted rack of lamb with red wine sauce. Our dinner began with an eggplant and gorgonzola crostini served with red onion pesto and a zesty caesar salad, both served on black octagonal plates. The shrimp margarita was flamed in tequila and served with avocado cream sauce and roasted tomato salsa, while the herb-roasted cornish game hen rested on a bed of caramelized vegetables on a parsley-flecked plate. For dessert, we enjoyed an upside-down fig cake and pecan-praline cheesecake. The live piano music emanating from the lobby imparted a glamorous air.

(609) 884-5700 or (800) 732-4236. Entrées, $28 to $34. Dinner nightly, from 5:30; fewer days in off-season.

The Pelican Club, 501 Beach Ave.

You want to dine with an ocean view? The Craig family of Cape May's renowned Washington Inn restaurant (no view) obliged, taking over the penthouse restaurant in the oceanfront Marquis de Lafayette Hotel. Long and narrow with a vaulted ceiling, the vast sixth-floor establishment has 50-foot walls of windows onto the beach on one side and the Victorian townscape on the other. The Craigs describe their refurbished South Beach decor as "retro 1940s Miami." Displaying their priorities, they installed a glass-enclosed wine cellar to separate the dining room from the bar. Live jazz is played most nights in what has become Cape May's most urbane entertainment venue. The Cuban cookery that influences executive chef Walter J. Jurusz shows up in his signature dish, grilled Cuban-rubbed pork chop with red wine-infused pork jus, served with whipped sweet potatoes and plantain chips. He gives tropical and Asian accents to pan-seared Atlantic salmon with citrus beurre blanc, almond-crusted halibut with light curry cream and grilled yellowfin tuna with coconut-lemongrass sauce and mango-jalapeño salsa. Appetizers could be a crispy seafood spring roll with hoisin-ginger sauce or crab and shrimp cake with roasted yellow pepper aioli over mixed greens. Worthy desserts are mango-macadamia cheesecake and a coconut mandarin napoleon with passion fruit sauce.

Incidentally, you can "breakfast with the dolphins" in season, watching them feed and frolic in the shallow tides off the beach while enjoying a lavish buffet (adults $9.95, children $5.95).

(609) 884-3995 or (800) 257-0432. Entrées, $21.95 to $25.95. Breakfast daily, 7:30 to 11. Dinner nightly, 5 to 9.

Aleathea's, 601 Beach Ave.

Part of the cavernous ground floor of the old Colonial Hotel, now the Inn of Cape May, has been given over to this restaurant with a water view. The pillared Victorian dining room is dressed in dusty rose, but the seats of choice are on the big wraparound porch with a view of the beach and ocean a few hundred feet away. This is also a favorite haunt for oceanfront cocktails. Those who stay for dinner find main courses like soy-lacquered salmon fillet, flounder française, grilled swordfish with tequila-lime butter, veal chop sauced with crab and cheese, prime rib au jus and grilled filet mignon with a merlot demi-glace. Starters could be shrimp and crab parfait, mushrooms stuffed with crab imperial and oysters rockefeller. The chef's favorite dessert is a chocolate conch filled with seasonal berries.

(609) 884-5555 or (800) 582-5933. Entrées, $19.50 to $39. Lunch daily, noon to 3. Dinner nightly, 5 to 9:30. Weekends only from late October to late April. Closed January-March.

The Mad Batter, 19 Jackson St.

Since 1976, some of the most creative meals in town have been served here in the covered sidewalk café, the large dining room or on the rear porch amid white garden furniture, statues and greenery. We found the sidewalk café warm enough for candlelight dining on an early May night – a special treat, what with the view of the passing scene, the roar of the surf muted by classical music, and food so assertive that we returned the next morning for breakfast. We really liked the dancing devil shrimp stir-fried with pecans, kumquats and black bean sauce, and fettuccine tossed with snails, asparagus and baked garlic. Recent dinner entrées ranged widely from the signature crab cakes with rémoulade sauce and Asian-style grouper to jerked pork tenderloin and New Zealand rack of lamb. Breakfast produced a gorgeous fruit plate and excellent whole wheat peach pancakes. But the eclectic fare varies. We came for lunch a year later and found the food bland almost)beyond redemption.

(609) 884-5970. www.madbatter.com. Entrées, $19 to $32. Breakfast-brunch-lunch, daily 8 to 2:30. Dinner, 5 to 9. Closed Monday in spring and fall, also January to early February. BYOB.

Martini Beach, 429 Beach Ave.

"Upstairs/downstairs…together again," advertised this newcomer that took over the space long known as Restaurant Maureen. The beachfront establishment now called Cabanas offers dining in an upstairs venue called Martini Beach and a downstairs family restaurant and bar with an extensive casual menu. For years, the bar and restaurant had been separate – sometimes to the detriment of both. The new owner integrated the two floors, but retained separate themes. A South Beach-style menu is featured upstairs, and there are few better close-up ocean views in Cape May than from the enclosed porch out front. A varied list of starters and tapas runs from sesame-crusted rare tuna and grilled asparagus and crab salad to potato pierogis and rum-glazed chicken tenders. Typical entrées are roasted grouper with mango and shrimp salsa, cioppino, lump crab cakes, spice-rubbed flank steak and filet mignon with cabernet demi-glace. The downstairs combines casual family dining by day with late-night music and food into the wee hours.

(609) 884-4800. Entrees, $19 to $27. www.cabanasonthebeach.com. Martini Beach: lunch, Friday and Saturday from 11:30; dinner nightly, from 5. Cabanas: Lunch and dinner noon to 9 or 10, daily in summer, Thursday-Monday in off-season. Closed January-March.

McGlade's On the Pier, 722 Beach Ave.

Chef Mickey McGlade calls this the best-kept secret in Cape May. The rustic, beach-cottage kind of place is indeed hidden behind Morrow's Nut House near Convention Hall, and only because of an innkeeper's tip did we find it. But what a view of the ocean! And what food! We went for breakfast and thoroughly relished a shrimp and garlic omelet ($8.95) and Uncle Tuse's bacon, tomato and cheese omelet ($7.50), from a large menu on which everything appeared to have zip. The omelets (big enough for two to share, which we did on a subsequent trip) were accompanied by fresh fruit garnishes and great hash browns with lots of onions. A surprise treat was the school of dolphins that passed just offshore on their way to and from breakfast; although folks were watching from the breakwater, we on the canopied rear deck had the best view of all. The waitress advised that the dolphins pass each morning and afternoon. At lunch, the crab cakes are superb, and the salads are as enticing as the breakfast fare. We know innkeepers who come here for a casual dinner by the water to feast on shrimp rosa (with mushrooms and garlic over linguini), grilled salmon steak and the crab au gratin.

(609) 884-2614. Entrées, $16.95 to $19.95. Breakfast daily in summer, 7 to 3. Lunch, 11:30 to 3. Dinner, 5 to 9. Fewer days and no dinner in off-season. Closed October-May. BYOB.

The Lobster House, Fisherman's Wharf.

One of the largest enterprises of its kind, this includes an enormous restaurant, an outdoor raw bar, the schooner American, a take-out counter and one of the best seafood markets we have ever seen. We never visit Cape May without a cooler in which to bring some of the goodies home. The inside is a tourist zoo, jammed for lunch and dinner. Once we lunched on the 143-foot-long schooner anchored on the inland waterway, and felt somewhat on display for those at window tables inside. The schooner menu is rather limited and not too interesting. Most people go there for drinks, and we found the tuna melt and shrimp salad croissant mundane at best. Better is the raw bar – crab soup, steamed shrimp and crabs, and a clambake dinner. Even better is the Dockside Take-out, offering goodies from the seafood market like snapper soup ($3.75), soft-shell crab sandwich ($7.75 and delicious), and a broiled seafood combination platter ($13.95). Here's the place for a good, quick lunch on the dock as you watch the boats parade by. Inside, the oversize menu offers something for everyone in the old-school tradition, from crabmeat au gratin and baked stuffed flounder to a broiled fisherman's platter. The seafood is fresh off the establishment's own fleet of boats. The house specialty is lobster tails, scallops and shrimp served over linguini with garlic butter.

(609) 884-8296. www.thelobsterhouse.com. Entrées, $18.25 to $30.75. Lunch daily, 11:30 to 3. Dinner, 5 to 10, Sunday 2 to 9.

Henry's on the Beach, 702 Beach Ave.

Teresa and Ed Henry, who opened Zoe's for breakfast across the street, saw a niche for a casual family restaurant beside the ocean. They took over the old Promenade restaurant and offer a soup-to-nuts menu, from meat loaf to chicken to pastas to surf and turf. You can find simple fried and grilled seafood plus three nightly specials with a bit of innovation, as in mahi mahi with Polynesian sauce. Dinner entrées come with salad and biscuits. The remodeled 100-seat dining room is a mix of booths and tables, with windows onto the beach and ocean. An additional 100 seats are offered seasonally outside on a canopied deck over the sand.

(609) 884-8826. www.henrysonthebeach.com. Entrées, $10.95 to $19.95. Lunch daily in summer, 11 to 3. Dinner, 4:30 to 9:30. Closed Monday-Wednesday in off-season. BYOB.

The Cove Restaurant and Seaside Deck, 405 Beach Ave.

Picnic tables on the porch of this casual establishment at the south end of Beach Avenue are covered with oilcloth. The porch, almost over the water, affords a superb view down the curving beach toward the Cape May lighthouse. Manhattan clam chowder, crab cake sandwiches, and platters of fried seafood with french fries and coleslaw are featured. Dinners with salad bar are priced from $9.50 to $16.75. We enjoyed breakfast here – especially the creamed chipped beef on toast ($5.25). It's open daily in summer, 7:30 a.m. to 8 p.m.; BYOB at dinner.

FOR MORE INFORMATION: Cape May Chamber of Commerce, 609 Lafayette St., Cape May, N.J. 08204, (609) 884-5508. www.capemaychamber.com.

Mid-Atlantic Center for the Arts, 1048 Washington St., Cape May, (609) 884-5404 or (800) 275-4278. www.capemaymac.org.

Landmark St. Catharine's Church faces parkland across Spring Lake.

Photo by Bud Benz

Spring Lake, N.J.

Among the seaside towns strung out along the Jersey Shore is one that stands apart. No neon lights. No boardwalk bric-a-brac. No honky-tonk. No video arcades. No hangouts for young singles.

Spring Lake planned it that way. More than a century of tight zoning regulations and community resolve produced a genteel enclave of substantial homes, manicured lawns, a tree-lined shopping district, a pristine boardwalk and not one but three lakes a stone's throw from the ocean.

Enterprising developers launched Spring Lake in the late 19th century. They planned four neighboring towns, each having its own railroad station and a lavish hotel catering to a wealthy clientele from New York, northern New Jersey and Philadelphia. Additional hotels, large guest houses and elegant estates followed. The four communities united to become Spring Lake, which celebrated its centennial in 1992.

Situated in the most exclusive stretch of the northern Jersey Shore, Spring Lake is a town where time seems to stand still. The Warren Hotel held fast to its summer social season through 2000, when its owners reluctantly sold it for development of luxury private homes. The stately Spring Lake Community House accommodates a library and theater groups in manorial surroundings. The recreation commission sponsors summer concerts at the park gazebo and model-boat regattas on Spring Lake. The 1992 Centennial Clock, with benches and colorful flowers at its base, would be at home in a European town square.

The town was settled by affluent Irish families and still is known fondly as "The Irish Riviera." It remains an eminently livable community for those who can afford houses starting at $300,000-plus and oceanfront properties of $1 million or more. No chain motels are among the roughly two dozen lodging establishments, ranging from old hotels to B&Bs, and no more can be licensed. The number of rooms has declined recently from 1,000 to 500, so the population of 3,500 year-round increases only to about 5,000 in summer.

The two-mile shoreline is pristine, and the longest non-commercial boardwalk in New Jersey is interrupted by nothing more than a few covered benches and pavilions containing swimming pools at either end. Weeping willows frame and wooden footbridges cross Spring Lake, the meandering, natural spring-fed lake in the center of town. It and Lake Como at the north end of town and Wreck Pond at the south end yield a landscape rare for a seaside community.

The beach, the boardwalk, the lakes and the serene residential ambiance are the draws for visitors. As a New York Times article claimed, "it's not so much what there is to do, it is what there is not to do that makes Spring Lake special."

Getting There

About 35 miles due south of New York City as the gull flies, Spring Lake is some 75 roundabout miles by car. Take the Garden State Parkway south to Exit 98, and Route 34 to the traffic circle. Follow Route 524 (Allaire Road) east to Spring Lake and the ocean. Frequent bus and train service is provided from New York City.

Where to Stay

No Jersey Shore town except Cape May offers a wider selection of inns and bed-and-breakfast facilities than Spring Lake. They help make Spring Lake a vacation destination primarily for adults.

Small Inns and B&Bs

Hollycroft, 506 North Blvd., Box 448, Spring Lake 07762.

This 1908 mountain-style hunting lodge, hidden behind a curtain of holly in a wooded residential area, is unique in the area. You'd expect to find it in the Adirondacks, perhaps, but not at the Jersey Shore. When you're sitting in the living room paneled in knotty pine, the log-beamed dining room or the brick-floored sun porch beside the flagstone terrace, you can look out across Lake Como and see the Atlantic beyond. You feel as if you're in the mountain woods, but with the ocean at hand. Architect-owner Mark Fessler and his wife Linda offer seven comfortable guest quarters, all with private baths and eclectically furnished in country style. All but two contain king or queen beds and four have fireplaces. The most deluxe, Spring Lake's largest suite, is bigger than many a guest's Manhattan apartment. It's a cathedral-ceilinged beauty with a queensize canopied French iron bed, a chaise and two leather chairs facing a massive stone fireplace, a small sitting room with TV and wet bar, a bathroom with a separate shower and a soaking tub for two beside an arched window looking onto the lake, and a wicker-furnished screened balcony facing the lake. Mark painted clouds and sky on the bedroom ceiling. Linda stenciled pansies on the walls of Ambleside, which also has a water-view porch with a hanging swing seat. Unusual touches abound: a custom-made iron bed with a twig bird cage atop the canopy and lace curtains around the headboard in the Grassmere room, a twig accessory hanging from the rafters and

on the wall behind the queen bed in the Somerset. Each room comes with bottles of Perrier and the Hollycroft's own soaps. Sherry is offered in the living room. The Fesslers put out a substantial buffet breakfast in the cheerful dining room or on the water-view flagstone terrace. Besides juices and fruit, it might include black-raspberry crumbles, Irish soda bread, raspberry-chocolate chip muffins and creamy scrambled eggs or ham and cheese egg strata.

(732) 681-2254 or (800) 679-2554. Fax (732) 280-8145. www.hollycroft.com. Five rooms and two suites with private baths. Doubles, $165 to $215. Suites, $255 to $345.

Sea Crest by the Sea, 19 Tuttle Ave., Spring Lake 07762.

This inn on a residential street half a block from the ocean caters to what owners Fred and Barbara Vogel call "adult fantasy and romance." That translates to a winter wonderland in the Sleigh Ride Room, a Victorian fainting couch in the Victorian Rose Room and a whirlpool tub beside a fireplace and a window seat in a cathedral-ceilinged room devoted to the purpose in the expansive Norwegian Wood suite. A hammock for two is in the ocean-view sitting room of the prime Captain's Quarters, which comes with two fireplaces, a steam shower and a private deck with ocean views. Dolly's Boudoir also has a balcony with ocean view. Every accommodation comes with a fireplace, TV/VCR and a whirlpool tub for two. Featherbeds or DUX beds are the norm. Common areas include a graceful living room and a dining room with a majestic French oak table and sideboard. The Vogels serve a bountiful gourmet breakfast. Fresh fruit, homemade granola, muffins and scones precede the main course, which could be frittata, featherbed eggs or french toast. Afternoon tea is served beside the player piano. Guests may enjoy it outside on the luxurious wraparound veranda.

(732) 449-9031 or (800) 803-9031. Fax (732) 974-0403. www.seacrestbythesea.com. Three rooms and five suites with private baths. Doubles, $350. Suites, $400 to $475.

Normandy Inn, 21 Tuttle Ave., Spring Lake 07762.

Haute Victoriana reigns inside this five-tone olive green and gold Italianate villa with Queen Anne accents – the only Spring Lake B&B to be listed on the National Register. New innkeepers Mark and Christine Valori set the mood in a pair of fancy pink and red common rooms containing a rococo damask parlor set, an antique English tall case clock and marble sculptures. A Chickering grand piano occupies center stage in the huge, pillared dining room, where there's an extensive breakfast menu as well as daily specials for house guests. Complimentary wine is available all day on the side sun porch, a comfy retreat with wicker furniture. Upstairs on the second and third floors are air-conditioned guest quarters with crocheted bedspreads and lace curtains. Victorian lamps, old portraits and antique furnishings dignify the rooms, all of which now have telephones and televisions. Some on the third floor are rather small, although two at the rear have been turned into the Audenreid Suite with a sitting area, a gas fireplace, a kingsize bedroom and a soaking tub. A large main-floor room with a fireplace has an impressive bathroom with peacock wallpaper, a marble jacuzzi tub and separate shower.

(732) 449-7172 or (800) 449-1888. Fax (732) 449-1070. www.normandyinn.com. Seventeen rooms and one suite with private baths. Doubles, $142 to $292. Suite, $392.

Ashling Cottage, 106 Sussex Ave., Spring Lake 07762.

Hundreds of windowpanes in the gazebo-shaped solarium in front of this engaging Victorian B&B yield views onto the tranquil lake that gives Spring Lake its name and a glimpse of the ocean a block away. The eye-catching solarium is the site of an extravagant breakfast served by owners Joanie and Bill Mahon. "You couldn't face a better way to start the day," says Bill. The fare includes fresh fruit compote, cereal, banana-nut bread and perhaps waffles or a crêpe dish. The Mahons returned to the Jersey Shore, where he grew up, to renovate and refurbish the 1877 house. They refinished the original floors, redecorated the rooms and lightened up the decor in what Bill calls "fresh beach style." Two guest rooms yield views of the water and two have fireplaces. Ten hold queensize beds and one has a king. Updated bathrooms, ceiling fans and air conditioning are standard. Room 4 on the third floor, up in the treetops with a view of the lake, is a guest favorite. Most in demand in summer is a rear first-floor room with a private porch. Common areas include a living room with fireplace and a large-screen TV/VCR. Guests enjoy wicker rockers and loveseats on the airy front porch shaded by century-old sentinel sycamores. Bicycles, beach equipment and an outdoor shower for returning beach-goers are among the amenities.

(732) 449-3553 or (888) 274-5464. Fax (732) 974-9067. www.ashlingcottage.com. Nine rooms with private baths and two rooms with shared bath. Doubles, $145 to $295.

The Sandpiper Inn, 7 Atlantic Ave., Spring Lake 07762.
Built in 1888 by a Spanish ambassador as a summer residence, this four-story structure with a restaurant on the lower level had been an inn and hotel for 50 years before falling upon hard times. A frequent guest, Harvey Mell, rescued it from dereliction in 1994, renovating five of the fifteen bedrooms most in need and improving the rest. The breezy wraparound second-floor porch offers wicker chairs and tables and a good view of the ocean. Six guest rooms afford ocean views and two get a glimpse. The generally spacious, high-ceilinged rooms are individually decorated in light summer colors, predominantly pinks and greens, with carpeting and formal window treatments. All have modern baths, five with European-style whirlpool tubs, plus TV/VCRs and mini-refrigerators. Rosemary Richards, the affable innkeeper, says the Taj Mahal in front on the top floor is the most requested room; it has a king bed, two swivel chairs facing oceanfront windows and a double bathroom, each with its own vanity sink. The king-bedded Seaview on the second floor also has a direct ocean floor. On the ground level is a glass-enclosed indoor swimming pool unique in staid Spring Lake. Fresh fruit, pastries and breads are offered for continental breakfast in the large and formal Victorian parlor or outside on the porch.

(732) 449-6060 or (800) 824-2779. Fax (732) 449-8409. www.sandpiperinn.com. Fifteen rooms with private baths. Doubles, $199 to $279.

Spring Lake Inn, 104 Salem Ave., Spring Lake 07762.
New windows in the cylindrical roof of the turret give the Tower View suite here one of the best ocean views of any accommodations in Spring Lake. Resting beneath a chandelier, the queensize sleigh bed is literally surrounded by windows, and on the level below is a sitting room colorful in raspberry-mauve. The flair and colors are typical of the way in which the old, seasonal Spring Lake Hotel was transformed into a classy, year-round B&B. Spacious rooms on the second and third floors, most with queensize beds, are strikingly different from each other. The Morning Glory is painted purple, even in the bathroom, while the ocean-view Sunrise is a vivid yellow. The Claddagh yields a view through a trapezoid window, but you have to be standing up to see it. The Moonbeam is wine-colored, the Americana blue, and the Garden Delight electric green. The second-floor Seraphim, painted a deep burgundy, has a corner fireplace, a loveseat and an armchair for a living-room type setting. A full living room is part of a queen suite on the main floor. New owners Barbara Garcia and Andrew Seaman added fireplaces in seven guest rooms. They

also added digital cable TV to an inn that did not have television. Although the rooms are thoroughly up to date, the 80-foot-long Victorian porch lined with rockers and the large lobby full of rich wood harken back to the 1888 hotel's past. So does the vast square dining room alongside, a beauty with a twelve-foot-high ceiling and a handful of tables for a hearty breakfast. The handsome rear parlor with wainscoting is furnished with oriental rugs and a mix of traditional and contemporary seating.

(732) 449-2010. Fax (732) 449-4020. www.springlakeinn.com. Fourteen rooms and two suites with private baths. Doubles, $199 to $299. Suites, $359 and $499.

Hotels

The Hewitt-Wellington, 200 Monmouth Ave., Spring Lake 07762.

This Victorian condominium hotel was totally renovated in 1988 into one of the more inviting of Spring Lake's small hotels. Twenty-nine guest accommodations are offered in two three-story wings connected by a breezeway beside a small heated pool. Suites consist of a bedroom and a living room with a queensize sofabed and can accommodate four persons. Most of those in the east wing face a park and afford views of the lake and the ocean. Rooms are light and airy, all decorated in similar style with Drexel-Heritage furniture, thick carpeting and queen beds. TVs, mini-refrigerators, telephones and marble baths with brass fixtures are the rule. A complimentary continental breakfast is served in season. Dinner is available in the hotel's leased restaurant, **Whispers** (see Where to Eat).

(732) 974-1212. Fax (732) 974-2338. www.hewittwellington.com. Twelve rooms and seventeen suites. Doubles, $165 to $270. Suites, $250 to $305.

The Ocean House, 102 Sussex Ave., Spring Lake 07762.

You can't miss this handsome boutique hotel, transformed from the old Colonial Hotel and dating to 1878. The exterior is painted a Bermuda pink that stands out blocks away. Longtime Spring Lake residents Nancy and Dennis Kaloostian said it was "under the weather" when they bought the place. They proceeded to redo all 35 guest rooms, creating stylish and comfortable quarters, all with TVs and telephones. All have king, queen or twin beds, most got updated baths and eight in the Taylor Hall wing have partial ocean views. Six rooms are called mini-suites with queen beds and sitting rooms. Two suites have two bedrooms and two baths each. In a reversal of the usual decorative technique, Nancy picked the varied paint colors for each room and then coordinated interesting fabrics and carpets to match. Furnishings include antiques from several periods. The rambling hotel has a formal living room, a comfortable library, a dining room where a full buffet breakfast is put out for guests and a broad porch wrapping around the front and side to catch the ocean breezes.

(732) 449-9090 or (888) 449-9094. Fax (732) 449-9092. www.theoceanhouse.net. Twenty-seven rooms, six mini-suites and two suites. Doubles, $200 to $250. Suites, $275.

The Chateau, Fifth and Warren Avenues, Spring Lake 07762.

Located at the foot of Spring Lake and overlooking two parks and the town gazebo, this hotel dating to 1888 has become less hotel-like and more like a large B&B under owner Scott Smith. Thirty-six guest rooms and suites are in three buildings characterized by lots of public spaces, from decks to porches to a second-floor gazebo. Ceiling fans, wicker furniture and Waverly fabrics are the common denominator in each room. All also have TV/VCRs, refrigerators, wet bars, marble bathrooms and two phones with data ports. The ultimate are ten luxury suites with fireplaces and jacuzzis or soaking tubs for two. Some of these have private balconies or porches. We were happy to be ensconced in a large "classic parlor" with a sitting area, wet bar and two double beds in the Villa facing the town gazebo. The hotel's main lobby has been expanded to include a showy breakfast area, full of chintz floral armchairs at pink-linened tables. Continental breakfast is offered here – free midweek in the winter and $5.50 the rest of the year.

(732) 974-2000 or (877) 974-5253. Fax (732) 974-0007. www.chateauinn.com. Twenty-nine rooms and seven suites. Doubles, $189 to $279. Suites, $269 to $309.

The Breakers Hotel, 1507 Ocean Ave., Spring Lake 07762.

Totally refurbished in recent years under the ownership of Cosmo Scardino, this oceanfront hotel is Spring Lake's most posh – in a showy nouveau way. It was also the first to stay open year-round, starting something of a trend in town. Off a mirrored foyer are a piano bar, a glamorous dining room facing the ocean, and an enclosed veranda for breakfast and lunch overlooking a heated swimming pool and hot tub. Sixty-seven accommodations, from small to spacious, are on the second, third and fourth floors. Many yield ocean views. Each has air conditioning, TV, mini-refrigerator and telephone and is decorated in pastel pinks and greens. Eleven rooms have whirlpool tubs. One "luxury deluxe room" boasts a kingsize bed, fireplace, marble floor and circular whirlpool bath surrounded by mirrors. The tower suite has a round kingsize bed and windows on all sides.

(732) 449-7700. Fax (732) 449-0161. www.breakershotel.com. Sixty-five rooms and two suites. Doubles, $215 to $435.

Seeing and Doing

The prime attractions for visitors are the pristine beach flanked by a quiet boardwalk, plus the verdant parklands surrounding the town's namesake lake.

One could spend hours walking the streets and admiring the gardens and manicured lawns of Spring Lake, where commercial lawn services must rank as the town's single most prosperous business niche. Those and gardeners, whose talents are everywhere evident. Check out the manicured masterpiece surrounding the residence at 301 West Lake Drive. The whole lawn is clipped to one-fourth inch high and maintained daily like a putting green.

THE OCEAN. Two miles of wide beach (continually restocked with fresh sand) and New Jersey's longest non-commercial boardwalk separate the Atlantic Ocean from small sand dunes and Ocean Avenue. Spring Lake's boardwalk contains only a few pavilions with benches and two larger pavilions harboring saltwater pools, rest rooms and food stands at either end. The limited parking and need for beach passes deter transients and teenagers. Most hotels and inns include beach badges in their rates or sell them at a discount to guests. The boardwalk is great for strolling. Even on chilliest days, lots of people walk or jog on the boardwalk.

Beyond the town's limits, the beaches are less refined (although beach passes again are usually needed in summer). South of Spring Lake, the beach at Sea Girt is pleasant but quite a bit smaller. The lively, mile-long boardwalk at Point Pleasant Beach is flanked by Jenkinson's Park, an old-fashioned amusement park with rides and concession stands as well s Jenkinson's Aquarium. The Manasquan Inlet here provides boats to get out to the ocean.

Along Ocean Avenue north of Spring Lake, a large pair of brick pillars marks the entry to Belmar, a different world of taffy, frozen custard and a McDonald's on the beach. In the evening and on weekends, young singles cruise the beaches with beers in hand, and rock music pounds from cars and boom boxes. The visitor quickly realizes the beach action is in Belmar and beyond in Avon-by-the-Sea and Bradley Beach.

THE LAKES. Fed by underground springs in the center of town, Spring Lake is tranquil and picturesque. Weeping willows line portions of the shore, and the waters are populated by ducks and swans. Benches overlook the lake at intervals. The lake is long enough to require two ornate wooden bridges for pedestrians to shortcut from one side to the other. On the north side of town is Lake Como; on the south, Wreck Pond, a favorite for fishing.

St. Catharine's Church, Third and Essex Avenue. Built beside the lake between 1901 and 1907 by a wealthy resident as a memorial to his daughter, this striking edifice resembles the Romanesque St. Peter's Basilica in miniature and is well worth a visit. Two 800-year-old bronze standards from Rome line the entrance to the church. The high altar is made of the same Carrera marble used by Michelangelo and the stained-glass windows were made in Bavaria. A professor from Rome painted the interior frescos. The church is one of two in the same parish in Spring Lake, a heavily Roman Catholic community.

Theater. The Spring Lake Theatre Company, (732) 449-4530, stages six shows year-round in the Spring Lake Community House at Third and Madison avenues. The handsome English Tudor building built in 1923 by a former mayor and state senator includes a library and a 360-seat theater. Tickets are in the $18 to $24 range and sell out early.

Gazebo Concerts. The town recreation commission sponsors outdoor concerts in Potter Park on varying nights roughly every other week in summer. Jazz bands, the Atlantic Wind Ensemble, the Ocean Grove Band, the Happy Days String Band, a folksinger and an Irish balladeer were among recent performers. Townspeople and visitors bring chairs or blankets and nearly fill the park.

Sea Girt Lighthouse, corner Ocean and Beach avenues, Sea Girt. Just south of Spring Lake is the only lighthouse on this portion of the Jersey Shore. Atop a brick house, the light beamed from 1896 to 1955. The restored lighthouse, though not open to the public, is a favorite background for photographers.

BOAT RIDES. River Belle Cruises, 47 Broadway, Point Pleasant Beach, (732) 892-3377, offers sightseeing and dining excursions. A small replica of a Mississippi riverboat, the River Belle, cruises the calm inland waters of the Manasquan River, Point Pleasant Canal and Barnegat Bay. Two-hour sightseeing cruises are offered afternoons and some evenings from late June through Labor Day; adults $15, children $8. Other cruises include lunch on Wednesday and Thursday, pizza and fireworks on Thursday and brunch on select Sundays. Hours and prices vary. The related **River Queen** also offers charter and meal cruises from Bogan's Basin, 800 Ashley Ave, Brielle, (732) 528-6620.

OTHER ACTIVITIES. The level terrain of the area is good for **bicycling.** Bicycles are allowed on boardwalks from 6 to 10 a.m. Oceanfront parasailing out of Ken's Landing in Point Pleasant Beach is offered by **Point Pleasant Parasail,** (732) 714-2359. Public golf courses include the **Bel-Aire Golf Club,** Allaire Road and Highway 34 in Alllenwood, and the **Spring Meadow Golf Course,** 395 Allaire Road, Allaire.

Historic Allaire Village, Allaire State Park, off Route 524, Wall.
Listed on the National Register, this mini-Sturbridge is part of 3,000-acre Allaire State Park just west of Spring Lake. The outdoor living-history museum re-creates the days of New Jersey's early iron industry, the source of raw materials for marine engine manufacturer James P. Allaire's New York business. Interpreters dressed in the work clothes of the 1830s portray the daily life and times of early iron workers

and their families at the historic Howell Works, an industrial community established between 1822 and 1850 when bog ore was smelted. They demonstrate early crafts and open-hearth cooking in some of the twelve houses and buildings in a restored village. Other buildings include a snack bar and a general store/museum shop. The Pine Creek Railroad displays six antique trains, two of which offer ten-minute rides. *(732) 938-2253. www.allairevillage.org. Grounds open year-round, 8 to dusk. Village open Wednesday-Sunday 11 to 5, Memorial Day to Labor Day; Saturday-Sunday 10 to 4 in May and September-December. Parking, $5 weekends in season.*

SHOPPING. Four blocks of tree-lined Third Avenue and a section of Morris Avenue are home to small stores run by committed owners. One of the biggest drawing cards is the **Irish Centre,** which features all kinds of Irish imports reflecting the resort's heritage. Another is the old-fashioned **Spring Lake Variety Store** filled to the brim with all kinds of things, including beach chairs hanging from the ceiling. Clothing and accessories are more sedate specialties of **The Camel's Eye, Village Tweeds** and **Courts & Greens,** whose names indicate their priorities. Unusual clothing, accessories and handmade jewelry are featured at **Dreamkeeper.** Adorable bears clad in little smock dresses are in the windows of **Teddy Bears by the Seashore,** where two former Macy's buyers offer discounted clothing for children and their parents. We admired the cute clothes at **Samantha's. Spring Lace** is a mercantile confection full of lace and Victoriana (much of the Victorian lace on windows and tables at local inns was obtained here). Some of the most sophisticated cards, stationery, books and desk accessories we've seen are stocked at **Noteworthy By-the-Sea**.

New stores and galleries seem to pop up at every visit. We know innkeepers who covet every single item at **Kate & Company,** where English and Irish country pine furniture and home accessories are imaginatively displayed. Fine American crafts are among the "irresistibles," some made by the owners, at **The Moon & Sixpence.** Linens and soaps are featured with home and garden accessories at **Whimsicality.** Art enthusiasts admire the offerings of the **Spring Lake Gallery, Evergreen Gallery, ArtEffects** and **Thistledown Gallery.** At **Weekend Outfitters,** you can rent a kayak, canoe or a bicycle built for two, and you can even order a gourmet picnic with linens and china. The **Third Avenue Surf Shop** caters to the surfing lifestyle with equipment, apparel and home accessories.

For sustenance while shopping, consider **Who's on Third** for deli food and **Spring Lake Gourmet Pizzeria,** a sleek place that lives up to its claim of being "not just another pizzeria." Sweets lovers get their fill at the **Third Avenue Chocolate Shoppe** and **Jean Louise Homemade Candies,** where the day's special at one visit was chocolate-covered grapes. Snacks are available to eat in or take out next door at **Freedman's Bakery.** Gourmet pizzas and sophisticated entrée specials are offered at the **Spring Lake Gourmet Pizzeria.** The **Spring Lake Bottle Shop** is the place to pick up a good bottle of wine for restaurants where you bring your own.

A SPECIAL PLACE. Ocean Grove, an oceanfront religious community that still clings to its Methodist past, is a ten-minute drive north of Spring Lake via Ocean Avenue or Route 71. Look at all the tiny gingerbread houses, the larger gingerbread boarding houses and hotels and the colorful tents in season around the Great Auditorium dating to 1894. Consider the street names: Pilgrim's Pathway, Mount Tabor Way, Mount Carmel Way and broad Ocean Pathway, the last said to be New Jersey's most photographed street. Visit the showplace, 6,500-seat auditorium where religious meetings are still held Sundays throughout the summer; religious programs are scheduled each weekday, and name secular entertainers perform in the acoustically perfect amphitheater on Saturday nights – among them recently, the Kingston Trio, Frankie Valli and the Preservation Hall Jazz Band. The entire square-mile town, which claims the largest aggregate of Victoriana in the country, is designated a National Historic District. Not long ago nicknamed "Ocean Grave," it has risen from near-dereliction in the late 1980s to become a happening place. Jack Green, the Ocean Grove Camp Meeting Association president whose tent was featured on a house tour, set the pace with plans to restore the prime Queen Hotel, a decrepit landmark at the corner of Ocean Pathway and Ocean Avenue. A wall blew over in a windstorm in the middle of restoration and the plans were scrapped. Meanwhile, his son and daughter-in-law, Jack and Valerie Green, opened the Ocean Plaza, a Victorian B&B with eighteen summery bedrooms and private baths, at 18 Ocean Pathway. Many others followed suit, and the owners of the Raspberry Café struck culinary pay dirt with the opening of their acclaimed Moonstruck restaurant, which moved in 2002 to larger quarters just across the city line at 517 Lake Ave., in Asbury Park, overlooking narrow Wesley Lake and the Victorian landscape of Ocean Grove.

Where to Eat

For a town close to and oriented toward the ocean, Spring Lake has precious few good dining places beside the water. The choices are limited by zoning regulations and a lack of liquor licenses. But there are plenty of water-view options nearby.

Whispers, 200 Monmouth Ave., Spring Lake.

New owners have upgraded the small but highly regarded dining room in the Hewitt-Wellington hotel, across from the lake but without a water view. Instead, the focus is on the food and on the serene ambiance. The cream-colored room with burgundy accents is a picture of French elegance with a marble floor, upholstered armchairs, and four crystal chandeliers that coordinate with the long-stemmed crystal vases and wine glasses on the tables. Chef Scott Giordano took over in 2004 following the departure of chef-partner Mark Mikolajczyk, who wanted his own enterprise after making the restaurant one of New Jersey's best during a six-year tenure. The signature dish is panko-crusted swordfish stuffed with lump crabmeat and topped with crispy shrimp. Another favorite is Norwegian salmon served with cream cheese and chive whipped potatoes and a carrot purée. Other main courses could be pork tenderloin with peach barbecue sauce, veal chop with porcini mushrooms and herb-crusted rack of lamb. Start with a crab and brie quesadilla, stuffed ostrich or the "panache of appetizers:" a jumbo lump crab cake beside a duet of grilled shrimp and a wild mushroom salad. Desserts could be a fresh berry beggars purse, chocolate soufflé or tarte tatin. For a sample of Whispers at its best, try the chef's extravagant six-course tasting menu ($60).

(732) 974-9755. www.whispersrestaurant.com. Entrées, $25 to $33. Dinner nightly, 4:30 to 10. Closed Monday and Tuesday in off-season. BYOB.

Black Trumpet, 7 Atlantic Ave., Spring Lake.

Ensconced in the walkout lower level of the century-old Sandpiper Inn is this 96-seat gem, a U-shaped room that's mostly windows, with a glimpse of the ocean in the distance. One side is the patio room with an original Spanish tiled floor, live plants and even a bird feeder to convey the feeling of being outdoors. Innkeeper Rosemary Richards designed the club room on the other side to impart a golf club atmosphere in forest green and creams. Both are soothing settings for the refined fare of chef Mark Mikolajczyk, who trained at the New York Restaurant School before working at the famed Bouley in Manhattan. He took over the inn's restaurant in late 2004 in partnership with Dave McCleery, his longtime sous chef and former pastry chef at Whispers. They named their new endeavor for Mark's favorite mushroom. The black trumpet figures in his signature appetizer, pan-seared scallops over a rock shrimp potato pancake. The crab spring roll with a spicy vegetable vinaigrette is another favorite. The chef's signature entrée, nori-crusted swordfish on a tower of crabmeat, spinach and potato, came with him. Updated entrées include pan-seared fluke with brown butter sauce, de-shelled lobster in saffron beurre blanc in an egg-roll pastry, pesto-stuffed pork tenderloin and grilled New York strip steak in a port-wine demi-glace. Desserts might be tarte tatin, a trio of crème brûlées served with sugar cookie spoons and "a tasting of chocolate" – a warm bittersweet chocolate tart served with a minted chocolate hand-rolled truffle and homemade white chocolate ice creams.

(732) 449-4700. www.theblacktrumpet.com. Entrées, $16 to $29. Dinner nightly, from 5. BYOB.

The Mill at Spring Lake Heights, Old Mill Road, Spring Lake Heights.
Overlooking its own mill pond and with especially good water vistas from its main dining room and outdoor deck, the former Old Mill Inn is known for Spring Lake's most appealing waterfront dining – even if it is only a view of a lake. A classic on the Jersey Shore, it was rebuilt and enlarged following a fire in 1985 and underwent another facelift in 2003, plus a name change that recognized the fact it really wasn't an inn with overnight accommodations. The lobby, bigger than many a restaurant, opens into an elliptical bar and lounge area, surrounded by two large dining rooms. The main dining room is elegant with a high coffered ceiling and upholstered chairs at well-spaced tables, many with great views of the water. Best of all at midday is a window table in the lounge, away from the hubbub and seemingly perched over the water beside a flotilla of ducks. We enjoyed a spicy Manhattan clam chowder, an abundant arugula and endive salad with shaved pears and candied walnuts, and two crab cakes on a pool of herbed cream sauce, nicely presented with a side of vegetables. For dinner, owners Tamar Tolchin and Anthony Cirillo recommend any of the fresh seafood dishes, the extra-crispy roast duck with raspberry-port wine sauce and the prime rib with horseradish sauce. The choices are legion – nineteen entrées on the regular menu plus 21 more on a "comfort menu" that's amazingly affordable ($12.95 to $17.95) and available any night but Saturday. Start with lobster bisque, carpaccio or a lump crabmeat cocktail. Finish with the specialty cheesecake, chocolate-raspberry cake or key lime pie. The wine list is extensive.

(732) 449-1800. www.themillatslh.com. Entrées, $17 to $35. Lunch, Monday-Saturday 11:30 to 2:30. Dinner nightly, 2:30 to 10 or 11. Sunday, brunch 11 to 3, dinner 11 to 9. Closed Monday except in December.

The Breakers Hotel, 1507 Ocean Ave., Spring Lake.
The Seashell Room at the ocean end of The Breakers Hotel is Spring Lake's most glamorous dining scene. It also has the best head-on ocean view of any restaurant in town. The room is summery in beige and salmon with unusual carved shell-back cushioned chairs at crisp-linened tables bearing Lalique-style glass candle holders. The local consensus is that the food plays second fiddle to the setting. The extensive Italian/continental menu has stayed proudly the same since 1982 because, the chef says, "we know it works for our clientele." And it works for him, embracing all the standards from flounder française and shrimp marinara to lobster fra diavolo, from steak giambotta to veal rollatini. Combo platters pair boneless chicken with

veal marsala and shrimp parmigiana with veal parmigiana. There are basic pasta dishes, and predictable appetizers like hot antipasti, shrimp cocktail and eggplant rollatini. Chocolate-banana-daiquiri layer cake is the most exotic dessert. A pianist entertains nightly in the lounge. Breakfast and lunch are served poolside on The Veranda.

(732) 449-7700. Entrées, $16.95 to $23.95. Lunch daily from 11:30. Dinner nightly, 4:30 to 10 or 11.

Avon Pavilion, 600 Ocean Ave., Avon-by-the-Sea.

Hot dogs and hamburgers are the daytime fare at this stark white pavilion right over the beach in a posh little oceanside enclave a few miles north of Spring Lake. At night, the summery interior in sand and green colors is dressed with tablecloths and candlelight for fine waterside dining. The appealing menu is "dedicated to those who cherish the simple but divine pleasures of the seashore." The lapping waves are the backdrop for interesting pastas and main dishes. A cup of New "Joisey" clam chowder could start your meal. "Bay and Booze Shrimp" is the most popular appetizer (the shrimp are steamed in beer, Old Bay seasoning and butter, from Grandma Roxie's secret recipe). Herb-coated broiled salmon fillet with a lemon-lime sauce and a New York strip steak smothered with a mushroom and vidalia onion demi-glace are a couple of the entrée mainstays. A special might be pan-seared chicken breast and sautéed broccoli rabe with semolina rigatoni in a zesty chicken broth. Instead of a house salad, the place serves a tomato concoction with olives and onions in which to dip your bread. Finish with key lime mousse, perhaps, or toll house pie à la mode. Pancakes with Jersey blueberries, the ultimate omelet (everything but the kitchen sink) and veggie homefries au gratin are a few of the breakfast choices, and eggbeaters and sugar-free syrups and jellies are available.

(732) 775-1043. Entrées, $18.95 to $23.95. Open daily, Mother's Day through Labor Day: Breakfast, 7:30 to 11:15. Lunch, noon to 3:30. Dinner, 5:30 to 9 or 10. BYOB.

Matisse, 1400 Ocean Ave., Belmar.

The "art of dining" is proclaimed by chef-owner Anthony Wall at his winner in a small, unassuming place with a great view of the ocean. The chef, a veteran of Hyatt Hotel restaurants, returned to his home territory to prepare what he calls new continental cuisine. A stellar sundried tomato oil to be slathered on bread arrives with the menu. It starts with appetizers like goat cheese raviolis with basil and grape confit, braised mussels with ginger and sweet chiles, and crispy shrimp with orange-radish dipping sauce. Or you can sample the chef's selection of three appetizers. Main courses range from seared red snapper with ginger and cilantro soy to rosemary-crusted rack of lamb with burgundy jus. The portobello wellington with goat cheese and spinach, the braised chicken with olives and tomatoes in a spicy pepper broth, and the angus ribeye steak with parsley-shallot butter come highly recommended. The dessert selection includes a selection of cheeses and fruit as well as a hazelnut bombe with mango and a trio of crème brûlées. A seasonal outdoor deck offers a café menu.

(732) 681-7680. www.matissecatering.com. Entrées, $21.95 to $26.95. Dinner nightly, 5:30 to 9:30. Sunday brunch, 10:30 to 3. Closed Monday and Tuesday in off-season. BYOB.

Klein's Waterside Café, 708 River Road, Belmar.

The 75-year-old seafood market in front displays fish as fresh as can be. Behind is a covered deck with picnic and plastic tables as well as an open deck right beside the busy Shark River, where you can watch the fishing boats unload. Owner Ollie Klein's café is a fun, casual, no-frills place – the kind the area should have more of.

At night, candles flicker in glass holders on the tables, but you may find it disconcerting to be eating on paper plates with wimpy plastic utensils. The seafood is fairly priced, and you can bring your own wine. The menu has been expanded lately from the fish specialties to include chicken française, baby back ribs, New York strip steak and various pasta dishes. We started with succulent oysters on the half shell, which proved a better choice than the oysters casino. We also found the grilled salmon steak with coleslaw and rice pilaf better than the fried oysters with waffle fries that had perhaps seen better days. The entire menu is available to eat in as well as to take out. Klein's also operates a sushi bar next door, where you might be enticed by the all-you-can-eat sushi for $26.95 on Monday nights.

(732) 681-1177. www.kleinsfish.com. Entrées, $15.95 to $19.95. Lunch daily, 11 to 4. Dinner, 4 to 9 or 10. BYOB. No credit cards.

Jack Baker's Wharfside, 101 Channel Drive, Point Pleasant.
Overlooking the busy Manasquan River channel, this restaurant is one of several in New Jersey and Florida spawned by the one started by Jack Baker, son of a fisherman. Another is the **Lobster Shanty** next door to the Wharfside in Point Pleasant. Particularly popular with tourists, the two Point Pleasant restaurants provide standard water lovers' fare: a good range of seafood, a water view, bustling conviviality, a small section for outside dining, and affordable prices. The Wharfside is usually packed. The Lobster Shanty, which is so huge as to make its name laughable, is a bit more open, with a slightly better view and a fireplace ablaze in the off-season. The menus, virtually identical, include broiled scallops, stuffed flounder, baked scrod and seafood fettuccine. More adventurous palates may be served with mussels zinfandel, bourbon-glazed grilled salmon and basil-encrusted haddock served over a bed of roasted garlic and tomato pesto. Corn fritters and garlic bread come to the table in a basket and are quite tasty. The meal also includes coleslaw, rice or potato, and chowder or a tossed salad mixed at table by a "salad bar waitress" and served with the house Italian dressing.

(732) 892-9100. Entrées, $16 to $34. Open daily, 11:30 to 9:30 or 10:30.

Red's Lobster Pot, 57 Inlet Drive, Point Pleasant Beach.
Locals in the know prefer this little dockside shack to the larger, better-known establishments all around. They say the food prepared by fisherman Red Stillufsen's wife and daughter is better, and the blackboard specials quite creative. In season, you can wait outside at a raw bar or eat at a handful of tables beside the water at **Red's Lobster Dock**, an old-fashioned lobster pound. Inside, you're seated at one of twelve tables in a small, brightly lit room that is intimate, to say the least. Besides lobster, the all-seafood menu offers quite a range from mussels marinara to lobster fra diavolo and zuppa de pesce. The family not only catch their own fish but grow their organic herbs. Look for things like bluefish with mustard sauce and flounder française. Broiled lobster, flounder and shrimp are apt to be stuffed with the chef's special Canadian crabmeat stuffing. Calamari salad, scallops provençal, clams oreganata and lobster ravioli are among the appetizers. Key lime pie, peanut butter silk pie and amaretto cheesecake are good desserts. The brief lunch menu ($5.95 to $8.95) includes a free beverage and, for what it's worth, if you arrive by bicycle, you get a $1 "environmental discount" off your dinner order.

(732) 295-6622. www.redslobsterpot.com. Entrées, $13.95 to $23.95. Open daily, noon to 9. Closed Tuesday in off-season and November to late March. BYOB.

FOR MORE INFORMATION: Greater Spring Lake Chamber of Commerce, 1218 Third Ave., Spring Lake, N.J. 07762, (732) 449-0577. www.springlake.org.

Famed Montauk Lighthouse is landmark at tip of Long Island.

Montauk, Long Island

They call Montauk "The End," not the skeptics who think that's appropriate but because it is at the very tip of Long Island – a world apart for the New Yorkers who swell its 3,800 year-round population to some 40,000 in summer.

For the visitor, there are at least two Montauks. One is the rugged ocean shore with sand dunes and cliffs up to 200 feet high, calling to mind visions of the Oregon coast. The other is the sheltered interior of lake, bay, harbor and undulating topography that challenges nearby Block Island's designation as the Bermuda of the North.

But Montauk – voted one of the Last Great Places by the Nature Conservancy – differs in one remarkable respect from others. More than half its land is undeveloped and open to the public.

Montauk stretches between the Atlantic Ocean and Block Island Sound at the easternmost tip of Long Island – beyond the Nassau County suburbs, the Suffolk County exurbs and the moneyed Hamptons.

Officially, it is part of the Hamptons, the high-powered summer playground of New York's rich and famous. But in every sense other than its tax district, Montauk could be another planet. Where the Hamptons is Gucci, Montauk is more grunge. And that's the way they want to keep it.

Here is a sandy expanse once envisioned by Carl Fisher, the multi-millionaire industrialist who first developed Miami Beach, as the most luxurious summer resort of the western world. His faded English Tudor hotel atop Signal Hill, built in 1927 and now condominiumized, is all that remains of his dream.

Montauk remains essentially a beachy, boating and fishing mecca of the old school. Montauk's western gateway is Hither Hills State Park with miles of public beaches and hiking and biking trails. It ends at the easternmost point in New York State, another state park where the landmark Montauk Light has been a beacon for ships for more than 200 years.

Between these parks lies a small oceanside village built around a circular plaza, where the streets begin with the letters D, E or F and none of the national fast-food or motel chains has sullied its character. A few miles across the peninsula on the north shore is Montauk's busy deep-sea harbor, really an inlet from Block Island

Sound. The inlet opens into Lake Montauk, dredged by Carl Fisher to make a protected anchorage. For water lovers, Long Island's largest lake gives Montauk a dual ocean/lake perspective.

Montauk claims to be the sport fishing capital of the world. It also has some of the Northeast's best, most accessible beaches. Boat tours sail around the lake, harbor and beyond. Inland are a Robert Trent Jones-designed public golf course considered one of the nation's 50 best and horseback rides at the oldest working ranch in the United States. You can surf the waves or mountain bike alongside the dunes, feast on lobster or visit historic houses and museums.

If that's not enough – or if you simply get a rainy day – check out the reading rooms at the Montauk Library just east of the village center. The award-winning building tops a hill and has a commanding view of the ocean. You may not get much reading done, but you will enjoy one of the best water views around.

Getting There

Montauk lies about 135 miles east of New York City at the east end of the South Fork of Long Island. The Long Island Railroad, (631) 467-3210, serves Montauk from Pennsylvania Station, a trip of about three hours. The train station is located just north of the village center. The Hampton Jitney, (631) 384-4600, offers frequent trips between Manhattan and Montauk.

Motorists from the west and south take the Long Island Expressway (I-495) to Exit 70, which leads to the Sunrise Highway (State Route 27). From New England, the Cross Sound Ferry serves Orient Point on the North Fork from New London, Conn., (631) 323-2525 or (860) 443-5281; car and driver $37, adult passengers $10, children $5. Ferries connect Sag Harbor and the South Fork via Shelter Island.

Where to Stay

For waterfront accommodations, your decision will involve whether to be on the ocean, Lake Montauk or Block Island Sound. And your choice will be limited pretty much to cottages, motels and resorts, many of which have been condominiumized. Montauk's fishing and beach aura and its location at land's end account for a somewhat quirky ambiance. Check out the highly publicized but faded Montauk Manor hotel, the Shepherds Neck Inn, Ruschmeyer's Inn & Restaurant and the Crow's Nest Restaurant & Inn and you'll know what we mean.

The Panoramic View, 272 Old Montauk Hwy., Montauk 11954.

For ocean views from a lodging facility, there are none more dramatic in Montauk – or anywhere along the Mid-Atlantic/ lower New England coast – than here. Head down the main driveway and you think you're descending along California's Big Sur. Five white wooden buildings with green roofs, one or two stories each, are nestled at different heights along a steep, terraced hillside so that no one's view is blocked. At the foot is a 1,000-foot-wide strand of glorious beach. All with efficiency kitchenettes, the 120 units are categorized by elevation. You want

views from on high? Book a room at the 100-foot level in Highpoint or Valley View (which looks not on a valley but rather the open ocean). Midway down the hill are Hilltop and Point of View. Closest to the ocean are Salt Sea, two floors at the 25- and 35-foot level, and three "beach homes" with living room and wood-burning fireplace, two bedrooms, two baths, polished beechwood floors, porch and patio. Motel-type rooms with kitchenettes feature cathedral or raised ceilings, picture windows, carpeting, and natural cedar or white wood paneling. Suites add a separate bedroom and a living room with a sofabed. The accommodations are spacious and stylishly furnished, the balconies private, and the flowers and landscaping stunning. Nestled into the hillside at the 65-foot level is an attractive free-form heated pool, flanked by lounge chairs and lush greenery. In a way, its setting with ocean beneath looks like something out of the Caribbean. The wide, secluded beach is at its best here, and the Panoramic's beach boys provide chaise lounges and towels. The only downside is the strenuous climb back to your room, especially if you're nested at the upper levels. A plaque on a boulder at the entrance honors the establishment's 1958 founding by Earl Raymond French, "whose foresight and dedication led to the furthering of Montauk as a resort area." His family continues the tradition of T.L.C. and service here.

(631) 668-3000. Fax (631) 668-7870. www.panoramicview.com. One hundred seventeen efficiency units. Doubles, $176 to $294. Beach houses, $590 for four. Five-night minimum summer weekends. Closed early November to early April. No credit cards.

Gurney's Inn Resort & Spa, 290 Old Montauk Highway, Montauk 11954.
If money is no object and a social setting and spa facilities your priorities, this legendary resort dating to 1926 is for you. It's as close as Montauk comes to glitz. It also shares the same bluff-side perch as the Panoramic View, but – without the foresight of its neighbor – the views from some of its 109 rooms are obstructed by other buildings or sprawling concrete platforms in the middle. Some "view" rooms don't even have balconies. The best views are offered by the deluxe suites, staterooms and studios and five cottages, decorated in shades of beige, mauve and blue. The rooms we saw in the main Foredeck and Forward Watch ocean-view buildings were not as glamorous as those pictured in the showy brochure, although at least they had balconies. Despite the name, this is no inn but rather a hotel-style resort, lately converted like so many in Montauk to time-sharing or cooperative ownership. The main building has three restaurants, ranging from **La Pasticceria** where you can sip a $7 cup of cappuccino to the casual **Caffe Monte,** whose tables yield the best water views, to the vast **Sea Grille** dining room, with a bar and a grand piano in one section and windows onto a broad outside terrace, where the ocean looks as it would from an ocean liner. The 1,000-foot beach is a beauty in terms of facilities, from playground equipment to the Beach Barge set squarely in the middle to dispense drinks, box lunches and picnic fare. The international health and beauty spa – first on the East Coast and billed as the only sea water spa on this continent – offers a range of treatments and an indoor saltwater pool. The fitness center comes with views of the ocean. The gift shop is run by Summers of Montauk. Nightly entertainment varies from bingo to karaoke. Lola and Nick Monte, keepers of the inn, keep the place hopping with activities to appeal to mostly baby-boomer families and conventioneers.

(631) 668-2345 or (800) 848-7639. www.gurneys-inn.com. One hundred nine rooms and five cottages. Doubles, $360 to $465 MAP. Cottages for two to six, $675 to $1,595 MAP.

Montauk Yacht Club Resort & Marina, 32 Star Island Road, Montauk 11954.
Recently renovated and redecorated is the interior of this 22-acre waterfront

resort complex, off by itself on an island jutting out into Lake Montauk and accessed by a short causeway. The main resort is built around what was once a lighthouse. The waterfront consists of a 232-slip marina where many an impressive yacht is moored. The yacht club reference in the name is not literal, since this is a public marina and a full-service resort. The accommodations are among the most attractive and comfortable in Montauk. Eighty-four are in contemporary, two-story buildings, of which more than one-third face the harbor head-on. Rooms come with kingsize or two double beds (the kingsize having two club chairs rather than one). Our waterfront room in the South Forty wing faced a small beach from a delightful private balcony. In the room were a dressing table with a big mirror and a corner armoire with TV. The bathroom was actually four sections, including walk-in closet and built-in shelves. Toiletries and a mini-refrigerator came with. We felt quite luxurious in such fancy waterfront accommodations for a mere $79 a night, an off-season special, including breakfast. We would not have been as happy in units facing the pool or the parking area. Elsewhere on the property are 23 large rooms in "hideaway villas" fashioned from charming, Dutch-looking white stucco houses with green roofs and shutters. They were once owned by Flo Ziegfield of Ziegfield Follies fame. They have their own pool and tennis court, but are not as close to the water. Other resort facilities include an indoor and an outdoor pool, lighted tennis courts, fitness center and a gift shop. The main lodge holds the **Il Mare Ristorante** (see Where to Eat), a pleasant, rattan-furnished dining room with windows onto the water, and the more casual **Breezes Café.**

(631) 668-3100 or (888) 692-8668. Fax (631) 668-6181. www.montaukyachtclub.com. Eighty-four rooms and 23 villas. Doubles, $249 to $459. Closed Thanksgiving to mid-March.

The Surf Club, South Essex Street and Surfside Avenue, Box 1174, Montauk 11954.

Ostensibly the most luxurious of the condominium resorts that typify Montauk is this series of gray contemporary duplex townhouses at 8.5 acres at the edge of Montauk village. They're marked by sharply pitched lines and staggered placement and grouped around a landscaped courtyard with an angular pool. A boardwalk leads through the dunes to 550 feet of oceanfront beach. About one-third of the 92 units are oceanfront, and some others yield ocean views. Each has a small galley kitchen and a private balcony or deck. One-bedroom units have a queen bed up and a living room with sofabed down. Two-bedroom units have a queen bedroom on the first floor and twin beds in a loft, with a sofabed in the living room. The rooms we saw were compact and simply furnished, but serviceable. Village attractions are within walking distance.

(631) 668-3800 or (800) 527-8928. Fax (631) 668-9296. www.duneresorts.com. Ninety-two apartments. Doubles, $255 to $565. Four-night minimum weekends. Closed mid-November to mid-April.

Royal Atlantic Beach Resort, South Edgemere Street, Box 936, Montauk 11954.

This began as a motel and expanded into a "resort," with rooms, suites, condominiums, townhouses, a game room and a restaurant, in three complexes in the center of the village. It's the place for those who want to be on the beach, but with village action close at hand. The original motel with additions occupies the beachfront – literally. The balconies and decks of the 76 head-on view rooms open right onto the sand. Others are grouped around a beachside pool. Each of the 100 studio or bedroom units has an efficiency kitchen. Across the street and lacking any water view is Royal Atlantic North, suites of one and two bedrooms each with kitchens, looking out onto a second pool. The newest acquisition is Royal Atlantic

East, twelve two-story condominium units each with marble foyer, two kingsize bedrooms downstairs, jacuzzi bath, fireplaced living room and dining room upstairs and two oceanfront balconies. The property includes a restaurant and a beach bar. *(631) 668-5103. Fax (631) 668-4172. www.royalatlantic.com. One hundred fifty-two rooms. Doubles, $210 to $265. Suites, $260 to $295 for four. Condos, $575. Four-night minimum summer weekends. Closed November-March.*

Stone Lion Inn, 51 Edgemere St., Montauk 11594.

Sunset views across Fort Pond draw customers to this establishment, part of the old Windjammer motel and restaurant. New owner Bruce Bernacchia, who also has the acclaimed Harvest on Fort Pond restaurant, turned part of the Windjammer into the glamorous **East by Northeast** restaurant (see Where to Eat). The motel became an eleven-room "inn," open year-round. Each room has one or two queensize beds, TV and a coffeemaker. All have a deck or porch overlooking Fort Pond. Refurbishing of the rooms was in the plans for 2005. *(631) 668-7050. www.harvest2000.com. Eleven rooms with private baths. Doubles, $165 to $185.*

Sun 'N' Sound Waterfront Resort, 22 Soundview Drive, Box 34, Montauk 11954.

Most appealing of the motels on the north side of Montauk is this property facing Block Island Sound. Twenty-one of the 35 condominium units face a large waterside deck and a white sand beach. The rest look onto a large pool area. Most accommodations are one-room or bi-level units with lofts. Another option comes with bedroom and living room. Each unit has a full kitchen and a deck or balcony. Upper-level units seem more open, with vaulted ceilings and skylights. The beach here is tranquil, you can see boats coming and going from the nearby harbor, and the sunsets are compelling. *(631) 668-2212. www.sunnsound.com. Thirty-five rooms. Doubles, $150 to $250. Three-night minimum summer weekends. Closed late October to mid-March.*

Hartman's Briney Breezes Motel, 689 Old Montauk Hwy., Box 5020, Montauk 11954.

Set on a slope across the road from the ocean, this well-maintained motel is one of the more attractive of the old school. Still run by the Hartman family, it makes good on their claim of an ocean view from every room, or at least every terrace or balcony. All 44 recently renovated units, located in two-story buildings terraced around a pleasant pool area, come with kitchenettes and appear quite spacious. They vary from studio apartments with a sitting area to two-room suites with a bedroom. The furnishings are fresh and a cut above the rest. A pathway slices through the dunes to the beach. The Surfside Inn restaurant is next door. *(631) 668-2290. Fax (631) 668-2987. www.brineybreezes.com. Forty-four units. Doubles, $235 to $260. Suites for four, $295 to $350. Closed mid-November to mid-March.*

East Deck Resort Motel, 40 Ditch Plains Road, Box 5003, Montauk 11954.

You want basic accommodations on the beach, yet away from the fray? This low-slung, earthy motel tended by Alice Houseknecht is for you. Her one-story motel, founded by her late husband's grandparents, was one of the first in Montauk. It's on five acres in a residential area, right beside the Ditch Plains Beach, where surfers in wet suits ply their luck year-round and people pay top-dollar for a parking permit (East Deck guests get free access). Occupants of the 24 motel units share a common deck that wraps around the side and front. From it you can see the ocean, if not the beach. These pine-paneled rooms have a double and a twin bed, refrigerator and coffeemaker, and some add kitchenettes. Their cottagey decor looks like something out of the 1950s era – no TVs or microwaves or whirlpool tubs here. Along the rear of the property are six one-bedroom apartments, each again with a double and a twin bed as well as a high-riser day bed that opens up to sleep two. These have decks overlooking the olympic-size pool and playground in the middle, but are not as ocean-oriented as the motel units. "We're not condominiumized," says Alice, who professes not to know why so many of her colleagues have gone that route. Her clientele likes it that way. And they love that large and convivial common deck.

(631) 668-2334. www.eastdeckmotel.com. Thirty units with private baths. Doubles, $150 to $210. Three-night minimum in summer. Closed early November to mid-April.

Burcliffe By the Sea, 397 Old Montauk Hwy., Montauk 11954.

This pleasant little complex is hidden amid trees on a hill across the road from the ocean. Paula and John Burke offer four studio-efficiency motel units atop the slope, as well as a pair of two-bedroom cottages and a one-bedroom cottage. The cottages come with fireplaces, TV, kitchens and private patios. The studios sleep up to four. "Small, pretty and tranquil – that's what we are," says Paula, who's been keeping it that way for more than twenty years.

(631) 668-2880. Four efficiency units and three cottages with private baths. Doubles, $170. Cottages, $260 to $320. No credit cards.

Lenhart Cottages, 421 Old Montauk Hwy., Montauk 11954.

Across a side street from Burcliff, this cottage colony also is across the highway from the ocean on a hill. There are no trees here to block the view, and most of the cottages occupy a lofty perch. Fireplaces are an asset to ward off any chill in the studio and one- and two-bedroom cottages. Each also has TV/HBO, kitchen and air conditioning. Cottages at the top of the property overlook the swimming pool.

(631) 668-2356. Twelve cottages with private baths. Doubles, $220 to $295. Cottages for four, $350 to $495.

CAMPING. A 165-site campground beside a 2.5-mile ocean beach with access to 1,755 acres of parkland operates at Hither Hills State Park from mid-April through mid-November. The campground, one of the biggest draws in the New York State park system, includes picnic areas, a children's playground, general store, a freshwater pond, hiking and nature trails. Reservations can be made up to a year in advance at (800) 456-2267. Only seven-day reservations can be made between June and mid-September. Campers may reserve three to fourteen days the rest of the season. The charge is $24 nightly for New York State residents, $48 for non-residents.

Seeing and Doing ⸮⸮⸮

The ocean and Montauk Lake set the tone, and give Montauk a decidedly beachy fisherman aura. Active water sports and fishing prevail in season.

On or Near the Water

BEACHES. Montauk's broad beaches, stretching along the open Atlantic nearly fifteen miles from Napeague State Park to Montauk Point, are among the world's most beautiful. The land behind changes from rolling sand dunes to spectacular 70-foot-high cliffs near Montauk Light.

Hither Hills State Park is on the ocean, four miles west of the village. It has lifeguards, changing facilities, a restaurant, a playground and the largest parking lot in the area. Parking is $7 a day.

Montauk's four village beaches are accessible to walk-ons but cars require parking permits or fees. Annual permits are available from the Town Hall Annex next to the Chamber of Commerce, across from the village green. Many lodging establishments offer day passes for guests. Lifeguards are on duty weekends starting Memorial Day and daily 9 to 6, late June through Labor Day.

Kirk Park, at the western edge of the village, is the principal village ocean beach, the only one available to motorists without a beach parking permit. Parking is $10 per day. A picnic area is across the street from the beach in Kirk Park, where the signs at a recent visit said the park is "going native." That means it was being enhanced with indigenous plantings.

Ditch Plains Beach, two miles east of the village on the ocean, is the best for surfing. Spectacular cliffs rise at its western end. There are lifeguards, restrooms and a concession stand.

Gin Beach, on Block Island Sound at the east end of East Lake Drive, is the favorite bay beach for families and small children. They like the warm waters and small waves as well as watching all the boats coming in and out of Montauk Harbor.

Southlake Beach is a small, gentle beach on the south end of Lake Montauk. The sheltered waters are shallow and warm.

OTHER WATER SPORTS. Because of its consistent, well-formed waves, Montauk is known as the East Coast capital for serious surfing year-round. Ditch Plains is a favorite spot, both for surfers and spectators, and Turtle Cove is another. Beach diving by snorkelers looking for fish, lobster and crabs is popular off the jetties at Gin Beach. Diving among the shipwrecks off Montauk is a challenge for scuba divers. Windsurfing is great along Napeague Bay. Lake Montauk is the place for water-skiing.

BOATING. You can rent a boat from **Uihlein's Marina,** West Lake Drive Extension, Montauk Harbor, (631) 668-3799. It offers hourly and daily boat rentals, jet skis, water-skiing, parasailing, canoes and sea kayaks. **Montauk Kayak & Outfitting Company,** (631) 668-2964, rents kayaks and leads tours. Sailboats, pedal boats, rowboats, kayaks and canoes for use on placid Lake Montauk are available from **Puff & Putt Family Fun Center,** Main Street, (631) 668-4473, which is also a miniature golf course.

Scenic harbor cruises are offered hourly starting at 11 a.m. from Gosman's Dock by **White Swan Harbor Cruises,** (631) 668-7878. Participants see the commercial fishing fleet, private yachts, shipyards, the Coast Guard Station and harbor wildlife. White Swan also has a marine life excursion that includes pulling of lobster traps, daily at 9 a.m.

WHALE WATCHING. From mid-May into October, the **Viking Fleet,** West Lake Drive, (631) 668-5700 or (888) 358-7477, sails out to sea to find whales, porpoises and other forms of marine life. Trips leave at 10:30 and return at 5, Wednesday-Sunday in July in August and weekends in June and September; adults $36, children $18.

FISHING. The "cod ledge" and feeding grounds in the waters off Montauk give it claim to being the fishing capital of the world. Montauk holds 30 of the world's records for sport fishing. The public is welcome on most of the more than 50 charter boats that call Montauk home port. **Charter boats** generally take up to six passengers and offer everything from a $32 mini-hop to catch flounder and sole, up through bass, cod and pollack, to the $1,000 a day charters that chug out toward Martha's Vineyard and Nantucket in search of swordfish, marlin, sharks and tuna. The Star

Island Yacht Club & Marina, (631) 668-5052, claims Montauk's largest charter fleet and urges, "bring the family and see the catch at 4 p.m. every day." We can attest to the ten huge blues and fluke laid out on the docks off Flamingo Road near Dave's Grill by one of a dozen charter boats upon its noontime return – the participants were telling prospects they'd had "a good day." **Party boats,** a more economical alternative, leave Montauk every morning in season. The Viking Fleet, West Lake Drive, (631) 668-5700 or (888) 358-7477, is the largest. It offers half-day, full-day, two-day and night bass-fishing trips. Half-day trips are offered by Flying Cloud, (631) 668-2026; Marlin V, (631) 668-2818, and Lazybones, (631) 668-5671. The latter bills its 1 p.m. outing is "a Montauk tradition – bring your lunch and catch your dinner." Surfcasting is popular, especially in fall. Surfcasters, who congregate around Montauk Point, generally catch striped bass and bluefish. The striped bass swim every summer from Long Island Sound out past Montauk to the open ocean in one of the world's largest annual migrations.

Other Attractions

Montauk Point Lighthouse Museum, Montauk State Park.

The country's fourth oldest active lighthouse, this was the first federal lighthouse built in the United States, commissioned in 1790 by George Washington and finished six years later. It recently underwent a half-million-dollar restoration, and the sponsoring Montauk Historical Society is exceedingly proud of it (its Montauk Point Lighthouse Cookbook, with nearly 800 local recipes, sells for $12 in the Overlook Café and Gift Shop). The summer 2000 edition of its newspaper, The Beacon, detailed visits by New York Gov. George Pataki and by former Israeli Prime Minister Benjamin Netanyahu, as well as several hundred ordinary folks who turned up to greet the sunrise at the dawn of the millennium. You can climb the 137 steps to the enclosed top of the 100-foot-high tower for a panoramic view, which on clear days takes in the North Fork of Long Island, the Connecticut and Rhode Island shores and Block Island, R.I. The museum in the old 1860 keepers' house traces the history of the lighthouse in photos, a video and displays of navigation aids and lenses. An interactive diorama fifteen feet long and four feet wide depicts 28 lighthouses from Manhattan to Point Judith, R.I. The 724-acre state park flanking the lighthouse offers a picnic area and five miles of hiking trails.

(631) 668-2544 or (888) 685-7646. www.montauklighthouse.com. Open daily, 10:30 to 5 or 6, mid-May through October, weekends 10:30 to 4:30 in the off-season, holiday weekends in winter. Adults $6, children $3. Parking $5.

HIKING AND BIKING. Exercise your feet or rent a bike for a tour of Montauk and environs. Wide side lanes on most highways make bicycling on the East End safe and enjoyable. Scenic and more strenuous trails over thousands of acres of parkland offer the best mountain biking on Long Island. Some of the trails are original Indian paths. Others were cut by the first English inhabitants, shepherds from the Hamptons who drove their cattle and sheep onto Montauk in May and off in November. The Montauk segment of the Paumanok Path that starts in Napeague and continues to Montauk Lighthouse was finished in 1998. It's part of a network of hiking and biking trails that will eventually stretch across Long Island.

The folks at **Montauk Bike Shop,** Main Street, Montauk, (631) 668-8975, tout the trails at Hither Woods Preserve, north of Montauk Highway between Napeague and Montauk. Some 30 miles of trails crisscross 3,000 acres of diverse ecosystems – oak woods, grass lands, walking dunes, valleys, ridges and bluffs. They are the best way to experience this area as the first English settlers found it – wild and beautiful

While in the vicinity of Hither Hills State Park, hike out to the Walking Sand Dunes on the east side of Napeague Harbor. They're three large, U-shaped, 100-foot-high dunes that are slowly moving southeast, uncovering "phantom" forests as they go. The dunes yield good views of Napeague Harbor and Gardiner's Island.

Montauk State Park and the adjacent Theodore Roosevelt County Park offer a newly marked hiking trail from Third House east to Montauk Light. Considered the most spectacular stretch of the Paumanok Path system, it passes Oyster Pond, the Point Woods forest (one of the oldest on Lond Island) and 200-foot bluffs beside the ocean. The Roosevelt County Park also has hiking trails in the vicinity of Gin Beach, Big Reed Pond and Shagwong Point.

GOLF. The eighteen-hole, 6,860-yard public course atop a knoll at **Montauk Downs State Park,** (631) 668-5000, is ranked by Golf Digest as one of the nation's 50 best. Designed by Robert Trent Jones, it couples a challenging layout with smashing views of the surrounding bays and ocean. It includes a pro shop, restaurant, snack bar, putting green, driving range, tennis courts and an Olympic-size outdoor pool. Reservations for tee times may be made four days in advance at (631) 668-1234. Greens fees for New York State residents are $36 weekends, $30 midweek; $72 and $60 for non-residents.

HORSEBACK RIDING. You can ride throughout the area where the first cowboys tended their cattle in America. **Deep Hollow Ranch,** (631) 668-2744, the nation's oldest working cattle ranch (1658) off the Montauk Highway near Third House, offers trail rides daily along the beach and across parklands. Children's activities include a petting farm and pony rides. Texas-style barbecues and Wild West shows are offered nightly in summer. **Rita's Stables,** (631) 668-5453, off the Montauk Highway near West Lake Drive, has trail rides on a private trail system, special half-hour rides favored by families with children age 4 and up, and cowboy-style barbecues. Reservations are advised for both ventures, which are open year-round.

Historic Houses. The **Third House Museum,** (631) 852-7878, situated within the Theodore Roosevelt County Park three miles east of the village, was built in 1747 as the third of three homes for the keepers who took care of the cattle when Montauk was a summer pasture land for the East Hampton proprietors. A rambling building houses park offices and a portion of the Third House, plus photographs of Teddy Roosevelt and his Rough Riders, who were stationed at Montauk after the Spanish-American War. It's open Wednesday-Sunday 10 to 5; free.

Just west of the village on Montauk Highway is the **Second House Museum,** (631) 668-5340. Operated by the Montauk Historical Society, it's a late 1746 weathered Cape farmhouse also used by the cattle keepers. Among its attributes are historical exhibits, a school room in which Montauk's children were first educated and a fine herb and rose garden. Open Thursday-Tuesday 10 to 4, Memorial Day to Columbus Day; adults $2, children $1.

SHOPPING is not of interest to most beachgoers or fishermen, so don't expect to find the suave mercantile possibilities of, say, Amagansett and the Hamptons just to the west. Most stores are clustered along a couple of blocks of Main Street and flank the circular plaza in the village center. Among the biggest are the **Montauk Clothing Co., the Montauk Beach Store** and **White's Drug & Department Store. Claudia's Carriage House** is chock full of collectibles. **Summers** offers summer wear next door. Gifts are featured at **Willow** and the **Montauk Carriage House.** Produce, baked goods, prime meats and takeout meals are available at the indoor **Ocean View Farmers Market.** The **Montauk Artists Association** has turned the old railroad station into a community arts center. More sophisticated shopping is to be found out by the harbor in the Gosman's Dock complex. Look for **Irish Country Loft, Pier Group Montauk** (for men's casuals, yacht club style), **Summer Stock** for women, **Capt. Kid** for children and **Home Port** for accessories.

Where to Eat

Dave's Grill, 468 West Lake Drive.

Montauk's top-rated restaurant in terms of food is this unassuming looking establishment, a proper sea shanty with outdoor patio seating amid the fishing docks on Montauk Harbor. The outside masks an upscale interior, smart in white and blue, holding six booths for four and five nicely spaced tables for two. The place is small, but same-night reservations are taken starting at 4:30. Book a table and enjoy inspired seafood prepared by chef-owner David Marcley, who converted the place from a greasy-spoon fisherman's haunt in 1988. His menu changes weekly to include starters like "Chinese" spare ribs and lump crab cake with black bean and roasted corn salsa, but popular appetizers remain, among them coconut fried shrimp, mussels provençal, clams casino, fried calamari and lobster salad. Dave's signature cioppino is a favorite of Gourmet magazine, and his grilled pork chops are considered the best on the East End of Long Island. Other entrée standbys include flash-fried flounder with an onion and potato crust, oven-steamed halibut over swiss chard with a citrus-beet syrup, and grilled yellowfin tuna with a ginger-scented plum wine and lemongrass sauce. Almost everyone orders the chocolate bag for dessert. It's a lunch-size bag of belgian chocolate, filled with vanilla ice cream and whipped cream on a puddle of tangy raspberry sauce. The New Orleans bread pudding with bourbon sauce and the brownie club sandwich are other favorites. Dave's wife Julie, a classical jazz singer, is the hostess, wine sommelier and occasional entertainer.

(631) 668-9190. www.davesgrill.com. Entrées, $21.95 to $32.95. Dinner from 5:30, nightly in summer, fewer days in off-season. Closed November-April.

Harvest on Fort Pond, 11 South Emery St.

Nestled beside Long Island's second largest freshwater pond is this winning establishment where you might spot a heron on the dock stretching into the pond. There are a couple of attractive side patios beside a showy, expansive herb garden, which produces "a harvest of flavors." And a skylit porch wrapping around the interior dining room takes full advantage of the watery prospect. The highly rated food is robust American with a Tuscan flair. It's served family style, portions are huge and designed to be shared – which accounts for what appears to be the menu's lofty price structure. You could start with bruschetta with mixed seafood, pan-seared tuna with green tomato and grilled corn tapas or one of the grilled pizzas. Consider a pasta dish, perhaps fusilli with scallops and bacon or rigatoni with lamb and broccoli. Main courses could be pan-seared swordfish with spinach beurre blanc, hazelnut-crusted roast pork with grand marnier sauce and lamb T-bone with polenta and escarole. The night's specials might add a whole sizzling red snapper and grilled duck breast with a blood orange sauce. Substantial sides and salads are extra, but again meant to be shared. The dessert favorite is the Harvest brownie with hazelnut biscotti ice cream.

(631) 668-5574. www.harvest2000.com. Entrées, $26 to $36. Dinner nightly, 5:30 to 10 or 11. Closed January to mid-March.

East by Northeast, 51 Edgemere St., Montauk.

Fort Pond is on view in all its glory from a curved wall of windows in this hot new pan-Asian restaurant. The owners of the Harvest restaurant undertook a million dollar renovation of the old Windjammer Restaurant and Inn, producing a sleek, 150-seat dining room of Italian cherrywood, tile and glass allowing a panoramic look at the sunset shows. A wine room of stone and a comfortable bar-lounge accompany, and the motel next door is undergoing upgrades as the Stone Lion Inn. The menu takes a culinary journey from the Northeast to the Far East, with an emphasis on the latter. Chef Anthony Silvestri presents small and large plates designed to be shared. His signatures are Japanese hot rock (raw filet mignon slices that you sear on a hot stone and dip in sweet soy sauce) and shabu-shabu teapot (assorted raw seafood that you cook in a shiitake mushroom broth and flavor with various dipping sauces). Among numerous small plate choices are Peking duck tacos with hoisin sauce and avocado salsa, pork and shrimp spring rolls with three-citrus ponzu sauce and mixed grill satays with spicy peanut sauce. Share large plates of potato-crisped Montauk fluke, caramelized Chilean sea bass with mango salsa, soy-marinated London broil or roasted lemon-thyme chicken. Dessert could be a ying-yang parfait of peanut butter and chocolate, warm apple and cinnamon spring rolls with calvados-caramel sauce or a sampler of crème brûlées.

(631) 668-2872. Small plates, $14 to $20; large plates, $22 to $36. Dinner nightly, 5 to 10 or 11; off-season, Wednesday-Sunday 5 to 9 or 10.

Gosman's Dock, 500 West Lake Drive.

"Montauk is easy to find, it's right next to Gosman"s," proclaim the ads for this local institution – and it's not that much of a stretch, at least for those who arrive by boat. Located on the docks at the head of the harbor, the large complex is a mix of restaurants, clam bar, seafood market, ice cream shop and retail stores, all going under the umbrella of Gosman's Dock. That accounts for some of the confusion surrounding the correct names for the restaurants, which grew out of a chowder stand started in the 1940s by fish packers Robert and Mary Gosman. The huge, more formal Gosman's Restaurant has tables on two levels and windows on three sides. It specializes in fresh seafood caught by the Gosman fleet, lobster and prime rib. In an adjacent building, the outdoor Clam Bar serves lobsters, clams, burgers and franks at colorful umbrella-topped picnic tables beside the water. Next door, the Ice Cream Shop dispenses cones, sundaes, frozen yogurt and iced cappuccino. Overhead is the Topside Café and Bar (also called the Inlet Café), which offers some interesting fare, such as a grilled swordfish fajita. Beside it is what the staff said was the Fish Deck, a waterside deck where we were happy to have lunch on a sunny spring day. Whatever its name was, we liked the chicken caesar salad and the lobster roll, as well as the watery ambiance. Cheeky gulls, looking for handouts, perched almost too close for comfort, and the harbor inlet was busy with yachts and the fishing fleet cruising in and out. Both the food and service were good, considering the volume (the complex serves 2,000 dinners on summer nights).

(631) 668-5330. www.gosmans.com. Entrées, $14.95 to $24.95. Clam Bar, $5.95 to $9.95. Lunch daily, noon to 5. Dinner, 5 to 10. Closed mid-October to mid-April.

Oyster Pond, 4 South Elmwood Ave.

A tan building beside the dunes at the edge of downtown Montauk holds this newish restaurant, which has a beachy sun room off the bar for casual dining and a warmer, nautical-looking room with booths dressed in white butcher paper over white cloths on the street side. Chef-owner Lonny Lewis offers an extensive menu of contemporary American cuisine. The menu includes "just plain food" (plain old lobster, pan-seared fluke, linguini with tomato sauce and grilled chicken pizza) as well as "not every day food" (macadamia-crusted monkfish, grilled filet of ostrich, pan-seared duck paillard, and crispy whole daurade royal, a flaky white fish flavored with hot and sour ginger sauce). There are creative pizzas, pastas, salads (fire-roasted octopus or crispy shiitake mushrooms and goat cheese), a raw bar and a dozen appetizers. The Oyster Pond pu pu platter is a sampling of appetizers, including grilled oysters, spring roll, coconut shrimp, cured salmon and seared sea scallops.

(631) 668-4200. Entrées, $19 to $30. Dinner nightly, from 5. Closed Tuesday and Wednesday in off-season.

Il Mare Ristorante, 32 Star Island Road.

The base of the lighthouse at the Montauk Yacht Club Resort & Marina holds the six-sided Lighthouse Bar with a pub menu and big windows onto the busy marina and the adjacent Il Mare Ristorante. Here is an expansive dining room outfitted in rattan and conveying a plush yacht club feeling. It proves a pleasant setting for a satisfying dinner. One of us made a meal of a couple of appetizers – a selection of raw oysters with pickled ginger mignonette granita and a tian of grilled vegetables and goat cheese over field greens drizzled with pesto sauce. The other enjoyed an assertive pasta dish of sautéed manila clams with garlic and oregano wine sauce served over black pepper and herbed linguini. Other choices ranged from Maine lobster served with herb tagliatelle to tagliolini topped with ragu of lamb and wild mushrooms and veal porterhouse steak with cabernet wine sauce. A trio of sorbets made a fine ending. In season, the adjoining **Breezes Café** provides a casual alternative, as well as an outdoor bar beside the pool.

(631) 668-3100. Entrées, $21.50 to $28.95. Lunch daily, 11 to 2. Dinner nightly, 5:30 to 9 or 10.

Navy Road Restaurant, 16 Navy Road.

This hard-to-find place, on the other side of the tracks in an industrial section, is worth seeking out for its terrific location fronting on the rugged beach of Fort Pond Bay. The interior bar and dining rooms are set with white tablecloths, but the tented deck beside the beach is the venue of choice. The menu features contemporary American regional cuisine. Typical entrées are local flounder stuffed with crabmeat, almond-crusted grouper with grilled banana and melon-mango-papaya salsa, Long Island duck glazed with peaches, herb-rubbed filet mignon and prime rib au jus. One of the pastas "from across the sea" is seafood ravioli with grilled asparagus and frizzled leeks in a tomato-basil cream sauce. Seafood bruschetta, backfin crab cakes and coconut shrimp with raspberry-mustard sauce are among the starters.

(631) 668-1064. Entrées, $18.95 to $27.95. Dinner nightly from 5. Closed November-April.

Lenny's On the Dock, 494 West Lake Drive.

Chef Lenny Delfino, something of a celebrity with a local TV variety show, took over the former Johnny Marlin's restaurant in 1999. The casual, family-style main room with bar, blond wood and vaulted ceiling has fish models on the wall. Tables on the canopied and semi-enclosed outside harborfront deck wrapped in plastic were going begging the coolish spring day we arrived for lunch. All it took was someone to pave the way, apparently, for soon others followed. It turned out to be a salubrious setting for a thick and spicy New England clam chowder, a shrimp roll and a hefty grilled yellowfin tuna sandwich. The extensive all-day menu has something for everyone. Appetizers run from onion rings and chicken wings to clams casino and shrimp cocktail. There are cold, fried, grilled and broiled seafood and chicken platters as well as "house specialties," among them shrimp scampi over rice or pasta, stuffed flounder, lobster, and surf and turf. Lenny sometimes plays the accordion for the crowd.

(631) 668-2500. Entrées, $11.95 to $18.95. Lunch and dinner daily in season.

Nick's, 148 South Emerson St.

This is the only oceanfront restaurant in Montauk village. The question is what to make of it all. The signs out front variously proclaim restaurant, nightclub, kids' menu and best frozen drinks on Long Island. There's no denying the beach and water views from the outdoor Beach Bar or the upstairs dining area, a vast solarium-type affair with plants hanging from the crossbeams beneath a transparent ceiling. Nick Deane and his wife Claire took over what he said had been "a kids' bar" in 1998 and elevated the culinary aspirations with the hiring of a chef who had worked with Emeril Legasse in New Orleans. That explains the Bourbon Street barbecued shrimp, the oysters bienville and the spicy clams casino offered as appetizers on the ambitious dinner menu. Main courses range from Louisiana stuffed shrimp to filet mignon with mushroom-cabernet sauce, although local seafood predominates. The downstairs bar and Caribbean Club swing until 4 in the morning.

(631) 668-4800. Entrées, $18.95 to $29.95. Breakfast in summer, 7:30 to 11:30. Lunch, 11:30 to 5:30. Dinner, 5:30 to 10. Closed midweek in off-season and Columbus Day to May.

The Crow's Nest, 4 Old West Lake Drive.

Here's another waterside restaurant that the first time-visitor may not know quite what to make of. The entry path borders on the gaudy, the quirky reception area is plastered with clippings telling how owners Don and Astrid Torr met Hillary and Bill Clinton, and the two-level, nautical dining room has lots going on (window tables yield views of Lake Montauk). A Great Barrier Reef aquarium is full of exotic fish and, during the dinner hour, you can watch the hosts feed John and Elsie, "pets" billed as Montauk's only live captive sharks. If that's not enough, the 2,000-gallon lobster tank is full of "cute crustaceans just waiting to jump into the pot and onto your plate" – yeah, right. Said lobsters are supposedly legendary, but you also can get local seafood, prime steaks and chops. Fried clams, penne à la vodka, lobster ravioli, sole nantua, grilled whole red snapper, chateaubriand – you name it, this quirky place probably has it. At lunch, the offerings range from a grilled cheese and tomato sandwich for $7.95 to a lobster bake for two, including a four-pound lobster and a bottle of Dom Perignon, for $190. Now that's the good life.

(631) 668-2077. www.crowsnestrest.com. Entrées, $17.95 to $29.95. Lunch and dinner daily in season, noon to 11. Sunday brunch, noon to 3.

The Lobster Roll Restaurant/Lunch, 1980 Montauk Highway, Napeague Beach.

"Lunch," proclaims the sign above this unassuming looking gray seafood shack sandwiched beside the dunes four miles west of Montauk. It might as well say "Stop," for that's what everyone in the know seems to do. It's a true place, one that claimed to have been reviewed "no less than 63 times" by leading magazines and newspapers. It has appeared in three movies and one novel, and boasts one of the longest lists of celebrity patrons in all of the Hamptons. Partners Andrea and Fred Terry and Paul DeAngelis run such a professional establishment that they teach restaurant management courses in the off-season. Their know-how pioneered lobster rolls in the area. But they also were the first to offer swellbellies, marinated charbroiled fish, pecan sole, shrimp rockefeller, seafood caesar salad and crab cakes. The prices on the extensive menu rarely change, the namesake lobster roll going for $8.95 last we knew. That and the casual atmosphere help explain the lineups of people waiting for seats at peak periods.

(631) 267-3740. www.lobsterroll.com. Entrées, $8.95 to $19.95. Open daily 11:30 to 9 or 10, May-October, weekends in off-season.

FOR MORE INFORMATION: Montauk Chamber of Commerce, Main Street, Box 11954, Montauk, NY 11954, (631) 668-2428. www.montaukchamber.com.

Lake George landmark Sagamore resort occupies island off Bolton Landing.

Bolton Landing/Lake George, N.Y.

It's called the "Queen of American Lakes," this 32-mile-long expanse of azure blue contoured by verdant mountains brimming with firs, pines and spruce. No less an authority than Thomas Jefferson hailed Lake George as "without comparison the most beautiful water I ever saw."

Lake George is indeed beautiful. You might not readily think so if you arrive, as do most, at the busy southern end, where Lake George village and its approaches from the south impart a carnival atmosphere. It's full of amusement parks, mini-golf courses, ice-cream stands, seasonal motels, jet ski rentals and tourists on parade. The main drag is Canada Street, its honkytonk demeanor neither reflective of nor complimentary to its neighbors to the north.

Go beyond Lake George village, however, and things quickly change. The mountainous east side of the lake is relatively inaccessible and undeveloped. The west side is only marginally more accessible and developed. Here, along 109 miles of lakeshore and amid 300-odd islands, is where you find beauty and serenity away from the hordes.

Head up the west shore along Lake Shore Drive (Route 9N) past Diamond Point to Bolton Landing, a proud, low-key village scenically situated at the widest point of Lake George, just below where it funnels into the Narrows. The ten-mile shoreline between Lake George and Bolton Landing ends in a stretch known as Millionaires' Row. Resort status came early to "Bolton," as the locals call it. City-slickers seeking refuge from summer's heat flocked to its lakeside hotels in an era known as "The Great and the Gracious," and Bolton became a mecca for composers and opera stars as well as wealthy New York and Philadelphia families. Today, only the Sagamore among the large hotels remains, grandly restored on its own private island outside

Bolton Landing. Lacking chain franchises and reflecting the Adirondack great camp tradition, Bolton Landing stands diametrically opposed to Lake George village.

Farther north is Hague-on-Lake-George, a time warp of a remote mountain hamlet whose quirky commercial side street resembles that of a ghost town out of the old West. The "Lake George Monster" created a stir here in the early 1900s, and not much has happened since. Beyond is Ticonderoga, best known for its historic fort that fell to the British in 1777. It stands in majestic and remote contrast to Fort William Henry at the south end of the lake, which is dwarfed by its surroundings in Lake George village.

Yes, Lake George beyond the eponymous village is where you will find the Lake George of magazine covers and one's dreams. Bolton Landing represents the best of an understated resort area that is uncrowded and unspoiled.

Come here for swimming, boating, fishing, hiking and other watery pursuits in a spectacular mountain setting. There's action aplenty to the south around Lake George village for those who want it. We focus on the other Lake George, where a more tranquil life prevails.

Getting There

Interstate 87 (the Adirondack Northway) passes the southern end of Lake George (and yields a good view) on its way from New York City to Montreal. Take Exit 22 onto Route 9 into Lake George village. Scenic Lake Shore Drive (Route 9N) follows the western shore of the lake, north of the village, to Diamond Point, Bolton Landing, Hague and Ticonderoga. Amtrak trains and buses stop nearby on their runs from New York to Montreal. Major airlines fly into Albany, an hour's drive south.

Where to Stay

The Sagamore, 110 Sagamore Road, Bolton Landing 12814.

Literally an island unto itself, this year-round resort is the ultimate waterside escape. The 72-acre private Green Island, accessed by a short causeway from Bolton Landing, manages through design to be at once busy yet tranquil. Built in the grand manner of the late 19th century and restored to the tune of $75 million for its centennial in 1983, the sparkling white main hotel looks south down the lake – and is as much a visible presence from the lake and the rest of Bolton Landing as the lake is from most of Green Island. Behind the hotel, dark wood lodge buildings,

separate and tiered for privacy, spread along hillsides sloping to the water. The main hotel, listed on the National Register, holds 54 rooms and 46 suites. Most have king or queen beds. Decor is traditional and the furnishings sumptuous. The seven lodge buildings, scattered among the trees near water's edge, include a total of 120 rooms and 120 suites. The latter come with wood-burning fireplaces and idyllic lake-view balconies. The Hermitage is a self-contained executive retreat with ten bi-level suites overlooking the lake. The Wapanak Castle, a renovated English Tudor stone structure on the lake beside the main hotel, accommodates up to twelve. It has six bedrooms, four baths, seven fireplaces, living room, dining room and family room and rents for $3,000 a night.

The Sagamore's dining options are many and varied: **Trillium** (see Where to Eat) for contemporary gourmet fare at dinner and Sunday brunch, the **Sagamore Dining Room** for continental cuisine at breakfast and dinner, **Mister Brown's Pub** for snacks and light meals, the glass-enclosed **Veranda** for continental breakfast and afternoon tea and drinks, the **Club Grill** at the golf course for hearty continental dishes at lunch and dinner, the **Pool Terrace** for alfresco lunch and light snacks and beverages, and nightly dinner cruises on **The Morgan,** a replica of a 19th-century touring vessel.

The property offers everything a water lover could want, from landscaped terraces to a marina to a small lakefront beach with an enclosed swimming area. Steve and Doris Colgate's Offshore Sailing School gives sailing classes on Lake George. The Sagamore Spa offers sauna, whirlpools and European-style spa service. Also on the island are a fitness center, indoor tennis and racquetball courts, an indoor pool, and nature and jogging trails. The Sagamore's eighteen-hole championship Donald Ross-designed golf course is nearby.

(518) 644-9400 or (800) 358-3585. Fax (518) 743-6036. www.thesagamore.com. 180 rooms and 176 suites. Rates, EP. Doubles, $269 to $450. Suites, $490 to $745.

Canoe Island Lodge, 3820 Lake Shore Drive (Route 9N), Box 144, Diamond Point 12824.

This charming place of history and tradition started with an island. In 1943, Albany native Bill Busch bought the island, named for the 1880 meeting of canoeists who formed the American Canoe Association there, located three-quarters of a mile offshore. Three years later he built six log cabins on the mainland and opened a resort that now serves 175 guests in 65 different accommodations: a main lodge, log cabins, lakefront chalets, hillside villas and a gracious carriage house. Newly retired, Bill and Jane Busch have turned operations over to their daughter and son-in-law, Carla and Tom Burhoe. The five-acre island, which has a south-facing crescent beach, is still the heart of the complex. The boat staff shuttles lodge guests to the island several times daily, and the Busch family hosts a chicken barbecue for guests there on Thursday evenings. Early traditions continue to this day: the chef's gala Sunday buffet, movie night, singalongs and dancing in the oak-paneled Tyrolean tavern. Meals are served with a view – through the treetops in the main lodge and at water level in the Windjammer restaurant on a vast platform over the boat docks. The waterfront is a beehive of sailing and fishing activity, reflecting two of Bill Busch's passions. Three new sloops highlight a fleet that would do a yacht club proud. Staying in one of the log structures spread seemingly at random across the steep hillside complex is like having your own summer house, except that meals are communal and family activities are planned. Accommodations vary, but comfort is a common denominator. The three-level Chalet Erika is the most luxurious, with king beds, fireplaces and large waterfront decks. Duplex redwood cottages and log cabins offer rooms with varying bed configurations. All have private baths, some have fireplaces and all but a couple of cozy main lodge rooms have TVs. A steep one-way road winds through the complex. Those with physical limitations may find getting about difficult. The more adventurous can hike uphill twenty minutes beyond the lodge to the Ledges for an awesome lake and mountain view. Rates in summer include breakfast, dinner and most lodge activities. Off-season rates include three meals daily and all activities. German specialties are featured in the dining room. The season begins with a Maifest and ends with four Oktoberfest weekends. *(518) 668-5592. Fax (518) 668-2012. www.canoeislandlodge.com. Sixty-five rooms and cottages with private baths. Rates, per person: $642 to $1,142 MAP weekly in July and August; $105 to $178 AP daily in off-season. Closed mid-October to mid-May. No credit cards.*

Melody Manor Resort, 4610 Lake Shore Drive, Box 366, Bolton Landing 12814.
Set well back and beneath the road on a large sloping property is this inviting motel-style resort with a serene view down Huddle Bay toward the Sagamore resort. It's lovingly run by Rose Alessi, daughter of retired owner Marzella Hamm, who gave it a German/Bavarian flavor. Rose married into a large Italian family from Naples, whose heritage is evident in the acclaimed Villa Napoli restaurant on the site. The location is quiet and the accommodations comfortable and up-to-date. The quality of the entire complex represents good value, and people of different ages and interests have plenty of room in which to spread out. From their hilltop perch, two-thirds of the rooms in three stuccoed sections yield direct lake views, enjoyed from patios or private balconies. The rest offer partial lake views through front windows, but no balconies. Three end units in the otherwise partial-lakefront Section B, extra-spacious and outfitted with private balconies and two queen beds, are as good as they get. All 24 rooms in the lakefront Section C offer full water views. TVs, telephones and air conditioning are standard. Bolton Brook rushes along one side of the property. A clay tennis court and a heated pool occupy portions of the upper property. Below is a 300-foot lakefront with lawns, beach, and free rowboats and canoes. Breakfast and dinner are available in **Villa Napoli** (see Where to Eat).
(518) 644-9750. www.melodymanor.com. Forty-one rooms with private baths. Doubles, $175 to $210. Closed November-April.

Boathouse Bed & Breakfast, 44 Sagamore Road, Box 1576, Bolton Landing 12814.
"The only B&B directly on Lake George" was the billing for this newcomer. And how! The 1917 summer home of speedboat racer George Reis stretches over the water above a two-slip, stone and wood boathouse along Millionaires Row. The front porch and side balconies and decks take full advantage, as do windows in the beamed and vaulted great room, where breakfast is served in the dining half and guests gather around a fireplace in the living area. Joe Silipigno and Patti Gramberg bought the place in 1997 for a summer home and decided to share their good fortune with B&B guests. They offer five guest rooms in the boathouse, all with TV, telephone and refrigerator. Two with king beds face the lake and open onto balconies. Two with queen beds are on the land side. The best of the lot is the Reis master bedroom with kingsize bed and a private sun porch onto the lake. Two large new guest rooms with kingsize beds in the carriage house add fireplaces, double whirlpool tubs, microwaves and lakefront balconies. The other bedrooms are upstaged by the rest of the property – especially that great second-floor porch offering a breathtaking view "that makes you feel like you're on a cruise without leaving shore," in Joe's words. Off a deck on the boathouse level, beside the boats moored inside, is a secluded deck with oversize wicker chairs for two. The lakeside lawn is dotted with lounge chairs and a spa. Patti prepares a full breakfast of "whatever moves me," perhaps pancakes, waffles or quiches.
(518) 644-2554. www.boathouseBB.com. Seven rooms with private baths. Doubles, $175 to $375.

Ruah Bed & Breakfast, 9221 Lake Shore Drive, Hague 12836.
This lake-view house, built in 1900 and one of northern Lake George's "Great and Gracious," was featured in a six-page spread in House Beautiful in 1996. Step inside

and you'll know why. The front of the house, on a hillside facing the lake across the road, is an awesome, 80-foot-long expanse of windows. The light and airy living room, 50 by 30 feet, comes with an antique grand piano, paintings and furnishings original to the house, and a massive fieldstone fireplace in the style of the Adirondack great camps. It's open to the dining room, which has a coffered ceiling and a showy south wall of windows brightened by colorful cut glass collected by owners Judy and Peter Foster. They bought the stately stone and white-pillared house in 1984 and, after raising their family, opened it as a B&B. They named it for an Old Testament word meaning, according to Judy, "a gentle breeze, a breath of life." Breeze and life are evident throughout the house, as well as on the wide front veranda, the balcony above and the gardens all around. The four second-floor guest rooms take their names from the cluster of small islands on view outside. All have gas fireplaces and king or queensize beds, and three open onto the front balcony. The Queen of the Lakes master bedroom is the largest, with kingsize bed, a luxurious settee by the front window, and an unusual bathtub encased in coral that matches the coral beneath the window seat. The Waltonian opens onto two balconies. Comments in the guest book, displayed along with magazine articles on a large table in the living room, single out the Fosters' graciousness and lively hospitality. Judy prepares an abundant buffet-style breakfast, which culminates in a main dish like a soufflé, waffles, pancakes or frittata. Peter, a landscape architect, has served his own property well. The house, incidentally, was designed by Stanford White for artist Harry Waltrous, a colorful character whose most famous prank was the Lake George Monster, created in his studio here. The "monster" appeared off and on in 1906 off Waltonian Island and the hoax was reported in the New York Times.

(518) 543-8816 or (800) 224-7549. www.ruahbb.com. Four rooms with private baths. Doubles, $145 to $200.

Trout House Village Resort, Lake Shore Drive, Hague 12836.

Four hundred feet of waterfront and sandy beach enhance this pleasant complex of "country inn," log cabins, cottages and motels, all facing the lake down a sloping lawn. The Patchett family bought the place in 1971 and turned its facilities dating to the 1890s into, yes, a small resort village covering many bases. The homespun main lodge is billed as a nine-bedroom country inn with individual decor and the occasional canopy bed, along with private baths, TVs and telephones. An apartment flavor is imparted in rooms with kitchens, dining areas and varied bed configurations. Most in demand are fourteen efficiency log cabins. Updated, they vary in size from one to three bedrooms and some add dual-view fireplaces and jetted tubs. Favored by families in summer, they morph into couples' getaway destinations the rest of the year. Three seasonal cottages and four motel units are advertised as basic and simple. The buildings are nicely spaced and most enjoy head-on views of the lake. Accommodations are rented weekly in summer, nightly the rest of the year. Besides the usual waterfront activities, the lawn offers a putting green, games area and barbecue grills. Scott and Alice Patchett and their four children live on the property, and their care shows.

(518) 543-6088 or (800) 368-6088. www.trouthouse.com.. Twenty-four units in lodge, log cabins, cottages and motel. Doubles, $650 to $2,350 weekly in summer, $69 to $275 daily in off-season.

Hilltop Cottage, 4825 Lakeshore Drive, Bolton Landing 12814.

Guests in this modest farmhouse across the road from the Marcella Sembrich Memorial Museum can relive some of the late opera diva's experiences. For this was the caretaker's cottage for her lakeside estate along Millionaire's Row and Mme.

Sembrich put up some of her vocal students for the summer in its second-floor guest rooms. Her music studio is now an opera museum (see Seeing and Doing) and this is the home of its director, Anita Richards, and her husband Charlie, both retired educators. They have furnished the house with family items and antiques reflecting Anita's German background and their association with the estate. They occupy the main floor and put up guests Thursday-Sunday in the two recently renovated upstairs bedrooms, both homey and rather European looking. The front Bay View Room has a queen bed and adjacent private bath, while the rear Meadowcamp Room has a queen bed, twin bed and an en-suite bathroom. They also offer Ballymore, a pine-paneled cabin behind the house with queen bed, TV, small refrigerator and microwave, available by the week. Anita serves an ample breakfast of quiche or German apple pancakes at a table for six on the vine-shaded screened porch in front of the house.

(518) 644-2492. Fax (518) 644-2191. www.hilltopcottage.com. Two rooms and one cabin with private baths. Doubles, $80, Thursday-Sunday. Cabin, $80 (three-night minimum), $450 weekly. Closed November to mid-May.

The Lodges at Cresthaven Resort, 3210 Lake Shore Drive, Lake George 12845.

New two-story log cabins on a bluff, built for time-share purchases as well as rentals, are offered at this thirteen-acre complex about one and one-half miles north of Lake George village. All polished logs inside and out, the two-bedroom, two-bath lodges are decorated in lodge style and come with full kitchens, entertainment centers, gas fireplaces, outdoor grills and covered porches with great views of the lake. Studio units and two-room efficiencies are offered in a carriage house overlooking the pool. Besides the large heated pool and deck area, amenities include a lakeside beach and a wading pool. The Boathouse Restaurant is next door.

(518) 668-3332 or (800) 853-1632. Fax (518) 668-0324. Forty-two lodges and rooms. Lodges, $3,200 to $3,700 weekly in summer, $250 to $450 nightly in off-season. Studios and efficiencies, $850 to $1,350 weekly in summer, $75 to $150 nightly in off-season. Closed November-April.

Clinton Inn, 3250 Lake Shore Drive, Lake George 12845.

This lakefront complex has been upgraded and expanded lately into "Lake George's Newest All-Season Resort," although the season seems to be short (it was not yet open at our May visit). Nestled among tall pines on the site are two-story motel buildings in a U-shaped configuration around an attractive courtyard with a large, L-shaped swimming pool. Scattered down a shady hillside toward the lake are sixteen housekeeping cottages, some of them new, each with one or two bedrooms. Refurbished motel rooms have two queen beds; others have one king or queen bed and a queen sofabed. All rooms have TV and a refrigerator. A path descends to the lakefront and a private sandy beach. Also available are tennis, basketball and volleyball facilities, an eighteen-hole putting green, coffee shop and store, a playground, picnic tables and barbecue grills. Complimentary continental breakfast is offered to motel guests at the adjoining Hearthstone Restaurant.

(518) 668-2412. www.clintoninn.com. Fifty-four rooms and sixteen cottages. Doubles, $159 to $199. Efficiency cottages, $1,095 to $1,395 weekly. Closed mid-October to mid-May.

CAMPING. Adirondack Forest Preserve Camping offers camping areas right on the water. Most in demand is **Lake George Islands Public Campground,** which consists of 387 shoreline sites on 47 state-owned islands in the middle of the lake, available mid-May to mid-September. All sites have a boat dock, a fireplace, picnic table and toilet facility. The campsites are located in three major areas. Two are reached by boat from Bolton Landing and their sites rent for $16 nightly: Glen Island Group, with 212 sites east of Bolton Landing, and the Narrow Island Group with 85 sites in the northern part of the lake. The Long Island Group with 90 sites ($14 nightly) is at the southern end of the lake. **Hearthstone Point Public Campground,** (518) 668-5193, has 250 waterfront sites on the mainland along Route 9N, two miles north of Lake George village, available mid-May through Labor Day. Its campsites are $14 nightly. Reservations for each campground are booked through a toll-free reservation system that applies to all New York State campgrounds, (800) 456-2267.

Seeing and Doing

The focus is on the lake, but the mountains make a difference. Fed by mammoth underground springs, the 32-mile-long lake is at its widest at Bolton Landing. The mouth of the lake is at Lake George village at the southern end. Its outlet at the northern end flows through Ticonderoga Creek into Lake Champlain, which – surprise – is 210 feet lower than Lake George, making for a gradual descent greater than Niagara Falls.

On the Water

BOAT TOURS. Because of the mountainous setting and their relative inaccessibility, the lake's shoreline and islands are best viewed by boat.

Lake George Steamboat Company, Steel Pier, Beach Road, Lake George.

The major player among excursion boat companies, this company has been transporting passengers on Lake George since 1817. One-hour sightseeing cruises are offered seven times daily aboard the steamboat paddlewheeler **Minne-Ha-Ha,** built in 1969 on Lake George. Its engine room is enclosed in glass so passengers get to see the boiler and engine at work. The steam calliope on the top deck plays merrily away, powered by steam from the boat's own boiler. Adults $9.50, children $5.75.

The smaller, two-deck **Mohican,** said to be the oldest operating excursion boat in America, gives morning lake cruises all the way up to Ticonderoga and back, leaving at 9, stopping in Bolton Landing at 9:40 and 12:45 and returning to Lake George village at 1:45; adults $18.75, children $8.75. Its afternoon Paradise Bay cruise leaves at 2:30 and covers the southern half of Lake George; adults $14.75, children $7.50. The boat, built in 1908, was designed specifically to be able to enter the Paradise Bay section of the lake, turn entirely and exit.

The newest and largest of the company's three boats is the awesome, four-deck **Lac du Saint Sacrement** (bearing the lake's early French name before it was renamed in 1775 for King George III). It offers buffet luncheon, dinner and Sunday brunch cruises. You can take a cruise only without meals, but most opt for the food service. The two-hour lunch cruise leaves daily at noon; adults $24.75, children $14.25 (cruise only, adults $14.75, children $6.75). Dinner cruises leave nightly at 6:30 for 2¼ hours; adults $34.75, children $19.75.

(518) 668-5777 or (800) 553-2628. All tours daily late June to Labor Day, most tours weekends only in spring and fall. Lunch cruise daily, May-October.

Shoreline Cruises, 2 Kurosaka Lane, Lake George.

Scenic, narrated one-hour cruises depart approximately every half hour from 10:30 to 7 on small tour boats that hug the shore, offering passengers an opportunity to see secluded islands and million-dollar mansions up close (adults $8.75, children

$4.75). The larger, three-deck wood yacht **Horicon** has two-hour lunch cruises Thursday-Sunday at 12:30, with snacks available à la carte (cruise only, adults $13.95, children $6.95). The Horicon also gives sunset happy hour cruises nightly from 6:30 to 8 (adults $10.95, children $5.95). Dinner cruises are offered Thursday-Sunday at 6 (adults $29.95, children $19.95) on the new 400-passenger **Adirondac**, a 155-foot-long vessel designed after late 19th-century touring ships. Also available are moonlight entertainment cruises, with live music and dancing, from 9 to 11 on Friday, Saturday and Monday (adults $14.95, children $7.50).

(518) 668-4644 or (888) 542-6287. www.lakegeorgeshoreline.com. Tours daily, May-October.

BOAT RENTALS. Bolton Landing has no fewer than eight marinas. **Chic's Marina,** next to the Algonquin Restaurant on Lake Shore Drive a mile south of the village, (518) 644-2170, offers Boston Whalers, powerboats, cabin cruisers, canoes, water skis, jet skis and other boats from April through November. Outboard rentals are featured at **Water's Edge Marina,** (518) 644-2511, and **Norowal Marina,** (518) 644-3741, both on Sagamore Road near the bridge to Green Island. Water's Edge has a lakeside store and caters to spring and fall fishing parties. Norowal has a minimarket, laundromat, showers and other services for boaters. Outboards, canoes and kayaks are among the rental offerings of **F.R. Smith & Sons,** Sagamore Road, (518) 644-5181.

Kayaking has taken off on Lake George, as elsewhere. Hourly and overnight rentals of sea kayaks are available from **Lake George Kayak Co.,** which has a large sporting goods store on Main Street in downtown Bolton Landing and a kayak rental center at 3 Boathouse Lane, Green Island, (518) 644-9366. Owner Ike Wolgin cites the peace and quiet of a kayak experience on the northern end of the lake as opposed to the noise and interference by motor boats, jet skis, parasailers and big tour boats that monopolize the south end of the lake.

DIVING. Several sites in the lake have been identified for viewing "sunken fleet" vessels dating to the 1700s when the French and the British were competing for North America. The Lake George region was a focal point for the struggle from 1757 to 1760. Intermediate and advanced diving sites are maintained by the state under its Submerged Heritage Preserve program, (518) 897-1200 or 891-1370. One dive is in 107-foot-deep water to a "land tortoise," one of a class of military vessels unique to Lakes George and Champlain in the 18th century, intended to serve as a floating artillery platform.

FISHING. Lake George is a favorite of fishermen. Lake trout, largemouth and smallmouth bass, landlocked salmon, yellow perch and northern pike are among the species found. Many charter boats take visitors out to fish on the lake. **Ted's Charter Fishing Service** at 3940 Lake Shore Drive, Diamond Point, (518) 668-5334, offers four-hour trips for salmon, lake trout and bass.

SWIMMING. Most lodging establishments mentioned here have their own lake access and beaches for guests. Lifeguards staff public beaches in Bolton Landing and Lake George village. Rogers Park and Veterans Memorial beaches in Bolton Landing are free if you walk; the parking fee is $4.50. A special treat is a boat ride out to an island for swimming and picnicking. Speaker Heck Island has day-use sites, and there are more sites for island picnics in the Narrows.

Other Activities

Hiking and nature trails. Classified as a "Forever Wild" forest area, the east side of Lake George is great for hiking. Extensive trail networks lead up mountains and through forests for lake and pond views. The Buck Mountain Trail from Pilot Knob, a 6.6-mile round trip, rewards the energetic with panoramic views of Lake George from its open rock peak. For rock climbers, Rogers Rock at the north end of the lake rises straight above the lake. It's best approached by canoe, and several routes of moderate grade go from 200 to 400 feet high.

Up Yonda Farm, 5239 Lake Shore Drive, (518) 644-9767, is an estate bequeathed to Warren County as an Environmental Education Center. Its 73 acres offer nature trails that include a butterfly garden, a working beehive and views of Lake George. A museum contains wildlife exhibits and a diorama with native mammals and birds in various habitats. It's open daily in summer 8 to 5, to 4 rest of year. Parking, $3.

If you crave lake and mountain views but aren't up to the climb, drive up the **Prospect Mountain Veterans Memorial Highway.** The 2,030-foot summit of **Prospect Mountain** is reached via a 5.5-mile-long scenic drive off Route 9 near Lake George village. There are three overlooks along the way and picnic tables at the top. It's open daily 9 to 5, Memorial Day to late October; vehicles, $6.

Bolton Auto and Walking Tours. To mark its Bicentennial in 1999, the Town of Bolton produced an informative if not very user-friendly map outlining a one-mile walking tour of the village and a ten-mile driving tour. Both tours point out historic and sightseeing attractions big and small, some of them privately owned and some involving the successors to long-gone hotels and mansions.

Much of Bolton Landing's lakeshore is known as **Millionaires Row.** It starts at the Lake George Club, organized in 1908 by mansion owners for social and sports purposes. Nearby is Homer Point, site of the summer home once owned by Mme. Louise Homer, contralto for the Metropolitan Opera, who is remembered for her hymn sings at the Lake George Club. Her composer husband Sidney was a cousin of artist Winslow Homer.

Marcella Sembrich Memorial Studio, 4800 Lakeshore Drive, Bolton Landing.

If Bolton Landing has a tourist attraction, this is it. The quaint, pink stucco teaching studio of the Metropolitan Opera diva Marcella Sembrich on Sembrich Point is one of the few structures open to the public from Lake George's Great and Gracious period of the early 20th century. The opera singer summered in a family mansion here and her vocal students from the Julliard School of Music trained in the studio at the southern end of the fourteen-acre estate. Following her death, the family established it as an opera museum, which has been open each summer since 1937. The museum holds mementos of her operatic career, a 1905 Steinway piano used by Paderewski, elaborate performance gowns, a photo of Enrico Caruso autographed "to my greatest Gilda, from her Duke," plus signed photos from Puccini, Toscanini, Mahler, Strauss, Brahms, Verdi, Rachmaninoff and others. Visitors may walk along nearly a quarter mile of shoreline paths amid towering white pines and lake vistas in what was part of Mme. Sembrich's beloved woodland retreat.

(518) 644-9839 or 644-2492. Open daily, 10 to 12:30 and 2 to 5:30, mid-June to mid-September. Adults, $2.

Bolton Historical Society Museum, Lake Shore Drive, Bolton Landing.

This 1890 structure beside the library served as a Catholic church until it became a museum for the historical society founded in 1970. The museum was renovated inside and out for the town's 1999 Bicentennial. Photos of 19th-century Lake George hotels convey the Gilded Age. The collection of local artifacts, furniture, clothing and the like recall the town's status as the summer home for musical celebrities.

(518) 644-9960. Open in July and August, Monday-Friday noon to 5 and 7 to 9, Saturday noon to 5. Free.

Bolton's musical heritage continues to this day with the annual **Barbershop Quartet Singing Festival** around Labor Day weekend. More than 100 amateur quartets sing in the streets of Bolton Landing on Saturday morning as people await three weekend concerts in which some of the world's top professional quartets entertain.

Rogers Memorial Park is hidden off Lake Shore Drive behind the Bolton Free Library. It offers tennis courts, swings, a picnic area, bandstand and, best of all, a beautiful sandy beach. Steamboat Pier is where the Mohican tour boat stops to pick up passengers at 9:40 and returns at 12:45.

SHOPPING. Lake George village is the mecca for shoppers in search of T-shirts and souvenirs. South of the village is a group of factory outlets, including Polo, Jones of New York, Nautica, Timberland, Etienne Aigner and others of the familiar ilk. A couple of miles south toward Glens Falls is **Suttons Marketplace,** an extraordinary complex with a great array of crafts, furniture, clothing and gourmet foods plus a café in an upscale country-store atmosphere.

In the center of Bolton Landing, the shops are few but select. **Trees** is the place for Adirondack-made items and books, from twig signs to bark lampshades. A canoe full of colorful pieces is the centerpiece of **Finishing Touches,** stocking linens, accessories and gourmet foods. The **Blueberry Basket** is a cottage full of gifts, and **Black Bass Antiques** speaks for itself. More gifts are available at **The Gift Box. Boyd's Bears & Friends** offers bears and banners. **Bolton Bay Traders** carries a Bolton Landing T-shirt along with casual clothes and Adirondack books and gifts. The **Indian Teepee Gift Shop** is chock full of collectibles.

Hague. This up-lake mountain town was the home of the **Lake George Monster** hoax in 1906. Hague at the time was the summer home of two prominent New Yorkers, publisher William Mann and artist Harry Watrous. Mann owned a home on Waltonian Island and Watrous lived in a mainland mansion (now Ruah Bed & Breakfast) across from the island. The pair competed to see who could catch the season's largest trout. When Mann took the lead with what Watrous considered a fake, Watrous fashioned a sea monster from a pine log, painted it green and gave it two green eyes. With a pulley system from shore, he could raise it to the surface or submerge it. The monster frightened residents as well as tourists and made waves in the New York press. The monster is now at the Lake George Historical Museum in Lake George village, but local boosters hoped to bring it home to Hague.

Where to Eat

The Algonquin, Lake Shore Drive, Bolton Landing.
This is the premier dining establishment on all of Lake George, according to local consensus. Happily, it's on a hillside right beside the water, a mile south of Bolton Landing, and takes full advantage of its lakeshore location. A large outdoor patio holds tables topped by cheerful umbrellas. Inside, the barstools face the lake in the main-floor **Pub Room,** which has vinyl-cloth-covered tables and an informal menu. Upstairs is **Topside,** with wraparound windows, white-clothed tables and bentwood chairs, open for dinner only. Boaters pull right up to the docks in front, and there's lots of lakefront activity to entertain diners at all hours. The Pub Room's all-day menu includes six kinds of burgers, salads and sandwiches. The "fresh catch salad" (swordfish when we were there) is billed as the house favorite. We made a fine lunch of the grilled salmon croissant with citrus mayo and the Mexican burger accompanied with guacamole, jalapeño peppers and fries. Dinner entrées range widely from grilled salmon béarnaise and seafood au gratin to chicken saltimbocca

and prime rib au jus. Greek shrimp with feta cheese and tomatoes in a cream sherry over linguini is a house specialty. Appetizers include creamy house pâté with toast rounds, chicken wings, baked brie and crab cakes with rémoulade sauce. Homemade desserts include banana cream pie, white chocolate éclair cake, frozen peanut butter mousse pie and five layers of something called a chocolate confusion layer cake.

(518) 644-9442. www.thealgonquin.com. Entrées, $17.99 to $24.99. Lunch daily in season, 11:30 to 5. Dinner nightly, from 5. Closed mid-October to late April.

Villa Napoli, 4610 Lake Shore Drive, Bolton Landing.

The attractive restaurant on the side of the Melody Manor Resort property is considered one of the area's best. It takes its name from the Villa Marie Antoinette mansion next door as well as from the Neapolitan heritage of Damian Alessi, husband of owner Rose Alessi. A jaunty front patio catches a glimpse of the lake. Inside the alpine-looking structure with timbered walls and mini-gabled roof are an atmospheric bar and lounge and an elegant, pine-paneled dining room lit by authentic lamps saved from the main house at Villa Marie Antoinette. A fireplace with a hand-carved marble front, also saved from the villa, adds warmth. The restaurant is known for its Tuscan grilled specialties, saltimbocca, osso buco, cioppino, pastas and gourmet pizzas. "We have to offer your basic chicken parm because some people want the familiar," says Rose, "but it's the best" and the emphasis is more on high-style, northern Italian cuisine. You might start with shrimp and scallop spiedini, clams and mussels sautéed in garlic butter or an antipasto platter large enough to share. Pastas lean to the heavier Neapolitan style, including a rich lasagna and eggplant parmigiana. The kitchen extends its reach with secondi like the day's seafood catch steamed in parchment paper on a bed of herbs and vegetables, sautéed chicken in lemon cream with artichoke hearts and roasted peppers, and veal marsala.

(518) 644-9047. Entrées, $21 to $25. Dinner nightly, 5 to 10, mid-June to Labor Day, weekends in off-season. Closed Columbus Day to mid-May.

The Trillium, The Sagamore, Bolton Landing.

The 120-seat dining room is the most luxurious of the six restaurants at the fabled Sagamore resort on a private island on Lake George. Corinthian columns, beige walls and window treatments, brass chandeliers, pink upholstered chairs and Austrian china on pink tablecloths set the scene for contemporary regional cuisine The menu is at the cutting edge, and service is solicitous. A five-course tasting menu for the entire table features the best of the evening's offerings. Expect starters like Hudson Valley foie gras au torchon and baked oysters with salmon roe. Main dishes could be crispy fillet of Alaskan halibut with saffron-shellfish emulsion, Argentinean-style mixed grill and peach-lacquered veal tenderloin. Warm chocolate cake with chambord raspberry confit and chocolate ice cream might be the finale.

(518) 644-9400. Entrées, $29 to $35. Dinner nightly by reservation, 6 to 9:30; jackets required. Sunday brunch in season, 10 to 3.

The Boathouse Restaurant, 3210 Lake Shore Drive, Lake George.

"Difficult to find, but worth it," says the menu. It's difficult only because it's in what used to be an authentic boathouse, situated down a hill beside the Cresthaven Resort. Only the sign is visible from the road. Waves lap at the docks next to the outdoor tables, which on a hot summer afternoon are a good place for lunch right beside the water. Many of the tables inside the pleasant pine interior get water views as well. The extensive menu offers something for everyone, and a light menu is available day and night. You might lunch on a nacho platter, chicken caesar salad or a blackened fish or grilled prime rib sandwich. The dinner menu adds things like blackened salmon, shrimp scampi, chicken stuffed with prosciutto and provolone, filet mignon and New York strip steak. A raspberry chicken sandwich is featured anytime. Cheesecake and carrot cake are among the desserts.

(518) 668-3332 or (800) 853-1632. Entrées, $18.95 to $24.95. Breakfast daily, 8 to 11:30. Lunch, noon to 4. Dinner, 5 to 10. Sunday brunch, 10 to 2. Closed November-April.

Contessa Restaurant, 5102 Lake Shore Drive, Bolton Landing.
The lake is on view only in the distance and from the deck out back, but this Brooklyn-style Italian restaurant that's part of the Contessa Resort Motel complex high above the lake is popular with locals. Pizzas are made according to customer whim. The house special is one with a "choice of seven toppings." Family pizza nights (all you can eat) are featured Monday-Thursday. Regular dinner entrées include the usual suspects, from shrimp marinara to chicken francese to veal parmigiana. But it's the pizzas and pastas like baked ziti, tortellini with pesto and penne with vodka sauce that are bestsellers here. Brooklyn cannolis, stuffed to order, are the signature desserts.

(518) 644-2960. www.contessamotel.com. Entrées, $13.95 to $18.95. Open daily, noon to 10. Closed Columbus Day to May.

The View Restaurant at Indian Kettles, 9580 Lake Shore Drive, Hague.
The oldest established restaurant on Lake George, this large place with a soaring ceiling has been family-owned and operated since 1947, and the Whisher family is continuing the tradition following the retirement of the founding family in 2001. The place takes part of its name from the holes cut by glaciers in boulders found along the shore below, which made natural cooking pots for early Indians who lived in the area. Bradley Whisher has substituted Adirondack decor for the former Indian motif. The huge rear deck, with a ten-mile view down the lake, is particularly appealing. Prime rib is the house specialty. Expect the likes of pan-seared trout with citrus vinaigrette, bacon-wrapped pork tenderloin, and a mixed grill of lamb, lacquered duck breast with raspberry demi-glace and filet mignon. Strawberry shortcake and cheesecake head the dessert list.

(518) 543-8038. www.indian-kettles.com. Entrées, $19.95 to $31.25. Breakfast on summer weekends, 7:30 to 11:30. Lunch daily, 11:30 to 4, Memorial Day to mid-September. Dinner nightly, 5 to 9:30, Memorial Day to mid-September. Closed Tuesday-Thursday in off-season and November-April.

Stone Manor Restaurant, 4436 Lake Shore Drive, Diamond Point.
Part of the evolving, six-acre Blue Water Manor "resort," the restaurant that looks like a stone manor right beside the shore was in flux at our 2004 visit. Owners Daniel and Dr. Ellen Nichols were playing musical chairs with the venues, moving the formal dining area into what had been the bar in the main-floor manor room with a huge stone fireplace. The Blue Moose Tavern was moving downstairs, joining a waterside dining area with upholstered chairs at tables on a covered patio. The same menu is served in both places. It's detailed in cutesy terminology ("the one and only filet sandwich – Dan and Ellen say 'you deserve it.'") There's really something for everyone, from "true caesar salad" to steak au poivre. The "famous mixy-matchy grill" yields twin petite filet mignon, barbecued chicken breast and lobster tail. Desserts include tiramisu and our favorite Nuns of New Skete cheesecake.

(518) 644-2535 or (800) 299-8938. www.bluewatermanor.com. Entrées, $15.95 to $27.95. Lunch on weekends, from 11. Dinner nightly, 4 to 10. Closed mid-October to mid-May.

FOR MORE INFORMATION: Bolton Landing Chamber of Commerce, Box 368, Bolton Landing, NY 12814, (518) 644-3831. www.boltonchamber.com.

Lake Placid, N.Y.

Mere mention of the name Lake Placid conjures up images of the Winter Olympics, Whiteface Mountain, skiing, skating, sports – and snow. Hardly a vision of water. But the famed winter sports capital takes its name from a mountain lake and is actually a summer resort of long standing, at its busiest in July and August and in the early fall.

Lake Placid (the lake that adjoins the village) and Mirror Lake (the smaller in-town lake that first-time visitors invariably think of as Lake Placid) give the village a watery presence that distinguishes it from other Eastern mountain towns. And the scenic mountains all around distinguish Lake Placid from other water places.

Located on a lofty plateau 1,744 feet above sea level, the village of 2,700 hardy souls is ringed by the highest of the Adirondacks' High Peaks – Mount Marcy, Algonquin and Whiteface among them.

Nature's endowments influenced Lake Placid's development as one of the premier summer and winter resorts in the Northeast. Grand hotels were built overlooking Mirror Lake. In 1904, the Lake Placid Club imported 40 pairs of skis from Norway and introduced winter sports to North America. Less than three decades later, Lake Placid was chosen to host the 1932 Winter Olympic Games, the first in North America. Its Olympic stature was reinforced in 1980 when it again hosted the Winter Olympics – best remembered for the "miracle of Lake Placid." People danced in the streets after the upstart American hockey team defeated the Soviets on their way to the gold medal.

Lake Placid has acquired an enviable Olympic heritage, both in sports personalities and venues. The village has placed more than 60 competitors on Olympic teams, on every Winter Olympic team and in every event. The visitor's first out-of-the-ordinary sight is apt to be the ski jump towers, rising like high-tech grain elevators southeast of town. Upon entering the village, one quickly senses the importance of athletics – from stores to clinics to doctors specializing in sports injuries. And in the heart of Lake Placid, beneath flags of all participating countries flying alongside the Olympic Arena, in the middle of summer you might find a pile of what looks like snow. Some guess that it consists of mounds of ice shavings from the skating rink, but young and old alike pause to make a few snowballs or cool off on a hot day.

The mountains and the athletic atmosphere make Lake Placid a mecca for mountain climbers, hikers and cyclists. The lakes and rushing streams make it popular with boaters, swimmers, fishermen and anyone else who likes to be near the water.

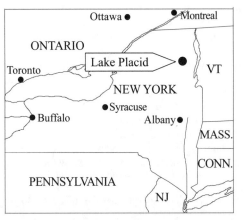

There are boat excursions, paddleboats, gorge trips, carriage rides around Mirror Lake, airplane rides over the lake and concerts beside the lake. The village's charming little library backs up to the lake. And when the excellent Lake Placid Sinfonietta presented a lakeside summer program "Down by the Water," featuring musical compositions inspired by water, many concert-goers attended in boats.

The village is in the heart of Adirondack Park, an area of forever-wild wilderness larger

Mirror Lake in heart of Lake Placid is on view from balcony at Mirror Lake Inn.

than Massachusetts. This is where the Adirondack great camps and lodges are centered, and the home of the Adirondack chair and birch-bark furnishings. The Adirondacks exude a distinct sense of place. At the heart of it all is Lake Placid.

Getting There

Lake Placid is located in the northeastern Adirondacks, about 130 miles north of Albany and 125 miles south of Montreal. Most motorists approach from the south via I-87 (the Adirondack Northway). Take Exit 30 at Underwood for Route 73, heading 28 miles northwest to Lake Placid.

Adirondack Trailways buses serve Lake Placid from Albany and New York City, and Champ Express serves Lake Placid from Plattsburgh. Amtrak trains operate between New York and Montreal with a stop at Westport, 40 minutes to the east. Lake Placid Airport has daily charter services. USAir commuter planes from metropolitan centers fly into nearby Saranac Lake's airport.

Where to Stay

The area offers resorts, motels, ski chalets and a growing number of small B&Bs. Here we concentrate on those on or near Mirror Lake or Lake Placid. Throughout this chapter, note the distinction between Mirror Lake, the small lake in the village, and Lake Placid, the larger, less accessible lake that leads to the base of Whiteface Mountain.

Lodging rates vary dramatically between high season (summer and winter) and off-season.

Lake Placid Lodge, Whiteface Inn Road, Box 550, Lake Placid 12946.

The owners of The Point, the extravagant world-class resort on Upper Saranac Lake, took over the old-favorite Lake Placid Manor and renamed it a lodge. With the deft touch that made The Point the epitome of sybaritic comfort in the Adirondack great camp style, David and Christie Garrett transformed the manor into a comparable but less daunting refuge. It's a Point for mere mortals, worthy of its recent elevation to Relais & Châteaux status. Off by itself on the forested edge of Lake Placid, several miles from the village hubbub, the lodge is blessed (or cursed, depending on your stamina for stairs) with a hilly location overlooking lake and mountains. The reception lobby sets the stage: Ahead and below, visible down several long flights of twig-lined stairs tunneling step by step toward the lakeshore, are the dining rooms and common areas. Fifteen rooms are in the main lodge, a couple of side lodges and a lakeside lodge below. Seventeen more are in cabins along the lakeshore. The establishment is furnished with the largest collection of Adirondack furniture in the country, all of which is available for purchase.

The accommodations, named for the region's high peaks and lakes, are best described as plush. All have ample bathrooms, most with deep soaking tubs and dual-head showers, and contain substantial, raised fieldstone fireplaces (three suites contain two each). The walls in some are paneled in board and bead wainscoting. Mounds of pillows and rich fabrics top the plump king and queensize feather beds. There are sumptuous armchairs, rustic twig and birch-bark furniture, Native American rugs or oriental carpets on the floors and original local art on the walls. Oversize pin cushions wrapped in birch bark as sewing kits are in each room. So are Crabtree & Evelyn toiletries, bottled Adirondack mineral water and fresh fruit. Peanut-butter cookies wrapped in doilies are presented at turndown. Most rooms afford water views, but the ultimate is the lakefront Whiteface Suite upstairs in the main lodge. It's endowed with a lavish sitting area, a private balcony, a canopied king bed against the window and a deep soaking tub from which you might see Whiteface Mountain out the adjacent window. Another prize is the Birch Cottage with his and hers bathrooms, walk-in closet and large porch with lake view. The nine rooms and suites in the Lakeside lodge face the water. Their balconies and decks are nicely partitioned by stacks of firewood, as much a decorative signature of the lodge as all the twig furnishings and birch-bark mirrors. The newest accommodations are in fifteen log cabins a short walk from the main lodge, just steps from the lakeshore. Outfitted in similar fashion to the lodge, they have beamed and arched ceilings, tall stone fireplaces, wet bars and large baths with twig-framed soaking tubs and separate showers. From the picture windows and Adirondack chairs outside the doors, the lake and mountains are on full view. Owl's Head Cabin, the most luxurious, has a king bed, oversize jacuzzi, dry sauna and a six-headed steam shower.

As at The Point, dining is a highlight (see Where to Eat). Breakfast and afternoon tea are included in the rates. The hearty Adirondack breakfast incorporates juices, smoked fish, homemade pastries and a hot entrée. Off the entry lobby is the Gallery Shop, full of distinctive Adirondack and antler-related furnishings, apparel and dinnerware. The property comes with a sandy swimming area and a large deck and lawn for sunbathing. A pontoon barge gives sightseeing cruises around the lake. Eighteen holes of golf and four tennis courts are offered at the adjacent Whiteface Club.

(518) 523-2700 or (877) 523-2700. Fax (518) 523-1124. www.lakeplacidlodge.com. Eleven rooms, four suites and fifteen one- and two-bedroom cabins. Doubles, $400 to $475. Suites, $650 to $900. Cabins, $625 to $1,300.

Mirror Lake Inn Resort and Spa, 5 Mirror Lake Drive, Lake Placid 12946.
This four-diamond resort and spa facing Mirror Lake has long been known for the ultimate in taste and low-key elegance. Though the main inn was destroyed by fire in 1988, its successor built by owners Ed and Lisa Weibrecht looks as if it's been there forever. The resort has 128 rooms, sixteen of which are suites in the main building. A few are in two houses by the lakeshore and in a hilltop conference

center. The rest are in two structures behind the inn and connected to it by enclosed walkways. The public spaces, which are uncommonly plentiful, are sights to behold. The fireplaced library is a richly paneled room accented with stained glass and heads of trophy animals. Complimentary tea, cookies and tea breads are served in a corner sitting area, off which is a plush sunroom/lounge with big windows toward the lake. Every table in the swank, formal **Averil Conwell Dining Room** has a water view, and casual fare is served at **The Cottage** beside the lake (see Where to Eat). Downstairs is a full-service salon and spa, complete with exercise room, sauna, a huge whirlpool and a 60-foot lap pool with a waterfall at one end. The inn's fitness-minded staff and its emphasis on wellness are inspired by Lisa Weibrecht, who was the U.S. Women's national luge champion in 1977 and in 1995 was inducted into the 46ers Club after climbing all 46 Adirondack peaks above 4,000 feet. The sixteen Placid suites, all with whirlpool baths, are luxurious indeed. They range from large rooms with sitting areas and private balconies to split-levels, each with a living room and a spiral staircase leading to a king-bedded loft. Less regal are the majority of rooms in the two motel-style buildings behind the inn. Every room faces the lake and most have private balconies, kingsize beds, bathrooms with hair dryers, wet bars and mini-refrigerators, clock-radios, TVs, padded hangers and photos of old Lake Placid. Rooms in two houses by the lake are closest to the water, but are older, smaller and furnished in early American style. They're billed as the most economical way to enjoy the ambiance of the inn. Although guests tend to gather around the outdoor pool, the inn's beach is good for swimming. Rentals are available at the boathouse.

(518) 523-2544. Fax (518) 523-2871. www.mirrorlakeinn.com. One hundred twelve rooms and sixteen suites. Rates, EP. Doubles, $260 to $340. Suites, $465 to $825.

Interlaken Inn, 15 Interlaken Ave., Lake Placid 12946.
Exceptionally attractive from the outside with gardens and terraces all around, this in-town inn is on a residential side street linking Mirror Lake and Lake Placid, both within easy walking distance. It's attractive inside as well, as renovated and enhanced in 2002 by new owner Mary Neary. She produced two new suites, the Equestrian decorated in umber toile with king sleigh bed and whirlpool tub and the Cornucopia with a queen poster bed and private balcony overlooking Whiteface Mountain. Private balconies also enhance the spacious Red Toile Room with king bed and the English Country Room done in vintage florals. The preceding rooms have TVs, but five smaller rooms with queen beds – one on the third floor with a clawfoot tub beneath a skylight – do not. All are appointed with Frette linens and robes, down duvets and Aveda bath products. A two-story carriage house in back has a living room with sofabed, kitchen and dining area, and an upper bedroom with kingsize rattan bed and balcony. Common rooms on the main floor of the inn bear high embossed tin ceilings, paneled walls and Mahinda rugs over birch floors. The fireplaced living room is a gathering place, while nooks and crannies provide secluded retreats. One side of the main floor is given over to a fine-dining restaurant (see Where to Eat). The other side has a handsome pub with a wine cellar and dining area. A full breakfast is offered in the morning.

(518) 523-3180. Fax (518) 523-0117. www.theinterlakeninn.com. Seven rooms, two suites and one carriage house with private baths. Doubles, $155 to $225. Suites, $225 to $275. Carriage house, $350.

Hilton Lake Placid Resort, 1 Mirror Lake Drive, Lake Placid 12946.
Don't be deceived by the street address. Most of this 179-room hotel is located across Main Street in a five-story, U-shaped high-rise built around a swimming

pool. The Hilton is where the action is, around the indoor and outdoor pools, in the Dancing Bears lounge, the meeting and banquet facilities, and the **Terrace Dining Room.** Standard hotel rooms (they're called "super deluxe") have private balconies, but Mirror Lake can barely be glimpsed across the rooftops from the lower floors. We far prefer the motel-style rooms closer to the lake, 44 cheaper units in the older Lakeview building across the street and 30 of the most expensive right on the waterfront. Six are in a three-story building from which one could fish off the balconies and the rest are nicely hidden from public view in a one-story strip under the parking lot, facing grass, docks and a pool at water's edge.

(518) 523-4411 or (800) 755-5598. Fax (518) 523-1120. www.lphilton.com. One hundred seventy-nine rooms. Doubles, $159 to $289.

Best Western/Golden Arrow Hotel, 150 Main St., Lake Placid 12946.

It's not the Hilton, but this Best Western is located right on the shore of Mirror Lake and appeals more to water-lovers. The lobby with soaring windows framing the view hints at what's in store. Half the rooms face the lake a stone's throw away. Most have balconies. A few offer fireplaces, whirlpool tubs and kitchenettes, and six have two bedrooms. The two four-story buildings screen the sights and sounds of Main Street from guests sunning on the striking, pure-white sand beach below, a popular place for swimming, paddleboating and canoeing. The recently renovated rooms are furnished in typical hotel style. There's plenty of action in the indoor pool, fitness center, the restaurant, the lounge and nightclub.

(518) 523-3353 or (800) 582-5540. Fax (528) 523-8063. www.golden-arrow.com. One hundred thirty-three rooms and eight suites. Doubles, $109 to $199. Suites, $139 to $349.

Lake Placid Resort/Holiday Inn, 1 Olympic Drive, Lake Placid 12946.

High on a hill overlooking the village and Mirror Lake, this motor inn with the ever-changing name is the starting point of local entrepreneur Serge Lussi, who since has acquired the old Lake Placid Club property with its 45 holes of golf, a restored clubhouse and residential development. Formerly the SunSpree Resort, this now bills itself as a resort hotel and golf club. Whatever, the lodging facility has a view that lives up to the name of its predecessor, the Grand View Hotel. The owner redid the lobby entrance to capitalize on the view. The lake is visible from front rooms on the second, third and fourth floors; those in back face the High Peaks. Newer mini-suites are angled for the best views. All rooms have refrigerators and coffeemakers. Chalets come with fireplaces and jacuzzis. Other attractions are an indoor pool, fitness room with sauna and whirlpool, tennis courts, a trout stream for fishing, a private beach on Mirror Lake, the golf courses and a cross-country ski center. Three meals a day are served in **Arturo's Ristorante.** Formal dining is offered at the inn's **Veranda** (see Where to Eat), a summery house across the road. Lunch is available in season at the stunning **Golf House Restaurant** in the clubhouse and beside the lake at the **Boat House Restaurant.**

(518) 523-2556 or (800) 874-1980. Fax (518) 523-9410. www.lpresort.com. Two hundred eight rooms. Doubles, $109 to $259.

Wildwood on the Lake, 88 Saranac Ave., Lake Placid 12946.

Twelve of the 35 units at this motel and cottage complex face Lake Placid and are quite appealing with private decks or balconies and a view onto the shady lawn. Most rooms contain two double beds, two chairs, a table, TV, telephone, a small refrigerator and a coffeemaker; a few have two queen beds and jacuzzis. An efficiency suite offers a kingsize bed, fireplace and whirlpool tub for two. This part of the lake is too shallow for swimming, but there's a quite charming little pool by the road, filled with lake water that trickles down a waterfall, with a slide and a small beach at one end. Also available are a small heated pool up a hill beside some poolside units with private balconies, and an indoor hot tub and sauna. Rowboats, canoes and paddleboats are complimentary for guests. Owners Horst and Edith Weber are responsible for the Tyrolean look of the place. A cottage overlooking the pool has a king bedroom, fireplace, whirlpool tub and balcony, while a fireplaced cottage with kitchenette accommodates up to six. The lakeside lawn is a beauty (many people were reading in loungers at our visit), and there's a game room for rainy days.

(518) 523-2624. www.wildwoodmotel.com. Thirty-one rooms and four cottages. Doubles, $58 to $118. Suite, $128 to $168. Cottages, $68 to $195.

Paradox Lodge, 2169 Saranac Ave., Lake Placid 12946.

This small inn backing up to Paradox Bay on Lake Placid is run very personally by chef Moses "Red" LaFountaine and his wife Nan. They took over an abandoned house built in 1899 and created an intimate restaurant on the main floor (see Where to Eat) and four upstairs guest rooms furnished with Adirondack-style furniture the owner made himself. The rear Treetop Suite has a queen bed and a sunken sitting room with a head-on lake view. Another lake view is available in the Bay View Room with an antique oak double bed. A remarkable Averil Conwell mural fills one wall of the double-bedded Daisy Room. Guests gather in the front living room, a quirky clutter of antiques, pennants, snowshoes and what-have-you, which opens into the similarly quirky dining room. In 2005, the LaFountaines expanded by renovating a house next door. Named for its cedar interior, their new Cedar Lodge has four large rooms with kingsize beds, sitting areas, gas fireplaces and whirlpool tubs. A full breakfast in the main lodge is included in the rates.

(518) 523-9078 or (877) 743-9078. Fax (518) 523-0029. www.paradoxlodge.com. Seven rooms and one suite with private baths. Doubles, $110 to $295. Suite, $140.

Seeing and Doing

The lakes and the mountains in such close proximity make a fortuitous combination – to our minds, the best of its kind in the Northeast. One can fish, hike, climb the High Peaks or play golf in the morning; go boating, swim or tour the Olympic sites in the afternoon, and go to a cultural event in the evening – all within a few miles of Lake Placid.

Touring Lake Placid

Placid Xpress, (518) 523-2445 or (800) 447-5224, is a free park and ride shuttle service available daily during the summer and weekends in spring and fall. A trolley or bus stops at signed pickup points around the village every 15 to 20 minutes.

Walking Tour. In summer, everyone seems to be walking (or jogging or biking) around Mirror Lake on a new sidewalk constructed, rather lavishly, of brick pavers. The 2.5-mile loop passes the storied Lake Placid Club resort property and Mirror Lake Inn and allows one to see the lake, fine homes and the downtown area close up. In town, take Parkside Drive by the beach and the toboggan slide. Head up Main Street, catching glimpses of the lake between shops and through their rear windows. A pleasant vantage point is Bandshell Park, with its Paul White Bandshell across from the beautiful Episcopal Church.

The **Peninsula Nature Trails** off Saranac Avenue, behind the Howard Johnson Resort Inn, is an arboretum in which forest growth is marked for identification. Its network of trails reaches to the shores of Lake Placid.

Boat Tours. Paddle boats, canoes, rowboats and sailboats may be rented at several places along Main Street, including P.K.'s Boats Inc., for use in Mirror Lake, where power boats are banned. **Lake Placid Marina,** (518) 523-9704, offers hour-long, sixteen-mile cruises of Lake Placid in an enclosed tour boat. Boats pass three large islands, many private estates and the base of Whiteface Mountain. Most of the lake frontage is accessible only by boat, leaving much of the wilderness in its pristine state. Tours at 10:30, 1, 2:30 and 4 daily in summer, fewer trips daily in late spring and early fall. Adults $7.50, children $5.50. **Jones Outfitters Ltd.,** 331 Main St., (518) 523-3468, has canoe, kayak and pedal boat rentals as well as fishing trips and guide service.

BIKING AND BIKE TOURS. Billed as a mountain adventure center is **High Peaks Cyclery,** 331 Main St., (518) 523-3764. It has all kinds of rentals and information on guided or self-guided tours. Bikes and information also are available from **Placid Planet,** 51 Saranac Ave., (518) 523-4128. The **Mountain Bike Center** at the Olympic Sports Complex rents bikes for rides on the cross-country ski trails around Mount Van Hoevenberg.

FISHING. The state record lake trout was hauled out of Lake Placid in 1986. Rainbow trout and bass are also caught, and Mirror Lake is popular for small-scale fishing. Nearby mountain streams like the Ausable River are renowned for fly-fishing.

HIKING AND MOUNTAIN CLIMBING. The Adirondack Mountain Club and local sports shops have information on trails and tours. The AMC's summer information center is on Cascade Road, six miles southeast of Lake Placid. Many of the High Peaks trails start at the Adirondack Loj, eight miles southeast of the village. The casual visitor would barely get a leg up on the 46 High Peaks, which take most mountaineers years to conquer all. But in our younger days the men in our weekend party managed a day's climb to the summit of Mount Marcy, New York's highest, while the women shopped in Lake Placid and brought a steak back to the campground to barbecue for dinner.

Airplane Rides. Adirondack Flying Service, Lake Placid Airport, Route 73, (518) 523-2473, gives two twenty-minute scenic flights: one over the Olympic venues, village, Whiteface Mountain and Cascade area, and the other over the Adirondack High Peaks, including Mount Marcy. Adults $25; two-person minimum.

Olympic Site Tour

The Olympic Regional Development Authority, (518) 523-1655, oversees the sites of the 1932 and 1980 Winter Olympic Games, many of which are open to the public. The Lake Placid Olympic Site Tour is a self-guided driving tour of the Olympic facilities, available from mid-June through early October at a reduced price, $19. Among the facilities:

Olympic Center, the largest ice complex of its kind in the world, is the main landmark in the center of town at 218 Main St. Four ice rinks are housed under one roof, and at least one is open for public ice-skating in the summer. Figure skating shows featuring world-class performers are presented most Saturday nights in summer at 7:30 in the arena; adults $6, children $4. A main-floor location is the site of the **1932 and 1980 Lake Placid Winter Olympic Museum.** Exhibits include video highlights, athletes' uniforms, hometown heroes, sports equipment, Olympic memorabilia and historical information about all local Olympic sites. Museum open daily 10 to 5. Adults $4, children $2.

MacKenzie-Intervale Olympic Jumping Complex, (518) 523-2202, off Route 73 at the southeast entrance to town, is notable for two towers that look a bit like high-tech grain elevators from afar. Ski jumpers train and compete year-round on special surfaces that simulate snow conditions when wet. You can take a chairlift (or drive around) to the 120-meter ski jump tower, where a glass-enclosed elevator rises 26 stories to a wraparound observation deck affording a panorama of the Lake Placid area and the High Peaks. At the tower's base is a grandstand-type affair from which you can watch jumpers plummet down the in-run and soar off the jump onto a plastic-covered outrun. At the foot of the jumping complex is the **Kodak Sports Park,** a U.S. Freestyle Ski Team aerial training center. In summer, aerialists perfect their technique, jumping off plastic-covered ramps and being propelled 50 feet into the air. They do twists and flips before landing skis first in a seventeen-foot-deep pool of water, to the delight of the crowds that are always present, whether during daily practices or special competitions. Open daily, 9 to 4; adults $5, children $3; add $3 and $2 respectively for chairlift and elevator ride.

Verizon Sports Complex at Mount Van Hoevenberg, (518) 523-4436, off Route 73 seven miles southeast of town, includes a new, state-of-the-art combined bobsled/luge/skeleton track that debuted in 2000 during the inaugural Winter Goodwill Games. A dedicated bobsled run, a mile long with sixteen turns, is said to be the most perilous in the world. A trolley takes visitors up a service road to the top every fifteen minutes; our driver volunteered that the run was redone because the athletes said it had become too fast and too dangerous. You can walk down the inside of the bobsled run or return by trolley. The intrepid can try the summer bobsled ride in a wheeled bobsled at speeds up to 50 miles an hour, Wednesday-Sunday 10 to 4, for $30. Displays and films of bobsledding are shown in the bobsled finish building at the base. Open daily, 10 to 4; adults $3, children $2. The complex also has a biathlon range and a mountain bike center.

Whiteface Mountain Highway and Gondola, Wilmington. Opened in 1935, the easy, eight-mile drive up the north face to the 4,867-foot summit of Whiteface offers spectacular vistas. On a clear day, you can see Lake Champlain, Vermont's Green Mountains and the Montreal skyline. The two-lane road has only two hairpin turns as you near the top of the only Adirondack High Peak accessible by car. It ends at a stone castle with a cafeteria, gift shop and parking area. The last portion of the trip up New York's fifth highest peak is accomplished by climbing a stone stairway or riding a 276-foot-high elevator, cut through the top of the mountain and reached through a cold, dank tunnel. The latter is not for the claustrophobic. At the top, you can clamber up and around the rocks to the summit, unencumbered by any fences.

The way to see the Whiteface ski area, the lower east face of the mountain that was the site of the Olympic competitions and still known for good but often windblown skiing, is from the base parking area off Route 86. A gondola takes sightseers to the top of 3,600-foot Little Whiteface; adults $12, children $8. Highway open daily mid-May to mid-October, 8:30 to 5 in summer, 9 to 4 before July 1 and after Labor Day; car and driver $9, passengers $4.

U.S. Olympic Training Center, 421 Old Military Road, (518) 523-2600. The $13 million training center dedicated in 1990 has two clusters of housing for 200 athletes and one of two U.S. Olympic Committee gift shops selling items with the Olympics logo; the other is at Hilton Plaza on Lake Placid's Main Street. The gymnasium complex includes three basketball courts, weight rooms and facilities for volleyball and handball, plus outdoor playing fields. The center attracts large numbers of summer athletes to Lake Placid because of the additional space and sports programs. Self-guided tours, daily 9 to 6, Sunday noon to 5.

Other Attractions

John Brown Farm, 2 John Brown Road, Lake Placid, (518) 523-3900. This state historic site represents the last home and burial site of abolitionist John Brown – remember the song: "John Brown's body lies a-moldering in the grave?" The unassuming farmhouse is furnished as it was in the 19th century. It includes documents and mementos of an eccentric who came to the Adirondacks in 1848 and whose ideas rank with those of the world's leading thinkers. A self-guiding farm trail passes through the grounds. House open Monday and Wednesday-Saturday 10 to 5, Sunday 1 to 5, May-October. Admission $2.

High Falls Gorge, Route 86, Wilmington, (518) 946-2278. Proclaimed as "the ancient valley of foaming waters," this privately owned gorge drops 120 feet in a cascading series of falls, potholes and whirlpools just off Route 86. A large gift shop and restaurant are at the entrance. Visitors take a half-hour walk a quarter of a mile down and back along groomed paths, railed platforms and steps. A self-guiding tour map and recorded messages detail some of the interesting geology and plant life. Open daily, 9 to 5:30 in summer, 9 to 5 rest of season, early May to late October; 8:30 to 4:30 in winter. Adults $9.95, children $5.95.

GOLFING. Golf Digest called Lake Placid's courses "a formidable lineup." The town-owned **Craig Wood Golf Course,** Cascade Road off Route 73 east of town, welcomes the public. The **Lake Placid Resort Golf Club** has reopened 45 holes of the former Lake Placid Club courses. Golf Digest likens it to "Scotland without the air fare." The **Whiteface Club & Resort** offers an exceptionally scenic, eighteen-hole championship course beside woods and Lake Placid.

ENTERTAINMENT. Lake Placid considers itself the summer entertainment capital of the Adirondacks, and was among contenders to become the summer home of the New York Philharmonic. Concerts like New Kids on the Block have been presented at the Olympic Center. The **Lake Placid Film Festival** takes place annually in early June. Two major horse shows are scheduled in late June and early July. Ice skating, hockey, freestyle skiing and ski jumping competitions are held throughout the summer.

Lake Placid Center for the Arts, 93 Saranac Ave., (518) 523-2512, offers live theater, concerts, dance performances and films. Exhibitions in its Fine Arts Gallery and North Gallery are open free Monday-Friday 10 to 5 and weekends 1 to 5.

You'd expect to find music in the air in a town with a Paul White Memorial Bandshell, a street named Victor Herbert Road and the former summer home of Kate Smith. **The Lake Placid Sinfonietta,** founded in 1917 at the Lake Placid Club, is considered one of the best small orchestras in the East. Each summer, the 20 professional musicians present a six-week Sunday evening series called Music in the Mountains at the Lake Placid Center for the Arts, plus free Wednesday evening Pops in the Park concerts at the Paul White Memorial Bandshell beside Mirror Lake. Many concert-goers attend by boat.

Nineteen big-name rock groups appeared in the first **Songs at the Lake** benefit outdoor music festival weekend in July 2004 at the Olympic Oval.

SHOPPING. If you want athletic equipment or apparel, you will be sure to find it in Lake Placid. **High Peaks Cyclery** at 331 Main St. is a sports store deluxe; we're told that if the folks at L.L. Bean don't have it, they refer people to H.P.C. **Eastern Mountain Sports** is one of the increasing numbers of chain and outlet stores settling along Main Street, among them Benetton, The Gap, Van Heusen, Bass, Izod and Geoffrey Beene.

The famed Adirondack Museum of Blue Mountain Lake has opened a terrific new store and gallery called **Adirondack Museum on Main** at 75 Main St. It features distinctive crafts, home accessories, clothing, prints and books selected for their connection to regional history and culture.

We also love the **Adirondack Store & Gallery** at 109 Saranac Ave., where we wandered amid the birch bark baskets, the twig furniture, the balsam pillows and the pine cone china used at the Lake Placid Club. The **Adirondack Craft Center** at the Lake Placid Center for the Arts, 93 Saranac Ave., is a treasure trove of the works of more than 300 area artisans. Beautiful quilts, jewelry and pottery are shown; we admired a metal armadillo that we would have liked to put in our garden, but its $300-plus cost discouraged us. Twig furnishings, bark frames and the like are shown on three floors at **Adirondack Decorative Arts & Crafts,** billed as the largest store on Main Street. Contemporary crafts are featured at **Moon Tree Design.**

Ruthie's Run at 11 Main St. is about the best place for clothes of the Geiger ilk and zillions of sweaters. **Great Range Outfitters,** 71 Main, purveys classic casual and outdoor clothing for men and women. There's a pond filled with koi amid all manner of educational things at **Nature Unlimited. With Pipe & Book** specializes in old and rare books about the Adirondacks as well as pipe and tobacco products.

Where to Eat

Lake Placid offers endless places to eat, many of them of the traditional tourist variety. The focus here is on those with water views.

Lake Placid Lodge, Whiteface Inn Road, Lake Placid.

Go here for the ultimate in Adirondack great camp experiences and perfectly executed contemporary American food. Dine on the wide lakefront porch and watch the moon rise over Lake Placid, or inside the glamorous, lodge-style dining room to admire the remarkable wood wall murals carved by a Tupper Lake logger. New executive chef Ken Ohlinger, recently arrived from a Relais & Chateaux inn in eastern Tennessee, added a Southern accent to the Adirondack menu. Dinner in the 70-seat restaurant is prix-fixe, $70 for three courses (a five-course tasting menu is $110, available for the entire table only). A typical meal might start with a choice of cream of jerusalem artichoke soup with morel mushrooms, a watercress salad or beef carpaccio. The main course could be seared yellow-eye snapper with spring onion broth, crisp roasted chicken with pommery mustard jus, sirloin of Colorado lamb or carpetbagger filet of beef. Desserts include "inverted lemon meringue pie" and chocolate molten cake with tiramisu ice cream. A pub menu is offered from noon to 9. A 4,000-bottle wine cellar is the setting for special wine-tasting dinners.

(518) 523-2700. Prix-fixe, $70. Lunch, noon to 2:30. Dinner nightly, 6 to 9 or 9:30.

The Interlaken Restaurant, 15 Interlaken Ave., Lake Placid.

Some of the most inspired food in town is served at the recently renovated restaurant and pub in the Interlaken Inn. Under new ownership, the kitchen is overseen by executive chef Richard Brosseau, a Whiteface ski instructor who formerly owned Richard's Freestyle Cuisine in town. His cutting-edge menu here might start with such appetizers as rabbit schnitzel with German potato salad, Thai curry-glazed nuts tossed with asparagus set in a parmesan cheese cup, and a goat cheese crêpe topped with cabernet-onion sauce. Main courses vary from salt and pepper tuna steak served over Asian slaw to grilled lamb loin served over a crispy pita topped with lemon-garlic mashed potatoes. Dessert could be Richard's triple chocolate sin, warm almond cake topped with maple ice cream, or biscotti with vidal icewine. About 40 diners can be seated in the airy main dining room, notable for a stunning Adirondack mural that wraps around the walls above the wainscoting, and on an adjacent sun porch. Light fare is offered in the inn's charming pub.

(518) 523-3180. Entrées, $24 to $30. Dinner by reservation, nightly except Monday, 5:30 to 9:30.

Mirror Lake Inn, 5 Mirror Lake Drive, Lake Placid.

The murals of early Lake Placid on the walls of the **Averil Conwell Dining Room** were done by the local artist of that name, who died in 1990. At age 94, she had restored the paintings saved from the inn's fire in 1988. The expansive room on two levels has windows facing Mirror Lake across the road and every table gets a view. Most in demand are the handful of tables on a screened porch. Co-owner Lisa Weibrecht, the U.S. women's national luge champion in 1977, is into fitness and health, which accounts for the spa and wellness menu offered at dinner. The regular menu features game dishes like coffee-encrusted venison loin, pan-seared buffalo ribeye steak and roasted rack of wild boar. Other choices include prosciutto-wrapped swordfish drizzled with a tomato and basil butter sauce, shrimp and scallop scampi, and roasted rack of Colorado lamb with a dried cranberry and roasted hazelnut reduction. Three-onion tart and pan-seared foie gras head the appetizer list. Peanut-butter and walnut pies are favored desserts. A pianist entertains on weekends. In the morning, recorded classical music is the backdrop for an extensive breakfast buffet taken by the sunny windows. A full buffet is available, but we were quite satisfied with the continental buffet with lots of fresh fruit, cereals and muffins.

(518) 523-2544. Entrées, $22.95 to $30.95. Breakfast daily, 7:30 to 10, to 11 weekends. Dinner nightly, 5:30 to 9.

The Cottage, 5 Mirror Lake Drive, Lake Placid.

Operated by the Mirror Lake Inn, this pleasant café is across the street and right beside Mirror Lake, with windows onto the water and a popular side deck that catches the breezes beneath the shade of birch trees. It's perfect for lunch, a light supper or drinks into the wee hours. On a sunny afternoon, three of us enjoyed the roast beef sandwich special, the drunken knockwurst dog steamed in beer and a gloppy taco salad. Heaping sandwiches and salads are the rule, but you also will find a veggie burger, nachos, steamed shrimp, a cheese board, quiche and specials.

(518) 523-9845. Prices, $6.25 to $9.95. Open daily in summer, 11:30 to 10.

Veranda Restaurant, 1 Olympic Drive, Lake Placid.

This high-style, seasonal restaurant is part of Serge Lussi's Lake Placid Resort/ Holiday Inn enterprise. There's no denying the charm of the summery house on a hilltop with a glimpse of distant Mirror Lake through the trees. It takes its name from the front veranda, full of rattan tables and chairs that are popular commodities on mild evenings. Inside, past the bar built around a fieldstone fireplace, is the main Hearthside Room, with fabric panels on the upper half of the room. Upstairs is the beautiful Birch Room, trimmed in birch logs, which also has a fieldstone fireplace. Peach and white linens are topped with the original service plates that came with the house. French chef Claude Gaucher from Dijon might offer such entrées as tuna steak niçoise, dover sole meunière, sautéed duck breast with green peppercorn sauce, steak au poivre and rack of lamb provençal. Start with escargots bourguignonne or seafood vol-au-vent. For dessert, we hear good things about the strawberry tart, meringue glacé, chocolate mousse cake and tarte tatin.

(518) 523-3339. Entrées, $18.95 to $29.95. Dinner, Tuesday-Sunday 5:30 to 9:30.

The Boat House, Mirror Lake Drive, Lake Placid.

This expansive place is right over Mirror Lake, with a covered deck beside the water, an open deck over the beach and a smashing view of the town across the way. The Boathouse is part of the Lake Placid Resort, and is located beside the resort's beach. We stopped here at a recent visit for lunch, only to find lunch service discontinued to favor the resort's new Golf House Restaurant – too bad, for we water-lovers prefer this vista to the mountain views, however breathtaking, from the Golf House. The Boat House claims the only sunset view across the water in Lake Placid. Floral cloths brighten the tables, but otherwise the decor is simple so as not to compete with the watery surroundings. The dinner menu is extensive and varied. Crab cakes garnished with shrimp and rémoulade sauce is a local favorite. Other entrées range from trout fillet roasted with enoki mushrooms in parchment and cedar-planked salmon to chicken pancetta, veal piccata and filet mignon. Appetizers, sushi, California rolls, salads and pastas are also offered.

(518) 523-4822. Entrées, $12.25 to $27.95. Dinner in summer, Wednesday-Monday from 5

Freestyle Cuisine, 51 Main St., Lake Placid.

A glamorous spot overlooking Mirror Lake, this has the right ingredients: location, style and an innovative menu. The canopied outdoor patio beside the water and the urbane contemporary interior are designed to impress. So is the distinctive menu written in free style, as in first courses: "the duck" (confit with fennel and red onion salad and a truffle vinaigrette) and "the brie" (wrapped in prosciutto and pan-seared with cucumber-basil salad and melon coulis). For main courses, consider "the salmon" (grilled with lemon grass consommé and gingered purple sticky rice) or "the steak" (Niman Ranch hanger, pan-seared with jerk seasoning). The place was opened by free-wheeling chef Richard Brosseau and bore his name until 2004 when he moved to the Interlaken Restaurant, leaving sidekicks Tim Loomis and Danielle Pageau to carry on. They offer a short bar menu, an award-winning wine list and some fantastic desserts.

(518) 523-5900. www.freestylecuisine.com. Entrées, $22 to $27. Dinner nightly, 5 to 9:30.

Paradox Lodge, 76 Saranac Ave., Lake Placid.

Dine beside the open kitchen as chef-owner Moses "Red" Lafountaine prepares a meal to remember. The chef, who closed his famed Steak and Stinger restaurant to open an inn, offers an extensive continental menu for eighteen diners in a convivial, almost family-style setting at four rustic tables (made by the chef and offered for sale) amidst a veritable trove of collectibles and clutter. The dining-room windows are onto the side lawns, rather than onto Paradox Bay in back, although you could start with cocktails in the back yard. Inside, you'll feast on starters of stuffed wild boar sausage, smoked trout or grilled foie gras. Main courses run from seared Maine diver scallops to chicken marsala, pork normandy, grilled veal chop and filet mignon au poivre. Desserts follow the continental classic theme.

(518) 523-9078. Entrées, $17.95 to $36.50. Dinner nightly except Monday, 5:30 to 8:30.

Caffé Rustica, 211 Saranac Ave., Lake Placid.

This small, wildly popular café features rustic Italian and Mediterranean fare prepared in a wood oven in an open kitchen. Kevin Gregg, who trained at the Culinary Institute of America, opened following a stint as chef at the Interlaken Inn when his mother owned it. Here, hidden at the side of the Price Chopper shopping plaza, he seats 30 in snug quarters inside and more outside in summer on a terrace beside a showy hillside rock garden. Although wood-fired, thin-crusted pizzas are featured, there's much more: exotic handmade pastas and risottos, salads, and grilled fish and meats. Folks rave about the cedar-planked salmon, the chicken saltimbocca and the filet au poivre with a cognac cream demi-glace. Orange crème brûlée, chocolate truffle cake and homemade sorbets are among the desserts.

(518) 523-7211. Entrées, $14.95 to $23.95. Lunch, Monday-Saturday 11:30 to 3. Dinner, Monday-Saturday 5 to 9 or 10.

The Brown Dog Café & Wine Bar, 3 Main St., Lake Placid.

A whimsical canine motif is evidence that this long and narrow storefront café chooses not to take itself too seriously, except perhaps during the dinner hour. By day, it offers traditional deli fare – build-your-own sandwiches, soups and salads. Come night, a bistro menu presents innovative specials, perhaps prosciutto-wrapped sea scallops with artichoke-citrus pesto and New York strip steak with portobello-shallot butter. The bar menu features things like duck quesadilla, crab cakes with lime-cilantro rémoulade and a filet mignon sandwich. Owner Bill Tennant pours more than 50 premium wines by the glass. The tables of choice are four by the rear windows overlooking Mirror Lake.

(518) 523-3036. www.thebrowndogs.com. Entrées, $16.95 to $21.95. Lunch daily, from 11. Dinner nightly, 5 to 10.

The Great Adirondack Steak & Seafood Company, 34 Main St., Lake Placid.

Longtime local restaurateurs Joan and Ed Kane closed their other establishments to concentrate on this, a huge place serving a huge menu for three meals a day in season. They seat 120 in a pair of Adirondack-themed dining rooms and a brew pub plus an expansive outdoor patio with a glimpse of Mirror Lake through the Village Bandshell Park across the street. The eight-page dinner menu offers all kinds of appetizers, pastas, five versions of chicken as well as seafood and grill selections and combinations thereof, both standard and creative. Each is paired with one of the beers or ales produced in the on-premise brewery.

(518) 23-1629. Entrées, $15.95 to $35.50. Breakfast weekends and summer, 8 to 11. Lunch daily, 11:30 to 3:30. Dinner daily, 3:30 to 10.

Charcoal Pit Restaurant, Saranac Road (Route 86), Lake Placid.

The parking lot always seems to be packed at this local institution on the west side of town, and with good reason. Everyone says the food is excellent, it's fairly priced and the atmosphere is a cut above what you'd expect from a place that's been around since 1957. We're partial to the greenhouse room, pretty in pink and green with a solarium along one side looking onto splendid illuminated gardens that outshine even the notable Adirondack sunsets. Traditionalists like the original, darker dining room, where tiny white lights outline the crossbeams and plants are everywhere. Owner Jim Hadgis is Greek, which accounts for such items on the oversize menu as Greek salad, Greek shrimp and Greek lamb chops (as well as a painting of a Greek wedding by local artist Averil Conwell and a stunning stained-glass piece representing Greek mythology). But beef is the biggest seller, followed by fish, veal and rack of lamb. Altogether there are some 30 possibilities, from seafood newburg to filet mignon au poivre. The dessert cart might harbor banana-chocolate chip or Heath bar crunch pies.

(518) 523-3050. Entrées, $12.95 to $29.95. Dinner nightly, 5 to 10. Closed Wednesday in off-season.

FOR MORE INFORMATION: Lake Placid/Essex County Visitors Bureau, Olympic Center, Lake Placid, NY 12946, (518) 523-2445 or (800) 447-5224. www.lakeplacid.com.

Canadian spans of Thousand Islands Bridge link islands with mainland at right.

The Thousand Islands, N.Y.-Ont.

The quaint overhead "welcome" signs at the entrance to each village in the Thousand Islands region are distinctive.

Until lately, Alexandria Bay's sign lit up in neon, a garish reminder of the resort heritage of this touristy village, which, though tacky, is somewhat endearingly so. The signs for Clayton and Gananoque are old-fashioned wood, reflecting a more low-key tradition. The small sign at the entrance to the hamlet of Rockport has a homemade look, evidence of a simpler way of life.

The Thousand Islands region is a watery venue of rocky, forested islands straddling two nations and marking the beginning of the storied St. Lawrence River as it leaves Lake Ontario to flow hundreds of miles northeast into the Atlantic Ocean in eastern Quebec.

Some of the Thousand Islands – officially they number 1,864 – are mere rocks with a couple of trees, too small for habitation, though some hold a single cabin. Others are large enough for many cottages, and busy Wellesley Island contains a Victorian village, several state parks, a golf resort and hundreds of summer homes. The largest, Ontario's charming Wolfe Island, supports a year-round farming population of nearly 1,500.

The region's vacation centers are as varied as the islands themselves. The focus on the American side is Alexandria Bay, locally called Alex Bay or simply the Bay. Here is an old-fashioned, once-moneyed resort in the genre, perhaps, of parts of the Jersey shore. To the west is Clayton, its poor-boy cousin lately on the upswing, an historic riverfront community that's a mecca for fishermen, campers and museum-goers.

The Canadian side is generally more low-key and more scenic. Its focus is Gananoque (GAN-a-NOK-kwee, or Gan, as the locals call it), an up-and-coming town of inns and restaurants (and a new casino), where the annual ten-day Festival of the Islands in mid-August has become one of the biggest family celebrations in Ontario. To the east, tiny Ivy Lea and Rockport retain the look of generations ago.

In the heart of the area, Wellesley Island in New York and Hill Island in Ontario provide bridge and highway links between two nations and two very different shores.

Fishing and boating are the islands' chief attractions for many. Bass, walleyed pike and muskies keep the anglers happy. More than 75 excursion boats full of sightseers ply the river waters.

You can ride on a tour boat or rent a houseboat. Watch hulking ocean-going freighters pass along the St. Lawrence Seaway. Go scuba diving to look at underwater shipwrecks. Attend vesper services by boat. Take a shuttle boat to shop at the Boateak on Bluff Island or a ferry to dine at an inn on Wolfe Island. Stay overnight at a B&B on a boat or an island. Camp in a cabin on Canoe Island or a tent on Mary Island, and island-hop between campsites in Canada's St. Lawrence National Park.

You can visit North America's largest freshwater maritime museum, see first-rate theater at a playhouse beside the water, visit a nature center on Wellesley Island, reminisce in the Victorian homes and ambiance of Thousand Island Park, relive the past on Wolfe Island, and enjoy the local Thousand Island salad dressing and River Rat cheese.

And everyone ogles Boldt Castle, the $2.5 million monument to a man's love and a broken heart on Heart Island, an omnipresent landmark off Alexandria Bay.

Just as the islands and towns vary, so do the people who populate or visit this busy summer vacation area. All types can find their place among the myriad islands and attractions of the mighty St. Lawrence.

Getting There

The Thousand Islands region is located approximately 100 miles north of Syracuse, 200 miles east of Toronto and 100 miles southwest of Ottawa. The closest cities, Watertown, N.Y., and Kingston, Ont., are each about 30 miles away. North-south Interstate 81 and the east-west Trans-Canada Highway 401 are the main access routes to the area. The two soaring spans of the Thousand Islands International Bridge connect the American and Canadian shores (one-way toll, $2).

Prices are quoted in local currency. American funds stretch farther in Canada, but hefty federal and provincial taxes eat up part of the difference.

Where to Stay

What you do and how you enjoy the Thousand Islands likely will depend on your choice of accommodations, which vary from resort to motel to B&B to cabin to campsite. The area is highly seasonal, and generally battens down the hatches for the winter.

Resorts

Riveredge Resort Hotel, 17 Holland St., Alexandria Bay, N.Y. 13607.

Following a 1988 fire, Jim Donegan's Riveredge motel re-emerged in the Islands' most glamorous reincarnation: a four-story, four-diamond extravaganza with two atriums, elevators, a concierge floor with loft suites and turndown service, corner jacuzzi rooms, a fourth-floor gourmet restaurant (see Where to Eat) and valet parking. (The last is a necessity because parking is limited and casual visitors are discouraged.) The rooms are Alexandria Bay's most luxurious, with Chippendale-style furniture, concealed TVs, two chairs and a table and balconies –only a railing separates each from the next and you can see every other balcony along your floor, which makes for some convivial gatherings. Ten rooms face the St. Lawrence head-on; the rest have side views of the river, although those on the west side look across a small harbor to downtown Alex Bay. The fourth-floor concierge suites consist of sitting rooms with loft bedrooms up a spiral staircase, two TVs and three telephones. Some have whirlpool tubs. Live music wafts from the RiverWatch Lounge into the pool area and lobby and even outside during happy hour. The indoor pool area has a large jacuzzi and sauna, plus a Nautilus facility. There's an outdoor pool by the marina.

(315) 482-9917 or (800) 365-6987. Fax (315) 482-5010. www.riveredge.com. One hundred twenty-nine rooms. Doubles, $179 to $318. Loft and jacuzzi suites, $239 to $338.

The Edgewood Resort, Edgewood Park Road, Box 99, Alexandria Bay, N.Y. 13607. This storied resort has had its ups and downs over its history as northern New York's oldest resort, dating to 1885. A Syracuse investor teamed up with Richard Thomson of the ubiquitous local lodging family to rescue it from bankruptcy in 1997. He spent lavishly to refurbish the far-flung accommodations and open a new waterside restaurant. A large carved black bear at the entrance to its own 75-acre peninsula across the bay from downtown sets an Adirondack theme more in keeping with the area than the garishness of other local resorts. All 125 refurbished rooms in a variety of motel and lodge buildings are clustered around a central clubhouse. The prime Black Bear Lodge closest to the riverfront appeals with an Adirondack lodge look and twig balcony railings. That's the motif as planned for all the buildings, we were told, but further enhancements as well as a planned conference center have been on hold. The rooms we saw had Stickley-style furniture inside and molded green Adirondack chairs on the outside. Deluxe jacuzzi suites come with kingsize beds; other rooms have king or two queen beds. Three meals a day are served in the **Riverfront Café,** fashioned from the historic Baker Cottage at river's edge, which boasts the Islands' first wood-fired brick oven. The spacious restaurant is a beauty with an interior bar, lodge-style dining around much of the perimeter beside big windows onto the water and an enormous outdoor deck with umbrella-topped tables. The with-it menu of pizzas, salads, pastas and grilled or oven-roasted entrées appealed the evening we were there; the music blaring from the bar did not.

(315) 482-9922 or (888) 334-3966. Fax (315) 482-5210. www.theedgewoodresort.com. One hundred twenty-five rooms. Doubles, $129 to $299. Closed November-March.

Pine Tree Point Resort, 70 Anthony St., Alexandria Bay, N.Y. 13607. This 50-year-old resort, on a 40-acre peninsula thick with pines, has what we consider the most alluring public setting in the islands. That may compensate for

fading upkeep and, at our latest summer Sunday afternoon visit, an eerie sense of quiet, even emptiness – as if both staff and guests had left for the day. Still overseen by the founding Thomson family and situated off by itself away from town, the complex consists of a main inn with 21 guest rooms, a cocktail lounge and dining rooms (see Where to Eat), plus cottages and motel-style buildings (many with waterfront balconies). Also available are a picturesque outdoor dining terrace with a smashing view down the St. Lawrence, a quiet cove for boats and a shady area with a tepid swimming pool and a jacuzzi. The corner Victorian room and the 22 balconied Cliffs units at water's edge are most prized, though ours suffered somewhat from wear and outdated decor.

(315) 482-9911 or (888) 746-3229. Fax (315) 482-6420. www.pinetreepointresort.com. Ninety-six rooms and cottages. Doubles, $119 to $209. Closed late October to May.

Glen House Resort and Motel, Thousand Islands Parkway, Box 10, Gananoque, Ont. K7G 2T6.

The Canadian side's largest resort, this rustic complex owned since 1963 by the Seal family sprawls in motel-style on either side of the main, turn-of-the-century Glen House along the quiet riverfront, away from the parkway. Most rooms have water views, but only eight open onto traditional balconies or patios. The balconies for the rest, our top-priced room included, are oddly enclosed so that only one sliding screen door can open to let in air from the outside. We did not care to sit there on a hot evening, with the air-conditioner sound magnified from the inside and a large tree screening the view, so the best option was to relocate to tipsy chairs on the sloping back lawn. Other accommodations include two-bedroom chalets, fireplaced rooms and jacuzzi suites. There are a small heated pool at river's edge, a larger indoor pool and sauna, a large and rather brightly lit dining room with a salad bar and abundant but so-so food, and a cocktail lounge with panoramic water views. It wasn't until after we paid for room and dinner separately that we found we could have booked the MAP plan for less.

(613) 659-2204 or (800) 268-4536. Fax (613) 659-2232. www.glenhouseresort.com. Eighty-one rooms and four two-bedroom chalets. Doubles, $125 to $175.

Inns and B&Bs

The Gananoque Inn, 550 Stone St. South, Gananoque, Ont. K7G 2A8.

Massed flowers front and back indicate the care that has gone into the rejuvenated Gananoque Inn under new owners. Innkeeper John F. Keilty invested big bucks to restore the waterfront property into the jewel that it once was. Nicely situated on the river a few blocks south of downtown, the complex has 29 rooms in the hundred-year-old main structure plus fourteen "waterfront units" that began life as a motel, ten rooms in an annex and two deluxe suites in an adjacent Victorian house called Cedar Knoll. Most in demand are the waterfront units, each with a king or two queen beds and a couple with jacuzzi tubs. Motel units never looked so good. They face lush gardens, lawns and the riverfront, and command top dollar. Four rooms upstairs in the annex also enjoy great water views from balconies, as do six rooms in the main hotel, especially end rooms with large balconies, king beds and jacuzzi tubs, and the two Cedar Knoll suites. Half the inn rooms offer fireplaces. Updated baths, air conditioning and TVs in armoires are modern touches in a building that occasionally shows its age, although refurbished rooms are quite luxurious and stylish. The newest accommodations are two with jacuzzis and fireplaces in the Caverly Cottage, a renovated Victorian house at the edge of the property. Three meals a day are served seasonally in the elegant restaurant (see Where to Eat). A dark and atmospheric pub is open year-round.

(613) 382-2165 or (800) 465-3101. Fax (613) 382-7912. www.gananoqueinn.com. Fifty-nine rooms and suites with private baths. Doubles, $155 to $279. Suites, $355.

Hart House Inn, 21979 Club Road, Wellesley Island, NY 13640.

A heart is engraved in the sidewalk leading to the most tranquil and deluxe B&B in the Thousand Islands. It conveys the idea of romance, one of the themes of a

B&B that incorporates LOVE in its phone numbers and whose ebullient innkeeper likely will give you a hug as you depart. You'll also depart with myriad memories: a sumptuous house that has been grandly restored, good views of river and golf course, some of the best gourmet breakfasts ever and pampering touches by doting innkeepers who care. "People tell us they find this a sanctuary," says the Rev. Dudley Danielson, innkeeper with his wife Kathy. That pleases him no end, since he was called to the Christian ministry after seventeen years as a one-man show as publisher of a seasonal newspaper for Thousand Islands vacationers called Relax! It also pleases Kathy, a former Toronto interior designer who spent summers as a child helping her grandmother run an inn in her native Hungary. She's been a master at hospitality since opening a deluxe B&B in Gananoque in 1986. (Indeed, that's how the couple met. He stopped at her B&B to solicit an advertisement, and says "life hasn't been the same since.") They bought the abandoned 30-room Hart House, which hotelier George Boldt had cut in half and moved to the site to make room for his castle a century ago. Rescuing it from planned demolition, they opened in 1995 with one guest room, adding roughly a room each year. Giving credit to 240 "angels" who helped in various ways, they were up to eight rooms at our visit. Five are large luxury rooms with king or queen beds and whirlpool tubs, and three have fireplaces. Three are smaller – one, the River Room, big enough only for a pineapple-framed double bed and a fireplace. Five offer glimpses of the river; three look onto the surrounding Thousand Islands Country Club fairways. The ultimate quarters are in the sumptuous main-floor Kashmir Garden Suite, as elegant and comfortable as they come. Its faux-leather walls enclose a dramatic kingsize canopy bed, leather sofa and chair, a TV in a French armoire, a private patio and a see-through fireplace into the soaring bath, which holds a corner whirlpool tub and a separate rainforest shower. The main-floor common rooms at the rear of the house can best be described as majestic: A large living room opens to a big sun porch and the wall is mirrored so the space seems even larger. Another curving section of the wraparound sun porch serves as the staging area for a breakfast to remember. The leisurely repast is spelled out daily on a blackboard. It begins at 9 with a choice of exotic juices and remarkable pastries, in our case a pear and cherry crisp, raspberry danish and English almond loaf. We sampled Dudley's specialty peach and blueberry pancakes, light as a feather, before digging into Kathy's Russian eggs, a dish that her grandmother had served in Hungary. Dudley performs weddings in the substantial Grace Chapel with its beautiful stained-glass cross, flanked outside by tiered decks, a waterfall and Japanese garden. Nearly three acres of lawns and gardens, a wildflower expanse, humming birds and even a stunning, five-foot-wide birdhouse built as a replica of the Hart House add to the ambiance of a place that soothes the soul.

(315) 482-5683 or (888) 481-5683. www.harthouseinn.com. Eight rooms and suites with private baths. Doubles, $135 to $315.

Trinity House Inn, 90 Stone St. South, Gananoque, Ont. K7G 1Z8.
Yachtsmen who often sailed in the Thousand Islands while vacationing from Toronto, Jacques O'Shea and the late Brad Garside opened this uncommonly urbane small inn in a dignified 1859 house, whose bricks imported from the Trinity district in Scotland account for its name. "We're not on the water," acknowledges Jacques, "so we had to bring the water to us." That accounts for the tiered lily pond, waterfall, fountains and water garden in the showy back yard – a lush, floral, watery oasis shutting out the sights and sounds of busy Gananoque just outside. Inside, part of the main floor is given over to an elegant restaurant (see Where to Eat), which showcases some of the art works from the downstairs art gallery. Lately, the gallery has been reduced in size to accommodate the plush Prince Regent Suite, all dark

and intimate with exposed limestone walls, queensize bed, wet bar with mini-fridge and sitting area, double jacuzzi and separate shower. The six upstairs guest rooms are named after favorite islands. Jacques collects the beautiful oriental screens that accent some of the rooms, which are handsomely furnished with splashy oriental and Victorian touches. All are centrally air-conditioned and have TVs, though the tiny Georgina is so cramped its TV can be viewed only from the inn's sole double bed. Abundant amenities include bath gels, toiletries, crystal ice buckets, hair dryers, irons and ironing boards. Next door in the building that held the old jail is "The Lock-Up," a four-person suite with kitchen, dining area and private balcony. A screen of cranes, a masterpiece in the downstairs hall of the main house, has been supplemented by two bronze sculptures of blue herons the partners brought back from Key West. Inn guests enjoy a stunning parlor with a shiny black floor, white rug and white sofas, and a rear deck and patio with umbrellaed tables overlooking the gardens. The complimentary breakfast includes juice, fruit salad, a basket of homemade muffins and breads, plus hot and cold cereals. By reservation, Jacques takes guests on cruises through the Islands aboard his 30-foot yacht, Lady Trinity.

(613) 382-8383. Fax (613) 382-1599. www.trinityinn.com. Six rooms and two suites with private baths. Doubles, $120 to $194. Suites, $194 and $243. Closed briefly in winter.

GrayRock B&B, 13 Connor Dr., R.R. 2, Gananoque L7G 2V4.

Backing up to the Thousand Islands Parkway with a glimpse of the river beyond is this elegant contemporary in a residential area of large new homes. Joyce Burgess, who was "born on one of the thousand islands," and her husband Rick, owner of a medical supply company in Kingston, built the home in 1992 and opened it as a B&B in 1998 when they became empty nesters. They retreated to the 3,000-square-foot lower level and turned their master bedroom on one side of the main floor into a luxury room with a king bed, a large built-in TV over the fireplace, two club chairs and an enormous, six-piece bathroom with – count 'em – jacuzzi tub, walk-in shower, bidet, toilet and twin vanities, plus a walk-in closet. Upstairs are three more rooms, each with queensize bed and opening onto a rear balcony overlooking two acres of manicured lawns with the river visible across the parkway. Two rooms join to make a family suite with a skylit bath between. All have TVs, thick carpeting, walk-in closets and a comfortable air. Ditto for the fancy living room, off a soaring entry hall tiled in marble. Breakfast is served at a table for eight in the formal dining room or in the rear courtyard. The fare includes fresh fruit, specialty breads and perhaps bacon and eggs or french toast.

(613) 382-1255. www.grayrockbandb.com. Two rooms with private baths and two rooms with shared bath. Doubles, $95 to $195.

Rockport Boathouse Country Inn, 19 Front St., Rockport, Ont. K0E 1V0.

This is foremost a restaurant right on the water in the placid hamlet of Rockport (see Where to Eat). But there's an attractive small motel with "garden rooms" in back and two quite luxurious B&B rooms upstairs over the restaurant. Both have queen beds, gas fireplaces, balconies overlooking the river, air conditioning and satellite TV. Room 1 in the motel offers a queen bed, private balcony, and whirlpool tub for two. A full breakfast is included in all the rates. Young proprietor Erich Prohaska, who's also known for his cooking, ranks his rooms with the best in the Islands. Breakfast is offered in the restaurant, and there's no more appealing waterside venue than the canopied deck jutting over the river.

(613) 659-2348 or (877) 434-1212. www.boathousecountryinn.com. Eight motel rooms and two B&B rooms with private baths. Doubles, $135 to $185 in motel, $175 and $200 in inn. Closed mid-October to late April.

The Chateau, 29621 State Route 12, Clayton, N.Y. 13624.

The facade of this "new country inn" built in 1922 is modeled on that of a European chateau and backs up to the St. Lawrence from a residential section one mile east of Clayton. David Kay's grandfather bought the property known as the Chateau cottages in the 1950s. David and his wife Virginia, who live on the ground floor, offer four second-floor bedrooms and a common area. Two have king beds, one a queen bed and one has two double beds. A one-bedroom efficiency suite on the third floor with queen bed comes with a living room, kitchenette and patio. The Chateau also offers a waterfront cottage 25 feet from the river with a living room, kitchen and second-floor bedroom. An expanded continental breakfast of cereals, fruit, muffins or bagels is served on a rear veranda overlooking the waterfront. Guests enjoy a swimming pool and a boat dock. The Kays call their accommodations "plain and simple," and they represent good value.

(315) 686-4217. www.chateatucountryinn.com. Five rooms and one cottage with private baths. Doubles, $75 nightly, $400 weekly.

Islander Marina Lodge, 500 Theresa St., Clayton, N.Y. 13264.

The second-floor of a marina was renovated in 2003 to produce seven contemporary bedrooms and a large balcony overlooking the bay and riverfront. Motel-style rooms go off either side of a corridor that runs the depth of the building, so water views are oblique except from the far-end Beau Rivage and Maple rooms, but everyone gets to enjoy the attractive balcony in good weather. The modern rooms have queen beds, TVs and updated baths with showers. Rates vary by room location and size.

(315) 686-1100. www.islandermarina.com. Seven rooms with private baths. Doubles, $125 to $150.

On the River – Literally

Houseboat Amaryllis B&B, Box C-10, Rockport, Ont. K0E 1V0.

Moored alongside the private 4½-acre Alimar Island about ten miles off Rockport is this 100-foot-long, double-deck houseboat built in 1920 as a hunting and fishing lodge. Pieter and Karin Bergen share their ten-room "floating summer house" with up to ten guests, many of whom are attracted by their guided kayak, sailing and biking tours called Amaryllis Adventures. Three guest rooms and a suite overlooking the water are equipped with twin or queen beds and private baths. Each accommodates up to three people, and the suite adds a sitting room. Common facilities include a living room with fireplace, a dining room and a wraparound veranda, and there's space left over for the Bergens and their two children. Pieter usually picks up overnight guests in Rockport after dinner, although the couple offer dinner by arrangement. Omelets or pancakes are standard fare for breakfast. During the day, Pieter leads eco-tours by bicycle, sailboat and foot, "exploring the micro-climate where river and forest meet." He planned to set up an educational nature center on their semi-wild island, a refuge for wildlife. The widely traveled Bergens work in education in the off-season in Toronto, where he teaches part-time and she's with the famed McMichael Canadian Art Collection galleries in suburban Kleinburg.

(613) 659-3513. Winter phone: (416) 767-6464. www.bbamaryllis.com. Three rooms and one suite with private baths. Doubles, $105 to $130. Closed mid-October to May.

Island Boathouse B&B, Fishers Landing, N.Y. 13641.

After operating a B&B in New York's Hudson Valley for four years, Phyllis Gardner returned to her home area to open a B&B in a boathouse on her family's private

Occident Island off Fishers Landing. Guests, who arrive via their own boat or are shuttled over by the hostess, occupy the top floor of the boathouse. It includes a small double bedroom plus a bathroom and a large room holding a sofa and two double beds. The facility accommodates two to six people. A spacious deck overlooks the Rock Island Lighthouse and the seaway shipping channel. A microwave and refrigerator are provided, but no cooking is allowed. The gregarious innkeeper serves a full breakfast by the wood stove in the main house. It begins with a platter of ten kinds of sliced fruit and culminates in a main course of perhaps blueberry pancakes or french toast. No other meals are served, but Phyllis will shuttle guests to the mainland for lunch or dinner. Swimming, sailing and water skiing are the activities of note here.

(315) 686-2272 or (800) 686-6056. www.1000islands.com/occident. Two rooms with bath. Double, $170; $20 each additional. Closed November-April.

Houseboats accommodating up to six adults can be rented by the weekend or week from Remar Rentals, 510 Theresa St., Clayton, N.Y. (315) 686-3579; Houseboat Holidays Ltd., R.R. 3, Gananoque, Ont. (613) 382-2842, or River Queen Houseboating, 505 Thousand Islands Pkwy., Ivy Lea, Ont. (613) 659-3310 or (877) 659-3310.

Motels

Capt. Thomson's Resort, 45 James St., Alexandria Bay, N.Y. 13607.

The Thomson family, who also own Pine Tree Point Resort and the adjacent Captain's Landing floating restaurant here, run this motel, where the riverfront (Main Channel) rooms are blessed with an unbeatable location right over the water with a view across to Boldt Castle. As you watch all the boating activity or take in the sunset, the waves lap at the rocks and birds land on your private balcony (and at one point the hook – with worm – on the fishing line of the young lad fishing from the balcony next door swung around and embedded itself in our balcony as well). The recently renovated rooms are spacious and comfortable; ours had a full bathroom with an extra sink, but also had those skimpy linen-service towels that you can almost read through. New rooms offer jacuzzi tubs. There's a small heated pool out front beside the parking lot and restaurant.

(315) 482-9961 or (800) 253-9229. www.captthomsons.com. Sixty-eight rooms. Doubles, $75 to $179. Closed mid-October to May.

The Ledges Resort Motel, 71 Anthony St., Box 245, Alexandria Bay, N.Y. 13607.

Its location set back from the riverfront near Pine Tree Point rates this small motel a cut above many of the Bay's others. Don't be put off by the rear, L-shaped facade as you arrive; things look much more inviting from the river side. There are broad lawns, the swimming pool has a water slide, and guests can fish from the docks. Bed configurations vary from one double or king to two doubles. The chalet, a floating house in the water, offers three bedrooms and two baths, kitchen and fireplace. There also are newer efficiencies ranging from one to three bedrooms, and a kingsize suite. Every room has TV, telephone, refrigerator and microwave. Rates include continental breakfast.

(315) 482-9334 or (877) 233-9334. www.thousandislands.com/ledges. Twenty-five units. Doubles, $88 to $148. Suite, $125 to $175. Efficiencies by the week, $625 to $1,500; chalet, $1,800. Closed mid-October to May.

Fisherman's Wharf Motel, 16 Sisson St., Alexandria Bay, N.Y. 13607.

All rooms are within 25 feet of the waterfront in this downtown motel, hidden along a side street overlooking the town pier. The 24 rooms are modern and comfortable, with one or two double beds and a few with queensize waterbeds. Most open to the second-floor balcony or a ground-level wharf containing tables and chairs right beside the water. No wonder guests seem to hang out here all day. But unless you close the windows and run the air-conditioner, late-night noise can be a problem, especially on weekends, when young carousers make merry in downtown Alex Bay.

(315) 482-2230. www.thousandislands.com/fwharf. Twenty-four rooms. Doubles, $75 to $99. Closed mid-October to mid-April.

Torchlite Motel & Efficiencies, 19159 Peel Dock Road, Wellesley Island, N.Y. 13650.

Eighteen comfortable motel and efficiency units are available at this secluded waterfront location, on Wellesley Island almost beneath the American span of the Thousand Islands International Bridge. The head-on river view is what sells the snug, two-story place, although free coffee and donuts and a pleasant swimming pool area help.

(315) 482-3550. Winter (315) 682-6330. www.thousandislands.com/torchlite. Eighteen rooms. Doubles, $70 to $90. Closed November-April.

West Winds Motel & Cottages, 38267 Route 12E, Clayton, N.Y. 13624.

Sloping lawns down to the river, a large and attractive pool, a versatile picnic and recreation area, and comfortable motel furnishings make this a good bet in the Clayton area. Twelve remodeled motel units have one or two queen beds. Eight good-looking housekeeping cottages with screened porches are spaced well apart, two near the water, on the tranquil five-acre property. A fishing pier, boat rentals, horseshoe courts and a putting green are among the amenities. Families on extended visits were much in evidence at our stay.

(315) 686-3352 or (888) 937-8946. www.thousandislands.com/westwinds. Twelve rooms and eighteen cottages. Doubles, $58 to $78. Cottages for two to six, $615 to $1,010 weekly. Closed November to mid-May.

Camping

STATE PARKS. Some of New York State's finest parks are in this area and offer campsites among their facilities. **Wellesley Island State Park,** (315) 482-2722, is by far the largest, with 430 campsites and a public golf course. From a marina here you can rent a boat to get to campsites on Canoe or Mary islands. One of the more pleasant sites is **Keewaydin State Park,** (315) 482-3331, a 179-acre former private estate sloping down to the river west of Alexandria Bay off Route 12 and boasting an Olympic-size pool and a marina among its amenities. It's also the headquarters of the Thousand Islands regional state park office, where camping reservations are computerized through Ticketron, (800) 456-2267.

Those who prefer not to rough it in tent or camper may rent cabins by the week at DeWolf Point and Canoe Island. One of us happily spent many a childhood vacation at **DeWolf Point State Park,** (315) 482-2012. Fourteen two-room cabins for four are scattered along the Lake of the Isles shoreline. They're basic and bare, with little more than a refrigerator, bunk beds and two electric lights. Weekly rentals are $94, usually booked well in advance.

Primitive camping is offered in **St. Lawrence Islands National Park,** a UNESCO-designated biosphere reserve. Canada's smallest national park, it consists of 21 islands and Mallorytown Landing on the mainland northeast of Rockport in Mallorytown, (613) 923-5261.

A number of large, privately owned campgrounds are available as well.

Seeing and Doing ———————————— ∽∽∽

On the Water

BOAT TOURS are *the* thing in the Thousand Islands, and more than 75 tour boats from eight cruise lines offer trips up to 52 miles long as often as every hour in season. Sometimes it seems there are more tour boats than private craft in this area seemingly made for powerboats. Sailboats are far less in evidence. Also noticeable are the enormous lakers and ocean-going freighters plodding to and from the Great Lakes through the St. Lawrence Seaway via the American Narrows off Alexandria Bay.

Tour boats vary in size and duration of trip (one to three hours). Some, particularly **Parkway, Rockport** and **Heritage 1000 Islands Cruises** in Canada, boast of small boats that go where the larger ones can't. The three-decker **Gananoque Boat Line** vessels out of Gananoque and Ivy Lea and the large **Uncle Sam Boat Lines** boats out of Alexandria Bay and Clayton let people move around for various vantage points. Tour high points are the millionaires' row cottages around Alex Bay, the Canadian palisades area where the greenish waters are 250 feet deep, and some of the smaller, fancily landscaped islands containing a single home and boathouse. Youngsters might get bored after awhile, but we thoroughly enjoyed hearing all the tidbits about who owned the houses and islands. Uncle Sam's Seaway Island Tour, upwards of three hours long and encompassing both Canadian and American channels between Alex Bay, Rockport and Clayton, is the most comprehensive tour. Trips aboard Parkway's 48-passenger Island Cruise double-decker are said to be the most interesting. You also can take lunch and dinner cruises, and shuttles to Boldt Castle. Basic tour prices are in the $14 to $20 range and include unlimited stopovers at Boldt Castle.

Boldt Castle, Heart Island, off Alexandra Bay, N.Y.
This was to be the testament of the love for his wife of George C. Boldt, a Prussian immigrant who became the most successful early hotel magnate in America, owning the Waldorf-Astoria in New York and the Bellevue-Stratford in Philadelphia. He had spent $2.5 million on a six-story, 120-room Rhineland-style castle with enormous boathouse and power plant when she died in 1904. No one ever tells the cause, although our young boat guide suggested cancer. Work was stopped and visitors wander through the huge, mostly empty rooms, imagining what might have been. Since 1977, the Thousand Islands Bridge Authority has been restoring the castle to the way it was the day she died, and the results are quite impressive, especially the grand staircase of marble. Main-floor exhibits portray the story of George and Louise Boldt and the development of the Thousand Islands. The second floor contains a working craft studio. Visitors on self-guided tours see a fifteen-minute video and explore the Power House and Clock Tower accessed by a stone arch bridge, the Alster Tower (a "playhouse" containing a dance hall and bowling alley), the Hennery, the palatial stone Arch entry and a stone gazebo. The recently restored **Boldt Yacht House,** reached via ferry from the castle or by car on Wellesley Island, is a beauty. The awesome structure holds a collection of antique wooden boats, including some from the original Boldt fleet. The family's three yachts and huge houseboat were moored in slips 128 feet long. The castle is reached by boat tours or shuttles from Alex Bay.

(315) 382-9274 or (800) 847-5263. www.boldtcastle.com. Open daily, 10 to 6:30, mid-May to mid-October, castle to 7:30 in July and August. Heart Island, adults $5.25, children $3. Yacht House, $3 and $2.

Singer Castle on Dark Island, off Chippewa Bay, N.Y.

Self-made New York millionaire Frederick Gilbert Bourne surprised his family in 1904 with this 28-room hunting "retreat" on eight-acre Dark Island. After 100 years as a private residence and a site for weekly religious services, the new owners, a German investment group, opened the turreted, terra cotta-roofed granite castle for tours in 2003 to help fund continuing restoration. The castle includes an elaborate five-story clock tower with Westminster chimes and comes with three boathouses (Bourne, fourth president of the Singer Sewing Machine Co., served many years as commodore at the famed New York Yacht Club). His was the only river castle to be finished and occupied at the beginning of the last century. The architectural marvel was designed by architect Ernest Flagg and modeled on Sir Walter Scott's Woodstock castle in Scotland. Guides in medieval costumes show four floors filled with furnishings and artifacts original to the castle. The labyrinth of secret passageways with metal grates for spying on visitors, turret rooms, a two-story ice house, an indoor squash and basketball court and even a dungeon are highlights. The castle is accessible by personal watercraft and tour boat lines in Alexandria Bay, N.Y., Rockport and Brockville, Ont.

(315) 324-3275 or (877) 327-5475. www.singercastle.com. Tours on the hour daily 11 to 5, late June to September; Thursday-Sunday in off-season. Open Memorial Day to Columbus Day. Adults $12, children $5.

You also can see the Thousand Islands by water taxis, day sailing expeditions, U-Drive Boats, helicopter tours, hot-air balloons and from the 400-foot-high **Thousand Islands Skydeck** on Hill Island (adults, $7.95). The best auto route is along the scenic Thousand Islands Parkway on the Canadian side, with beautiful vistas and frequent picnic spots. The American side is nearly devoid of river views from the main Route 12.

Guided **sea kayaking** expeditions through the islands are led by T.I. Adventures, 38714 Route 12E, Clayton, (315) 686-2000. Full-day and half-day trips, including lunch and equipment, are scheduled. In Ontario, sea kayaking equipment and tours are offered through Misty Isles Lodge, 25 River Road, Lansdowne, (613) 382-4243, and 1000 Islands Kayaking Co., Gananoque, (613) 329-6265.

SPORT DIVING has become big in the Thousand Islands, thanks to recent water purification efforts and the accidental introduction of zebra mussels by freighters from the Black Sea. The region now claims to have some of the best freshwater scuba diving in the world, because of clear water and the number of wrecks that rest on the bottom of the St. Lawrence. Horizontal visibility of 50 to 70 feet in 100-foot depths is not unusual. The St. Lawrence has been a major shipping route since the 1700s, and the numerous shoals have turned mariners' misfortune into a diver's delight. Shipwrecks range from three-masted schooners and pleasure craft to commercial freighters. More than a dozen dive shops in the area rent equipment and offer instruction. Package tours on the region's only Coast Guard-certified diving boat are offered by 1000 Islands Diving Adventures, 335 Riverside Drive, Clayton, (315) 686-3030 or (800) 544-4241.

FISHING is popular, especially around Alexandra Bay ("bass fishing capital of the world") and Clayton. Our boat tour guide said 85 species, from pan fish to sturgeon, have been caught, and the world's biggest muskie was landed in the Shoals region. Numerous guides lead fishing parties on chartered boats.

Half Moon Bay Vesper Services. Since 1887, non-denominational vesper services have been conducted by visiting ministers in a secluded bay off Bostwick Island near Gananoque. The congregation arrives and remains in small boats, including canoes, for an hour of hymns and meditation at 4 p.m. on summer Sundays amid a natural water setting gouged in granite by the glaciers. Ushers in canoes distribute hymnals and collect offerings. Boats for people requiring transportation leave at 3 and 3:30 p.m. from the Gananoque Bay Dock.

A fun day trip from stateside is by ferry to **Wolfe Island,** largest of the Thousand Islands, and then on to waterside Kingston, Ont., the Islands' largest city. We started from Cape Vincent, N.Y., arriving at 1:55 for the 2 p.m. ferry, only to be told by the Customs official that the boat operator had left two minutes earlier – "2 o'clock, according to his watch." An hour later, we boarded the next ten-vehicle ferry ($8), run by the same family since the 18th century. It was a ten-minute ride to the island, a time warp of rolling farmlands, waterfront cottages, a little village called Marysville, an excellent restaurant and nearly 1,500 permanent residents. A free, much larger provincial ferry completes the twenty-minute ride to **Kingston,** a prosperous university city of museums, suave shops and good restaurants.

Waterside Attractions

The Antique Boat Museum, 750 Mary St., Clayton.

Started in 1964 as the outgrowth of the nation's oldest annual antique boat show and auction (still held here the first weekend in August), this former lumberyard has grown into the largest freshwater maritime museum in the United States. Boating enthusiasts have a field day exploring nine new and restored riverfront buildings along the two-acre waterfront complex. They contain all manner of wooden boats, the local St. Lawrence skiffs, old birch-bark canoes, an Adirondack guide boat, exotic yachts, runabouts, outboard motors and such. Proclaimed "the most impressive collection of antique boats in the world," the more than 200 small craft show the ingenuity of builders in adapting to the tricky St. Lawrence waters, our informant said, and you'll marvel at the importance that boating has had here over the years. A yacht in the Cleveland Dodge launch building rests on blocks so visitors can peer under as well as inside via ramps. The Stroh beer family's commuter boat was being readied to go back in the water at one of our visits. A couple of buildings are employed for classes run by the museum's Boat Building School staff. The fine River Memories shop carries books and nautical gifts. The Seagull, a 40-foot cruiser built in 1935, takes up to twelve passengers on 50-minute trips around the islands on the hour for $12. Speedboat rides in a triple cockpit runabout cost $10. The museum, earlier considered a sleeper with great potential, has realized its potential as a destination site.

(315) 686-4104. www.abm.org. Open daily 9 to 5, mid-May to mid-October. Adults $8, children $4.

Minna Anthony Common Nature Center, 44927 Cross Island Road, Wellesley Island State Park.

Eight miles of trails and walkways crisscross through 600 acres of wooded wetlands, marshes, swamps and rocky knobs for close-up views of varied wildlife – perhaps a thorny porcupine in a tree, beavers splashing in ponds or white-tailed deer loping into the woods. The center's staff offers special trail hikes and nature walks. Perched on a plateau of the reddish-brown Potsdam sandstone characteristic of the area, the museum includes live collections of fish, reptiles and amphibians, plus mounted waterfowl and a beehive with live bees.

(315) 482-2479. Open daily in summer, 8:30 to 8:30, Sunday to 5; rest of year, 8:30 to 4:30, Sunday 10 to 4:30. Parking, $7 in season, free rest of year.

The Gardens at Landon Bay, 302 Thousand Islands Pkwy., Gananoque, (613) 382-2719. Called a unique blending of nature and nurturing, this 175-acre environmental learning center and ecological reserve is just across the parkway from Landon's Bay. Part of the Landon Bay Centre with a 125-site campground, it's home to dozens of themed gardens, walkways, nature trails and such, developed by a variety of community groups. Visitors can wander for hours amidst the flora and fauna. Promoters claim the Lookout Trail has the best natural views of the Thousand Islands. There are butterfly havens, Canadian bogs, hummingbird gardens, birdhouses, osprey nests and more. Open daily mid-May to mid-October, 8 a.m. to 9 p.m. Adults, $4.

The much-used **Thousand Islands Bikepath** parallels the Thousand Islands Parkway (unfortunately for users, on the far side of the highway from the river) on the Canadian side for 22 miles from Gananoque to Brockville. The paved path is popular with joggers, walkers and rollerbladers as well as cyclists. There are frequent rest areas with picnic tables and restrooms, swimming beaches and plenty of vantage points for viewing the river.

Thousand Island Park. Established in 1875 as a church colony, this slice of Victoriana at the west end of Wellesley Island is on the National Historic Register and reminiscent of the Methodist campground at Oak Bluffs on Martha's Vineyard. It's worth a visit for a look at the colorful old cottages and the spacious green with a tabernacle at the far end. Stop at the quirky boutiques upstairs in the restored Wellesley Hotel or at The Guzzle, an old-fashioned ice cream parlor and sandwich shop across the street.

WATER CULTURE. Boaters dock at the highly regarded **Thousand Islands Playhouse,** (613) 382-7020, fashioned from the old Gananoque Canoe Club building, which is right on the river at the foot of Charles Street in Gananoque. Five plays a season are produced in the 350-seat Springer Theatre. The shows, mostly comedies and musicals, are scheduled for about a month each from mid-May through October. A more intimate, 120-seat Firehall Theatre opened in 2004 with two productions. The casts are professional, curtain is Tuesday-Saturday at 8 (also matinees at 2:30 on Wednesday, Saturday and Sunday). Tickets, $25 to $32.

The Historic Thousand Islands Village Foundation has revived part of Gananoque's riverfront along Water Street. Its focal point is the **Arthur Child Heritage Centre of the 1000 Islands,** 125 Water St., (613) 382-2535 or (877) 217-7391. The landmark two-story Victorian "Grand Cottage" with verandas and widow's walk is full of interesting art exhibits, the Canadiana Gift Shop and interpretive displays of the area's natural and cultural history; open daily May-October, admission $2.

SHOPPING has not been among the area's strengths. Downtown Alex Bay is full of ice cream parlors, candy stores and trinket, T-shirt and curio shops, plus a gaudy riverside arcade called the Supercade. It also has **Riverbank Gallery** with good local art, the adjacent **Summers Boutique** for gifts and a small nook dispensing cappuccino and espresso, a shop called **Thousand Islands Originals,** and casual and resort wear at **Bay Trading Clothing Outlet.** Local items and historical memorabilia are on view and for sale at **Cornwall Brothers Store,** run by the local historical society.

On Route 12 between Alex Bay and Clayton is **Captain Spicer's Gift Shop and Gallery,** with gifts, nautical books, clothing, birdhouses and a good selection of marine and local art. In Clayton, the **Gold Cup Farms** store at 242 James St. is a favorite; we passed on the squeaky fresh cheese curd but bought the local River

Rat cheddar cheese (the extra-sharp is great) and tried a couple of the good chocolate cordial candies, tasting of various liqueurs. River art by Michael Ringer is shown at the **St. Lawrence Gallery** on Riverside Drive. Furnishings and decorative accessories geared to cottage living appealed at **Porch & Paddle.**

For a different experience, consider **The Boateak,** a shop above a boathouse on Bluff Island off Clayton. Reached via a free shuttle boat by appointment, (315) 686-3190, it features American arts and crafts from 300 artisans and antiques, including Sid Bell wildlife jewelry, Adirondack chairs, stuffed animals and pierced lampshades.

Serious shoppers find lackluster most places along Gananoque's main street, though often Americans are intrigued by Canadian stores, and English china and woolens are priced lower than in the States. Of more interest are the shops in the new Historic Thousand Islands Village along the restored Water Street riverfront. It includes picturesque buildings housing **River Myst Clothing Co., Leeds County Bookstore, Island Beach Co.** and **Gallery Vaga.**

Where to Eat

Dining in the Thousand Islands region adheres to the surf-and-turf syndrome with, surprisingly, Maine lobster and prime rib heading the list. Local fish is rarely on restaurant menus; even Thousand Islands dressing is seldom mentioned.

The Best for Food

Casa Bella, 110 Clarence St., Gananoque, Ont.

The region's most sophisticated dining unfolds in three cozy dining rooms seating 50 at this, the worthy successor to the long-running regional Canadian restaurant known as The Cook Not Mad. Chef-owner Stev George and his wife, Deanna Harrington, took over the Victorian house a block from the water in 2002 and restored the dining operation as well as the original B&B. Both culinary school graduates who have cooked at leading restaurants across Canada, the young couple are serious about Mediterranean cuisine, as attested by the exotic tasting menus and à-la-carte dinners, plus off-season cooking classes and wine tastings. The changing offerings might begin with housemade tagliatelle with asparagus, fiddleheads and sturgeon caviar or pan-seared Quebec foie gras with corn pancakes and balsamic syrup. Main courses range from grilled Pacific sockeye salmon with mascarpone risotto to wild caribou with elderberry sauce. Dessert could be madagascar vanilla bean crème brûlée or panna cotta with berries and lemon vincotto. The night's table-d'hôte menu ($38) represents good value, and separate five-course tasting menus ($65) feature meat and fish. Upstairs are four overnight guest rooms, one with private bath and a distant river view, renting for $85 to $160 a night.

(613) 382-1618 or (866) 382-1618. www.eatatbella.com. Entrées, $24 to $35. Dinner, Tuesday-Saturday from 5:30 May-October, Friday-Saturday in off-season. Closed January and February.

The Gananoque Inn, 550 Stone St. South, Gananoque, Ont.

The best riverfront view in Gananoque opens up from the dining room and a pleasant outdoor deck at this rejuvenated inn. A couple of new executive chefs have elevated the food to match. At noon, sitting beneath colorful umbrellas on the geranium-bedecked balcony, we enjoyed a stellar lunch of mussels and spinach ravioli stuffed with a delicate tomato and herb cream sauce that cried out for sopping up with a fresh loaf of bread (complimentary on request) as well as an appetizer of bruschetta of tomatoes, garlic and cheese on a baguette, accompanied by a pricey little green salad. Our accommodating college-age waitress turned out to be the daughter of the owner, who has markedly upgraded the entire dining and lodging facility. The dinner menu ranges widely from cornmeal-encrusted pickerel fillet with apple-cider mayonnaise and mushroom-crusted salmon with lemon-caper vinaigrette to chicken breast stuffed with goat cheese and grilled veal chop with marsala-peppercorn sauce. The seafood chowder splashed with pernod makes a good starter. The main dining room is pristine in white linens. Food also is available in a dark and rustically old-school pub, **Muskie Jake's Tap & Grill,** which also offers a balcony overlooking the water.

(613) 382-2165 or (800) 465-3101. Entrées, $21.99 to $26.99, pub $14.95 to $18.95. Lunch, 11:30 to 2. Dinner, 5:30 to 10, weekends only in winter. Pub open daily year-round.

Trinity House Inn, 90 Stone St. South, Gananoque, Ont.

A more glamorous setting for dining in these parts is hard to come by. Innkeeper Jacques O'Shea upgraded what started as a small bistro into a full-fledged dinner operation in two formal dining rooms and an enclosed veranda. Seating is on comfortable upholstered armchairs or cushioned bentwood chairs at well-spaced tables dressed in black, red and green floral cloths. A large deck and patio overlooking a waterfall and colorful gardens offer al fresco dining in season. Jacques oversees a chef and staff working out of an incredibly tight kitchen space and, at one visit, had just made a refreshing mandarin mousse cake for dessert. He calls the basically continental fare "modern country house cuisine," with an emphasis on garnishing and presentation. That translates to main courses like farm-raised trout with cucumber-caper salsa, lemon-garlic shrimp, chicken and pork roulade, confit of duck with mandarin orange and ginger glaze and pecan-crusted rack of lamb with raspberry-mint demi-glace. Start with baked brie, mussels marinière or a smoked duck and citrus salad. Finish with hazelnut truffle mousse, deep-dish Georgia pecan pie or any of the chef's special concoctions.

(613) 382-8383 or (800) 265-4871. Entrées, $18.95 to $29.95. Dinner, Tuesday-Sunday from 5:30. Closed weekdays, November-April.

The General Wolfe Hotel, Wolfe Island, Ont.

People on both sides of the border consider this little-publicized spot among the tops for dining in the Islands. The fact that it's on an island, reached by a free twenty-minute ferry ride from Kingston and a two-minute walk from the landing, adds to its appeal. The exterior of the renovated 1853 structure looks like a typical Canadian village roadhouse/hotel, but three formal dining rooms with a glimpse of the water are country pretty, and a pianist entertains weekends in summer. Eliska Ismail continues the tradition launched by her late father, ex-Czech hotelier Miroslav F. Zborovsky. She and her staff maintain his ambitious "continental nouvelle" menu that ranges widely from dover sole, coquilles St. Jacques and frog's legs to duck à l'orange, chateaubriand and steak diane. Those in the know go for his specials of the day, a complete table d'hôte dinner for a bargain $32.95. You might start with French onion soup au gratin and caesar salad, select from a choice of grilled tuna garnished with citrus wedges and cilantro, roasted pheasant with burgundy sauce, sirloin steak with lemon-parsley butter or rack of lamb, and end with crème brûlée or French pastries and coffee. Wines are pleasantly priced by Ontario standards, starting at $24. Upstairs are nine air-conditioned bedrooms with private baths and TV, with double, queen or kingsize beds and five with jacuzzi tubs, priced accordingly, $55 to $115.

(613) 385-2611 or (800) 353-1098. www.generalwolfehotel.com. Entrées, $21.95 to $35.95. Dinner by reservation, Tuesday-Sunday 5:30 to 8:30. Casual tavern dining open daily. Closed January-March.

The Wellesley Hotel and Restaurant, 42809 St. Lawrence Ave., Thousand Island Park, Wellesley Island, N.Y.

The ever-so-quaint, Victorian-relic community of Thousand Island Park is home of the old Wellesley Hotel, which has a seasonal restaurant on the main floor, a second floor of Victorian boutiques and a wing of eight bare-bones hotel rooms of the old school, now rented as suites with a bedroom and sitting room with a bath in between. The lessees seem to come and go, but we had one of our better meals on the summery dining porch here a few years back. In 2003, the restaurant and hotel operation was leased to Gerry and Diane Brinkman, who upgraded the accommodations as best they could and whose food was an instant hit. The couple, who owned the former Rochester Club Restaurant in Rochester for eleven years, offer a short, affordable menu in the main-floor dining porch with a view of the river. Expect starters like crab cakes rémoulade, yellow perch cocktail, escargots in a skillet with roasted garlic and blue cheese or a rustic steak and spinach tart. Entrées range from Thai sea scallops with a spicy Asian garnish to grilled New York strip steak. Cherry-wood planked salmon and Tuscan-style pork chops are specialties.

(315) 482-3698. www.wellesley-hotel.com. Entrées, $18.95 to $22.95. Dinner nightly, 5 to 9 or 10. Pub daily, noon to 11 or midnight. Closed early October to late May.

The Clipper Inn, 126 State St. (Route 12), Clayton, N.Y.

Locals are partial to the Simpson family's restaurant beside the highway east of Clayton. The exterior and the menu could be anywhere, but the interior, the food and the service are quite distinguished. The dining rooms are contemporary with stained glass, skylights, hanging plants, and cane and chrome chairs at pink and mauve-linened tables spaced well apart, particularly in the dark and intimate room where we were seated. A freebie starter of pasta salad with roasted red peppers, a basket of rolls and bread, and an unusual house salad combining everything from niçoise olives to pepperoni to mandarin oranges hinted of pleasures to come. Among entrées, we lucked out with two specials: the smaller portion of prime rib, a man-size slab of perfect rare beef with horseradish sauce, and garlic-crusted rack of lamb, an extraordinary presentation of nine chops, french fries and broccoli with hollandaise sauce, a serving so abundant that even the lamb-lover among us could not finish. An excellent, modestly priced French cabernet accompanied from a wine list priced from yesteryear. We tried to save room for one of the great-sounding desserts, but could only manage a shared dish of raspberry twist frozen yogurt. Two mints gilded the bill – it was the best $50 dinner we'd had in a long time. Over more than two decades, chef Mike Simpson has deservedly garnered a loyal following for his continental/American fare, especially his shrimp scampi. You can't go wrong with anything on the extensive menu. Skip an appetizer or you'll never finish.

(315) 686-3842. www.clipperinn.com. Entrées, $14.95 to $29.95. Dinner nightly in summer, 5 to 10; Wednesday-Sunday in off-season. Closed November-March.

Jacques Cartier Dining Room, Riveredge Resort Hotel, 17 Holland St., Alexandria Bay, N.Y.

Alex Bay's most glamorous hotel claims its most glamorous restaurant, a fourth-floor beauty in blue and white with windows onto the water on three sides. Elaborate rattan chairs are at tables set with Steuben crystal, alstroemeria and frosted-glass oil candles. A pianist or harpist entertains in season. A team of chefs executes a pretentious French menu that changes every two weeks. Caesar salad and flambéed desserts are prepared tableside. Items like slow-roasted lobster tail, loin of venison and rack of lamb are cooked on a French rotisserie in a space open to the room handsomely bordered with blue and white tile. Other choices range from seafood medley over lemon pepper linguini to filet mignon and grilled veal chop. Appetizers include escargots served in a garlic cream sauce over snow crab and mesclun greens, chiffonade of lobster and wild mushrooms in puff pastry, and sliced caramelized muscovy duck breast with baby spinach and candied pecans. Desserts run to chocolate and strawberry gâteau and grand marnier torte. Three meals a day are available in the hotel's **Windows on the Bay** restaurant on the ground floor, where we gobbled up the specialty strawberry pancakes for breakfast.

(315) 482-9917. Entrées, $28 to $35. Dinner nightly, 6 to 9:30. Closed mid-October to mid-May.

On the Riverfront

Pine Tree Point Resort, Alexandria Bay, N.Y.

We can think of no better riverside setting for the $16.95 New Orleans-style Sunday jazz brunch than the outdoor terrace surrounded by pines and water or, for dinner, the small Sunset Room off the larger Voyageur dining room at Pine Tree Point. Here, amid half a dozen tables, we watched freighters pass and the sun set as we warmed up at the salad bar and sampled an adequate rack of lamb and a filet mignon, each garnished with grapes and a good, zesty mix of tomatoes and zucchini. We thought the highly touted pastry cart ordinary, but liked the crème de menthe parfait, big enough for two. Choices ranged from no fewer than four kinds of chicken (the alexandria sautéed with mushrooms and white wine is the house specialty) to garlic rib steak, prime rib and haddock oscar. At a subsequent visit, we enjoyed the Friday night seafood buffet, an all-you-could-eat extravaganza of appetizers (the smoked salmon with proper accompaniments was excellent), hot dishes like grilled tuna and king crab legs, excellent roast beef and lamb, and a table of so-so desserts.

(315) 482-9911. Entrées, $16.95 to $22.95. Dinner nightly, 6 to 10. Sunday brunch in summer, 10 to 2. Open mid-May to mid-October.

Captain's Landing, 49 James St., Alexandria Bay. N.Y.

We ate dinner here, and breakfast, too – such is the watery allure of this floating barge with a restaurant right at river's edge. As you approach, you think you're about to enter a shingled house on a pier between two sections of the Capt. Thomson motels. Inside, you realize you're right on the water when the restaurant pitches slightly as waves from a passing freighter roll in. The Thomson family's latest hit, this has a pleasant candlelit, two-level dining room (all tables with views of the water) on the ground floor and an upstairs lounge with old postcards inlaid in the tables. Both levels come with decks at one end and a couple of open alcoves for outdoor dining. For dinner, we enjoyed poached salmon béarnaise and pork cutlets with a good mushroom-leek sauce. And, because of a kitchen delay on the salmon dish, we took them up on their offer of free desserts (raspberry sherbet and a dense chocolate chambord cake, which went particularly well when mixed together). The extensive dinner menu seems to have lost some of its zip lately in favor of the tried and true, from broiled haddock, seafood pasta and chicken tenders to prime rib and filet mignon. At breakfast, we enjoyed eggs benedict at a table for two in our own outdoor alcove beside the water. The all-you-can-eat breakfast buffet for $6.95 is a popular item these days.

(315) 482-7777. www.captthomsons.com. Entrées, $12.95 to $23.95. Breakfast daily, 7 to 1. Lunch, from 11. Dinner, 5 to 9 or 9:30. Closed mid-October to early May.

Riverside Café, 506 Riverside Drive, Clayton, N.Y.

The large rear deck beside the river is the place of choice for lunch or dinner at this casual storefront establishment that succeeded the innovative Wild Goose Café when it closed. Owners Roger and Cheryl Wakeel scaled down the menu and reduced the hours to the point they had just closed when we arrived for dinner at 7:40 on a summer Sunday. We had planned to try a couple of Greek "specialties:" shrimp à la grecian and chicken souvlaki. Otherwise the dinner menu is Italian/American, ranging from fried clam strips and stuffed sole with basil sauce to prime rib and steak. At another visit, a couple of lunch specials proved adequate: a haddock sandwich and a crab cake sandwich on homemade french bread.

(315) 686-2940. Entrées, $12.95 to $19.95. Open daily, 11:30 to 8 or 8:30, Sunday noon to 7:30. Closed November-April.

Harbor Inn, 625 Mary St., Clayton, N.Y.
Across the street from the Antique Boat Museum complex is this funky, restored 1860s riverfront home with a glimpse of the river. New chef-owners Roger and Vicki Hyde dropped the "diner" from the name, which harked back to the seats around a central dining counter. Theirs is more of a restaurant with assorted tables topped with vinyl cloths, a few tables with water views on the front deck, and a collection of old tools, bottles and such on the walls. We had a good lunch here of monkfish chowder, vegetable quiche and cobb salad, accompanied by a mason jar full of iced tea, the biggest drink we ever saw for 85 cents. For breakfast, you can order Texas french toast with toasted almonds or choose among ten omelets. Roger's background as executive chef for large Texas hotels shows in his dinner specials. Served with soup or salad, they are quite innovative for the area, perhaps sautéed Canadian walleye pike fillets with lemon and sherry, sautéed chicken with asparagus and white wine, and blackened sirloin with sautéed mushrooms and mustard-garlic sauce. The Hydes also offer a large guest rooms and two suites with views of the river, good values at $83 a night.

(315) 686-2293. Entrées, $9.44 to $11.97. Open daily, 6 a.m. to 9 or 10 p.m.

Boathouse Restaurant & Tavern, 19 Front St., Rockport, Ont.
Right on the water in the tiny hamlet of Rockport is this restaurant with indoor tablecloth dining in two rooms and a nifty, 90-seat deck with a striped blue and white canopy at water's edge. People came and went by boat as we lingered on a sunny Saturday a few years back over a hamburger plate with fries and cucumber coleslaw and a good but not very ample caesar salad. There's a vaguely alpine flavor here (oompah music playing at our latest visit), so one is not surprised to find that the owners, the Prohaska family, are from Austria. Son Erich, the executive chef who makes desserts like green tomato pie, apple strudel and fresh raspberry pie, says the Boathouse specializes in "country cottage cuisine." That translates (we guess) to a Maryland crab burger, Mediterranean plate, steamed mussels and breaded zucchini sticks with tzatziki. Fish and chips, chicken fingers, jumbo shrimp on a skewer, grilled salmon, stirfries, and German and Greek specialties are among the offerings. All-natural lagers and ales from the Upper Canada Brewing Company are on tap in the Boathouse Tavern, an adjacent riverfront building featuring pub fare

(613) 659-2348. Entrées, $10.95 to $19.95. Breakfast, lunch and dinner daily, 9 a.m. to 9 p.m., May to early October. Tavern, 11 to 11 daily, year-round.

FOR MORE INFORMATION: Thousand Islands International Tourism Council, 43373 Collins Landing, Alexandria Bay, NY 13607, (800) 847-5263. www.visit1000islands.com.
Alexandria Bay Chamber of Commerce, 7 Market St., Alexandria Bay, NY 13607, (315) 482-9531 or (800) 541-2110. www.alexbay.org.
Clayton Area Chamber of Commerce, 517 Riverside Drive, Clayton, NY 13624, (315) 686-3771 or (800) 252-9806. www.1000islands-clayton.com.
Thousand Islands/Gananoque Chamber of Commerce, 10 King St. East, Gananoque, ON K7C 1E6, (613) 382-3250 or (800) 561-1595. www.1000islandsgananoque.com.

Youngsters cavort in waters of Havana Glen.

Watkins Glen/Seneca Lake, N.Y.

Think of Watkins Glen and car racing probably comes to mind. But think again. The Glen – as the village, a state park from which it takes its name and an auto racetrack are called almost interchangeably – is more than a one-track place. Blessed with a scenic location at the foot of the most sparkling of the Finger Lakes, it has attractions galore.

Not the least are its natural assets, among them Seneca Lake (the deepest, widest and next to longest of the picturesque Finger Lakes), and a hilly terrain of cascading waterfalls, awesome gorges and placid glens. To these scenic and recreational attractions add the two dozen-plus wineries that proliferate across the hillsides on either side of Seneca Lake. They represent the biggest concentration of vineyards in what is now the nation's second largest wine-producing region, and add a new dimension to tourism in what had been primarily a racetrack town.

Watkins Glen's lakefront is enlivened by a 150-slip marina, a 330-foot-long fishing pier crowned with a Victorian gazebo and the Seneca Harbor Park. The park hosts special events like the Watkins Glen Waterfront Festival in late May, launching the summer season with nautical displays, a parade of boats and even a cardboard boat regatta. Excursion boats and a restored schooner ply the southern end of the lake. The downtown is spruced up with plantings, cobblestone walkways and Victorian-style street lamps.

The problem of housing visitors adequately is just being addressed. Most of the area's lodging facilities were built prior to the 1960s in the early years of auto racing here and show their age. A couple of dozen small bed-and-breakfasts have popped up in the last 25 years. But until a private developer or a chain motel operator enters this area where the only non-indigenous establishments are a Burger King, a Subway and a Pizza Hut, visitors will find the lodging and dining choices surprisingly slim for a resort area.

That's unfortunate, because, as local boosters say: the southern Finger Lakes area is "a paradise untapped." And Watkins Glen is at the heart of it all.

Getting There

Watkins Glen is at the southern end of Seneca Lake, about 80 miles southeast of Rochester and 75 miles southwest of Syracuse. From the New York Thruway, take New York Route 14 south from Geneva. Watkins Glen also can be reached from the south via Route 14 off the east-west Route 17 expressway at Elmira-Horseheads.

Where to Stay ────────── ♫♫♫

Accommodations are varied but limited, considering the number of visitors to this area in summer and early fall.

Motels and Lodges

Longhouse Lodge Motel, 3625 State Route 14 at Abrams Road, Box 111, Watkins Glen 14891.

The Mobil and AAA raters like this unpretentious motel high above Seneca Lake two miles north of town, and so do we. It's the only local place of its type making a concerted effort to keep up with the times, and there's luxury B&B lodging in the related Longhouse Manor astride the hill beyond (see below). The motel offers plenty of space for relaxation: on deck chairs outside each unit, on lawn chairs facing each other in a gazebo, and on loungers beside the small heated pool. The spacious rooms are better outfitted than most in the area, and include mini-refrigerators and air conditioning. Some have king or queensize beds. Eight newer deluxe units come with vaulted ceilings, microwaves and TV/VCRs. One efficiency unit has two beds and a pullout sofa to sleep six. Work out on the exercise equipment on the deck at the end

of the deluxe units and enjoy a distant view of the lake. Owners Jim and Mary Franzese offer a complimentary continental breakfast of bagels and English muffins. *(607) 535-2565. Fax (607) 535-5415. www.longhouselodge.com. Twenty-one units. Doubles, $69 to $139*

Glen Motor Inn, 3380 Route 14, Watkins Glen 14891.

This full-service lodging and dining establishment has 40 motel units in two buildings separated by a swimming pool and a third building one level higher. Located down a sharp hillside and shielded from the highway above, the rooms overlook a parking area and Seneca Lake some distance below. Thirty units have water-view balconies, and all have cable television. Rooms are relatively small and spare; we had to bring in a chair from the balcony in order to seat a guest. Run by five generations of the Franzese family, the motel started with a two-bedroom flat rented for $3 a couple in 1937, according to Victor Franzese, a race-car driver of some repute and owner today with his wife Linda. His late mother, Helen Franzese, who called herself "the momma to all the racers," was fond of telling about all the racing celebrities they've entertained over the years in their **Montage** restaurant. *(607) 535-2706. Fax (607) 535-7635. www.glenmotorinn.com. Forty units. Doubles, $88 to $98.*

Rainbow Cove Resort Motel and Restaurant, 3482 Plum Point Road, Himrod 14842.

Twenty-four rooms in two structures have patios or balconies and access to pleasant, shaded grounds leading to the lakefront across Plum Point Road. Our room in the "economy" one-story section dating to 1950 was smaller than the rooms in the "deluxe" two-story section built about 1970. Access to the lake and an impressive pool behind the restaurant are distinct pluses; the folksy atmosphere and stable prices remain from yesteryear. At breakfast, others are likely to join your table in a dining room looking across the lawn to the lake. Dinner is rather more formal. The restaurant recently dropped its traditional prix-fixe meal served family style at 7 in favor of an à la carte menu featuring most of the longtime specialties. Expect choices like spaghetti and meatballs, broiled scallops, chicken parmesan, ham steak with homemade raisin sauce and New York strip steak. Owner Jeff Ripley tells the story of how the original house and the Four Chimneys winery homestead up the road were part of a Hollywood retreat envisioned by Mary Pickford and Douglas Fairbanks Jr. It seems early movie stars made this part of the lake the "Gold Coast" after black and white films were launched in nearby Ithaca. *(607) 243-7535. Twenty-four units. Doubles, $60 to $85. Dinner nightly, 5 to 8. Entrées, $8.95 to $14.50. Closed late October to early May.*

Inns and B&Bs

The Inn at Glenora Wine Cellars, 5435 Route 14, Dundee 14837.

Behind and beneath the winery, this new inn straddling a hillside overlooking Seneca Lake offers upscale guest rooms, a restaurant called **Veraisons** (see Where to Eat) and a conference center. The view of the lake and vine-covered hills is spectacular. Winery principal Gene Pierce designed the low-slung, spread-out board and batten building as a country hotel "to fit in with the architecture of upstate farm country" and to blend into the vineyard. Rooms go off an interior corridor on two floors. Each has a private balcony or patio with a view over vineyards down to the lake. The interior incorporates Stickley mission furniture, including an armoire containing an entertainment center and refrigerator. Our deluxe "Vintner's Select" room was one of ten with a king bed and a corner fireplace, plus a spacious bath with whirlpool tub, separate shower and pedestal sink. Others have two queen beds, but no whirlpool tub nor fireplace. Each room comes with a coffeemaker, hair dryer and a chilled bottle of our favorite Glenora riesling. At breakfast, the Veraisons poached eggs, topped with crabmeat and hollandaise sauce and served over herbed risotto cakes, was first-rate.

(607) 243-9500 or (800) 243-5513. www.glenora.com. Thirty rooms with private baths. Doubles, $139 to $235, EP.

Idlwilde Inn, 1 Lakeview Ave., Watkins Glen 14891.

The biggest house in town – occupying a 2.5-acre hilltop site with a view of Seneca Lake in the distance – was restored to its former glory in 1999. Now an elegant, European-style B&B, it offers spacious public rooms, a nifty wraparound porch furnished in rattan, and a variety of guest accommodations ranging from small to grandiose. The eighteen-room Shingle-style mansion, beige with a red slate roof, was built as a summer home in 1892 by Long Islanders. They gave it the same name (but different spelling) as the old Idlewild airport. Long occupied by the family of local salt industrialist W.W. Clute, it was in rundown condition when it was acquired by John van den Hurk, a Dutch-born former J.C. Penney Co. executive, and his Italian wife Maria. They oversaw the painstaking restoration and are on hand full-time, assisted on weekends by her brother and sister-in-law, Carlo and Nancy Castellana of Stamford, Conn. Guests enter through a large hall, one side of which opens into a music room and a dining room big enough to seat 30. Nine guest units offer lake views, a couple from private balconies. The biggest is the master suite, an awesome second-story space with a step-up kingsize bed, two decorative fireplaces, a front sitting room, a side sun porch and a private balcony curving around a cupola, not to mention a bathroom with one of the largest walk-in showers we ever saw. Also popular is a third-floor suite, fashioned from a former ballroom. It has a queen poster bed and its balcony is higher, thus yielding the best lake panorama in the house. (A good lake view also is offered from the window seats and sitting area of a new room added across the lawn in the carriage house.) The west wing of the house contains another suite with a bathroom that Maria bills as "like a cruise to nowhere," given its circular windows resembling those in a ship. Two tiny rooms here share a hall bath, and a fourth room on the main floor is handicapped-accessible. Decor is formal and understated in the European tradition, with an emphasis on large and sturdy antiques. One of the two living rooms holds a TV. For breakfast, fruit salad, pastries and cereals might be followed by scrambled eggs, pancakes, french toast or cheese strata. Outside are a sunken garden with a fishpond and a dollhouse that looks like a gazebo.

(607) 535-3081. www.idlwildeinn.com. Five rooms and three suites with private baths and four rooms with shared baths. Doubles, $90 to $185. Suites, $210 to $235.

Nautical Nights Bed & Breakfast, 4280 Locust Road, Dundee 14837.

Squeezed on the shore beneath Seneca Lake and a 100-foot cliff is this wonderful and deluxe new B&B. Michelle and Brad Carman bought an 800-square-foot cottage and spent seven years renovating and expanding before opening in 2003. At water's edge, a broad, 125-foot-long deck wraps around the interior, which is blessed with floor-to-ceiling windows and doors that take full advantage of the view. Two guest rooms with queen beds on the main floor have a corner jacuzzi tub in one case and a two-person shower in the other. Upstairs is the enormous Heron's Roost, named for the herons that nest nearby and "put on quite a show for guests," according to Michelle. Bigger than the original cottage, it has a kingsize bed at one end and a queen bed at the other, with windows opening onto a 34-foot balcony. Just outside is the snug Beach Bungalow, a honeymoon hideaway with its own deck. All rooms have hardwood floors, tiled baths, TVs and contemporary lodge decor. On the main floor, a common living room opens onto an enclosed porch where a buffet breakfast is put out. Fruits, yogurt and cereal preceded orange-pecan french toast the day of our visit. The only downside is the incredibly steep driveway that cuts through the 25-acre wooded property off State Route 14 and drops down the cliff. Once you descend, you may never want to leave.

(607) 243-7703. www.nauticalnights.com. Three rooms and one cottage with private baths. Doubles, $140 to $235. Closed November to Memorial Day.

Magnolia Place, 5240 Route 414, Hector 14841.

Seneca Lake is on view in the distance from the hilltop location of this renovated 1830s farmhouse redesigned for comfort and romance by innkeeper Theresa Kelly Remmers. There are new wraparound decks on two floors, guest rooms with fireplaces and soaking or whirlpool tubs, lacy canopy beds and – quite a sight – an attached new building with a four-foot deep swimming pool, skylights and a wall of windows and columns. There's a king bed in the Orient room, but the rest are queen beds. Rooms vary from the airy front-corner Pink room with a glass table and two ice-cream parlor chairs in the bay window opening onto a wide deck to the side Rose room, which appears dark and formal in contrast. The rear Magnolia room has a queensize bed draped in sheer white lace, a fireplace and a jacuzzi for two in the corner, with a shower in the bathroom. More lace envelops the queen bed in the new front Champagne room, whose occupants at our visit liked its jacuzzi tub and its access to a deck and hailed the breakfasts as "unbelievable." Local fruits, homemade granola and pastries precede the main course, perhaps the specialty baked blueberry french toast or corn fritters with smoked salmon, crème fraîche and a poached egg. Said breakfast is taken in a country kitchen big enough for a harvest table set for eight with two extra side tables for two. More seating is available in the formal dining room, the front living room and the side porch.

(607) 546-5338. Fax (607) 546-5339. www.magnoliawelcome.com. Eight rooms with private baths. Doubles, $130 to $200.

Sunset on Seneca, 3221 Route 414, Burdett 14818.

Without so much as a sign or other identification, this contemporary-style house with decks and docks onto Seneca Lake looks rather like a yacht club. But Donna and Frank Davis converted the former physician's home into a low-key B&B. Their two-story house of weathered clapboard is right on the shore at the southern end of the lake, facing the sunsets to the west from an expansive wraparound deck. "You enjoy the whole lake – not just a lake view," says Donna. Lounge chairs await on the deck, along with tables and a seven-person hot tub. The enclosed sun porch is furnished in rattan. An open stairway from an atrium-style living room leads to a large reading/game room upstairs. Each guest room has a queen bed and satellite TV with DVD. Donna serves a full breakfast at a table for eight beside the open kitchen or on the outside deck. The fare might be omelets to order, quiche, lox and bagels or stuffed French toast. The large docking area that made us think this was a yacht club includes two boat lifts and two jet-ski ramps.

(607) 535-6973 or (800) 233-5752. Fax (607) 535-9219. One room with private bath and two rooms with shared bath. Doubles, $135 to $185.

Longhouse Manor, 3137 Abrams Road, Watkins Glen 14891.

Bill and Carol Franzese, who got their start at the Longhouse Lodge Motel, opened some of the area's fanciest B&B accommodations in the lower level of their sprawling three-level house on a slope above the motel. With their son Jim and daughter-in-law running the motel, they concentrate on the B&B. Four large rooms are individually decorated, carpeted in green and furnished in the hotel style. A couple have kingsize poster beds, while a third offers two iron canopied double beds. Pull-out sofabeds are standard. TVs and telephones are among the room amenities. A large common recreation room/lounge with a pool table and a wood stove is popular with guests. So is the manor's new swimming pool beside a landscaped garden, overlooking the lake in the distance. There's also a putting green. Lounge furniture invites relaxation around the pool (the expansive deck that caught our eye off the first floor is reserved for family). The Franzeses put out a continental breakfast at 8, and offer a full breakfast at 8:30.

(607) 535-2565. Four rooms with private baths. Doubles, $119 to $249.

The Seneca Lake Watch, 104 Seneca St. (Route 14), Watkins Glen 14891.
A wraparound veranda and a couple of upstairs porches called "watchtowers" afford views of Seneca Lake from this ornate Queen Anne Victorian home on a hillside on the northern outskirts of town. George and Julie Conway, who took over from his parents, pamper guests in five bedrooms and a couple of antiques-filled common rooms. Two front bedrooms, the Keuka with king bed and balcony and the Cayuga with queen bed, open to a tiny balcony affording lake views. Two other queen-bedded rooms and a large room with a king bed and a twin bed are in back. They are furnished with floral comforters and wicker chairs. Guests help themselves to coffee and tea in an upstairs kitchen. The first risers in the morning get to enjoy a cup of coffee on the second-floor watchtower; the rest may go to the spacious sun deck in back. Breakfast is served at a lace-covered table beneath three original, back-lit stained-glass windows in the dining room overlooking a small garden fountain and a busy bird feeder. The fare is elaborate: perhaps sour-cream coffee cake, broiled grapefruit and sausage patties with apple pancakes or a scrambled egg dish with whipped cream cheese. The sound effects are music and – a new one on us – the singing of the birds amplified through a microphone in the feeder.

(607) 535-4490. Five rooms with private baths. Doubles, $85 to $130.

The Manor Bed & Breakfast at Castel Grisch, 3390 County Route 28, Watkins Glen 14891.
Founded by a Swiss family because its hillside location reminded them of their native land, this substantial B&B is part of an estate winery with a picturesque restaurant overlooking Seneca Lake. New owners Christopher and Erin Schiavone carry on the European traditions of their predecessors. They offer four bedrooms for overnight guests in a distinctive stucco and timbered manor house laced with vines at the crest of the property. A tiled entrance leads to the octagonal living room furnished in rattan; a sunroom adjoins. Upstairs, the Champagne Room, with its own little balcony overlooking the vineyards and the lake, has a kingsize bed and a large bath with double vanity. Two other rooms with queen beds also have balconies. The Riesling Room has a king bed and a tiled bath with a whirlpool tub. The manor has a common sitting room with fireplace and TV and a new hot tub and exercise room. A three-course breakfast might yield scrambled eggs with cheddar cheese and chives, blueberry pancakes or apple-walnut-raisin french toast.

(607) 535-5457. www.themanorbandb.org. Four rooms with private baths. Doubles, $139 to $169.

South Glenora Tree Farm B&B, 546 South Glenora Road, Dundee 14837.
Up quiet South Glenora Road beside Glenora Glen, a couple of miles above the lake, is this tranquil winner of a B&B fashioned from two old dairy barns. Inside,

you'd never know you were in a barn. You cross a wraparound porch full of wooden rockers and gliders to enter a wide-open common area with living room, dining table and guest kitchen running the width of the front of the structure. Doors open unobtrusively off the common area to four guest rooms, all nicely outfitted in country style. Three have queensize beds and the Cherry Room has a king bed and gas fireplace. The prize accommodation is the Willow Suite in the smaller barn above the quarters of owners Steve and Judi Ebert. It offers a small living room with sofabed, a large bath and an airy bedroom with a gas-fired stove, a TV/VCR and a freestanding queensize bed facing a private balcony and a grand view across the 140-acre tree farm. The entire place is centrally air-conditioned, a blessing on the record-hot night we stayed here. The outdoor picnic pavilion with refrigerator and barbecue was a pleasant spot for a takeout dinner. The next morning we were sent on our way with a communal breakfast of juice, fresh fruit, hot oatmeal with the proper brown sugar, and carrot bread and cinnamon rolls.

(607) 243-7414. Four rooms and one suite with private baths. Doubles, $119 to $129. Suite, $149.

Reading House B&B, 4610 Route 14, Box 321, Watkins Glen 14891.

Four guest rooms with oversize beds covered with antique quilts, ample common rooms and a rural property with two farm ponds and all manner of fruit trees commend this rambling white B&B opened in 1990 in Rock Stream by Rita and Bill Newell. A view of Seneca Lake that reminds Bill of his native Hudson River area doesn't hurt. You can sit under an arbor atop the hillside garden and watch guests trying to negotiate the meadow maze with a panoramic view of the lake as a backdrop. Built in 1820, the Federal-style farmhouse has been expanded and embellished with Greek Revival and Victorian touches. A stunning quilt made locally covers almost an entire wall of one of the two nicely furnished parlors. Two rooms have king beds and two have queens, one of the latter with an extra double bed. We like best the quiet, rear-corner guest room with a king bed and water view. Colorful area rugs and dried flowers enhance all the rooms. The Newells prepare a bountiful breakfast: juice, fruit salad and cereal followed perhaps by mushroom omelet, cheese quiche, frittata, buckwheat pancakes with local sausage or french toast made with french bread. Then they and their guests may take leftover bread to feed the small fish that crowd their ponds.

(607) 535-9785. Four rooms with private baths. Doubles, $75 to $95.

The Inn at Chateau Lafayette Reneau, Route 414, Box 238, Hector 14841.

This restored 1911 farmhouse next to a winery occupies a hillside location overlooking Seneca Lake. A large rear deck and most of the rooms take full advantage of the view. Winery owner Dick Reno bills his inn as a place for a romantic getaway. The five bedrooms are named for wines. The Chardonnay, Cabernet Sauvignon and Riesling have double in-room jacuzzis. Rooms come with polished oak flooring, lace curtains and bed linens, and antique furnishings. A cook prepares hearty breakfasts to order for guests.

(607) 546-2062 or (800) 469-9463. www.clrwine.com. Five rooms with private baths. Doubles, $120 to $150.

Camping

Campgrounds are numerous. **Warren W. Clute Memorial Park** at the southern end of Seneca Lake has complete facilities. Managed by the village (303 Franklin St., Watkins Glen, 535-4438), it offers 90 tent and trailer sites by the day, week or season and a free boat launch to the lake. South of town, fourteen campsites are available at the Town of Montour-owned **Havana Glen Park,** Route 14, Montour Falls, (607) 535-9476, and 110 wooded and open sites are available at the **Watkins Glen KOA,** Route 414 South, Watkins Glen, (607) 535-7404. Sites along the canal leading to Seneca Lake are available through **Montour Marina and Campsites,** Route 14, Montour Falls, (607) 535-9397. North of town are 160 sites in **Paradise Park and Campground,** Route 14A, Reading Center, (607) 535-6600, and the municipally owned **Smith Park & Campground,** Peach Orchard Point, Hector, (607) 546-9911, with lakefront campsites along 2,000 feet of shoreline available by the day or week.

Seeing and Doing

Seneca Lake is flanked by scenic hills that are highest at the southern end around Watkins Glen. The hillsides make perfect growing sites for the vineyards and orchards that crisscross their slopes, creating an unforgettable canvas. Creeks that slice through crevices as they rush toward the lake have forged waterfalls and glens, no fewer than 400 in the southern Finger Lakes area alone.

The Lake and the Glens

Watkins Glen State Park, Franklin Street (Route 14), Watkins Glen.
This is the biggest and best-known of all the gorges. Stone walkways and trails traverse the gorge, which drops nearly 700 feet in two miles from the park's upper entrance to a tunnel entrance south of downtown Watkins Glen. Locally called the eighth wonder of the world, the gorge has sheer, 200-foot-high cliffs, rock caverns, grottos and eighteen waterfalls and cascades. It's an easy, though sometimes wet and slippery walk with 832 steps, most at the lower end. For those who want to walk only one way, a shuttle bus runs between the two entrances every fifteen minutes until 6 p.m. A shorter version of the walk goes as far as the South Entrance. At the South Entrance, the state park has 305 campsites in forests above the gorge as well as an Olympic-size swimming pool with a reported capacity of 2,000 people. The pool costs 50 cents for adults, 25 cents for children.
(607) 535-4511. Park open daily, 8 a.m. to dusk, mid-May to mid-October. Parking fee, $7.

Other Falls. Four nearby falls and glens have their devotees, too. **Chequagua Falls** tumbles 186 feet – just eight feet short of Niagara – into downtown Montour Falls, presenting a startling sight at the end of the village's Main Street. Just south of Montour Falls is **Havana Glen,** a village park with 37 waterfalls. There's an open glen where youngsters wade in a pool and cavort behind a 75-foot-high waterfall. Along Seneca Lake are two other glens and falls, which are less accessible to the public. **Hector Falls** tumbles 165 feet in several cascades above and below Route 414 in Hector. The privately owned **Glenora Glen** meanders through cascades and swimming holes from Route 14 down to one last waterfall in the lakefront hamlet of Glenora.

Captain Bill's Seneca Lake Cruises, North Franklin Street, Watkins Glen, (607) 535-4541. Hour-long boat cruises have been popular for years on the 49-passenger vintage steamer that lives up to its name, Stroller IV. They've been augmented lately by the Columbia, a sprightly blue and white double-decker vessel with a capacity of 150. It offers a two-hour lunch cruise, a three-hour dinner cruise, a late-evening cocktail cruise lasting close to midnight on weekends, and even a Monday night teen dance cruise (which we, on our balcony at the Glen Motor Inn, could hear coming from a long way away). Capt. Bill Simiele gives sightseeing cruises on the Stroller IV, hourly from 10 to 8 in summer; adults $9, children $4. Columbia cruises by reservation: Lunch, Wednesday and Saturday noon to 2, $23.95; dinner, Tuesday-Friday 7 to 10 and Saturday-Sunday 6 to 9, $32.95 (Saturday, $36.95).

Seneca Day Sails, (607) 535-5253, offers sails aboard the vintage schooner yacht **Malabar X** three times daily from the Fishing Pier on the Watkins Glen waterfront. Scheduled cruises are from 10 to noon (fee, $27) and from 1 to 4 and 5:30 to 8, ($37).

Kayaks, canoes and bicycles are rented by Terrapin Outfitters, 219 North Franklin St., Watkins Glen, (607) 535-5420. Guided kayak tours are available, including one three-hour trip through the Queen Catherine Marsh every Sunday starting at 7 a.m. Kayaks may be rented from Kayak Rentals at the Yak Shack, Village Marina at 1 Seneca Harbor, (607) 535-7912. Boat rentals are available at Anchor Inn & Marina, 3425 Salt Point Road, (607) 535-4159 or 535-4759.

The Wineries

Seneca Lake's deep waters and steep hillsides have produced a winegrowing region that has been called "the American Rhineland." The majority of the roughly two dozen wineries are clustered along the lake's west side – the densest concentration outside California's Napa Valley. All are relatively small to mid-size and specialize in European and California-style viniferas. They are open for wine tastings and sales (most for a price – refundable with purchases – ostensibly to discourage freeloading tipplers).

The largest producer of classic vinifera wines in the East is **Glenora Wine Cellars,** which has grown from 5,000 cases in 1977 to 40,000 cases today. It's known for prize-winning chardonnays and dry rieslings, and has started making sparkling wines. It offers an audio-visual presentation and tastings in the expanded showroom, or you can feast on wine, food and view at its new Veraisons restaurant.

Farther up the lake's west side, the winery at the **Hermann J. Wiemer Vineyard** is very small and very serious, and has many national awards to show for it. **Four Chimneys Winery** at Himrod produces organic wines, including an Eye of the Bee blend of Concord grape and honey. Views of Seneca Lake are afforded from six small wineries along Route 14: **Lakewood Vineyards, Hickory Hollow Wine Cellars, Torrey Ridge Winery, Seneca Shore Wine Cellars** and **Fox Run Vineyards.**

Castel Grisch, which looks more like a chalet, is close to Watkins Glen on the lake's western shore. It offers tastings in a showroom and meals in a large, European-appearing café and restaurant with outdoor deck overlooking Seneca Lake.

The largest winery on the east side of the lake is **Wagner Vineyards** in Lodi. Owner Bill Wagner uses well a spectacular vineyard setting overlooking the lake. Here are an architecturally striking octagonal winery, a microbrewery and an adjacent restaurant and open deck perfect for sipping wines with lunch or a snack.

Five smaller wineries on the east side of the lake also are worth a visit. **Chateau Lafayette Reneau** offers a substantial tasting room and gift shop in a restored barn with a great picnic deck overlooking the lake, plus a B&B next door. **Red Newt Cellars** in Hector has a good bistro. **Logan Ridge Wine Cellars** affords a panoramic lake view from its hilltop perch, plus fine dining at Petioles Restaurant. **Standing Stone Vineyards** has won numerous awards and is augmented by the Smokehouse Café. An architecturally stunning Greek Revival barn is the stylish setting for production and tasting of fine wines at **Lamoreaux Landing Wine Cellars.**

Other Attractions

Bird and wildlife watching is offered in **Queen Catherine Marsh,** an 890-acre state-owned wetland, fish and wildlife preserve. It's accessible by boat, foot or car off the east side of Route 14 between Watkins Glen and Montour Falls.

Hiking and camping are popular in the **Finger Lakes National Forest,** which embraces 13,000 acres of wildlife and forestry management land in Hector. The forest offers 25 miles of trails (part of the 650-mile Finger Lakes Trail network) for hikers and horseback riders. Nine primitive campsites are available at the Blueberry Patch Campground, a wooded area beside five acres of blueberries. The Catherine Valley Trail offers thirteen miles of hiking and biking terrain between Seneca Harbor Park in Watkins Glen and the Mark Twain State Park.

Watkins Glen International, Box 500, Watkins Glen, (607) 535-2481. The widely known Watkins Glen auto races started in 1948 and became world-famous for the annual Grand Prix, a three-day weekend of Formula One racing. Rescued from bankruptcy in 1983 by a subsidiary of the nearby Corning Glass Works, the hilltop racetrack is now owned by the corporation that runs the Daytona 500. Six major racing weekends are scheduled from June through September. The racing crowd, upon which the town depends, is a mixed blessing. Upwards of 150,000 fans descend upon the area and fill the business coffers while disturbing the area's peace and quiet. Race schedule and prices vary.

Watkins Glen Grand Prix Circuit Tour. Historical signs have been placed along the original 6.6-mile route of the Grand Prix race, which started and ended in front of the Schuyler County Courthouse and went up hill and across dale. With a brochure available from the Chamber of Commerce, you can trace the original course used from 1948 to 1952. As the brochure claims, for those who were here in the early days, it is a sentimental journey and for those who have never been here, it is a lesson in motor racing history. The annual Watkins Glen Grand Prix festival the weekend after Labor Day starts Friday in downtown Watkins Glen and celebrates the heritage of road racing.

The new **International Motor Racing Research Center and Museum** at 610 South Decatur St., (607) 535-9044, appeals to racing fans. Its exhibits and collections of fine art, racing posters, race programs, periodicals, photographs and memorabilia document the history of motor sports. Open Monday-Saturday 9 to 5, free.

Racing memorabilia is displayed in nearly every restaurant and tavern hereabouts. The Seneca Market, the old three-story Frost Machine Shop foundry that had been a keystone of the lakefront development inspired by the Rouse Company, failed after a decade or so. Its space was taken over by Watkins Glen International as a retail area called **The Shop.**

SHOPPING. The choices are limited, unless you go on wine-buying sprees at the vineyards. The biggest store in town is **Famous Brands Outlet** at 412 Franklin St., with good discounts on Woolwich, Levi's, Wrangler, Timberland, Dexter and the like. Other shops come and go along Franklin Street, but one we hope will make it is **Seneca Lake Jewelry and Pottery,** whose wares are suave in an area otherwise lacking. A Chamber of Commerce source said there are enough antiques shops "to make a serious antiquer comfortable," although we were hard-pressed to find more than one of note. **Sullivan Homemade Candies** sells candies cooked in copper kettles and dipped in chocolate. A coffee bar is featured at **Glen Mountain Market,** which offers baked goods.

Out of town, the seasonal **Skyland Farm Craft Gallery & Café** is a must stop at 4966 Route 414, Hector. In a 200-year-old barn built around a tree, potter Barbara

Hummel displays her own work along with items from 150 regional artisans. A spiral staircase winds around the two-story-high oak tree to a viewpoint overlooking the extensive gardens, farmyard animals and Seneca Lake. The café offers light lunches and fifteen flavors of Italian gelatos, and we're told the baked desserts are to die for.

Where to Eat

Food with a View

Seneca Harbor Station, 3 North Franklin St., Watkins Glen.

The best up-close views of Seneca Lake are offered at this jaunty newcomer fashioned from the old train station. Co-owners Mark Simiele and his sister Gina, whose father launched Captain Bill's Seneca Lake Cruises next door, restored the station inside and out. The interior seats 100 in a light and airy nautical theme. The covered outdoor platform with a bar holds another 90 for lakeside dining and imbibing. Mark bills the food as "casual resort dining." The extensive menu starts with shrimp gumbo, steamed clams, potato skins, Buffalo wings, fisherman's salad and the like. Seafood pastas are the signature dinner entrées. Others vary from rainbow trout florentine, lobster and snow crab to St. Louis pork ribs, prime rib, grilled filet mignon with garlic butter and combos like steak and crab. Dessert could be orange-raspberry rum cake, caramel apple pie or Irish whiskey fantasy.

(607) 535-6101. www.senecaharborstation.com. Entrées, $13.99 to $24.99. Lunch daily, 11:30 to 3:15. Dinner nightly, 4:30 to 9 or 10. Closed December-March.

Veraisons Restaurant, 5435 Route 14, Dundee.

This large restaurant – part of the Inn at Glenora Wine Cellars – yields smashing views of Seneca Lake from its handsome dining room as well as its expansive outside deck overlooking vineyards and valley. The interior has a vaulted ceiling, white walls with wood trim and well-spaced tables decked out in green and beige. We booked a table on the deck for a dinner that began with a complimentary tapenade with crackers. A loaf of bread sliced on a board and a choice of excellent salads (one bearing grapes, toasted pine nuts and shaved ricotta on baby greens) came next. Main courses were excellent Montauk scallops served with a corn salsa and herbed risotto cake and succulent medallions of grilled Chilean sea bass, sauced with herbed pinot blanc and served with roasted Israeli couscous. Dessert was a flavorful port-poached pear and ice cream. Executive chef Arthur Kelly Jr. also offers pan-seared duck breast with peach-mandarin orange compote, apricot-stuffed brace of quail in a phyllo nest and Kansas City strip steak with meritage demi-glace. The interesting lunch menu might include a pork tenderloin salad, a bison burger and a broiled crab imperial "disc" sandwich with chardonnay mayonnaise on grilled sundried tomato bread. Linger with a bottle of Glenora chardonnay and you might never want to leave.

(607) 243-9500 or (800) 243-5513. Entrées, $19 to $27. Lunch daily, 11:30 to 3. Dinner, 5 to 9 or 10.

Castel Grisch, 3380 County Route 28, Watkins Glen.

Founded by a Swiss couple who built the beautiful manor house (now a B&B) glimpsed as one enters the property, this winery restaurant is notable for its alpine ambiance. Two large European-looking dining rooms dressed in burgundy and pink have full-length windows onto a large, partly canopied deck strung with tiny white lights. Beyond is a view of Seneca Lake beneath steep hillsides. The lunch menu is unusual for the area, from the Hungarian goulash soup to the duck salad and salade niçoise. Among open-face sandwiches are wiener schnitzel and bratwurst, served with warm German potato salad. Or you can get a winemaker's fruit and cheese plate. Expect some of the same at night, plus pasta dishes (spaetzle or pasta provençal) and entrées like wiener schnitzel, sauerbraten, broiled halibut, roast duck and delmonico steak with roesti potatoes. A German buffet is a draw on Friday nights for $18.95. Desserts include apple strudel and chocolate-raspberry mousse with chardonnay topping.

(607) 535-9614. Entrées, $15.95 to $21.95. Lunch daily, 11 to 4. Dinner, Friday-Saturday 5 to 9, Sunday 3 to 7. Sunday brunch, 11 to 2. Closed November to mid-May.

Petioles Restaurant, 3800 Ball Diamond Rd., Hector.

Wine-inspired regional cuisine is featured at this large restaurant on the main floor of the sprawling Logan Ridge Wine Cellars facility, formerly the contemporary mansion of a local contractor, high above Seneca Lake. William Cornelius, well-known area chef, took over in 2004 as executive chef here and media chef for its companion Glenora Wine Cellars. Tables in the formal main dining room are well spaced (make that *very*); the large canopied outdoor deck is more convivial. The dinner menu is ambitious and changes frequently. Typical appetizers are calypso shrimp flamed in dark honey rum and crab and stilton croquettes with loganberry-hoisin wine sauce. Entrées could be mesquite-rubbed sea scallops with an avocado ragu, free-range chicken breast in a cappuccino-brandy cream sauce and twin tournedos wrapped in bacon and served on a warm caesar salad. At lunchtime, expect soups, salads, sandwiches (we liked the oyster po-boy) and pastas. The place serves lunch daily, but lends itself to large functions, which is why no dinner is served on Saturdays.

(607) 546-6600 or (866) 546-6486. www.loganridge.com. Entrées, $17.95 to $29.95. Lunch, Monday-Saturday 11 to 4. Dinner, Wednesday-Friday 5 to 9. Sunday brunch, 11 to 3. Closed November-March.

The Bistro at Red Newt Cellars, 3675 Tichenor Road, Hector.

Local caterer Deb Whiting and husband Dave, the winemaker, opened a spacious dining room and covered deck as part of their winery named for the Eastern red spotted newt. The innovative food received enthusiastic reviews, and the white-linened dining room offers a view of the Seneca Lake valley (but not the lake itself). Mushroom turnover, salmon cakes with ramp cream sauce, and a spinach and arugula salad are among starters on the changing menu, whose ingredients are furnished by local purveyors. Lunchtime might yield a turkey sandwich with avocado and green chile cream cheese on focaccia, an open-face prosciutto sandwich with grilled tomatoes and provolone, or a phyllo strudel stuffed with chard, asparagus, Aztec rice and roasted red peppers. The dinner menu adds entrées like flounder stuffed with asparagus and red pepper, seared duck breast in a blueberry port sauce, grilled pork tenderloin with rhubarb sauce, and bacon-wrapped beef tenderloin with tarragon pesto. Dessert could be chocolate-covered cherry cheesecake or a lemon mousse and blueberry napoleon.

(607) 546-4100. www.rednewt.com. Entrées, $2 to $24. Lunch, Thursday-Sunday noon to 4, weekends in off-season. Dinner, Thursday-Sunday 4 to 9. Closed in winter.

The Stonecat Café, 5315 Route 414, Hector.

The unknowing passerby would likely never stop at this former garage and fruit stand with a garage door in front and funky dining rooms inside. But the local winery crowd cherishes the hip little café next to the obscure Bloomer Creek Vineyard. Ex-Washington, D.C., chef Scott Signori and his wife Jessica dispense their own smoked foods and organic regional cuisine in two laid-back dining areas and a canopied deck where diners enjoy spectacular sunsets across the Seneca Lake valley. The smoked pulled-pork barbecue is the signature item here, served with Carolina-style barbecue sauce, black-eyed peas, dill coleslaw and cornbread. Cornmeal-crusted catfish finished with a smoked tomato coulis, sausage and chicken braised in Northern Italian gravy and served over polenta, and peppercorn-crusted strip steak finished with dijon-thyme cream sauce typify other possibilities. Start with a smoked fish plate of Alaskan salmon and black tiger shrimp over greens or a grilled tofu satay. Tapas are on the lunch menu along with salads, sandwiches and cheese boards. Live music is featured Wednesday and Saturday nights, with jazz at Sunday brunch.

(607) 546-5000. www.stonecatcafe.com. Entrées, $14 to $22. Lunch, Thursday-Saturday 11 to 3. Dinner, Wednesday-Sunday 5 to 9. Sunday jazz brunch, 10:30 to 3. Closed in winter.

Other Choices

Wildflower Café, 301 North Franklin St., Watkins Glen.
Local entrepreneur Doug Thayer has a winner in this storefront café and the adjacent Crooked Rooster Pub. Fifty diners can be seated at a mix of booths and pine tables beneath a pressed-tin ceiling. Posters enhance the brick walls. Fresh seafood and interesting meat presentations range from bouillabaisse to crisped duck breast with chipotle-port glaze. We can vouch for the Wildflower pizza ($9), big enough that three shared it as an appetizer and still had leftovers. Among entrées, we enjoyed the maple-glazed salmon fillet, the pork anjou with pears and walnuts, and a special of fettuccine with anchovies, mushrooms and more. The Glenora seyval blanc was a bargain (as are most local wines in restaurants hereabouts) and the apple crisp with whipped cream was fine. The price was right, the ambiance spirited and casual, and the menu more appealing than most in town.

(607) 535-9797. www.wildflowercafe.com. Entrées, $14.95 to $19.95. Lunch daily, 11:30 to 2, to 4 on weekends. Dinner, 5 to 10 or 11.

Chef's, Route 14 South, Watkins Glen.
"Smoking or non-smoking, folks?" barked the hostess as we arrived for breakfast. She seated us at a table, poured coffee and went on to the next party. "Smoking or non-smoking, ladies?" The old-school waitresses at this diner-grown-large are as much the show as the food, which is basic, bountiful and downright cheap. Our griddle cakes ($2.50) and a western omelet ($4.40) arrived almost as we placed our order. The 130-item menu lists dinners from meatloaf with gravy, made from Grandma's recipe, to grilled tuna steak to mesquite chicken to angus beef steaks. Grandma's rice pudding heads the area's largest dessert menu. Although known for its unusual burgers, Chef's added a low-carb menu in 2004. When Tony Pulos took over the business in 1949, he couldn't afford a sign so kept his predecessors' name. We learned from John Pulos that his father's long hours at the diner had put him through Hobart College up the lake in Geneva, that John served on the Hobart board of trustees and that Chef's is the "official restaurant" of the Hobart soccer team, as it seems to be of so many people in Watkins Glen. They pack it at all hours and call it "a little piece of culinary Americana," and rightly so.

(607) 535-9975. www.chefsdiner.com. Entrées, $5.95 to $14.99. Open daily from 6 a.m., to 8 p.m. weekdays and 9:30 Friday and Saturday.

FOR MORE INFORMATION: Schuyler County Chamber of Commerce, 100 North Franklin St., Watkins Glen, NY 14891, (607) 535-4300 or (800) 607-4552. www.schuylerny.com.

Old Fort Niagara in New York is on view across mouth of river through town park gazebo.

Niagara-on-the-Lake, Ont.

Think Niagara and most people think of Niagara Falls. But there's much more to Niagara than the falls. Devoted locals cling to the belief that the real Niagara is Niagara-on-the-Lake, a once-sleepy hamlet that has blossomed into a world-class destination resort at the point where the Niagara River meets Lake Ontario.

Though a scant dozen miles distant from touristy Niagara Falls, Niagara-on-the-Lake is a world apart. Here is a lovely, sedate town dating to the late 1700s when it was settled by United Empire Loyalists and became the first capital of Upper Canada. However, the British relocated the capital to Toronto before the War of 1812. Shipping interests moved west with the opening of the Welland Canal to bypass the falls and link Lakes Erie and Ontario. The town's role later in the 19th century as a lakeside summer resort and home of a Canadian version of Chautauqua, the traveling cultural and spiritual program, was short-lived.

Niagara-on-the-Lake languished until the summer of 1962, when a local attorney began mounting George Bernard Shaw plays. They were the precursor of the famed Shaw Festival, which now produces a dozen plays by Shaw and his contemporaries in three theaters from April into November. Theatergoers came from near and far for the plays, but also found a quaint town of great beauty and architectural merit, steeped in history and British Loyalist tradition. Within a distance of fifteen miles are some of the finest parklands in the world and at least 43 scenic or historic sights, according to one tour guide. Also here are a fruit-growing and wine-producing region of great note.

Niagara-on-the-Lake – or NOTL, as it's abbreviated, and Niagara, as it's called – is buttressed by two of the Great Lakes. On the north is Lake Ontario, from the shores of which on a clear day you can see the skyline of Toronto 30 miles across the lake. On the east is the Niagara River, whose shores quickly fold into the majestic gorge ending at Niagara Falls. On the other two sides are scenic parklands and more vineyards and orchards than we've encountered before in such proximity.

The falls are a must-see, of course. Americans have long considered the Canadian side of the falls and its surroundings more scenic and well kept up than the American side. Head up the Niagara River Parkway to Niagara-on-the-Lake and you'll find that NOTL is nicer yet.

The parkway lives up to its billing as 35 miles of remarkable scenery, interspersed with historic houses, gorges and glens, and glorious gardens. The view of the Niagara River from Queenston Heights reminds some of Europe. The "lake effect" tempers the climate and helps produce abundant fruit and grapes for award-winning wines. The Welland Canal offers views of ocean-going vessels, and the early harborfront lives on in Old Port Dalhousie.

All the while, Niagara-on-the-Lake remains poised beside river and lake, secure in its own charms and drawing increasing numbers of visitors to share them.

Getting There

Niagara-on-the-Lake is situated on the south shore of Lake Ontario, across the Niagara River from New York State. It's roughly 30 miles north of Buffalo and 85 miles south (by road around the lake) from Toronto. Both cities are major ports of entry for air, rail and bus passengers.

Motorists arriving by the New York Thruway or Ontario's Queen Elizabeth Way take the Niagara River Parkway or Route 55 to NOTL.

Where to Stay ———————————— ⟋⟋⟋

First-time visitors often expect to be able to stay on the water in a place called Niagara-on-the-Lake. But residential development, parklands and the Niagara Golf Club occupy the choicest locations. Those accommodations on or near the water are few and far between—and very much in demand.

Hotels and Motels

Queen's Landing Inn & Conference Resort, 155 Byron St., Niagara-on-the-Lake L0S 1J0.

The town's largest hostelry occupies a prime location atop a slope overlooking the river across the Niagara-on-the-Lake Sailing Club's busy marina. The original owner of the Pillar and Post, which started Niagara's inn boom in the 1970s, gave the structure a Georgian facade. So it looks as if it's been around awhile. But it's been upgraded and enhanced by new owner Si Wai Lai, who fled China in 1967 by swimming to Hong Kong and now has bought up much of Niagara-on-the-Lake. Although the Prince of Wales Hotel is her most showy extravaganza, the Queen's Landing is no slouch. You know you're in one of Si Wai's hotels from the showy floral arrangements

everywhere, not to mention all the gardens outside. About half the rooms have river views. All have kingsize or two double beds, large-screen TVs in armoires, floral draperies and comforters, two wing chairs and closets with irons and terrycloth robes. Forty have jacuzzi tubs and three dozen have gas fireplaces. Four suites by the harbor have been fashioned from the 1835 dockmaster's office, built when Niagara was one of the busiest ports and shipyards in Upper Canada. They have been restored recently for luxurious lodging, as have a waterfront cottage and a lakeside villa. The restaurants with outdoor terraces (see Where to Eat) look across a marina to the river. The lower floors, built into the side of the slope, include a light and airy area with a large indoor swimming pool and a health facility with lap pool and whirlpool.

(905) 468-2195 or (888) 669-5566. Fax (905) 468-2227. www.vintageinns.com. One hundred thirty-seven rooms and five suites. Doubles, $225 to $430. Suites, $425 to $530.

Harbour House Hotel, 85 Melville St., Box 760, Niagara-on-the-Lake L0S 1J0.

The river is on view across and down the street from this deluxe new boutique-style urban hotel. But as designed by owner Susan Murray's husband, an architect, it lacks any balconies or even a riverfront orientation. Instead, this newly constructed, shingled Cape Cod-like structure with a gambrel roof is turned inward as if to avoid the sights and sounds from the busy marina across the street. All is sumptuous and high-end, from the restful Library Lobby with oriental rugs and a fireplace to the beautiful conservatory dining room beside a garden patio. Decor is understated nautical with a lighthouse table here, a ship's painting there. Rooms on the second and third floors have kingsize feather-top beds dressed with 300 thread-count linens and down duvets, gas fireplaces, TV/DVD players in armoires and marble bathrooms. Most have California whirlpool tubs, except for a few that have oversize glass showers with multiple jets. One second-floor corner suite with a harbor view has a sofabed in the living room, three TVs and a double whirlpool tub. The best harbor view – if you're inclined to stand and look out the window – is from the third-floor honeymoon suite. Guests enjoy general manager Timothy Taylor's "famous cheese dips" at the wine tasting daily at 4 in the library lobby. An extensive European-style breakfast in the conservatory is complimentary in the morning.

(905) 468-4683 or (866) 277-6677. Fax (905) 468-0366. www.harbourhousehotel.ca. Twenty-eight rooms and three suites with private baths. Doubles, $275 to $360. Suites, $375 to $415.

South Landing Inn, 21 Front St., Queenston L0S 1L0.

Good values as well as good views are offered from this historic inn and newer motel-style annex in Queenston, Niagara's hilltop neighbor. The values are rooms priced half again lower than they would be in NOTL; the views are of the Niagara River from the inn's front verandas and the annex's private decks. The main house, built as an inn in the early 1800s, is the town's oldest building. Its five rooms have private baths, are furnished in Canadian pine, and have TV and air conditioning. Since 1987, guests have enjoyed rooms on two floors of the annex across the street. Four suites on either end are most prized, particularly those on the river end with private decks. Standard rooms have two double beds; those on the second floor have ceiling fans and better views over and around the main inn toward the river. Innkeeper Tony Szabo proudly shows the remarkable needlepoint pictures, one a large portrait of the Rockies, done by his wife Kathy and now gracing the second-floor foyer of the main inn. Breakfast is available in a small restaurant on the inn's main floor.

(905) 262-4634. Fax (905) 262-4639. www.southlandinginn.com. Nineteen rooms and four suites with private baths. Doubles, $95. Suites, $125.

The Anchorage Motel, Bar & Grill, 186 Ricardo St., Box 233, Niagara-on-the-Lake L0S 1J0.

The town's only waterfront motel faces the river opposite the sailing club marina. Most rooms in the L-shaped, 1950s-style motel have one queen bed, but three of the larger have two. "We're the economy lodging in town," the manager affirmed. Rooms are small but serviceable and nondescript, with white walls, original blue tiled baths, one wicker chair and a TV on a high corner shelf. Eight rooms on the second floor get better water views than those on the ground floor. In-room continental breakfast is included in the rates. The restaurant offers dinner and an appealing water-view patio bedecked with flowers. The extensive menu is predictable, from pizzas and pastas to chicken wings, ribs, seafood and steaks. Food reports at our visit were mixed, and the emphasis may be more on the large bar and cocktail lounge.

(905) 468-2141. Fax (905) 468-0841. www.theanchorage.ca. Twenty-two rooms with private baths. Doubles, $125 to $155.
Entrées, $12.95 to $26.95. Lunch daily in summer, 11:30 to 4:30. Dinner, 4:30 to midnight.

King George III Inn, 61 Melville St., Box 1215, Niagara-on-the-Lake L0S 1J0.

The rooms pictured in a glass case in front of this unassuming riverfront establishment may not do them justice. They appeared quite basic, so we were surprised to find eight fairly spacious rooms, individually outfitted with pretty wallpapers, quilts, TV, clock radios, hair dryers and coffeemakers. The two largest have queen beds plus a queen sofabed. Four rooms have covered balconies facing the river across the Niagara Sailing Club marina. One at the end has a big side balcony that those in smaller rooms get to use as well. There's a separate entrance for the rooms from the downstairs whirlpool jet boat headquarters. A continental breakfast is put out in the upstairs foyer. Guests are encouraged to take it out onto the balcony to enjoy the passing scene.

(905) 468-4800 or (888) 438-4444. www.niagarakinggeorgeinn.com. Eight rooms with private baths. Doubles, $99 to $129. Closed November to mid-April.

Inns and Bed & Breakfasts

The Oban Inn, 160 Front St., Niagara-on-the-Lake L0S 1J0.

If you want to be near the water in historic surroundings, the Oban Inn is for you. The landmark inn facing Lake Ontario across a strip of golf course has been around since 1824 and looks it, so seamless was the rebuilding after the original burned to the ground on Christmas Night in 1992. A favorite of traditionalists, the local icon is the latest of Niagara's four major hostelries to be acquired by Si Wai Lai, the Chinese-born hotelier. She took over in late 1999 with a pledge to keep it the same (except for an increase in prices) while exercising her proclivity for upgrades. The best rooms are considered to be the six looking onto the lake in the adjacent Oban House and the Greenview Estate, transformed in 2000 from the former owner's residence. The rest of the rooms go off narrow corridors adorned with ornate paintings on the second and third floors of the main inn. Those in front looking toward the lake are larger and have queen or twin beds, gas fireplaces and plush armchairs or a loveseat facing a TV. A second-story balcony, outfitted with chairs and plants, goes off the rooms at the back of the inn and is available to all house guests, as is a library/sitting room with TV and gas fireplace. Three meals a day are served in the historic restaurant and tavern (see Where to Eat).

(905) 468-2165 or (888) 669-5566. Fax (905) 468-4165. www.vintageinns.com. Twenty-four rooms and one suite with private baths. Doubles, $225 to $375. Suite, $475.

Lakewinds, 328 Queen St., Box 1483, Niagara-on-the-Lake L0S 1J0.

Four rooms and suites in this sumptuous manor house face Lake Ontario across the golf-course fairways. Owners Jane and Stephen Locke not only share their home with B&B guests, they offer a swimming pool and stunning, intricate gardens on nearly two acres in an area of substantial residences. The prime accommodations are kingsize suites, including Heaven, a third-floor hideaway where a loveseat and window seat offer a bird's-eye view of the lake and the bath contains a jacuzzi tub. We also like the second-floor Venetian suite, so named for all the silver and glass and the hand-painted mirrored furniture, with double whirlpool tub and separate shower. Other rooms bear furnishings appropriate to their names: Florentine, Singapore and Algonquin. Comments in guest diaries embellish on three themes: sumptuous surroundings, gourmet breakfasts and personable hosts. The main floor holds a solarium and a formal living/dining room in which the Lockes serve breakfasts to remember. Ours began with apple-cassis juice, cantaloupe with port and berries and five varieties of breads. The main course was leek and sage quiche with roasted red pepper coulis, teamed with a crostini bearing sautéed mushrooms, pesto, tomato and goat cheese. The wraparound veranda is a place to take in the lake breeze and enjoy the tranquil surroundings. At our latest visit, Jane proudly showed off the new flagstone terrace and landscaping around the back-yard pool, as well as a European-style piazza, a fish pond and showy cutting and herb gardens.

(905) 468-1888 or (866) 338-1888. Fax (905) 468-1061. www.lakewinds.ca. Three rooms and three suites with private baths. Doubles, $165 to $295.

The Old Bank House, 10 Front St., Box 1708, Niagara-on-the-Lake L0S 1J0.

Nicely located across from a park and facing Lake Ontario, this historic B&B dates to 1817. It has been vastly upgraded since our first stay here when it was one of the few B&Bs in town. Judy and Michael Djurdjevic offer nine comfortable bedrooms furnished in elegant European style with king or queen beds or two double beds and TVs in armoires. Three rooms have direct views of the lake through the park, and three rooms have access to a balcony. Everyone enjoys the flower-bedecked front veranda and a huge living room. The foyer is brightened with the stunning artworks of Adrian Milankov, a friend of the family. Breakfast is served at individual tables in a sunny conservatory that opens onto a side patio. The morning of our visit yielded a fruit cup with ladyfinger biscuits in crème anglaise and omelets laden with cheese, mushrooms and ham.

(905) 468-7136. www.oldbankhouse.com. Nine rooms with private baths. Doubles, $145 to $225.

Riverbend Inn & Vineyard, 16104 Niagara River Pkwy., Box 1560, Niagara-on-the-Lake L0S 1J0.

The Wiens family, who sold the Prince of Wales Hotel here to cap Si Wai Lai's lodging empire, re-emerged in 2004 with this luxury inn in a stately 1860s Georgian mansion with later additions in the midst of thirteen acres of grape vines, making theirs the closest vineyard to the river. John Wiens, his wife Jill and his father Henry Wiens are actively involved in running the endeavor, as they had been at the Prince of Wales. Here they offer 21 sizable rooms and suites and a small, elegant restaurant serving three meals a day. Guest rooms on three floors are furnished in formal Georgian style, with queen or two double beds, sitting areas with gas fireplaces, flat-screen TVs hidden in armoires, and standard bathrooms. Seven rooms, including one massive affair near the board meeting room, come with stand-up balconies or decks. The restaurant at the rear of the mansion includes an elegant 1890s salon/bar flanked by marble pillars, a 26-seat dining room with windows onto the Peller Estates vineyard and a 40-seat dining patio. The contemporary regional menu is as creative as those of its winery dining peers and more affordably priced. An appealing grill and terrace menu is available all day. Expect entrées like pan-seared red snapper with tarragon coulis, cider-braised lamb shanks and roast rack of Canadian venison in the $16 to $29 range. The inaugural wines from the inn's grapes were being produced by the neighboring Reif Winery under the inn's own label.

(905) 4688-8866. Fax (905) 468-8839. www.riverbendinn.ca. Twenty rooms and one suite with private baths. Doubles, $195 to $325 EP.

Somerset B&B, 111 Front St., Box 929, Niagara-on-the-Lake L0S 1J0.

This imposing beige brick manor house backs up to Lake Ontario and takes full advantage. Three comfortable suites each offer two double beds, a sitting room with TV and a private balcony overlooking the lake. The master suite adds a jacuzzi tub in the bathroom. Managers Walter and Betty Andres cosset guests for owners from Germany, who were originally silent partners in the Prince of Wales Hotel here. Their "extended continental breakfast" turns out to be quite a meal in a formal dining room open to a contemporary living room with big windows onto a pillared veranda overlooking the lake. The fare the day we visited included french toast, while tomato strata was on tap the next morning. Besides the view from their suites, guests enjoy a manicured rear lawn sloping to the lakeshore.

(905) 468-5565. Fax (905) 468-8899. www.somersetbb.info. Three suites with private baths. Suites, $270 and $320. Closed January-March.

The River Breeze, 14767 Niagara Pkwy., Niagara-on-the-Lake L0S 1J0.

Exceptional landscaping beautifies this substantial gray brick house, set well back from the parkway on an acre of gardens and trees, several miles south of town. Bert and Mimi Davesne, originally from France, designed and built the house in 1975 and decided to share it with overnight guests after they became empty-nesters. Three of their four queen-bedded rooms offer views of the Niagara River, and two have balconies. Our room, one of the latter, was rather confining, so we were glad to have the extra balcony space. Repeat guests, who are legion, come back for his wife's breakfasts, says Bert. The fare ranges from quiche to crêpes to croissants and buns, prepared and served in the French manner. Guests gather in a handsome living room or on the back terrace, atop a bluff with a view onto the river. They also enjoy a swimming pool surrounded by tropical plants and potted palms.

(905) 262-4046 or (866) 881-7536. Fax (905) 262-0718. Four rooms with private baths. Doubles, $120 to $150.

House on the River, 14773 Niagara Pkwy., Niagara-on-the-Lake L0S 1J0.

Also high above the river with a view to match is this vaguely alpine-looking contemporary with vaulted roof, owned by Marybeth and Jay Moyer. They share it with guests in two "view" rooms on the walkout lower level and two main-floor rooms opening onto a swimming pool at the front and side. All have queensize beds and private entrances, and one has a wood stove. The lower-level rooms open through large sliding glass doors onto a patio and the riverbank, with lawn chairs scattered about. Above is a patio where guests enjoy breakfast under an umbrella on nice days. Fruit salad, cereal and croissants precede the main course, perhaps yogurt pancakes or french toast. The Moyers offer complimentary bicycles for guests to use on the Niagara bike path out front.

(905) 262-4597 or (877) 213-0089. Fax (905) 262-06875. Four rooms with private baths. Doubles, $110 to $135.

Grand Victorian, 15618 Niagara Pkwy., Niagara-on-the-Lake L0S 1J0.

Across the parkway from the river and screened by trees is this large B&B that's a work in progress. The imposing white stucco landmark – very grand and very Victorian – is next to Reif Estate Winery, whose wines innkeeper Eva Kessel pours for guests in the evening. Five second-floor rooms have fireplaces and ornate, oversize beds. The River Room yields a view of the river and has a kingsize canopy plantation bed reached by a small stepladder. The Porch Room offers a screened porch onto the side yard and river. The North Suite on the main floor offers a step-up bed canopied in beige brocade and buried in pillows, plus a sitting room with a river view and a bath with clawfoot tub. Breakfast is served in a round conservatory. The fare could be quiche, orange french toast or waffles with fruit. There's plenty of space for guests to spread out in the main-floor common rooms and the flower-bedecked front veranda. In back are a pool and a tennis court and proliferating gardens that are Eva's pride and joy.

(905) 468-0997. Fax (905) 468-1551. www.grandvictorianbandb.com. Five rooms and one suite with private baths. Doubles, $170 to $200. Suite, $225.

Seeing and Doing

The Shaw Festival is the attraction for most here. But there are plenty of water pleasures as well as historical, sightseeing, winery and farm-market attractions.

Shaw Festival, 10 Queen's Parade, Box 774, Niagara-on-the-Lake L0S 1J0.

Twelve plays of George Bernard Shaw and his contemporaries are staged in three theaters from April to late November. One of the world's largest permanent ensembles of actors is led by new artistic director Jackie Maxwell. The 869-seat Festival Theater, built in 1973, showcases the larger epic works and musicals. The 327-seat Court House Theater presents smaller works of Shaw and the more intimate American and European dramas of the period. The 328-seat Royal George Theater houses smaller musicals and mysteries.

(905) 468-2172 or (800) 511-7429. www.shawfest.com. Performances, Tuesday-Sunday at 2 and 8. Tickets, $30 to $82.

Touring

It's best to have a car, both to get around town and to see the sights, although sometimes it's more fun to take to a bicycle.

The **Niagara River Parkway,** a 35-mile-long drive along the river between Niagara-on-the-Lake and Fort Erie, is incredibly scenic and generally tranquil, except near the falls. "The prettiest Sunday afternoon drive in the world" is how Winston Churchill described it. The northern end from NOTL south to Queenston is the most attractive section, with orchards and substantial homes generally on the west side and treed parklands to the river on the east. Picnic tables and river vistas abound. Meandering beside the parkway is the wonderful **Niagara River Recreation Trail,** a paved path for bicycling, jogging and walking, which gets lots of use. The Georgian-style **McFarland House,** restored and furnished to the War of 1812 period, backs up to the river and is open to the public for tours and tea. The **Gen. Isaac Brock Monument** dominates the Queenston Heights Park, just above the charming, historic riverside hamlet of Queenston. South of Queenston, in rapid scenic fashion, come the **Niagara Parks School of Horticulture** gardens, a 100-acre riot of color in season; the famed **Floral Clock,** formed by about 20,000 plants that change every year, and the **Niagara Glen Nature Area,** an unexpected treat with picnic tables overlooking the gorge and nearly three miles of trails along the gorge wall and river bank. It's a 45-minute walk down and back, but worth it for the flora and fauna and rock formations. (Park naturalists guide free nature walks in season.) Beyond are the **Niagara Whirlpool,** crossed by a Spanish cable-car ride, and the **Great Gorge Adventure,** a boardwalk along the fierce rapids, reached by elevator and tunnel. The Canadian and American Falls are best viewed from the Canadian park system, if you don't get up close via the Maid of the Mist boat tour. Why anyone would pay to go up one of the high-rise observation towers, we don't know. Whenever our family visited Niagara Falls during the time we lived fairly nearby in Rochester, N.Y., we took a quick look at the falls and then headed for the super swimming holes and picnic areas of **Dufferin Islands** sequestered just south, away from the hordes.

Other Drives. Niagara Boulevard along the lakeshore and outer Queen Street are waterside streets lined with beautiful homes. Almost every street in what's called the Old Town holds architectural treasures as well. Just west of town between Niagara Boulevard and Lakeshore Road lies Chautauqua Circle, where monster trophy homes have sprung up among the quaint bungalows and Victorian gingerbread cottages built during the heyday of the Chautauqua campground here. Lakeshore Road cuts through vineyards and orchards, seldom yielding a view of the lake, although you can detour down any of the Fire Line roads that end at the water. Other than the Niagara River Parkway, we think the area's most scenic route is Route 81 along the Niagara Escarpment. It's a twisting, hilly, mostly rural road full of surprises, with far different vistas and topography from those of the flatlands below.

Tours of Old Town in **horse-drawn carriages** leave from the main corner of King and Queen streets. Providers include Sentineal Carriages, (905) 468-4943, and Queens Royal Tours, (905) 468-1008.

BICYCLING. Bicycles are not only a pleasant but at peak times the most practical way of getting around town. Cyclists get to savor the architectural and landscaping treasures on every side street, which motorists are prone to miss and most pedestrians don't get to. You also can bike along the Niagara River Recreation Trail, with lots of sightseeing and picnicking opportunities along the way. Rentals are available from Zoom Leisure, 275 Mary St., (905) 468-2366.

Niagara Wine Tours International, 92 Picton St., offers guided cycling tours with visits to wineries and lunch in a private vineyard daily, (905) 468-1300 or (800) 680-7006.

WALKING. Niagara-on-the-Lake seemingly was made for strolling, perhaps because of its age and penchant for a slower pace. The main street, Queen changing to Picton, is peopled by hundreds of pedestrians at all hours, enjoying the shops and historic sites – not to mention the oversize spheres of flowers, two hanging from every lamppost, the hibiscus blooming in outdoor planters and the abundant gardens all around. Detours onto the side streets and parallel streets are worthy diversions. Simcoe Park and Queen's Royal Park, where the river meets Lake Ontario, are full of treats.

Recreation

Niagara River Whirlpool Jet Boat Tours, 61 Melville St., Niagara-on-the-Lake.
People watch a series of videos as they debate where to sit – or, in some cases, whether even to go – on this breathtaking ride through the famed Niagara River rapids and gorge. Once decided, they don yellow splash suits and life preservers and line up on bleachers alongside the King George III Inn for a pre-trip safety orientation prior to boarding an open, 48-seat jet boats designed for the purpose. The beginning of the hour-long, twelve-mile round trip into the Devil's Hole Rapids

above the Queenston bridge is scenic and relatively tame. But you likely will get wet and swallow some water as you gape open-mouthed in awe (or fright) in the face of the increasing rapids, the fastest, deepest and largest in the world in terms of water volume and pressure. A guide narrates the details through a megaphone as the diesel-powered jet boat scuds across the rapids like a spinning top. Then, as a cable car crosses overhead, the jet boat skims into the famed Niagara Whirlpool, flitting about at will in the maelstrom where many daredevils have lost their lives. The experience is considered more thrilling than dangerous. The wind blow-dries your hair as the boat returns at speeds up to 40 miles an hour.

(905) 468-4800 or (888) 438-4444. www.whirlpooljet.com. Trips hourly by reservation, daily 10 to 7, April-October. Adults $54, children $44.

SWIMMING. Public swimming facilities are sadly lacking, which may be why so many residents have their own pools. We found a little beach in NOTL's riverfront Queen's Royal Park, but nobody was swimming ("pollution," the natives advised, though we've seldom seen such clear, appealing water and have never hesitated to swim in Lake Ontario). A small lakefront beach and picnic area are available at picturesque Ryerson Park off Niagara Boulevard in the Chautauqua section. Good swimming of the pond and creek types is available in Dufferin Islands, part of the Niagara Parks Commission just south of the falls.

GOLFING. Of the two dozen golf courses in the Niagara Region, three are in Niagara-on-the-Lake. Most historic is Niagara-on-the-Lake Golf Club, a nine-hole course by river and lake in Old Town. Opened in 1875, it said to be the oldest in North America. There's a new clubhouse and pro shop, with a waterside restaurant and lounge serving three meals a day. The public is welcome, as well as at other, less expensive nine-hole courses at St. Davids and Queenston.

Other Attractions

Historic Sites. As the first capital of Upper Canada and one of Ontario's oldest towns, Niagara-on-the-Lake is full of history. Forty historic points of interest are noted in the town's "Historic Guide," a handy pamphlet and map. We won't begin to duplicate it, but will steer you to the **Niagara Apothecary Museum,** the restored first pharmacy at Queen and King, and **St. Mark's Anglican Church** and graveyards, a shady retreat facing Simcoe Park, away from the crowds. The locally prized **Niagara Historical Society & Museum** at 43 Castlereagh St., the first in Ontario built solely for use as a museum, houses room settings, displays and more than 20,000 artifacts. It's open daily 10 to 5:30 May-October, 1 to 5 rest of year; adults $5, children $1. The **McFarland House,** a mile south of town along the Niagara Parkway, is a restored Georgian house used as a hospital in the War of 1812, open daily 10 to 5 in summer, weekends to 8; adults $3.50. The **Laura Secord Homestead** in Queenston houses a fine collection of early Upper Canada furniture and artifacts appropriate to the woman known as the Paul Revere of Canada. Tours daily in summer, 10 to 5; adults $2, children $1.

Fort George National Historic Site, Queen's Parade, Niagara-on-the-Lake.
Dating to 1797, this was the principal British fort on the Niagara Frontier and looks much as it did during the War of 1812 when the United States tried to capture Canada. It helped prevent the Niagara area and all of British North America from falling into American hands. A National Historic Site following reconstruction in 1939, it's worth touring for a look at the officers' quarters, soldiers' barracks,

blockhouses, carpenter shop, powder magazine and the other trappings of a major fortress. Costumed interpreters perform daily tasks. In the summer there are fife and drum drills and infantry and cannon firings at various times.

(905) 468-4257. www.parkscajnada.gc.ca,k. Open daily 10 to 5, April-October. Adults $10, children $5.

The Welland Canal, just west of town at the entrance to St. Catharines, is one of Canada's engineering marvels and the second most visited attraction in the region after Niagara Falls. Opened in 1932, it is the fourth in a series of canals built since 1829 so Great Lakes ships could bypass the falls to go between Lakes Erie and Ontario. Huge lakers and ocean-going vessels are raised and lowered a total of 330 feet in a series of eight locks. The best vantage point is the lookout platform at the Welland Canal Viewing Center at Lock 3 (just off the Queen Elizabeth Way at Glendale Avenue, Route 89). The site contains an information center, audio-visuals, the St. Catharines Museum, a canal-side restaurant and the Welland Canal Gallery, which has a large, hands-on working model of the canal's lock system.

SHOPPING. A large branch of **Crabtree & Evelyn,** which looks right at home along Queen Street, is the town's only chain store other than a **Dansk Factory Store.** An increasing number of sophisticated, one-of-a-kind shops are found along Queen and a couple of side streets.

The **Old Niagara Bookshop** has plenty of local lore and Canadiana. **Loyalist Village** offers distinctively Canadian parkas, gloves, shearling hats – all that heavy gear for northern winters – as well as cottons and jewelry. **Just Christmas** is just that. Clothing boutiques range from **Casual Country** to the high-fashion **Great Things** and **El du Monde.** Two stores of interest to those partial to the British Isles are **Scottish Loft** and **Irish Design,** while **Something Different** offers fashions from Down Under. **L'Esprit Provence** is a haven of pottery, bowls, posters, kitchen gadgets and more from the South of France.

Greaves Jams & Marmalades, which occupies a prime downtown corner at 55 Queen St., looks just as it must have 50 years ago. Bins of jams, shelves of jams, boysenberry, peach, raspberry, red and black currant – you name it, they have it, and they use no pectin, preservatives or coloring. The chocolate aroma is almost overpowering at **Maple Leaf Fudge,** which offers flavors from Irish cream and rum-almond to amaretto.

Many of the watercolors and vivid floral designs you see around town emanate from **Angie Strauss,** a shop that's a riot of color and good taste at 125 Queen St. Her staff of 25 Mennonite women put Angie's designs on everything from high-fashion sweatshirts in the $50 range to gifts, cards, wine labels and kitchen accessories. We acquired a couple of refrigerator magnets and a large print at a fraction of the cost of one of her lovely originals ($2,000), and thus qualified for a pair of free sweatpants at her Fashion Outlet, where discontinued patterns are sold.

Barbara Zimmermann's work appeals at **Lakeside Pottery,** 755 Lakeshore Road, especially her pots in a celadon green tint. She also does nice soup bowls, piggy banks, jewelry and buttons.

The Artists' Loft at 188 Victoria St. is a potpourri of fine art and crafts from local artisans. The **Romance Collection Gallery** in a handsome restored Victorian house at 177 King St. features the art of Trisha Romance. The **Doug Forsythe Gallery** at 92 Picton St. is home of the famous dory planter, and the **Chantal Poulin Art Gallery** at 153 King St. shows the works of the ex-Montreal artist. Local artists exhibit at the restored **Pumphouse Visual Arts Centre** at 247 Ricardo St., which overlooks the river.

RiverBrink/The Weir Foundation, 116 Queenston St., Queenston.

Best of all for serious art lovers may be this little-known treasure beside the river, just off the Niagara River Parkway. A lawyer from London, Ont., Samuel E. Weir built the brick house called RiverBrink in the 1960s as a gallery and library in which to exhibit and store his impressive collection. It's full of predominantly Canadian paintings, sculptures and furnishings, with an emphasis on the Group of Seven and the history of the Niagara Peninsula. The upstairs, with furnishings labeled and clothing and neckties hung in a bedroom closet, looks much as he left it upon his death in 1981. The walls are paneled and the shades drawn, so the gallery is rather dark, but the connoisseur should feel at home.

(905) 262-4510. Fax (905) 262-4477. www.riverbrink.org. Open Wednesday-Sunday 10 to 5, mid-May to early October. Adults $5.

The Wineries

The Niagara Peninsula has become one of North America's leading wine producers in the last 25 years. It is known for its rieslings and chardonnays, as well as a local eiswein ("ice wine") made from grapes that are pressed frozen in winter, producing a sweet dessert wine that promises to become as Canadian as hockey, in one wine writer's estimation. The vineyards are concentrated on the flatlands and on what locals call "the Bench" of the Niagara Escarpment (the seat of the long, tiered ridge shaped like a bench above Lake Ontario).

Reif Estate Winery, the closest to river and town, is known for wines in the German style, particularly dry riesling and gewürztraminer. All North American grapes were uprooted in favor of European vinifera and premium French hybrids on the 130-acre estate behind the winery. Nearby at 290 John St., off the Niagara River Parkway, is **Peller Estates Winery,** the high-end winery and restaurant recently opened by the owner of Hillebrand Estates Winery.

Hillebrand Estates Winery, Highway 55, calls itself Canada's most award-winning winery and its largest estate winery. Associated with sister wineries in Germany's Rhine Valley, it is known for its lively and informative tours and an excellent restaurant. Its showroom looks like a big retail wine store, which it is.

Licensed as Ontario's first cottage winery in 1975, **Inniskillin Wines Inc.,** Line 3 Road, is considered by many to be Canada's finest winemaker. Visitors may take a 45-minute tour and taste wines in a 1930s barn, the ground floor of which has been transformed into a sparkling showroom.

Wines in the German style are featured by Herman Konzelmann at the **Konzelmann Estate Winery,** 1096 Lakeshore Road. The dry riesling and gewürztraminer are especially good here, and you can see the rows of grapes, all labeled, growing primly along the lakeshore. **Strewn Winery** at 1339 Lakeshore Road is home to the Wine Country Cooking School and Terroir La Cachette Restaurant and Wine Bar.

Where to Eat ⎯⎯⎯⎯⎯⎯⎯⎯⎯⎯⎯⎯⎯ *♪♪♪*

Water Views

Tiara at the Queen's Landing, 155 Byron St., Niagara-on-the-Lake.

This elegant hotel restaurant offers some of Niagara's best food in its most appealing surroundings. Large and pillared, it is a majestic oval of soaring windows onto the Niagara Sailing Club marina. Outside are a wonderful dining terrace repeating the curve of the dining room, as well as a new patio with an outdoor grill. Fine dining is offered on one side outdoors, and a lounge menu on the other. Executive chef

Stephen Treadwell is known for strong flavors and complex cooking. The changing menu ranges widely from sea salt-crusted Bay of Fundy salmon with sake and peanut hoisin to Australian rack of lamb with chanterelles and port wine jus. Typical starters are a tarte tatin of goat cheese, caramelized onions and frisée and tempura soft-shell crab with a pea shoot and pine nut salad. We sampled the chef's eight-course tasting menu ($85), an exceptional four-hour feast from foie gras terrine through the signature "symphony of desserts." The exotic Tiara lunch menu is served all day in the Bacchus Lounge and adjacent terrace. Amidst landscaped surroundings overseen by a giant statue of David, you can eat quite well on a range from daily sandwich ($12) to fire-roasted lamb sirloin with truffle jus ($26).

(905) 468-2195. Entrées, $30 to $45. Lunch daily, noon to 2, Dinner nightly, 5 to 10. Lounge menu, 11:30 to midnight.

The Oban Inn, 160 Front St., Niagara-on-the-Lake.

The Oban has long been considered the quintessential Niagara experience, as it was when we had dinner there with visiting parents on our first visit to NOTL to see a Shaw play back in the '60s. It seemed a bit dated then, but no more. Since local hotelier Si Wai Lai took over in late 1999, the menu has undergone a transformation. Only prime rib with Yorkshire pudding remained from the traditionally English dinner fare. In place of dover sole you might find pan-roasted fillet of char with lemon and garlic oil. The short menu starts with a shrimp cocktail with smashed avocado and grapefruit chutney and crunchy camembert with red pepper jelly on baked garlic focaccia. Stout-marinated breast of chicken and espresso-grilled strip loin with "simple maple jus" typify the new-look main courses. The signature meringue chantilly, Oban hot fudge sundae and English trifle continue on the dessert menu. All is served amid pristine white linens in formal dining rooms and glassed-in garden dining porches. Still ever-so-British-looking is the rich tartan **Shaw's Corner** piano bar and pub, stunning in dark red and hunter green. Here you can order such traditional favorites as welsh rarebit, hot roast beef on toasted French bread or steak and kidney pie. The staff wears tartan vests, reflecting the inn's start as a private home built by one Captain Duncan Milloy from Oban, Scotland. The outdoor terrace – surrounded by flowers and offering a view of Lake Ontario – is popular in summer for lunch, tea and drinks.

(905) 468-2165. Entrées, $26 to $43. Lunch daily, 11:30 to 2. Dinner nightly, 5 to 9.

The Queenston Heights Restaurant, Queenston Heights Park, 14276 Niagara Pkwy., Queenston.

We figured this old-timer, operated by the Niagara Parks Commission, would be charming and quaint in the old Oban Inn style. How wrong our expectations! The dining room is glamorous, the cuisine quite contemporary and the view – well, you might think you were high on a slope gazing down at the Rhine. From the heights above the river, you can see all the way down the Niagara to Lake Ontario. Everything appealed on the inspired regional menu at a summertime lunch on the expansive outdoor terrace until we discovered that the power had gone off and only cold meals were available. One of us made a lunch of two appetizers: a tomato and eggplant salad and smoked salmon carpaccio, garnished with shavings of romano cheese, herbs and flowers. The other settled for a sandwich of smoked turkey breast with cranberry mayonnaise stuffed inside a whole wheat croissant. A glass of the local Inniskillin brae blanc was a good choice from a wine list strong on Canadian whites and reds. From the dessert cart we picked a magnificent chocolate-strawberry charlotte with curls of chocolate as we savored the afternoon sunshine. The contemporary dinner menu is short and to the point: perhaps fillet of sole and salmon served on a basil potato cake, pork tenderloin en croûte and mignon of veal topped with smoked salmon and lemongrass sauce. The Riverview Patio lately has been covered and expanded. The formal main dining room is Tudor in feeling with a high timbered ceiling, armchairs at well-spaced tables dressed in white, and a painting of Niagara Falls above a huge stone fireplace. The expansive windows looking to the north are the dominant feature, and most diners can't take their eyes off the view.

(905) 262-4274 or (877) 642-7275. www.niagaraparks.com. Entrées, $20.95 to $29.95. Lunch daily, 11:30 or noon to 3, summer Saturdays from 11. Dinner nightly, 5 to 9 or 10. Sunday brunch, 11 to 3. Closed mid-January to late March.

Vineland Estates Winery Restaurant, 3620 Moyer Road, Vineland.

Lake Ontario and the Toronto skyline are visible in the distance from the expansive deck outside this elegant restaurant. There's no more pleasant a setting on a nice day for lunch or dinner, although the handsome interior with its dressy staff has its devotees. So does the food of talented chef Mark Picone, a pioneer in the contemporary regional cuisine. The fare has become far more ambitious than in the early days, when we lingered over platters of cheeses and pâtés for lunch and, more recently, a supper of bruschetta, caesar salad with Canadian bacon and a platter of smoked salmon. Now expect lunch to be of dinner aspirations and prices, and dinner to be, well, an event. How could it be otherwise with – and we quote from one seasonal menu – starters like a trio of warm jumbo scallops in brilliant saffron milk with curly endive seedlings and cumin crisps or a clay pot of cured trout and Carol's premium goat cheese on Windy Farm's baby beet tops with snappy croutons? Or entrées of seared halibut on braised onion and lemon shavings with caperberries in a sauvignon blanc/mussel sauce or a longbone chop of red deer from Lakeland, marinated in hard cider on new potatoes and Dan's vitamin greens? Or desserts of raspberry napoleon with crème fraîche or almond milk crème brûlée with dulce de leche ice cream? You get the idea. When the lunch menu opens with an East Coast lobster martini with fennel and red onion shavings, berries and tomato-paprika aioli for a cool $25, it's got to be a gastronomic experience. If you can't bear to leave, the winery offers a little stucco cottage B&B down the driveway called **Wine 'n Recline,** available nightly for $150.

(905) 562-7088 or (888) 846-3526. www.vineland.com. Entrées, $30 to $40. Lunch daily, 11 to 3. Dinner, 5 to 9.

Other Choices

Hillebrand's Vineyard Café, Highway 55, Niagara-on-the-Lake.

The stylish and widely acclaimed restaurant at Hillebrand Estates Winery is a beauty, with a wall of windows opening onto the barrel-aging cellar along one side and taller windows in back yielding views of a California-look deck and vineyards beyond. Menus neatly bound with grapevines detail some exotic fare. One of us lunched on the day's cold cucumber soup garnished with smoked salmon and a salad of arugula and radicchio with a confit of tomatoes and smoked scallops. The other liked the penne pasta tossed with smoked chicken, caramelized onions and roasted garlic in a spicy tomato sauce. Dinner fare is similarly elaborate, with a changing menu ranging from pan-seared Pacific halibut fillet with morel cream to organic ribeye steak with cabernet truffle sauce. Can't decide? Try the Tour of Niagara, a sampling of regional specialties for $40. Typical desserts are mango and cardamom crème brûlée and a trio of seasonal sorbets.

(905) 468-7123 or (800) 582-8412. www.hillebrand.com. Entrées, $25 to $36. Lunch daily, 11:30 to 5. Dinner, 5 to 11.

Peller Estates Winery Restaurant, 290 John St., Niagara-on-the-Lake.

Handsome murals and big windows onto the vineyard distinguish the large and suave restaurant that's the culinary showcase of the Peller Estates Winery. An outdoor patio and wine garden is appealing in season. Chef de cuisine Jason Rosso offers a concise but ambitious menu of "regional wine country cuisine." At lunch, that ranges from an omelet of house-smoked chicken and Quebec brie to "surf and turf" – pan-seared scallops on a salad of rabbit confit and red potatoes with house-made tartar sauce. We enjoyed a leisurely midday repast of a Quebec duck breast salad with celery root, duck confit and belgian endive and Pacific salmon tartare with cucumber and peppercorn chutney. Dessert was coffee brûlée with hazelnut jaconde, espresso poached pear and granite with cardamom sauce anglaise in a side espresso cup – very good and very precious, like the rest of the meal. For dinner, expect such entrées as pan-seared diver scallops with ginger essence, duck three (cardamom-crusted Quebec magret, escalope of liver and confit leg in icewine tea broth) and the Peller version of "tournedos rossini" – roasted veal tenderloin with foie gras and cabernet truffle gastrique.

(905) 468-4678 or (888) 673-5537. www.peller.com. Entrées, $27 to $38. Lunch daily, noon to 3. Dinner, Sunday-Thursday 5:30 to 8:30, Friday and Saturday 5 to 9.

Shaw Café & Wine Bar, 92 Queen St., Niagara-on-the-Lake.

This striking circular restaurant is part of a Victorian shopping complex built by hotelier Si Wai Lai, who's also into good food. It juts onto the downtown sidewalk, its dining terraces flanked by fountains and statuary, looking like something out of modern-day Italy. The interior has cafe-style tables around a circular staircase leading to an upstairs wine bar, a prominent pizza oven and open kitchen, and a patisserie case laden with some of the best-looking desserts we've seen. The all-day menu is trendy and enticing, from a mushroom and asiago sandwich to a potato and artichoke salad. Shaw's version of meatloaf is a blend of pork and lamb with a truffled mushroom ragoût. Desserts like grand marnier cheesecake, vanilla mille-feuille and kirsch and blackberry mousseline are to die for. Espressos and lattes, wines and beers round out the offerings.

(905) 468-4772. Entrées, $14.85 to $21.95. Open daily, 10 to 9, weekends to midnight.

The Epicurean, 84 Queen St., Niagara-on-the-Lake.

This appealing cafeteria-style eatery has a lengthy display case holding tempting choices for eating inside a cheery, buttercup yellow dining room or outside on a leafy side patio. Soups could be Mexican chicken or gazpacho. You might order a sandwich of seafood and avocado or eggplant with roasted peppers and chèvre, or you might want a smoked salmon and asparagus quiche, moussaka or chicken and feta pie. We liked the curried chicken and cashew sandwich and a medley of three salads served with pita bread.

At night, the cafeteria turns into **The Grill at the Epicurean,** with an innovative dinner menu ranging from yellowfin tuna with sesame-soy vinaigrette to steak frites. The food ranks with the best in town and represents good value.

(905) 468-0288. www.epicurean.ca. Lunch, $5.75 to $8.50; Grill, $17 to $22. Lunch daily, 11 to 5:30. Dinner nightly, 5:30 to 9 or 10.

FOR MORE INFORMATION: Niagara-on-the-Lake Chamber of Commerce, 153 King St., Niagara-on-the-Lake, ON L0S 1J0, (905) 468-4263. www.niagaraonthelake.com.

Yacht is moored in Connecticut River beside landmark Goodspeed Opera House.

Lower Connecticut River, Conn.

Traveling along the lower Connecticut River in 1771, John Adams exclaimed, "I have spent this morning riding through paradise. My eyes have never beheld so fine a country."

Were he alive today, he'd likely still agree. As it nears the end of its 400-mile journey from the Canadian border, New England's longest river wends and weaves beneath majestic hillsides before emptying into Long Island Sound. The steep, forested and undeveloped terrain makes the river unusual. So does the fact that its mouth is unsullied by industrial development. A sand bar blocked the kind of encroachment that has urbanized other rivers where they meet the ocean. Indeed, the Connecticut is the nation's biggest river without a major city at its mouth.

Its unspoiled nature, its verdant banks and steep hillsides, and the historic small towns that grew up beside it make the lower Connecticut River estuary a national treasure. Indeed, it is one of 40 areas in the world that the Nature Conservancy included on its list of "Last Great Places" worth protecting.

Protected it always has been, fortunately. You can tell from the lack of development all along the lower river where you might otherwise expect it. At the mouth of the river on one side is the borough of Fenwick, an old-line Yankee enclave of substantial summer homes and a golf course that occupies the choicest piece of real estate in Connecticut. On the other side are the tidal marshlands that serve as a refuge for wildlife and inspired the late resident birder Roger Tory Peterson.

Geography and the powers-that-be have protected the lower river valley since it was settled in the 17th Century. Historic Essex was settled in 1635, its harbor a haven for shipbuilding long ago and for yachting in modern times. Lately it was named "the best small town in America." Across the river in Old Lyme, artists gathered at the turn of the 20th century and founded the American Impressionist movement, and the arts flourish to this day. Upriver are Deep River, Chester and East Haddam, unspoiled towns steeped in history.

Besides scenery, the attractions for water-loving visitors include a Victorian opera house producing top musicals, a hillside medieval castle reminiscent of those along the Rhine, a vintage railroad and an ancient car ferry, maritime and art museums, good restaurants and choice places to stay.

Getting There

The lower Connecticut River is about 20 to 40 miles southeast of Hartford. The Route 9 divided highway parallels the river on its west side from I-91 north of Middletown to I-95 in Old Saybrook. No through routes flank the undeveloped east side of the river. Major airlines fly into Hartford. Amtrak trains stop at Old Saybrook.

Where to Stay

Saybrook Point Inn & Spa, 2 Bridge St., Old Saybrook 06475.

The honor of best commercial waterfront location, bar none, goes to this glamorous resort hotel and marina on a point near where the Connecticut River meets Long Island Sound. Developer Louis Tagliatela Sr. sank $25 million into rebuilding the old and rather infamous Terra Mar resort from the ground up, and recently added more luxury rooms and a destination spa. On three floors, the hotel now has 81 sumptuous rooms and suites, most quite a bit larger than the industry norm and two-thirds with water views across the busy marina. Most have small balconies (although some are so cramped you can barely stand on them). Fifty come with fireplaces and sixteen have jacuzzis. All are outfitted with kingsize or two double beds, 18th-century reproduction mahogany furniture, wet bars and ahead-of-their-time bedside consoles that "do everything but send faxes," says operations director Stephen Tagliatela, the owner's son. They control the lights and air conditioning, display directions in several languages and tell the current times around the world. Italian marble glistens in the bathrooms as well as in a lobby bearing hand-loomed carpets from England. An indoor pool looks through a wall of glass onto an outdoor pool near the water. Beside the indoor pool are a jacuzzi, steam room and a well-equipped health club facility. Twelve spa rooms and a dedicated lounge area were added in 2000. At the other end of the U-shaped hotel is the **Terra Mar Grille,** an elegant waterside dining room and lounge (see Where to Eat).

(860) 395-2000 or (800) 243-0212, Fax (860) 388-1504. Seventy-six rooms and four suites. Doubles, $219 to $389. Suites, $449 to $799.

Bishopsgate Inn, Goodspeed Landing, Box 290, East Haddam 06423.

Situated down a long driveway a block from the Goodspeed Opera House, this 1818 Colonial house was built by an Essex shipbuilder and once occupied by a Goodspeed. Now it's lovingly run by energetic Colin and Jane Kagel, who first became acquainted with Connecticut while he was with the U.S. Submarine Service in Groton, and their son Colin, wife Lisa and young son. "Ours is a real family enterprise," says Jane. And a winning one, at that. The house is full of books, artworks and family collections. Among them are Jane's silver urns in an open cupboard above the huge fireplace in the living room and Colin's prized canvas-backed working decoys on a shelf in the upstairs sitting room. The six guest rooms with featherbeds and antique furnishings are decorated with character. Four have working fireplaces. The most dramatic is the Director's Suite, with a beamed cathedral ceiling, a kingsize brass and iron bed, its own balcony and a dressing area off a theatrical bathroom with lights around the mirror of the double vanity and its own sauna. Jane and Lisa cook full breakfasts in the former 1860 kitchen, which has a small fireplace and baking oven. Their crustless spinach quiche is a favorite, as are the stratas and waffles. All are served by candlelight at a long table in a beamed dining room where there's a lot to look at.

(860) 873-1677. Fax (860) 873-3898. www.bishopsgate.com. Six rooms with private baths. Doubles, $110 to $145. Suite, $175.

Gelston House, 8 Main St. (Route 82), East Haddam 06423.

Although best known as a restaurant, this 1853 landmark next to the Goodspeed Opera House offers four restored guest rooms of recent vintage. Two are on the second floor and two on the third, and are accessed by a long flight or two of stairs. All have queen beds and TV. Two suites with sitting rooms have fine views of the Connecticut River and the swing bridge at Goodspeed Landing. The smaller rooms look onto the village and are less in demand. Furnished with antiques and decorated with fancy fabrics, the accommodations appear a bit formal and stiff, as is typical of the genre. The suite we were shown had Victorian sitting-room furniture around the perimeter, nothing in the center and nary a good lamp to read by. But the river view out the bedroom window compensates. A complimentary continental breakfast comes in a basket. The main floor is given over to the restaurant and lounge.

(860) 873-1411. www.gelstonhouse.com. Two rooms and two suites with private baths. Doubles, $100. Suites, $225. Closed Monday and Tuesday.

Riverwind, 209 Main St. (Route 9A), Deep River 06417.

A sense of history pervades this charming, atmospheric B&B, which has been nicely redecorated in a country Shaker look by new owners Roger and Nicky Plante. A rear addition of recent vintage was built to look 100 years older than the existing 1850 inn, seamlessly blending old and new. Riverwind is unusual in that it offers eight guest rooms and an equal number of common areas that afford space for mingling or privacy. The heart of the house is the beamed keeping room and dining room with a huge fireplace in the new/old section at the rear. In front, the Plantes brightened up the living room and rejuvenated the library and game room, as well as an upstairs sitting room with a fireplace and herbs hanging from the beams. The enclosed front porch has been opened to the outside and made more welcoming with a lineup of white rocking chairs. Bedrooms on two floors vary in configuration and style. Most have queen beds and all are appointed with period antiques and stenciling. The rear Champagne and Roses Room comes with a queensize half-tester canopy bed, fireplace, a Japanese steeping tub and a private balcony nestled in the treetops. The new, third-floor Moonlit Suite has a mission-style queen bed (with an extra sleigh bed in

an alcove), a brick fireplace, double whirlpool tub and satellite TV. From a twelve-foot stone cooking fireplace in the atmospheric keeping room come a variety of fancy breakfast treats.

(860) 526-2014. Fax (860) 526-0875. www.riverwindinn.com. Six rooms and two suites with private baths. Doubles, $135 to $210. Suites, $165 to $225.

Griswold Inn, 36 Main St., Essex 06426.

A block from the water and nautical through and through, the Gris – as it's fondly called – has historic charm matched by few inns in this country. There's the requisite taproom containing a steamboat-Gothic bar, potbelly stove and antique popcorn machine. Copious meals and a celebrated hunt breakfast are served in four dining rooms that are a kaleidoscope of Americana (see Where to Eat). And the floors in some of the guest rooms list to port or starboard, as you might expect of an inn dating to 1776, when it was built as Connecticut's first four-story structure. When commandeered by the British during the War of 1812, the inn was found to be long on charm but short on facilities. Today, all 31 guest accommodations in the main inn, the annex and in houses across the street come with private baths, air conditioning and telephones, and all but nine in the annex have been enhanced cosmetically of late. That means updated bath fixtures, fabric window treatments and wide-plank hardwood floors with oriental rugs. Rooms we saw upstairs in the inn covered a range from standard facing the street (twin beds and a small bathroom with shower) to a suite with queen bed, and a sitting alcove with a convertible loveseat lit by a lamp so dim as to be useless for anything but romance. Six suites with fireplaces across the street in a retail complex known as Griswold Square are the most deluxe, in a comfortable and historic way. A complimentary continental breakfast buffet is put out in the Steamboat Room section of the restaurant.

(860) 767-1776. Fax (860) 767-0481. www.griswoldinn.com. Fourteen rooms and sixteen suites with private baths. Doubles, $100 to $220. Suites, $160 to $370.

Deacon Timothy Pratt House B&B, 325 Main St., Old Saybrook 06475.

This 1746 center-chimney Colonial listed on the National Register once was the home of the deacon at the pillared Congregational meetinghouse across the street. It served five generations of Pratts and now houses an expanding B&B. Former electrical engineer Shelley Nobile opened with four guest quarters and in 2003 added three more rooms in the former James Pharmacy building she acquired next door. Each room has a queensize canopy or poster bed, working fireplace, bath with whirlpool tub, TV, telephone and stereo/CD player. A fishnet canopy bed is angled from the corner in the Sunrise Room, which has two Queen Anne wingback recliners and an oversize jacuzzi. The premier accommodation in the main house is a suite with a carved four-poster rice bed, working fireplace, french doors opening onto a TV room with a day bed and an extra-large bathroom with a double jacuzzi. A pleasant living room is furnished with period pieces and decorative accents characteristic of the rest of the house. A full breakfast is served by candlelight on weekends in a formal dining room with an extra-long table for sixteen. A continental breakfast buffet is offered on weekdays. Next door, Shelley operates the James Gallery, a gift shop and an old-fashioned ice cream parlor and soda fountain.

(860) 395-1229. Fax (860) 395-4748. www.pratthouse.net. Five rooms and two suites with private baths. Doubles, $110 to $200.

Copper Beech Inn, 46 Main St., Ivoryton 06442.

Long known for its restaurant (see Where to Eat), the Copper Beech has upgraded its lodgings, both in an imposing white mansion shaded by the oldest copper beech tree in Connecticut and in a nicely secluded carriage house out back. New innkeepers Ian and Barbara Phillips started with the guest quarters upstairs above the restaurant, refurbishing three period rooms and a kingsize suite overlooking the rear gardens. The most deluxe is the sumptuous front master bedroom, big enough to include a kingsize carved mahogany poster bed, a couple of sitting areas and a new gas fireplace. Its renovated bath has been tiled in marble and boasts a hydro-massage tub and a heated floor. We still like best the nine rooms in the carriage house. Each has a jacuzzi or hydro-massage tub and french doors onto an outdoor deck or balcony overlooking the gardens. Second-floor rooms retain their original vaulted ceilings with exposed beams. Mahogany queensize or kingsize beds, club chairs, TVs and telephones are the norm. Guests relax in an elegant, wraparound atrium/ solarium in the front of the inn. A continental-plus breakfast buffet has been augmented lately with a couple of prepared egg dishes like quiche or coddled eggs.

(860) 767-0330 or (888) 809-2056. www.copperbeechinn.com. Twelve rooms and one suite with private baths. Doubles, $150 to $335.

Bee and Thistle Inn, 100 Lyme St., Old Lyme 06371.

Stately trees, gardens all around and a flower-bedecked entrance welcome visitors to this cheery yellow inn, set on five acres bordering the Lieutenant River in the historic district of Old Lyme. Built in 1756 with subsequent additions and remodeling, the structure is a charming ramble of parlors and porches, dining rooms and guest rooms. Eleven upstairs rooms come with period country furnishings. They vary widely in size from small with double or twin beds to large with queensize canopy beds and loveseats. Room 2 with a queen bed has a new gas fireplace and Room 3 has a new kingsize bed. Four-poster, fishnet canopy and spool beds are covered with quilts or afghans. Nooks are full of games and old books are all around. Breakfast in the inn's acclaimed restaurant (see Where to Eat) is complimentary for guests. It's taken on the inn's sunny dining porches, a great place to start the day.

(860) 434-1667 or (800) 622-4946. Fax (860) 434-3402. www.beeandthistleinn.com. Eleven rooms and one cottage with private baths. Doubles, $110 to $219.

CAMPING. For a true watery experience, camp on an island in the Connecticut River. Park your car at Gillette Castle State Park and paddle a canoe downriver to Selden Neck State Park in Lyme. Or put your small boat in at Salmon River Boat Launch, just north of East Haddam, and head up the Connecticut to Hurd State Park. Both riverside campsites are on islands accessible only by boat. Selden Neck, the largest island in the state, has room for about 50 campers, and Hurd can handle twelve. Available May-September, island campsites must be booked in advance at (860) 626-2336. The fee is $4 per camper nightly.

Wolf's Den Campground, 256 Town St. (Route 82), East Haddam 06423, (860) 873-9681, rents 205 sites from May-October.

Seeing and Doing

To the casual passerby, much of the Connecticut River appears inaccessible. You simply have to know where to look.

On the River

Essex Steam Train & Riverboat, 1 Railroad Ave., Essex.

They call it a journey into yesteryear, but it's also a great way to see and savor the area. With its whistle tooting and smokestack spewing, the Valley Railroad Company's marvelous old steam train runs from the old depot in the Centerbrook section of

Essex through woods and meadows to the Connecticut River landing at Deep River. There it connects with the three-deck Mississippi-style riverboat MV Becky Thatcher for an hour's cruise up past Gillette Castle to the Goodspeed Opera House and back. Narration highlights the history, folklore, flora and fauna along the way. The two-hour trip into the past is rewarding for young and old alike. Railroad buffs enjoy the working railroad yard, vintage rail cars and exhibits gathered around the National Register landmark depot. For hikers, the railroad on its first two excursions of the day offers a connection to Gillette Castle, with a stop at the Ferry Road landing in Chester, a ride on the Chester-Hadlyme Ferry and a moderately strenuous hike up to the castle. The Essex Clipper dinner train runs two-hour excursions on weekends in a vintage luxury dining car, Friday at 7:30, Saturday at 7 and Sunday at 4, June-October. The fare with dinner is $60.

(860) 767-0103 or (800) 377-3987. www.essexsteamtrain.com. Train and Riverboat trips run at 11, 12:30, 2 and 3:30, daily in summer, Wednesday-Sunday in October and Friday-Sunday in late spring and early fall. Train and boat, adults $24, children $12. Train only, adults $16, children $8.

Connecticut River Expeditions, Steamboat Dock, Essex.

The public gained more access to the lower Connecticut River with the launching in 2004 of this outfit's R/V River Quest, in cooperation with the Connecticut River Museum. The 60-passenger vessel – "new, quiet and environmentally friendly" – explores the tranquil, protected waters on everything from public cruises to special birding expeditions. The 75-minute narrated tours are offered twice daily of Essex Harbor and the lower river, pointing out historical and ecological attractions along the way. Early sunset cruises for adults (BYOB and picnic baskets) are offered Monday-Friday at 6:30 in summer and Friday-Sunday at 4:30 in fall. The River Quest also provides special bird-watching and environmental excursions sponsored by the Connecticut Audubon Society's new eco-travel office in Essex.

(860) 662-0577. www.ctriverexpeditions.org. Daytime cruises at 1 and 3 daily in summer, weekends in early spring and late fall; adults $12, children $8. Sunset cruises, $15.

Sightseeing and specialized excursions along the Connecticut River on a 400-passenger boat are offered from Goodspeed Landing by **Camelot Cruises Inc.,** 1 Marine Park, Haddam, (860) 345-8591 or (800) 522-7463. Brunch buffet cruises are scheduled from noon to 2:30 Sundays from May-October for $29. Camelot also offers three-hour murder mystery dinner cruises Fridays and Saturday nights from 7 to 10 for $59.75 each. New Orleans luncheon cruises are available on selected Thursdays in summer. Fall foliage lunch cruises are offered in the fall.

Savor the past aboard the tiny **Chester-Hadlyme ferry,** which has plied the river between Chester and Hadlyme since 1769. The second oldest continuously operating ferry service in the country (after one upriver between Rocky Hill and Glastonbury), it carries up to nine cars and 49 passengers on each four-minute trip and operates "on demand," April-November. Vehicles $3, passengers $1.

Public boat launching sites along the river are located at the Salmon River in East Haddam, Haddam Meadows in Haddam, the Hadlyme ferry landing in Lyme, the Town Dock at the foot of Main Street in Essex, and beneath the Baldwin Bridge at Old Saybrook. There are many private marinas, as well.

Near the River

Goodspeed Musicals, Goodspeed Landing, East Haddam.

The past is present at this restored 1876 Victorian opera-house confection built by shipping magnate William Goodspeed on the banks of the Connecticut River.

The opera house – a national treasure – produces uplifting musicals, revivals and new tryouts. Each is top flight – 43 have been world premieres and sixteen have gone on to Broadway, including "Annie," "Man of La Mancha" and "Shenandoah." The three shows each season run for about three months each. You climb endless flights to reach your seat in tiered intimacy. At intermission, munch popcorn from the old-fashioned machine and sip champagne by the glass in the Victorian bar or on the veranda high above the river. You'll think you've died and gone to the nineteenth century. Since 1984, Goodspeed has developed three new musicals annually and fostered emerging artists on a second stage, Goodspeed-at-Chester/ The Norma Terris Theatre.

(860) 873-8668. www.goodspeed.org. Shows are Wednesday at 2 and 7:30, Thursday at 7:30, Friday at 8, Saturday at 4 and 8:30 and Sunday at 2 and 6:30, April-December. Tickets, $24 to $53.

Gillette Castle State Park, 67 River Road, East Haddam.

This picturesque, 164-acre park was the former estate of William Gillette, the Hartford-born actor and playwright known for his portrayal of Sherlock Holmes. He designed the house of his dreams after medieval castles in Germany and had it built starting in 1914 on the last of a series of seven hills at a bend in the Connecticut River. His fertile imagination is revealed in each of the 24 rooms of the fieldstone castle. Gillette designed the furniture, including built-in couches and a dining room table that moves on metal tracks on the floor. Other than the intriguing castle, his chief legacy was a three-mile-long narrow-gauge railroad he designed and operated around his property. The train has been moved and most of the tracks dismantled, but his "Grand Central Station" survives as a depot in a picnic area and the state planned to restore a small loop of the railroad. A guided walk through the castle takes about a half hour. You can enjoy stunning views of the water below, walk along the river and picnic at tables scattered throughout the park. The best waterside picnic spots are along sandy beaches just above the Chester-Hadlyme ferry landing.

(860) 526-2336. Park open daily, 8 to dusk; free. Castle open daily 10 to 4:30, Memorial Day to Columbus Day. Castle tours $5, children $3.

Connecticut River Museum, 67 Main St., Essex.

Restored in 1975 from an 1878 steamboat warehouse, this interesting, cupola-topped structure at Steamboat Dock is living testimony to the maritime, economic and cultural heritage of the Connecticut River Valley. The site has been significant for nearly 400 years. It is where Native Americans pulled their dugout canoes ashore, where Colonial shipbuilders debated revolution, and where travelers boarded steamboats on the way to Hartford or New York. The river's story is highlighted in changing exhibits on the main floor. A recent one focused on "Fenwick-on-the-Sound: From Public Playground to Private Borough" and paid tribute to the late Katharine Hepburn, the borough's "most famous" resident. Another consisted of small boats from the museum's collection, including a shad boat that worked on the river and a birch bark canoe owned by the late newsman Charles Kuralt, who lived in Essex. Upstairs, where windows on two sides and a balcony afford sweeping views of the river, is the permanent shipbuilding exhibit. The highlight is a full-size replica of the first American warship, David Bushnell's strange-looking Turtle, built here in 1776 as a secret weapon to win the Revolutionary War. There's also a model of a Dutch explorer ship that sailed up the river in 1614. Boats built and used on the river are displayed in the boathouse. The foundation property also includes a small waterfront park with benches and the 1813 Hayden Chandlery, now the Thomas A. Stevens maritime research library. Newly berthed at Steamboat Dock is the 54-foot environmental research vessel R/V River Quest, which offers afternoon and sunset cruises for museum visitors and the public.

(860) 767-8269. www.ctrivermuseum.org. Open Tuesday-Sunday, 10 to 5. Adults $6, children $3.

The Essex Waterfront. As a living and working yachting and shipbuilding town, the Essex waterfront is a center of activity, and you'll find marinas all around. For yachtsmen, Essex holds some of the same cachet as Marblehead, Mass., or Oxford, Md. Just south of Steamboat Dock along Novelty Lane are the century-old Dauntless Club, the Essex Corinthian Yacht Club and, on an ever-so-watery point between the river and Middle Cove, the posh Essex Yacht Club. The historic structures here and elsewhere in town are detailed in a walking map.

Uptown Essex. Besides the waterfront area, Methodist Hill at the other end of Main Street has a cluster of historic structures. Facing tiny Champlin Square is the imposing white **Pratt House** (circa 1732), restored and operated by the Essex Historical Society to show Essex as it was in yesteryear (open June-Labor Day, weekends 1 to 4, $2). The period gardens in the rear are planted with herbs and flowers typical of the 18th century. The society also operates the adjacent **Hill Academy Museum** (1833), an early boarding school that now displays historical collections of old Essex. Next door in the academy's former dormitory is the Catholic Church and, next to it, the Baptist Church, one of only two Egyptian Revival structures in this country.

Old Saybrook grew inland from the point where in 1614 the Dutch explorer Adriaen Block became the first white man to enter the river Quonitocutt, or "Long Tidal River." **Fort Saybrook,** Connecticut's first military fortification, was built near the river's mouth in 1636 by the British. What once served as protection from the Pequot Indians is now an 18-acre historical park created by the Fort Saybrook Monument Park Association. Shore portions yield panoramic views of the river and storyboards depict the history of the original Saybrook colony, one of Connecticut's first.

Old Lyme. One of Connecticut's prettiest towns has a long main street lined with gracious homes from the 18th and 19th centuries, including one we think is particularly handsome called Lyme Regis, the English summer resort after which the town was named. Lyme Street, over the years the home of Connecticut governors and chief justices, is a National Historic District.

Ferry Point State Park, Ferry Road, Old Lyme. If you crave peace and quiet alongside the water, this little-known park is for you. Leave your car in the parking lot beside the state Department of Environmental Protection's Marine Headquarters and enjoy a handful of picnic tables and a gazebo beside the Connecticut River. Follow the boardwalk south underneath the railroad bridge and leave the busy marinas and the roar of I-95 behind. Walk alongside the river and marshlands a few hundred yards to a twenty-foot-high observation platform. You're in another world, with scarcely a sign of civilization in your panoramic vista. Here you can see the marshland reclamation project and peer across a channel to an osprey nest on the Great Island Wildlife Management Area. Look past the mouth of the river and across the Sound to the North Fork of Long Island. Plaques along the way identify ducks, herons and anadromous fish, among others. You may be joined by fishermen, birders and a kayaker or two. Park open daily, dawn to dusk.

Florence Griswold Museum, 96 Lyme St., Old Lyme.

This is the pillared 1817 landmark in which the daughter of a boat captain ran a finishing school for girls and later an artists' retreat, with most of the rooms converted into bedrooms and studios in the barns by the Lieutenant River. Now run as a museum interpreting its early status as a boarding house for artists and the home of American Impressionism, it has unique painted panels in every room. Especially prized is the dining room with panels on all sides given over to the work of the Old Lyme artists, who included Childe Hassam. Across the mantel the artists painted a delightful caricature of themselves for posterity. The arts colony thrived for twenty years and its works are on permanent display in the second-floor galleries. They include major works by Childe Hassam and John Henry Twachtman, and the largest collection of Willard Metcalf paintings in the world. Also on view are selections from the priceless Hartford Steam Boiler Collection of American art, recently donated to the museum by the insurance company. Changing exhibitions are produced in the striking new Krieble Gallery, a modernist, white and silvery series of barn-like buildings backing up to the river. Three soaring, skylit galleries were showing variations of a world-class exhibit called "The American River" at our latest visit. Both the building and its contents elicited a pertinent comment in the guest book: "Wonderful views, inside and out."

(860) 434-5542. www.flogris.org. Open Tuesday-Saturday 10 to 5 and Sunday 1 to 5; Griswold House closed Sunday January-March. Adults $7, children $4.

The **Lyme Art Association Gallery**, 90 Lyme St., next door to the Florence Griswold Museum, is headquarters of the Lyme Art Association. Founded in 1902, it is said to be the nation's oldest summer art group to have held continuous exhibitions in its own gallery. It exhibits seven major shows each season (Tuesday-Saturday noon to 4:30, Sunday 1 to 4:30, most of year; admission $4).

At 84 Lyme St. is the handsome, Federal-style **Lyme Academy of Fine Arts,** with changing exhibits by local artists and academy students (Tuesday-Saturday 10 to 4 and Sunday 1 to 4; donation). The works of Lyme's American Impressionists also are hung in the Town Hall, and the public library often has exhibits.

SHOPPING. The choicest shopping opportunities for visitors are in Essex and Chester.

The **Talbots** store confronting visitors head-on as they enter the downtown section of Essex sets the tone. Also fashionable in different ways are **Silkworm, J. Alden Clothier, Stonewear Clothing** and a colorful place called **Equator. A Pocketful of Posies,** billed as a shabby chic boutique, opened in 2004 in the quarters of the late Clipper Ship Bookstore. Pillows and tableware are featured among home accessories at **Portabella. Fenwick Cottage** stocks unusual gifts and decorative accessories. Jewelry, incense, candles and gifts are the specialty of **Scensibles.** Another concentration of stores is farther down Main Street at Griswold and Essex squares. **Red Balloon** offers precious clothes for precious children. Lilly Pulitzer is featured at **The Yankee Palm.** At **Red Pepper,** we saw items we had never seen anywhere else, among them interesting glasses and goblets in all kinds of colors made in Upstate New York, and cat pins by a woman who lives on a farm with seven cats. The shop carries clothing from small designers, almost all made in this country – which is unusual these days. **Hattitudes** stocks more kinds of hats than we ever expected to see. The **Essex Coffee & Tea Company** dispenses fancy beverages. Behind it is **Sweet P's,** a candy and ice cream shop. Also here is the **Essex Mariner** with model boats, carved shore birds and nautical brass. Nearby is **Olive Oyl's** for carry-out cuisine and specialty foods.

Lately, Chester has become a destination for shoppers, especially those with an interest in the esoteric. We like the colorful Italian tableware and pottery at **Ceramica** and the French-inspired fabrics and pottery at **Souleiado en Provence.** Traditional and contemporary local crafts are exhibited at **Connecticut River Artisans.** All things herbal are featured at **R.J. Vickers Herbery.** Leif and Katherine Nilsson show their contemporary paintings at **Nilsson Spring Street Studio & Gallery.** Kathryne Wright's **Hammered Edge Studio & Gallery** specializes in unusual jewelry and wearable art. Special interests are served at **Willow Tree** (vintage clothing), **Dino Varano** (crafted artware) and **One of a Kind Antiques.**

Where to Eat ⟋⟋⟋

Water Views

Gelston House River Grill, 8 Main St. (Route 82), East Haddam.

The Carbone family of Hartford restaurant fame took over this landmark white confection at Goodspeed Landing and succeeded where others have failed. With a sensational riverside location and a captive audience from the Goodspeed Opera House next door, the re-christened River Grill has not only satisfied and survived but also has expanded. Lately it expanded into the gift shop at the side of the building to add a dining room off the lounge. The new room lacks the view of the elegant main dining room, a huge enclosed porch with big windows on all sides overlooking the river. But the food is the same, and generally praised – no mean feat for a busy place subject to the demands of theater-goers. Recent starters on the short contemporary menu were two salads, a wild mushroom risotto, salmon cake with spicy rémoulade and mussels provençal. The six entrées ranged from salmon fillet with tomato aioli to New York strip steak with compound butter. The lunch menu is twice as extensive. In season, the outdoor Beer Garden is popular for lunch and casual suppers.

(860) 873-1411. Entrées, $19 to $27. Lunch, Wednesday-Saturday 11:30 to 2:30. Dinner, Wednesday-Saturday, 5:30 to 9. Sunday, brunch 11 to 2:15, dinner 4 to 8.

The Blue Oar, 16 Snyder Road, Haddam.

Who'd ever think a former snack bar at river's edge overlooking a marina would dispense good, innovative fare? Third-generation restaurateur Jim Reilly saw the possibilities for the one-room shack at the Midway Marina off Route 154 north of Tylerville. He painted picnic tables in rainbow colors on the grounds, installed chairs at a counter running around the perimeter of a wraparound porch, hung blue oars overhead and built a makeshift pavilion outside. You bring your own bottle, review the blackboard menu, place your order and find a table. Jim cooks "whatever's fresh that day" on a six-foot industrial grill on the porch with sauces he prepares ahead. The five-item menu at our October visit listed the likes of braised tilapia with roasted tomatoes, artichoke hearts and saffron rice; grilled salmon with white wine sauce over a warm black bean and corn salad, and grilled rosemary pork loin with orange-cranberry sauce and mashed potatoes. Starters are simple: chowders, potato-cheddar-bacon soup and steamers. Desserts, displayed in a pastry case at the counter, might be key lime mousse, white and dark chocolate mousse tower and strawberry-rhubarb tart. The snack bar heritage is evident in burgers, deli sandwiches and hot dogs, available day or night. Dinner is by candlelight, and the setting by the river, though very much weather-dependent, is pleasantly rustic and refreshing.

(860) 345-2994. Entrées, $15.95 to $18.95. Lunch, Tuesday-Sunday 11:30 to 5. Dinner nightly, 5 to 9. Closed Columbus Day to Mother's Day. BYOB. No credit cards.

Terra Mar Grille, Saybrook Point Inn, 2 Bridge St., Old Saybrook.

There may be no more glamorous dining room on the Connecticut waterfront than this L-shaped room wrapping around an interior bar, with windows onto the mouth of the river beyond a marina. Cushioned rattan chairs are at generally well-spaced tables dressed in heavy cream-colored cloths and lit by shaded gas lamps. It's a formal, special-occasion place, although the outdoor tables appear more casual. The food here generally measures up to the view. For lunch, the breast of chicken stuffed with spinach, roasted peppers and mushrooms and topped with a whole-grain mustard and garlic sauce proved exceptional. The whole wheat pasta primavera with a julienne of vegetables seemed dull only in comparison. The dinner menu yields about a dozen main courses, from seafood paella, blackened escolar and tilapia meunière to chicken breast stuffed with wild mushrooms and goat cheese, grilled pork chop with cabernet demi-glace and filet mignon with port wine demi-glace. The seafood crêpe and the grilled shrimp wrapped in pancetta are good starters. Dessert could be warm apple napoleon, chocolate bourbon cake or a trio of crème brûlées.

(860) 395-2000. Entrées, $21.95 to $33.95. Lunch daily, 11:30 to 2. Dinner nightly, 6 to 9 or 10. Sunday brunch, 11 to 2.

Dock & Dine, 145 College St. (off Route 154), Saybrook Point, Old Saybrook.

With windows onto the water on three sides, this long-running restaurant claims Connecticut's best riverfront location, an open vista where broad river meets Long Island Sound and boats of all kinds frequently pass by. The food has been upgraded under owner Jon Kodama, who has forged a chain of coastal restaurants from his base in Mystic, but the view remains its chief asset. You're so close to the water that you almost feel you're on a ship. A huge carved fish hangs in the center of the dining room. The large lounge also has nautical accents. The only outside dining is a small seasonal deck off the lounge. The lunch menu is heavy on typical touristy shore food: peel-and-eat shrimp, nachos, fried calamari, burgers and tuna melts, fried clams and scallops, fish and chips, and chicken teriyaki. The dinner menu has some of the same plus more adventurous fare: lobster ravioli and seafood-stuffed mushrooms for appetizers, sautéed lobster cakes, bouillabaisse, grilled swordfish with mango-papaya salsa, chipotle-glazed grilled pork loin and New York sirloin for main courses.

(860) 388-4665 or (800) 362-3625. Entrées, $12.95 to $26.95. Lunch daily, 11:30 to 3, to 4 in lounge. Dinner nightly, 4 to 9 or 10. Closed Monday and Tuesday in off-season.

Sage On the Waterfall, 129 West Main Street, Chester.

This was a Chart House restaurant until 2000, and the chain sure knows how to pick waterside locations. So when this Chart House and one on the New Haven harborfront were targeted for closing, some of its managers bought up the sites and repositioned each as an American bar and grill. This one on a wooded site overlooking the Pattaconk River on the outskirts of Chester was once the Rogers & Champion Brushworks factory. Diners enter via a covered wooden footbridge across the little river beside a waterfall and find themselves in a lively, atmospheric bar and lounge. Upstairs are three dining rooms with white-cloth and paper-covered tables, barnwood walls and old mill works overhead. A main-floor dining room off the lounge is perched right beside the waterfall, with outdoor decks on either side – each an appealing place for drinks or dinner. The extensive menu remains in the Chart House idiom, particularly strong on steaks and prime rib, served with house salad and artisan breads. Side vegetables are extra. You'll also find shrimp scampi, herb-crusted baked salmon, sautéed scallops and four presentations of chicken.

Four dinner sandwiches are served with coleslaw and french fries. Mini lobster rolls, steamed mussels, baked brie and spicy chicken skewers with blue cheese dip make good starters. Vanilla bean crème brûlée, dark chocolate mousse and creamy cheesecake are favorite endings.

(860) 526-4847. www.sageamerican.com. Entrées, $14.95 to $30.95. Dinner nightly, 5 to 9, 10 or 11.

Crow's Nest Gourmet Deli, 35 Pratt St., Essex.

This deli and bakery in the Dauntless Shipyard claims the only waterfront dining in Essex. It's not exactly riverfront, set well back in a marina. But the water can be glimpsed and boats are everywhere on view from the wide second-floor deck outside, so it's a favorite of visiting yachtsmen and yacht watchers. Owners Mark and Judi Mannetho are caterers, too, so the food should be a cut above the standard fare listed on the extensive printed menu. Perhaps it is the blackboard specials that give the place its gourmet claim. Mark advised that the "crabby patty" (Maryland crab cake on whole wheat with saffron aioli, tomato and sprouts) posted at our visit had become such a hit it would gain a regular place on the menu. The lobster roll proved disappointing. Better settle for one of the fancy sandwiches or, our other choice, a bread bowl filled with seafood bisque. Corned-beef hash with poached eggs is a highlight on the breakfast menu.

(860) 767-3288. Sandwiches, $5 to $8. Breakfast daily, 7 to 11:45, weekends to 1. Lunch daily, 11:45 to 4 in summer, to 3 in winter. Closed Tuesday in winter.

Other Choices

Restaurant du Village, 59 Main St., Chester.

The hostess greets you with a cheery "Bon Soir" at this charming restaurant, as authentic as any you'd find in a rural French village. Alsatian chef Michel Keller and his Culinary Institute-trained American wife Cynthia run their top-rated establishment very personally. Through a cozy bar-lounge, decorated with plump piggies (the logo of the restaurant) with a few tables for overflow, you reach a small dining room with white curtains on the windows, French oil paintings on the walls, and white linens, carafes of wildflowers and votive candles on the tables. Meals begin with what may be the best French bread you will taste in this country. Among the short list of appetizers, standouts are the cassoulet, a small copper casserole filled with sautéed shrimp in a light curry sauce; the croustade with grilled vegetables, and escargots with wild mushrooms in puff pastry. We also like the baked French goat cheese on herbed salad greens with garlic croutons. Entrées might be pan-seared tuna steak topped with tapenade, rabbit flamande, roast duck with kumquats and Cynthia's specialty, a stew of veal, lamb and pork with leeks and potatoes. Desserts change daily and are notable as well. Michel might prepare an open fruit tart with blueberries and peaches in almond cream, a gratin of passion fruit and paris-brest, in addition to his usual napoleons, soufflés glacé and crème brûlée.

(860) 526-5301. Entrées, $27 to $32. Dinner, Tuesday-Saturday 5 to 9, Sunday 5 to 8.15. Closed Tuesday in winter.

Copper Beech Inn, 46 Main Street, Ivoryton.

Surrounded by gardens and shaded by the largest copper beech tree in Connecticut, this venerable inn offers high-style dining in three elegant, refurbished dining areas. The chandeliered main Ivoryton Room conveys a rich, sumptuous Victorian motif. The paneled and beamed-ceilinged Comstock Room retains the look of the billiards parlor that it once was. Between the two is a pretty garden porch with a handful of romantic tables for two. The formal, contemporary French fare has been refreshed by executive chef William Von Ahnen and his wife Jacqueline, the pastry chef, who moved to the Copper Beach after a long tenure at the famed Chantecleer in Nantucket. The menu ranges widely from fillet of gray sole stuffed with a scallop mousse and served with a lobster claw and a lobster-ginger sauce to roasted rack of Colorado lamb with a rich red wine sauce. Indeed, all the food tends to be rich here, from the house-made lobster and sole sausage with truffle beurre blanc to the sautéed foie gras with a caramelized blackberry-chardonnay sauce. The lobster française, a house specialty deglazed with madeira, brandy and cream and garnished with black truffle risotto, is fabulous. So is the magret and confit of duck with armagnac-laced dried plums and the grilled veal chop with marchand du vin sauce. Finish with one of Jacqueline's spectacular desserts, perhaps the chocolate tasting for two, a creamy mixed-fruit tart or a light and ethereal tarte tatin with cinnamon ice cream.

(860) 767-0330 or (888) 809-2056. Entrées, $26 to $38. Dinner, Tuesday-Sunday 5:30 to 9:30.

Gabrielle's, 78 Main St., Centerbrook.

This Victorian-era house with a gazebo-like front porch has been a culinary landmark in the area since 1979. A trio of new owners tore down walls of what had been Steve's Centerbrook Café and created more open dining areas that are suave in ecru with white trim, accented by stunning art works and greenery. It's a stylish setting for the contemporary and artistic American fare created by talented chef Daniel McManamy, veteran of many an area restaurant. A perfect lunch here brought the signature mussels and frites, incredibly thin fries that were addictive when paired with the tarragon aioli dip, and cornmeal-crusted fried oysters with chipotle aioli. These and other mainstays on the lunch menu turn up as appetizers and small plates at night. The fairly extensive dinner menu also offers salads, thin-crust pizzas and fifteen entrées from grilled brook trout with shiitake mushrooms in a carrot-ginger sauce to grilled New York sirloin steak with roasted walnut-gorgonzola butter. A dish called lobster in vatapa (simmered with shrimp and scallops and served in a spicy sauce over rice), Indian-spiced breast of duckling and chicken in green mole indicate the kitchen's range. Desserts might be white and dark chocolate mousse, crème brûlée, linzer torte and apple-almond tart with french vanilla ice cream.

(860) 767-2440. www.gabrielles.net. Entrées, $18 to $25. Lunch, Tuesday-Friday and Sunday 11:30 to 3. Dinner, Tuesday-Sunday from 5 to 9 or 9:30.

Griswold Inn, 36 Main St., Essex.

Some things seldom change, and the immensely popular Gris is one of them, having been going strong since 1776. The always-crowded Tap Room is a happy hubbub of banjo players and singers of sea chanteys, and everyone loves the antique popcorn machine. A meal at the Gris is an experience in Americana. There's much to see in four dining rooms: the important collection of Antonio Jacobsen marine oils in the dark paneled Library, the Currier and Ives steamboat prints in the Covered Bridge Room (actually fashioned from a New Hampshire covered bridge), the riverboat memorabilia in the Steamboat Room, the musket-filled Gun Room with 55 pieces dating to the 15th century. Together, they rank as one of the outstanding marine art collections in America. The menu is a mixed bag of seafood, meat and game, ranging from pesto-crusted sea bass to chicken pot pie, prime rib and New York strip steak with house-made worcestershire sauce. Three versions of the inn's patented 1776 sausages are served as a mixed grill with sauerkraut and German potato salad at dinner. They're in even more demand for lunch, when you also can get eggs benedict or Welsh rarebit, a goat cheese and arugula salad or yankee pot roast. At our latest lunch, a wicker swan full of packaged crackers helped sustain us as we waited (and waited) for our orders of crostini and shepherd's pie. The oil lamps were lit at noon, the place was hopping and the atmosphere was cheery on a dank autumn day. That we remember, more than the food. The ever-popular Sunday hunt breakfast ($16.95) is an enormous buffet of dishes ranging from baby cod and creamed chipped beef to scrambled eggs and a soufflé of grits and cheddar cheese.

(860) 767-1776. Entrées, $18.50 to $28. Lunch, Monday-Saturday 11:45 to 3. Dinner, 5:30 to 9 or 10. Sunday, hunt breakfast 11 to 2:30, dinner 4:30 to 9.

Bee and Thistle Inn, 100 Lyme St., Old Lyme.

This cheery yellow inn's restaurant consistently wins statewide awards for "romantic dining" and "best desserts." Dining is in country-pretty enclosed porches on either side of the inn as well as in a room linking the two in back. Luncheon choices are generally of the brunch and dinner variety. Instead of soups and sandwiches expect substantial salads and entrées from mushroom strudel and seafood stew to fillet of sole and grilled tournedos of beef. In the traditional inn style, regulars like to start with cocktails in the living room as they peruse the menu proposed by innkeeper Philip Abraham, the Culinary Institute of America-trained chef. His short dinner menu ranges widely from grilled yellowfin tuna with apple-beet salsa to seared venison medallions with gin-juniper gravy. Our crab cakes with chipotle rémoulade and the filet mignon were sensational, their simple names failing to do justice to the complexities of their preparation or that of their accompaniments. We also enjoyed the thin-sliced, rare breast of duck served on a passion-fruit puree with a spiced pear beggar's purse. You might start with the cured salmon napoleon, the breast of turkey terrine studded with sundried cherries and pistachios or the pan roast of oysters with minced root vegetables in puff pastry. Finish with a triple-nut bourbon tartlet, a ginger-scented pear dumpling or one of the homemade ice creams and sorbets.

(860) 434-1667 or (800) 622-4946. Entrées, $26 to $34. Lunch, Wednesday-Saturday 11:30 to 2. Dinner, Wednesday-Sunday from 5:30. Sunday brunch, 11 to 2.

The Black Seal, 15 Main St., Essex.

Come to this appealingly nautical "seafood grille" for casual dining and local color. All the decorative items hanging along the walls and from the ceilings of the front tavern and the rear dining room could distract one from the food, of which there's something for everyone day and night. Basically the same fare is offered at lunch and dinner, though lunch brings more sandwiches and dinner more entrées. Graze on things like chili nachos, fire-pot chili, stuffed potato skins, cajun shrimp, Rhode Island clam chowder, California burgers, and cobb and caesar salads anytime. At night, entrées could be grilled brook trout topped with crabmeat, pan-roasted snapper fillet finished with tomato-cumin vinaigrette and steak au poivre, along with the predictable assortment of fried seafood dinners. Desserts include chocolate mousse terrine, pumpkin-praline torte and chocolate-raspberry cake.

(860) 767-0233. www.theblackseal.com. Entrées, $12.95 to $21.95. Lunch, daily 11:30 to 3:30, weekends to 4. Dinner, 5 to 9:30 or 10. Sunday brunch, 11:30 to 2.

FOR MORE INFORMATION: Central Regional Tourism District – Connecticut's Heritage River Valley, 31 Pratt St., Hartford, CT 06103, (860) 244-8181 or (800) 793-4480. www.enjoycentralct.com

More localized information may be found at www.essexct.com, www.chesterct.com and www.oldsaybrookct.com.

Mystic, Conn.

Think of Mystic and the word "seaport" comes to mind. For this is the home of famed Mystic Seaport, the nation's premier maritime museum. Ponder some more and you might add shipbuilding, whaling, fishing, clipper ships and sea captains' homes. You might even think of tourism, now the area's biggest business.

Although Mystic is a mere village and a post-office address straddling the Mystic River – a political nonentity enveloped in the larger towns of Groton and Stonington – it is important beyond its size.

Historically, Mystic has been a site for shipbuilding since the 17th century. In the mid-1800s, the village of 1,500 owned eighteen whalers and the boatyards produced 22 clippers, some of which set sailing records that have never been equaled. Later, many of the nation's fastest sailing yachts and schooners were built here, and submarines still are made along the banks of the Thames River on the western side of Groton.

Today, Mystic thrives on its legacy of having produced more than 1,000 sailing vessels, more noted captains and more important sailing records than any place of its size in the world.

Its quaint neighbor to the southwest, Noank, reflects its heritage as both a home of shipbuilders and a lobster fishing port. To the southeast, the charming borough of Stonington – as historic a seaside enclave as you'll find along the East Coast – is the home port for about 30 draggers and lobster boats, Connecticut's only surviving commercial fishing fleet.

With a notable maritime tradition chronicled by Mystic Seaport, Mystic has long been the state's prime tourist destination. In addition to the Seaport, visitors are drawn to the recently expanded Mystic Aquarium and Institute for Exploration, the submarine Nautilus and the U.S. Naval Submarine Base in Groton, and the U.S. Coast Guard Academy across the Thames River in New London.

Lately, another draw has been the wildly successful Foxwoods Resort Casino, the world's largest, and the nearly as large and more showy Mohegan Sun Casino. The Indian-backed ventures continue to expand with more slots as well as hotels, restaurants, theaters, an arena and even a museum.

All of these tourist magnets have resulted in a mix of hotels, motels and B&Bs, seafood restaurants and fast-food eateries, eclectic boutiques and factory outlets, and other attractions that bring still more tourists.

In the midst of it all is busy downtown Mystic, the only place we know of where U.S. Route 1 traffic is stopped hourly while the rare bascule bridge over the Mystic River is opened to let sailboats pass. But then, Mystic is also one of the few places we know where motorists stop all along Main Street for pedestrians – tourists, many of them – to cross.

Getting There

About 50 miles east of New Haven, the Mystic area stretches along Long Island Sound in southeastern Connecticut from Groton to the Rhode Island border. U.S. Route 1 meanders through the heart of Mystic, while Interstate 95 crosses its northern edge. State Route 27 links the two. Regular

Visitors to Mystic Seaport stroll along maritime museum's waterfront.

train service is provided by Amtrak, whose shoreline route between Noank and Stonington is one of the more scenic around. Major airlines fly into Hartford and Providence – locals tout the latter's airport as particularly convenient.

Where to Stay

Accommodations in Mystic are numerous and diverse, but few are on or near the water. Rates vary widely from weekend to midweek as well as by season.

Water Views

Steamboat Inn, 73 Steamboat Wharf, Mystic 06355.

You're so close to the water, you feel as if you're on board ship at this luxurious B&B beside the Mystic River (indeed you are, on the luxurious Valiant "boat and breakfast" moored outside). Named after ships built in Mystic, all ten inn rooms have whirlpool baths and televisions hidden in cupboards or armoires. Six on the second floor have fireplaced sitting areas facing the river. They're outfitted in lavish style: mounds of pillows and designer sheets on the queensize canopy or twin beds, loveseats or sofas and a plush armchair in front of the fireplace, mantels and cabinet work that make these rooms look unusually homelike. The most smashing views are from Mystic, a room in the center, although our favorites are the second-floor rooms at either end, brighter and more airy with bigger windows onto the water and half-cathedral ceilings. Four rooms on the ground floor are suite-size in proportion and come with double whirlpool tubs and wet bars with microwaves, but are on view to the constant stream of passersby on the wharf unless the blinds are drawn. Guests have little reason to leave their rooms, but there's a common room on the second floor. It has all the right magazines, and glass tables for continental breakfast. Homemade breads and muffins are put out each morning, and tea and sherry in the evening. Lately, co-owner John McGee added the charter vessel **Valiant,** custom-built in New Orleans. An avid boatsman, he docks it alongside the inn and, when in port, offers five outside staterooms for bed and breakfast at $195 to $250 a night.

(860) 536-8300. Fax (860) 536-9528. www.steamboatinnmystic.com. Ten rooms with private baths. Doubles, $195 to $300.

The Inn at Stonington, 60 Water St., Stonington.

The old Harborview Restaurant was destroyed by fire, and from its ashes in 2001 rose this luxury B&B facing the waterfront, the first good place to stay in the borough. New owner Bill Griffin, also a partner in the Whaler's Inn in Mystic, spared no expense in producing a handsome gray and white-trimmed, three-story inn up against the sidewalk in front, with nothing but docks and water behind. All twelve guest rooms in the main building come with fireplaces and ten have jacuzzi tubs. Beds are queensize except for two kings, and furnishings are "very high-end," Bill said. Six have water views and french doors leading onto private balconies. The best view may be from the third-floor sitting area with a common balcony. Six larger rooms with high ceilings are available in a new brick annex next door. All come with jacuzzi tubs and five have kingsize beds and fireplaces. The two seaside rooms contain small sitting areas and refrigerators. One is a deluxe room offering a large balcony with a view of the harbor. On the main floor of the main inn are a living room/dining area where a substantial continental breakfast is served. Complimentary wines and cheese are offered in the afternoon. The inn includes a basement exercise area and has kayaks and bicycles for guests. Meals are available at Skipper's Dock (see Where to Eat), the nicely renovated year-round establishment at the rear of the property, which has been leased to a well-known local restaurateur.

(860) 535-2000. Fax (860) 535-8193. www.innatstonington.com. Eighteen rooms with private baths. Doubles, $175 to $395.

The Whaler's Inn, 20 East Main St., Mystic 06355.

The folks from the luxury Steamboat Inn across the Mystic River acquired and upgraded this venerable inn and motel in the heart of town. There are 41 rooms in the older main building and nearby houses, and two newer motel buildings surrounding a courtyard. The newest accommodations are eight upscale rooms with whirlpool tubs, fireplaces and partial water views in a building called the Hoxie House on the river side of the property. It was nicknamed the Jimmy Carter Wing after former the former president and his party booked it in 2004 during christening ceremonies in Groton for a new nuclear-powered submarine bearing his name. Rooms throughout the complex vary. All come with TVs and phones. Motel units in the Noank House have one or two double beds and showers; those in the Stonington House, bathtubs. Rooms in the inn and the 1865 House next to it are decorated traditionally and most have queen beds. These and the new luxury rooms are the higher-priced accommodations. The small lobby is nicely outfitted with wing chairs and oriental carpets. Continental breakfast is offered in a common hospitality room. On the main floor is Restaurant Bravo Bravo, serving lunch and dinner.

(860) 536-1506 or (800) 243-2588. Fax (860) 572-1250. www.whalersinnmystic.com. Forty-nine rooms with private baths. Doubles, $139 to $249.

The Inn at Mystic, Route 1, Mystic 06355.

Although this nicely landscaped, thirteen-acre complex atop a hill beside Pequotsepos Cove includes a fine inn in a white-pillared Colonial Revival mansion and deluxe inn-style rooms in its East Wing, it began as a motor inn and is, we think, the area's nicest. It's the only motor inn overlooking the harbor and Long Island

Sound and at least looks like New England, with brown shingles and blue shutters. The rooms vary from good to spectacular. Twelve deluxe units in the renovated East Wing come with queensize canopy beds, wing chairs and fireplaces, plus balconies or patios with views of the water. Six rooms here have huge jacuzzis in the bathrooms with mirrors all around. The complex takes its name from the 1904 mansion atop the hill, which has five large and antiques-decorated guest rooms, some with fireplaces and all with whirlpool tubs. In summer on a wicker rocker on the inn's spacious veranda, gazing out over English gardens and orchards toward Long Island Sound, or in winter sitting deep in a chintz-covered sofa by a fire in the drawing room with its 17th-century pine paneling, you may feel like a country squire. Behind the inn, the gatehouse has three attractive fireplaced accommodations done in a Ralph Lauren country look. Humphrey Bogart and Lauren Bacall stayed here on their honeymoon, we're told. Rooms in the original two-story motor inn are handsomely furnished as well. In yet another building on the property is the inn's **Flood Tide Restaurant** (see Where to Eat). A tennis court, a small pool, two putting greens and use of canoes, kayaks and rowboats in the cove are other pluses here.

(860) 536-9604 or (800) 237-2415. Fax (860) 572-1635. www.innatmystic.com. Sixty-seven rooms with private baths. Doubles, $160 to $295 EP.

Taber Inne & Suites, Route 1, Mystic 06355.

Located in a quasi-residential area east of town, this expanding establishment includes a renovated motel, a restored 1829 guest house, and a couple of new buildings with deluxe jacuzzi rooms and townhouse suites whose balconies overlook the Mystic River. Twelve rooms have water views when the leaves are off trees that screen the two-acre compound from Williams Beach, according to owner Tom Taber. In the motel are twelve rooms with a kingsize bed or two doubles. Four rooms in the 1829 Cavan House come with queen beds, whirlpool baths and private decks. Four more rooms in the Wexford House building that replaced an old farmhouse have fireplaces and double whirlpool tubs and three on the second floor have water views. A water view is also offered from one of the eight Waterford townhouse suites out back, each with two bedrooms, living rooms with fireplaces, wet bars and whirlpool tubs. The six latest rooms with fireplaces and whirlpool tubs are in a new East Wing structure holding a fitness center and an indoor pool.

(860) 536-4904 or (866) 466-6978. Fax (860) 572-9140. www.taberinn.com. Twenty-six rooms and eight suites with private baths. Doubles, $169 to $210. Two-bedroom suites for four, $345 to $425.

Orchard Street Inn, 41 Orchard St., Stonington 06378.

Three plush and private B&B accommodations in a bright yellow cottage along the ocean marsh emerged in 2003 in a tightly zoned town where such uses are not encouraged. The use of the old Lasbury Guest House was grandfathered, which explains how New York building contractor Richard Satler and Regina Shields gutted the interior of the old guest house to produce a seaside B&B. Each section of the cottage has its own entrance off a private patio, a queensize bed, all-new bath, TV with DVD player, mini-refrigerator and loveseat. The spiffy, summery decor is best in the rear Delphinium Room, with vaulted ceiling, high queensize poster bed, wicker loveseat and a larger patio facing the wetlands. Their cottage accommodations completed, the couple were planning some changes in the main house, where they live. In the reception area, they have bistro tables where Regina offers a full breakfast – fruits, muffins, croissants and perhaps an omelet.

(860) 535-2681. www.orchardstreetinn.com. Three rooms with private baths. Doubles, $160 to $175.

Other Choices

Hilton Mystic, 20 Coogan Blvd., Mystic 06355.

Opened in 1986 to the tune of $15 million, this is not your typical Hilton in terms of head-on, high-rise architecture. Across from the Mystic Aquarium, its low red-brick exterior and peaked roofs emulate the look of 19th-century mills and warehouses. Inside, all is luxurious, from the Mooring restaurant to the grand piano in the fireplaced lobby with intimate sitting areas next to an open courtyard in which a dolphin sculpture resides. The Soundings lounge offers a cozy fireplace and an all-day bar menu. The spacious guest rooms have two doubles or one kingsize bed and are decorated in rose and green, each bearing two large prints of Mystic Seaport scenes commissioned from artist Sally Caldwell Fisher. Five deluxe rooms have queen beds and a sitting area plus big jacuzzi tubs in the extra-large bathrooms. They also have separate vanities and enormous closets. The meandering, angled layout puts some rooms an inordinate distance from the elevators but also contributes to peace and quiet; we walked the equivalent of a couple of blocks to our corner room, but never heard a sound all night. Facilities include a small and shallow indoor-outdoor pool and a fitness center.

(860) 572-0731. Fax (860) 572-0328. www.hiltonmystic.com. One hundred seventy-six rooms and six suites. Doubles, $159 to $279.

The Old Mystic Inn, 52 Main St., Box 733, Old Mystic 06372.

The sweet aroma of apple-cranberry coffeecake baking in the oven greeted our arrival at this historic hostelry near the head of the wide Mystic River. Innkeeper Michael Cardillo Jr., a Culinary Institute of America-trained former private chef, treats overnight guests to afternoon cakes, brownies and popcorn. They bed down for the night in four antiques-furnished guest rooms in a red and white 1784 Colonial house up against the rural road and four newer rooms in a blue carriage house built out back in 1988. Rooms are named after New England authors (the house at one time was the antiquarian Old Mystic Book Shop). All have queen beds, and three in the main house have working fireplaces. Two larger rooms in the carriage house have gas fireplaces and whirlpool tubs, canopy beds, and a loveseat and two wing chairs in one, a loveseat and a wicker chair in the other. The main house has pleasant sitting rooms upstairs and down, a front porch and an atmospheric front dining room where four tables are set for breakfast. Michael calls his fare "country gourmet." You might have baked stuffed french toast with maple-walnut syrup, caramel-apple pancakes or herbed scrambled eggs in puff pastry with smoked gouda mornay sauce and steamed asparagus. The deep back yard includes perennial gardens and a gazebo.

(860) 572-9422. Fax (860) 572-9954. www.oldmysticinn.com. Eight rooms with private baths. Doubles, $145 to $185.

Mystic Seaport Inn, 6 Coogan Blvd., Mystic 06355.

Its location back from the highway and high atop a hill overlooking the Olde Mistick Village shopping complex sets this recently renovated and expanded motor inn apart from all the chains along motel row. One of the original two-story brick and wood-frame buildings in back retains 44 guest rooms (some nicely sheltered facing the woods), but the front building with motel entries off the corridor gave way to a new three-story building with faux gables and dormers and 75 larger rooms of interior corridors. Called suites, each has a kingsize or two queen beds and pullout sofa. Each comes with flat-screen TV, refrigerator and microwave. The old outdoor pool is gone, but there's an indoor pool and hot tub and a new fitness center

Continental breakfast is complimentary in a dining area off the sparkling lobby. Jamms Restaurant next door serves lunch and dinner daily.
(860) 536-2621 or (877) 523-0993. Fax (860) 536-4493. www.mysticseaportinn.net. Forty-four rooms and seventy-five suites. Doubles, $119 to $169.

CAMPING. Seaport Campgrounds, Route 184, Box 104, Old Mystic 06372, (860) 536-4044, is a 130-site family campground with hookups and separate tenting area two miles north of I-95. Attractions include a swimming pool, pond fishing, recreation room, playground and miniature golf. Closer to the highway is **Highland Orchards Resort Park,** Route 49, North Stonington 06359, (860) 599-5101 or (800) 624-0829, a large RV area with two pools, fishing pond, playground, basketball court, miniature golf, fireplace lounge, camping cabins and a few wooded tent sites.

Seeing and Doing

Fish and Ships

Mystic Seaport, 75 Greenmanville Ave. (Route 27), Mystic.

From a local marine historical museum with one building in the old Greenman family shipyard in 1929, Mystic Seaport has evolved into the nation's largest maritime museum, an impressive testament to the lure, the lore and the life of the sea. The seventeen-acre site along the Mystic River contains more than 60 historic buildings, 300 boats, a planetarium and significant collections of maritime artifacts and nautical photography. Together they create a mix of a working seaport village, a preservation shipyard, a museum of massive proportions and a must-visit attraction for any seaman worth his salt.

Even landlubbers enjoy the re-creation of a 19th-century seafaring community. Trades of the era are demonstrated in the cooperage and shipsmith, shipcarver and model shops. You can poke through the Mystic Bank and shipping office (the second oldest bank in Connecticut), see handbills being published in the Mystic Press print shop, and visit the hardware store, schoolhouse, the drugstore and doctor's office, and the delightful little Fishtown Chapel. Guides cook on the open hearth of the Buckingham House kitchen, sing chanteys and demonstrate sail-setting, whaleboat rowing and fish salting.

Everyone climbs aboard the Charles W. Morgan (1841), the last of America's wooden whaleships afloat and a remarkable example of the seaport's ship restoration efforts; the full-rigged training ship Joseph Conrad (1882), and the 1921 fishing schooner L.A. Dunton. More than 400 small wooden craft, the largest such collection in the country, are on display in the Small Boat Exhibit and North Boat Shed. Others are afloat along the seaport's docks or can be seen from a visitors' gallery as they undergo repairs in the Henry B. duPont Preservation Shipyard, where the freedom schooner Amistad was built.

The Seaport's signature exhibition, "Voyages: Stories of America and the Sea," fills all three floors of the Stillman Building with art, artifacts and interactive multimedia presentations illustrating how Americans have been and still are connected to the sea. Themes of the decade-long exhibition change each year to cover immigration, recreation, foreign trade, Navy life, fisheries and rivers, among others. The shipping and shipbuilding businesses are explained in the Mallory Building, and other collections are displayed in more buildings than you can possibly comprehend in a day.

Don't miss the wonderful scale model of Mystic as it appeared in the mid-19th century. Take a ride on the steamboat Sabino (see below). See the stars at midday in a planetarium show. Visit the excellent Museum Store, which offers all kinds of nautical items, an art gallery, baked goods, housewares and one of the best maritime bookstores anywhere.

Meals are served in the Seamen's Inne Restaurant & Pub, located at the north entrance. Seasonally, you can enjoy a light meal served with 19th-century flair at the Schaefer Spouter Tavern, or get a snack at the Galley.

(860) 572-0711 or (888) 973-2767. www.visitmysticseaport.com. Open daily, 9 to 5 April-October, 10 to 4 rest of year. Adults $17, children $9.

Mystic Aquarium & Institute for Exploration, 55 Coogan Blvd., Mystic.

A $52 million expansion has transformed the Mystic Marinelife Aquarium into one of the best anywhere. Only the exhibit building and theater remain from days gone by. Now you'll be amazed by the spectacular outdoor Alaskan Coast habitat where beluga whales and harbor seals swim about or bathe and bark, as the case may be. You'll love the penguins passing by like so many little fish in an aquarium in the Roger Tory Peterson Exhibit. And you'll marvel at the dizzying, high-tech audio-visuals of Challenge of the Deep, home base of ocean explorer Robert Ballard's Institute for Exploration.

Even the original exhibit building erected only a few decades earlier has a new look. Now called Sunlit Seas, it features 40 new fish and invertebrate exhibits. They include a tidal salt marsh that's home to flounder, puffers and crabs and the colorful Coral Reef, a 30,000-gallon habitat with 16 viewing windows onto 500 varieties of exotic fish, sharks, stingrays and moray eels. California sea lions replaced the dolphins in the renovated marine theater. Now you're more apt to be impressed by the huge Alaskan Coast habitat, a meandering rock outcropping beside an 800,000-gallon pool where you can watch sleek beluga whales from above and below – a series of three 20-foot-long windows offers a whale's-eye view of the goings-on. The same goes for the adorable African black-footed penguins in the Peterson exhibit, on view both inside and outside, above and below. You can touch a cownose ray as it swims past your fingertips in the new Ray Touch Pool. As you follow the Marsh Walk between the fur seals and Steller sea lions of the Pribilof Islands section and the stranded mammals undergoing rehabilitation in the Seal Rescue Clinic, you're only a stone's throw from passing traffic on I-95.

Enter the doors of the R/V Discovery for an eight-minute theater presentation that may or may not orient you for the mind-boggling multimedia exhibits and interactive displays in the Challenge of the Deep. It presents fascinating deep-sea findings and shipwrecks, including Ballard's discovery of the sunken Titanic and his most recent archaeological expeditions, including one in 2000 to the Black Sea. In the new Immersion Theater, you might see an interactive show like one on "Dinosaurs: Beyond Extinction" or watch Ballard's 2003 expedition to the Titanic wreck. The visitor finds this section involves work and concentration, as opposed to the more passive exhibits and activities that precede it. Emerge from the dark into the open and a manmade pond, flanked by outdoor tables beside the Waterfront Café. You'll never again think of Mystic as just another aquarium. The whole atmosphere and experience are more like something you'd expect of Disney's Epcot Center transferred up north.

(860) 572-5955. www.mysticaquarium.org. Open daily, 9 to 6, shorter hours (10 to 5 weekdays December to March. Adults $16, children $11.

Historic Ship Nautilus/Submarine Force Museum, Naval Submarine Base, Crystal Lake Road, Groton.

The storied Nautilus, the world's first nuclear-powered submarine, was built a

Groton's General Dynamics Electric Boat Division shipyard in 1954. Returned to its birthplace, it has been opened to visitors after cruising faster, deeper, farther and longer than any craft in history. A recent $4 million expansion has doubled the size of the submarine museum, which contains the world's finest collection of submarine artifacts. It traces the history of underwater navigation, showing a submarine control room, working periscopes and models depicting submarine style and development. Films of submarines past and present are shown in a 70-seat theater. The expansion includes a museum store, a cut-away model of a 688 Los Angeles Class sub, a ballistic missile, Cold War exhibits and a library with sitting-area views of the Thames River. Outside are four mini-submarines. The highlight for most remains a self-guided tour of portions of the 519-foot-long Nautilus, berthed beside a dock in the Thames. The lines may be long, but you get to see the control room, torpedo room, attack center, officers' and crew's quarters and dining areas.

(860) 694-3174 or (800) 343-0079. www.ussnautilus.org. Open Wednesday-Monday 9 to 5 and Tuesday 1 to 5, mid-May through October; Wednesday-Monday 9 to 4, rest of year; closed first full week of May and the third full week of October. Free.

Boat Tours

S.S. Sabino, South Gate, Mystic Seaport.

The 57-foot, two-deck Sabino is the last coal-fired passenger steamboat operating in the country. Built in 1908 in East Boothbay, Me., and long used on Maine's Damariscotta River, it was acquired in 1974 by Mystic Seaport for passenger excursions. Half-hour river cruises are available for 100 Seaport visitors on the half hour from 10:30 to 3:30; adults $5.25, children $4.25. The Sabino is at its best after hours when it gives 90-minute evening cruises down the Mystic River past Noank and Masons Island to Fishers Island Sound. Along the way, you'll wait for the Mystic bascule bridge to rise and pass the place in Noank where workers built the original engine, which you can see for yourself in the boat's exposed engine room.

(860) 572-5731. Evening cruises, daily at 4:30, also Friday and Saturday at 6:30, mid-May to mid-October. Adults $10.25, children $8.75.

Project Oceanology, 1084 Shennecossett Road, Groton.

The public may participate in two-and-one-half-hour educational cruises from mid-June through Labor Day aboard a 55-foot research vessel departing from the University of Connecticut campus at Avery Point. EnviroLab expeditions teach passengers how to identify fish, measure lobsters, examine bottom mud and collect water samples. They're scheduled daily at 10 and 1, mid-June through August. Harbor tours to the landmark New London Ledge Lighthouse, which is explored inside and out, leave Tuesday, Thursday and Saturday at 4, mid-June to late September. Seal watch tours are scheduled weekends in February and March.

(860) 445-9007 or (800) 364-8472. www.oceanology.org. Adults $19, children $16. Reservations recommended.

Mystic Whaler Cruises, 15 Holmes St., Mystic, (860) 536-4218 or (800) 697-8420. Come aboard Capt. John Eginton's 110-foot schooner **Mystic Whaler,** which offers popular seagoing vacations on board. There are occasional five-hour day sails around Fisher's Island Sound ($80 per person) and more frequent lobster dinner cruises (up to four evenings a week, $75), scheduled around longer cruises. Trips of two to five days may go to Newport, Block Island, Shelter Island, Sag Harbor, Cuttyhunk or Martha's Vineyard, the destination determined by the captain based on winds and tides. Rates vary from $280 to $405 for two days to $700 to $810 for five days.

Voyager Cruises, 15 Holmes St., Mystic, (860) 536-0416. The 81-foot, gaff-rigged schooner Argia gives scenic half-day sails daily at 10:20 and 2:20, May-October, and sunset cruises nightly from 5:30 to 7:30; adults $36, children $26. Shorter tours around Mystic harbor and the Mystic Seaport Museum complex are offered daily at 1:30; adults $25, children $15.

Mystic River Tours, 31 Water St., Mystic, (860) 536-9980, offers scenic 90-minute tours of the Mystic Harbor aboard for up to six passengers aboard electric boats that are both quiet and environmentally friendly. Tours leave hourly from 10 to 5 for $25 per person. Sunset cocktail cruises may be arranged at night.

A 40-foot motorsailer, **Mystic Jitney,** 31 Water St., Mystic, (860) 460-3105, offers three-hour sails for walk-on passengers ($75) when it is not booked for private charters.

Mystic River Kayak Tours, 15 Holmes St., Mystic, (860) 536-8381, rents kayaks, bicycles and mopeds. Kayak rentals and tours and moonlight paddles are offered by **King Cove Marina,** 926 Stonington Road, Stonington (860) 599-4730.

Walking Tours

In Mystic, walk along the boardwalk on the east bank south from the downtown drawbridge and enjoy the new Mystic River Park. Another favorite walk passes stately old homes along Gravel Street on the west bank of the river north of downtown.

Denison Pequotsepos Nature Center, 109 Pequotsepos Road, Mystic, (860) 536-1216, is a nature museum and 300-acre wildlife sanctuary. It offers seven miles of trails through woodland, wetland and meadow habitats and is a wonderfully quiet place to walk. More than 150 species of birds have been identified within the sanctuary. Non-releasable raptors reside in outdoor aviaries near a natural history museum of native wildlife, where you can view live turtles, owls, frogs, salamanders, snakes and more up close. Sanctuary open daily, dawn to dusk. Center open Monday-Saturday 9 to 5, Sunday 10 to 4; adults $6, children $4.

STONINGTON. There's no tour as such, but a stroll along Water and Main streets and cross streets of Connecticut's quaintest seaport is a must. The Stonington Historical Society has marked with signs many 18th- and 19th-century structures, including the home where the mother of artist James Whistler and later poet Stephen Vincent Benet lived and the birthplace of Capt. Nathaniel Brown Palmer, discoverer of Antarctica. The 1852 **Palmer House,** a fine example of a prosperous sea captain's home, is open seasonally for tours – its cupola yields a panoramic view of the sea. The borough is full of large homes crowding their lots right up to the sidewalks; the architecture is an intriguing mix of gambrel roofs, old Cape Cod and pillared Greek Revival. Today, Stonington is home to a number of celebrities who cherish its quiet charm, which you can best appreciate by walking its streets. At the end of Water Street is the picturesque **Old Lighthouse Museum,** the first government lighthouse in Connecticut (1823). On two floors it houses the Stonington Historical Society's collection of photos of old Long Island Sound lighthouses, an ice-harvesting exhibit, whaling and fishing gear, articles from the Orient trade and an exquisite dollhouse. Climb the circular stone staircase to the top of the tower for a panoramic view of three states and Long Island Sound. The museum is open daily 10 to 5, May-October; adults $54, children $2.

Other Attractions

SWIMMING. Most of the shorefront in this area is privately owned, and beaches are few. A Connecticut Supreme Court ruling in 2002 opened town beaches to all, bu allowed towns to charge non-residents a premium. For surf swimming, head across the Rhode Island state line to Watch Hill and Misquamicut, which face the open ocean. A protected beach called **Esker Point** at Groton Long Point has picnic tables in the trees; there's no surf, but it's uncrowded and open to the public. **Williams Beach** in Mystic is accessible through hotels and motels that provide passes.

WINERIES. Southeastern Connecticut's mild climate and its proximity to water make fertile territory for vineyards. **Stonington Vineyards,** 523 Taugwonk Road, Stonington, offers tours daily at 2 and wine tastings and sales from 11 to 5. You also can tour the winery and sample the first production from the new **Jonathan Edwards Winery,** 74 Chester Maine Road, North Stonington, open Wednesday-Sunday 11 to 5.

ART. Enjoy water views while exploring regional art at its best at the **Mystic Art Association Galleries and Studios,** 9 Water St. Beside the Mystic River, it features changing exhibitions and special events in the summer. The **Mystic Seaport Museum Store** has an art gallery and a variety of nautical arts and crafts. Mystic hosts the annual **Mystic Outdoor Art Festival,** scheduled the second weekend in August and considered one of the largest and best in the East.

GAMING. For anyone who hasn't experienced them, the rise of the Indian casinos and related development in this area in little over a decade borders on the incredible. The **Foxwoods Resort Casino,** Route 2, Ledyard, (860) 885-3000 or (800) 752-9244, run by the Mashantucket Pequots, is a hugely profitable enterprise hulking out of the rural forests north of Mystic. Tastefully done (surprisingly so, given its nature), the six casinos are open 24 hours a day year-round. The 6,500 slot machines are the major draw for those who, like us, can't part with more than a quarter at a time. Also draws are big-name entertainment, 24 restaurants and three hotels with more than 1,400 rooms, including the eighteen-story, Grand Pequot Tower.

The **Mohegan Sun Casino,** 1 Mohegan Sun Blvd., Uncasville, (860) 646-5682 or (888) 226-7711, is close on the heels of Foxwoods as the world's second largest casino and, suddenly, one of its most spectacular. Compared with Foxwoods, the Mohegan tribe's nicely themed casino looked at the start more like a shopping mall with its direct-access highway, five-story parking garage and giant food court. Its gaming was in the Casino of the Earth, a huge circular room patterned on the four seasons, each distinguished by different Indian designs, traditions and imagery. Recent additions include the world's largest planetarium atop the new Casino of the Sky, celebrity-chef restaurants, a 10,000-seat arena and a glitzy, 34-story, 1,200-room luxury hotel – Connecticut's largest – beside the Thames River.

SHOPPING. Mystic has an uncommon concentration of interesting stores. **Olde Mistick Village,** Route 27 at I-95, offers 60 shops in a landscaped, built-to-look-old complex. Here is a catch-all of boutiques, gift shops and such designed to appeal to tourists. The carillon music from its Anglican chapel lends a happy air and the ducks in a pond beside the water wheel keep youngsters amused.

Downtown Mystic. Stores here are increasingly upscale and of appeal to residents as well as visitors. **Whyevernot** has unique items, from jewelry to fabrics to clothing. **Bank Square Books** is a well-stocked bookstore. **McMonogram for Kids** has children's clothes. **Mark, Fore & Strike** offers fine clothing. **The Bermuda Shop** shows classic, elegant apparel for women. **Jackeroos** sells men's and women's clothes from Australia, New Zealand and the South Sea Islands. **Mildly Wild Sportswear** has "original Mystic designs created, printed and stitched by us." **Peppergrass & Tulip** offers a potpourri of things for the boudoir, apparel, preserves, wood carvings and such. **Comina** has exotic international furnishings and accessories. **The Finer Line Gallery/Framers of the Lost Art** is one of several galleries, and we like almost everything at **The Company of Craftsmen**. **Good Hearted Bears and More** has them in all guises, even in reindeer outfits at Christmas. Jewelry inspired by the sea is featured at **Mermaid's Cove Jewelers**. The best ice cream in town is dispensed at the **Mystic Drawbridge Ice Cream Shoppe**. **Mystic Pizza**, established in 1973, produces the pizza made famous in the 1988 hit movie.

In Stonington, more shops pop up every time we visit. Among the best antiques shops are **Grand & Water, Orkney & Yost** and **Devon House Antiques. Quimper Faience** has firsts and seconds of the popular hand-painted French china at this, its flagship store and world administrative headquarters. We're partial to the **Hungry Palette**, whose screened fabrics are turned into colorful skirts that match the wall hangings displayed in the window; we coveted some of the corduroy ones for winter. **Cumulus** carries handcrafted jewelry and gifts, while **Findings** is a good interiors store. **Solomon's Mines** purveys fine jewelry. High fashion apparel and accessories are offered by New York fashion designer Narua Barraza at her new store, **Barraza**. **Luli** advertises beautiful wordly clothes.

Where to Eat

Water Views

Skipper's Dock, 66 Water St., Stonington.
The folks who made the Harborview into one of the great restaurants in the state returned to its last remaining adjunct, the Skipper's Dock on the water at pier's end in Stonington harbor. Ainslie Turner and her late husband Jerry turned the place into a cheery, year-round restaurant and tavern with fireplaces ablaze in cool weather and lots of nautical memorabilia and nostalgia. The result is a happy cross between the haute Harborview (since destroyed by fire and rebuilt as the Inn at Stonington) and the casual Skipper's Dock of old. The food is more than a mix, with a decided emphasis on the side of the Harborview's creativity. Yes, you can still get a mug of creamy clam chowder and cherrystone clams or blue point oysters on the half shell. You also can get stuffed quahogs Portuguese and the specialty oysters Ainslie, toasted with garlic aioli and panko crumbs. And wild mushroom and sausage strudel, baked escargots, and crab cakes in tequila-lime cream sauce. These are just for starters. Main dishes include the Harborview's classic Marseilles-style bouillabaisse, a savory array of choice seafood in a tomato-fennel-saffron broth, panko-crusted ahi sesame tuna and a pair of old specialties, coquilles St. Jacques and grilled filet mignon with gorgonzola and garlic butter. The dessert list might feature the Harborview's signature grasshopper pie, a Vermont maple-pecan pie and crème brûlée with fruit. The food and service seem to be best at lunch, when some of the same treats are available along with eggs benedict and an exotic pan-seared duck breast and warm goat cheese salad. The fried oysters with french fries and slaw and the Grand Central pan roast, a seafood sauté with an addictive sauce, were first-rate though pricey treats at our latest lunch. They're also offered day and night in the Harbar, a high-style pub with framed magazine covers on the walls and boating gear hanging overhead. The best place for all this good eating, of course, is on the expansive deck right out over the water.

(860) 535-0111. Entrées, $16.95 to $25.95. Lunch daily, 11:30 to 4. Dinner nightly, 4 to 9:30 or 10. Closed Tuesday in winter and month of January.

Flood Tide, Route 1, Mystic.
Large windows overlook Pequotsepos Cove out toward Long Island Sound from the hillside perch of the Inn at Mystic's renovated restaurant. An even better view

is offered from window tables in the more casual dining area off the lounge. A new exhibition kitchen with a clay-pit brick oven along one side may take some diner's eyes off the view in the formal dining room, whose setting is one of updated nautical elegance. We were impressed with the $15.95 daily luncheon buffet, which at our visit yielded everything from seviche, caviar, seafood salad, eggs benedict, seafood crêpes and fettuccine with lobster alfredo to bread pudding and kiwi tarts. You can also order from an à la carte menu. In the evening, the brick oven is put into play with entrées categorized as wood grilled, wood-burning oven roasted and on the wood-burning turn spit. Expect things like grilled Stonington fluke with lime butter, lobster pot au feu, bouillabaisse, orange-honey brined chicken with thyme jus, cinnamon-rubbed pork rack with calvados demi-glace, filet mignon, even a roasted vegetable mille-feuille. Châteaubriand is finished tableside for two. Start with oven-roasted mussels basted with hazelnut-garlic butter, fried oysters with roasted garlic aioli or lobster cappuccino. Lavender crème brûlée, bananas foster and flamed mango parfait are extravagant endings. An outdoor patio is popular in summer.

(860) 536-8140. Entrées, $22 to $35. Lunch, Monday-Saturday, 11:30 to 2:30. Dinner nightly, 5:30 to 9:30 or 10. Sunday brunch, 11 to 2.

The Fisherman Restaurant, 937 Groton Long Point Road, Noank.

A great view of the water and an elegant nautical decor are offered at this locally popular restaurant and lounge. About 150 diners can be seated at widely spaced tables in three dining rooms. The side room with the best view of the waters around Esker Point is handsomely outfitted in blue. The larger rooms to the rear are in gray and burgundy. Once you sit in the unusual cushioned chairs that swivel and rock, you may never want to get up. Entrées on the extensive dinner menu range from fish and chips, fried clams and a fried seafood platter to bouillabaisse, baked salmon, seafood kabob, stuffed chicken breast, prime rib, sirloin steak and combinations thereof. Salad, vegetables and starch come with, and no one leaves hungry. Lobster madeira is a pasta specialty. Appetizers are of the grilled mussels and chicken teriyaki variety. Old-fashioned desserts include parfaits, bread pudding with bourbon sauce and chocolate cream pie. The lounge menu, offered all day, offers good values.

(860) 536-1717. Entrées, $14.95 to $26.50. www.fishermanrestaurant.com. Lunch, Monday-Saturday 11:30 to 3. Dinner nightly, 4:30 to 9:30 or 10; Sunday, dinner and lounge menu, 11:30 to 9.

S&P Oyster Company, 1 Holmes St., Mystic.

There's no better view of the Mystic River and the goings-on near the busy drawbridge than from this establishment with a prime downtown location. Part of a chain, the restaurant consists of two levels of dining and a bar, all of which have lots of windows onto the water. Upstairs, a brightly striped spinnaker is stretched across the ceiling, and old photographs of Mystic line the wall. A pleasant side patio beside the river provides downtown Mystic's only outdoor riverfront dining. The all-day menu features the usual seafood and steak house suspects, but not the oyster theme that you would expect from its name. Oysters come as appetizers – on the half shell, fried or baked with cheese. The house specialty is a cull lobster and a cup of Rhode Island clam chowder for $18.99. Otherwise, expect a wide variety of seafood items from fried fisherman's platter to Alaskan king crab legs and twin stuffed Canadian lobster tails. Wood-grilled yellowfin tuna with a wasabi-soy-ginger glaze, blackened tilapia with pineapple salsa and bouillabaisse are among the possibilities. Grilled strip sirloin and petite filet mignon also are available.

(860) 536-2674. www.sp-oyster.com. Entrées, $12.99 to $24.99. Lunch daily, 11:30 to 4. Dinner, 4 to 10 or 11 in summer, 4 to 9 or 10 rest of year.

Boom, 194 Water St., Stonington.

This trendy establishment occupies a prime harborfront location in the Dodson Boatyard. Alas, the outdoor deck that made its predecessor, the late Boatyard Café, so popular has been fully enclosed for year-round dining. That negates much of the appeal for water lovers and makes this simply another restaurant with a modest water view, mostly of boats and the booms from which it takes its name. Tables in the dining room with wraparound windows are topped by nautical charts covered by glass. A noisy bar is a focal point. Chef-owner Jean Maude Fuller-Gest's menu is short but sweet and her food has been well received of late. For lunch, our party of four sampled the Carolina clam chowder (a bit odd with diced sweet potatoes) and roasted tomato soup. The fried oyster sandwich and the scallop taco were better than the bland portobello mushroom and grilled chicken sandwiches. The BOAT sandwich (bacon, olive tapenade, arugula and tomato) is a better choice these days. Chocolate ganache, key lime pie and mango sorbet were good desserts. At night, look for main courses like pan-seared salmon with artichoke hearts and diced tomatoes, Stonington scallops with roasted red pepper curry sauce, native flounder with a tomato-basil coulis and kalamata olive tapenade, and black angus sirloin with house-made steak sauce on the side. In 2002, Boom opened a larger sibling at Brewer's Pilots Point Marina in Westbrook, and that one capitalizes on its nifty outdoor dining deck with a water view.

(860) 535-2588. www.boomrestaurant.net. Entrées, $17.50 to $22.50. Lunch, Tuesday-Saturday 11:30 to 2:30. Dinner, Tuesday-Sunday 5 to 9. Sunday brunch, 11 to 2.

Abbott's Lobster in the Rough, 117 Pearl St., Noank.

It's altogether fitting that this old lobstering town would be the home for more than 50 years of a lobster pound like those you dream of (and occasionally find) in Maine. Right beside the Mystic River as it opens into wide Fishers Island Sound, Abbott's is casual as can be with gaily colored picnic tables resting on mashed-up clam shells. You order at a counter inside and get a number – since the wait is often half an hour or more and the portions to come are apt to be small, we bring along drinks and appetizers to keep us going. Lobster, last we knew, was $14.95 for a one-and-one-quarter pounder. It comes with a bag of potato chips, a small container of coleslaw, melted butter and a paper bib. Also available are steamers, clam chowder, mussels, shrimp in the rough, lobster or crab rolls and a lobster feast. Adjacent shacks dispense desserts and shellfish from a raw bar. If you seek more basic (and fried) fare, head for Abbott's sibling **Costello's Clam Shack,** an open-air place beneath a blue and white canopy right over the water beyond the Noank Shipyard.

(860) 536-7719. www.abbotts-lobster.com. Entrées, $14.95 to $22.95. Open daily, noon to 9, May to Labor Day; Friday-Sunday noon to 7, Labor Day to Columbus Day. BYOB.

Other Choices

Restaurant Bravo Bravo, 20 East Main St., Mystic.

Contemporary Italian fare is delivered at this convivial, 50-seat restaurant on the main floor of the Whaler's Inn. Diners at close-together tables may see the bascule bridge through large glass windows, but the watery ambiance was lost when the inn took over the outdoor Café Bravo space for expansion. Chef-owner Carol Kanabis continues to offer an extensive menu that rarely changes but offers plenty of excitement, especially among the specials. For dinner, sirloin carpaccio, grilled shrimp wrapped in prosciutto with skewered artichokes, seafood sausage stuffed with lobster and scallops, and baked mozzarella skewered between croutons topped with a savory garlic sauce make good starters. Typical entrées are crab cakes topped with lobster-chive sauce, a saffron-seasoned seafood stew, osso buco and braised lamb shanks. Grilled local ostrich with a watermelon barbecue and sweet corn sauce was a special at one visit. The lengthy dessert roster includes the obligatory tiramisu as well as tartufo, fruit napoleon with mascarpone cheese and ricotta cheesecake with grand marnier sauce.

(860) 536-3228. Entrées, $16.95 to $24.95. Lunch, Tuesday-Saturday 11:30 to 2:30, also Sunday in summer. Dinner, Tuesday-Sunday 5 to 9 or 10.

Captain Daniel Packer Inne, 32 Water St., Mystic.

Once a stagecoach stop on the New York to Boston route, this shingled gray building with red door dating to 1756 is across the road from the river. Everyone enjoys the crowded tavern downstairs, where a light pub menu is served amid the original walls of brick and stone and a fire blazes in the huge fireplace three seasons of the year. The main floor exudes history in a couple of handsome dining rooms with working fireplaces and bare tables topped by formal mats portraying sailing ships. Longtime owners Richard and Lulu Kiley offer a varied lunch menu of chowders, salads, burgers, grilled pizzas and seafood, beef, poultry and pasta entrées in the pub. The dinner menu upstairs adds some twists, especially in terms of seafood: baked codfish with grilled pineapple chutney, roasted Atlantic salmon with basil sauce and red pepper confit, and grilled swordfish stacked with caramelized onions and fennel and finished with roasted red pepper coulis. Other entrées are more traditional: veal homard, sliced lamb with a raspberry-veal demi-glace and angus strip steak with a truffle demi-glace. All come with garden salad, baguettes and roasted garlic. Bailey's cream cheese cheesecake, turtle pie, double chocolate mousse and gelatos are favored desserts. A pub menu similar to that offered at lunch is available in the pub at dinnertime.

(860) 536-3555. www.danielpacker.com. Entrées, $19.95 to $29.95. Lunch daily, 11 to 4. Dinner, 5 to 10. Pub daily from 11.

Noah's, 113 Water St., Stonington.

This endearing restaurant – long known for good food, casual atmosphere and affordable prices – has been gussied up a bit lately. The once-funky double storefront now has fine art on the walls of the main dining room, where cherry booths beneath paddle fans and a tin ceiling draw the locals for three meals a day. A front room with a handsome horseshoe-shaped mahogany bar offers a bar menu. Contemporary international specials are posted nightly to complement traditional dinners on the order of broiled flounder, cod Portuguese, pork chops and grilled chicken. The night's numerous specials have been upscaled lately and are a tad pricier, as you'd expect for dishes like prosciutto-wrapped monkfish with chianti sauce, spice-rubbed mako shark, grilled bluefish with mango-lime relish, grilled rare salmon with wasabi and pickled ginger, and lobster and monkfish sauté. Seafood is featured, but you might find grilled brace of quail with chardonnay cream sauce or veal flank steak with pinot noir sauce. Save room for the scrumptious homemade desserts, perhaps chocolate-yogurt cake, bourbon bread pudding, or what one local volunteered was the best dessert he'd ever had: strawberries with Italian cream made from cream cheese, eggs and kirsch.

(860) 535-3925. www.noahsfinefood.com. Entrées, $12.25 to $23.95. Breakfast, 7 to 11, Sunday to noon. Lunch, 11:15 to 2:30. Dinner, 6 to 9 or 9:30. Closed Monday.

FOR MORE INFORMATION: Mystic Chamber of Commerce, 14 Holmes St., Box 143, Mystic, CT 06355, (860) 572-9578 or (866) 572-9578. www.mysticchamber.org. Mystic and Stonington are part of the Connecticut East Convention & Visitor's Bureau, 470 Bank St., New London, CT 06320, (860) 444-2206 or (800) 863-6569.

Bathers frolic in water and on sand at Narragansett beach.

Narragansett, R.I.

Although few people realize it, the Narragansett of more than a century ago was a society resort rivaling Newport.

The New York Times commented in 1877 that Narragansett was "an American watering place in the truest sense of the term." A writer for Harper's Weekly added in the late 1800s: "The habitués of the place are, in general, people of the same social standing as those of Newport and have in the main less money."

Aristocratic vacationers from New York, Philadelphia and points south frequented no fewer than ten major hotels, built summer "cottages" only slightly smaller than Newport's, and reveled in the recreational and social goings-on at the Stanford White-designed Narragansett Casino. They enjoyed what they considered a simplicity and lack of pretension, as opposed to the more affluent Newport visible across Narragansett Bay.

A fire in 1900 destroyed the large Rockingham Hotel and the adjacent casino. More fires, financial difficulties and changing vacation patterns wiped out the other hotels in the first part of the 20th century. The hurricanes of 1938 and 1954 left standing only a few reminders of the resort's colorful past.

The landmark granite Towers spanning Ocean Road at the entrance to the old Casino and the high-rent districts along Ocean Road and Gibson Avenue remain as symbols of the Narragansett that was. So do a number of oft-hidden mansions of modern-day Newport proportions.

Today, with less of an identity and "less money" than Newport, as the Harper's writer put it, Narragansett is often overlooked by out-of-staters. It's a mecca for Rhode Islanders who cherish its beaches, its boating and its fishing and the kinds of tourism that accompany them.

Narragansett actually encompasses several areas, each quite different from the others: There's the historic and busy Pier area, which passes for downtown Narragansett. The mansion and beach area along Ocean Road to the south toward Point Judith and along Boston Neck Road north toward Wickford. The working fishing village of Galilee – "tuna capital of the world." And the outlying commercial areas and highway maze bordering adjacent Wakefield.

Amid nature's splendors are remnants from the area's 370-year history. The Narragansett Indian Statue, the Old Narragansett Church, the Gilbert Stuart Birthplace and Snuff Mill, the 1750 Casey Farm, the Point Judith Lighthouse, the quaint living-museum village of Wickford and the fishing harbor at Galilee are reminders of another era.

Getting There

At the southwest entrance to Narragansett Bay opposite Newport, Narragansett is located on Scenic Route 1A off U.S. Route 1. It is fifteen miles east of Interstate 95 and 30 miles south of Providence.

Where to Stay ──────────────── ∽∾∾

This is a highly seasonal area geared to beach-goers, and lodging establishments respond accordingly. Summer weekend rates are highest; midweek and off-season are usually lower. Some of the larger, more visible establishments are not up to snuff and some that claim ocean views are stretching. A number of small, seasonal B&Bs are away from the water and operate principally on weekends.

Silver Lake Cottage, 361 Woodruff Ave., Wakefield 02879.

The waterfront Colonial Revival mansion built as a summer home by the Welch grape juice family of Western New York is now the Narragansett area's most appealing B&B. Susan and Bob Clendenen of Greenwich, Conn., retired from corporate life in New York and Southern California to the head of Silver Lake, a privately owned, mile-long lake hidden in woodlands at the edge of busy Wakefield, They bought the three-acre property – still called Silver Lake Cottage from the era when mansions in Newport were cottages – to share as a B&B. The house, shaded by one of the oldest copper beech trees in the state, faces the lake and a park-like setting designed by the Olmsted brothers. The heart of the house is an enclosed sun porch, complete with blooming hibiscus plants, running the width of the house. It opens onto a huge stone patio, with a "meander" path down to the lake. Inside, guests also have use of a formal living room, a den/office and an upstairs library. Upstairs also are five spacious guest rooms, all with their own bathrooms and

closets and all but one with views of the lake. They're comfortably furnished in traditional style with king, queen or twin beds, but none of the contemporary amenities such as jacuzzis, fireplaces and entertainment centers. "This is an old-fashioned house where you step back in time," the hostess advises – as if you're a guest of relatives in a grand but understated mansion near the shore. Susie serves an elaborate breakfast from her butler's pantry and enormous kitchen, where she employs an AGA stove. Breakfast at our visit, served in a formal dining room, was an assorted fruit platter, rhubarb coffee cake and a version of eggs benedict with mushroom and bell pepper sauce.

(401) 782-3745. Fax (401) 792-2292. www.silverlakecottage.com. Five rooms with private baths. Doubles, $155 to $195.

The Richards, 144 Gibson Ave., Narragansett 02882.

Repeat customers fill this substantial yet low-key B&B, named for the owners and lacking a sign or even a brochure. They like the welcome and the run-of-the-property philosophy of owners Nancy and Steve Richards, deans of local innkeepers. The couple started in 1981 with a modest B&B now known as Pleasant Cottage. Six years later, they became only the third owners of the landmark 1884 stone castle called Druid's Dream, built by Joseph Peace Hazard of an illustrious local family after whom the nearby hamlet of Peace Dale was named. The house and yard were derelict when the Richardses bought, but they have fully restored and updated the property. The 8,500-square-foot house, off by itself behind high hedges in a posh residential area, once presided over a 200-acre estate and was built of Narragansett granite quarried on the property. It reflects the builder's fascination with England, which accounts for the windows recessed in eighteen-inch-thick walls. Upstairs are four handsome guest quarters, each stylishly decorated and full of creature comforts. The Blue Room comes with a crown-canopied kingsize brass bed, velvet loveseat and one of the working fireplaces found throughout. Two accommodations have queen canopy beds. One is the Hydrangea Suite, named for a favorite painting of an hydrangea above the fireplace and painted to match. It has a clawfoot tub and a sitting room with a second fireplace. A suite in what was the servants' quarters contains one room with a king bed, another with a queen bed and a sitting room with fireplace. On the main floor, guests enjoy a comfortable living room and a chandeliered dining room, where soufflés and strudels are typical breakfast fare. They also enjoy a rickety, open two-passenger elevator, on which Nancy may give her guests a ride. Our ride was fun, and so is the house where she keeps changing things to surprise returning guests.

(401) 789-7746. Two rooms and two suites with private baths. Doubles, $115 to $165. Suites, $155 and $220.

Ocean Rose Inn, 113 Ocean Road, Narragansett 02882.

A rose in the beveled glass door and a front patio beside a rose garden set the stage for this upscale inn, with the ocean on full view across the street. It was beautifully transformed in 1999 from the old Pier House Inn and motel by a Cranston-based group that owns small New England hotels, for whom this is its first "Victorian inn." Theirs is more contemporary than Victorian, despite its 1897 pedigree, and more of a richly appointed small hotel. The staff oversees nine inn rooms, five with water views, and a two-story, eighteen-unit motel in back, most with good views, especially from the upper balconies. A wide veranda wraps around much of the inn's main floor, part of which is leased out to a restaurant called **Turtle Soup** (see Where to Eat). That may account for the sign posted in the pleasant, paneled living room with ocean view, "Please do not move the furniture." It's also why there are coffeemakers in each room – this isn't a B&B, we were informed. All inn rooms have kingsize beds and are surprisingly large. The modern bathrooms also are large, so it's a mystery why all but two have showers only. The prime rooms we saw are outfitted with shiny wood floors, poster beds, wicker chairs, TVs and colorful sea garden paintings. Their walls are painted whimsically in lavender and pale yellow, and windows accented with sheer pink or green curtains. Four second-floor rooms have private ocean-view decks. Three are in front, but the best is a larger side room with a bigger corner deck and a marble bathroom.

(401) 783-4704. www.oceanroseinn.com. Nine inn rooms with private baths and 18 motel rooms. Rates, EP. Doubles, $199 to $329, $119 to $179 EP in motel.

Dunmere Gatehouse, 560 Ocean Road, Narragansett 02882.

A turreted granite entryway, its iron gates closed to keep out the curious, leads to the gatehouse built in 1883 as part of the estate of the Dun of Dun & Bradstreet. Some gatehouse. A stone building topped by a circular tower in an area of palatial houses, it's the home of physician Bob O'Neill and his wife Linda, who redid the walkout lower level for a daughter's wedding and opened it to guests as a B&B of sorts. With a private entrance, the guest suite looks out on an idyllic, terraced landscape through gazebos and balustrades to a clay tennis court, pond and the ocean below. The suite has a mini-kitchen, bedroom, sitting area, TV and telephone. Linda stocks the refrigerator with the makings for a continental breakfast of fresh fruit and homemade baked goods.

(401) 783-3797. One suite with private bath. Double, $125 to $195. Two- or three-night minimum.

The 1900 House, 59 Kingstown Road, Narragansett 02882.

Here's an eclectic Victorian B&B full of personality. Innkeepers Sandra and Bill Panzeri share their home with guests in three second-floor accommodations. Airy rooms with double beds, antique furnishings and TVs reflect some of Sandra's collections of quilts, document boxes, sewing kits and what-not. "Give me two of something and it's a collection," explains Sandra. A side bedroom, called the Morning Room, connects through its bathroom to a front-corner sitting room with a sofabed and can become a family suite for four. Guests gather in the cozy Victorian living room or on a wraparound screened porch full of wicker. They enjoy a multi-course breakfast by candlelight beside a wood stove in the dining room. Sandra goes all out with the likes of fruit parfait, homemade cinnamon-pecan muffins and belgian waffles topped with blueberries and strawberries. Upon departure, guests are apt to leave with bounty from Bill's prolific back-yard garden.

(401) 789-7971. www.1900houseri.com. Two rooms and one suite with private baths. Doubles, $125. Suite $150.

Four Gables Bed & Breakfast, 12 South Pier Road, Narragansett 02882.

This B&B offers ocean views from the guest suite, the dining room and the wonderful, curved brick patio where breakfast is served. A fine example of a classic New England shingle-style summer home with an Arts and Crafts interior, it has a massive cross-gambrel roof, four fireplaces, various nooks and crannies, and a back yard that shows the landscaping talents of Barbara Higgins, innkeeper with her husband Terry, an attorney. They recently turned two upstairs bedrooms that shared a large hall bath into a suite. The bedroom has a king-size bed, while the sitting room has a TV, refrigerator, chaise lounge and a sleep sofa for one or two. The wall between entry and sitting area is filled with a massive, mirrored hall seat from their former Victorian house in East Greenwich – "this was the only place it would fit here," explains Barbara, and it is a tight but beautiful fit. Downstairs are a small living room and an unusual dining room, with a plant-filled alcove opening onto the garden patio, enclosed in a curved brick wall and with a view of the ocean down the street. The table here is big enough for four for afternoon wine and for two at breakfast. Omelets, crêpes or stuffed french toast might be the fare.

(401) 789-6948. One suite with private bath. Double, $125 to $145.

Summertime House, 19 Chestnut St., Narragansett 02882.

A block from the ocean is this recently restored Victorian house with an annex for overnight guests in a handsome new wing at the back, facing a side street. Bearing an "established 1999" sign at the separate entry, it's a first-class set of accommodations. Innkeeper Alison Kutcher offers more than 1,000 square feet of private living space on two floors, plus a veranda with rocking chairs. The main floor holds a combination living room/dining area with TV, a galley kitchen and a full bath. The living room has a full-size futon for sleeping. The upstairs has a large room with queen bed and a day bed and a second full bath. It opens onto a sun deck/balcony. The two rooms are rented together as a suite. A continental breakfast is offered in the dining area.

(401) 782-2274. Fax (401) 782-1254. One two-bedroom suite with two private baths. Doubles, $195.

Scarborough Beach Motel, 901 Ocean Road, Narragansett 02882.

There are larger and more visible motels in Narragansett, even some with better ocean views. But the best run and most appealing may be this modest old-timer, lately enhanced with interesting landscaping by someone with an interest in exotic bushes and trees. A three-building complex in an otherwise residential neighborhood, it faces Ocean Road and the open ocean, with pristine Scarborough State Beach across the road. Four second-floor units, Nos. 24 to 27, in a newer building enjoy the best views from their shared balcony. Rooms underneath are next in popularity. Other rooms are in one-story buildings of older vintage, some with water views. Rooms offer one, two or three double beds. Efficiencies include a double bed, sofabed and kitchenette. Coffee is available in the morning, and donuts are added on weekends.

(401) 783-2063. Fax (401) 782-0138. www.scarboroughbeachmotel.com. Twenty-seven rooms. Doubles, $129 to $174 weekends, $95 to $135 midweek.

CAMPING. Long Cove Marina Family Campsites offers 150 sites at Long Point Marina, 325 Point Judith Road (Route 108). **Fishermen's Memorial State Park** has 147 trailer and 35 tent sites near the beaches at 1011 Point Judith Road. **Worden Pond Family Campground** boasts 200 wooded sites on the state's largest freshwater pond at 416A Worden's Pond Road, South Kingstown.

Seeing and Doing

A walk along the seawall hugging Ocean Road allows views of open ocean and crashing surf.

THE BEACHES. These are the big attractions, and the natives consider them the best in New England. There's one for every taste: quiet beaches, noisy beaches, people beaches and secluded beach. The **Narragansett Pier Town Beach** in the Pier area in the center of town is the most crowded. Near the entrance to the old Casino at the heart of the Victorian-era resort, its patrons have long since traded parasols for surfboards. The beach, known for the best surfing in New England, is the site of regional competitions. There are two pavilions, changing rooms and concessions. Daily admission is $5 and parking $6. **Scarborough State Beach** to the south along Ocean Road and the **Roger W. Wheeler State Beach** at Sand Hill Cove are less crowded, sandy beaches. Scarborough is especially appealing in separate North and South complexes, with landscaped pavilions and beach houses; if ever a beach could be called elegant, it is this, although members of the Dunes Club adjacent to the town beach might disagree. Tiny **Salty Brine State Beach** at Galilee, protected by breakwaters, is good for family swimming and you can watch the Block Island ferry as it comes into the channel. Parking for non-residents at the state beaches is $14 weekends, $12 midweek.

WATER SPORTS. Kayaking and canoeing are special on the Narrow River, a unique mix of tidal inlet, wildlife refuge, salt marsh, estuary, a fjord-like pond and a river that empties into Narragansett Bay. Canoes and kayaks are available from **Narrow River Kayaks,** 95 Middlebridge Road, (401) 789-0334. Professionals lead bird-watching tours to nearby Gooseberry Island and salt flats on weekends. Surfboards and related equipment may be rented from **Warm Winds Surf & Sport,** 26 Kingstown Road, (401) 780-9040, which bills itself as the largest surf shop in New England. Surfboards also may be rented from **Gansett Juice,** 74 Narragansett Ave., (401) 789-7890. The **Narragansett Pier Dive Shop**, 145 Boon St., (401) 783-2225, rents diving and snorkeling equipment and conducts daily wreck charters; it also rents kayaks and canoes.

FISHING. Some of the world's most fertile fishing grounds are found off the Rhode Island coast, particularly the famed Block Island and Cox's Ledge areas. Galilee is known as the tuna capital of the world, and the annual late-August tuna festival is a major attraction. The area is the third largest exporter of lobster in the world. It is the second largest fishing port in New England and has one of the oldest fishing co-ops in New England. Other catches include bluefish, cod, flounder, shark, swordfish and marlin. A number of large open party boats sail daily at 6 a.m. and charge by the person. Charter boats are reserved for the day. The Chamber of Commerce lists nine charter and party boats, most sailing from Galilee or Point Judith.

BOATING. You can rent a boat from a number of marinas to sail the waters made famous by the America's Cup races off Newport. You also can take a ferry from Galilee for a day trip to Block Island.

Rhode Island's only whale watch excursions are offered from 1 to 5:30 daily in summer by the **Frances Fleet,** 33 State St., Port of Galilee, (401) 783-4988 or (800) 662-2824; adults $35, children $25. Finback whales are normally sighted off the Rhode Island coast.

Southland Riverboat, State Pier, Galilee. (401) 783-2954. Eleven-mile narrated sightseeing cruises on the two-decker Southland are offered in season out of Galilee. The 149-passenger boat goes through the Galilee Breachway into the protected Harbor of Refuge, on to the historic Point Judith Lighthouse and back past Jerusalem and Snug Harbor into the Great Salt Pond. Sunset cruises are available Thursday-Saturday at 7; adults $14, children $8. Sightseeing cruises run daily in summer at 11, 1 and 3; adults $12, children $6.

Interstate Navigation Co., State Pier, Galilee. (401) 783-4613. www.blockislandferry.com. One-hour cruises to Block Island are offered on the auto ferry seven times daily in peak season. The island is one of the most beautiful in the Atlantic and makes a good day trip or overnight excursion. Its long shoreline contains good beaches and one of the best harbors in the Northeast. Bicycling is a favorite pastime. The town of Old Harbor is fun to explore. Same-day round trips, adults $15.15, children $7.10.

A quicker trip is offered by **Block Island High Speed Ferry,** State Pier, Galilee, (877) 733-9425. www.islandhighspeedferry.com. The largest and fastest passenger catamaran in Rhode Island gets from Galilee to Block Island in 30 minutes. The ferry runs roughly every two hours; round trip, $29.

Historic Attractions

The area is steeped in history, although it doesn't flaunt it.

The most visible is **The Towers,** the last remaining section of the famed Narragansett Pier Casino, which in its heyday was the center of the summer social season. Under restoration, it's home to the Narragansett Historical Society and a gift shop, and used primarily for functions and a Thursday evening concert/dance series in summer. The **Narragansett Indian Monument** at the junction of Kingstown Road and Strathmore Street is one of a series throughout the country honoring Native Americans. The 23-foot sculpture was carved by artist Peter Toth from a single Douglas fir.

Another landmark is the **Point Judith Lighthouse,** 1460 Ocean Road, an octagonal brick building erected in 1816. Visitors may tour the grounds and pause on benches at the adjacent **Rose Nulman Memorial Park,** a scenic overlook above the ocean.

South County Museum, Strathmore Street off Boston Neck Road (Scenic Route 1-A), Narragansett.

Nearly 20,000 artifacts relating to early Rhode Island life are on display on Canonchet Farm, across from the Narragansett town beach. The 174-acre park is a 19th century working mini-farm with a wildflower garden, nature trails and several farm buildings on the grounds of the former Gov. William Sprague mansion. A cemetery with graves dating to 1700, a one-room schoolhouse, a country kitchen and a general store also are of interest. The museum has an extensive collection of tools, farm implements, utensils, toys, vehicles and mechanical devices depicting life a century ago. An old print shop shows how newspapers were produced at the turn of the last century.

(401) 783-5400. www.southcountymuseum.org. Open Wednesday-Saturday 10 to 4 and Sunday noon to 4, July-August; Friday-Saturday 10 to 4 and Sunday noon to 4, May-June and September-October. Adults $5, children $2.

Gilbert Stuart Birthplace, 815 Gilbert Stuart Road, Saunderstown.

Born here in 1755, Gilbert Stuart was the foremost portraitist in early America, best known for his portrait of George Washington. His dark red, Dutch Colonial-style house is turned away from the road to face a mirror-like millpond reached by a footbridge. The National Historic Landmark house, which contains few of his art works, is maintained more as a Colonial house museum than an art gallery. An operating snuff mill with water wheel, the first in America (1751), is on the lower level of the house. Guided tours are given on the hour.

(401) 294-3001. Open Thursday-Monday, 11 to 3, April-October. Adults $5, children $2.

Casey Farm, 2325 Boston Neck Road (Route 1-A), Saunderstown.

A 300-acre working farm that was the site of Revolutionary War activity, this is one of the original plantation farms of the Colonial era. Still functioning as a community-supported farm, it has a fine collection of barns, organic gardens and an assortment of animals. The 1750 Casey Homestead overlooks Narragansett Bay and Conanicut Island. The house museum displays memorabilia interpreting several generations of the Casey family who were leaders in the U.S. military and Army Corps of Engineers. Now owned by the Society for the Preservation of New England Antiquities, the house contains original furniture, family paintings, prints, china, and military and political documents over a span of more than 200 years from the 18th through the 20th centuries.

(401) 295-1030. Open Saturday, 11 to 5, early June to mid-October. Adults $4, children $2.

WICKFORD. The entire village of Wickford is worth exploring. Old churches, quaint shops, beautiful gardens and historic homes combine to present an image of life unchanged over the years. Established in 1641 and laid out in 1707, this is our idea of the ideal New England seaside village – historic through and through, and made all the more charming by the glimpses of Wickford Cove here and there. A stone walkway behind the pharmacy on Grown Street is flanked by benches from which to enjoy views of the harbor. The **Old Narragansett Church** (1707) on Church Lane is the oldest Episcopal Church standing north of Virginia. Its organ, the oldest in America, dates to 1680. The church is open for tours in summer, Thursday-Monday 11 to 4. North of town off Route 1 is **Smith's Castle,** one of America's oldest plantation houses built in 1678. Consumed interpreters conduct guided tours of the recently restored National Register historic building and archeological site in summer, Thursday-Monday 12:15 to 3; adults $5, children $1.

SHOPPING. What passes for downtown Narragansett is a landscaped shopping plaza named the Pier Marketplace. Shops come and go and are mainly of the basic tourist or local service variety. Among them are **Christine's Casuals, Special-T Shop,** the **Shell Boutique, The Victorian Lady** for home and garden accessories and, across the street, **Flowerthyme.** The main commercial area is around Mariner Square, heading west toward Wakefield.

To our minds, Wickford has the area's most interesting shops. We particularly like the **Wickford Gourmet Foods and Café** complex. **Robin Hollow Outfitters** is Rhode Island's largest Orvis dealer. **Wilson's of Wickford** has a tradition of fine clothing since 1944. Newer women's boutiques are **Green Ink** and **Pink Pineapple.**

Where to Eat ⁓⁓⁓

Spain of Narragansett, 1144 Ocean Road, Narragansett.
Here is one beautiful restaurant, with food to match . The pale yellow dining room looks ever-so Mediterranean with arches and a waterfall trickling down one wall. The large outdoor Spanish courtyard off the bar appeals for a drink or Sunday dinner. Also appealing is the canopied deck off the upstairs dining room. Both yield a glimpse of the ocean. Almost universally acclaimed as the best local restaurant, it's better than ever since relocating in 1997 from its original quarters in the Village Inn at Narragansett Pier. Chef-owner Salvadore Gomes plies his legions of customers with gargantuan portions of Spanish food and drink. Spanish music plays in the background as diners sample typical Spanish appetizers, from grilled smoked chorizo and shrimp in garlic to the signature pan-fried calamari with a blend of mild and hot peppers. Entrées include two versions of paella and two of the shellfish casserole mariscada, plus basque-style fillet of sole, four chicken and three veal dishes, pork chops and a Spanish steak dish served for two: sliced tenderloin with artichoke hearts and mushrooms in a rioja wine, dijon and garlic sauce. Flan and chocolate truffle mousse cake are favored desserts. The drink list features sangria and Spanish wines, brandies and cognacs.
(401) 783-9770. www.spainri.com. Entrées, $11.95 to $18.95. Dinner, Tuesday-Saturday 4 to 10, Sunday 1 to 9.

Turtle Soup, 113 Ocean Road, Narragansett.
The restaurant in the recently restored Ocean Rose Inn maintains a low profile locally. But it seems to pack in the passersby who view it from the seawall, stop perhaps for a drink on the rose garden patio or the broad veranda, and stay for a

meal. The restaurant is leased to Linda Cinco, who used to own the Duck Soup Deli in Warwick, and Amy Streeter. "We have zero turtle on the menu," admits chef Leigh Ann Saunders, except for a "turtle salad" that's really chicken. What they do have is a lengthy list of appetizers, salads, pastas and entrées. The latter include lobster ravioli with vodka cream sauce, grilled salmon with balsamic-raspberry glaze and toasted walnuts, chicken roulade, pork au poivre and grilled sirloin marinated in ale. The cooks and the staff have fun and there's a lively bar. The two-level white dining room with a bead-board ceiling is mostly windows to take advantage of the ocean views. The prices are a pleasant surprise, given the million-dollar location.

(401) 792-8683. www.turtlesoupri.com. Entrées, $13 to $24. Lunch in summer, Tuesday-Sunday 11:30 to 4. Dinner, Tuesday-Sunday 4 to 10.

Coast Guard House, 40 Ocean Road, Narragansett.

Lunching on the expansive upstairs deck beside the ocean is fun, watching all the swimmers in the distance on the Narragansett Town Beach and all the windsurfers riding the waves. In fact, one of us had his first lobster dinner here as a child and gave it short shrift to escape outside onto the rocks with his kid brother to watch the pounding surf. The oceanfront setting in the National Register-listed landmark beside the Towers is usually better than the fare, although that situation is said to have improved lately. There are big wraparound windows onto the ocean. A large canopied rooftop bar is popular with the beach crowd. At our latest lunch on the deck, we enjoyed a lobster roll ($12.50) and a chicken caesar wrap sandwich. Dinner is served by the windows in the long and narrow Oak Room. The menu offers a Mediterranean seafood stew, a veal and lobster sauté and rack of lamb amid the more plebian choices of baked scrod, baked stuffed shrimp, grilled seafood and steaks. Key lime, toffee and coconut cream pies are touted for dessert. The Sunday brunch buffet for $16.95 packs in the non-beachgoers.

(401) 789-0700. www.thecoastguardhouse.com. Entrées, $15 to $24. Lunch, Monday-Friday 11:30 to 3. Dinner nightly, 5 to 9 or 10, Sunday 4 to 9. Sunday brunch, 10 to 2.

Amalfi Mediterranean Restaurant, 1 Beach St., Narragansett.

The second best water view (after the Coast Guard House) is offered on the breezy outdoor deck with a bar at this restaurant beside the Village Inn at Narragansett Pier. Here is where Spain got its start locally, to be succeeded by a number of lessees who have come and gone. Amalfi's has gotten better reviews under chef-owner Kenneth Young, both from the restaurant critics and from the young beach crowd that favors the place. The bar and deck are where the action is and frankly appeal more than the lineups of close-together tables packed into the vast white-clothed dining room, where big windows yield views of the beach scene. Chef Young includes in his Mediterranean theme the cuisines of Greece and Morocco, with an assist from new chef de cuisine Gene Allsworth, formerly of Narragansett's acclaimed but short-lived Trieste Café & Trattoria. Start with their garlic and mint tzatziki or perhaps mussels provençal to accompany your seafood paella, pork shank osso buco or seared lamb saltimbocca. Grilled striped bass with lobster-basil butter sauce, seafood paella and grilled filet mignon with cabernet demi-glace are regular features. The ganache-filled chocolate dacquoise is a stellar dessert.

(401) 792-3999. www.amalfiri.com. Entrées, $18.95 to $29.95. Lunch daily, noon to 4. Dinner nightly, 4 to 10.

Basil's, 22 Kingstown Road, Narragansett.

This tiny, dark Victorian charmer – stuck in a time warp of 1950s French and, for most, pleasantly so – is lovingly run by Vasilios (Basil) and Kathleen Kourakis.

Formerly a chef in Vail, Colo., Basil took over the quarters once occupied by our favorite Le Petite France in 1984 (to be closer to Europe, he said). Here he does all the cooking himself, shunning the robust flavoring of today's cooks for a more refined, restrained style. He offers a French-continental menu of steak and veal dishes, including his specialty veal medallions topped with a light cream and mushroom sauce. Poached salmon, scampi provençal, chicken piccata, duck à l'orange and beef stroganoff are traditional favorites, done to perfection. Escargots bourguignonne and frog's legs are among starters. Dessert could be a smooth chocolate mousse, coupe Basil, a French-style parfait or baked alaska. The service is professional and the wine list is good. The pretty dining room is intimate (make that very), with banquettes along the walls and tables lushly dressed in white linens over print cloths.

(401) 789-3743. Entrées, $17 to $35. Dinner, Wednesday-Sunday 5:30 to 10.

Woody's, 21 Pier Marketplace, Narragansett.
Chef-owner Ted Monahan lost his restaurant lease in Westerly and moved into this pint-size place in the heart of Narragansett. He seats only 24 or so at close-together tables dressed with white linens and striking blue service plates, beneath a candle-lit chandelier and beside windows shielded with white lace curtains. The short menu is categorized by tapas, greens and, for entrées, "birds, grains, animals and swimmers." Except for specials, it's also basically unchanging, even for the quirky prices ending in odd numbers (the popular brick-seared free-range chicken with wild greens and smashed potatoes went up less than 20 percent from $13.33 to $15,97 in Woody's first eight years). Folks rave about the seared sea scallops with capellini and Thai vegetables in a spicy tomato broth, the pistachio-encrusted spring lamb with pomegranate sauce and the grilled filet of beef with walla walla onions and horseradish. Nearly half the entrée choices accommodate vegetarians, as in roasted vegetable papoli with couscous and grilled flatbread drizzled with roasted tomato vinaigrette. Good tapas are the roasted garlic shrimp with sundried tomatoes and herbs, the roasted squash and red pepper quesadilla with jack cheese and chipotle-lime crème fraîche, and the grilled portobello and goat cheese pizza. Desserts include strawberry shortcake made with buttery shortbread cookies rather than biscuits and a heavenly chocolate mousse cake with a light chocolate meringue crust. The wine list has been honored by Wine Spectator.

(401) 789-9500. Entrées, $15.77 to $25.41. Dinner, Wednesday-Sunday from 5:30.

Crazy Burger Café & Juice Bar, 144 Boon St., Narragansett.
Go here for local color, quirky ambiance, lots of fun and just plain good food. Not to mention more than twenty varieties of burgers, the best sweet potato chips, fruit smoothies, chai teas and espresso. Chef-owner Mike Maxon used to come up with exotic burgers when he created the day's specials at Rue de L'Espoir in Providence. So when the opportunity arose to take over the old Seaside Diner here, the name was already a given. He offers mad cow burgers, vegan burgers, a luna-sea salmon burger, a great baa-baa lamb burger and what have you, with "crazy sides" like orzo salad, bangkok slaw and poundies (Irish mashed potatoes). Breakfast fare is inventive as well – how about a crab benny: Moroccan crab cakes with poached eggs on a bolo? Dinner choices vary from Osaka salmon, swordfish teriyaki and Chinese fried tilapia to chicken framboise, vegetable gateau and Israeli couscous with vegan meatballs. When we were there, the borderline ravioli was a powerful special of black bean-scallion ravioli topped with blackened scallops in a smoked yellow tomato-corn-asparagus salsa. In summer, Mike reports, some visitors come for

three meals a day – "it's like going to three different restaurants." You can sit inside at a counter or booths in a small room that defines funk, or outside on a rear patio surrounded by rampant gardens lovingly tended by Mike's wife.

(401) 783-1810. Entrées, $12,95 to $18.95. Breakfast daily, 8 to 4. Lunch daily from 8. Dinner nightly, 4 to 9 or 10. BYOB.

Champlin's Seafood Deck, 256 Great Island Road, Narragansett.

For seafood in a casual setting beside the water, this gets the area's highest recommendations. With a retail seafood store below and an upstairs location above the docks at the entrance to the harbor in the fishing hamlet of Galilee, you know the seafood has to be fresh off the boat. Champlin's is a bit more basic than its reputation had led us to expect, with a rustic ramble of decks and interior rooms holding picnic tables – some protected from the elements, and some totally open to the sun and sea. It's also much larger and busier, and you're apt to find beachgoers eating in their bathing suits and children feeding the gulls. You line up to place your order at the upstairs window, take a number and find a seat, preferably near the channel where you can watch fishermen unloading their catch and see the Block Island ferry come and go. The fried shrimp and scallops are reputed to be the best around. We were certainly impressed with the lobster salad roll ($10.99), a knife-and-fork affair loaded with succulent lobster and the only "salad" evidence a piece of lettuce tucked in the bun. Dinners come with coleslaw and a choice of red or french fried potatoes. Besides the usual suspects, you might find charbroiled swordfish, baked scallops and baked stuffed shrimp. The seafood platter ($16.99) yields fried clams, clam strips, fish, scallops and shrimp. The place has a full liquor license. For dessert, the Down Under shop on the ground level offers ice cream, fudge, and chocolates shaped like lobsters and crabs.

401) 783-3152. Entrées, $5.49 to $16.99. Open daily, 11 to 9.

Aunt Carrie's, 1240 Ocean Road, Narragansett.

Another glorified seafood shack, this one is away from the harbor fray and has indoor seating with a view of the dunes and open ocean. The dining room of the weather-worn, shingled beach house seats 150. Open and airy, it is cooled by sea breezes drifting through screened windows. Aunt Carrie's been going strong since 1920, and looks it. It lives up to its name, the fourth generation of the original family tendering food and service in the style of a favorite aunt. You can eat quite well here on fried dinners of clams, scallops and shrimp, served with fresh-from-the-oven breads, a cup of chowder, a green salad, french fries and – as your aunt would have it – a slice of warm apple pie. There are shore dinners with lobsters, too, as well as the usual clam cakes, fried clams and the like. Save room for the legendary afore-mentioned pie, cinnamon-scented. The menu says that if you get there early in the morning, you can watch the cooks peeling apples for the pies and preparing the raisin bread.

(401) 783-7930. Plates, $7.25 to $16.95. Complete dinners, $12.25 to $23.95. Open daily except Tuesday in summer, noon to 8; Friday-Sunday in shoulder season. Closed Sept. 20 to late May.

FOR MORE INFORMATION: Narragansett Chamber of Commerce, 36 Ocean Road, Narragansett, RI 02882, (401) 783-7121. Fax (401) 789-0220. www.narragansettri.com/chamber.

South County Tourism Council, 4808 Tower Hill Road, Wakefield, RI 02879, (401) 789-4422 or (800) 548-4662. www.southcountryri.com.

The Breakers is Newport's largest mansion facing ocean along famed Cliff Walk.

Newport, R.I.

As America's yachting capital, an historic seaport and the birthplace of the U.S. Navy, Newport is a nautical city like no other.

After its founding in 1639 at the tip of Aquidneck Island as a religious refuge (the first Quakers and Jews in the New World settled here), Newport was one of the nation's leading ports in the 17th and 18th centuries. The first Navy boats sailed from its harbor into Narragansett Bay and the Atlantic. In the 1800s, the Vanderbilts, the Astors, the Morgans and others of America's 400 created a seaside summer resort unmatched in opulence. In the last century, the Navy increased its Newport presence to the point where it became the area's largest employer, with 10,000 military and civilian personnel at 32 commands and installations.

The Newport-to-Bermuda races, the Tall Ships and the America's Cup extravaganzas solidified Newport's place on the international maritime map.

The nautical presence is pervasive. You sense it amidst all the wharves – both old and quaint, and rebuilt and trendy – along Thames Street. It's glittering and glamorous along the Cliff Walk behind the Bellevue Avenue mansions, where the society's famed 400 summered. It's more rugged along the ten-mile Ocean Drive around the peninsula where some of today's wannabe 400 live. There are sailboats everywhere and regattas all season. The beaches are fine for swimming and surfing. The Museum of Yachting, the Newport Yachting Center and the International Yacht Restoration School promote things nautical.

Newport's Yellow Pages devote three pages to boating, from building to rentals. Restaurants and stores take up the theme in their names: The Mooring, the Pier and the Rhumbline, the Armchair Sailor Bookstore, Cast Offs and JT's Ship Chandlery.

Myriad pleasures are to be found by anyone interested in the water: history, sports, good living, shopping and fine dining. What more could one want?

Getting There

Newport occupies the southwest tip of Aquidneck Island, the point where Narragansett Bay meets Rhode Island Sound. Some 40 roundabout miles south of Providence, it's reached via Routes 114 or 138 from the north and east; via I-95 or Route 1 and Route 138 across the Jamestown-Newport Bridge from the west.

Where to Stay——————————————— *ՐՐՐ*

Newport has an incredible range and number of accommodations, from some two dozen hotels and motels to more than 200 inns and B&Bs at last count. Establishments detailed here have a water view or orientation, which is not the case with most Newport accommodations.

Hotels/Motels

Hyatt Regency Newport Hotel & Spa, 1 Goat Island, Newport 02840.

The most watery location in Newport is offered by the rejuvenated Hyatt, located just offshore on a small island in Narragansett Bay. Born as the Sheraton Islander and later a Doubletree, this became a Hyatt in 2000 and completed $12 million of renovations in 2003. It remains Newport's all-around large resort hotel, from its banquet room, conference center and underground garage to its indoor and outdoor pools, tennis courts, spa, and health club. That it happens to be away from the hubbub on narrow Goat Island between the Jamestown-Newport Bridge and Newport Harbor and surrounded by the water on three sides (the other end of the island has marinas and condominiums) is a distinct advantage. A disadvantage is that you have to use your car or walk quite a distance to visit the rest of Newport, except in summer when there's a harbor shuttle. Most of the rooms on six floors of a brick structure that looks at first glance like a grain elevator afford views of the water. Ours didn't, unless you consider the indoor pool a water view. That huge pool area is light and airy with high arched-glass roof and a busy cocktail area where imbibers can watch the swimmers. There's also an outdoor saltwater pool beside the tennis courts. We enjoyed perfect water views during a subsequent conference when we were put up in the newer Captain's Quarters, where nearly half the 47 more deluxe rooms open right onto the bay. The hotel's spa offers a variety of treatments and packages. In 2004, the hotel completed a major facelift to its **Windward Grille** to show off its waterfront location. Light fare is available in the **Auld Mug Lounge.**

(401) 851-1234. Fax (401) 851-3201. Two hundred forty-six rooms and eighteen suites. Doubles, $189 to $365.

The Chanler at Cliff Walk, 117 Memorial Blvd., Newport 02840.

A boutique hotel and restaurant, the reborn Chanler occupies Newport's most dramatic oceanside location and makes the most of it. The extravagant French Empire-style showplace, enveloped in lush landscaping behind a sweeping stone entry identified only by a plaque, is situated on four acres at the terminus of the Cliff Walk and

overlooks Easton's Beach and the open ocean. Built in 1865 as the summer home of Congressman John Winthrop Chanler of New York, it was renovated to the tune of $10 million plus by John and Jean E. Shufelt, who undertook a similar renovation earlier at the Mission Point Resort on Michigan's Mackinac Island and own the La Farge Perry House, a small Newport B&B. Twenty sumptuous guest rooms are furnished and decorated to different eras, among them Renaissance, Greek Revival, English Tudor, Louis XIV, Colonial, Federal, French Provincial, Victorian and Mediterranean. All have plump king or queensize beds and jacuzzi baths and all but two have gas fireplaces. Most come with crystal chandeliers, fine paintings, flat-screen TVs, DVD players and wet bars. Many offer water views. The best are the largest (Renaissance) with a rooftop deck in the main house and three villas in the east wing with ocean-facing decks with hot tubs and a more casual New England island theme. Three garden villas in front with floral names and themes have both baths with jacuzzis and private garden courtyards with hot tubs under pergolas and two sitting areas to compensate for their smaller size and lack of ocean views. Three meals a day are served with a view in **The Spiced Pear,** the hotel's luxurious restaurant (see Where to Eat). The mahogany paneled lounge and the adjoining outdoor terraces overlooking the ocean also provide food and drink.

(401) 847-1300. Fax (401) 847-3620. www.thechanler.com. Twenty rooms with private baths. Doubles, $895 to $1,095.

Newport Harbor Hotel & Marina, 49 America's Cup Ave., Newport 02840.

After the former Treadway hotel/motor inn fell on hard times, new owners changed the name and undertook renovations of rooms on four floors. The first-floor rooms were completed first, with end walls of windows and sliding glass doors onto the harbor. We water lovers would still opt for the fourth-floor rooms with private balconies; seven face the harbor head-on. Views from eight balconies on the sides vary; those on the north side offer only glimpses of water at best. About half the hotel's rooms face the harbor, but most do not open to the outside; the rest overlook the parking lot and the city. Each has a kingsize or two double beds. Rooms were totally refurbished in 2003 to convey a Newport nautical theme in navy and gold. Baths were remodeled to include marble floors, tub surrounds and pedestal sinks. Facilities include an indoor pool, saunas and a 60-slip marina, flanked by a new harborfront boardwalk and marina deck behind the hotel. The location is one of Newport's best, beside the water and in the thick of the downtown action near Bowen's and Bannister's wharves. Three meals a day are served in **Waverleys,** with a few window tables and a canopied sidewalk terrace in summer. There's frequently live entertainment in the lounge.

(401) 847-9000 or (800) 955-2558. Fax (401) 849-6380. www.newporthotel.com. One hundred thirty-three rooms. Doubles, $159 to $399.

Newport Marriott, 25 America's Cup Ave., Newport 02840.

Newport's biggest hotel opened in 1988 on Long Wharf, next to the Gateway Center transportation and information complex and with the harbor across the street. Billed as one of the Marriott chain's top resort hotels, it has 319 guest rooms arranged around a five-story atrium. They tend to be on the small side; the place was started as a Holiday Inn Crowne Plaza, and the rooms are not as large as Marriott would have built. Best are those with harbor or city views; others look over the atrium or the parking garage. The top floor is a deluxe concierge level. Facilities include an indoor pool, sauna, whirlpool, fitness center and four racquetball courts. Dine in **Fathoms,** lately refurbished in sea colors with sculptures of fanciful fish around the room and curved panels that impart the sensation of being on a ship. Window tables and the eye-catching bar/lounge afford views of the harbor.

(401) 849-1000 or (800) 458-3066. www.newportmarriott.com. Three hundred twelve rooms and seven suites. Doubles, $145 to $350.

Long Wharf Resort, 5 Washington St., Newport 02840.

This is the newest of a growing roster of time-sharing resort properties headquartered in Newport. It's quite a spread, built in the shingle style with a circular tower to resemble the landmark Newport Casino and facing the harbor across the street. This one is all small condo-style units of two and three bedrooms, nicely furnished with everything a family might need for a week's vacation. Half the units on the L-shaped structure's second, third and fourth floors get water or courtyard views, although there are no balconies upon which to take advantage. The rest face a parking lot or the Marriott. The master bathrooms contain single whirlpool tubs. The main floor includes a lounge area with a fireplace and a small pool in which any swimmers are on full view with a trickling waterfall as a backdrop. The pool opens through plastic flaps to a much larger pool area outdoors, and a third pool was under construction in 2004. There's also a small theater in which movies are shown nightly. There's no meal service, but guests can prepare their own.

(401) 847-7800 or (800) 225-3522. Fax (401) 845-0127. Eighty-two suites. Rates, $335 to $460.

Inn on Long Wharf, 142 Long Wharf, Newport 02840.

Blessed with a great waterfront location, all 40 suites in this time-sharing resort built in 1985 face directly onto the harbor. It's across the street at an angle from its newer, larger sibling, the Long Wharf Resort, and shows its age, at least in comparison. But the "inn" is all one-bedroom units facing the harbor – if you open the sliding glass doors, only a railing separates you from a spill into the drink. Rooms on four floors open off a corridor into the bedroom; beyond are a bathroom with a double whirlpool tub opposite a small kitchenette equipped with refrigerator and microwave, and beyond that a comfortable living room with a sofabed, chair, TV and that sliding door onto the water. Although the suites lack balconies, there's a sundeck on the roof. The former Long Wharf Steak House had morphed into a business lounge or conference room at our latest visit. We couldn't determine exactly which, since the front desk was unmanned. A customer seated in the lobby advised that check-in was across the street at a common visitor reception building.

(401) 847-7800 or (800) 225-3522. Forty suites. Doubles, $235 to $315.

The Newport Bay Club and Hotel, 337 Thames St., Box 1440, Newport 02840.

Probably the nicest of the many harborfront time-sharing resorts not directly facing the water, this has 36 large and luxurious units, ranging from one-bedroom suites to two-bedroom townhouses. It's sited perpendicular to the water at the busy downtown intersection where Thames Street, America's Cup Avenue and Memorial Boulevard intersect. The old General Electric mill retains its high wood ceilings and paneling. Each condominium-style unit contains a kitchenette or full kitchen, a large living room with pullout bed and dining area, a queensize bedroom and a marble bathroom with whirlpool tub. The fourth-floor townhouses have balconies upstairs and down, with side views of the harbor if you're standing up. Continental breakfast is served. Downstairs in the Perry Mill Marketplace are retail shops and nightclubs.

(401) 849-8600. Fax (401) 846-6857. One-bedroom suites, $199 to $409; two-bedroom suites and townhouses, $299 to $599.

Seaview Inn, 240 Aquidneck Ave. (Route 138A), Middletown 02842.

A good view of Easton's Pond and the ocean from a hilltop back from the road commends this motel of 1950s vintage, which dropped the motel from its name and fancied itself as an inn under new owners. It's the only one of the Newport area's many standard motels that's close to the ocean – others farther out Routes 138 or 114 in Middletown could be in Anytown, but the prices are lower than in Newport proper. This has accommodations on two floors, all with balconies or patios to enjoy the view. Adirondack chairs are placed strategically around the lawn. Rooms have paneled walls, two double beds, color TV and a couple of wood and leather motel chairs. A complimentary continental breakfast is served in the coffee shop.

(401) 846-5000 or (800) 495-2046. Fax (401) 848-0873. www.seaviewnewport.com. Thirty-nine rooms and two suites with private baths. Doubles, $129 to $219.

The Inn at Newport Beach, Memorial Boulevard at Wave Avenue, Newport 02840.

Formerly Easton's Inn on the Beach and later The Greenhouse Inn and Restaurant, this semi-old-timer was rescued from foreclosure by the owners of the local Comfort Inn and became affiliated with Historic Hotels of America. All rooms underwent renovations, and furnishings are a cut above. The four-story hotel is right across from the very swimmable Easton's Beach in a busy area that can be noisy by day and evening. The twenty air-conditioned rooms along the front offer water views. Deluxe rooms on the recently installed fourth floor have modern baths (several with whirlpool tubs), antique reproduction furniture and are quieter. All have TV/DVDs, refrigerators, microwaves, hair dryers and Caswell-Massey bath amenities. A complimentary continental breakfast is available in the solarium dining room.

(401) 846-0310 or (800) 786-0310. Forty-five rooms and five suites with private baths. Doubles, $159 to $379.

Inns/B&Bs

Castle Hill Inn & Resort, 590 Ocean Drive, Newport 02840.

While retaining its grand oceanside setting on a 40-acre peninsula at the west end of Ocean Drive, the old Inn at Castle Hill has a new name, refurbished accommodations and a new vitality that has vaulted it into the rarefied realm of the world's top small hotels as anointed by travel magazines. The locally owned Newport Harbor Corp. reassumed control of the landmark Victorian property and vastly upgraded the accommodations that had become outdated. Water lovers particularly enjoy the outlying Harbor House units with open porches overlooking Narragansett Bay and the enlarged beachfront efficiency lodgings right at water's edge. Traditionalists and romantics might opt for the eight Victorian guest rooms and three suites in the main inn or adjacent Swiss-style chalet, the former laboratory of original owner Alexander Agassiz, the Harvard marine biologist. All recently refurbished, most have king or queen beds, double whirlpool marble baths, fireplaces and original antiques. The opulent 30-foot-high Turret Suite includes a deep soaking tub beside the window on the main bedroom level, which is joined by a winding mahogany staircase to a loft sitting area with a 360-degree view. Besides their porches overlooking the bay from a cliff about 30 feet from the mansion, each of the six Harbor House units has a kingsize bed, gas fireplace, whirlpool bath and television. Latest to be redone were some of the eighteen spartan Beach House rooms. The first eight to be enlarged and refurbished – four each in two buildings – now rank with the best beachside cottage accommodations in southern New England. They are elegant with vaulted ceilings, beadboard paneling, gleaming hardwood floors and beachy decor. Each has a kingsize bed, TV/VCR and a distressed leather couch that converts into a queen bed in the sitting area, gas fireplace, granite-counter galley kitchen, double whirlpool tub and separate marble shower, and an outdoor deck facing the ocean. From the whirlpool tub in several, you can look out onto the beach – and be there in no time. A complimentary breakfast with a choice of juices, fruits and entrées is served to overnight guests in the mansion's Sunset Room, part of its main-floor restaurant (see Where to Eat). The fare includes lobster omelets, eggs benedict, French toast made with raisin challah and smoked salmon with breakfast garnishes.

(401) 849-3800 or (888) 466-1355. Fax (401) 849-3838. www.castlehillinn.com. Fourteen rooms, three suites and eight cottages with private baths. Doubles, $395 to $850. Suites, $850 to $1,450. Cottages, $5,075 weekly in summer.

Cliffside Inn, 2 Seaview Ave., Newport 02840.

This Victorian charmer is among the most luxurious of Newport's upscale B&Bs, although top honors may be shared with its over-the-top sibling, the Abigail Stoneman Inn. This one, however, has the advantage for water lovers of a location a short block above the Cliff Walk, with a glimpse of the ocean from the front veranda, plus three suites in the Seaview Cottage with an ocean view at the foot of the property. Low-key Victoriana and creature comforts prevail throughout the main house, a Second Empire summer villa built in 1880. As restored by late owner Winthrop Baker, each of its thirteen accommodations has one or two working fireplaces. Their "bathing salons" – eleven with whirlpool tubs – are some of America's most glamorous. The cottage adds three suites, each with three fireplaces and sound-system bathrooms. The Seaview on the lower floor is a stone-walled hideaway with an antique French kingsize bed and wood-burning fireplace. Its plush sitting room shares a see-through gas fireplace with the marble bathroom, which has an Allure bath, shower and sound system to end all systems. Upstairs, the queensize Atlantic enjoys an ocean view as well as a sitting room with a media center sporting LCD TV, DVD, VCR, CD and multi-room stereo system. The kingsize Cliff has "his and her" sitting rooms, one a living room and the other a study. Besides offering every amenity one could want, the Cliffside pampers guests with exotic afternoon tea service in the inn's formal parlor or on the wide front veranda. In the morning, the staff serves up a lavish breakfast, which culminated at our visit in eggs benedict with a subtle hollandaise sauce. There's food for thought here, too, in the more than 100 paintings of reclusive artist Beatrice Turner, onetime owner of the house, whose life story and background are full of mystery.

(401) 847-1811 or (800) 845-1811. Fax (401) 848-5850. www.cliffsideinn.com. Eight rooms and eight suites with private baths. Doubles, $245 to $425. Suites, $375 to $575. Add $50 weekends, May-October.

The Francis Malbone House, 392 Thames St., Newport. 02840.

Good harbor views across the street, a large rear courtyard and lawn, commodious common rooms and elegant guest rooms make this an exceptional B&B choice in downtown Newport. It bears the name of the shipping merchant for whom the house was built in 1760. The main house has eight corner bedrooms on the second and third floors plus a main-floor suite, all with updated baths and six with fireplaces. The four front rooms are bigger and yield harbor views. Each is handsomely furnished with antique queen beds covered by monogrammed duvet comforters. A rear addition has nine larger rooms, each with a kingsize bed, fireplace, jacuzzi and bigger vanities and closets – "all the things we wanted but couldn't have in the old house," according to innkeeper Will Dewey. The four rear rooms in the newer wing share two private garden courtyards, both unexpectedly verdant retreats in downtown

Newport. The most luxurious are two new suites in the 1750 Benjamin Mason House at the rear of the property. The downstairs holds a living room, dining room, kitchen and sunroom with a courtyard. Upstairs are two spacious bedrooms, each with king bed, fireplace and jacuzzi tub and TV in the bathroom. Occupants join other guests for tea and breakfast in the main inn. All guests enjoy a large fountain courtyard between the buildings, and share a couple of elegant, high-ceilinged front parlors and a library with TV. The wing also holds a 40-seat breakfast room, where guests partake of a gourmet breakfast, from eggs benedict to belgian waffles.

(401) 846-0392 or (800) 846-0392. Fax (401) 848-5956. www.malbone.com. Sixteen rooms and four suites with private baths. Doubles, $245 to $345. Suites, $395 to $475.

Admiral Fitzroy Inn, 398 Thames St., Newport 02840.

The harbor is on view from a rooftop terrace and two rooftop guest rooms at this B&B, newly billed as "a European-style hotel in the heart of Newport" by the Newport Harbor Corp., also owner of the posh Castle Hill Inn & Resort. Two rooms with kingsize beds and whirlpool tubs on the roof open onto private decks, while the rooftop terrace is available to all guests for sunning during the day. Guests are cosseted comfortably in seventeen bedrooms that belie the 1854 structure's not-so-distant status as the St. Mary's Church convent. A plain, shingled box on the outside, it's quite appealing inside, especially the striking hand-painted decorative touches everywhere. Done for the former innkeeper by a young artist, they vary from borders to murals and entire walls and are worthy of a gallery. An elevator serves guest rooms on three floors, most of them quite spacious by Newport standards and artfully furnished with antique queensize or king beds, white duvet comforters, and upholstered or wicker loveseats and chairs. All have TVs and small refrigerators, some hidden in hand-stenciled armoires. An electric kettle with the fixings for tea or coffee is in each room. Room 10's large mural of an apricot tree in a clay pot is so realistic it even shows bugs and a butterfly. A European continental breakfast is taken at individual tables in the cheery main-floor dining room, its walls highlighted by hand-painted garlands of flowers. Besides the usual you might find warm ham and cheese croissants or hard-boiled eggs.

(401) 848-8000 or (866) 848-8780. Fax (401) 848-8006. www.admiralfitzroy.com. Sixteen rooms and one suite with private baths. Doubles, $165 to $305.

Sanford-Covell Villa Marina, 72 Washington St., Newport 02840.

The only Newport B&B directly on the water, this Victorian mansion has a wide piazza on three sides from which to take in the view of the harbor. An old-fashioned glider hangs on chains from the ceiling of the rear porch. Beyond is a small lawn with a heated saltwater pool and a jacuzzi, and beyond that a dock stretching into the harbor. That's enough for us, but the inside is an architectural dream – shortly after it was completed in 1870 by Boston architect William Ralph Emerson (cousin of Ralph Waldo Emerson), a Boston newspaper called it "the most elegantly finished house ever built in Newport." The four-story tower entry hall rises 35 feet to the ceiling above the fourth floor; small balconies project at several levels, and the stenciling is incredible. The original woods remain, as do many of the furnishings, including a dining set once owned by the founder of the U.S. Naval Academy at Annapolis. Seven rooms, including a two-bedroom walk-out basement apartment, have private baths. Three on the second floor have king beds, fireplaces and water views. The third-floor Kate Field Room has a cushioned window seat in the bay window and a blackboard upon which guests write whimsical messages. It and the Playroom share a bathroom with marble sinks and a wood-trimmed clawfoot tub overlooking the Goat Island lighthouse. A continental breakfast is served at a huge table in the dining room beneath a ceiling bedecked with silver stars. Both guest rooms and public rooms are richly furnished by Anne Ramsey Cuvelier, descendant of an early owner, who moved lately from California to be in residence year-round.

(401) 847-0206. www.sanford-covell.com. Seven rooms with private baths and two with shared baths. Doubles, $165 to $325. www.sanford-covell.com.

Adele Turner Inn, 93 Pelham St., Newport 02840.

The folks from the Cliffside Inn acquired the Admiral Benbow Inn, upscaled and refurbished it with the predictable amenities, and named it for the mother of local artist Beatrice Turner. The 1855 sea captain's home, listed on the National Register, is along a prime residential street descending to the waterfront. The panoramic water view from its rooftop deck has been rated one of Newport's best. Three of the three-story inn's thirteen rooms are suites. The Tycoon on the third floor with a 43-foot-stretch along the front of the house has a water view and one of the inn's three double whirlpool tubs. The best view of all is from the deck off the rear queen-bedded Harborview Spa room, which gained an outdoor hot tub. Working gas fireplaces were installed in every guest room, and the front parlor has two. King and queensize beds, elegant quilts and window treatments, new rugs and carpeting, TV/VCRs and telephones are common to all. The pampering service, gourmet breakfast and elaborate tea service for which the Cliffside is known are duplicated here. There's also an afternoon wine and food tasting, plus nightly turndown service with treats. The stunning Victorian parlor is furnished with period antiques, rich fabrics and four large portraits of Adele Haas Turner, painted by her daughter Beatrice when the family summered in the house that became the Cliffside Inn.

(401) 847-1811 or (800) 845-1811. www.adeleturnerinn.com. Ten rooms and three suites with private baths. Doubles, $195 to $455. Suites, $395 to $480. Add $50 weekends, May-October.

Mill Street Inn, 75 Mill St., Newport 02840.

Inn purists might find this inn austere, but we rather like its European atmosphere and its water views. A 19th-century brick mill restored in 1985 and listed on the National Register, it offers 23 guest suites. The vast expanses of white walls are fine backdrops for contemporary paintings and posters, modern sofas and chairs, industrial gray carpeting, vases filled with fresh flowers, wet bars and television sets. In a few rooms, original brick walls and beams tone down some of the white. Beds are queensize, fans whir on the ceilings, and baths are gleaming and white-tiled with pedestal sinks. Eight duplex townhouses on the second floor have a living room down and a bedroom above, opening onto private decks raised just enough so you can sit on the chairs and see the distant harbor and the Jamestown bridge. An extensive continental breakfast is served summer mornings on the rooftop deck with a view of the harbor. In cooler winter, breakfast and afternoon tea are offered in a charming basement room.

(401) 849-9500 or (800) 392-1316. Fax (401) 848-5131. www.millstreetinn.com. Twenty-three suites with private baths. Doubles, $195 to $365.

Seeing and Doing

On or Near the Water

America's Cup Avenue and Thames Street are a sea of humanity in summer, as boat people and tourists jam the streets and the wharves that jut into the harbor at every opportunity. The harbor and Narragansett Bay are filled with powerboats and sailboats. Regattas are scheduled summer weekends and sometimes during the week. The Newport Yachting Center off America's Cup Avenue is the scene of boat shows and special events, and even operates an outdoor ice-skating rink à la Rockefeller Center in winter.

HARBOR CRUISES. Viking Tours, 23 America's Cup Ave., (401) 847-6921, offers one-hour sightseeing cruises on its 140-passenger Viking Queen four times a day in summer from the Goat Island Marina; adults $11, children $6. The **M/V Amazing Grace,** Sayer's Wharf, (401) 847-9109, gives one-hour narrated cruises of Newport Harbor and Narragansett Bay from Oldport Marine adjacent to the Mooring restaurant six times a day in summer; adults $10, children $7. Billed as Newport's most luxurious excursion vessel, the **M/V Spirit of Newport,** (401) 849-3575, sails from Bowen's Wharf six times a day in summer; adults $12, children $6. It also hosts sunset music cruises Wednesday from 8 to 10; adults $15.

Sightsailing of Newport, (401) 849-3333 or (800) 709-7245, offers a variety of 75-minute cruises on small sailboats six times daily from 32 Bowen's Wharf for $20 to $30. **Classic Cruises of Newport,** (401) 847-0298 or (800) 395-1343, has sailing excursions aboard the 72-foot schooner Madeleine as well as cruises on the high-speed Prohibition-era motor yacht Rumrunner. Both depart five times daily from Bannister's Wharf; sails run $25 to $30 and the yacht $17 to $22. The 78-foot schooner **Adirondack II,** (401) 846-3018, sails from the Newport Yachting Center with up to 60 passengers on four trips daily, $23 to $30. The 57-foot catamaran **Flyer,** (401) 848-2100 or (800) 863-5937, offers two-hour sails four times daily ($30 to $35) from the Inn on Long Wharf. Leisurely one-hour sailing tours for $20 are offered by Newport Sailing School and Tours, Goat Island Marina, (401) 848-2266. **Sail Newport,** (401) 849-8385 or 846-1983, rents sailboats at Fort Adams State Park.

The **Jamestown & Newport Ferry,** (401) 423-9900, offers passenger service every 90 minutes between Newport and Jamestown. Regular stops in Newport are at Bowen's Landing, Perrotti Park and Goat Island. Passengers may stop on request at Fort Adams and the Rose Island Lighthouse and stop for lunch in Jamestown. Eight round trips operate daily from 9:50 to 8, July to Labor Day. An all-day pass costs $14.

Adventure Sports Rentals, 142 Long Wharf, (401) 849-4820, rents outboard boats, sailboats, kayaks, inflatable dinghies and bicycles. It also offers fishing trips and parasailing tours. Kayak rentals and tours also are available from **The Kayak Center,** 518 Thames St., (401) 848-2920, and **Kayak Newport,** 365 Thames St., (401) 848-9249.

The Museum of Yachting, Fort Adams State Park.

A special place for yachtsmen is this museum housed since 1985 in a 19th-century granite building on a point at the end of Fort Adams in Newport Harbor. The goal was to have a center of yachting beside the harbor, which is in fact the center of yachting, according to museum officials. Yachting costumes, memorabilia, photos, paintings and models trace the history of sailing inside what was once an Army mule barn. The fascinating photo exhibit called "The Mansions and the Yachts" focuses on the sailing roles of the Vanderbilts, Astors and Morgans ("while the women were here for the social life, this is what the men did," our guide explained). The Small Craft Gallery displays old wooden boats beneath a model of the boat that won the first America's Cup perched near the ceiling. Upstairs is the Single-Handed Sailors Hall of Fame, honoring transatlantic and round-the-world solo feats, and a library detailing ocean voyages. Located in the museum's boat basin are classic yachts dating from the late 1800s to 1965, restored by the museum and actively sailed by volunteers throughout the summer. Among them is the flagship Courageous, winner of the America's Cup in 1974 and 1977, and Dennis Connor's Freedom (1980). The museum is small, but it's designed to appeal to laymen as well as sailors. Even if you're not into sailing, you'll get a feel for part of Newport's heritage, and the hilly waterside site is spectacular.

(401) 847-1018. www.museumofyachting.org. Open daily 10 to 5, mid-May through October. Adults $5, children $4.

International Yacht Restoration School, 449 Thames St.

Local yachtswoman Elizabeth Meyer spearheaded the 1996 opening of this $7-million venture housed in an 1831 stone mill building and an adjacent generating plant on the former electric company site along the waterfront on lower Thames Street. The public can watch student shipwrights refurbishing some of the world's biggest yachts. The premier restoration project is the 1885 schooner Coronet, a 167-foot beauty called the last remaining great American yacht. All restoration work is viewable from walkways at several levels in the 40-foot-high restoration hall. Exhibits and galleries help explain the proceedings.

(401) 849-5777. www.iyrs.org. Open daily 10 to 5; closed Sunday in off-season. Free.

Fort Adams, in Fort Adams State Park off Harrison Avenue.

The nation's largest coastal fortification and guardian of the head of Narragansett Bay from 1799 to 1945 is open to the public for picnicking, fishing, swimming and guided tours. Named for President John Quincy Adams, the fort was designed to accommodate 2,400 soldiers and 468 mounted cannons, and the fortifications can still be seen. The hilly point juts into the bay and provides as good a vantage point today for yacht-watching and the Newport skyline as it did for soldiers defending their country. The fort has been reopened for scheduled tours, and garrison drills and camp reenactments are given at times. Visitors can see the casements where big guns once roared, some recently restored to display exhibits from the Naval War College Museum, which was closed to the public after the 2001 terrorist attacks. And the intrepid can venture into the listening tunnels beneath the fort's walls. Also in the 80-acre state park is Eisenhower House, the summer White House of President Eisenhower (not open for tours).

(401) 847-0707. www.fortadams.org. Guided fort tours on the hour, daily 10 to 4, mid-May through Columbus Day; adults $6, children $3 to $5.. Park open daily from sunrise to sunset; parking $2.

Rose Island Lighthouse, Narragansett Bay.

A mile offshore, this restored 1912 operating lighthouse welcomes visitors for tours in summer. It's reached via the Jamestown & Newport Ferry, which stops on demand eight times a day. In addition to the $14 ferry fee, the $3 landing fee includes a lighthouse tour and use of the picnic tables and grounds for beachcombing, bird watching, fishing and swimming. After the lighthouse museum closes each day, the two keeper's bedrooms on the first floor become available for those who want a novel B&B experience offshore (doubles, $185). "It's back to basics," according to lighthouse officials. There's no running water and you bring your own food. But it has appeal. The better-furnished upstairs keeper's apartment is manned by families who pay from $900 to $2,000 weekly to be working keepers of the week – an experience booked up to three years in advance.

(401) 847-4242. www.roseisland.org. Rose Island Lighthouse Foundation office at 365 Thames St., Newport, open daily 9 to 1. Lighthouse tours daily 10 to 4, July to Labor Day.

The Norman Bird Sanctuary, 583 Third Beach Road, Middletown, (401) 846-2577, is a 450-plus-acre wildlife refuge with more than seven miles of hiking trails. It's a sleeper, offering the region's best birding and wildlife viewing possibilities.

Visitors can enjoy a leisurely stroll through fields and woods or hike over craggy ledges to the top of Hanging Rock for a good view of the ocean, Second Beach, marshlands and Gardiner's Pond. A trailside natural history museum and the Barn Owl Gift Shop are available for browsing. Open daily, 9 to 5. Adults $4, children $2.

Train Excursions. Relive the past on a scenic nine-mile train ride along the Narragansett Bay shoreline via the **Old Colony & Newport Railway,** 19 America's Cup Ave., (401) 624-6951. Ride behind a vintage diesel in a turn-of-the-last-century passenger coach or one of the oldest operating parlor cars (1884). You'll see the Newport Naval Base, ships sailing in the bay, rocky beaches and varied wildlife. A one-hour, ten-mile trip departs Sunday at 11:45 and 1:45, mid-January to mid-November. Parlor car, $11. Coach, adults $7.50, children $5.

The Newport Dinner Train, 19 America's Cup Ave., (401) 841-8700 or (800) 398-7427, carries passengers in modern comfort along Narragansett Bay on lunch and dinner excursions, plus murder mystery and cabaret dinners with singing conductors. Schedules vary, but lunch excursions are generally Thursday and Saturday at noon, $32.95. Dinner excursions are Friday and Saturday at 6:30, $49.95 to $59.95.

Brenton Point State Park, Ocean Avenue. Benches are placed strategically all along a bluff for contemplating the ocean in this scenic prize of a park. Stairs lead down to the rocks, an area popular with fishermen, sunbathers and divers. The grounds along the shore contain parking lots, and picnic areas with grills and restrooms. On good days, kite fliers are out in droves.

Ten-Mile Drive. Also called the Ocean Drive, this is the East Coast's version of California's Seventeen-Mile Drive in Carmel. It meanders along Newport's southern shore past rocky points with crashing surf, spectacular scenery that provides an awesome setting for equally spectacular mansions and contemporary homes, and a couple of beach clubs including the fabled Bailey's Beach where society's 400 sun, swim and socialize.

The Cliff Walk. For an intimate look at the ocean and the backs of the mansions, the 3.5-mile Cliff Walk along Newport's southeastern shore is a must. The walk, designated the first National Recreation Trail in New England, begins at the western end of Easton's Beach (Newport's First Beach). Although you can get onto the walk at several points, we like to start at the foot of Narragansett Avenue, where you walk down to the ocean on the Forty Steps. The first couple of miles are well-maintained and quite easy; the last part past Marine Avenue and around the point near East Bailey's Beach requires good shoes and a stout heart since the path disappears and the going is rocky. You also must pass through a couple of dark, damp tunnels. And a few years ago we were greeted outside the fenced-in Doris Duke estate by a surly guard and the fiercest watchdogs ever. The faint-hearted might better take the first half of the walk and retrace their steps.

Harbor Walk along the northwestern shore is the latest in Newport's efforts to open its waterfront to the public. A brochure and map, sponsored by the Friends of the Waterfront Harbor, gives details. Two walks start at Perrotti Park, a new public park with benches and a striking sculpture along America's Cup Avenue, opposite the Gateway Information Center. Harbor Walk North covers Long Wharf and the historic Point residential section, the original Colonial center of the city and waterfront. The walk follows Washington Street and the public rights of way called driftways to the water. Harbor Walk South heads south past Newport's active harborfront and wharves extending off Thames Street as far as King Park. Treats along this portion included restored wharves, mini-parks, a bandstand, statue and the Ida Lewis Yacht Club. The club is named for America's first female lighthouse keeper, who tended the light on the site a century ago.

BEACHES. Most of the Ocean Drive beaches are private, but you can sunbathe in Brenton Point State Park. Those in the know also go to **Gooseberry Beach,** a privately owned beach open to the public on Ocean Drive just west of Bailey's Beach; this family-oriented place with little surf charges $10 for parking. For surf swimming, head for **Easton's Beach** (also known as First Beach), a wide and sandy three-quarter-mile strand along Memorial Boulevard from the Cliff Walk to the Middletown line. The surf action lures surfers from far and wide in the off-season. There are boardwalks, an amusement rotunda and the Newport Aquarium, and cabanas may be rented. Parking costs $8 on weekdays, $15 on weekends. Beyond Easton's Beach in Middletown are **Second Beach** (where surfing is permitted) and **Third Beach,** parking at both, $10 on weekdays, $15 on weekends). **King Park** along Wellington Avenue in Newport is on a sheltered harbor with pleasant lawns, a pier, a good supervised beach for children, a raft with slides and a free bathhouse. **Fort Adams State Park** has a free beach with a small roped-off area for swimming; parking $2. At all beaches, lifeguards work weekends starting Memorial Day, and daily from mid-June to Labor Day.

Other Attractions

Mansion Tours. The Preservation Society of Newport County, 424 Bellevue Ave., (401) 847-1000, offers guided tours of its nine mansions and a topiary garden. The most visited is the 72-room **Breakers,** the 1895 seaside summer home of Cornelius Vanderbilt II, patriarch of America's wealthiest family. The most opulent of Newport's "cottages," it resembles a northern Italian palace and the vast lawn stretches down to the Cliff Walk. From its upper loggias, you can see the Elizabeth Islands far out to sea on a clear day, and you get to tour the kitchens and butler's pantry – an area larger than most houses. A private collection of Vanderbilt memorabilia is on display at the Breakers Stable and Carriage House.

Other choices are romantic **Rosecliff** of "The Great Gatsby" fame, whose living room doubled as a ballroom; William K. Vanderbilt's **Marble House,** where the hostess once gave a ten-course dinner party for 100 of her friends' dogs, and the museum-like **Elms,** with the finest of Newport's grounds. Also open are the 1852 **Chateau-Sur-Mer,** the 1866 Italianate villa **Chepstow,** the shingle-style 1881 **Isaac Bell House** (a restoration work in progress), the 1748 **Hunter House** in the historic Point section and **Green Animals** overlooking Narragansett Bay in nearby Portsmouth, considered the best topiary garden in the country. If you've seen the grander mansions, you may like best the 1839 **Kingscote,** a charming Victorian that looks lived in and livable.

Mansion schedules vary: open 10 to 5 (Breakers 9 to 5), all open daily mid-June to mid-September; major mansions open daily mid-April to mid-November; Breakers, Elms and Marble House open daily, mid-November to Jan. 2; Rosecliff open daily and Breakers and Elms open weekends, January to mid-April. Admission: Breakers (including Stables), adults $15, children $4. Any other single property, adults $10, children $4. Combo tickets to five properties, adults $31, children $10.

Several other mansions are open under private ownership. **Astors' Beechwood,** 580 Bellevue Ave., (401) 846-3772, is perhaps the most extravagant. It's an 1851 Italian-style seaside villa that was home to the woman who coined the term "400" for the number her New York ballroom would comfortably hold. Insisting upon being called "The Mrs. Astor," she had 281 diamonds in her stomacher and looked like a walking chandelier, according to our guide. Open daily 10 to 5 May-October, Friday-Sunday 10 to 4 in February-April, and special Victorian Christmas hours, early November to mid-December; adults $15, children $10. The 60-room **Belcourt**

Castle, 657 Bellevue Ave., (401) 846-0669, is the home of the Tinney family, whose collection includes art and antiques from 33 countries. Hour-long guided tours, daily noon to 5; adults $10, children $5 to $7. Candlelight or ghost tours are given nightly except Tuesday, $15.

Rough Point, 680 Bellevue Ave.

This impressive mansion on a windswept oceanfront promontory near the far end of the Cliff Walk was left by her father in 1925 to twelve-year-old Doris Duke, his only child and considered the richest heiress in the world. It became one of her private retreats and the public was never allowed inside until 2000. Now it's open for 90-minute guided tours under auspices of the Newport Restoration Foundation, founded and funded in 1968 by Doris Duke. The foundation eventually preserved 84 houses and now administers the **Samuel Whitehorne House Museum** and **Prescott Farm.** Unchanged since Miss Duke's death in 1993, the huge mansion remains a time capsule, reflecting her extraordinary collections of fine and decorative arts and furniture, displayed in their original setting. Rough Point is not accessible by auto. A courtesy shuttle bus departs every twenty minutes from the Gateway Visitor Center, where tickets are obtained

(401) 847-2448 or (401) 849-7300. www.newportrestoration.org. Tours, Tuesday-Saturday 10 to 3:20, mid-May to early November. Admission, $25.

Historic Sites. Newport has more than 400 structures dating from the Colonial era on Historic Hill and the Point. Among them: the 1763 **Touro Synagogue,** the oldest house of Jewish worship in the country; the Christopher Wren-inspired **Trinity Church** (1726), which has the second oldest organ in the country; the 1739 **Old Colony House,** locally believed to be the real Independence Hall (Rhode Island was the first colony to separate from Britain and the Declaration of Independence was read from its balcony); the 1748 **Redwood Library,** oldest in the country; the **Old Stone Mill** that some believe was built by Norsemen in the 11th century in Touro Park, and the 1741 **Newport Artillery Company Armory and Museum,** headquarters of the oldest militia organization in America.

SHOPPING. The main shopping area is along Thames Street, Brick Market Place, and Bowen's and Bannister's wharves. Lately, the hot spots are along Lower Thames Street, where shops are burgeoning out to the new Wellington Square and beyond, and Spring Street, home of exotic galleries and boutiques that seem to come and go each year. Bellevue Avenue near Memorial Boulevard is where the 400 used to shop and some still do.

Downtown Newport lately acquired a **Banana Republic,** the **Gap for Kids, Rockport Company Store** and **Claire Murray Lifestyles,** but we prefer browsing the indigenous shops along the wharves. Favorites are **Scrimshanders** with scrimshaw and Nantucket lightship baskets, **Collage** for jewelry and gifts, **Marie-Luise** for blown glass, **Primavera** for unusual gifts and garden accents, the **Roger King Gallery of Fine Art, Michael Hayes** for men's and women's fashions, and **Irish Imports Ltd.** for handknits and crafts. Head to the **Rue de France** retail store for furnishings and accessories inspired by the French countryside. Look for resort wear at the **Sail Loft** and the **Upperdeck Clothing Co.,** and handcrafted furniture at **The Ball & Claw,** the showroom of Jeffrey P. Greene, specialist in Newport's famed Goddard and Townsend designs. **Onne van der Wal Gallery** shows award-winning nautical photography. The **Museum Store** of the Preservation Society of Newport County stocks local books, jewelry and nautical memorabilia. **Mark Fore & Strike** carries men's and women's sportswear, while **The Narragansett** offers fine clothing for men and women. Pick up a T-shirt or sweatshirt, most with Newport insignia, at **Newport Breeze.** Lower Thames is well worth a stroll, too, with lots of new (and ever-changing) shops. **JT's Chandlery** is the place for nautical gifts, ship models, sailing supplies and apparel. We liked the painted fish-shaped clocks and dinner plates at **Thames Pottery,** the colorful windsocks at **Flying Colors Ltd.,** the herbal products at **Tea & Herb Essence,** and the hand-blown glass fish creations at **Thames Glass.** Books of nautical interest are a specialty of the **Armchair Sailor.**

Where to Eat ⏤⏤⏤⏤⏤⏤⏤⏤ ♪♪♪

Newport's concentration of yachtsmen, big-spenders, high society and tourists has spawned an enormous range and number of restaurants, with new ones popping up every year. We focus on those near the water.

The Black Pearl, Bannister's Wharf.
Our favorite all-around restaurant in Newport – and that of many others, judging from the crowds day and night – is the informal tavern, the outdoor deck with umbrella-topped tables and the elegant Commodore Room that comprise the Black Pearl. The Commodore Room, whose small-paned windows overlook the harbor, dispenses contemporary continental cuisine (dinner entrées from gray sole meunière and grilled swordfish with tomato-beurre blanc to breast of pheasant with perigeux sauce and dry-aged sirloin steaks obtained from a New York butcher). More casual is the cozy and noisy tavern, where people line up at lunch for the great clam chowder ($6.50 a bowl, and seemingly better every time we order it), crab benedict, a tarragon chicken salad and the famous pearl burger in pita bread with mint salad ($8.25). Most popular in summer is the outdoor patio on the wharf, where you sit beside the water under colorful umbrellas and watch the world go by. You can get most of the tavern fare outside, with heartier entrées (baked cod with pepper jack cheese, 21 Club chicken hash and grilled calves liver) available inside at both lunch and dinner. Desserts are few but scrumptious. Although the service may be so fast as to make you feel rushed (the world's smallest kitchen serves up to 1,500 meals a day in summer), we've never been disappointed by the fare.

(401) 846-5264. Entrées, $19 to $38; tavern, $15.50 to $28. Dinner in Commodore Room, 6 to 11. Tavern and outdoor café open daily from 11. Closed six weeks in winter.

The Mooring, Sayer's Wharf.
Ensconced in a building that once served as the New York Yacht Club station house, this has arguably the best harborfront location in town. An outside patio right by the water and window tables in the dining room as well as a new bar/lounge created by enclosing an upper deck take advantage of the view. That the food is so good is a bonus. We've been pleasantly surprised by the quality every time we've eaten here. For a late lunch on a summer Saturday, our party of four had to wait only ten minutes for a table on the breezy patio as we eyed the entrée salads and hefty sandwiches passing by. We sampled the warm salmon salad, the seafood quiche with coleslaw, steamed mussels with garlic bread, half a dozen littlenecks, and a terrific scallop chowder we deemed even better than the award-winning clam chowder. A recent winter lunch produced aforementioned clam chowder, better than ever, as well as an open-faced, knife-and-fork concoction that lived up to its billing as the ultimate grilled cheese sandwich. We also were smitten by the day's blue-plate special ($12.95): a cup of chowder, succulent grilled salmon with tomato-basil sauce, french fries and coleslaw. Dinner choices are as basic as fish and chips, fried clams and baked haddock and as elevated as charbroiled swordfish with

lemon-tarragon butter, flame-grilled tiger shrimp, seafood mixed grill and a rich seafood pie. The interior décor is nautical with old photographs and prints, and the dark tables are bare. The Mooring's more casual annex, the seasonal **Smokehouse Café,** is known for its smoked foods, chowders and barbecued ribs and wings.

(401) 846-2260. Entrées, $14.95 to $29.95. www.mooringrestaurant.com. Lunch and dinner daily, 11:30 to 10 or 11.

The West Deck, 1 Waite's Wharf.

Exciting bistro cuisine at refreshing prices draws those in the know to this waterside spot beside the harbor, a century-old structure that once served as a garage for an oil company. Here, in an airy, garage-like space that's one-third cooking area, 30 diners can be seated at tables dressed in white and ten more cozy up to an L-shaped eating bar facing the open kitchen. A long sun porch alongside nearly doubles the capacity, and more can be accommodated seasonally on a super outside patio where there's a wood grill. The menu is printed nightly, and at our latest visit offered a dozen entrées from sesame-crusted mahi mahi with coconut-curry sauce and banana chutney to grilled filet mignon with stilton cheese and port wine sauce. The night's terrine of duck, rabbit, quail and foie gras with hazelnuts and port wine glaze proved fabulous. So was a superior leg of venison with sundried cherry sauce, served with thyme-mashed potatoes, although a couple of elements in the signature mixed grill of petite filet, lamb chop, chicken and andouille sausage proved surprisingly tough. A couple of the rich desserts – grand marnier crème brûlée and cappuccino-praline mousse with espresso sauce – compensated. In season on the waterfront deck, the outdoor grill furnishes the bulk of the dishes on a simpler, all-day menu that ranges from burgers and a fish sandwich to teriyaki steak and lobster.

(401) 847-3610. Entrées, $22 to $32. Lunch menu outside in summer, noon to 9. Dinner nightly, 5:30 to 10 or 11. Off-season, dinner Wednesday-Sunday, 5:30 to 9 or 10.

The Spiced Pear, 117 Memorial Blvd., Newport.

The drama of the ocean views from the chic new restaurant in the restored Chanler at Cliff Walk boutique hotel is matched by the culinary theatrics emanating from its exhibition kitchen. The view goes almost without saying, so perfectly situated is the serene main dining room at the far end of the establishment, with floor-to-ceiling windows onto the Atlantic on two sides and an idyllic garden terrace for outdoor dining alongside. The theatrics are the forte of chef Richard Hamilton, a Cordon Bleu graduate who delivers inspired regional American fare with a nod to his Southern heritage. The bill of fare is exotic and complex, as in our appetizers of lobster "pudding" with truffle oil and chives, peeky toe crab on green papaya puree, foie gras with grape jelly, and diver scallops with ossetra caviar and champagne. The signature lamb loin with tomato-mint relish and the venison with mushrooms and garlic proved excellent main dishes. But the real hit of the evening was the buttery poached lobster paired with "macaroni and cheese," actually a creamy orzo rice laced with shallots, mascarpone cheese and truffle oil. The pastry chef's desserts included a tarte tatin prepared with mango rather than apple, a delicate chocolate cake surrounding a smooth mousse and cherry filling, and a trio of chocolate, vanilla and hazelnut ice creams. As the chef fiddled with the format, the original à-la-carte dinner menu was changed to a variety of prix-fixe tasting menus, each with several choices and some bearing substantial surcharges. The standard was $59 for three courses, but there were a six-course tasting menu ($95) and a twelve-course chef's table menu for $145.

(401) 847-2244. Prix-fixe, $59. Entrées, $26 to $58. Lunch daily in season, 11:30 to 2:30, weekends in off-season. Dinner nightly in season, 5:30 to 10, Wednesday-Sunday in off-season.

The Clarke Cooke House, Bannister's Wharf.

Long considered one of Newport's fanciest and with an attitude to match, the venerable Clarke Cooke House converted its downstairs dining rooms into the **Candy Store** café, a summer sushi bar and a porch with water view, as well as a mid-level Grille, a middle-of-the-road bistro offering lunch and dinner with the Candy Store menu. The result is more space for casual fare at somewhat more down-to-earth prices. Upstairs is a formal dining room called the **Skybar,** colorful in green and white, with banquettes awash in pillows beneath a beamed ceiling. In summer it opens to a breezy but elegant canopied upper deck called the **Porch** with a great view of the waterfront. Chef Ted Gidley's contemporary French entrées here range from fillet of sole lyonnaise and native halibut embellished with caviar vin blanc and lobster vinaigrette to molasses-cured breast of magret duck, steak au poivre and roast rack of lamb persillade. Carpaccio of yellowfin tuna, raviolis of lobster and morels with champignon sauce and pan-seared breast of squab with foie gras "au torchon" are typical appetizers. Dessert might be hazelnut, chocolate and caramel nougatine mousse cake, and a chocolate-studded triumph called "snowball in hell."

(401) 849-2900. www.clarkecooke.com. Entrées, $27 to $39. Dinner nightly in season, 6 to 10 or 10:30, weekends in off-season. Candy Store and Grille, entrées $17.95 to $32.95. Lunch daily, 11:30 to 5, weekends in winter; dinner nightly from 5, Wednesday-Sunday in winter.

22 Bowen's Wine Bar & Grille, 22 Bowen's Wharf, Newport.

One of the best locations of any steakhouse is claimed by the latest restaurant venture of the Newport Harbor Corp. (that of the Mooring and Castle Hill Inn fame). It's right on the wharf, in the building formerly occupied by the Chart House restaurant. The large, two-floor dining room is elegant with rich mahogany, white tablecloths and leather seats. Expect the usual steakhouse fare of raw bar and seafood appetizers, hefty slabs of prime beef flown from Chicago, pricey sides and rich desserts. The steaks, chops and grilled fish are offered with a choice among three mustards, three butters and three sauces. And there are variations from the usual: tempting salads, an array of house specials from seared tuna over rice noodles to Mediterranean-roasted chicken and, on weeknights in the off-season, an enticing seasonal menu of "upscale comfort food, priced for more casual, spontaneous dining" ($15.95 to $19.95). In summer, lunch and evening appetizers are offered at the outdoor Portside bar on the wharf.

(401) 841-8884. www.22bowens.com. Entrées, $23.95 to $43.95. Open daily, 11:30 to 10, weekends to 11.

Cheeky Monkey Café, 14 Perry Mill Wharf.

The owners of Providence's acclaimed Gatehouse Restaurant branched out with this small, two-level dining room, bar and an upstairs cigar lounge with a view of the harbor. Named for the British expression for a fun-loving, devilish person, this has a dark and vaguely jungle-look decor of black wood tables and faux-leopard skins on the benches and wainscoting. Dining is on two levels, facing an open kitchen. The short dinner menu might start with coconut-red curry mussels, crispy sea scallops with a "cheeky" tartar sauce and a panko-crusted tuna nori roll with a tamari dipping sauce. The lobster bisque might be garnished with "a tarragon black pepper monkey tail cracker." Main courses range from grilled Moroccan salmon fillet and house-smoked pork tenderloin with banana-plantain gravy to grilled filet mignon topped with lobster-peppercorn butter sauce. Dessert could be bananas foster, chocolate truffle cake or assorted sorbets.

(401) 845-9494. www.cheekymonkeycafe.com. Entrées, $21.95 to $29.95. Dinner nightly, from 5:30.

Castle Hill Inn & Resort, 590 Ocean Drive.

There's no more posh setting for waterside dining than at this storied inn, atop a hill out in the Ocean Drive mansion area overlooking Narragansett Bay. Especially salubrious is the oval Sunset Room, a windowed porch just across from the mahogany bar and lounge and jutting out toward the bay. Redecorated with a billowing cream-colored canopy on the ceiling, this is the place for Castle Hill's long-popular Sunday brunch. The kitchen is under the tutelage of Casey Riley, who transferred here after opening Agora at the Westin Hotel in Providence. The food aspires to the heights. Consider recent autumn main courses like wild coho salmon grilled with toasted coriander and lemon in a lemongrass-ginger broth and roasted Colorado rack of lamb with garlic-parsley crust, acorn squash bread pudding, toasted chanterelles and imported Devon cream. Even the lowly chicken is a whole petit poussin stuffed with dried fruits, glazed with apricots and elevated with foie gras sauce. You might start with the foie gras of duck, pan roasted with dried fruit flapjacks, toasted pecans, balsamic syrup, micro greens and Normandy butter. Dessert could be banana-walnut soufflé with espresso crème anglaise, an "autumn fancy" assortment of three desserts or the chocolate signature, an assortment of five. A grill menu is offered from 3 until sunset in summer on the bay-view cabana terrace with an outdoor bar.

(401) 849-3800 or (888) 466-1355. Entrées, $24 to $39. Lunch, 11:30 to 3 Monday-Saturday in summer, Friday-Saturday in off-season. Dinner nightly, 5:45 to 9:30; jackets requested. Sunday brunch, 11 to 3.

Le Bistro, 41 Bowen's Wharf.

An airy, elegant decor in the second-floor and third-floor dining rooms with windows toward the water make this fancier than the usual French bistro. Under new management, the food may not reach its previous heights, but we've enjoyed a fine salad niçoise and a classic bouillabaisse with rouille from a luncheon menu on which there's much to appeal to the occasional francophile. At night, the fare has lost some of its Burgundian charm. Look now for regional fare like local cod with a honey-caramelized scallion glaze, sea scallops sautéed with prosciutto and brandy, roasted free-range chicken with garlic-basil butter and sirloin steak with mushroom-bourbon sauce. When the menu says the steak comes with "our authentic" french fries cooked in peanut oil, you wonder. Start with mussels marinière or escargots bourguignonne. Finish with creole-style bread pudding. The amiable bar on the third floor serves light fare and is usually crowded day and night.

(401) 849-7778. www.lebistronewport.com. Entrées, $16.95 to $28.95. Lunch daily, 11:30 to 5. Dinner, 5 to 11.

Asterisk, 599 Lower Thames St.

One of Newport's more trendy and eclectic restaurants is run by the scion of a family of Danish restaurateurs. John Bach-Sorenson alighted from Copenhagen in Newport – "it reminded me of home" – and looked for a restaurant site. He found it in a working auto-repair garage, now transformed into a airy and colorful space with a part-open rear kitchen and a remarkable handcrafted bar along one side. A romantic, dimly lit salon look is conveyed by shaded gas lamps flickering on close-together white-linened tables beneath a high, industrial-look ceiling. Garage doors open onto an enclosed, canopied sidewalk café out front. The continental-Asian menu ranges widely from potato-wrapped grouper and sole meunière to pork chops with melted brie and peaches, veal scaloppini and steak au poivre. You can opt for mussels marinière with frites or "le petite asterisk:" one-half lobster, ten oysters, four shrimp, and eight clams and mussels ($42). Frozen tiramisu parfait, raspberry crème brûlée and profiteroles are favorite desserts. The place is named for one of John's favorite French comic-strip characters, known for fighting the bureaucracy, which he had to do to win a wine and beer license. He also runs Boulangerie, a bakery and sandwich shop at 382 Spring St., and lately took on La Petite Auberge, a classic French restaurant at 19 Charles St.

(401) 841-8833. Entrées, $19 to $32. Dinner nightly, from 5.

The Atlantic Beach Club, 55 Purgatory Road, Middletown.

Run by Greek brothers Peter and Harry Kyriakides, this recently renovated and expanded veteran merges the late Johnny's age-old seafood house and more contemporary dining areas seating a total of 450 with a raw bar and an outdoor terrace for up to 500 people right over the sand beside Easton's Beach. That's a capacity of nearly a thousand people, so you can imagine the summertime scene. But the functions are blessedly out of the way from the surprisingly calm and elegant main dining room, which has windows on two sides onto the beach. A dozen bartenders and rock bands keep the local crowd happy at what local skeptics call a gin mill with food. Tourists like the enormous, all-things-for-all-kinds menu. In the quieter off-season, you can lunch inside as we did, at a window table at beach's edge, and watch surfers in wet suits cresting the waves. The seafood chowder was surprisingly good; ditto for the caesar salad with chicken and plenty of crunchy french bread. The grilled marinated vegetables with goat cheese and olive tapenade was less successful, being too oily. The huge dinner menu ranges from baked scrod and broiled sole to duck breast pinot noir, veal saltimbocca and lobster thermidor.

(401) 847-2750. www.atlanticbeachclub.com. Entrées, $15.95 to $27.95. Lunch daily, 11:30 to 4. Dinner, 11 to 11. Sunday brunch, 10:30 to 2.

Flo's Clam Shack & Raw Bar, 4 Wave Ave., Middletown.

A fisherman in a yellow slicker stands sentinel on the roof of this glorified clam shack, which is dwarfed by the Atlantic Beach Club kitty-corner across the street and the Inn at Newport Beach next door, opposite Easton's Beach in Newport. Flo opened the real thing here a few years back after 30 years in Portsmouth. From the rear parking lot, you walk along a path through what appears to be a bamboo grove to the outdoor counter, where you place your order. Although clams are the specialty, Friday evening's prime rib night for $9.95 seems to get equal billing. The lengthy menu is otherwise basic, a fisherman's platter topping the list for $16.95. Place your order and receive a rock with your number painted on it. Start with the signature clam cakes, "chowda," fiery stuffed quahogs from an old Portuguese recipe or "a Greek salad made by a Greek." Choose a fried clam roll or the "no-nonsense, all-lobster-meat lobsta roll" ($14.95). There are a dozen choices for seafood platters. Pitchers of beer and wine splits are the beverages of choice, but you can splurge for "two gourmet hot dogs and a bottle of Moet" champagne for $50. There are a few rustic tables inside, with more out front in a tiki-bar terrace up against the street. The Topside Raw Bar on the second-floor deck yields a good view of the beachfront action.

(401) 847-8141. Seafood platters, $7.75 to $16.95. Open daily 11 to 9, Memorial Day to Labor Day, Thursday-Sunday in off-season. Closed January and February. No credit cards.

FOR MORE INFORMATION: Newport County Convention & Visitors Bureau, Gateway Visitor Information Center, 23 America's Cup Ave., Newport, RI 02840, (401) 845-9123 or (800) 976-5122. www.gonewport.com.

Sailboat passes Woods Hole landmark Nobska Light.

Falmouth Chamber of Commerce Photo

Falmouth/Woods Hole, Mass.

The beaches and rural charm that draw people to Cape Cod are not readily apparent in Falmouth. That's because the Falmouth that most people see is viewed from the main roads, usually as they rush to the ferry for their destination, Martha's Vineyard.

Falmouth indeed is the embarkation point for the Vineyard, a few miles offshore and accessed by ferry from Falmouth and Woods Hole. But some visitors stray from the tourist route and pause here for a look around. They like what they see and decide to return. If you get off the beaten path, you might well be smitten, too.

Settled by Quakers in 1661, Cape Cod's second largest town has the most shoreline of any Cape Cod town. Away from the mainstream are 68 miles of coastline, about twelve miles of it public beach area. There are conservation lands, wildlife sanctuaries, inlets and ponds, plus fourteen harbors that convey a yachting air.

The far-flung town consists of eight villages, each with its own identity. North Falmouth and West Falmouth, both historic and charming, face Buzzards Bay to the west. East Falmouth is residential and commercial, and its harbors face south toward Vineyard Sound. The heart of Falmouth is Falmouth Center, spreading outward from the historic village green. This is the Falmouth that most visitors see.

The other Falmouth they may know is salty Woods Hole, the principal ferry departure point for Martha's Vineyard. Woods Hole is also a busy marine research center that is home to four major scientific institutions, including the National Marine Fisheries Service, the Woods Hole Oceanographic Institution and the Marine Biological Laboratory. Their facilities and personnel give it something of the look and feel of a government installation. Much of Woods Hole is surrounded by water and in its center is Eel Pond, a saltwater harbor filled with a variety of boats big and small. They sail in and out of Vineyard Sound, stopping traffic on the main street as a hand-operated drawbridge is raised to let them through.

There are also neighborhoods, which impart still more flavors to the mix that is Falmouth. Tony Falmouth Heights, one of the oldest planned recreational communities in the country, has parklands and grand Victorian summer homes and cottages along the ocean beach. Also catering to the beach crowd are some of the typical Cape cottage colonies along the sands in Falmouth and East Falmouth. Quissett, Sippewisset and the Oyster Pond section are more rural enclaves, where substantial Cape Cod houses on lush, wooded properties are cooled by the ocean breezes.

More than most Cape towns, Falmouth is home to year-round residents and businesses, which give it a stability that evades fleeting summer communities. For many, that is part of Falmouth's appeal. To see what else is so attractive, you have to shun the beaten path and get close to the water.

Getting There

Falmouth is at the southwestern corner of Cape Cod. From the mainland, take the Bourne Bridge onto the Cape and Route 28 south to Falmouth and Woods Hole.

Where to Stay

There are many places to stay, especially in and around Falmouth Center. But as in many Cape Cod towns, precious few are close to the water or enjoy water views. Those that do are concentrated in Falmouth Heights, around Falmouth Inner Harbor and in Woods Hole.

Inn on the Sound, 313 Grand Ave., Falmouth Heights 02540.

On a bluff across the road from Vineyard Sound in the posh Falmouth Heights beach section, this modern-looking B&B offers the nicest and most stylish accommodations hereabouts. Renee Ross, a former interior designer and manager of an art gallery, and her brother David Ross, a theater lighting expert, turned the century-old, shingle-style structure into a retreat of distinction and comfort. They offer ten attractive rooms with queensize beds, TV, plump chairs or settees and a dramatic flair. Four have oceanfront balconies and five more yield water views, as does the common deck in front. Most rooms have whitewashed ceilings of beadboard. The Silver Harbor comes with a parquet floor and a shower for two. Rooms are done in shades of white, beige and taupe, except for one room in nautical blue. The living room, sleek in danish modern, is open to a sunroom with wicker furnishings and a stone fireplace. The rear breakfast room, stunning in white, contains four tables set for four. Soft music plays as guests sample fresh fruit from a buffet and breakfast pastries from a three-tiered platter. The main course could be crêpes, quiche or a different version of french toast layered with ham and cheese. Lately, the inn· added a two-bedroom kitchenette rental accommodating up to four for up to $3,500 a week.

(508) 457-9666 or (800) 564-9668. Fax (508) 457-9631. www.innonthesound.com. Ten rooms with private baths. Doubles, $150 to $295. Three-night minimum summer weekends.

Baileys By the Sea, 321 Grand Ave., Falmouth Heights 02540.

Four years of renovations transformed what owner Liz Bailey called "a dump of a lodging house"

into a B&B taking full advantage of its oceanfront location overlooking Martha's Vineyard. Liz and her husband Jerry offer six rooms named for places they lived during his career as an IBM executive. All rooms have ocean views and come with TVs, hair dryers and good reading lights. The largest is the aqua-blue Tokyo, full of Asian influences reflecting their eight years in Tokyo. It has a queen bed, a day bed and two rockers facing the water – which Liz reports that guests feel is like "rocking on water" – plus a whirlpool tub and separate shower. Two wing chairs face the bay window in the front queensize room called Traverse City, where their daughter was born. The twin-bedded Worcester opens onto an ocean-view deck and adjoins the Calgary, where Jerry grew up. Those two and another pair of rooms share baths and are usually rented as suites. Guests enjoy a fireplaced living room furnished with American and Asian antiques, a formal dining room and a wraparound sun porch filled with wicker, but usually join Liz in the open kitchen as she prepares breakfast. The meal might start with a Bailey's blend smoothie and cantaloupe with blueberry sauce. The main event might be apple pancakes or a rolled omelet with hash browns and homemade bread. "If they have to eat again before 3 in the afternoon, I've failed," says Liz. At day's end, she serves cookies, wine and cheese, or a glass of Bailey's.

(508) 548-5748 or (866) 548-5748. www.baileysbythesea.com. Two rooms and two two-bedroom suites with private baths. Doubles, $180 to $265.

The Scallop Shell Inn, 16 Massachusetts Ave., Falmouth Heights 02540.
Here's a B&B with a difference – quite a few, in fact. You can tell from the front yard (all parking area), the huge Brazilian mahogany deck and the wraparound entry hallway that leads who knows where? Designer/architect Betsey Cogliani sold her business and spent some of the proceeds turning this into her idea of a 21st-century B&B: "the charm and flavor of an era gone by with sensitivity to the needs and necessities of today's lifestyles." That translates here to a beachy setting combined with raised fireplaces, whirlpool tubs, extravagant decor, even in-room wall safes. From mahogany balconies, four of the seven rooms offer water views, somewhat condensed by buildings in front. Other rooms are sequestered unto themselves with private entrances, gas fireplaces and whirlpool tubs in the bedrooms. Each has a plump feather bed laden with down pillows, TV/VCR and marble bathrooms with hand-painted vanities or pedestal sinks, robes and imported toiletries. Although most beds are king or queensize, that in the Periwinkle is a canopied double, with a two-person whirlpool tub beside the fireplace nearby. What is billed as a three-person whirlpool tub is beneath a skylight in the vaulted ceiling of the Parrot Perch, whose king bed is brightened by colorful tropical covers and pillows. The Sea Biscuit offers two double beds "for a family of four or two couples" and a whirlpool tub. The prized Crow's Nest on the third floor, stylishly outfitted mainly in white with floral print accents, has the best view from its balcony. The mahogany vanity comes with a marble counter with a hand-painted sink and a built-in television. Its queen bed is "fully automated with a massage option." The five-course breakfast is served any time of day in a light and airy morning room and prepared, Betsy says, "on site from old family recipes." The main course could be a lobster and asparagus omelet, crème brûlée french toast, eggs benedict or steak and eggs. Complimentary beverages and snacks are available 24 hours a day in the guest kitchenette, and guests have free use of the appliances in the cedar linen room and "laundry center." Although there's no guest parlor as such, there's a fireplaced billiards and sitting room dominated by a pool table and a wet bar with free drinks. In other words, you make yourself at home and indulge.

(508) 495-4900 or (800) 249-4587. Fax (508) 495-4600. www.scallopshellinn.com. Seven rooms with private baths. Doubles, $285 to $360. Three-night minimum in season.

The Seaside Inn, 263 Grand Ave., Falmouth Heights 02540.

New owners poured big bucks into the renovation of the old Oceanside Inn, creating an attractive and versatile compound of three nicely landscaped buildings around and behind their popular beachside pub restaurant, the British Beer Company. The lodgings and motif are more motel-style than inn, but are perfect (and perfectly located) for those who want to be near the beach. There's even a grassy park beside, for youngsters who tire of the sand. Ten rooms have good water views and about half have kitchenettes. Standard rooms have one double or queensize or two double beds, a chair, telephone and TV. The efficiencies are a bit larger, given their kitchenettes and dining tables. Four quarters are suites. One is a family suite with two double beds in the front room and a queen bed in the rear room with a kitchenette. The top floor of one building contains two jacuzzi suites, one with two bedrooms and the other with two double beds in the main room. Both have large outdoor balconies for savoring the views.

(508) 540-4120 or (800) 827-1976. www.seasideinnfalmouth.com. Nineteen rooms and four suites with private baths. Doubles, $119 to $259.

Woods Hole Passage, 186 Woods Hole Road, Falmouth 02540.

Part of this attractive, barn-red structure was once the stable for the estate next door, although you'd hardly guess it today. Innkeeper Deb Pruitt has outfitted a carriage house addition to the stable section with four guest rooms and added a fifth bedroom and a large common room with fireplace in the former stable. The common room looks through big windows onto a two-acre back yard, a quiet retreat away from the busy road, surrounded by gardens and shade trees. There, guests may take breakfast on the terrace or saunter down the lawn and through the woods to the beach. All rooms have queensize beds and their bathrooms have showers with seats. The two upstairs rooms we saw in the addition have vaulted ceilings and handsome bed quilts. Breakfast is a hearty affair, beginning with a fruit dish and homemade breads or scones. The main course could be mexicali eggs or crème brûlée french toast. The repast could energize you for a ride on one of Deb's complimentary bicycles along the Shining Sea bike trail nearby.

(508) 548-9575 or (800) 790-8976. Fax (508) 540-4771. www.woodsholepassage.com. Five rooms with private baths. Doubles, $125 to $195.

Sands of Time, 549 Woods Hole Road, Box 106, Woods Hole 02543.

This modern motor inn and the more old-fashioned Harbor House behind are beautifully situated, on a hillside overlooking what innkeeper Susan Veeder calls Woods Hole's picturesque "Little Harbor" across the road. The establishment is also exceptionally nice, flanked by lovely gardens in front and a secluded pool in back. The rooms we saw had kingsize beds, two club chairs, floral wallpapers, shag carpeting and upscale furnishings. Each of the twenty motel units on two floors opens through sliding glass doors onto a patio or balcony. Above and in back of the motel is the large, rambling 1870s Harbor House, open year-round with thirteen guest rooms, eight with working fireplaces and most with water views. Rooms here are appointed with four-poster brass and wrought-iron beds and wicker sitting areas. Some rooms have kitchenettes for longer stays. All have TVs and telephones. Complimentary coffee and donuts are offered in the lobby in the morning.

(508) 548-6300 or (800) 841-0114. Fax (508) 457-0160. www.sandsoftime.com. Thirty-three rooms with private baths. Doubles, $150 to $200. Motel closed mid-November to mid-April.

Nautilus Motor Inn, 539 Wood Hole Road, Box 147, Woods Hole 02543.

Sharing a driveway with the Sands of Time next door, this also shares its water views, although some are angled or obscured and not many are head-on. It conveys a busier atmosphere, with a clubby lobby where coffee is complimentary in the morning, two tennis courts and a large deck surrounding the swimming pool. On two floors in several buildings, most rooms come with two double beds against paneled walls, two plump club chairs and balconies overlooking the pool scene. Rates vary by location and view. On the premises is the Dome Restaurant and Lounge, the first geodosic dome designed by Buckminster Fuller. Although away from the water, it offers an atmospheric venue for steak and seafood dinner fare.

(508) 548-1525 or (800) 654-2333. Fax (508) 457-9674. www.nautilusinn.com. Fifty-four rooms. Doubles, $119 to $225.

The Tides Motel, Grand Avenue, Falmouth 02541.

You want water views? Up close? Open ocean or sheltered harbor? A private sandy beach outside your door? This low-key old-timer may suffice. It doesn't advertise and doesn't need to. The Tides is located on a point at the entrance to the Falmouth Inner Harbor, just beyond the yacht club and across the harbor from the old Regatta restaurant. Those in the know cherish it for its location and value. On two floors, twenty rooms face the ocean head-on. Those on the ground floor open onto a red cement-block patio where the white lounge chairs literally are at beach's edge. Upstairs units enjoy more privacy and uninterrupted views. Eight units on the side have side views onto the ocean across a parking area and a glimpse back toward the sheltered inner harbor. Twenty rooms come with kitchenettes – actually counters and appliances up against the bathroom wall and beside one of the two double beds. The accommodations are white and so squeaky clean we thought (wrongly) that they'd just been freshly painted. A suite with two bedrooms, sitting room and kitchen sleeps six and, for $205 a night, may well be the best waterside bargain on Cape Cod.

(508) 548-3126. Twenty-nine rooms. Doubles, $150 to $160. Suite, $205. Three-night minimum weekends; two-night minimum in summer.

Red Horse Inn, 28 Falmouth Heights Road, Falmouth 02540.

Fastidious owners Eleacia and Robert Fredette run this highly rated in-town inn and motel across from the ferry docks. It's the one to which local innkeepers direct people seeking motel accommodations, because they are rather inn-like. The 22 individually decorated rooms are located in a two-story motel building or in the main building, which was renovated from the original inn. Most have a queensize bed (some have two), and a new fireside room offers a gas fireplace, hardwood floors and a whirlpool tub for two. A modern cottage room has a kingsize bed. All have TVs and small refrigerators. The beautifully landscaped property has won awards for its gardens. There's a secluded patio swimming pool. The Red Horse offers parking permits for some of Falmouth's best beaches and free parking for guests on day trips to the islands.

(508) 548-0053 or (800) 628-3811. Fax (508) 540-6563. www.redhorseinn.com. Twenty-two rooms. Doubles, $145 to $225.

Green Harbor Waterfront Lodging, 134 Acapesket Road, East Falmouth 02536..

A sandy beach on a saltwater inlet and all kinds of waterfront activities make this old-timer popular with families. Nestled along a woodland hillside, the place has standard motel rooms on three levels, with sliding doors opening onto patios or balconies facing the water. Most have one queenize and one double bed. Half have microwaves and refrigerators and the other half have full kitchens with dining areas. Eight of the most popular beachside units are right at water's edge. The others are on a slope back from the water, facing the large heated pool and a kiddie pool. A three-bedroom cottage is suitable for large families or three couples. The inlet's muddy bottom is fine for boating – there's a private boat ramp and dock. Youngsters like to crab and clam from the beach. Rowboats and paddleboats are available free.

(508) 548-4747 or (800) 558-5556. www.gogreenharbor.com. Thirty-seven rooms. Doubles, $118 to $170. Closed November-April.

CAMPING. Sippewisset Campground & Cabins, 836 Palmer Ave. (Route 28), Falmouth 02540. (508) 548-2542 or (800) 957-2267, www.sippewisset.com. One hundred campsites accommodate everything from tents to trailers at this wooded property close to town and beaches. There's also a cabin colony of eleven Cape Cod-style housekeeping cabins, sleeping two to eight, rented by the week for $365 to $675.

Seeing and Doing

Falmouth and Woods Hole are busy in season, when the population triples to 100,000. Because they are year-round communities, they offer frequent special events and more than the usual roster of band concerts, house tours, road races, boat trips, antiques shows, flea markets, church suppers, lectures and such.

The **Whoosh Trolley,** (800) 352-7155, starts at Falmouth Mall and stops at fourteen points of interest around the area. It makes a circuit every twenty minutes daily from 9:30 a.m. to 9 or 10 p.m., late May to late September; adults $1, children 50 cents. Parking at beaches is restricted and difficult in Woods Hole, where meters gobble up quarters every fifteen minutes. Bicycling is a better way for visitors to get around, and many bicycle routes are marked.

Activities

BEACHES. Nearly twenty percent of Falmouth's coastline is beach area accessible to the public, and the waters are warmer than farther out on the Cape. The average summer water temperature of about 70 lasts into late September. Public beaches with parking available for a nominal fee are Surf Drive Beach in Falmouth, Menauhant Beach in East Falmouth and Old Silver Beach in North Falmouth. Falmouth Heights Beach in Falmouth is open to the public, but parking is by beach sticker only. Bathhouse facilities are available at Menauhant, Old Silver and Surf Drive beaches. Daily parking passes are available from many inns and motels.

Parasailing is popular in Falmouth Harbor. **Gold Coast Parasailing Corp.,** (508) 693-3330, takes adventurers for rides above the harbor in summer. **Windsurfing** is allowed from beaches only before 9 and after 5 for public safety.

BOATING. Falmouth Harbor is the embarkation point for frequent day excursions across Vineyard Sound to Martha's Vineyard. **The Island Queen,** 297 Dillingham Ave., (508) 548-4800, ferries passengers to Oak Bluffs in 35 minutes. Round-trip fares: adults $12, children $6, bicycle $6, parking $15. The Falmouth-Edgartown Ferry Service, 278 Scranton Ave., (508) 548-9400, takes passengers by reservation on the Pied Piper from Falmouth Marine to Edgartown in 45 minutes. Round-trip fares: adults $30, children under 5 free, bicycle $8, parking $15.

Steamship Authority auto ferries, (508) 477-8600, leave Woods Hole for 45-minute rides to Vineyard Haven on Martha's Vineyard. One-way fares: cars $62, adults $6, children $3.25, bicycles $3.

Patriot Party Boats, (508) 548-2626 or (800) 734-0088, offers sunset cruises, sailing, fast-ferry service and deep-sea fishing trips from the Town Marina, 180 Scranton Ave. Two-hour sunset cruises along Falmouth's shoreline pass six lighthouses. Trips leave at 6:30 in July and 6 in August; adults $15, children $10. Two half-day deep-sea fishing trips are scheduled daily at 8 and 1; adults $30, children $20. Two-hour day sails aboard the schooner Liberté are offered in summer. Patriot boats also provide year-round fast-ferry service to Martha's Vineyard.

Ocean Quest, Water Street, Woods Hole, (508) 385-7656 or (800) 376-2326. Naturalists give interesting 90-minute oceanography cruises around the waters of Woods Hole. Their hands-on discovery cruise is oriented to families. Participants pull lobster traps, drag a plankton net and use a discovery scope to see microorganisms collected. They get to operate the oceanography instrumentation and equipment in the bow, and in the cabin they explore the chemistry of seawater. Trips depart Monday-Friday at 10, noon, 2 and 4; adults $20, children $15.

Waquoit Kayak Co. at Edwards Boatyard, 1209 Route 28A, by the Childs River in East Falmouth, (508) 548-9722 or 548-2216, rents canoes and kayaks and gives lessons and tours. Rates range from $35 for a single kayak for a half day to $59 for a double kayak all day. Tours and and rentals are offered by **Cape Cod Kayak** at 1270 Route 28A in Cataumet, (508) 563-9377.

BIKING. A former railroad track has been turned into the sparkling **Shining Sea Bicycle Trail.** The paved path extends 3.9 miles from the Ice Arena in Falmouth to the Steamship Authority in Woods Hole, with several access points en route. One of the best of its genre, it winds close to the ocean beside surf, beaches and woodlands. Bikers share it with joggers, walkers and roller-bladers, all of whom were out in force the day we tried it. The name honors the memory of Katharine Lee Bates, who was born in Falmouth and wrote "America the Beautiful." The trail connects with other marked bicycle routes to the north and east.

RUNNING. Falmouth has long been known as "a running town." It hosts a number of challenging road races, including the world-renowned, seven-mile Falmouth Road Race in late August and the Cape Cod Marathon in late October. The former is the event of the year in Falmouth, attracting 8,000 participants and thousands of spectators along the race route from Woods Hole to Falmouth Heights. Among the scenic places to run is the Shining Sea Bicycle Trail. Many runners jog along residential streets and near the beaches along Surf Drive, Grand Avenue and Menauhant Road.

Places of Interest

Falmouth's historic **Village Green** is a picturesque, triangular-shaped parcel on which the militia trained for the American Revolution and the War of 1812. The Colonial, Federal, Greek Revival and Italianate houses bordering it are attractive – some have been converted into B&Bs. The First Congregational Church facing the green at 68 Main St. harbors a bell commissioned by Paul Revere. The bell still tolls on the hour. Its receipt, dated 1796, is on display.

Museums on the Green, 55-65 Palmer St., Falmouth.

The Falmouth Historical Society opens two restored houses on the village green for guided tours. The **Julia Wood House** was built in 1790 by Falmouth's famous early physician, Dr. Francis Wicks, known for his work with smallpox inoculations. The Georgian-style house has one of the town's few remaining widow's walks. Among its displays are the original 18th-century scenic wallpaper brought from Paris, period furniture, antique hooked rugs, a handmade quilt collection, clothing and toys, and a restored kitchen with fireplace and early utensils. The Hallett Barn out back displays early tools and farm implements and houses the society's gift shop. Next door, the 1724 **Conant House** contains memorabilia of whaling days, a military exhibit, a shell collection and a large collection of china, silver and glass. The Katharine Lee Bates Room houses the society's collection of books and pictures pertaining to her song, "America the Beautiful." A placard identifies the private home at 16 Main St. in which the composer was born in 1859.

(508) 548-4857. Open Tuesday-Saturday 10 to 4, late June to late September, also weekends 1 to 4 in spring and fall. Historic house tours: Adults $5, children free. Hallett Barn Visitor Center and exhibits open free.

Spohr Gardens, 45 Fells Road, Falmouth.
Hidden among the homes and wooded properties in the Oyster Pond neighborhood is this little-known treasure shared by Charles and Margaret Spohr and, since their deaths, by the Spohr Charitable Trust. The six-acre garden surrounding their residence slopes down to Oyster Pond, where you're apt to be greeted by swans as graceful as the gardens are tranquil. The gardens are at their best in spring, when 700,000 daffodils launch a showy procession of magnolias, azaleas, rhododendrons, hydrangeas and lilies. Wide grassy paths wind through the gardens, with nautical artifacts, sculptures and benches here and there. Signs point out rock gardens, hillside walks and more. A huge boulder bears the carving, "Spohr Gardens, 1950." A sign notes that contributions for the gardens' continuing maintenance are gratefully accepted.

(508) 548-0623. Gardens open daily, 8 a.m. to 8 p.m. Free.

Hiking and Nature Trails. Wooded trails winding through the neighborhoods of Falmouth offer a look at salt marshes, tidal ponds and beaches and provide opportunities for beachcombing, bird-watching, hiking and mountain biking. A favorite footpath leads from picturesque Quissett Harbor through thirteen wooded acres of **The Knob,** a wildlife sanctuary and rocky beach outcrop stretching into Buzzards Bay. The **Salt Pond Areas Bird Sanctuaries,** 881 Palmer Ave., Falmouth, (508) 548-8484, offers 44 acres of orchards, fields and wooded trails around a 1775 landmark farmhouse known as Bourne Farm. The **Waquoit Bay National Estuarine Research Reserve,** 149 Waquoit Hwy. in East Falmouth, (508) 457-0495, consists of 2,500 acres of barrier beaches, marshlands and uplands. It operates eleven campsites on Washburn Island.

Marked trails wind through 49 acres of holly and franklinia preserves around Grassy Pond at the **Ashumet Holly & Wildlife Sanctuary,** 286 Ashumet Road, East Falmouth, (508) 563-6390. Operated by the Massachusetts Audubon Society, it is known for the holly collection assembled by the late Wilfred Wheeler, the first state agriculture commissioner. You'll find more than 1,000 holly trees, including eight different species and 65 different varieties. The area is also known for its large resident colony of barn swallows, observable in summer. Open daily, dawn to dusk. Adults $3, children $2.

WOODS HOLE. A world center for marine and environmental research, Woods Hole is home to the world's oldest fisheries research facility, the laboratory of the National Marine Fisheries Service founded here in 1871. The village now contains two large private laboratories (the huge Woods Hole Oceanographic Institution and the Marine Biological Laboratory) and a second government facility (the U.S. Geological Survey's Science Center for Coastal and Marine Geology). Together, these institutions occupy some 170 buildings and operate a dozen research vessels and collecting boats. They employ more than 1,300 people, for whom most parking areas in Woods Hole seem to be reserved.

National Marine Fisheries Service Aquarium, Water and Albatross Streets. This is about the only institutional building of general interest. Harbor seals splash in a pool outside the aquarium, the nation's first when it opened in 1871. Feeding times are 11 and 4 p.m. Inside are local and commercial species in their water tanks. In the "Behind the Scenes" area out back, you can see an enormous blue lobster, look at a starfish under a microscope and touch all sorts of sea life, including hermit crabs and horseshoe crabs. Cape Cod Life magazine calls the aquarium "the best rainy day activity on the upper cape."
(508) 495-2001. Open daily in summer 11 to 4; rest of year, Monday-Friday 10 to 4. Free.

Woods Hole Oceanographic Institution has an information office at 93 Water St. and a small Exhibit Center in a former church at 15 School St. The latter has videos and displays about its vessels and scientific research as well as a gift shop. The most interesting display features Alvin, the tiny submarine that allowed WHOI researchers to explore and photograph the remains of the Titanic in 1986. Visitors can step inside a full-size model of the inner sphere of Alvin and imagine life at the ocean floor while watching vivid footage taken at deep-sea hydrothermal vent sites. An interactive exhibit features whale and dolphin research and explores the roles sound and hearing play in the lives of marine mammals. The exhibit center is open Monday-Saturday 10 to 4:30 and Sunday noon to 4:30, Memorial Day through Labor Day; closed Monday in May and September-October; donation, $2.

The **Marine Biological Laboratory** has a visitor center and gift shop at 100 Water St. Exhibits show living marine organisms at play and tell why they are important in biomedical research. The laboratory offers three hour-long tours weekdays in summer, starting at 1 p.m. Tours include a video presentation, a visit to the Marine Resources Center for a look at marine animals and a walking tour of the campus.

The **Woods Hole Historical Museum,** 573 Woods Hole Road, (508) 548-7270, displays local watercraft, ship models and a diorama of Woods Hole as it was in 1895. Its library is strong on maritime subjects. A boat museum features local small craft. The staff gives a free 90-minute walking tour around Eel Pond on Tuesday at 4 in July and August. Open Tuesday-Saturday 10 to 4, mid-June through Columbus Day.

Other points of interest in Woods Hole are **St. Joseph's Bell Tower,** Millfield Street, and the **St. Mary's Garden** beside Eel Pond. The **Church of the Messiah** on Church Street has an herb meditation garden and a cemetery in which nine Nobel Prize winners are buried. Farther out Church Street is **Nobska Light,** which commands a high vantage point on a bluff. Its beacon is visible seventeen miles out to sea. This is a good place to see the "hole" for which Woods Hole was named, the north shore of Martha's Vineyard (appearing surprisingly close by on a clear day) and the Elizabeth Islands. More than 30,000 boats of various kinds pass by annually.

SHOPPING. The center of Falmouth offers stores of interest to visitors as well as residents. **Maxwell & Co.** purveys fine men's and women's clothing and **Rosie Cheeks** specializes in women's fashions. **Bean & Cod** stocks colorful dishware along with specialty foods and has a deli. **The Nantucket Trading Company** offers gourmet kitchen and tableware. Global gifts and clothing are featured at **Port Cargo. Twigs** is an interesting home and garden shop. Along Palmer Avenue is **Howlingbird Studio,** which silkscreens T-shirts and offers unusual women's sportswear. **Oolala** has paper goods and home accessories. You can take a coffee break next door at **Coffee Obsession.**

In Woods Hole, **Handworks Gallery,** a cooperative, has a variety of handicrafts and fine art. More art is available at **Local Colors Gallery.** The **Howlingbird Studio** specializes in scientific and nature designs on its screen-printed T-shirts and hats. **Liberty House** sells contemporary women's clothing, jewelry and gifts. **Under the Sun** features gifts, shoes, contemporary crafts and jewelry.

Where to Eat

Landfall, 2 Luscombe Ave., Woods Hole.

This institution of more than 50 years is aptly named – it could not be closer to the water and still be on land. In fact, its large wraparound rear dining room seating 180 is built out on piers. Run by the sons of founder David Estes, it's an upscaled seafood haunt with wood tables and captain's chairs, wood floors, a bar made from a dory, beams taken from a Gloucester dock, buoys and lamps and even a Grecian urn hanging from the ceiling. French doors across the rear open onto the water. The food is predictable, from fried native clams and broiled scrod to grilled swordfish, broiled Chatham scallops and seafood newburg. Lobster savannah and bouillabaisse are signature dishes. Chicken française over linguini, broiled sirloin steak and filet mignon are non-fish choices. The land and sea combo here is sirloin steak and two baked stuffed shrimp. Hot Portuguese toast with garlic butter, house salad and choice of garlic mashed potatoes, french fries or baked potato accompany.

(508) 548-1758. Entrées, $19 to $29.50. Lunch and dinner daily in summer, 11 to 9 or 10; Thursday-Sunday in off-season. Closed late November to early April.

Fishmonger's Café, 56 Water St., Woods Hole.

This natural-foods restaurant beside the Woods Hole drawbridge and harbor is beloved by vegetarians. But there's plenty of international fare to appeal to others, especially if you consider the specials list. The interior of the weathered gray building blends California hippie and New England nautical ambiance. It's plain as can be with simple wood chairs at bare, polyurethaned wood tables. Fresh flowers and candles in hurricane chimneys add a touch of class. And the food is worth seeking out amidst the sea of sameness of many Woods Hole eateries. For dinner, you might start with garlicky mussels steamed in beer with green chiles and onions, Thai spring rolls or the sundried tomato caesar salad. Vegetarians favor the guacamole tostada, the Middle Eastern plate and the tofu with vegetables. Others go for the fisherman's stew in an herbal tomato broth, and the chicken California (grilled or fried and covered with guacamole, melted muenster cheese, tomatoes, sour cream and sprouts). Specials could be grilled halibut with lemongrass tomato broth over couscous and grilled tuna with Portuguese sauce and saffron polenta. Homemade pies and cakes are good desserts.

(508) 548-9148. Entrées, $18.95 to $24. Breakfast daily, 7 to 11. Lunch 11 to 4. Dinner 5:30 to 10. Closed Tuesday in off-season and mid-December to mid-February.

Shuckers World Famous Raw Bar and Café, 91A Water St., Woods Hole.

Dining is mostly on a large outdoor deck overlooking Eel Pond at this casual haunt, a local favorite. But there are a handful of tables by the bar inside, where the specialty is Nobska Light beer brewed to owner Kevin Murphy's specifications. The place proved perfect for lunch, when we enjoyed a zesty seafood chowder, an ample seafood salad and a tasty seafood salad sandwich, although everyone else seemed to be ordering the stuffed tomatoes. The raw bar is popular at night, as is the lobster boil complete with steamed clams, mussels and corn on the cob. You'll also find a broad array of treats from scrod au gratin, scallops pesto and shrimp

provençal to mesquite-grilled swordfish, pina colada chicken, barbecued ribs and sirloin steak. Dessert favorites are chocolate volcano cake and ice-cream pie.
(508) 540-3850. Entrées, $14.95 to $19.95. Lunch and dinner daily, 11 to 11. Closed November-April.

Phusion Grille, 71 Water St., Woods Hole.
Of all the places with water views in Woods Hole, this offers the best, especially its side deck built right out over the water at the drawbridge. Partly open and partly canopied, it's a perfect place to watch all the watery goings-on. The food situation has improved since proprietor Carol Grieger took over the old Black Duck restaurant in 2003, gave it a new name and offered creative food with an Asian accent. She enhanced the decor, imparting a beachy bistro look, but the waterfront deck is the venue of choice when the weather cooperates. On the menu are the likes of ginger and soy marinated salmon wrapped in nori seaweed, garlic-rubbed pork tenderloin drizzled with ginger-soy glaze, baked prawns stuffed with lobster and sea scallops, and grilled filet mignon with sundried tomato and port wine demi-glace. Dinner might start with cajun fried calamari, chicken and Chinese sausage fried dumplings or a margarita pizza. Desserts could be raspberry crème brûlée, berry strudel with vanilla bean gelato or banana bread pudding with rum sauce.
(508) 457-3100. Entrées, $21 to $27. Dinner nightly in summer, 5 to 10. Closed in winter.

Captain Kidd Restaurant, 77 Water St., Woods Hole.
Although the front is nondescript, this establishment offers some of the best water views of Eel Pond out back. It actually comes with two faces – a year-round tavern spreading onto outdoor tables on docks in the pond in summer, and a fancier, seasonal waterfront dining room. The popular watering hole is named for the pirate who supposedly spent time around Woods Hole. In the atmospheric tavern, a whimsical pirate mural hangs above barrel-style bar tables and seats, across from a long mahogany bar. The enclosed patio with a wood stove is cozy in chilly weather. The tavern is pubby, good for lunch or a casual supper. Among favorites are pizzas, burgers, fish and chips, the fried fisherman's platter, baked scrod and teriyaki chicken. Upscale dining is featured in the dining room, again oriented toward the rear and Eel Pond. Expect entrées like grilled swordfish braised with mango and papaya, seafood en croûte, filet mignon and rack of lamb.
(508) 548-8563. www.thecaptainkidd.com. Dining room entrées, $20 to $30; nightly 5:30 to 11, June to mid-September. Tavern entrées, $12.95 to $18.95; lunch daily 11:30 to 3, dinner 5 to 9.

The Flying Bridge, 220 Scranton Ave., Falmouth.
Even with upwards of 1,000 seats, this touristy place gets crowded in season, given its prime location beside the yachts on the west side of Falmouth's busy Inner Harbor. Tables are arranged in a ramble of patios and boardwalks, lower decks and upper decks framed in festive blue and white awnings as well as beside floor-to-ceiling windows in interior dining rooms. The downstairs is a little more casual in feeling, with a large bar to one side. Upstairs, rattan chairs flank wood tables lit by candles. The all-day menu offers something for everyone, from sandwiches, salads and appetizers to seafood specials, steaks and lobsters. Seafood may be grilled, pan-seared or blackened. Mud pie and ice cream puff are typical desserts.
(508) 548-2700. Entrées, $16 to $26. Open daily, 11:30 to 9 or 10. Closed December to April.

The British Beer Company, 263 Grand Ave., Falmouth Heights.
One of a local chain and here part of the Seaside Inn compound, this fun place opened in an old seafood restaurant across from the beach. It's the busiest location

around – in fact, the finish line of the Falmouth Road Race is conveniently out front. The interior is a modern mix of nautical and British pub decor. The British theme is carried out in the British beers, of which eighteen are on draft, and the wry aphorisms inscribed on the ceiling beams and around the bar, plus a handful of "traditional specialties" such as fish and chips, cornish pasties, banger and mash, bubble and squeak, and shepherds pie. We had a quick lunch in the bar at the side, yielding the window tables across the front to diners with more time. The choices on the extensive all-day menu are snacky and pubby, augmented by homemade pizzas and a handful of entrées like Caribbean chicken, pot roast and filet mignon. The burgers are billed as the biggest this side of the English Channel. We can vouch for the roast beef sandwich, which turned out to be a whopper of a club sandwich, accented with cheese and horseradish sauce. It arrived in an oversize basket loaded with more french fries than one person could possibly consume.

(508) 540-9600. www.britishbeer.com. Entrées, $8.95 to $23.95. Open daily, from 11.

Chapaquoit Grill, 410 West Falmouth Hwy. (Route 28A), West Falmouth.

Although it's not on the water, people wait up to two hours for one of the 95 seats in this trendy but affordable grill. They come for wood-fired pizzas from a huge brick oven that occupies an open room off the entry, "big-flavored" appetizers and entrées, specials that are really special and a good wine list. Unassuming on the outside, "Chappy's" is much bigger than it looks with a bar and waiting area and a large rear dining room. The last has a vaguely Caribbean theme: splashy patterned cloths on the widely spaced tables, colorful sea prints on the salmon-colored walls and the odd fish silhouette hanging from a trellis screening the two-story-high ceiling. The printed menu offers appetizers like littleneck clams steamed Portuguese style, deep-fried calamari, caesar salad and the chef's antipasti. Entrées range from penne ala vodka and wild mushroom ravioli to cioppino. The specials board generates the most excitement. Consider one night's selections: grilled salmon fillet over radicchio-endive salad with white peach-tarragon vinaigrette, grilled sirloin marinated in tequila and cilantro with a chipotle demi-glace, and baked manicotti stuffed with lobster, shrimp, scallops and ricotta. "We keep things changing so people will come back," says chef Carl Bonnert. That they certainly do.

(508) 540-7794. Entrées, $15 to $26. Dinner nightly, 5 to 10.

Coonamessett Inn, Gifford Street at Jones Road, Falmouth.

Beautifully landscaped grounds backing up to secluded Jones Pond enhance the view from the main dining room of this large, barn-red, traditional New England property dating to 1796. The view is grand from the Ralph Cahoon Room, hung with the late folk artist's paintings. You'll miss it if you're seated in the fireplaced Vineyard Room, which is strung with white lights in grape vines along the beams, or the casual Eli's Lounge in front, where a tavern menu is served. Try for the Cashoon Room or the rear Garden Room and enjoy New England specialties, some of which have been updated lately with contemporary accents to draw a younger crowd. The old-timers to whom the Connamessett caters like the traditional shrimp cocktail, baked cod and lobster newburg. But also expect things like chicken saltimbocca, grilled ribeye steak and rack of lamb.

(508) 548-2300. Entrées, $18 to $30, Eli's $12 to $16. Lunch, 11:30 to 2:30. Dinner, 5:30 to 10.

FOR MORE INFORMATION: Falmouth Chamber of Commerce, 20 Academy Lane, Falmouth. MA 02541, (508) 548-8500 or (800) 526-8532. www.falmouthchamber.com. More information is available at www.woodshole.com.

Cape Cod Bay and much of Provincetown are on view from deck at Land's End Inn.

Randall Perry Photo

Provincetown, Mass.

Henry David Thoreau considered the beaches of Cape Cod a place where "a man may stand and put all America behind him." Nowhere is that more true than in Provincetown, the storied town poised on a fragile sandbar at the very tip of the Cape.

Cape Cod's last town is also its first town – the Pilgrims on the Mayflower landed here in 1620 and stayed five weeks before sailing across Cape Cod Bay to find shelter and fresh water at Plymouth. The town was settled in the mid-1700s by Portuguese fishermen and their families. In the 20th century, artists were drawn by the "Cape light" that is strongest in Provincetown. They found it "a place hard to get to and hard to get out of," as Eugene O'Neill famously described it. Free-living and free-thinking, they cast a spell over Provincetown that pulsates to this day.

Now a town of 3,200 year-round inhabitants, the population increases ten-fold in summer. The populated part of P-town, as it's called, three miles long and generally two blocks wide, curves cheek-by-jowl for three miles around the harbor facing sheltered Cape Cod Bay. On the north side are the towering dunes and beaches of the Cape Cod National Seashore and the open Atlantic.

The combination of edgy town, turbulent seas and shifting sands seems to release people from their past. They come here for a new beginning in an open community, free of constraints and conformity, much as in Key West, that other land's end down the East Coast. The result is a unique mix: artists and actors, a gay majority (both male and female), a fishing community, the Portuguese, townies, summer residents and tourists.

The East End, relatively quiet and residential, houses many year-round residents and art galleries. If Provincetown has a center, it's MacMillan Wharf and, around the corner, the Town Hall. Park yourself on a bench in front of Town Hall and observe the passing parade – people watching seems to be even more popular than whale watching, the official No. 1 tourist attraction here. Beyond the center is the West End, which yields to a more leisurely flow of guest houses, restaurants and private residences, some of them quite substantial and contemporary.

From the busy wharves come and go commercial fishing boats, plus excursion boats and an express catamaran to and from Boston. Whale watching tours started on the East Coast here in 1975, taking advantage of the fertile feeding grounds of the Stellwagen Bank sanctuary offshore.

Away from the fray are the moors at the far West End and the National Seashore parklands along the north side. Golden dunes, nature trails, bike paths and wide-open beaches invite exploration. Mother Nature upstages the human show.

Getting There

Provincetown is located at the end of Cape Cod. From the Sagamore or Bourne bridges, Route 6, the mid-Cape Highway, goes all the way out to Provincetown. Bus service is available from New York and Boston. Two passenger ferries from Boston, one a high-speed catamaran and the other a larger three-decker, operate under auspices of Bay State Cruise Co., (617) 748-1428. They run daily in July and August, and weekends in June and September. You can fly to and from Provincetown via Cape Air, (800) 352-0714.

Where to Stay

Visitors should be aware that, except for larger motels and resorts, most lodging establishments cater to gays or lesbians or welcome them. As the manager of the Watermark Inn advised, "everyone who comes here should be open-minded." Her inn's clientele is "mixed," meaning a mix of straights, gays and lesbians. Others run a broad range of mixed (those included here) to strictly gay or lesbian. The *Out and About* testimonials (or lack thereof) reprinted in brochures and the rainbow flags flying in front of guest houses speak volumes.

Watermark Inn, 603 Commercial St., Provincetown 02657.

Pair an innovative architect with a terrific bayfront location in the primarily residential East End and you get this shingled, contemporary beach house, one of Provincetown's largest and most luxurious. From Commercial Street, the front attracts as a refuge with a weathered Cape Cod shingle look and a small but pleasant yard and gardens. The rear opens up onto two levels of full-length decks, the lower one right out over the water at high tide, which rises several feet up the steps from the beach. The tide rises and falls nine feet, so when the tide is out guests enjoy a sandy beach. They also can walk fifteen minutes into the center of Provincetown. Kevin Shea and his wife, Judy Richland, bought a former inn-turned-restaurant in 1986 and transformed it into a summery haunt perfect for the Cape. Six of the ten one-bedroom suites offer head-on bay views and private decks. Four on the side yield "oblique" glimpses, but are only steps away from the common deck on the main level, dotted with umbrellaed tables and chairs. All suites

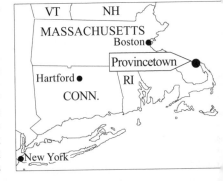

have kitchenettes and one has a full kitchen. Telephones and small TVs are standard. Two have working fireplaces. Beds are king or queensize and covered with quilts. Furnishings are contemporary, with plump sofas and chairs upholstered in grays or taupes to contrast with white walls and ceilings. Sliding glass doors, large windows, vaulted ceilings and skylights make each living area bright and airy, oriented toward the water. Bedrooms are darker and located toward the street side. Suite 7, the most expensive, offers a corner view toward Provincetown and sunset from its two-sided deck as well as a water view from its kingsize bed. Rates are generally by the week (Saturday to Saturday) in summer, booked far in advance, and nightly the rest of the year. Although the Sheas are in residence in summer, a manager is on hand at other times. No food is served; guests may do as they wish with their kitchenettes. There's parking for guests – a sought-after commodity in Provincetown. Most don't venture far, however, from their beachfront paradise with all the comforts of home.

(508) 487-0165. Fax (508) 487-2383. www.watermark-inn.com. Ten suites with private baths. Doubles, $190 to $400 nightly, $1,200 to $2,510 weekly in summer; $85 to $290 nightly rest of year.

The Red Inn, 15 Commercial St., Provincetown.

The historic Red Inn, long known for its restaurant, now offers prime waterfront accommodations as well. A quartet of four men from varied backgrounds took over the establishment in 2001 and added two "residences" to the lineup of six rooms right beside the beach in a prime West End residential section. The main, barn-red 1805 sea captain's home contains the restaurant and four guest rooms and two suites. Bay windows yield head-on views of the water at the far end of rooms that are decorated to the elegant hilt. The Harbor's End quasi-suite has an oversize chair for two in the front section and a pillow-top queen bed beside the water-view patio in back. Decor is formal and sumptuous, the kind that might appeal more to vacationers in the off-season than to beachgoers in summer. The three accommodations on the ground level open onto a sandy seawall, where Adirondack chairs await. Next door, an enormous deck serves guests in two cottage-style residences, both with kitchens and fireplaces. The living room of the Delft Haven, with windows onto the water on two sides, holds a baby grand piano in one corner. Continental breakfast is provided in the morning, and for dinner you only have to book a table in the dining room (see Where to Eat).

(508) 487-7334 or (866) 473-3466. Fax (508) 487-5115. www.theredinn.com. Four rooms, two suites and two residences with private baths. Doubles, $210 to $295. Residences, $425 and $485. Five-night minimum stay in summer.

Anchor Inn Beach House, 175 Commercial St., Provincetown 02657.

A $5 million renovation turned this aging waterfront Victorian on the bay side of Commercial Street into one of Provincetown's more luxurious B&Bs, now run by the holding company that also owns the Red Inn. Rooms feature whirlpool baths or deluxe showers and all but three have gas fireplaces. All rooms come with TV/VCR, twin-line telephone with dataport, wet bar with refrigerator, and bath amenities such as robes and hair dryers. Most deluxe are rear rooms facing Cape Cod Bay. They include four ground-floor cottage rooms with private entrances, decorated like early 19th century cottages with wicker furniture and cozy porches. Nautical themes prevail in the first-floor "yacht cabins," furnished to the 1930 period with boat beds and wood cabin walls. Six deluxe captain's suites offer kingsize beds, double whirlpool tubs and french doors onto a balcony overlooking the harbor. These are decorated in English chintz or with handmade furniture from the West Indies. Three rooms in the tower on the east side of the house offer balconies with side water views, four-poster beds and sitting areas. Six rooms facing Commercial Street have large front balconies. Their decor ranges from a yacht cabin to a paneled library, which has a water view from a private balcony. Guests enjoy an expansive foyer that doubles as a living room and dining area. The staff puts out a continental breakfast of muffins, pastries, cereals and yogurt.

(508) 487-0432 or (800) 858-2657. Fax (508) 487-6280. www.anchorinnbeachhouse.com. Seventeen rooms and six suites with private baths. Doubles, $175 to $375.

The Masthead, 31-41 Commercial St., Provincetown 02657.

A variety of attractive accommodations and a verdant and waterfront setting in the quiet West End are hallmarks of this family-run resort. Houses with inn rooms and apartments, cottages, studios and efficiencies are strung out in weathered Cape Cod structures along a wide lawn with a 450-foot-long sun deck above the beach. Accommodations vary from surprisingly large (most cottages and efficiencies) to two "inn rooms" with lavatories and a shared shower and a decidedly small inn room with a double bed on the street side renting for $99 a night in peak season. Paneled cottages of one to three bedrooms face the water and each has a large living-room picture window. They are nicely furnished – some with antiques and oriental rugs, original art and walls of books – in early American style. The prized Helena Rubenstein Cottage has kingsize and twin bedrooms plus a luxury kitchen, cathedral-ceilinged living room and dining room and private veranda on the water. Once its namesake's summer cottage, it also was formerly Enrico Caruso's home. A room named for Mrs. Bob Hope has a seven-foot window overlooking the bay and dramatic rheostat wall lighting. Picture windows also enhance the studio suite and kitchen in the Captain's Quarters. Queen, double and twin beds are the norm, and accommodations serve from two to four. Rooms come with refrigerators, telephones and TVs; larger quarters add kitchens. Roses and other flowers perk up the grounds, which end at the bayside sun deck, where the water laps at the pilings below at high tide. The beach emerges as the tide goes out. Lounge chairs and charcoal grills are at the ready. Cottages and apartments are booked by the week in summer, but rooms and one garden-view efficiency are available nightly. Rates quoted for four are for families only. Valerie and John Ciluzzi, joined by one of their three sons in summer, have run the place with T.L.C. since 1959.

(508) 487-0523 or (800) 395-5095. Fax (508) 487-9251. Nineteen units with private baths and two with shared shower. Doubles, $99 to $328 nightly and $1,491 to $2,324 weekly ($2,016 to $2,906 for four).

The Land's End Inn, 22 Commercial St., Provincetown 02657.

A place unto itself atop Gull Hill, the highest point in Provincetown's West End, this exotic inn commands panoramic views of town, dunes and Cape Cod Bay. The views inside the weathered wood structure with a cupola-topped turret are exotic, too. Make that *very*. Ditto for the ambiance. Reached from a small parking lot in back or by a set of stairs winding up from Commercial Street, the main floor is a showy clutter of architectural refinements and collections too abundant to enumerate or fully take in. Many are original to the house, built as a summer bungalow at the turn of the last century by Boston merchant Charles Higgins. The stained glass, Asian wood carvings and antiques like a "grandmother's clock" are notable. If the interior looks like an art deco museum, the exterior is idyllic: wraparound porches and alcoves, studded with heavy wood and log tables and chairs, with water views that won't quit. Prolific gardens add to the setting, although since longtime owner David Adam Schoolman's death, they have been toned down and manicured and the jungle of plants removed from the interior. Lately owned by former Ritz-Carlton hotelier Michael MacIntyre of the Brass Key guesthouses in Provincetown and Key West, the inn offers sixteen accommodations with queen or king beds. They vary widely, but each is a mini-museum of antiques and collections. Several have private decks or balconies. Three apartments with cooking facilities accommodate up to four. Rising above the house are three tower rooms and the Schoolman Suite. Two of the latter plus a kitchenette apartment are rented only by the week in summer. Guests mix in the ramble of living-room areas. They gather for continental breakfast at individual tables in the dining room or take it to the porch.

(508) 487-0706 or (800) 276-7088. www.landsendinn.com. Sixteen rooms and suites with private baths. Doubles, $245 to $445 nightly, $1,350 to $2,875 weekly. Closed late November to early May.

BayShore & Chandler House, 493 Commercial St., Provincetown 02657.
Nineteen apartments are available in the waterfront BayShore and its companion North Houses across the street, whose water views are good to nil. Formerly known as the Hargood Guest House and long run by Ann Maguire and Harriet Gordon, it has been condominiumized but facilities are rented out daily or weekly as available. The BayShore complex has five Cape-style houses converted to two studios and fourteen one-bedroom and three two-bedroom apartments, all but one with private decks or patios and some with fireplaces. Each living room contains a sofabed and TV. Rates vary with proximity to the water. The lodgings are grouped around a green lawn with a sunken garden and a terrace with umbrellaed tables and loungers overlooking the beach. All have private entrances, modern baths and complete kitchens (with everything from dishwasher to stemware and china and a garlic press). Fully renovated in 1997 is Chandler House, four doors closer to town. It has an expansive two-bedroom Gallery apartment with a huge fireplaced living room and deck, plus a one-bedroom Beach House cottage with fireplace and deck at water's edge. In the Captain's House are four apartments with fireplaces, including the one-bedroom Penthouse with cathedral ceiling and sweeping water view. Beds are generally queensize, except for one king in the Gallery and a few twins.

(508) 487-9133. Fax (508) 487-0520. www.bayshorechandler.com. Twenty-four apartments and one cottage with private baths. Doubles, $1,200 to $2,300 weekly in summer, $105 to $230 nightly (two-night minimum) rest of year.

Provincetown Inn, 1 Commercial St., Provincetown 02657.
No more watery location is offered by any Provincetown motel than this, which occupies its own isthmus surrounded by water on three sides. It calls itself a seaside resort and conference center. Both aspects are true, and its public facilities are home to the Provincetown Theater Company for nightly performances in summer. But this is essentially an aging motor inn, especially its one-story U-shaped buildings facing Cape Cod Bay on the outside and a parking lot in the inside. The water views from the subdivided patios are awesome; the inside corridors off the parking lot are not. Rooms in the priciest Cape Tip cross-section of the U face south. The Harborside section faces the pool area and Provincetown, while the Breakwater section looks toward the breakwater leading to Long Point and the dunes beyond. Corner accommodations in the Cape Tip section are suites: the Honeymoon has a king bed and sitting area, while the Captain's Suite has a queen bedroom, living room, dining area and eat-in kitchen. A two-story motel section along Commercial Street (called Pine and Perry, for the wood and man who built them, we were told) looks onto a pool area and the beach, although some rooms here face the street. The place has history. It's located opposite the little Pilgrims First Landing Park in the West End traffic rotary, where the pilgrims landed in America, and bears hand-painted murals

depicting the history of Provincetown. Cocktails and lunch are served at the Pilgrim Pool Bar & Grill around the Olympic-size pool in season. The Inn Pub offers appetizers, sandwiches and light entrées as well as Keno. When we were here at midweek in late May, the place seemed eerily quiet with only a few rooms occupied. It was advertising romantic bed and breakfast getaways in advance of the hordes of summer. A continental breakfast buffet is included in the rates.

(508) 487-9500 or (800) 942-5388. Fax (508) 487-2911. www.provincetowninn.com. One hundred rooms and two suites with private baths. Doubles, $139 to $219. Suites, $259 to $369. Waterfront units closed November to mid-April.

Best Western Tides Beachfront, 837 Commercial St., Provincetown 02657.

Nicely located along the shore Route 6A on the eastern outskirts of Provincetown, this is set well back from the road on six acres. It's right on Cape Cod Bay near the Provincetown border with Truro. A 600-foot-wide beach expands with the receding tide, and guests like to walk the flats amid the undulating sandbars. Taken over by Best Western, the old Tides resort was designed for self-sufficiency. A small breakfast and lunch restaurant is part of the resort. The grounds are landscaped, the lawns are lush and the outdoor pool is heated. All rooms in the main two-story motel have sliding doors opening right onto the beach or upstairs balconies. Only a couple of end units in a ten-room, one-story building at right angles to the beach get a glimpse of the water. Room furnishings are pleasant, and many units include a refrigerator. At the western end of town is the 54-room **Best Western Chateau Motor Inn** at 105 Bradford St. West, with similar rates. Its landscaped hilltop location offers great views of the dunes and distant waters surrounding Provincetown.

(508) 487-1045. Fax (508) 487-3557. www.bwprovincetown.com Sixty-four rooms with private baths. Doubles, $139 to $249. Closed late October to early May.

Surfside Hotel & Suites, 543 Commercial St., Provincetown.

New ownership has upgraded this property, which began in the early 1960s as a midrise motor inn typical of beach communities up and down the Atlantic coast but such an anomaly in Provincetown that it was dubbed "the green monster." Not much could be done to change the facades of the two buildings on either side of Commercial Street in the residential East End. But the gardens and landscaping have been enhanced, the rooms and baths refurbished, and the name changed from its earlier designations as motel and inn. Thirty-eight rooms and two suites in the four-story waterfront building face Cape Cod Bay, from ground-floor patios on the beach and shared balconies on upper floors, which are served by an elevator. Across Commercial Street is a three-story building where seventeen rooms face the street, seventeen face the parking lot and twelve look onto the pool and garden area. There are plenty of lounge chairs around the pool, which at our visit was heated to a sultry 86 degrees. Because of its setback, Surfside retains its beach even at high tide, when its neighbors lose theirs to the rising waters. All rooms in both buildings come with refrigerators and TV. Bed configurations vary from king and queen to one or two doubles. A complimentary continental breakfast is offered in the morning.

(508) 487-1726 or (800) 421-1726. Fax (508) 487-6556. www.surfsideinn.cc. Eighty-four rooms and two suites. Doubles, $140 to $340. Suites, $450 to $550. Closed mid-November to April.

Dyers Beach House Motel, 171 Commercial St., Provincetown 02657.

Right beside the water in the heart of town, this is located behind retail buildings, reached down a driveway so narrow that there's a small space alongside marked turn-around only. That's the only way a car could get back out, not that you want to leave this little bayside haunt located in the thick of things. The place lives up to its motto, "Sea for Your Self," as expressed by owner Mary Henrique, a Provincetown native. The structure right up against the water has three rooms up and two down, with an office across the parking area. Most rooms have two double beds or a double and a twin. All have TVs with VCRs. Their decks in back overlook the water, which at high tide laps against the building. Bookings are intended to be weekly in summer, but shorter stays may be available and are available in the off-season.

(508) 487-2061. www.provincetownescape.com. Five rooms with private baths. Doubles, $185.

Race Point Light, Cape Cod National Seashore.
For a different experience, families and groups may opt to stay in the lighthouse keeper's quarters at remote Race Point Light at the tip of Cape Cod. Guests are taken by four-wheel drive vehicle to the restored lighthouse, where they stay in three bedrooms sharing 1½ baths and a living room. For the length of their stay, guests live as a lighthouse keeper's guest would have back in the 1950s. Proceeds go the American Lighthouse Foundation for maintenance and continued restoration.

(508) 487-9930. www.lighthousefoundation.org. Rates from $105 nightly.

Seeing and Doing

The ocean, beaches and towering dunes that surround Provincetown on three sides are what make it so appealing for a waterside escape. Most beaches are part of the Cape Cod National Seashore, which provides diverse attractions for visitors.

Provincetown has only two through streets, Commercial and Bradford, which dead-end at the moors at the tip of the Cape. Parking can be a hassle. The same goes for driving, what with sauntering people turning Commercial Street into a pedestrian mall and bicyclists zigzagging through one-way traffic the wrong way. Visitors are advised to walk, bicycle or take the Breeze Shuttle, which circles the town and beaches every 20 minutes (single ride $1, day pass $3, children free).

The best way to get oriented is to take the **Provincetown Trolley,** (508) 487-9483, which gives 40-minute sightseeing tours around town and the National Seashore. Trolleys leave from Town Hall on Commercial Street between Ryder and Gosnold streets every half hour from 10 to 4 and hourly in the evening; adults $9, children $5. The tours are narrated and quite informative. More personalized tours are offered by horse-drawn carriages, also parked in front of Town Hall.

On or Near the Water

Cape Cod National Seashore.
The Cape's most expansive national treasure, the seashore was established in 1961 under the administration of President Kennedy, for whom Cape Cod was his summer home. The 43,500-acre seashore protects 40 miles of ocean beaches, rolling dunes, swamps, marshes, wetlands, pine barrens, forests, wildlife and historic structures, all culminating around the tip of the Cape at Provincetown. Self-guiding nature trails, as well as biking and horseback riding trails, wend through these landscapes. Guided walks and lectures are offered April-November. The Province Lands Visitor Center, Race Point Road off Route 6, dispenses information and shows a film on Provincetown, daily 9 to 5, early May to late October. From its upper-level observation deck you can look out across the dune and beach area.

(508) 487-1256. Open year-round. Free. Beach parking fee in summer, $10.

SWIMMING. When the tide is out, people swim along the bay beaches from Truro into Provincetown Harbor and the West End. Out on the seashore, Herring

Cove Beach is the best, according to locals. The Cape Cod Bay water is calmer and warmer than that on the ocean side. Signs at the entry warn "public nudity prohibited," although that's occasionally disregarded. Provincetown's most popular gay beach is to the left or south here. The first stretch is primarily lesbian, beyond is primarily male. The northern stretch has a family clientele. So does the north-facing Race Point Beach, where the ocean surf rolls in and the sand is smoother. Here is where the currents of ocean and bay meet in a boiling rush known as "The Race." The currents can be dangerous for small boats, and the Race Point Lifesaving Museum is located here. Both National Seashore beaches have lifeguards and bathhouses, and Herring Cove has a snack bar. To avoid the daily parking fee, those in the know buy a National Seashore season pass for $20, which gives free parking at all the beaches. Windsurfing within the National Seashore is permitted outside lifeguard-protected beaches.

For a change of pace, hike along the beach from the Herring Cove parking lot out to a smaller cove between Herring Cove and Race Point, called **Hatch's Harbor**. Once a raucous shantytown frequented by pirates and local renegades, today it is a smooth beach that fills up at high tide with warm pools in which youngsters like to paddle about.

HIKING AND BIKING. From the parking lot off Race Point Road in the National Seashore, hike the **Beech Forest Trail** into the heart of a picturesque beech forest. The one-mile loop skirts the shallow Beech Forest Pond and hugs dunes that are gradually engulfing parts of the forest. About eight miles of paved bicycle trails wind through the dunes. We enjoyed biking the 5.5-mile **Province Lands Trail** out to Race Point and Herring Cove beaches and returning past Pasture and Bennett ponds and beside Beech Forest. But watch out for sands shifting across the pavement. Unwary riders may find themselves suddenly upended.

In town, public landings every few blocks make the beach accessible to everyone. You can walk the beach along the harborfront at low tide for a boater's view of Provincetown. At high tide the gentle waves lap right up to the buildings on the south side of Commercial Street. Low tide exposes shifting sandbars or "flats," as the locals call them.

You also can hike out the rock breakwater from the West End rotary to Wood End and Long Point lights. The moors to the west, nearly dry at low tide, show the wildlife and ecology of the salt marshes. The mile-and-a-half walk is tricky and at times you have to hop from rock to rock. Parts of the breakwater may be submerged at high tides. **Long Point** itself is starkly beautiful – a place where you really are at land's end, but with Provincetown a comforting sight back in the distance.

Foss Woods in the East End, acquired by the town to preserve conservation land, surrounds the old railroad right of way. It now makes for a good walking trail.

Active hikers enjoy treks across high dunes from a couple of access points, and dune climbers are sometimes a startling sight for first-time visitors approaching along Route 6. At Snail Road and Route 6 in the East End, a fire road cuts into the scrub pine forest and leads to the dunes. At the Pilgrim Heights parking lot in Truro, another fire road heads out to the beach, just north of Head of The Meadow.

Old Harbor Lifesaving Station, Race Point Beach. The century-old station, floated here from Chatham in 1977, houses displays of shipwrecks and heroic rescues by the U.S. Lifesaving Service at sea. Every Thursday at 6, the staff re-enacts a 1902 rescue drill. Open daily except Thursday in summer, 3 to 5. Donation.

DUNE TOURS. The towering dunes give Provincetown its unique light and scope. For an entertaining look, hitch a ride with **Art's Dune Tours,** corner of Commercial and Standish streets, (508) 487-1950 or (800) 894-1951. Art Costa started giving dune tours in 1946 in an old Ford Woody. Today you'll likely be in a four-wheel-drive GMC Suburban van as you drive around the National Seashore through grasses and along cranberry bogs, pass the remains of the Peaked Hill life-saving station that rescued shipwrecks, and get a look at the famous dune shacks where artists and writers became inspired (and still are). The first was built in 1794 as a refuge for shipwrecked sailors. Now eighteen cottages, most built between 1935 and 1950, dot the ridges and valleys between Race Point and High Head in Truro. Part of the National Register of Historic Places, four are available each summer to artists and writers as retreats. Dune tours of one to one and one-half hours, daily 10 to 5:30; fares, $12 to $15.

HORSEBACK BEACH RIDES. Nelson's Riding Stables, 43 Race Point Road, (508) 487-1112, takes riders of all levels on one-hour tours through the dunes on horseback. You ride through woods, over sand dunes and through a wild cranberry bog. Guided beach and dune rides also are offered daily and at sunset by **Bayberry Hollow Farm,** 27 West Vine Extension (off Bradford Street), (508) 487-6584.

WHALE WATCHING. Whales, which played an important role in the Provincetown economy in the 19th century, now attract thousands of visitors who depart from Provincetown Harbor each year to observe, rather than kill, the now-endangered species in their natural habitat. The tradition began in 1975 when scientists from the Provincetown Center for Coastal Studies teamed with charter fishing boat captain Al Avellar to study the three species of whales found offshore. His **Dolphin Fleet,** (800) 826-9300, which launched the guided whale watching phenomenon on the East Coast, is considered the standard by which others are judged. Beyond Race Point back toward Boston is Stellwagen Bank, a newly proclaimed National Marine Sanctuary, the only one in the Northeast. It's a shallow, underwater plateau that is a rich feeding ground for whales, dolphins and seals, and Provincetown is its closest land neighbor, eight miles away. Whale watch excursions of three to four hours leave from MacMillan Wharf three times a day. More than 50 humpback, right and finback whales are often seen on a single trip. Naturalists from the Center for Coastal Studies add insights as they guide all Dolphin cruises. Three boats give morning, afternoon and sunset tours mid-April through October. Adults, $24.

Three-hour naturalist-conducted tours also are offered by **Portuguese Princess Excursions,** (508) 487-2651 or (800) 442-3188. Tours depart from MacMillan Wharf daily May-October, adults $19 to $22.

SAILING AND BOATING. Several schooners based on MacMillan Wharf offer daysails and sunset sails. Depending on the winds, they sail across Cape Cod Bay toward Truro and Wellfleet or around Long Point toward the Atlantic. **Bay Lady II,** (508) 487-9308, gives a two-hour sail on its 73-foot schooner.

Kayak tours and rentals are available through **Off the Coast Kayak,** 237 Commercial St., (508) 487-2692.

The **Viking Princess,** (508) 487-7323, a 40-foot yacht styled after the coastal steamers of a century ago, specializes in eco-tours departing from MacMillan Wharf. It offers narrated harbor tours and an interactive "critter" cruise exploring for birds, plankton, lobster, crabs, starfish and sometimes dolphins.

Town Attractions

Visitors should trace three strands of Provincetown's heritage that made it the melting pot it is today – the Pilgrims, the Portuguese fishermen, and the artists and free spirits.

The Pilgrims landed first not at Plymouth but in Provincetown. First Landing

Park, a small landscaped memorial in the middle of a traffic rotary in the West End, commemorates their arrival. It stands in quiet contrast to the hoopla surrounding Plymouth Rock. The drama of the Mayflower Compact is rendered in a bas-relief at the foot of the landmark Pilgrim Monument.

The influence of the Portuguese fishermen who settled the town in the mid-1700s is evident in the names of the fishing boats along Fisherman's Wharf, the Portuguese bakery on Commercial Street and the annual Portuguese Festival and Blessing of the Fleet in late June.

The artists who were inspired by the Cape Cod "light" and each other formed the nation's largest arts colony. You can see the dune shacks as well as some of their works in the town's museums and galleries.

Pilgrim Monument and Provincetown Museum, off Route 6 on High Pole Hill.

The monument, tallest granite structure in the country, offers a panoramic view of Cape Cod from its 252-foot-high observation deck. Designed like an Italian tower, you reach the top by walking up an inclined ramp and stairs. The monument was built in 1910 to honor the first landing of the Mayflower. At its base is a museum with a collection of artifacts that trace the history of the Outer Cape. Displays include dioramas, ship models, scrimshaw, a map of the Mayflower's route, whaling equipment, items salvaged from nearby shipwrecks and even preserved polar bears, part of an unusual North Pole collection in honor of native son Donald MacMillan, who explored the Arctic with Commodore Robert Peary. The Pilgrim Room contains Mayflower memorabilia as well as Colonial and Victorian china, silver and pewter.

(508) 487-1310. Open daily, 9 to 7 in summer, 9 to 5 in spring and fall. Closed December-March. Adults $7, children $3.

Provincetown Heritage Museum, 356 Commercial St.

Located in the former Methodist church built in 1860, this was established in 1976 by the town to depict the history of Provincetown. It holds one of the world's largest indoor models of a Grand Banks fishing schooner, the 66-foot-long Rose Dorothea. Other attractions range from one of the oldest library collections in the country and paintings by local artists to antique fire equipment and exhibits of marine gear, fishing equipment and harpoons.

(508) 487-7098. Open daily 10 to 5:30, Memorial Day to Columbus Day. Adults $4.

Expedition Whydah Sea Lab and Learning Center, 16 MacMillan Wharf.

This traces the story and displays the treasures of the pirate ship Whydah, which sank off nearby Wellfleet in 1717. "Black Sam" Bellamy's Whydah is the only pirate ship ever recovered from the deep. Visitors find cannons, jewelry and coins salvaged from the brig, as well as a working conservation library.

(508) 487-8899 or (800) 949-3241. Open daily 10 to 7 in summer, to 4 in spring and fall, weekends only Columbus Day to New Year's. Adults $8, children $6.

THE ARTS. The arts are integral to the Provincetown experience. The nation's oldest continuous arts colony dates to 1899, when Charles Hawthorne began teaching painting to hundreds of artists who flocked here to take advantage of the open air and changing light. Literally dozens of galleries flourish across the town, with a concentration in the East End.

Writers and playwrights soon joined the artists here. The famous Provincetown Players originated in 1916 when Eugene O'Neill's "Bound East for Cardiff" debuted on a foggy 1916 night in an old fishhouse-turned-stage on Lewis Wharf. They wintered in Greenwich Village and after several seasons relocated to New York. A plaque at 570 Commercial St. commemorates the Players and the first O'Neill production as the birthplace of modern American theater. O'Neill, Thoreau, John Dos Passos, Tennessee Williams, Edna St. Vincent Millay and Norman Mailer all found inspiration here.

Provincetown Art Association and Museum, 460 Commercial St.
The association was established in 1914, and by 1916 the Boston Globe ran a front-page article headlined "Biggest Art Colony in the World in Provincetown." Edward Hopper, Jackson Pollock and Robert Motherwell were among those who worked in town. The museum has a permanent collection of more than 1,500 works, shown throughout the year in four galleries. It also stages exhibitions of works by established and emerging artists.
(508) 487-1750. www.paam.org. Open daily noon to 5, Memorial Day to October, also 8 to 10 p.m. daily in summer and weekends in June and September; rest of year, weekends noon to 4. Adults $2.

SHOPPING. For most, the people-watching takes priority over shopping along tight, congested Commercial Street, the main drag (in more ways than one). Like so much else in Provincetown, stores come and go. They also tend to cater to the offbeat, as in **Freak Street Clothes and Accessories.** Standouts for us were **Utilities,** with good home accessories; **Impulse Gallery,** lots of colorful glassware; **D. Lasser Ceramics; Frenchware,** with clothing and dry goods for the Francophile, and the **Northern Lights Hammock Shop. Marine Specialties,** a warehouse of a place also known as the Army Navy Store, advertises demilitarized clothing, boots, boating gear and, more than anything, "good junk."

Where to Eat ⟶ ⌇⌇⌇

Provincetown offers more good restaurants per capita than anyplace on the Cape. Happily, some of the best are located on the waterfront, including all of these:

The Mews, 429 Commercial St.
Here is one dynamite waterfront setting – a romantic downstairs dining room that looks like an extension of the beach just outside its walls of glass. The designer even took samples of sand to Boston to match with the paint on the terra cotta walls, which are hung with changing abstract art. Floodlights illuminate the beach, and from virtually every white-clothed table you have the illusion of eating outside. Owner Ron Robin and executive chef Laurence de Freitas feature American fusion cuisine. Among appetizers, we liked the oysters with crabmeat béchamel and pancetta, albeit a precious little serving that we had hoped to share, and a classic caesar salad. Main courses range from mirin-glazed Atlantic salmon with rhubarb and cucumber yogurt to Mediterranean spice-rubbed rack of lamb. The smoked pork tenderloin with apricot-serrano chile sauce was served with sweet potato polenta, while the shrimp curry came in a puff pastry with black mission figs. Key lime pie was a hit from the dessert tray, as was coffee ice cream drizzled with hot fudge sauce. Service was polished and the food preparation more than competent, but the romantic beachside setting – illuminated as darkness fell – is what remains etched in our memories. Next time we might opt to eat in the lively upstairs bar area called **Café Mews,** which offers an American bistro menu of appetizers, sandwiches, pastas and lighter entrées. Here you'll also find a vodka bar, billed as the largest in New England if not the country, with more than 175 brands from 27 countries.
(508) 487-1500. www.mews.com. Entrées, $22 to $32. Dinner nightly, from 6. Sunday brunch, 11 to 2:30, Easter through October.

The Red Inn, 15 Commercial St.

Unimpeded water views are obtained from three dining areas strung out along the rear of this recently renovated 1805 sea captain's house that sports a polished, more contemporary look than its wide-board hardwood floors and beamed ceilings would indicate. The inn proclaims a gold medal award for "best water view dining on the Cape," and the new American cuisine is equal to the setting. One of the four owners, Phillip Mossy from Louisiana, is the head chef. Repeat diners tend to go for the raw-bar selections as preliminaries to the inn's "big 22-ounce porterhouse steak" or pepper-crusted filet mignon with Jack Daniels sauce. Others like to start with the spicy lobster corn chowder and perhaps a bacon-wrapped oyster brochette or lobster and artichoke fondue in a warm sourdough bowl, Chef Mossy imparts Louisiana accents to such main courses as shrimp and crawfish sautéed with mushrooms in a sherry-creole tomato cream sauce over pasta and creole-seasoned duck breast grilled with a passionfruit-maple glaze. His pan-roasted local cod might be served on a bed of rosemary potatoes and applewood bacon with a lemon-garlic confit.

(508) 487-7334. www.theredinn.com. Entrées, $22 to $42. Dinner nightly, 5:30 to 10, May-October; Thursday-Sunday in off-season. Brunch, Thursday-Sunday 10 to 2:30 in summer, weekends in late spring and early fall. Closed January to mid-April.

Martin House, 157 Commercial St.

New American cooking with international accents is served up in this shingled 1750 sea captain's house snuggling up to the harbor on the Atlantic Street Landing. Brothers Glen and Gary Martin offer six snug dining rooms with fireplaces upstairs and down (check out "the cave" where the three chimneys meet), plus a trellised garden patio beside the harbor holding a handful of tables for two. That's the best place for water views. The signature oysters Claudia on the half shell with a ponzu dipping sauce, wasabi and pickled ginger make a fabulous starter from a menu strong on first courses and small plates. Others could be smoked sea scallops with red chile sauce and poblano cream, and the house salad with organic greens, roasted cashews and papaya-lime vinaigrette. Executive chef Alex Mazzocca favors the local catch, and often buys whole fish fresh from the back beach minutes before the restaurant opens. Typical main dishes are tasso-wrapped halibut fillet, fennel-dusted salmon fillet with saffron cream and shellfish steamed in sangria with roasted vegetables and yellow rice. We were well pleased with the sautéed lobster topped with red pepper crème fraîche and the duck breast saltimbocca. Treats like roasted and stuffed green tomatoes in a spicy file tofu cream sauce impress vegetarians.

(508) 487-1327. www.themartinhouse.com. Entrées, $25 to $34. Dinner nightly, 6 to 10 or 11. Sunday brunch, 10 to 2. Closed Monday-Wednesday in the off-season.

Jackson's at the Flagship, 463 Commercial St.

Like the highly acclaimed restaurant Chester on the other side of the street, this newcomer in the old Flagship restaurant is named for the dog of one of its founding partners. Windows on three sides yield views of the water, framing a dark and nautical interior of booths and tables. The weathered but stylish East End space is popular for its original dory bar and fireplace, as well as its international fare. The short menu might begin with shrimp and cabbage dumplings, Thai-inspired mussels and sesame-crusted tuna sashimi. Main courses are as varied as a classic bouillabaisse and a "killer" meatloaf. Typical are tropical grilled halibut, crispy seared salmon with a jalapeño-peanut sauce, osso buco and peppercorn-coated sirloin steak with a roasted garlic demi-glace.

(508) 487-2813. www.jacksonsflagship.com. Entrées, $16.95 to $29.95. Dinner nightly, from 6. Closed mid-November to April.

Fanizzi's By the Sea, 539 Commercial St.

The tired old Pucci's Harborside restaurant gave way to this worthy successor, highly recommended by East End hoteliers for good Italian-American food, value and friendly service. The old waterfront deck is long gone, in favor of a renovated and enclosed sun-porch affair with windows on three and one-half sides. Owner Paul Fanizzi's repertoire is enormous – indeed, the day's specials list is longer than many a restaurant's regular menu. But the kitchen's reach does not exceed its grasp, as attested by a recent lunch: an oversize crab cake sandwich and the specialty burger marinated in ale and herbs and served with cheddar and bacon on an English muffin. Each was accompanied by a slew of french fries and a zesty coleslaw. The portions rendered desserts redundant and the prices were easy on the pocketbook. At night, you can choose among appetizers (from nachos to a Mediterranean platter), burgers, sandwiches and entrées ranging from fish and chips and roasted garlic chicken to mustard nut-crusted cod, veal dishes and grilled ribeye steak.

(508) 487-1964. www.fanizzisrestaurant.com. Entrées, $13.95 to $20.95. Lunch daily, 11 to 4. Dinner nightly, from 4. Sunday brunch, 10 to 2.

The Lobster Pot, 321 Commercial St.

Tourists rub elbows with locals at this institution known for consistent, abundant seafood. There's the typical lobster-pot decor, but not the typical menu. Some fairly sophisticated fare comes out of the rows of kitchens opening off the long corridor leading to the rear dining rooms, one on the main floor and one upstairs, both overlooking the water. We certainly liked executive chef Tim McNulty's prize-winning clam chowder, rich and creamy, and the mussels marinara with the plumpest mollusks ever. The shrimp chantilly tossed with spinach fettuccine is a lunchtime classic. Tortilla-crusted halibut, shellfish algarve, cajun bouillabaisse, cioppino and sole rockefeller are among the seafood offerings at dinner. Lobster comes in at least seven variations, from a clambake to lobster newburg. Run for more than 30 years by the McNulty family, the Lobster Pot also has a fish market, raw bar, bakery and gift shop.

(508) 487-0842. www.ptownlobsterpot.com. Entrées, $16.95 to $25.95. Lunch daily, 11:30 to 5. Dinner, 5 to 10 or 11. Closed January-March.

Sal's Place, 99 Commercial St.

This waterfront haunt with a touch of the Italian Riviera remains much as it was when Sal del Deo opened it in 1963. Upon retiring in 1989, he sold it to his longtime chef Jack Papetsas and his wife Lora. The old-fashioned, Southern Italian menu is virtually unchanged, except for a few more seafood items. Pastas and sauces are homemade and range widely from a simple yet tasty spaghettini with tomato sauce to more complex dishes with mushrooms, chicken livers or cheese. A specialty is spaghettini alla foriana, the traditional Ischian dish with raisins, pine nuts, walnuts and anchovies. The veal comes from Boston and any of its variations are first-rate. Salmon and shrimp are featured seafood items. Portions are huge, so only heavy-eaters are advised to start with one of the traditional antipasti, good as they are. Lora prepares desserts, including a stellar tiramisu and chocolate mousse topped with a strawberry. Most of the wines come from small Italian vineyards the owners visit in the off-season. Although the interior space can get cramped and stuffy, dining by candlelight on the canopied deck beside the water is a delight on summer evenings.

(508) 487-1279. Entrées, $16 to $22. Dinner nightly in summer, 6 to 10; Friday-Monday in off-season.

Ross' Grill, 237 Commercial St.

Some of the most interesting food in town is served up beside the water at this urbane and hip café and raw bar. The place is right above the beach, on the second level at the far end of a shopping arcade called Whaler's Wharf. The pity is it's so small and, for the not so hip, rather uncomfortable. Beneath a high jet-black ceiling stand eight bleached-pine tables, half of them of the high bar variety flanked by barstool perches. Thirteen more seats for dining line the central bar. From a tiny open kitchen beside the entry, chef-owner Ken Ross prepares the likes of crispy Tuscan cod, shellfish risotto, crab cakes with spicy rémoulade sauce, steak frites, and rack of New Zealand lamb. Start with escargots in puff pastry, chicken liver and pistachio pâté or even a basket of hand-cut french fries. Finish with a dessert from the pastry case beside the door. Cobb salad and oyster po-boys star on the lunch menu.

(508) 487-8878. Entrées, $16 to $30. Lunch, Wednesday-Monday 11:30 to 4. Dinner, Wednesday-Monday 5:30 to 9:30. Closed in February.

Bubala's by the Bay, 183 Commercial St.

The expansive sidewalk terrace out front is Provincetown's best for watching the passing parade, according to the folks who took over this colorful, funky and laid-back establishment. The exterior is painted bright yellow and topped by campy carved birds. But it's the interior with windows onto the harbor that appeals most to water-lovers. Although better known for its atmosphere than its food, the kitchen rarely closes, serving three meals a day into the wee hours. The chefs buy right off the boats, so the fish could not be fresher: perhaps sole poached in pinot grigio with shallots and mushrooms, grilled tuna wasabi, seafood cassoulet or cod steamed with lemon grass in parchment. The international menu entices the young crowd with fajitas, focaccia sandwiches, quesadillas, burgers and such. The wine list is bargain priced. The action around the U-shaped bar picks up in the evening. Come here the next morning for an eye-opening mimosa and three-egg omelets, bagels with smoked salmon or huevos rancheros.

(508) 487-0773. www.bubalas.com. Entrées, $12.95 to $25.95. Breakfast, lunch and dinner daily, 9 a.m. to 1 a.m.

Clem & Ursie's Seaside Lobsters, 205 Commercial St.

Hidden at the end of a shopping arcade is this new offshoot of the wildly popular Clem & Ursie's Restaurant & Market, an expanding venture that overlooks a commercial parking lot at 85 Shank Painter Road. Here is an unpretentious little takeout stand, dispensing many of the Silva family's favorites – lobsters, chowders, pot pies and casseroles, barbecued ribs, sandwiches, grilled seafood, "daily Jamaican specialties" and who knows what all? It's all to go, obviously, and there's no more eclectic waterfront place for the partaking than the picnic tables beside a funky seaside garden and a raised deck right beside the water. The sea clam pie and "Southern iced tea" really hit the spot.

(508) 487-6722. www.clemandursies.com. Entrées, $7 to $21. Open daily in season.

FOR MORE INFORMATION: Provincetown Chamber of Commerce, 307 Commercial St. at MacMillan Wharf, Box 1017, Provincetown, MA 02657, (508) 487-3424. www.ptownchamber.com. A comprehensive website is www.provincetown.com.

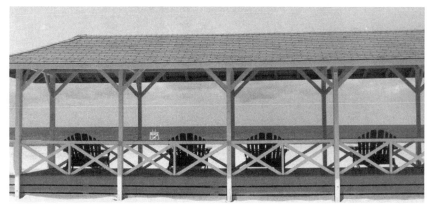

Pavilion facing ocean awaits swimmers at Cliffside Beach Club.

Nantucket, Mass.

Everything about Nantucket epitomizes an island at sea.

With 85 miles of coastline, no point on the fourteen-mile-long island is more than a mile or two from the water. From historic Nantucket Town to beachy Surfside across island, from quaint Siasconset on the east to remote Madaket on the west, you can feel the breeze and smell the salt air (and almost touch it in times of pea-soup fog). Nearly everywhere you see dunes, moors and heathlands honed by time and hear the sounds of the sea.

Here is an island of history and romance nearly 30 miles off Cape Cod, with no land visible on the horizon. It's home to the nation's largest concentration of eighteenth-century buildings as well as 65 miles of pristine beaches. Historically it has been known as the "Little Gray Lady of the Sea" (by edict, most houses must be allowed to weather to the gray patina that results from the salt air). But we think of Nantucket, too, in the preppy pink and green of its more contemporary veneer, as well as in the azure blue of its waters and the gold of its sandy beaches.

Nantucket was settled in the early 1600s, harbored fortunes as a whaling port in the 19th century, and with a year-round population of 10,000 carries well its history and affluence today. That's partly due to its relative isolation and an inherent sense of preservation, and partly due to the resources of Walter Beinecke Jr. of the S&H Green Stamps family.

Variously considered Nantucket's visionary or villain, Beinecke started in the early 1960s to turn the town around to face the waterfront that had been abandoned over the years. When he sold his holdings to First Winthrop Corp. of Boston a quarter century later, he had built or restored three leading lodging establishments, the Nantucket Boat Basin, 40 cottages on the wharf and 36 retail buildings in the downtown area. He created the Nantucket Historical Trust and co-founded the Nantucket Conservation Foundation, which set the twin themes for the preservation of Nantucket.

His efforts led to the preservation of 11,800 acres of open space – more than one third of the island's land total.

Recognizing the small size of the island and its finite quantities, Nantucket managed its growth by limiting access. It has become an upscale, year-round community, many of its houses owned by high-living mainlanders who fly in on private jets. Tourism has been nurtured and the season extended – starting with the annual

Daffodil Festival in late April and ending with the Nantucket Noel on New Year's Eve. The famed Christmas Stroll the first full weekend in December fills virtually every hostelry on the island.

Daytrippers do come to Nantucket. But they return on the late-afternoon ferry to Hyannis, leaving the island for those who are willing and able to pay upwards of $500 to eat and spend the night.

For the good life that Nantucket offers, many are willing to pay the price. Whether you're into beaching or boating, luxury lodging or fine dining, the arts, history or nature, Nantucket is one island that has it all.

Getting There

Nantucket is reached by ferries or airplanes.

The Steamship Authority, South Street Dock, Hyannis, (508) 477-8600, www.steamshipauthority.com. Called simply the Authority (in more ways than one), it has six trips a day in each direction in summer between Hyannis and Nantucket (about 2¼ hours). One-way costs are $175 for cars and $14 for adults, $7.25 for children. Auto reservations are imperative, far in advance. The Authority also has a "fast ferry" for pedestrians and bicycles. The hour-long trip is offered six times daily from Memorial Day through Jan. 3. Reservations are recommended: (508) 495-3278. One-way fares: adults $27.50, children $20.75.

Hy-Line Cruises, Ocean Street Dock, Hyannis, (508) 778-2602 or (888) 778-1132, www.hy-linecruises.com. Two-hour crossings for passengers only are provided by the smaller Hy-Line ferries, which have three sailings daily from Memorial Day to mid-September. One-way: adults $15, children $8. Hy-Line also offers high-speed catamaran service for passengers and bicycles, offering one-hour trips six times a day year-round, (800) 492-8082. One-way: adults $35, children $26. Round trip, adults $61, children $43.

Nantucket's airport is the second busiest in Massachusetts, serving commercial jets from Boston, New York and Newark, smaller airlines from Hyannis, New Bedford and Providence, charter aircraft and an inordinate number of private planes.

Once on the island, you can get around by taxi or the Nantucket Regional Transit Authority Shuttle, (508) 228-7025. Its buses cover most of the island, serving Madaket, Miacomet, Siasconset and Surfside and Jetties beaches. They run daily from 7 a.m. to 11:30 p.m., June-September. Frequency and fares vary, from $1 to $2.

Where to Stay————————————————/◌◌◌_

About 1,200 rooms available on the island vary widely in style and price. Most are in B&Bs and guesthouses that are converted homes of antique vintage. Many require minimum stays of two nights or more in peak season. Apartments, cottages and houses usually rent by the week or longer.

Near the Water, In Town

Cliffside Beach Club, 46 Jefferson Ave., Box 449, Nantucket 02554.

Nantucket's niftiest beachside accommodations are those at the old Cliffside Beach Club, dating to 1924 and located in a residential section on the north shore, away from downtown. Here on a glorious 400-foot strand, members used to wait years to reserve one of the prime sections of the west beach. The same umbrellas and chairs are still in the same spots, according to general manager/owner Robert F. Currie, whose grandfather founded the club. Some of the old-fashioned changing rooms have been transformed into fourteen airy, contemporary guest quarters with cathedral ceilings and modern baths. All the beds, tables, vanities, doors and even the pegs for the beach towels were built by Nantucket craftsmen. Angled wainscoting serves as the headboards for the built-in queensize beds. The woodwork from the old bathhouses is handsomely accented with dark green colors and prints by local artists. Nine beachfront studio apartments, each with a private deck and the phones and TVs characteristic of all the rooms, and several suites are of newer vintage. A new health club offers state-of-the-art exercise facilities. Lunch and dinner are available to guests and the public at **The Galley at Cliffside Beach** (see Where to Eat), situated between the club and the studio apartments. Continental breakfast is served in the club's spectacular lobby, full of smart wicker furniture and planters, and topped by quilts suspended from the beamed cathedral ceiling. Then it's off to while away the day on one of the best private beaches on the island.

(508) 228-0618. Fax (508) 325-4735. www.cliffsidebeach.com. Thirty-one rooms and suites with private baths. Doubles, $380 to $605. Suites, $730 to $1,485. Closed Columbus Day to Memorial Day.

The White Elephant, 50 Easton St., Nantucket 02554.

The White Elephant is no longer the "white elephant" of Nantucket. The image was acquired years ago based on the size and quality of the old-timer's rooms relative to their lofty prices. Lately it has been upgraded and expanded by the owners of the secluded Wauwinet, who earlier had taken one of the island's oldest hotels and transformed it into a Relais & Chateaux property. A superb harborfront location offers lush lawns, fancy walkways lined with hedges, and plantings that focus on a white elephant statue in the middle, two nine-hole putting greens and a pleasant pool to the side of the outdoor terrace and restaurant. The newest lodgings in the renovated hotel have kingsize beds, many have working fireplaces and some have harbor views, though rooms vary widely in terms of size and view. The interior design was overseen by the same New York firm that refurbished the Wauwinet. We're partial to the corner rooms with windows onto Children's Beach, although others might find them too public and cherish the privacy of the interior. The eleven rose-covered garden cottages scattered about the harborfront property have been redecorated. They offer one to three bedrooms and the living rooms of some have bay windows overlooking the water. Some have fireplaces and a few have kitchenettes. The Breakers annex, located on the White Elephant's grounds, is like a small inn. It offers 25 spacious guest rooms, many with harbor views and all with private patios or balconies. Breakfast may be enjoyed there or in the new harborside lounge. The main hotel includes a new fitness center and offers spa treatments. Breakfast is complimentary in the **Brant Point Grill,** which serves three meals daily (see Where to Eat).

(508) 228-2500 or (800) 475-2637. Fax (508) 325-1195. www.whiteelephanthotel.com. Twenty-two rooms, 31 suites and eleven cottages with private baths. Doubles, $450 to $600. Suites, $515 to $900. Cottages, $470 to $1,400. Closed late October to early May.

Nantucket Landfall, 4 Harbor View Way, Nantucket 02554.

Nantucket's first B&B situated close to the water was opened by Gail and David More in an old house with a great front porch furnished in white and navy wicker. All eight guest rooms come with updated baths, a couple of them ingeniously tucked into cubicles "because this is a small house and we had to use every inch," Gail relates. She made up for lack of space with interesting decor and colorful comforters. Two larger front rooms on the main floor – one with a king bed and the other with a queen canopy – face the water. The latter room has a light pine armoire, a bathroom with a clawfoot tub and chairs on the porch for enjoying the view of the harbor across Children's Beach. Two second-floor rooms have sitting areas overlooking the harbor. The Snuggery, a second-floor room with double bed and deck, must be the best value on the island at $110 a night. The third-floor Captain's Quarters has a king bed, a deck with water view and, in addition to a bathroom with shower, a bathtub secreted behind a screen in the bedroom. The living room of the B&B contains a fireplace and library, where Gail has compiled an enlightening scrapbook on the island's offerings. The Mores serve a continental-plus breakfast of fruit, bakery breads and occasionally extras like hard-boiled eggs, pineapple-blueberry cobbler and baked apples.

(508) 228-0500. www.nantucketlandfall.com. Eight rooms with private baths. Doubles, $110 to $310.

Cliff Lodge, 9 Cliff Road, Nantucket 02554.

This B&B's lofty rooftop deck is a great vantage point from which to enjoy a broad panorama of Nantucket Sound as well as the brilliant colors of sunrise and sunset. The 1771 sea captain's house in a residential neighborhood overlooking town and harbor offers twelve guest quarters, designed for comfort and decorated with a summery, beach look. Bedrooms are notable for spatter-painted floors, Laura Ashley wallpapers, frilly bedding, fresh flowers and antiques. Many have kingsize beds and fireplaces, and all have telephones and TVs nicely built into the walls or concealed in armoires. A main-floor apartment offers a kingsize bedroom, a queen sofabed in the living room, kitchen and private porch. Few B&Bs have so many neat places to sit and relax, inside or out. There are five sitting rooms on three floors, plus the rooftop deck, reading porches and a couple of brick patios beside lovely gardens. Innkeeper Sally Beck serves a buffet breakfast in one of the sitting rooms, or guests can adjourn to the side patio, where she matches the tablecloths with the flowers that are in bloom. Fresh fruit, cereal, muffins and Portuguese toasting bread are typical fare. Hot or iced tea and snacks like cucumber sandwiches and homemade cookies are offered in the afternoon.

(508) 228-9480. Fax (508) 228-0049. www.clifflodgenantucket.com. Eleven rooms and one apartment with private baths. Doubles, $195 to $280. Apartment for four, $450.

Nantucket Whaler Guest House, 8 North Water St., Nantucket 02554.

The harbor is on panoramic view from the newest penthouse suite at this hostelry launched in 2000 by two sophisticated women from Manhattan's Upper East Side. Buoyed by the success of their transformation of their original whaling captain's home into a luxury guest house, Calliope Ligeles and Randi Ott added the view suite and a guest room nearby at 4 Step Lane. The third-floor suite has a queen bedroom to go with the view. The Nantucket Yacht Club building and the Whaling Museum block water views from the original property, which concentrates its assets in the interior. As resurrected by the New Yorkers, the formerly rundown 1850 Greek Revival structure now has four studio rooms, three one-bedroom suites and three two-bedroom suites – all considered spacious by New York (and Nantucket) standards. Every suite has its own private entrance, and nearly all face a back yard landscaped with rhododendrons, antique roses and lilies. Suite 2 is the most private, with its own little white porch facing a quiet cobblestone street. Suite 4, the most romantic, has lovely views of the garden. Studio 7 occupies an entire corner of the second floor and opens onto an outdoor deck. Bedrooms are lavished with flowers, well-chosen antiques, fine linens and plush robes, and towels for the beach. The early American and English country furnishings, are augmented by modern conveniences like TV/VCRs, CD players, wet bars, refrigerators, microwaves and toaster ovens. No breakfast is included, but you can make your own or the owners will supply the makings in a "lite bite basket" ordered beforehand.

(508) 228-6597 or (800) 462-6882. Fax (508) 228-6291. www.nantucketwhaler.com. Five rooms and seven suites with private baths. Doubles, $325 to $425. Suites, $400 to $650.

The Veranda House, 3 Step Lane, Box 1112, Nantucket 02554.

Three wraparound verandas yield water views from this venerable hotel, reborn in 2003 from the old Overlook Hotel. Perched astride a small hill that rises above North Water Street and gave Step Lane its early name, the structure was nicely renovated as far as historic restrictions allowed by Ethan Devine, grandson of recent owners. Its 25 hotel-style rooms range from small and rustic with shared baths in the original 19th-century style to large and luxurious retreats with private balconies overlooking the harbor. None have telephones, let alone jacuzzi tubs, but a few have plasma-screen TVs and air conditioning. Beds in a variety of configurations from twin to kingsize are decked out in Frette linens and down comforters. Rooms are minimally furnished in light colors and decorated with antique photos. Best for water-lovers are four on the third floor with private baths and harbor views, especially queensize Room 23 with its own veranda (a feature repeated in the kingsize Room 11 on the second floor). Four other rooms on the third floor claim water views from their shared bathrooms. All guests get to see harbor views from the verandas that wrap around each floor. They also share a TV in the common room, and a European-style breakfast of frittata or quiche, cereals, fruits and cheeses.

(508) 228-0695. Fax (508) 374-0406. www.theverandahouse.com. Eighteen rooms with private baths and seven rooms with shared baths. Doubles, $135 to $165 shared, $175 to $350 private. Closed mid-October to mid-April.

Brass Lantern Inn, 11 North Water St., Nantucket 02554.

This in-town B&B is closest to the ferry docks – a consideration for luggage-toting visitors without cars. Redecorated by owner Michelle Langlois, the nine older guest rooms in the front of the 1846 Greek Revival house vary in size and two share a bath. All have the telephones and TVs common to all the rooms, and most beds are queensize. Rooms here are named for sailing ships. We stayed in one of the luxury rooms named for flowers in a two-story garden annex built by the contractor-son of a former innkeeper. Especially nice here are the two extra-large rooms with cathedral ceiling, queensize bed, and sitting area with two white wicker chairs, a skirted table and a sofabed. Guests have access to a living room with antiques and oriental rugs. A continental breakfast of granola and baked goods is served in a first-floor dining room restored with chair rail and recessed panel wainscoting or outside on the garden patio. Hors d'oeuvres are offered in the late afternoon, and the innkeeper throws a garden cocktail party on summer Saturdays.

(508) 228-4064 or (800) 377-6609. Fax (508) 325-0928. www.brasslanternnantucket.com. Fifteen rooms with private baths and two rooms with shared bath. Doubles, $165 to $325. Closed mid-December to February.

Cobblestone Inn, 5 Ash St., Nantucket, 02554.

There's a harbor view from the living room of the third-floor suite in this 1725 house beside a cobblestone street, which is also close to the ferry docks. Innkeeper Robin Yankow and her attorney husband Keith built an addition and in effect "turned the house around" to create more space for their growing family and better accommodations for their guests. What had been a tiny guest room on the third floor became a living room for the new suite, formed by joining it with another bedroom. They also added a room with queensize bed and an outdoor patio in a former shed. A second-floor room with a queen poster bed has a "split" bathroom with a chimney between. TVs, telephones and central air conditioning are other attributes of the guest quarters, whose wide-plank floors, narrow closets and tilted doorways testify to their age. All are nicely furnished with period pieces. Guests gather for continental breakfast, including fruit, cereal and homemade muffins or fruit breads. They also have access to a stocked pantry room off the kitchen.

(508) 228-1987. Fax (508) 228-6698. Three rooms and one suite with private baths. Doubles, $185. Suite, $250.

Union Street Inn, 7 Union St., Nantucket 02554.

This restored 1770 house, now a luxury B&B, offers twelve spacious accommodations close to downtown, the harbor and ferry docks. Rooms come with antique furnishings, scatter rugs on the original wide-plank pine floors and cable TV. The designer wallpapers, canopy beds, Frette linens and fluffy duvets convey elegance Six rooms have working fireplaces, including a suite with queen canopy bed, mini-fridge and sitting room with VCR and telephone. Another premier room has a king poster bed and fireplace. Others have queensize or two twin beds, except for one with a double bed. Because of its zoning, the Union Street can offer more than Nantucket's highly regulated continental breakfasts. Owners Ken and Debbie Withrow serve things like scrambled eggs and bacon, blueberry pancakes, french toast made with challah bread and, every fourth day, eggs benedict. The repast is taken in a large dining room or at three handsome garden tables on the side patio beneath an ivy-covered hillside.

(508) 228-9222 or (800) 225-5116. Fax (508) 325-0848. www.union-street-inn.com. Eleven rooms and one suite with private baths. Doubles, $275 to $410. Suite, $445. Closed December-March.

The Wharf Cottages, 1 Old South Wharf, Box 1139, Nantucket 02554.

Twenty-two harborfront cottages on Swain's and Old South wharves were nicely refurbished by the Walter Beinecke-inspired company that formerly owned the White Elephant and the Harbor House. They now are operated by its successor, Nantucket Island Resorts, which added eleven condo-style Harborview Cottages – many with water views – on the street leading up to the wharves. Celebrities often rent the Wharf Cottages by the month or season and three-night minimums are the norm in season, but single nights may be available (by chance and without reservations). Some transformed from old fishermen's shacks, the 22 cottages vary from studios to three bedrooms, and are right on the water amidst all the yachts in the boat basin. Each has a queensize master bedroom, kitchenette/dining and living area, telephone and cable TV. Some have skylights, living rooms with decks over the water, and brick patios. As the brochure says, "you're part of the scene, right on the harbor," with boats and boat people traipsing by, for better or worse.

(508) 228-1500 or (800) 475-2637. Twenty-two cottages. Studio and one-bedroom cottages, $280 to $630 daily. Two- and three-bedroom cottages, $430 to $940 daily.

On the Water, Out of Town

The Wauwinet, 120 Wauwinet Road, Box 2580, Nantucket 02554.

This restored "country inn by the sea" is among the most posh in New England. Boston developers Stephen and Jill Karp, longtime Nantucket summer homeowners, spared no expense in turning the age-old Wauwinet House into the ultimate in taste and comfort. The location is without peer – a private, parkland/residential area on a spit of land with the Atlantic surf beyond the dunes across the road in front, the waters at the head of Nantucket Harbor lapping at the lawns in back. Our room, one of 25 in the inn, was not large but was nicely located on a third-floor corner facing the harbor so that we were able to watch spectacular sunsets at night. It had a queensize bed with lace-trimmed pillows, wicker and upholstered armchairs, and a painted armoire topped with a wooden swan and two hat boxes (one of the inn's decorating signatures). All the rooms we saw had different, striking stenciled borders (some turning up in the most ingenious places), interesting artworks and sculptures, and such fillips as clouds painted on the ceiling. The deluxe rooms with kingsize or two queen beds included bigger sitting areas, but many did not seem to be as fortuitously located as ours. Every room holds a TV/VCR, tapes for which may be ordered from a library of 500, along with a bowl of gourmet popcorn. Courtyard cottages across the road contain five more guest accommodations. One is a four-bedroom cottage with kitchenette and fireplace. The inn's main floor harbors a lovely living room and library done in floral chintz, a back veranda full of wicker that you sink into, **Topper's** restaurant (see Where to Eat) and a small, classy lounge. A full breakfast is included in the room rate. Guests may order any item from strawberry and rhubarb pancakes to egg white omelet with spa cheese and fresh vegetables. Outside, chairs are lined up strategically on the back lawn, a croquet game is set up, drinks and snacks are available at a small beachside grill, and two tennis courts are tucked away in the woods. You can swim from a dock or a beach along the harbor, or walk a couple of minutes from the hotel through the dunes to the most gorgeous, unoccupied and seemingly endless strand on the Atlantic coast.

(508) 228-0145 or (800) 426-8718. Fax (508) 325-0657. www.wauwinet.com. Thirty-three rooms and two cottage suites with private baths. Doubles, $500 to $1,020. Cottage suites, $1,025 to $2,300. Four-night minimum in summer. Closed late October to early May.

The Summer House, 17 Ocean Ave., Box 880, Siasconset 02564.

Ten romantic, rose-covered cottages of the old school and an atmospheric restaurant present an idyllic oceanfront scene worthy of Bermuda on the south side of 'Sconset, as the islanders call it. Under a canopy of trees and ivy, the cottages are sweetly decorated with colorful wallpapers, eyelet-embroidered pillows, lace curtains, English antiques and such. Interesting roof lines, painted floors and chests, stained glass, leaded windows, stenciling, and little nooks and crannies add to the charm. Contemporary as can be are the newly remodeled bathrooms, all with marble jacuzzis. The Jimmy Cagney cottage, where the actor frequently was ensconced, offers two bedrooms, one with a kingsize bed with real ivy growing over it and another smaller room with a queen bed. Cottages have one or two bedrooms, two have kitchens, one has a sitting room and another a working fireplace (that's Penrose, which we found particularly attractive with barnwood walls, arched pickled wood ceilings and a kingsize bed). Our quarters had no good place to sit except on the front patio, where we felt rather on display as customers paraded up the path to the veranda-fronted main house, which houses the inn's office and a restaurant for dinner. A pianist entertains in the sophisticated restaurant (see Where to Eat). Continental breakfast is served on the veranda here to overnight guests. The property includes a heated pool halfway down the bluff across the road, beside the dunes leading to the open Atlantic, where the beach extends for miles in either direction. Guests enjoy tennis privileges at the Sconset Casino, a private club.

(508) 257-4577. Fax (508) 257-4590. www.thesummerhouse.com. Seven cottage rooms and suites and three two-bedroom cottages with private baths. Cottages, $575 to $675 for two, $775 to $925 for four. Closed January-March.

The Wade Cottages, Sankaty Avenue, Siasconset 02564.

Rooms, apartments and cottages are offered in this venerable, family-run summer compound atop 'Sconset's North Bluff, with a private beach below. Among the community's few public accommodations, they maintain the graciousness and informality of the village's summer homes. Old-fashioned chairs on the spacious lawn afford magnificent ocean views. Room guests are served continental breakfast in the Card Room of the beautiful main house, some of which is still occupied by the hospitable Wade family. Accommodations range from guest rooms with private or shared baths to apartments of one to four bedrooms (one with the tiniest kitchen ever) and housekeeping cottages with three to five bedrooms. Guest rooms look spare and cool with dark stained wood floors and simple bedspreads and decorating. The Greenhouse cottage is right on the water with great views of dunes and ocean. There's a play yard for children. The parking lot consists of crushed clamshells and the entire complex is enclosed in privet hedges.

(508) 257-6308. Fax (508) 257-4602. www.wadecottages.com. Eight rooms, six apartments and three cottages. Rooms, $145 to $240, three-night minimum. Apartments, weekly $1,840 to $2,840. Cottages, weekly, $2,970 to $3,670. Closed November-April.

Seeing and Doing ————————————— ⟋⟋⟋⟋⟍

What you do in Nantucket depends somewhat on where and how long you're staying. Daytrippers and weekenders generally remain close to Nantucket town. Those staying longer and those with cars can explore the island. Here is a sampling of its attractions.

Touring

Getting Around. Cars are discouraged, except for homeowners and those staying a long time. The heart of town is congested, streets are narrow and some are one way, parking is limited and the cobblestone streets are rough on the shock absorbers. Bicycles and mopeds are the preferred means of getting around, other than on your own two feet. You can rent a car in town from Affordable Rentals, (508) 228-3501 or (877) 235-3500; Nantucket Windmill Auto Rental, (508) 338-1227 or (800) 228-1227, and Young's Bicycle Shop, (508) 228-1151. Hertz, Budget and Thrifty and Nantucket Island Rent-a-Car, (800) 508-9972, offer car rentals at the airport. On one two-night working trip, we rented a clunker (and we do mean a clunker) for 48 hours (noon to noon) and covered all the island that we didn't walk or bike. There are taxis and the Nantucket Regional Transit Authority shuttle buses, and more bicycles and mopeds than you can honk your horn at.

SIGHTSEEING TOURS. The island is big enough and daunting enough that most first-timers need some orientation. **Barrett's Tours,** 20 Federal St., (508) 228-0174 or (800) 773-0174, offers three 90-minute bus tours daily, with stops in Siasconset. **Nantucket Island Tours,** Straight Wharf, (508) 228-0334, boards passengers on its mini-bus for an hour-long, 30-mile journey around the island. Operating as **Ara's Tours,** (508) 221-1951, photographer Ara Charder covers 30 miles of the island on 90-minute van tours three times daily and stops, of course, for photo-ops.

Informative walking tours are led by docents of the **Nantucket Historical Association**, (508) 228-1894. They start at the Nantucket Whaling Museum and cover the development of the downtown core from a Colonial outpost into an international whaling port and today's seasonal resort. The 90-minute tours are offered Monday-Saturday at 10:15, 11:15, 1:15 and 2:15 and Sunday at 2:15, Memorial

Day to Labor Day, and daily at 2:15 from Labor Day to Columbus Day. The $15 fee includes admission to the whaling museum.

Ninety-minute walking tours ($10) are led by **Dirk Gardiner Roggeveen,** (508) 221-0075, a twelfth-generation Nantucketer and island historian. He goes "where the buses don't," through hidden alleys and byways, all the while spinning tales of Nantucket lore. **Robert Pitman Grimes,** (508) 228-9382, also a Nantucket native, entertains visitors with interesting tidbits about island history on a nearly two-hour tour of the island in a suburban van. Ninety-minute van tours are offered three times daily by Gail Nickerson Johnson of **Gail's Tours,** (508) 257-6557. **Great Point Natural History Tours** are offered by the Trustees of Reservations, (508) 228-6799. The three-hour guided tour over ten miles of barrier beach includes a climb to the top of Great Point Lighthouse; adults $30, children $15.

BICYCLING. Bikes or mopeds are the best way to see the outskirts of Nantucket town (the cobblestone streets of downtown pose a problem there), and are a good way to get out to Surfside Beach. The ride is flat, on a path bordering the roadway. The most popular trip is out the bike path bordering the road to Siasconset, an easy (make that boring) eight-mile straightaway past the airport with the wind generally from behind. The beguiling east-end village perched on a rose-dotted bluff is very different from busy Nantucket town. The sand dunes, the turquoise ocean, the golf courses and the birds a-twitter between vine-covered cottages present "a magical setting like that of Bermuda," as a Summer House manager reminded us. Instead of retracing your path, return via the winding, sometimes up-and-down loop road past Sankaty Light, Quidnet and Polpis. Here you'll see cranberry bogs and ponds, striking homes and rolling moors, and you'll get a feel for the real island. The real island is also sensed from the bike path out to Madaket and you get the same kind of ups and downs and arounds on the pleasant, paved path beside the road – rather than being in the road, as on the Polpis loop.

Bikes and mopeds may be rented in the vicinity of the ferry landings from **Nantucket Bike Shop, Young's Bicycle Shop** and **Cook's Cycle Shop,** and from **Island Bike & Sport** at 25 Old South Road.

Church Tower Tour, First Congregational Church and Old North Vestry, 62 Centre St., is billed as Nantucket's "most unique tour." Church officials say that you get a bird's-eye view of town and can see the entire island from the church tower atop Beacon Hill. Open Monday-Saturday 10 to 4, mid-June to mid-October.

On or Near the Water

Nantucket Harbor Cruises, Straight Wharf, (508) 228-1444. If you've already arrived by ferry, this may seem redundant, but at least you find out what you were looking at. Lobstering cruises leave at 9:30 daily June to September; shoreline sightseeing cruises are offered three times in the afternoon and a sunset cruise is offered in the evening. Finally, at the end of the day, leaving at 8:45 from July 1 to Aug. 31 is a Harbor Lights cruise of 45 minutes. Costs range from $12.50 to $25.

SAILING trips are available through a number of enterprises based along Straight Wharf. Capt. James Genthner of **Endeavor Sailing & Excursions,** (508) 228-5585, offers a variety of cruises aboard his 31-foot Friendship sloop Endeavor. His 90-minute sails range from $25 to $35 per person. Themed trips with music, often with a fiddle player on board, are offered in the evening. Capt. Blair Perkins of **Shearwater Excursions,** (508) 228-7037, offers 90-minute eco-tours and wildlife excursions on a 26-foot catamaran.

BOAT RENTALS are available through Nantucket Boat Rental, (508) 325-1001; Nantucket Harbor Sail, (508) 228-0424, and Nantucket Kayak Rentals, (508) 228-7499.

FISHING CHARTERS. At least nine outfits offer sport-fishing trips. **The Albacore,** Straight Wharf, (508) 228-5074, has been involved in the catching of three world-record bluefish. Capt. Marc Genthner takes fishermen out on the **Just Do It Too,** (508) 228-7448. Several surfcasting charters are offered for the more adventurous.

BEACHES. The north shore beaches facing Nantucket Sound tend to be calmer and more tranquil than those facing the open ocean. On the south shore, the waters from the Gulf Stream are warmer (up to 75 degrees in summer), the ocean bottom slopes more gently and the beaches are wider. Just north of town is **Jetties Beach,** the best all-around for calm waters and named for the jetties that jut out into the ocean from its sandy shore. Bathhouses, lifeguards and a snack bar are available. **Children's Beach,** closer to the center off Harbor View Way, reflects its name and has a playground. More secluded and harder to reach on the north shore is **Dionis,** a harbor beach sheltered by dunes and favored by snorkelers and children. On the south shore, our favorite all-around is **Surfside,** four miles south of town. It has lifeguards, a food concession, bike racks, changing areas and an impressive surf – the beach is most expansive, of course, at low tide. Less crowded and more private is **Siasconset Beach,** a pleasant strand along the east shore. Heavy surf is featured at **Nobadeer, Miacomet** and **Cisco** beaches on the south shore. The beaches at **Great Point, Coskata** and **Coatue** are popular with those who can get to them, either by boat or jeep. At the island's west end is **Madaket,** a great place for sunset-watching and isolated beaching; here the water deepens rapidly.

Wildlife Refuges. Twenty-one miles of ocean, harbor and sound shoreline are protected by the Coatue, Coskata-Coatue and Great Point-Nantucket national wildlife refuges. Mainly barrier beaches, marshes and dunes, they harbor a variety of birds, shellfish and even jackrabbits. Visitors are welcome, but are warned that swimming may be dangerous. Coatue is part of the Nantucket Conservation Foundation, which has protected more than 6,100 acres of the island. Great Point is a remote and desolate stretch, reached by jeep or foot. You'll see clamming and oyster ponds, eagle and tern nesting grounds, and bayberry forests as you cross the dunes to the ruins of America's oldest working lighthouse, now being restored.

Other Attractions

Historic Nantucket. Dating to 1659 when Thomas Macy arrived as the first settler, Nantucket town has more than 2,400 historic houses, an extraordinary total. About 800 structures predate the Civil War (including several from the late 1600s), the greatest such concentration in the country. Walk up Main Street for a look at the impressive Three Bricks, Georgian mansions built by whaling merchant Joseph Starbuck. Twelve buildings of special significance are open to the public by the **Nantucket Historical Association,** 2 Whalers Lane, (508) 228-1894. They include two museums and five period houses of different eras. On the outskirts, don't miss the Oldest House (1686) on Sunset Hill, the Old Mill (1746) and the Old Gaol (1805). Buildings are open mid-June to Labor Day, Monday-Saturday 10 to 5 and Sunday noon to 5; shorter hours in spring and fall. Tickets may be obtained individually or in combination; adults $15, children $8.

Nantucket Whaling Museum, 15 Broad St.
The association's Whaling Museum is the town's largest attraction, as befits a community that was a major whaling port. That heritage is detailed in the inviting

red-brick building, a former candle factory, just off Steamboat Wharf. The museum opened in 1930 as an outgrowth of the private collection of summer resident Edward F. Sanderson and has expanded since. (It closed in 2004 for a year's restoration, reopening with a new "museum center" orientation and gallery building joining it to the Peter Foulger Museum next door). The Whaling Museum's extensive exhibit includes a 43-foot finback whale that washed onto the north shore in 1967, an eighteen-foot whale jaw, what's said to be the only candle press in existence, the original lens from the Sankaty lighthouse, a room full of a world-renowned collection of scrimshaw, whalecraft shops, whaling implements and whalers' finds, along with portraits and memorabilia of those who made Nantucket the third largest port in the United States at the time. Lectures on the history of whaling are scheduled three times a day. You leave the rambling structure via an outstanding museum shop.

(508) 228-1894. www.nha.com. Open daily 10 to 5, Memorial Day through October; weekends 11 to 3 in fall and spring. Adults $10, children $6.

Maria Mitchell Association, 1 Vestal St.

This complex consists of the birthplace of America's first woman astronomer, a small aquarium, a museum of natural history, an observatory and a science library. The woman who discovered the Mitchell comet was raised on Nantucket. Her home remains as it was in 1818 and features the only public roofwalk on Nantucket. Next door is a memorial observatory. The museum of natural history is housed in the Hinchman House, 7 Milk St. It contains many living island reptiles as well as preserved birds and fauna. Marine life indigenous to Nantucket's salt marshes and harbors is displayed in the quaint aquarium on the harbor at 29 Washington St.

(508) 228-2896. Open Tuesday-Saturday in summer, 10 to 4. Combination tickets: adults $10, children $7.

Nantucket Life Saving Museum, 158 Polpis Road.

This fascinating place is said to be the only one of its kind in the world. The new museum building is a re-creation of the original Surfside Station, built by the U.S. Life Saving Service in 1874. The drama of rescue at sea is presented through photos, original boats and life saving equipment, quarterboards of vessels wrecked around Nantucket and more. Featured are items recovered from the Italian liner Andrea Doria, which sank more than 40 years ago off Nantucket's southeast coast. Also exhibited is the top of the original Great Point Light and the original 1856 Fresnel lens from the Brant Point Lighthouse.

(508) 228-1885. Open daily 9:30 to 4, mid-June to Columbus Day. Adults $5, children $2.

SHOPPING. Nantucket is a paradise for shoppers, and every year new stores open (residents bemoaned the arrival of Benetton, the first mainland chain store other than the old Country Store of Concord and Crabtree & Evelyn, both of which passed muster). Fine small shops, boutiques and galleries are scattered along the wharves, Main Street and side streets. Specialty stores with names like **Nobby Clothes, Beautiful People, Nantucket Panache** and **The Cashmere Shop** compete with the more traditional like **Murray's Toggery Shop** and **Mitchell's Book Corner.** Among standouts are **Zero Main** for suave women's clothing and **Lilly Pulitzer Shop** for colorful apparel, **Rosa Rugosa** for painted furniture and household decorative items, and **Nantucket Looms,** with beautiful, whimsical woven items and a sweater in the window for "only $1,000." **The Lion's Paw,** one of the nicest gift shops we've seen, is too elegant for words; we especially like its pottery lines. **The Spectrum** is good for arts and crafts and **Claire Murray's** is a fantastic shop for hand-hooked rugs. **Majolica** offers colorful hand-painted Italian ceramics, and **L'Ile**

de France has china, pottery, collectibles and clothing. **The Hub** newsstand and sundry store on Main Street is a local institution.

Other local institutions are Nantucket faded pink pants ("Nantucket reds") worn by men, while women tote Nantucket's famed lightship baskets on their tanned arms. The baskets come in assorted shapes and sizes, and are carried in many shops. The Nantucket Lightship Basket Makers & Merchants Association produces an informative brochure, "A Guideline to Buying a Nantucket Lightship Basket." At **Michael Kane Lightship Baskets,** we looked at a small $800 number without the ivory, but decided to pass.

Where to Eat ———————————— *♪♪♪*

For an island with a year-round population of 10,000 (augmented by up to 50,000 high-livers and free-spenders in the summer), Nantucket has an amazing variety of good restaurants. Even the summer-long vacationer would be hard-pressed to visit them all – and might go broke in the process. Most of the top restaurants require or advise reservations; a few don't take them. Here we concentrate on those nearest the water, or those with a particularly summery air.

Straight Wharf Restaurant, Straight Wharf, Nantucket.

Chef Marian Morash of television and cookbook fame put this harborfront restaurant on the culinary map, but Steve and Kate Cavagnaro have kept it there. The Cavagnaros, owners of the much-acclaimed Cavey's restaurant in Manchester, Conn., spend the summer in Nantucket, he in the kitchen and she out front. The interior is a pristine palette of shiny floors and soaring, shingled walls topped by billowing banners and hung with striking paintings by an island artist. Beyond is a canopied, rib-lit deck overhanging the harbor, the place to eat if you want to be right beside the water. The other "in" place is the noisy side bar and grill, with crowds usually spilling outside onto a terrace in front. The same kitchen serves both, with a sophisticated seafood menu in the dining room and deck and more rustic, casual grill fare in the bar. We've tried both venues, and each has its place. Starters are standouts, among them the signature smoked bluefish pâté with focaccia melba toasts, a rich lobster bisque heavily laced with sherry, seared beef carpaccio with shards of parmigiano-reggiano, white truffle oil and mesclun, and local black bass with a vegetable mignonette. A sauté of halibut with lobster and morels and grilled rare tuna with white beans, escarole and roasted garlic proved excellent main courses. Choices range from pan-roasted local cod with clams and smoked sausage to rosemary-grilled rack of lamb with eggplant and lamb cassoulet. The dessert specialty is warm Valrhona chocolate tart with orange cardamom gelato.

(508) 228-4499. Entrées, $31 to $39. Dinner by reservation, Tuesday-Sunday 6 to 10:30. Open Memorial Day to late September. Grill, $16 to $22, no reservations.

The Galley on Cliffside Beach, 54 Jefferson Ave., Nantucket.

Nantucket diners have no better beachfront location than in this restaurant with a canopied, flower-lined deck right beside the ocean. Rimmed with red geraniums and hanging plants, the blue wicker chairs and white tablecloths make an enticing setting against a background of azure water and fine sand. We thoroughly enjoyed a couple of the best bloody marys ever before a lunch of salade niçoise and chicken salad Hawaiian. A jazz pianist plays at night, when the place conveys a clubby air. Executive chef Steven Polowy's seafood-oriented dinner menu ranges from pan-roasted halibut with a caviar beurre blanc, served over tiny French green lentils, to roasted lobster and local shellfish with riesling-braised leeks, fire-roasted baby corn and "young" potatoes. The only meat options on a recent menu were filet mignon with bordelaise sauce and basil-infused lamb loin. Start with the signature New England clam chowder with smoked bacon, a lobster spring roll, cornmeal-crusted calamari or shrimp tempura with Asian slaw. Finish with homemade cognac ice cream, blood orange meringue tart or chocolate-soufflé cake. Retired owner Jane Currie Silva's sons David, who used to be sous chef, and Geoffrey, the mâitre-d, oversee the front of the house.

(508) 228-9641. Entrées, $29 to $45. Lunch daily in summer, 11:30 to 2. Dinner nightly, 6 to 10, early June to mid-September.

Brant Point Grill, 50 Easton St., Nantucket.

A large harborfront terrace beside the pool – with a feeling rather like that of a yacht club – makes the restaurant at the White Elephant another good bet for lunch. At a recent visit, both the lemon angel-hair pasta with Nantucket scallops, lobster, shrimp and roasted artichokes and the asparagus salad with lobster and salmon caviar (for a cool $16) appealed. A light menu is available day and night, and a raw bar is featured in late afternoon on the terrace. The restaurant is billed as Nantucket's premier steak and seafood house, featuring native lobster, prime aged beef and gourmet chops. The casually elegant dining room occupies several levels, some with water views through a gently curved wall of large windows. You might start with a chilled shellfish sampler, kobe beef tartar or lime-marinated tuna atop a green wakame salad. Expect main courses like tuna steak rubbed with fennel and coriander, grilled swordfish with mushrooms and sherry beurre blanc, crisp Long Island duck with vanilla rum glaze, veal loin chop or chargrilled filet mignon enhanced with a house-made dried cranberry sauce. Desserts vary from a chocolate turtle cake on caramel-pecan sauce to cranberry bread pudding with citrus curd. The changing trio of sorbets is served in an edible cookie cup.

(508) 325-1320. www.brantpointgrill.com. Entrées, $28 to $45. Lunch daily, noon to 2:30. Dinner nightly, from 6. Closed late October to mid-April.

Oran Mor, 2 South Beach St., Nantucket.

Former Wauwinet executive chef Peter Wallace took over the old Second Story restaurant space with windows toward the harbor and renamed it for a Gaelic phrase meaning "Great Song," which is also the name of his favorite single-malt scotch. Three small, off-white dining rooms with seafoam green trim are dressed with paintings by local artists. Peter considers it a soothing backdrop for international cuisine that is at the cutting edge. For starters, we liked his champagne risotto with sweetbreads and wild mushrooms, and his Asian fried quail with sticky rice. Expect other choices like tuna tartare with essence of celery and ossetra, a Thai littleneck clam hot pot with somen noodles and a salad of soft-shell crab over field greens. Main courses vary from grilled halibut with chorizo and mahogany clam sauce to roast rack and grilled leg of lamb with mashed fava bean bruschetta. The grilled duck breast with local nectar jus is considered the best duck dish on the island. We enjoyed the seared tuna with shallot jus and spinach, and grilled swordfish with orange and black sesame seed butter. Wife Kathleen's desserts include fresh fruit croustade in a tulipe, quenelles of chocolate mousse topped with pralines, and molten chocolate cake with a trio of ice creams.

(508) 228-8655. Entrées, $25 to $34. Dinner nightly in season, 6 to 10. Closed Sunday-Wednesday in winter.

Topper's at the Wauwinet, Wauwinet Road, Nantucket.

Things sure have changed since the Wauwinet opened in the mid-1800s as The

Wauwinet House, a restaurant serving "shore dinners." Lunch on the outdoor terrace or dinner in the light and airy dining room here as the sun sets over Nantucket Bay is a special treat. For water lovers, an extra perk is boat service aboard the **Wauwinet Lady,** which takes people from downtown out to Topper's for lunch or dinner. The traditional à la carte service in the dining room was eliminated in 2004 in favor of prix-fixe dinners, $78 for three courses and $95 for six courses. Topper's bar offers light, casual meals daily from noon to 11. Executive chef Christopher Freeman's menu is creative and ever-changing. We liked the grilled quail on a toasted brioche and the mustardy lobster and crab cakes for starters. Typical main courses are a signature Nantucket lobster stew, caramelized sea scallops with french green lentils and seared foie gras vinaigrette, roast duck with seared black plums and rhubarb chard, and a superior roast rack of lamb with potato-fennel brandade. A seven-vegetable napoleon pleases vegetarians. The wine list, featuring more than 800 vintages and 18,000 bottles, is a consistent winner of the Wine Spectator Grand Award. After a meal like this, the homemade ice creams and sorbets appeal to us more than the richer pastries that catch many an eye. Service is friendly, the water comes with a lemon slice, the bread is crusty, and everything's just right. Could be that the location puts one in the proper frame of mind. Be advised, however, that many tables in the two side-by-side dining rooms don't get a water view. For that, you may just have to return for lunch on the terrace.

(508) 228-8768 or (800) 426-8718. Prix-fixe, $78 for three courses. Lunch, Monday-Saturday noon to 2. Dinner nightly, 6 to 9:30. Sunday brunch, noon to 2. Closed late October to mid-May.

The Chanticleer, 9 New St., Siasconset.

Renowned across the world for world-class dining, this elegant French restaurant on two floors of a large 'Sconset cottage has been considered tops since Jean-Charles Berruet acquired it in 1969. À la carte lunch (entrées $25 to $28) in the outdoor garden, at tables beneath trellised canopies of roses and beside impeccably trimmed hedges, is a 'Sconset tradition, as is an after-dinner drink accompanied by piano music in the beamed and nautical **Grille Room,** formerly the Chanty Bar. Amidst heavy silver and pretty floral china, dinner is served in the lovely fireplaced dining room opening onto a greenhouse, in the Grille or upstairs in a pristine peach and white room. Regulars put themselves in the hands of a knowledgeable staff to steer them to the right choices on an ambitious and complex menu. For appetizers, we liked the lobster and sole sausage poached with a puree of sweet red peppers and the oysters served in a warm mussel broth topped with American sturgeon caviar. From a choice of six entrées, the Nantucket-raised pheasant, stuffed with mushrooms and ricotta, and the roasted tenderloin of lamb served with a venison sauce were superb. The award-winning wine cellar contains 1,200 selections.

(508) 257-6231. www.thechanticleerinn.com. Entrées, $42 to $45. Prix-fixe, $75. Lunch in summer, Tuesday-Sunday noon to 2. Dinner, Tuesday-Sunday 6:30 to 9:30. Closed Monday, also Tuesday and Wednesday in off-season. Reservations and jackets required except in the Grille. Closed mid-October to May

The Summer House Restaurant, 17 Ocean Ave., Siasconset.

A more romantic setting for dining could scarcely be imagined than the front veranda of this low-slung, Southern-style house or its summery interior dining room. It's a mix of white chairs and painted floors, good 'Sconset oils and watercolors on the whitewashed walls, and fresh flowers and plants everywhere. We chose one of the handful of tables on the veranda yielding a view of the moon rising over the ocean that we could hear lapping at the foot of the bluff across the road. The setting remained etched in our memory longer than our dinner, which was more ordinary than the tab would have suggested. Reports suggest the food has improved lately. Typical appetizers might be a smoked salmon, lobster and scallop sausage with black caviar, and a spring roll of goat cheese, citrus, mint and snap peas with fennel and watercress. Assertive, complex flavors continue in such entrées as tuna nori and Szechuan seared tuna with tempura lobster tail, tangerine soy emulsion and grapefruit-braised greens; amandine roast trout and littlenecks with asparagus and truffle risotto, and grilled beef tenderloin with a jonah crab cake, marrow-crusted potato roesti and elephant garlic crème fraîche. A brandy tart with dollops of whipped cream, blueberries and slices of kiwi proved a memorable choice for dessert. Our meal was enlivened by piano music that makes you want to linger over one of the island's largest selections of single malts, cognacs and ports. Lunch is available at the **Beach Café** on a landscaped terrace beside the pool, sequestered halfway down the bluff in the dunes above the beach. Everything's pricey, but there's a good selection and the burger is advertised as the best on the island.

(508) 257-9976. www.the-summer-house.com. Entrées, $32 to $48. Café: Lunch daily in summer, 11:30 to 3; light menu and cocktails, 3 to 8. Restaurant: Dinner nightly in summer, 6 to 10:30. Closed Monday and Tuesday in off-season and mid-October to mid-May.

The Rope Walk, 1 Straight Wharf, Nantucket.

A serious restaurant or a singles bar? This establishment can't seem to make up its mind, or at least the customers can't. But you can't get much closer to the water than on the outdoor patio on the wharf, or for that matter the two interior dining rooms, where management says they serve more than 200 people daily for both lunch and dinner in season. No reservations are taken, and the scene gets crowded. If you can get in, and if it's not too noisy, you may be well satisfied with the grilled seafood and meats, some with creative twists. Consider some of the recent offerings: sofrito-baked swordfish with sweet and sour pepper relish, seafood jambalaya, halibut provençal and steak frites with herb butter. Starters are more basic: fried calamari, steamers, fried oysters with rémoulade sauce and Portuguese-style mussels.

(508) 228-8886. www.theropewalk.com. Entrées, $21.50 to $28. Lunch daily in summer, 11 to 3. Dinner nightly, 5:30 to 10. Closed November-April and Monday-Wednesday in off-season.

Bosun's Bistro, Old South Wharf, Nantucket.

Formerly the site of the Morning Glory Café (home of the famed morning glory muffin), this remains a good place for breakfast as well as for a casual lunch or dinner. It offers sheltered outdoor patio seating and an intimate interior (make that very). It's a wonder how the small kitchen can produce the variety it does, starting in the morning with a spicy "firecracker omelet" and raspberry-stuffed french toast. Lobster rolls are featured at lunch. At night, Bosun's short menu might begin with warm tomato bruschetta and a fire-roasted artichoke with roasted garlic and an assertive cracked-pepper and lemon aioli dipping sauce. Colorful and edible flowers garnish the entrées, among them sautéed jumbo shrimp, sesame-coated salmon fillet, grilled swordfish and rack of lamb. The chicken breast might be stuffed with spinach, crabmeat and smoked gouda cheese and sauced with sherried tomato cream sauce. Dessert favorites include New York-style cheesecake and a dense, heart-shaped brownie served on caramel sauce.

(508) 228-7774. Entrées, $18.95 to $27.95. Breakfast daily, 8 to 11. Lunch, noon to 2:30. Dinner nightly, 6 to 10. Closed mid-October to June.

FOR MORE INFORMATION: Nantucket Island Chamber of Commerce, 48 Main St., Nantucket, MA 02554, (508) 228-1700. The visitor information center is at 25 Federal St., (508) 228-0925. www.nantucketchamber.org. or www.nantucket.net.

Rockport's Motif No. 1 is on view front and center from Greenery restaurant.

Cape Ann, Mass.

Cape Ann is Massachusetts's quieter cape, as residents like to compare it to the better-known Cape Cod. A protuberance jutting into the Atlantic north of Boston, it is a heady mélange of rocky shores and sandy beaches, of working harbors and artist colonies, of quiet villages and a quirky city.

In 1604, French explorer Samuel de Champlain sailed into Gloucester Harbor and called it Le Beauport – "the beautiful harbor."

You can sense a uniqueness to the area when you arrive at Gloucester Harbor and spot the tourists gathered at the famous bronze statue, The Man at the Wheel, commissioned in 1923 in memory of the 10,000 Gloucester fishermen lost at sea. All around are the sights and smells of a true working harbor, the nation's first fishing port and still one of its largest. This is a city of 29,000 that clings to its roots, as depicted in the book and movie, *The Perfect Storm*.

Rockport, beyond Gloucester at the very tip of Cape Ann, is more of a village and a seasonal resort. Discovered by artists – and tourists – after the Civil War, it defines the word quaint, especially around Dock Square and famed Bearskin Neck, where centuries-old fishing shacks have been converted into art galleries, shops and restaurants.

Visitors are drawn to Cape Ann by the rocky coast more typical of Maine and a pervasive sense that this area is "different." That's certainly true of Gloucester, from its ungussied-up waterfront to the bohemian air of Rocky Neck, which calls itself the nation's oldest arts colony and looks it, to the oceanfront mansions of Eastern Point and Bass Rocks. Follow the self-guided Gloucester Maritime Trail to experience some of the many facets of America's oldest working seaport.

And there's no town quite like Rockport. Aptly named and an early producer of granite, it's a "dry" town in which Sunday evening band concerts are the major entertainment. An unassuming fishing shack on the wharf, called Motif No. 1, is outranked as an artist's image only by the Mona Lisa. Country lanes and charming homes hug the coast in neighborhoods from Land's End to Pigeon Cove. The twin lighthouses on Thacher Island are on view from houses and inns along winding Marmion Way. Yachts can be glimpsed from the narrow streets along the water in the quiet, English-looking hamlet of Annisquam.

On Cape Ann, you have a choice of inns or motels closer to the ocean and more affordable than at many East Coast destinations. The same goes for restaurants. There are good beaches, parks and picnic areas. Just offshore are two of the best whale feeding grounds in the Northeast, giving Cape Ann claim to being the Whale Watch Capital of the World. Attractions include museums, art galleries and historic sites.

Is it any wonder that those who live on Cape Ann think they have it all?

Getting There

Cape Ann is located about 30 miles northeast of Boston. By car, Route 128 and Route 133 lead to the Cape from U.S. Route 1 and Interstate 95. Commuter trains run from Boston to Rockport, one of the few shore towns that still has train service.

Where to Stay ⎯⎯⎯⎯⎯⎯⎯⎯⎯⎯⎯⎯ ⟋⟍⟋⟍

Inns and B&Bs

The Charles Hovey House, 4 Hovey St., Gloucester 01930.

The first summer house built in Gloucester (1845), this glowing peach-amber, Tuscan-style villa atop a bluff has a spectacular view of Gloucester harbor and an air of elegance and romance. "Why, even my 83-year-old mother said it was romantic, so it must be," quipped innkeeper Jane Daniel, owner with her husband, Robert Nickse. It's also elegant, from the marble fireplace and crystal chandelier in the living room, strikingly furnished in white, to the fine antiques throughout the house. "We're collectors," says Jane, "so the decor is always changing." At our visit, the master bedroom had a unique silver-chromed brass headboard behind the queen bed, a loveseat beside the working fireplace, a circular table in the front window overlooking the harbor and one of the eye-catching art deco bathrooms typical of the house, this one with a six-foot-long soaking tub. The front Lincoln Room was named for the antique carved double bed similar to one in the White House, according to Jane's father, retired White House correspondent Jim Daniel. It is part of a suite, with a funky bathroom on the lower level of the belvedere and a sitting room with a wraparound view on the upper level. The rear Ladies' Suite with sitting room and fireplace contains examples from Jane's oriental fan collection as well as portraits of favorite women behind the hefty brass queen bed. A simpler, rear ground-floor room with a quilt-covered queen poster bed has more of an early American look and paintings of seascapes to compensate for the lack of a water view. The dining room is enveloped in a wraparound mural of early Gloucester. Here is where Jane, a self-described "lifelong compulsive cook," puts out a breakfast buffet

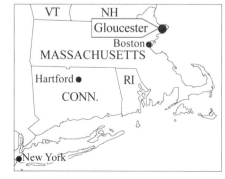

spread of regional treats. In addition to the usual preliminaries, you might find codfish cakes with baked beans and yankee corn pudding, blueberry crêpes or a frittata. In good weather, guests like to take it out to the wide front porch. There, Jane says, "they get mesmerized by the view" and find it hard to leave. We know.

(978) 281-7732. Fax (978) 281-7745. www.hoveyhouse.com. Three rooms and two suites with private baths. Doubles, $135 to $275.

The Inn at Babson Court, 55 Western Ave., Gloucester 01930.

It took seven years for Paul Jensen, a former theater set designer, and Donald Roby to restore this house across the street from the Gloucester harbor, and one visit to their rambling B&B will show you why. The building, dating to the 1600s and with multiple additions in its evolution as a four-family house, is a fantasyland of comfortable efficiency suites favored by families. Enter in back through an atrium and ahead is a wall of bookshelves. One section with a strategically placed doorknob swings open to reveal the front Fitz J. Babson Suite, a ground-floor space with a view from the parlor, a queen bedroom and the galley kitchen typical of each suite. The oldest section holds the side Cut Stevens Suite, a knockout space all in gray, from chairs to bedcovers, with a maze of rafters beneath the vaulted ceiling of original weathered pine, a loft sleeping area reached by a spiral staircase and a bathroom paneled in mahogany. The more feminine Nancy Proctor Suite in the rear has a lace canopy queen bed, a nursery, a living room with kitchen area and a deck overlooking the cloistered courtyard rose garden, where a fish pond gurgles and morning glories climb the trellis. The place has character, not the least of which is innkeeper Paul, whose eyes twinkle as he relates that "if you're good, really good," the muffin bunny will leave a basket of goodies at your door in the morning. He adds, "this house really envelopes you. We have five ghosts, and they only appear in the daytime." At night, what with all the decorative theatrics, they might lose their way.

(978) 281-4469. Fax (978) 281-3214. www.babsoncourt.com. Three efficiency suites with private baths. Doubles, $175 to $200.

Harborview Inn, 71 Western Ave., Gloucester 01930.

A pleasant little fountain garden and porch enhance the front of this three-story house up against the street, across from the harbor. The interior of the house, built in 1839 by descendants of the famed Gortons of Gloucester Seafood, is a beauty as well. Before John and Marie Orlando opened it as a B&B, it was decorated in 1994 by Better Homes and Gardens for coverage in one of its decorating editions. Four rooms have harbor views and all have TVs and telephones. Each floor contains a suite. The Magnolia on the top floor with queen bed and two futons in the sitting room and the Gloucester on the second floor with queen bed and fireplace offer the best views of the harbor. The main-floor Golub has a king bed and a sitting room with hand-painted wall murals. A continental breakfast is offered in the morning.

(978) 283-2277 or (800) 299-6696. www.harborviewinn.com. Three rooms and three suites with private baths. Doubles, $99 to $129. Suites, $149 to $159.

Eden Pines Inn, 48 Eden Road, Rockport 01966.

You can't get much closer to the ocean than on the rear patio that hovers over the rocks at this delightfully secluded B&B by the sea. The lodge-like front parlor with stone fireplace, the California-style side breakfast porch with white wicker furniture and picture windows, the rear porch full of wicker lounge chairs with a neat brick patio below, even a couple of bathroom windows take full advantage of the water view across to Thacher Island and its twin lighthouses. All six of the unusually spacious guest rooms upstairs come with idyllic private balconies overlooking the ocean. Four have king or queen beds and the others have two queen or two double beds. Decorator fabrics and marble baths are the norm. Owners Nicky and Michael Kern put out a self-serve continental breakfast, as well as mid-afternoon tea, lemonade and setups for drinks, along with cookies, wine and cheese. There are few more picturesque places for partaking than the patio with wicker lounge chairs smack beside the ocean.

(978) 546-2505. www.edenpinesinn.com. Six rooms with private baths. Doubles, $210. Closed January-March.

Seacrest Manor, 99 Marmion Way, Rockport 01966.

Guests get a sweeping ocean view from the spacious second-story sundeck above the gracious living room of this elegant, weathered-gray mansion in a prosperous residential area. They also get beautiful lawns and gardens and a breakfast to remember. Dwight B. MacCormack Jr., who has run the B&B since 1972, pampers guests in six rooms and a two-bedroom suite, most with ocean views. Each has twin/king or queen beds, color television, a clock radio, a couple of chairs and a desk, and numerous amenities, from bedside mints to overnight shoe shines. The living room, where afternoon tea is served, has a masculine feel. There are leather chairs, dark colors and fine paintings, as well as exquisite stained glass and tiny bottles in the bow windows through which the ocean may be glimpsed. The formal dining room is decked out in fancy linens, Wedgwood china and crystal glasses at five tables for a breakfast that Town & Country magazine called one of the 50 best in America. It begins with fruit cup and fresh orange juice, continues with spiced Irish oatmeal and bacon and eggs, and ends with a specialty like blueberry or apple pancakes, french toast or corn fritters. The two-acre property provides flowers for the numerous bouquets scattered about the inn as well as plenty of places for guests to relax and enjoy the ocean air.

(978) 546-2211. www.seacrestmanor.com. Six rooms and a two-bedroom suite with private baths. Doubles, $185 to $215. Suite, $185, or $98 individually with shared bath. No credit cards. Closed December to March.

Emerson Inn By the Sea, 1 Cathedral Ave., Rockport 01966

Rockers are lined up facing the ocean on the back porch of this recently renovated and grandly pillared Federal-style inn. One of a number of old-fashioned establishments in Rockport, this has been infused with a new energy and spirit by owners Bruce and Michele Coates. Rooms are in two sections on several levels, none of which seems to connect with the others, and reflect their 160-year-old heritage. The prime accommodations are eleven deluxe ocean-view rooms with kingsize beds and spa tubs. Two have small electric fireplaces and two have balconies – the one with both is "the best room in the house," says Bruce. The broad rear lawn leads to a small saltwater swimming pool at the edge of the ocean bluff. The spacious "grand salon" lobby holds a grand piano and a buffet table with a platter of cookies and coffee and lemonade in thermos jugs. Breakfast and dinner are served in **The Grand Café** (see Where to Eat). A full breakfast is included in the rates in season. Breakfast is continental in the off-season.

(978) 546-6321 or (800) 964-5550. Fax (978) 546-7043. www.emersoninnbythesea.com. Thirty-six rooms with private baths. Doubles, $145 to $379.

Yankee Clipper Inn, 96 Granite St., Box 2399, Rockport 01966.

One of Rockport's larger and older inns, the Yankee Clipper takes full advantage of a remarkable setting on a bluff, with beautifully landscaped lawns on a bit of a point jutting into the ocean. Randy and Cathy Marks took over the 1929 art deco Georgian mansion in which the Yankee Clipper got its start and now offer more contemporary rooms in the Quarterdeck next door as well. Six of the inn's rooms, all named after clipper ships, yield full ocean views – some bordering on the spectacular from sun porches or decks. Everyone shares a beauty of a deck off the third floor. The Quarterdeck, built in 1960 beside the water, features even more dramatic views. It has a knockout penthouse on the third floor with two double beds, a sofabed and velvet chairs facing floor-to-ceiling windows onto the ocean. Two ground-floor oceanfront lodgings look across gardens to the open sea. The inn's main floor holds a grandly furnished living room. The new owners closed the former restaurant on the porch to concentrate on functions. But the porch setting was retained for overnight guests, who enjoy a full breakfast in summer and a continental breakfast in the off-season. A heated saltwater pool is hidden from public view beneath the road on the landscaped, terraced grounds between the main inn and the Quarterdeck.

(978) 546-3407 or (800) 545-3699. Fax (978) 546-9730. www.yankeeclipperinn.com. Thirteen rooms and three suites with private baths. Doubles, $199 to $389. Three-night minimum weekends in summer.

The Captain's House, 69 Marmion Way, Rockport 01966.

A fabulous location at water's edge commends this white stucco mansion, billed as "a comfortable and casual guest house" by owner George Dangerfield. There's a wraparound porch, part of it open to the ocean and the rest enclosed for a library and TV. Inside are a huge parlor with beamed ceiling and fireplace, and a handsome dining room that catches a glimpse of the ocean. Two of the five upstairs bedrooms are particularly large, and those in front yield the best views. Each is done in turn-of-the-century wallpaper and has hand-creweled embroidery on the valances and reproduction Williamsburg furnishings. Sour cream blueberry coffeecake, muffins and fruit breads are served for continental breakfast in the dining room or on the porches, where guests "feel closer to the water," George says. They really feel close to the water in the lounge chairs spread out on neat little cement patios nestled here and there among the rocks along the craggy shore.

(978) 546-3825 or (877) 625-7678. www.captainshouse.com. Five rooms with private baths. Doubles, $150. Closed in January. Two-night minimum weekends.

Seaward Inn, 44 Marmion Way, Rockport 01966.

Facing the ocean on attractive grounds full of gardens, lawn chairs, boulders and stone fences, this complex includes the weathered main inn, a couple of outbuildings and four cottages generally rented by the week. Although refurbished, the last are likened to "the cottage you remember as a child," according to owner Nancy Cameron-Gilsey, daughter of the couple that ran the place for more than 50 years. The main inn offers ten old-fashioned rooms furnished with period pieces, vintage maple bureaus and desks, and the TVs and telephones common to all the accommodations. Adjacent is the Carriage House and Gull's Nest complex with five rooms, a pair of two-room suites with ocean vistas from new decks, and an oceanfront cottage. Other accommodations are in single or multi-unit, pine-paneled cottages with granite terraces. Guests may swim in a small spring-fed pond with a sandy beach, surrounded by beach chairs, situated on the property. Or they can enjoy the view of Sandy Bay from the lawns in front The **Sea Garden Restaurant** in the main inn serves breakfast (included in the rates) and dinner to the public (see Where to Eat).

(978) 546-3471 or (877) 473-2927. Fax (978) 546-7661. www.seawardinn.com. Fifteen rooms, two suites and six cottage units with private baths. Doubles, $149 to $239. Cottages, $179 to $324. Closed November to mid-April.

Motels

The Atlantis Motor Inn, 125 Atlantic Road, Gloucester 01930.

Rarely do you find waterfront motels so attractively situated as this and its neighbor, the Bass Rocks Ocean Inn. The ocean is right across the scenic shore road in a quiet, posh residential area known variously as Bass Rocks or Gloucester's Back Shore. At the Atlantis, 40 rooms on three floors look out at the surf crashing against the rocky coast. All basically the same, they have two double beds, Scandinavian modern furnishings and outdoor balconies. Those on the higher floors yield better views. Breakfast is available in the solarium coffee shop, furnished in rattan, which looks onto the ocean as well. There's a large pool and Good Harbor Beach is nearby.

(978) 283-0014 or (800) 732-6313. www.atlantismotorinn.com. Forty rooms. Doubles, $150 to $180. Closed November-April.

Best Western Bass Rocks Ocean Inn, 107 Atlantic Road, Gloucester 01930.

Handsome in brick, this white-columned Georgian Colonial style motor inn is of 1960s vintage. The sun porch of the adjacent 1899 Stacy mansion, accented with antiques and listed on the National Register, is the site for a complimentary cold breakfast buffet for overnight guests. Cookies and coffee or lemonade are served in the living room. Now affiliated with Best Western, it is run by fifth-generation hoteliers who have updated all the guest rooms with modern trappings while maintaining their traditional character. Rooms on two floors look across lawns and gardens onto the ocean. Sliding glass doors open onto balconies or porches. There's a small heated pool. Other amenities include a billiards room, a library and a rooftop sun and observation deck on the widow's walk atop the mansion. Some guests fish for striped bass off the rocks out front.

(978) 283-7600. Fax (978) 281-6489. Forty-eight rooms. Doubles, $155 to $285. Closed November-April.

Cape Ann Motor Inn, 33 Rockport Road, Gloucester 01930.

You can't get closer to the beach in Gloucester than at this motor inn, where the balconies literally hang over the southern end of Long Beach, an area flanked by summer cottages. The curving strand, one of Cape Ann's finest, literally is at your doorstep. And you've got free beach parking, to boot. Built in 1973 of dark brown wood, the three-story motel has fifteen efficiencies among its rooms. All rooms have one double bed, plus a sofabed and the usual motel amenities – plus sliding doors onto balconies over the sand, not far from water's edge. A fireplace takes the chill off cool mornings in the motel's new lobby, where a continental breakfast is complimentary. The motel's airy honeymoon suite is touted as the area's most luxurious. It boasts a kingsize bed, fireplace, hot tub, kitchen, entertainment center and "automated curtains."

(978) 281-2900 or (800) 464-8439. www.capeannmotorinn.com. Twenty-nine rooms and one suite. Doubles, $145. Efficiencies, $160. Suite, $250.

Good Harbor Beach Inn, 1 Salt Island Road, Gloucester 01930.

Right at the northern edge of Good Harbor Beach is this little compound, described by its owner as "like an old-time motor lodge." Its looks to us more like a cross between attached cottages and motel, especially out front as the units tiptoe unpretentiously up the hill. In back, the word "cute" could apply as the lodgings face every which way in buildings at different angles and none appears exactly the same. Each unit has a porch or balcony, and seven have better views than the others, since some are partially obstructed by those in front. Each has two double beds, TV and a refrigerator.

(978) 283-1489 or (877) 327-4355. www.goodharborbeachinn.com. Seventeen rooms with private baths. Doubles, $114 to $119. No credit cards. Closed November-March.

Captain's Bounty Motor Inn, 1 Beach St., Rockport 01966.

You can hear the surf rolling onto sandy Front Beach from the rooms at this no-frills oceanfront motel at the northern edge of downtown Rockport. There are two extra-large efficiency suites, each with two double beds and a sofabed, plus seven efficiency rooms. The rest are standard motel units. Each has a balcony with a head-on view of Sandy Bay. Front Beach has a raft for diving and a lifeguard on duty in summer. The rates – given the location – represent good value.

(978)-546-9557. Twenty-four rooms. Doubles, $130. Efficiencies, $145 and $160. Two-night minimum weekends. Closed November-April.

Bearskin Neck Motor Lodge, 64 Bearskin Neck, Rockport 01966.

New owners have upgraded this small motel, beautifully situated near the far end of Bearskin Neck. Rooms are on two floors and are rather basic, each with two double beds except for one with one double bed. The balconies are narrow and double as entry corridors, at least for the second floor. But there's a large common sundeck behind the adjacent gift shop and office, where continental breakfast is complimentary in the morning. And there's free parking – a premium amenity around here, according to co-owners Jack J. Byrd Jr. and Anthony Mancini. The rocky shoreline is outside your back door, and the shops of Bearskin Neck are out front.

(978) 546-6677 or (877) 507-6272. Eight rooms. Doubles, $149 to $159. Closed late October to late April.

Seeing and Doing

Gloucester, established in 1623 as the first fishing outpost in the Massachusetts Bay Colony, wears without pretension its title as America's oldest seaport. It's a busy, working, rather rough-edged city. Rockport is smaller, more refined and more touristy. Both have noted art colonies and close ties to the water.

On or Near the Water

WHALE WATCHING. Two of the world's best whale-feeding grounds, Stellwagen Bank natural marine sanctuary and Jeffrey's Ledge, are ten to twelve miles out to sea off Gloucester and Rockport. More than 500 finback, humpback, minke and right whales are said to migrate there annually.

Four major operators lead expeditions out of Gloucester. The oldest, **Cape Ann Whale Watch,** 415 Main St., (978) 283-5110 or (800) 877-5110, claims the largest and fastest vessel, the speedy Hurricane II. It also claims the most historic base, Rose's Wharf, home of the movie "The Perfect Storm," with the famous Crow's Nest Pub across the street. **Seven Seas Whale Watch,** Seven Seas Wharf, (978) 283-1776 or (888) 283-1776, boasts the newest and most elegant vessel north of Boston. Others are **Capt. Bill's Whale Watch & Deep Sea Fishing,** 33 Harbor Loop, (978) 283-6995 or (800) 339-4253; and **Yankee Fleet Whale Watch,** 75 Essex Ave. (Route 133), (978) 283-0313 or (800) 942-5464. Most trips leave twice daily in season at 8:30 or 9 and 1:30 or 2 and take about four hours. Reservations are suggested or required. Adults pay about $30, children $18.

FISHING AND BOATING. In a leading commercial fishing port you'd expect to find a number of deep-sea fishing excursions available. The most are offered by the **Yankee Fleet** (see above), which include all-day, morning and afternoon options for haddock, pollock, cod and halibut as well as evening blue-fishing trips and offshore excursions of one, two or three nights.

The **Salty Dog Water Shuttle** (fare, $3) operates in summer around Gloucester Harbor from Harbor Loop, (978) 314-9233. Trips leave from the Public Landing at the picturesque little Solomon Jacobs Park, beside the harbor master's office and the U.S. Coast Guard Station. The shuttle stops at St. Peter's Park, Ten Pound Island, Rocky Neck and Cripple Creek.

Narrated land and sea tours are available aboard the jaunty new amphibious vehicle **Moby Duck,** 75 Essex Ave., (978) 281-3825. After a 20-minute tour around town, the vehicle splashes into the water for a 35-minute harbor tour. Billed as "a whale of a ride," trips leave the Harbor Loop on Rogers Street hourly from 10 to 4 in summer, weekends in early June and in September; adults $16, children $10.

The 65-foot **Schooner Thomas E. Lannon** gives two-hour sails around Gloucester Harbor from Seven Seas Wharf beside the Gloucester House Restaurant, (978) 281-6634. The impressive schooner was built in 1997 in nearby Essex and named for owner Tom Ellis's grandfather, a Gloucester fisherman. It sails four times daily in summer; adults $30, children $20.

The 61-foot **Schooner Appledore III** offers three 90-minute afternoon sails and a sunset cruise from Tuna Wharf on Bearskin Neck, Rockport, (978) 546-7540; adults $25, children $20.

Lobstering and Island Cruises. Capt. Fred Nelson, (978) 546-3642, takes up to 22 passengers out on his 38-foot boat, **Dove,** from Rockport's Tuna Wharf. He offers 90-minute lobstering trips showing how lobsters are caught, measured and banded, as well as one-hour sightseeing tours around the islands of Sandy and Thacher bays. In Gloucester, **Harbor Tours Inc.,** 9 Harbor Loop, (978) 283-1979, offers narrated Cape Ann Lighthouse cruises around Rockport and Gloucester harbors and the Annisquam River daily in summer at 10 and 2:30; adults $21, children $12.

The **North Shore Kayak-Outdoor Center** at 9 Tuna Wharf, Rockport. (978) 546-5050, rents kayaks and bicycles and offers guided sea kayak tours.

Essex River Cruises, Essex Marina, 35 Dodge St., Essex, (800) 748-3706. Some of Cape Ann's more interesting and scenic nature cruises are offered by the 49-passenger Essex River Queen II pontoon boat through a pristine saltwater estuary to areas unreachable by car. Participants view lobstering, clamming, fishing and other river activities. Highlights include Crane Beach, a pristine barrier beach, Crane Wildlife Refuge and Hog Island, now a haven for migratory waterfowl and deer. Five 90-minute sightseeing cruises leave daily, May-October; adults $21, children $10.

THE BEACHES. The shores of Gloucester and Rockport are blessed with at least nine public beaches. The biggest is **Good Harbor Beach** on Thacher Road, Gloucester, near the Rockport line. The half-mile barrier beach is protected by sand dunes and has a bathhouse and a snack bar. **Wingaersheek Beach,** an open, breezy strand off Atlantic Street, Gloucester, is a local favorite. Parking fees at each are in the $10 range.

In Rockport, swimming is fine at sandy **Front Beach** and pebbly **Back Beach,** almost side by side in the center of town. **Long Beach** near the Gloucester line is another good strand. We also like the relatively unknown **Cape Hedge** and **Pebble** beaches at Land's End, **Old Garden Beach** along Sandy Bay, and the **Lanesville Beach** north of town. Parking can be a problem, but we've always lucked out.

Halibut Point State Park, Gott Avenue off Route 127, Pigeon Cove. On a clear day, you can see Crane's Beach in Ipswich, the Isles of Shoals in New Hampshire and Mount Agamenticus in Maine from this 54-acre park along the rocky coast. In the middle of the park is an abandoned, water-filled quarry from which tons of granite made their way to some of the more notable buildings across the Northeast. The granite ledges left behind are stunning against the ocean backdrop. A small visitor center and museum tells the story of Cape Ann's granite industry. The park is popular with hikers, birders and sunbathers. Hike out to the rocks for a picnic dinner followed by one of the best sunset views ever. Open daily in season, 8 to 8; parking, $2.

On Shore

The self-guided **Gloucester Maritime Trail** details four scenic journeys, each about a mile long, covering high points around Gloucester Harbor. A tour map is available at the seasonal Gloucester "Welcoming" Center, nicely perched on a bluff at Stage Fort Park, where picnic tables, a playground and gazebo look onto the harbor, with Half Moon Beach below. Signposts make the entire circuit easy to follow.

The **Settlers Walk** tour covers Stage Fort (the oldest defenses in the Massachusetts Bay Colony) and Stacy Boulevard/Western Avenue, site of the Man at the Wheel fishermen's memorial, a statue made famous in the movie, "Captains Courageous." It was sculpted by Leonard Craske in 1923 in his Rocky Neck studio on the occasion of the city's Tercentennial.

The **Downtown Heritage Trail** encompasses some of the city's oldest homes and landmarks, starting at St. Peter Square, site of the annual St. Peter's Fiesta and Blessing of the Fleet, which the local Portuguese celebrate with gusto. This trail includes the interesting **Harbor Loop** with the emerging **Gloucester Maritime Heritage Center;** the Fitz Hugh Lane House, the granite home of the famed seascape painter on a knoll with benches overlooking the water; the harborside Solomon Jacobs Park, and the 121-foot fishing Schooner Adventure (the last of Gloucester's great Grand Banks fishing schooners, open to the public on weekends). Here also is the Gloucester Marine Railways, part of the oldest continuously operating boatyard in America and a site used for the shore-side filming of Sebastian Junger's bestseller, "The Perfect Storm." Also on the Harbor Loop is the emerging Gloucester Maritime Heritage Center.

Farther out Main Street, the **Vessels View** tour focuses on the Inner Harbor, the headquarters and processing plant of Gorton's frozen fish products, aromatic (make that very) fishing docks and the eight-acre Jodfrey State Fish Pier. Along the way on Rogers Street opposite Rose's Wharf is the **Crow's Nest Pub,** gathering spot for crew and family featured in "The Perfect Storm." It was here that Ethel Shatford bade farewell to her son Bobby, lost at sea along with all hands aboard the ill-fated Gloucester fishing vessel Andrea Gail in a wild storm in 1991. Junger rented a room above this waterfront bar while he researched his book. Nearby is the beautiful Our Lady of Good Voyage Church, home church for Portuguese-American fishermen and their families.

In East Gloucester is **Painters Path,** which starts at the venerable North Shore Arts Association headquarters and traces the footsteps of famous artists along East Main Street and Rocky Neck, the oldest continuously working art colony in America. The neck protrudes out into Gloucester Harbor, creating Smith's and Wonson's coves and holding many a cottage and gallery.

Not part of the Maritime Trail but worth a look are the oceanfront mansions along Eastern Point and Bass Rocks, some of Cape Ann's most expensive real estate.

In **Rockport,** the charms extend far beyond Bearskin Neck, the mecca for tourists. You'll want to get out to the rocky point at the end of the neck for a panoramic view.

Or you can rest on a couple of benches off T-Wharf and admire Motif No. 1. The Rockport Rotary Club sign beckons, "This little park is just for you, come sit a while and enjoy the view."

Walk the **Old Garden Path** along the shore off Atlantic Avenue, past the Headlands and Old Garden Beach. Another, more rugged walk is the **Atlantic Path**, starting at Cathedral Rocks off Granite Street in Pigeon Cove. You'll find that Rockport is appropriately named – it has the rocky look of the Maine coast, in contrast with the sand dunes associated with most of the Massachusetts shore. Country lanes lined with wild flowers interspersed between interesting homes hug the rockbound coast and crisscross the cliffs and headlands in the area south of town known as Land's End. We like the California look of Cape Hedge Beach from the heights at the end of South Street, the twin lighthouses on Thacher Island as viewed from Marmion Way, and the ocean views all around Cape Ann, particularly the narrow streets along the water in picturesque Annisquam (stop for a lobster roll on the deck right over the water at the Lobster Cove).

THE ARTISTS. Gloucester and Rockport have drawn artists since the end of the Civil War, and by 1900 Rockport in particular became the place for artists to spend their summers painting. They set their easels up by the shore, watch the sea and coastline and capture the beauty of Cape Ann at all times of day and year. The more famous among them include Winslow Homer, Childe Hassam, Edward Hopper, Fitz Hugh Lane, Paul Manship and Milton Avery. Artists and their followers are clustered around Rocky Neck in East Gloucester and Bearskin Neck in Rockport.

The **North Shore Arts Association**, 197 Main St., East Gloucester, (978) 283-1857, exhibits paintings, sculpture and graphics of members in its two-story, barn-red structure on Reed's Wharf. Founded in 1922, it offers maps listing the homes of famous artists. Three major exhibits are mounted annually. Nearby is the **Rocky Neck Art Colony,** the oldest in the country. You'll know you're there when you see **The Ice Cream Gallery.** Located along Rocky Neck Avenue and down alleys and wharfs are countless galleries – most small, esoteric and, given their setting, ever so picturesque.

The **Rockport Art Association** at 12 Main St., Rockport, (978) 546-6604, offers changing exhibits and demonstrations year-round. Founded in 1921 as a means to exhibit their works, it has more than 250 artist members, most of whom live in Rockport. It also sponsors a four-week chamber music festival in June. Nearby is **Bearskin Neck,** the rocky peninsula that juts into the harbor, which was the original fishing and commercial center of the town. Today, most of the weather-beaten shacks have been converted into galleries, shops and eateries of every description. Arty photo opportunities abound as glimpses of Sandy Bay and the Inner Harbor pop up like a changing slide show between buildings and through shop doors and windows.

SHOPPING. Tourists tend to gravitate to the shops and galleries in Rockport, while Gloucester's downtown Main Street serves the needs of residents. But the latter has some choice destinations, especially **Pisces** at 96 Main for gifts and handicrafts, including nifty glass birds from Finland. **Stone Leaf** at 57 Main is another good shop.

In Rockport, T-shirt and souvenir shops abound on Bearskin Neck. Main Street and the Dock Square area generally have better stores. Colorful fused glass plates in the window drew us into **Square Circle,** where we marveled at incredible porcelain depictions of antipasto platters, fruit salad and the like, done by a woman from Virginia. We also liked the wares at **Too Fortunate Pottery. La Provence** offers great items from the South of France. The **Madras Shop, Enchanted Lady** and **Sand Castles** are known for clothing. Sportswear is offered by the new **Mark, Fore & Strike,** Rockport's first "chain" store. Proceeds from the well-stocked **Toad Hall Bookstore** in the old Granite Savings Bank building further environmental causes. Interesting casual clothing and jewelry are offered at **Willoughby's**, which has a cozy café in back.

Hannah Wingate House, two shops across the street from each other, and **Woodbine Antiques** are among the better antiques shops. The **Granite Shore Gallery** specializes in maritime art, decoys and fishing collectibles. Other good galleries include **An Artful Touch, Correale Gallery** and **Mosher Gallery.**

Historic Attractions

Beauport, 75 Eastern Point Blvd., Gloucester.

Interior designer Henry Davis Sleeper started building his summer home by the ocean in 1907 to house his collection of decorative arts and furnishings and just kept adding on. The result is a fantasy home of towers and gables that's as interesting inside as outside. Most of the 40 rooms are small, but each is decorated in a different style or period with a priceless collection of objects. Sleeper designed several rooms to house specific treasures: the round, two-story Tower Library accommodates a set of carved wooden draperies from a hearse; the Octagon Room matches an eight-sided table. One of the breakfast tables in the Golden Step Room is right against a window that overlooks Gloucester Harbor. After Sleeper's death in 1934, Beauport was purchased by Charles and Helena McCann, heirs to the Woolworth fortune. They preserved intact nearly all of his decorative schemes and arrangements. Their descendants gave Beauport to the Society for the Preservation of New England Antiquities as a public museum.

(978) 283-0800. Guided tours 10 to 4, Monday-Friday mid-May to mid-September, daily mid-September to mid-October. Adults $10, children $5.

Hammond Castle Museum, 80 Hesperus Ave., Gloucester.

Cross the drawbridge and be serenaded by pre-recorded organ music in this replica of a medieval castle. It was built in the late 1920s by inventor John Hays Hammond Jr. to house his collection of Roman, medieval and Renaissance art and objects. Visitors view the largest organ ever built in a private home. Its 8,200 pipes rise eight stories above the cathedral-like Great Hall. They also visit the unusual Renaissance dining room, Gothic and early American bedrooms, and an exhibit showing some of the inventions and patent models of a man reputed to be America's greatest inventor after Thomas Edison. Marbled columns and lush plantings watered by the castle's own rain system are on view in the Courtyard.

(978) 283-7673. www.hammondcastle.org. Open daily 10 to 5, Memorial Day to Labor Day; Saturday-Sunday 10 to 3, rest of year. Adults $8.50, children $5.50.

The Sargent House Museum, 49 Middle St., Gloucester.

This handsome, high-style Georgian house above the harbor was built in 1782 for Judith Sargent Murray, philosopher, writer, social activist and early champion of equal rights. She was the first woman to self-publish, the first woman playwright and the first woman to have a play produced on stage. Her recently discovered personal letters, many penned in rooms here, give a new eyewitness account of Revolution-era history. Her husband, the Rev. John Murray, was the founder of Universalism in America. The house, furnished as it might have looked in 1790, features fine collections of early American furnishings and textiles, China trade porcelain, oil portraits and personal items, from bed warmers to shaving stands. Visitors also see works by artist John Singer Sargent, whose roots were in Gloucester. *(978) 281-2432. www.sargenthouse.org. Open Friday-Monday noon to 4, Memorial Day to Columbus Day. Adults $5.*

OTHER MUSEUMS. In Gloucester, the **Cape Ann Historical Museum** at 27 Pleasant St., (978) 283-0455, celebrates both the area's art and maritime heritage. It exhibits the nation's largest collection of paintings and drawings by Gloucester artist Fitz Hugh Lane as well as works by other Cape Ann artists, decorative arts and antiques. The museum also displays artifacts and photographs from the continent's most productive early fishing port as well as the history of the area's granite quarrying industry. Visitors may tour the furnished home of Captain Elias Davis, built in 1804. Open March-January, Tuesday-Saturday 10 to 5; adults $7, students $4.50.

In Rockport, **The Sandy Bay Historical Society and Museum** at 40 King St., (978) 546-9533, shows early furnishings, collections and exhibits on shipping, fishing, the local granite industry and Rockport history in the Sewall-Scripture House built of granite in 1832, a new wing and in the Old Castle, a 1715 saltbox at Granite and Curtis street. The museum is open Monday-Saturday 2 to 5 in summer, $3. The **James Babson Cooperage Shop** (1658) on Route 127 near the Gloucester line, a small one-story brick structure with early tools and furniture, may be the oldest building on Cape Ann (open Tuesday-Sunday 2 to 5 in July and August, free). In Pigeon Cove at 52 Pigeon Hill St. is the **Paper House,** built 50 years ago of 215 thicknesses of specially treated newspapers; chairs, desks and other furnishings also are made of paper (open daily 10 to 5, April to mid-October; adults $1.50, children $1).

Where to Eat

Rockport is dry, but most restaurants invite patrons to BYOB. Good restaurants with liquor licenses are located in Gloucester.

Gloucester

Passports, 110 Main St., Gloucester.

"Opening doors to World Food in Gloucester." That's the theme of this lively establishment in the nation's oldest seaport, heretofore locked in a culinary time warp. Gloucester's top-rated restaurant is located in a couple of side-by-side downtown storefronts a block from the harbor. It takes a global theme in its stunning chinaware edged in maps, their subtle salmon and sage colors matching the curtains, carpeting and tabletops. The global theme continues on the ever-changing menu, which ranges widely from Asian spice-crusted tuna and tilapia crusted with Egyptian nuts and spices to slow-roasted pork shanks with Jamaican jerk spices, rahm schnitzel and steak au poivre. Even the local lobster is prepared with flair: poached, then grilled with orange-tarragon butter and paired with an apple and red onion salad. We got an enticing taste of chef-owner Eric Lorden's gutsy cooking at lunch. The sushi rolls were terrific. So was an ample if unconventional cobb salad, not composed but rather tossed with mesclun greens. Best of all was the yellowfin tuna burger paired with an interesting pasta salad. Dessert choices included chocolate torte and crème brûlée, both fixtures on the menu, plus apple-pear crumb pie and chocolate layer cake laced with kahlua. All this good eating takes place in two convivial rooms with high, pressed-tin ceilings, a small bar and a semi-open kitchen.

(978) 281-3680. Entrées, $14.50 to $22.50. Lunch, Monday-Saturday 11:30 to 4:30. Dinner from 5:30, Sunday from 5.

The Rudder, 73 Rocky Neck Ave., East Gloucester.

You know that Gloucester's culinary situation is changing – along with Rocky Neck's revival proclaimed out front – when The Rudder condenses its tired menu of boring seafood into an enticing compendium of contemporary fare. "House of big flavor," one menu called it. Right on the water in a building that was once a fish cannery, it oozes history, including the notation that in 1783 this was the first condemned house in America, according to a marker out front. It was salvaged lately by owner Jeanne Boland and chef Chris Wheeler. Look for starters like lobster ravioli, tuna tartare and Italian-style mussels. Main courses range from fish and chips to rack of lamb. The sesame-coated tuna and porterhouse veal chop are house favorites. The interior is a charming mélange of funky antiques, gadgets and photos from around the world, with windows onto Smith Cove. There's a small outdoor deck in back.

(978) 283-7967. Entrées, $17.95 to $26.95. Dinner nightly in summer, 4 to 10, Saturday and Sunday noon to 10; fewer nights in off-season. Closed Columbus Day to May.

The Madfish Grille, 77 Rocky Neck Ave., East Gloucester.

This colorful place has the best waterfront location in town – at the end of a walkway lined with quirky galleries, on a pier stretching out over Smith Cove. It also has an exciting menu of contemporary fare to go with the view. Although service can be inconsistent, chef Rob Hartley's food generally gets high marks. Beyond an outdoor terrace is a lounge with floor-to-ceiling windows onto the water. Around back is a two-level dining room with a shiny hardwood floor, crazy art on the yellow shingled walls, an open-hearth fireplace in the middle and tables covered in white butcher paper over white cloths, many right beside the water. The menu is categorized by apps, greens, pizzettes, noodles and grains, and entrées. Among the latter are tamari-seared bluefin tuna, Creole-spiced black grouper, prosciutto-wrapped lobster tail, house-smoked Thai free-range chicken in garlic sauce and wood-grilled chuck roast of buffalo. We know folks who make a meal of appetizers like a spicy tuna carpaccio roll, crab and chive cream cheese rangoons with two dipping sauces and crispy pork pot stickers. Or they simply stop by for the house-smoked barbecue platter, a steak sandwich or a margarita pizza.

(978) 281-4554. Entrées, $16.95 to $26.95. Lunch daily, 11:30 to 5. Dinner nightly, 5 to 10. Closed November-April.

Lobsta Land Restaurant, 10 Causeway St., Gloucester.

Good food served in abundant portions draws the locals to this all-day, family-style restaurant squeezed between Route 128 and salt marshes with water views in the distance. Seating is at oversize polished wood tables in three pine-paneled dining areas, two in back with large windows yielding a view, and in a front bar-lounge. The varied menu covers all the bases, from soups, innovative salads and sandwiches to fried seafood platters and interesting entrées. At lunch, the "cup" of clam chowder arrived in a bowl and the house salad was a huge platter of mixed greens tossed with apples, cranberries and blue cheese. The crab cake sandwich with zesty rémoulade sauce came with french fries. At night, about a dozen specials supplement the regular offerings that range from beer-battered scrod and fisherman's stew to chicken marsala and, of course, several versions of lobster. Be sure to inquire about the "market price." The lobster roll we almost ordered turned out to be a staggering $17.95.

(978) 281-0415. Entrées, $8.95 to $17.95. Open daily, 7 a.m. to 9 or 10 p.m. Closed December-March.

Rockport

My Place By-the-Sea, 68 Bearskin Neck, Rockport.

You can't get much closer to the ocean than at this stylish restaurant at the end of Bearskin Neck, handsomely refurbished by chef Kathy Milbury and hostess Barbara Stavropoulos, co-owners. A two-level outdoor porch wraps around the intimate interior, with an open lower level resting right above the rocky shore and a smaller side level covered by an awning and enclosed in roll-down plastic "windows" for use in inclement weather. Besides its idyllic waterfront setting, My Place is known for some of the best, most innovative dining on Cape Ann. Chef Kathy applies global accents to such seafood specialties as the signature baked swordfish with a tangy béarnaise sauce and pecan butter, pan-seared szechuan salmon on an Asian noodle pancake, poached halibut with spicy ginger-soy vinaigrette, crispy arctic char with smoked mussel velouté and Portuguese fisherman's stew in a fiery brodo. Starters range from shrimp and scallop tempura to poached mussels. The daily seafood tasting is a rewarding choice. Favorites among desserts are warm chocolate cake with maple-walnut ice cream and coffee panna cotta with vanilla rum anglaise.

(978) 546-9667. Entrées, $21 to $29. Lunch daily, 11:30 to 4. Dinner, 4 to 9:30 or 10. Fewer days in the off-season and closed November to mid-April. BYOB.

The Grand Café, 1 Cathedral Ave., Rockport.

French doors open onto a screened porch for outside dining with an ocean view at the historic Emerson Inn's refurbished, hotel-style dining room run by ex-Florida restaurateurs Bruce and Michele Coates. Their chef provides contemporary as well as classic cuisine. Starters might be crab cakes with mango-basil mayonnaise, crispy sweet and sour calamari with Thai chile paste and – billed as the "ultimate lobster cocktail" – a chilled lobster martini with sundried tomato rémoulade. Entrées range from grilled swordfish with corn salsa to porcini-dusted lamb loin finished with goat cheese and balsamic vinegar. Dessert mainstays are chocolate lava cake and crème brûlée. All is elegantly served, accompanied by live piano music on weekends.

(978) 546-9500. Entrées, $22 to $28. Dinner by reservation, Wednesday-Monday 6 to 9. BYOB.

Sea Garden Restaurant, 44 Marmion Way, Rockport.

The dining room at the old Seaward Inn has a new look and a new cuisine. Gone are the nightly choice of two traditional entrées and the wall strung with clothespins that held guests' napkins with their names over the years. Now the summery, wraparound dining rooms seat 75 people for fine dining, according to owner Nancy Cameron-Gilsey. The menu opens with items like Maryland crab cakes with roquefort aioli, seared diver scallops and Asian slaw with wasabi oil, lobster salad with sweet potato chips, and a wild mushroom ragoût. The six entrées range from sesame-encrusted salmon with orange-soy glaze to grilled filet mignon with port wine demi-glace. The lazy lobster casserole is a house favorite. Typical desserts are chocolate fudge cake with crème anglaise and lemon berry crème.

(978) 546-3471 or (877) 473-2927. Entrées, $18 to $28. Dinner, Tuesday-Sunday 6 to 9:30, Wednesday-Sunday in off-season. Closed November to mid-April. BYOB.

The Greenery, 15 Dock Square, Rockport.

The artists' favorite Motif No. 1 is on view across the harbor from the rear of the L-shaped dining room in this casual, creative establishment. And the view from the new upstairs dining room is even better. Seafood and salads are featured, as is a salad bar and an ice cream and pastry bar out front. Otherwise the fare runs from what owner Amy Hale calls gourmet sandwiches to dinner entrées like grilled catfish with homemade tartar sauce, poached salmon with mustard-dill sauce, "bouillabaisse linguini" and roasted raspberry-glazed duck with mango chutney. At lunch time, we savored the crab quiche with a side caesar salad and the homemade chicken soup with a sproutwich. The last was muenster and cheddar cheeses, mushrooms and sunflower seeds, crammed with sprouts and served with choice of dressing. We liked the sound of the crab and avocado sandwich, now a menu fixture, and overheard diners at other tables raving about the lobster and crab rolls. Apple-cheddar and chocolate-bourbon pecan pies, linzer torte and cappuccino cheesecake are listed in the dessert repertoire, most of which is available to go.

(978) 546-9593. Entrées, $14.95 to $20.95. Open daily, 8 to 9:30, 8 to 7 in winter. BYOB.

Brackett's Ocean View, 27 Main St., Rockport.

This locally popular family restaurant is simple as can be, except for the sweeping view of the water on two sides of the main dining room tucked around to the rear and not visible from the entry. The all-day menu is priced right and contains some interesting fare, including grilled portobello salad and a cajun chicken rollup. More substantial fare includes broiled sea scallops, fried seafood platters, baked scrod au gratin, codfish cakes, chicken parmigiana and grilled liver and onions. Start with the crispy thin fried onion rings – the best anywhere, according to a local innkeeper. Desserts of the day could be grapenut custard pudding and strawberry-rhubarb pie.

(978) 546-2797. Entrées, $9.95 to $25.95. Lunch daily from 11:30. Dinner from 4:30. Closed November-March. BYOB.

Ellen's Harborside, 1 T-Wharf, Rockport.

Wholesome food, reasonably priced. That's the attraction at this plain-jane, local institution with a front counter and tables and a rear dining room overlooking the water. Crowds start lining up for supper at 4:30 for what other restaurateurs call "total value." Except for the fried seafood platter and prime rib, almost everything on the dinner menu is priced in the single digits. The breakfast special could be eggs benedict for $3.95. You can get a clam roll or a cubano sandwich along with more mundane fare for lunch. Dinners run from fried squid to mixed grill or a full rack of barbecued ribs. Desserts like cranberry-raspberry and orange-pineapple cream pies and pineapple-tapioca pudding are in the $2 range.

(978) 546-2512. Entrées, $7.95 to $15.95. Open daily, 11:30 to 9. Closed November-March.

The Lobster Pool at Folly Cove, 329 Granite St. (Route 127), Rockport.

For casual seafood with no frills beyond a view, head out of town to the north, just past Halibut Point. Sit at one of the picnic tables on the lawn overlooking Ipswich Bay and, on a clear day, you can see the coast of New Hampshire. You can order lobster, clam or crab rolls, fried seafood plates bearing fries and coleslaw, burgers, salads, homemade desserts and pies. The lobster roll, seemingly brimming with lobster meat until you find it puffed up with considerable lettuce underneath, comes on a properly toasted hot dog bun. There are tables inside but, as at most lobster pounds, the experience is best when you can eat outside.

(978) 546-7808. Entrees, $8.95 to $15.95. Open daily, 11:30 to 8:30, mid-May to mid-October. BYOB.

FOR MORE INFORMATION: Cape Ann Chamber of Commerce, 33 Commercial St., Gloucester, MA 01930, (978) 283-1601 or (800) 321-0133. www.capeannvacations.com. Rockport Chamber of Commerce, 3 Main St., Rockport, MA 01966, (978) 546-6575 or (888) 726-3922. www.rockportusa.com.

Pier at North Hero House faces Green Mountains across Lake Champlain.

The Champlain Islands, Vt.

Its promoters call this area Vermont's West Coast, an appellation that's appropriate. Viewed from Interstate 87 above St. Albans, deep green islands, large and small, fill the expanse of Lake Champlain beneath a backdrop of towering peaks as far as the eye can see. Every time we pass this breathtaking vista it reminds us of a similar panorama of the San Juan Islands, viewed from Interstate 5 above Washington's Puget Sound.

They also call Lake Champlain the inland sea, which is not that far-fetched. After the Great Lakes, Champlain is America's sixth largest freshwater lake, its cool, crystal-clear waters compressed between the Adirondacks to the west and the Green Mountains to the east. But for the presence of mountains and the lack of tidal ups and downs, you could imagine yourself near the ocean in Maine's Casco Bay or Nova Scotia's Mahone Bay.

Given the "West Coast" and "inland sea" attributes, it's amazing how undiscovered – and unspoiled – the Champlain Islands are. Although barely fifteen minutes north of Burlington, Vermont's largest city, and an hour's drive south of Montreal, the islands convey a sense of isolation. This 27-mile stretch of rural retreat in the middle of the Northeast's largest lake is something of a never-never land near the international border, too distant for most Americans and another country for Canadians. It has been spared the onslaught that tarnishes similar waterways within development distance of three million people. Grand Isle County, Vermont's smallest, claims a year-round population of 5,000, tourist accommodations built years ago, summer cottages and campgrounds, rolling farmlands and apple orchards, abundant shoreline, and not much else.

U.S. Route 2 is the main road through the islands, from South Hero through Grand Isle, North Hero and Alburg. The islands, incidentally, were part of a charter granted in 1779 to Ethan Allen, Ira Allen and others of the Green Mountain Boys.

The grant was given the name Two Heroes, referring to the Allens, and some people still refer to the area as "The Heroes."

These little-known islands are replete with history and their own identity, as attested by the 470-page history of the Town of Isle La Motte, one of the more remote islands. "There is a certain indefinable spell about it," wrote author Allen L. Stratton. "It is a quietness, a sense of peace."

The islands are long and narrow, never more than five miles wide and sometimes, as at the portage point the Indians named Carrying Place, only as wide as the road separating lake from bay. They're connected by causeways, bridges and a sense of both peace and place.

Getting There

The Champlain Islands are in northern Lake Champlain, stretching from about fifteen miles north of Burlington to the Quebec border. From Vermont, they are reached via U.S. Route 2 from Interstate 89 near Colchester or State Route 78 from Swanton. From New York, take the Champlain exit off Interstate 87 east to Rouses Point and Route 2, or the Grand Isle ferry from Plattsburgh. Bus service to the area is provided by Vermont Transit. Amtrak trains stop in Plattsburgh, and major airlines fly into Burlington and Montreal. However, this is an area where you'll need a car.

Where to Stay

Inns and B&Bs

The North Hero House, Route 2, North Hero 05474.

This old lakefront hotel began serving guests who arrived by lake steamboat in 1891. But it was left to new owner Walter Blasberg, a New York investment manager who had vacationed on nearby Butler's Island for 30 years, to transform a place that had seen better days into the leading waterfront hostelry it was meant to be. He and decorator Beverley Camp of our favorite Hero's Welcome store have outfitted the 26 guest quarters in what she calls "comfortable antique lodge style." Eight rooms and the plush Gov. Thomas P. Salmon Suite are on the second and third floors of the main hotel, across the road from the lake. The second-floor corner suite is a beauty with an iron canopy queensize bed, double whirlpool tub, living room with gas fireplace and french doors onto a screened porch, where a hammock and wicker chairs look toward the lake. Seventeen more rooms – twelve with porches and even closer-up water views – are in three buildings clustered along the lakeshore. Our old favorite Cobbler's suite on the lower level of the Cove House has a foundation of Grand Isle granite, the original door and fieldstone walls three to four feet thick.

A tiled floor accented with oriental rugs leads to a living room with massive stone fireplace and a queen bed fashioned of pine logs. Occupants enjoy a screened porch and two chairs outside on a dock. All but four rooms in the back of the main hotel have water views. All rooms come with TV, telephone and featherbed mattress. Each four-poster or canopy bed is different, as are the color schemes, fabrics and wallpapers. All the antique

furnishings and collectibles came from island sources. Baths are updated, many with whirlpool tubs. The walls of the common rooms in the main building are hung with local art. The front porch of the main hotel has been enclosed, and a flower-bedecked terrace created in front. Boats moor at the old steamship dock, next to one of the lake's few sand-bottom beaches. Adirondack chairs are scattered along the shore for taking in the view. Breakfast in the hotel's refurbished restaurant (see Where to Eat) is included in the rates.

(802) 372-8237 or (888) 525-3644. Fax (802) 372-3218. www.northherohouse.com. Twenty-six rooms and suites with private baths. Doubles, $95 to $165. Suites, $165 to $295.

Shore Acres Inn & Restaurant, 237 Shore Acres Drive, North Hero 05474.

With 50 acres of rolling grounds and a half mile of private lakeshore, this appealing place is situated well away from the highway on the edge of a ledge beside Great East Bay. White with blue trim and blue awnings, it has nineteen lakeview rooms with waterfront decks in two one-story, motel-type wings on either side of the restaurant. Each room has TV, maple furniture and pine paneling, plus ceiling fans or air conditioning. A Vermont craftsman made most of the furniture. Rooms are enhanced by works of Vermont artists, framed by innkeepers Susan and Mike Tranby, who are picture framers in their spare time. Beds range from two twins to kingsize, and some have two queens. The Tranbys offer four newer, queensize rooms in a garden house annex that operates as a B&B in the off-season. Rooms here have decks or balconies with water vistas. Benches and lawn chairs are dotted about the nicely landscaped lawns for viewing the lake and Mount Mansfield beyond. Below are a pebbly beach and a raft. Breakfast and dinner are available in the restaurant (see Where to Eat).

(802) 372-8722. www.shoreacres.com. Twenty-three rooms with private baths. Doubles, $126.50 to $159.50 EP. Closed mid-October to May.

Ruthcliffe Lodge and Restaurant, 1002 Quarry Road, Isle La Motte 05463.

Isolated but on the lake, this lodge with restaurant and motel is particularly good for those who want to be away from it all. The waterfront location is one of the most appealing around, and Adirondack chairs are scattered about the lawns down to the rocky shore. It's a family operation, energetic innkeepers Mark and Kathy Infante having taken over from his parents who started the lodge in 1951. Meals are served in summer in the original lodge (see Where to Eat), which has a cathedral ceiling opening to a second-floor loft. Six attractive units in the adjacent motel look out onto the lake. Three have kingsize beds and two have two double beds. The end Sunflower Suite with two bedrooms and one and a half baths is good for families. Each unit has a ceiling fan and a clock-radio. Kathy hand-stenciled the walls of each and added her sister's wall quilts and memorabilia appropriate to the individual room's theme in an effort to "make this more like a B&B." A full breakfast of the guest's choice, from eggs benedict to belgian waffles, is served in the dining room or on the waterside deck. The common front veranda of the motel building facing the lake is paved with Vermont marble. Canoes and sea kayaks await at water's edge, and bicycles also are available for rent.

(802) 928-3200 or (800) 769-8162. www.ruthcliffe.com. Five rooms and one suite with private baths. Doubles, $108.50 to $112.50. Suite, $118.50. Closed Columbus Day to mid-May.

Thomas Mott Homestead, 63 Blue Rock Road, Alburg 05440.

Here is a B&B with a great waterfront location, spacious and comfortable guest rooms, homey common rooms and porches, and gourmet breakfasts. Innkeepers Susan and Bob Cogley took over the 1838 Shaker-style farmhouse in 2004. They offer four guest rooms, each furnished with antiques and quilts from different states. The downstairs Geoffrey-Kay Suite in which we stayed offers an antique iron queen bed, TV, vaulted ceiling and large walk-in closet. The ultimate accommodation is the Laurel Rose, sequestered beneath a cathedral ceiling with a queen bed, Shaker pegs, two comfy chairs in front of an angled fireplace and a balcony onto the lake, affording a view to Mount Mansfield and Camel's Hump. The moonlight over the water is magical, but the room is booked so far ahead that we've never managed to snag it for a night. Common areas include a fireplaced living room stocked with books and magazines, TV and games; a big side porch with a combination game and pool table, and two other porches. Antiques fill the expansive dining room, centered by an antique Canadian tailors' table and with a piano at one end. Here, the Cogleys serve a hearty breakfast culminating in eggs benedict, cheese soufflé, quiche or french toast. For afternoon or evening refreshments, Ben & Jerry's ice cream bars are always in the freezer. A gazebo overlooks the water, and there are a canoe and paddleboat for guests to use from a 75-foot swimming and fishing dock.

(802) 796-4402 or (800) 348-0843. www.thomas-mott-bb.com. Four rooms with private baths. Doubles, $115.

The Ransom Bay Inn, 4 Center Bay Road, Alburg 05440.

This stone house, an inn dating to 1810, has been renovated and upgraded by owners Richard and Loraine Walker. Made of gray marble quarried on Isle La Motte, it has four spacious, antiques-filled guest rooms with queen beds, hardwood floors and private baths. Guests have the run of a formal living room, a sunken living room with an all-slate floor and one of the inn's three fireplaces, and two dining rooms. In one, the Walkers serve a huge breakfast at a table big enough to seat everyone in the house and then some. The fare includes eggs, pancakes and french toast or combinations thereof. The specialty is omelets with portobello mushrooms, vidalia onions, red and green peppers and Vermont cheddar, served with bacon or ham, home fries and homemade croissants. "Once I get rolling," says Richard, who cooks at an old cast-iron wood stove, "I stuff people." He also offers dinner with advance notice, and was planning an addition for wedding receptions and functions. Guests enjoy access to seven acres and a semi-public beach.

(802) 796-3399 or (800) 729-3393. Four rooms with private baths. Doubles, $85 to $95.

Cottages

Cozy Cottages at Hislop's Landing, 505 West Shore Road, South Hero 05486.

Down a long hill off U.S. Route 2 are twelve cottages with decks overlooking the lake. The six on the shore are older; six behind them were built in 1979. One with three bedrooms includes a washer and dryer. The rest have two bedrooms, a day bed in the living room, shower bath, modern kitchen and front decks with picnic tables. Two of the roomiest by the shore have fireplaces. There's a sandy beach, and the protected bay called the Gut is fine for sailing and water skiing.

(802) 372-8229. Cottages, $650 to $750 weekly.

Fisk Farm, 8349 West Shore Road, Isle La Motte 05463.

Here is one of few lodging establishments with a "mission statement" – a seven-point mission statement, no less. That's because New Jersey transplant Linda Fitch feels a sense of attachment to the lakefront property her family acquired in 1970 and wants to share it with similarly inclined visitors. "This is an elegant place with a lot of history to it," she says. The farm, dating to 1776, once was the home of a Vermont lieutenant governor and it's said that Vice President Theodore Roosevelt was visiting when he received word that President McKinley had been shot. The setting today is rural, tranquil and close to nature, as the mission statement would have it – "a place of rest, respite and restoration for all who come." Guests stay in two cottages next to the main house fashioned from the estate's old store and post office that served the workers at the adjacent Fisk Quarry. The English-style Stone Cottage beside the house has a living room with sofabed, fireplace and kitchen and a loft with a queen bed. Beside the lake is the one-room Shore Cottage paneled in beadboard, with a kingsize bed, kitchenette and waterside deck looking across to the Adirondacks. The carriage barn is being restored for art shows, music and poetry readings. "We're musicians," advises Linda, who says the we includes several friends. The cultural events are scheduled on summer Sundays from 1 to 5, when tea is available in the garden.

(802) 928-3364. Two cottages rented by the week, June to mid-October, $600 and $800 weekly.

CAMPING is big in this area. In fact, there are far more campsites than there are guest rooms. Among the best:

Grand Isle State Park, Box 648, Grand Isle 05458, (802) 372-4300. Thirty-six lean-tos are included among the 156 tent and trailer campsites offered in this 226-acre park. Many sites are grouped around a big central lawn. More appealing are the eleven lean-tos on a shoreline ledge, most with views of the lake. The sites have no hookups, but shower and toilet facilities are available. A small playground is beside the beach, and there's a recreation hall. Tent sites, $16; lean-tos, $23.

North Hero State Park, North Hero 05474, (802) 372-8727. This 399-acre park has 99 campsites and eighteen lean-tos amid the trees along three well-spaced loop roads – none on the water, although within walking distance of the swimming and boat launch area. Shower and toilet facilities are available, as are boat rentals. A small gravel beach is popular with wind surfers, and there's a nature trail. Tent sites, $14; lean-tos, $21.

Among many private campgrounds, a location on a peninsula at the entrance to Mallett's Bay, with a panoramic view of the broad lake, is an asset of **Camp Skyland,** 398 South St., South Hero 05486, (802) 372-4200. Thirty-three campsites are located on six acres along the lakeshore. Also available are eight rustic single-room cabins and four housekeeping cottages.

Seeing and Doing _____ ♪♪♪

Water recreation reigns in this area, naturally. People are always on the lookout for Champ, the Lake Champlain sea monster whose sightings are front-page news in the Islander newspaper. "Champ must be touring the whole island, for just a few days ago 35 people reported seeing the creature off the YMCA Camp in South Hero," the Islander reported after two sightings off Grand Isle one summer. There are an eighteen-hole golf course at Alburg Country Club, two smaller courses and a few tennis courts. Visitors who get cabin fever can go off to Burlington or Montreal for the day.

On or Near the Water

BOATING. From canoes to luxury yachts, sunfish to schooners, boats ply the sheltered coves and bays around the Champlain Islands. Great East Bay, that part of the lake between the islands and the Vermont mainland, is generally more protected than the "broad lake" to the south and west.

There are no excursion boats in the Champlain Islands. The closest is the **Spirit of Ethan Allen III,** (802) 862-8300, which gives 90-minute scenic lake cruises daily at 10, noon, 2 and 4 from the impressive new Burlington Boathouse at the foot of College Street in downtown Burlington (adults $9.95, children $3.95, mid-May to mid-October). Lunch, brunch, dinner, sunset and moonlight cruises also are scheduled. Tour promoters tell visitors to look for Champ. In 1984, 70 passengers aboard the original Spirit of Ethan Allen made the largest mass sighting ever of the legendary creature.

The **Northern Lights Cruise Boat,** (802) 864-9669, leaves from Burlington's King Street ferry dock on 90-minute narrated tours along the Burlington waterfront, Sunday-Friday at 2 and 4; adults $8.95, children $3.95. It offers lunch cruises Monday-Friday at noon; adults $12.95, children $7.95. Weekend brunch cruises at noon cost $18.95 for adults, $10.95 for children.

Another way to see the lake is aboard the **Lake Champlain Ferries** run by the Lake Champlain Transportation Co., King Street Dock, Burlington, (802) 864-9804. The ferries connect Vermont and New York on three crossings: Grand Isle to Cumberland Head near Plattsburgh, Burlington to Port Kent and Charlotte to Essex. The Grand Isle crossing leaves from the heart of the Champlain Islands, is the shortest and runs the most frequently, roughly every twenty minutes around the clock in summer. It's the only ferry to run year-round. The twelve-minute trip costs $7.75 for car and driver, $2.75 for adult passengers; $16 maximum per car.

A number of marinas offer boat rentals. Kayaks, paddle boards and canoes are rented by **Hero's Welcome,** North Hero, (802) 372-4161. The newest fleet on the lake is advertised by **North Hero Marina** at Pelot's Point, (802) 271-5953. **Ladd's Landing,** at the bridge in Grand Isle, (802) 372-5320, has marina facilities and offers sailing instruction, charter services and boat rentals. The islands contain eight public boat launching areas from Keeler's Bay in South Hero to Kelly Bay at the Rouses Point Bridge in Alburg.

FISHING. Cool, clear and up to 400 feet deep, Lake Champlain is said to have as large an assortment of freshwater fish as any lake in the world. The annual **Lake Champlain International Fishing Derby** in mid-June helps raise funds for the lake restoration program, started in 1974 to restore fisheries for landlocked Atlantic salmon and rainbow trout. More than three million salmon and trout have been stocked in the lake and they're growing fast, according to LCI derby sponsors. In one derby, 1,099 fish were registered, among them 350 lake trout, 228 walleyed pike, 180 small mouth bass, 128 northern pike and 46 Atlantic salmon.

The **Ed Weed Fish Culture Station,** 14 Bell Hill Road, (802) 372-3171, next to the ferry terminal in Grand Isle, is the newest of five fish hatcheries maintained by the state to provide fish for public waters throughout Vermont. The multi-million-dollar facility is state of the art, raising salmon and trout to eight or ten inches, mainly for stocking Lake Champlain. A visitor center offers aquaria, displays on the lake's ecology and self-guided tours. Open daily, 8 to 4.

SWIMMING. Lake Champlain's water is so pure that people drink it and so refreshing that some swimmers find it chilly. We don't. Our only complaint is the dearth of sand beaches, as opposed to gravel or rock beaches. Often swimming is done from docks or rafts to avoid the stony bottom. Some of the best swimming is available in state parks. **Sand Bar State Park** at the causeway in Colchester is popular with daytrippers from Burlington; it has a long beach, shady areas with picnic tables, a snack bar and boat rentals. **Knight Point State Park** at North Hero offers a small, manmade sandy beach, picnic area and shelter, and boat rentals.

North Hero State Park has a small gravel beach and a few picnic tables for day use. The new **Alburg Dunes State Park** has a sand beach, dunes and a barrier island similar to formations found along ocean coastlines. You also can swim off a beach at St. Anne's Shrine. Windsurfing is offered by **Inland Sea Windsurf Co.** at its demonstration center at Sand Bar State Park, (802) 893-3011.

BIKING. The islands are relatively flat and most of the rural byways little traveled, so biking is popular. Five bicycle tours of island sites are outlined in an informative brochure and guide produced by the **Lake Champlain Bikeways Network.** Rentals are available from Hero's Welcome, North Hero, (802) 372-4161.

BIRDING. Nearly 300 species of birds have been recorded in the area, which lies on one of the major north-south flyways for migratory birds. Herons, eagles, falcons, ravens, osprey, hawks, snowy egrets, cormorants, ducks, geese and songbirds are among the finds. Birders say the **South Hero Swamp** and **Mud Creek Wildlife Area** in Alburg are particularly good sites. **Sand Bar Wildlife Refuge,** an 800-acre state wildlife management area across from Sand Bar State Park, is known for its duck population.

Other Attractions

Hermann's Royal Lipizzan Stallions, Route 2, North Hero.
Since 1992, the islands have been the summer home for the Royal Lipizzan Stallions of Austria, which winter in Myakka City, Fla. The sponsoring Lake Champlain Islands Chamber of Commerce has successfully capitalized on their appeal, although the relationship is on a year-to-year basis. The fourteen white purebred descendants of a line established in 1580 are known for their acrobatic leaps and other precisely executed maneuvers. From roughly early July to late August, they perform on an area field, most recently at the Islands Center for Arts and Recreation in Knight Point State Park. Spectators occupy folding chairs beneath a striped canopy or a couple of sections of open-air bleachers. The Lipizzans are owned and directed by Col. Ottomar Herrmann, who with his father and the help of General Patton smuggled their ancestors out of Austria during World War II. The Herrmann family chose this as their summer rest stop because it reminded them of their homeland. After the performances, the audience may visit the tent stables, meet the riders and even rub noses with the royal horses. They also can be viewed in their off-hours working out on the field. If you arise early, you might see the Lipizzans taking their morning baths in the lake.
(802) 372-8400. Summer performances Thursday and Friday at 6, Saturday and Sunday at 2:30. Adults $17, children $10.

St. Anne's Shrine, Isle La Motte.
Thousands of pilgrims find solace at the Edmundite Fathers' waterside shrine on the site of Fort St. Anne, Vermont's oldest settlement, where the first Mass in the state was celebrated in 1666. In keeping with island tradition, the shrine is rather primitive: a covered, open-air chapel where Eucharist celebrations are offered daily, an Italian marble statue of St. Anne housed in an A-frame, a grotto and the Way of the Cross, its stations nestled among tall pines beside the lake. A granite statue of Samuel de Champlain, sculpted in the Vermont Pavilion at Expo 67 in Montreal, now occupies the site where he landed in 1609. After a fire destroyed the original no-frills cafeteria, the indomitable shrine director raised funds to build a new one in 1995. The result is an architecturally striking, multi-purpose building up the hillside notable for beautiful stained glass. Visitors may swim from the beach, picnic on the grounds

or simply relax on a lovely, tranquil piece of land that is the islands' best-known visitor destination.

(802) 928-3362. www.sse.org. Shrine open daily, May 15 to Oct. 15. Free.

The Hyde Log Cabin, Route 2, Grand Isle.

If Grand Isle has a tourist attraction, this is it, the oldest log cabin remaining in the United States. Built in 1783 with an enormous fireplace at one end and an overhead loft, it housed the family of Jedediah Hyde Jr. and his ten children. Members of the Hyde family lived there for nearly 150 years. In 1945 the Vermont Historical Society acquired the cabin and moved it two miles to its present location along Route 2. Inside you see original furnishings, agricultural and household implements, bedspreads, clothing and such. A guide from the Grand Isle Historical Society informed us that more than two-thirds of the artifacts came from the Hyde family or their descendants and the rest from other pioneer families on the island. We felt we were part of an earlier era, listening to birds twittering out back through the open door and watching cows grazing on the next property. In 2004, the cabin complex was joined on one side by a mustard-yellow one-room schoolhouse. Alas, it is now overshadowed by a sprawling new school on the other side.

(802) 828-3051. Open Thursday-Monday 11 to 5, July 4 to Labor Day. Admission, $1.

Snow Farm Vineyard, 190 West Shore Road, South Hero.

Vermont's first vineyard and grape winery opened in 1996 near the lakeshore and – in the islands' idiosyncratic tradition – across the road from the Crescent Bay llama farm. Grapevines adorn the double doors and a side deck overlooks the vineyard. Owners Harrison and Molly Lebowitz sponsor Taste of the Islands food and wine pairings and a free Thursday evening summer concert series called Music in the Vineyard. South Hero, known at least locally as "The Garden Spot of Vermont," has a longer growing season than much of the state due to the moderating effect of Lake Champlain. That's good for grape-growing, and the first significant harvest was produced in 1999. Snow Farm's initial chardonnay quickly sold out, and the best-selling Snow White, a sweet blend of cayuga and seyval grapes, was down to the last six bottles at our visit. The 2002 estate riesling won a bronze medal, raising eyebrows of competitors like Kendall Jackson and Chateau St. Michelle, and the baco noir annually cops gold medals. The estate vidal ice wine is another winner. Besides wines, Vermont products are on sale and local artists show their works in month-long exhibitions.

(802) 372-9463. www.snowfarm.com. Open daily 10 to 5, May-December.

Old School House & Museum, Isle La Motte. Originally the South District schoolhouse (circa 1830), this small building now holds local artifacts, looms, spinning wheels and other items collected since 1925 by the Isle La Motte Historical Society. The island is noted geologically for having examples of every known geological period and a few specimens are here, according to the assistant curator, who lives in a house occupied by five generations of her family at the four corners. There are examples of the island's famed black marble that graces the U.S. Capitol and Radio City Music Hall, a piece of coral from a nearby farm field and two pages of Champlain's diary written upon his landing here. Open Saturdays from 1 to 4, July and August, or by appointment. Free.

Fisk Quarry Preserve, West Shore Road, Isle La Motte. A kiosk describes the history of the marble quarry, now a wildlife preserve and part of the ancient fossil reef that underlies the southern third of the island. Visible in the Fisk Quarry is the middle portion of the Chazyan Reef, formed 480 million years ago beneath a tropical sea in the present location of Zimbabwe. The oldest part of the reef is exposed in outcrops along the island's southern shoreline and the youngest part can be seen from the road to the north of the historical society building. At the quarry, you can see the famed stromatoporoids, fossils that appear as white rounded shapes on the quarry walls. The Isle La Motte Reef Preservation Trust purchased the quarry in 1998. Signage helps interpret for laymen one of the world's richest geological sites.

SHOPPING. Most stores are basic and the shops few and far between, except in North Hero, which has undergone a spurt of merchandising lately. An outgrowth of a century-old general store, **Hero's Welcome** is a complete, quite sophisticated general store, café and bakery, where people line up to buy the breads first thing in the morning and they're quickly sold out. Here you can find everything from books to carved decoys to good wines, gathered by owners Beverley and Bob Camp. We like to stop here in the morning for a cappuccino and a baked goodie. The shed in back has all you'd ever need for your boat. Next door is **The Back Chamber** with antiques and collectibles. Behind the relocated Chamber of Commerce office is the **Island Craft Shop.**

Stop for handmade chocolates in Grand Isle, the new home of the **Vermont Nut Free Chocolates** factory store and gift shop.

Apples are the theme at the **Apple Farm Market** along Route 2 in South Hero, from souvenirs to the real thing. Next door is a refreshment stand called, apparently, **Seb's French Fries,** where you can get a hot dog for $1.65 and a burger for $1.85. The "new" hot and spicy wings were being featured, but most folks seemed to be going for the ice cream, including the old favorite "rainbow sherbert." A six-foot-tall green frog is in front of **Green Frog Gifts & Clothing,** Route 314, South Hero. Inside is a little bit of everything from moccasins to Vermont food products, T-shirts to books, plus a large selection of frogs. Amid the array is an old refrigerator covered with "I Love Vermont" magnets.

In Alburg, the former Alburg Creamery is now the curiously named **New England Via Vermont,** a hodgepodge of Vermont memorabilia, from food products to sweatshirts, with a rear room labeled rummage and even a local history display. Outstanding solid wood furniture, including Shaker, Queen Anne, Chippendale, and Arts and Crafts styles, is produced by the **McGuire Family Furniture Makers** on Isle La Motte, located along Main Street in the center of town. There's a showroom here and at 44 Main St. in Alburg, which is also the home of the related **Vermont Clock Co.** Fifteen flavors of handmade chocolates are produced at **Shoreline Chocolates,** West Shore Road, Alburg, and dispensed with specialty foods from a little barn-board building Thursday-Sunday 10 to 4.

Where to Eat

Ruthcliffe Lodge, 1002 Quarry Road, Isle La Motte.

Some of the islands' best meals come from the kitchen of this small but venerable lodge, which also claims the islands' only waterside deck for outdoor dining. Chef-owner Mark Infante single-handedly mans the kitchen, preparing up three meals a day at peak times and serving far more food than most people can eat, which accounts for the inordinate number of doggy bags seen leaving the premises. On a calm summer evening, we found the deck beside the lake a magical setting for a dinner that began with mushroom-barley soup, tossed salad and good French bread (these come with the entrées, and no appetizers are offered). Choices range from shrimp scampi and chicken marsala to New York strip steak with peppercorn sauce. Mark is known for his herb-crusted rack of lamb, a hefty brace of eight chops. We liked a special of crab cakes with pasta and the signature shrimp marco, served over linguini with sundried tomatoes and shiitake mushrooms. Kathy Infante is responsible for most of the homemade desserts, including raspberry pie, blueberry bread pudding and amaretto cheesecake. Indoor dining is in a rustic, knotty-pine room with a cathedral ceiling that was rather brightly illuminated at our visit. Citronella candles provided all the light needed on a moonlit night outside.

(802) 928-3200. Entrées, $16.25 to $25.95. Breakfast daily, 8 to 10:30. Lunch in summer, Thursday-Sunday noon to 2. Dinner nightly in summer, 5 to 9, Thursday-Sunday 6 to 9 through Columbus Day. Closed Columbus Day to mid-May.

Shore Acres Inn & Restaurant, 237 Shore Acres Drive, North Hero.

The large, pine-paneled dining room dressed in subtle patterned cloths and fresh flowers has a stone fireplace and big windows onto Lake Champlain. Chef Dan Rainville's menu is short but sweet, and his fare consistent and highly regarded. He uses seasonal produce from a Grand Isle farm, buys the freshest of fish and prepares special dishes for vegetarians. The coconut beer-battered shrimp with apricot glaze is a favorite starter, as are maple-marinated sea scallops wrapped in smoked bacon. Main courses could be grilled tuna steak with mango chive butter, grilled swordfish with roasted peppers and pine nuts, seared polenta-crusted salmon with a roasted pepper coulis and grilled spice-crusted pork steak with chipotle-garlic sauce. Friends who stumbled onto the Shore Acres by chance raved about the beef tenderloin filet with a roast shallot sauce and the rack of lamb with garlic-port-rosemary sauce. The bread is homemade, as is the changing selection of desserts.

(802) 372-8722. Entrées, $16.95 to $23.95. Dinner nightly, 5 to 9, weekends only in off-season. Closed January-March.

The North Hero House, Route 2, North Hero.

The main dining room has been nicely upgraded in the restoration of this venerable hotel, and the lake is on view from a newly enclosed porch in front and a dining terrace outside. The dining room is handsome in Colonial style, with beige walls above white wainscoting and windsor chairs at nicely spaced tables dressed in blue and white. It's a stylish backdrop for contemporary American fare. The dinner menu might start with appetizers of crab cakes with chipotle rémoulade or a jerk-spiced swordfish kabob with red pepper relish. Typical main courses are cornmeal-crusted rainbow trout with shrimp creole sauce, stuffed pork loin with cabernet fig sauce, and mustard-crusted rack of lamb with red wine demi-glace. Desserts run from maple cheesecake with candied walnuts to crème brûlée. The rear Greenhouse Room is warmed by a wood stove in chilly weather. In summer, the enclosed front porch and the outdoor terrace are the venues of choice. A lobster buffet is featured on Friday evenings. Although lunch service has been discontinued, a "pier lunch" of lobster rolls and hamburgers on the grill is available in summer.

(802) 372-8237 or (888) 525-3644. Entrées, $17 to $30. Dinner nightly, 5 to 9 in summer, 5:30 to 8:30 in off-season. Lunch on pier in summer, noon to 5. Sunday brunch, 10 to 2. Closed Sunday-Tuesday, November-April.

Links on the Lake Restaurant, Alburg Country Club, 230 Route 129, Alburg.

When the old golf clubhouse burned down, a new one was built and included an expansive restaurant with a side deck, both with views of the lake. The public golf course and restaurant were upgraded in 2004 by new owners David Anderson, an Alburg summer resident, and his daughter, Kristin, in partnership with Vermonters Luke and Diane Bazin. A young chef from southern Vermont was getting good reports on his Italian-American fare. His opening menu included pasta dishes and such entrées as almond-crusted trout with lemon butter sauce, grilled chicken breast with pepper cream sauce, prime rib and grilled New York strip steak with horseradish sour cream. Fried calamari and shrimp risotto head the list of appetizers. Sandwiches, salads and "munchies" comprise the lunch menu.

(802) 796-3586. www.alburggolflinks.com. Entrées, $13.95 to $18.95. Lunch, Tuesday-Sunday 11 to 3. Dinner, Tuesday-Sunday 5 to 9 in summer, Friday-Sunday in late spring and early fall. Brunch on weekends. Closed mid-October to mid-May.

The Sand Bar Inn, 59 Route 2, South Hero.
The food has been upgraded lately at this traditional motel-restaurant, which draws regulars for its million-dollar view up the lake from the sandbar causeway. The dining room is attractive in blue and white, with a central stone fireplace open to tables on two sides and fresh flowers cut from the gardens outside. Candles flicker and the view of the lake across the road is impressive, to say the least. The menu has been updated to the point it was hardly recognizable at our latest visit. Gone were the old roast turkey, chicken cordon bleu and seafood newburg. In their place were the likes of almond-crusted salmon fillet served over soft polenta, Caribbean pork loin chop with mango puree, apricot duck breast and rack of lamb with shallot demi-glace. You could start with fennel-crusted sea scallops in saffron and white truffle oil, baked brie or escargots. Our New York strip steak and filet mignon dinners were so filling we had no room for dessert. The Sunday brunch packs in the locals. The adjacent Sandbar motel, a low-key favorite of ours over the years, had slipped seriously at our latest stay, but new owner Marco DiCarlo said renovations were in the works.

(802) 372-6911. Entrées, $15 to $25. Dinner nightly, 5 to 9. Sunday brunch, 9 to 1.

Hero's Welcome, Route 2, North Hero.
This stylish general store has a bakery and café up front. The aromas and the goodies defy the will of passersby who come in merely to browse. Stop for a breakfast of fresh-baked pastries (the oversize muffins are delectable), and then order one of the good deli sandwiches and head out for a day's touring or cycling. You can eat inside or take out to picnic tables on the lakeshore across the street.

(802) 372-4161. Prices, $1.50 to $4.99. Café open daily, 6:30 to 6, to 8 in summer.

St. Anne's Shrine Cafeteria, Isle La Motte.
From the ashes reborn in 1995, this curved hillside structure with picnic tables on wraparound outdoor decks with glimpses of the lake is more showy than its "cafeteria" fare. The food is a 1930s time warp of made-to-order hamburgers and hot dogs, the French-Canadian dish called poutine (french fries topped with gravy and cheese curds), coleslaw and macaroni salads, jello and tapioca puddings. At our latest visit, the day's specials were an egg salad sandwich ($2.75) and fried chicken with stuffing, potato pancakes and gravy ($6.50). We settled for a good turkey noodle soup and a couple of hot dogs, each $1.50. Another time, we tried the hamburger and the cheeseburger deluxe (the deluxe apparently referring to the huge slice of tomato). The woman next to us talked the counter woman into making a tomato and cucumber sandwich. Complete dinners are served on Sundays for $6.50.

(802) 928-3362. Prices, $1.50 to $6.50. Hours vary, weekdays from 10 to 2, weekends to 4.

FOR MORE INFORMATION: Lake Champlain Islands Chamber of Commerce, U.S. Route 2, Box 213, North Hero, VT 05474, (802) 372-8400 or (800) 262-5226. www.champlainislands.com.

Powerboats and wind surfers come and go from Wolfeboro town dock.

Wolfeboro/Lake Winnipesaukee, N.H.

Wolfeboro has laid claim to being America's oldest summer resort ever since its last English Colonial governor, John Wentworth, built in 1768 the country's first summer home, a palatial mansion on the shore of the nearby lake that bears his name. "Everybody in the country was talking about that house," advised our guide in the Wolfeboro Historical Society museum complex. "He summered here with his hunting and fishing cronies. He was one of those summer people!"

Sequestered between Lake Wentworth and Wolfeboro Bay, the eastern end of Lake Winnipesaukee, Wolfeboro has a year-round population of 3,000. That number triples in the summer, thanks to summer people plus as many tourists as can be accommodated in relatively limited facilities.

Though Wolfeboro is blessed with a magnificent location at the foot of mountains along New England's second largest lake, it maintains a sedate, small-town atmosphere. Brewster Academy opens its beach to the public in summer. Museums attract just enough visitors to make opening worthwhile. The mailboat delivers mail and passengers out to the islands. Between quick dips, a young swimsuit-clad peddler dispenses lunchtime hot dogs from a cart next to Cate Park at the town dock. There are benches for relaxation on the dock and along Main Street. Shopkeepers know their customers by name, and everyone on the street seems to know everyone else.

Happily, there's little schlock. Wolfeboro has resisted the honky-tonk that mars some other sections of Lake Winnipesaukee. Zoning is strict and shoreline property in such demand that the pressure of residential real estate has blocked commercial development. "What's hurting Wolfeboro is its lack of rooms," one innkeeper concedes.

That's just fine with most of the natives, the summer regulars and those visitors lucky enough to find accommodations. They enjoy the myriad pleasures of a lovely section of Lake Winnipesaukee, good restaurants and shops, two golf courses, cultural activities, a low-key social life, and the small-town atmosphere of one of New England's more pleasant villages.

Says Alan Pierce, owner of a bookstore and gift shop aptly named Camelot: "People come back to Wolfeboro every year and are so glad to see that it hasn't changed."

Getting There

Wolfeboro is about 45 miles northeast of Concord at the eastern end of Lake Winnipesaukee. From Interstate 93, take Route 28 directly to Wolfeboro, or take Routes 3 and 11 to Route 28.

Where to Stay

Its location is choice but its accommodations confined. The focus here is on Wolfeboro, but we add a couple of the nicer waterside facilities on Lake Winnipesaukee nearby. The "nice" and "waterside" criteria seem to be self-limiting. Those meeting both are relatively few and far between.

Wolfeboro

The Wolfeboro Inn, 90 North Main St., Wolfeboro 03894.

This venerable inn, built in 1812, was greatly expanded in 1988 to make 44 rooms, five with patios or balconies but, strangely for the location, very few with a good lake view. The layout is such that most rooms overlook the parking lot or village. Three end suites and three balconied rooms on the second floor appeal more to those seeking a view of the water. The main-floor suite we saw had a large, angled living room, a kingsize four-poster in the bedroom, Lord & Mayfair toiletries and a hair drier in the bathroom, a desk, two phones, TV in the armoire and a door to a small patio outside with a glimpse of the lake beyond a gazebo. Some of the original 1812 bedrooms retain their fireplaces and a sprightly country look. Although a bit removed from the lake, the inn has its own sand beach, docks, windsurfers and rowboats. It also runs the Winnipesaukee Belle excursion boat, a ride on which is complimentary for inn guests. The inn is a popular conference center, and a section of the lobby was given over to an artist's reception the afternoon we visited. Room rates include continental breakfast. Meals are served in the historic, locally popular **Wolfe's Tavern,** with dinner available in the formal dining room (see Where to Eat).

(603) 569-3016 or (800) 451-2389. www.wolfeboroinn.com. Forty-four rooms and suites with private baths. Doubles, $185 to $245. Suites, $265 to $305.

Topsides Bed & Breakfast, 209 South Main St., Box 416, Wolfeboro 03894.

This deluxe B&B with a nautical theme opened in 2004 in a restored dentist's home and office next door to St. Cecilia Catholic Church and Brewster Academy. Dennis and Cynthia Schauer retired to their favorite summer vacation spot from

Virginia, giving up foxhunting so Denny could pursue his interest in antique boats year-round. Five guest rooms with queen beds and TVs are on two floors. Three in the rear yield lake views in the distance, as does a great L-shaped porch full of wicker furniture in the back. Rooms are decorated according to their names. The main-floor Nantucket Room, fashioned from a former sun porch, and the second-floor Martha's Vineyard Room, light and airy with windows on three sides, sport a seashore theme. The main-floor Governor's Room testifies to the Schauers' former residence in a Virginia manor house, as does the Hunt Country Room, a private hideaway up a rear staircase with the largest bedroom and a small sitting room. Cynthia puts out breakfast on a counter made of a boat's top side between her kitchen and the dining room. The fare might be homemade coffee cake, egg casserole or pancakes.

(603) 569-3834. Fax: (603) 569-3835. www.topsidesbb.com. Five rooms with private baths. Doubles, $175 to $195.

The Lake Motel, 280 South Main St. (Route 28), Box 887-B, Wolfeboro 03894.

Among the Wolfeboro area's few motels, this is the best bet, thanks to its spacious property alongside tiny Crescent Lake. Situated well back from the road on sixteen acres, the motel opened in 1956 and has 650 feet of lake frontage. Each of the 30 rooms has two entries, one from an interior corridor and the other from the outside. The rear half face the water. All have two double beds, two upholstered chairs and cable TV. Our room was quite comfortable, but the best part was just outside: a broad lawn sloping toward a little beach popular with families, lawn games, a tennis court and boats for rent. Five housekeeping apartments rented weekly are located away from the water. **The Morrisey's Front Porch,** open for three meals daily in season at the entrance to the grounds, serves the most food for the money in town, according to motel owners Allan and Julie Bailey, who run their operation more like an inn than most motel keepers do.

(603) 569-1100 or (888) 569-1110. Fax (603) 569-1258. www.thelakemotel.com. Thirty rooms and five apartments with private baths. Doubles, $119 to $139. Apartments, $655 weekly. Closed mid-October to mid-May.

Piping Rock Resort, 680 North Main St., Wolfeboro 03894.

The name recently was upscaled to "resort," but this remains essentially a motel and cottage colony that has been condominiumized. The main eight-unit, two-story motel with balconies and decks overlooks a lawn sloping down to Lake Winnipesaukee. All now have kitchens, and one has two bedrooms. Our quarters were typical: a large room with futon sitting area, a queen bed, TV and kitchenette. Kind of a studio condo, it proved quite comfortable for the night, if not for longer. Available by the week are thirteen white and aqua housekeeping cottages with water views, two to three bedrooms and decks facing the pine trees. They are scattered about the hilly nine-acre property, and are more accessible to the water. There also are two three-bedroom suites that are considered apartments. By the shore are a sandy beach with a raft and boathouse. Those wanting to stay right on the water can book a small, two-bedroom facility on the second floor of the boathouse for $915 a week.

(603) 569-1915 or (800) 317-3864. www.pipingrockresort.com. Twenty-three units with private baths. Doubles in motel, $99 to $170. Cottages and apartments, $999 to $1,190 weekly; two-night minimum in off-season. Motel open year-round.

Pow-Wow Lodges & Motel, 19 Governor Wentworth Hwy. (Route 109), HC 69, Box 664, Wolfeboro 03894.

Hidden in a cool glen of lofty pines and hemlocks on a half-mile-long isthmus between Mirror Lake and Lake Winnipesaukee, this appealing little motel and cottage complex looks the way a lakefront lodge property should. "We cater to a quieter crowd," says Charlie Fairbanks, owner in residence with his wife Bev. Their four motel units and four cottages enjoy beautiful views across Mirror Lake, a private, spring-fed lake of not unsubstantial size beneath Mount Shaw. "You can go for hours without hearing the sound of a boat," says Charlie, although the silence is punctuated by passing auto traffic. Two of the four motel units come with two double beds and kitchen/living room areas; the others lack the kitchens but have porches. All have TVs and sundecks. Spaced well apart, the paneled, two-bedroom cottages contain combination living/dining/kitchen areas and screened porches. Each lodge has its own sandy beach with individual dock, from which one can swim to a large common raft equipped with lounge chairs. The fishing is great, says Charlie, and there's a recreation area for badminton, volleyball and horseshoes.

(603) 569-2198 in summer, (603) 225-2968 in winter. Four motel units and four cottages. Doubles, $105 to $115. Cottages, $1,100 weekly. Closed Columbus Day to May.

Clearwater Lodges, 704 North Main St., Wolfeboro 03894.

Opened in the late 1940s, this rustic resort run by run by new owners André and Aynne De Beer has fourteen housekeeping cottages on the Winnipesaukee shore about four miles north of town. The cottages are lined up along a road down a hill to the waterfront, where there are rental boats and a recreation hall with television and games. The pine-paneled, one and two-bedroom cottages have kitchens, fireplaces, shower baths and tiny porches.

(603) 569-2370. Fourteen cottages. Cottages, weekly $745 (one-bedroom) to $970 (two-bedroom). Daily rates available off-season, $115 to $130. Closed mid-October to mid-May.

Lakeview Inn & Motor Lodge, 200 North Main St., Box 713, Wolfeboro 03894.

Trees block whatever lake view this venerable establishment once may have had, but it clings to the name (although new owners did add "motor lodge" to the inn's name to portray its status more accurately). Three guest rooms are upstairs in the restored 200-year-old main building, which also houses a restaurant (see Where to Eat) and features a striking fan doorway with bull's-eye glass. The rest are on two stories of an attractive, air-conditioned motel annex with patios or balconies overlooking apple trees and a mountain. All have TV and thick carpeting, and four have kitchenettes. A continental breakfast is served to guests in the lounge.

(603) 569-1335. Fax (603) 569-9426. Seventeen rooms with private baths. Doubles, $90 to $100.

Brook & Bridle Summer Homes and Inn, Roberts Cove Road, Box 270-Mailboat, Wolfeboro 03894.

This unusual 30-acre complex along Lake Winnipesaukee has been accommodating guests since 1927. Only lately under the founder's granddaughter, Bonnie Dunbar, and her husband, Glen McLean, has it taken a higher profile, advertising its status as an inn and taking B&B guests in the off-season. Primarily, the couple rent ten handsome and versatile, architecturally different homes of one to five bedrooms scattered about their property, by the month in summer and weekly in spring and fall. "We create a neighborhood for the summer," says Glen. House occupants get acquainted at an introductory wine and cheese party at the beach house and spend the next four weeks as they please. Most don't venture far from their own porch or beach or the common, 400-foot beach, centered by an open cabana furnished with Adirondack chairs and dotted with umbrella-covered picnic tables and small boats. The summer house renters generate plenty of overnight guests for the substantial main inn high up the hill, which also takes in B&B guests for functions. In early fall, the inn offers seven bedrooms and a suite to transients. The original pine paneling is evident throughout the lodge-like home. All bedrooms but one face the lake. They contain king, queen or twin beds and look quite comfortable and stylish. Common facilities include a large beamed great room with a baby grand piano, a sunroom with a hot tub overlooking the gardens and, on the walkout lower level, a casual TV room with huge fieldstone fireplace and a snack kitchen opening onto a flagstone terrace. A full breakfast, often using seasonal berries picked on the property, is served at individual tables in the dining room.

(603) 569-2707. Fax (603) 569-6949. www.brookbridle.com. Ten houses, monthly in summer, $5,100 to $7,600; weekly in spring and fall, $1,375 to $2,150. Eight B&B rooms with private baths. Doubles, $185 to $205, September to mid-October.

CAMPING. Wolfeboro Campground, 61 Haines Hill Road, Wolfeboro, (603) 569-9881 or 569-4029, offers 50 campsites in the pines for trailers and tents. Family rates are $20 to $22 daily, mid-May to mid-October.

Willey Brook Campground, 883 Center St. (Route 28), Wolfeboro, (603) 569-9493, also has sites for tents and trailers, $20 to $28 daily.

Around the Nearby Winnipesaukee Lakeshore

Bay Side Inn, Route 11-D, Alton Bay 03810.

For location, this family-run establishment is tough to beat: right along the lakeshore in a residential section on quiet old Route 11-D (long since bypassed by the main highway). "As soon as people see the lakefront and then the mountains, the room is sold," says owner Stephen Rogers. His mother designed the complex and his father built it starting in 1949. Steve and his wife Raquel started major renovations and refurbishing when they took over in 1991. They offer pristine motel rooms, all with updated bathrooms, carpeting, cable TV, phones and ceiling fans, plus five two-bedroom hillside efficiency units of original vintage rented by the week. Twelve motel units, six up and six down, view the lake up close and head-on, with balconies and patios as vantage points. The upstairs units are reserved for adults as Steve seeks to convey a quiet, inn image. Complimentary continental breakfast is available in the fireplaced, lakeview common room of the owners' house, to which the motel units are attached. But it is the waterfront setting that makes this operation so appealing: shady, well-kept lawns along the 250-foot shoreline, a flower-bedecked and white-fenced lounging terrace, gas barbecue grills and a family-oriented waterfront with docks, raft and a paddleboat and water trampoline for guests' use, as well as kayaks and boats for rent. Steve even built a large, shaded sandbox with a small tent full of toys to keep youngsters occupied. The colorful plantings and the window boxes overflowing with impatiens outside each room indicate this is a place that cares.

(603) 875-5005. Fax (603) 875-0013. www.bayside-inn.com. Eighteen motel rooms and five efficiency units. Doubles, $125 to $175. Efficiencies, $775 to $925 weekly.

Belknap Point Motel, 107 Belknap Point Road, Gilford 03246.

Owners Elaine and Harry Blinn claim "the best view of the lake" for their off-the-beaten-path motel complex. There's a great view indeed from the eight upper units, perched high atop a steep hillside on two floors, Each has a queen or two double beds, a vanity outside the bathroom in the entry and a waterview balcony at the far end. A suite on one side with two double beds in the bedroom and a sofabed in the living room has a private sundeck. The upper complex is so high up you might be tempted to drive rather than walk down the steep rear driveway to the shore. There's a different lake view from the eight original efficiency units (two of them suites with a sofabed in the living room) in a building sandwiched between the road and the shore. The quarters here appear rather intimate, but there's no denying the lakeside location. One end suite has a private deck; the others are separated from the water by a cement deck and a ten-foot-wide strip of grass. A little sandy beach area fashioned amid the rocks, picnic tables and two boat docks await. All units include TV and telephone. Morning coffee is complimentary in the reception area.

(603) 293-7511 or (888) 454-2537. www.bpmotel.com. Sixteen units. Doubles, $100 to $110. Efficiencies, $110 to $120. Three-night minimum for efficiencies.

Seeing and Doing

Lake Winnipesaukee, obviously, is the main attraction. Glacier-formed and spring fed, it is flanked by three mountain ranges and dotted by 274 mostly uninhabited islands. The 26-mile-long lake, New Hampshire's largest and one of the busiest in New England, is more than 60 miles around. Wolfeboro Bay and environs are among the prettiest and quietest sections. Supposedly, more than 15,000 powerboats are registered on the lake, and you see far more of them than sailboats. As we dined by the water one night, we enjoyed the sounds and lights of motorboats after dark – a traditional lake effect we had forgotten after years of vacationing at the ocean.

One suggestion in a Chamber of Commerce handout entitled "50 Things for Families to Do in Wolfeboro" struck a chord: "Catch lightning bugs in a jar – a must for a child's summer memories." That seemed to capture the spirit of the place.

On the Water

The best way to see Lake Winnipesaukee and its generally sheltered shoreline away from the road is by boat.

M/S Mount Washington, Weirs Beach.

The hulk of this three-level excursion boat is far larger than you'd expect as it cruises ever so carefully up to the Wolfeboro town dock. On board, you're told that the ship was built in 1888 and traversed Lake Champlain from Burlington to Plattsburgh until 1940. Then it was moved to Winnipesaukee to replace the original 1872 sidewheeler Mount Washington. In 1982, the ship was cut in half and lengthened to 283 feet, for a capacity of 1,250. The three-hour cruise covers 50 miles and visits Weirs Beach, Wolfeboro and occasionally Center Harbor, Meredith and Alton Bay, boarding and disembarking passengers at each stop. The narrated cruise takes you through "The Broads," twelve miles long and five miles wide, beneath the Ossipee, Sandwich and Squam mountain ranges on the north, the Belknap Mountain range on the south and the White Mountains in the distance to the northeast. Powerboats come up close to ride the wake. The ship seldom gets close to shore, though you do get a good view of the rocks known as Witches Island and the exclusive Governor's Island community that housed the German Embassy prior to World War I. The sound of the ship's horn reverberates off the mountains as it prepares to dock at busy Weirs Beach, where most of the passengers board. Just before returning to Wolfeboro after a stop at Alton Bay, it crosses the longest section of the lake. There you can see twenty miles up to Center Harbor, and across the bay to the lawns and buildings of Brewster Academy, which identify Wolfeboro from afar. If you time it right, you may get a seat in the Flagship Lounge, where two could lunch on a roast beef sandwich, turkey club and a beer each for $20.

(603) 366-5531 or (888) 843-6686. Cruise leaves Wolfeboro at 11:15 Tuesday, Wednesday, Friday and Saturday. Departs Weirs Beach daily at 10 and 12:30 (also at 3:15 in July and August). Operates Memorial Day to late October. Adults $19, children $9.

The Winnipesaukee Belle, Wolfeboro Town Dock.

Run by the Wolfeboro Inn, this 65-foot-long, riverboat-style side paddlewheeler takes up to 70 passengers on 90-minute narrated cruises around the southern portion of Lake Winnipesaukee. Highlights include looks at one of the oldest boatyards on the lake, a loon refuge, the former Chiang Kai-shek estate and islands with interesting histories. The lower deck is enclosed and air conditioned. The upper deck is canopied and open to the breezes.

(603) 569-3016 or (800) 451-2389. Cruises leave daily at 10:30 and 12:30 (also 2:30 in summer), mid-May to mid-October. Adults $10, children $5.

BOAT RIDES AND RENTALS. Everybody seems to want to get onto this lake and you can, too. The **Millie B,** a ten-passenger antique speedboat owned by the Wolfeboro Trolley Co., (603) 569-1080, offers half-hour rides on demand from 10 a.m. to sunset from the Wolfeboro Town Dock; adults $15, children $7. **Wet Wolfe Rentals,** (603) 569-3200, offers paddle boats and pleasure boats in the Wolfe Town complex along Back Bay at 19 Bay St. Nearby, **Back Bay Marina,** (603) 569-3200, rents motorboats from 10 to 90 horsepower, as well as canoes and rowboats. One may take a lake tour on its antique wooden boat by reservation. More powerful runabouts are available by the day or week from **Goodhue & Hawkins Navy Yard,** 244 Sewall Road, (603) 569-2371. **Winnipesaukee Kayak** at 17 Bay St., (603) 569-9926, offers everything for the kayaker.

CANOEING. Along the lake's 183-mile shoreline are countless coves perfect for fishing, snorkeling, kayaking and canoeing. The Carroll County Independent newspaper advises canoeists: "Hug the islands and shore for a delightful paddle on the largest lake in the state. Keep out of the Broads, where the wind and big boats will swamp a canoe, and don't chase the loons."

SWIMMING. Most lodging establishments have their own beaches. The public is welcome at **Brewster Beach,** a fine little strand off Clark Road, operated by the town and made available by Brewster Academy. Another good town operation is **Carry Beach** off Forest Road. The Allen Albee Beach, off Route 28N, is a small, sandy strand on Lake Wentworth. Swimming and picnicking also are offered at **Wentworth State Park,** six miles east of Wolfeboro.

Other Attractions

Molly the Trolley makes its rounds hourly from 10 to 4 in summer, showing off the town and providing transportation to the downtown area from outlying parking lots. Narrated tours leave the town docks on the hour. All-day fares: adults $5, children $2.

RECREATION. Cate Park, a pleasant little waterfront park beside the town dock, is the site of Wednesday evening concerts by the Cate Park Community Band, and dances and art shows throughout the summer. **Back Bay Recreation Area** has a playground and four tennis courts that are lighted until 10 p.m. Golfers are welcome at the eighteen-hole **Kingswood Golf Club,** next to the Windrifter Resort off South Main Street, and at **Perry Hollow Golf and Country Club,** Middleton Road, Wolfeboro Falls. The **Wolfeboro Croquet Club** offers English-style croquet in the traditional all-white attire on the Clarke Plaza Green. Hikers of modest endurance enjoy the **Abenaki Tower Walk.** A gradual, one-third-mile climb through the woods off Route 109 north in Tuftonboro leads to the abandoned fire tower, now maintained by volunteers. Climb the 80-foot-high tower for a look at graffiti carved by youthful visitors over the years and a panoramic view of northern Lake Winnipesaukee and the Ossipee Mountains.

MUSIC. Since 1995, the **Great Waters Music Festival** has presented the Portland

Symphony Orchestra and other musical attractions on several summer Saturday nights in its new lakeside performance tent on the Brewster Academy Field. **The Friends of the Wolfeboro Community Bandstand** has augmented the traditional Wednesday evening band concerts with a series of free Saturday evening concerts by visiting bands, from jazz to bluegrass. Since 1937, **Wolfeboro Friends of Music** has sponsored visiting entertainers in ten concerts throughout the year. In 2004, the **Heifetz International Music Institute** occupied the Brewster Academy campus and presented a series of Friday evening concerts in St. Cecelia Church.

The Libby Museum, Route 109 North, Wolfeboro.
Across the road from the shore of Winnipesaukee stands the town-operated Libby Museum, started in 1912 by retired dentist Henry Forrest Libby to house his natural history collections. His original collection includes an alligator, a human skeleton, mummy hands, old surgeon's equipment and paintings from the campaigns of General Wolfe (for whom Wolfeboro was named). Visitors have added to the museum, which now has three main themes. There are nearly 600 animals, birds, fish and reptiles in its natural history collection, and 350 Native American artifacts, among them two dugout canoes found in Rust Pond. More than 800 pieces in the Newcomb collection form the basis of Northern New England country living artifacts, which include farm machinery, household items, pottery and Shaker implements. The museum has changing art exhibits, conducts an evening lecture series in summer, and schedules children's classes in enviro-arts, including Native American studies and local history. The museum's annual cocktail fund-raiser is considered *the* social event of Wolfeboro's summer.
(603) 569-1035. Open Tuesday-Saturday 10 to 4, Sunday noon to 4, June to mid-September. Adults $2, children $1.

Clark House Museum Complex, South Main Street at Clark Road, Wolfeboro.
Operated by the Wolfeboro Historical Society, this complex of three museums is well worth a visit. The Clark House (1778), a Revolutionary farmhouse, was home to three generations of the family that donated the house to the society in 1929. Everything in it is more or less original, according to our guide. That includes the first piano in Wolfeboro, an applewood four-poster bed, a dining room table from the Wentworth mansion, outstanding pewter, clocks and kitchenware. The one-room Pleasant Valley Schoolhouse (circa 1820) contains old school paraphernalia plus a replica of the Wentworth mansion (it burned to the ground in 1820, and there's considerable debate over what it was like). A copy of the New York Herald reporting Lincoln's death is at the door. A replica of the 1862 Monitor Engine Co. Firehouse was erected in 1981 to house an 1872 Amoskeag steam pumper, plus five pieces of apparatus, leather fire helmets and horse-drawn sleighs.
(603) 569-4997. Museums open Wednesday-Friday 10 to 4, Saturday 10 to 2, July to Labor Day, or by appointment. Adults $4, students $2.

Wright Museum, 77 Center St., Wolfeboro Falls.
A small tank seems to be crashing onto the street through the front brick wall of this relatively new museum devoted to the World War II era. The sight attracts passersby into a "museum of American enterprise," which showcases the nation's enterprising spirit as everyone rallied to the call to arms at home and abroad. It's a much expanded outgrowth of the collection of military vehicles owned by the Wright family of Worcester, Mass., who summer in Wolfeboro. Collector David M. Wright purchased the six-acre site of a former lumberyard and erected two buildings on the banks of the Smith River in 1994. The front building houses what he calls the

"home front" exhibits, which recreate life in America during the 1940s. Life magazine covers, an old kitchen with a single-door refrigerator and a Ford V-8 evoke nostalgia for anyone of the era, as does the dental office with a long-forgotten pulley drill and side rinse basin. A victory garden, most of whose vegetables seem to get eaten by scavenging animals, flanks the pathway to the rear building. Its main floor and mezzanine hold upwards of 40 military vehicles, including the largest American tank of World War II and a 1941 Ford jeep, "the oldest and rarest you'll ever see," according to the curator, who gave us a tour. Volunteers from town, all veterans clad in red, white and blue, help tell the story at this very personal place.

(603) 569-1212. www.wrightmuseum.org. Open Monday-Saturday 10 to 4, Sunday noon to 4, May-October; weekends April and November. Adults $6, students $3.

New Hampshire Boat Museum, 397 Center St. (Route 28), Wolfeboro Falls.
This peripatetic museum settled here in 2000 to be close to other museums after occupying sites in Meredith and Weirs. Its shed-style building, formerly a theater on the old Allen-A Resort property, showcases some of the beautifully crafted wooden boats that proliferated on Lake Winnipesaukee during the 19th century. Along with outboard motors, runabouts and speedboats, there are artifacts, race photographs and trophies tracing the state's boating heritage. Special events have included a summer lecture series, in-the-water boat shows and a vintage race boat regatta. A museum store features watercolors of boating activity on the lake by local artist Peter Ferber.

(603) 569-4554. www.nhbm.org. Open Monday-Saturday 10 to 4, Sunday noon to 4, Memorial Day to mid-October. Adults $5, children $3.

Hampshire Pewter Co., 43 Mill St., Wolfeboro.
Free half-hour factory tours are conducted at this pewter factory and showroom. Started in 1973 as a crafts shop, Hampshire Pewter has grown into a nationally known manufacturer of quality cast (rather than spun) pewter. A video presentation introduces the tours. The owners are proud that their firm has decorated New Hampshire's Christmas tree next to the White House every year since 1983. They say former President George Bush not only displays but uses his set of six wine goblets, a gift from Wolfeboro. You'll no doubt be impressed by the variety of 125 items of handmade pewterware, from Christmas tree ornaments to lamp bases, bells and even a loon. **Hampshire Pewter Etc.,** a shop at 7 North Main St., holds a smaller display of pewter, including wind chimes we coveted for a mere $32.

(603) 569-4944 or (800) 639-7704. www.hampshirepewter.com. Guided tours, Monday-Friday at 10, 11, 1, 2 and 3, Memorial Day to Columbus Day. Show room open Monday-Friday 9 to 5, also Saturday in summer and fall.

SHOPPING. Wolfeboro has shops of quite good taste along its Main Street, the Wolfeboro Marketplace, Mill Street and Railroad Avenue.
The Marketplace has two levels of oft-changing shops in an attractive, brick-walked complex that's nicely landscaped. The **Camelot Book and Gift Shop** across the street offers books, cheeses and gifts, and the cheddar cheese spread the owners make themselves is delicious. **Black's Paper Store & Gift Shop** has paper goods, newspapers and magazines, as well as gifts and interior accessories upstairs.
Stop at **Cornish Hill Pottery** to see fine stoneware pottery, from lamps to tableware, and you usually can watch the potters at work. The neat contemporary birdbaths caught our eye. **Made on Earth** showcases artisans from around the world. Handcrafts and collectibles are shown at **The Straw Cellar. Finely Crafted** offers home accents. Jewelry and works of 200 artisans are shown at **Kalled Gallery.**

The **Country Bookseller** offers books, as well as readings and a great little newsletter with contributions by local reviewers. For clothing and sportswear, head for **Wolfeboro Casuals. Milligan's Pendleton Shop** is New Hampshire's only licensed Pendleton specialist, outfitting "ladies and gentlemen."

The **Wolfeboro League Shop** of the League of New Hampshire Craftsmen at 64 Center St. is outstanding. Nearby, small wooden houses on the front lawn identify the **American Home Gallery,** which specializes in vintage items for home and garden.

Where to Eat

Waterside in Wolfeboro

Wolfetrap Grill & Rawbar, 19 Bay St., Wolfeboro.

Two red lobsters standing tall on the roof identify this popular seasonal place along Back Bay. Barbara and John Naramore borrowed the locally appropriate name from the Wolf Trap performing arts center outside Washington, D.C., where they used to live, and patterned it after a Maryland crab house, minus the emphasis on crabs. Here you'll find a stylish yet casual establishment with a large interior bar decked out in baseball caps, bar stools emblazoned with a wolf logo, an L-shaped dining room with butcher paper clipped to large tables, and a screened porch overlooking the water. On busy nights, upwards of 200 people are on the waiting list for one of the 98 seats. They wolf down raw bar items – from peel 'n eat shrimp to oysters on the half shell – the specialty lobster roll, served with fries and slaw, and a variety of seafood from the Naramores' adjacent **Wolfecatch** fish market. Not to mention the clam boil, the soft-shell crab dinner, the blue-plate special, the sundried tomato pesto with vegetables over pasta and the hand-cut steaks. Desserts run to homemade pies and ice creams. The wines and microbrewed beers are as eclectic as the rest of the place, all part of a marina complex called the Wolfetown Marketplace.

(603) 569-1047. www.wolfetrap.com. Entrées, $10.95 to $21.95. Lunch, Thursday-Sunday from 11. Dinner nightly, 4 to 11. Seasonal.

Garwoods Restaurant & Pub, 6 North Main St., Wolfeboro.

Aw shucks – they changed the name of our favorite Aw Shucks to the Oyster Club and then to Rumors, then The Pirates Den and finally, with another change in ownership, to Garwoods. The last seems to be the best, with the Roark family credited for turning what had become a bar into a more serious restaurant with a first-rate location. It remains a relatively casual place to drink and eat by the water, outside on a deck beside all the boat action or inside in a raftered bar. The front dining room has paneled and glass dividers in Victorian style with fishnets and nautical artifacts for decor. The menu offers something for everyone, from beer-battered chicken tenders and veggie quesadillas for starters to lobster casserole and filet mignon for main courses. There are five kinds of burgers and a signature sandwich of grilled chicken in a pineapple-teriyaki sauce, served on a toasted English muffin with curly fries. After dinner, we decided to forego desserts like mud pie and cheesecake. Instead we indulged in a couple of liqueurs as we lingered on the deck to watch the lights of boats darting to and fro after dark.

(603) 569-7788. www.garwoodsrestaurant.com. Entrées, $11.95 to $22.95. Lunch and dinner daily from 11 in summer. Closed Wednesday in off-season.

Jo Green's Garden Café, 33 Dockside St., Wolfeboro.

Wolfeboro Bay is on view from the third-floor Upper Deck with a large bar and game room favored by the young crowd, as well as the second-floor balcony off the

Secret Garden dining and banquet rooms and dance floor. On the ground floor are the garden café and an ice cream and coffee shop called Jo to Go. The name supposedly conveys the coffee and garden theme, which is otherwise obscure but for the prominent salad bar inside the entry and the floral wallpaper and garden trellis for decor. The expanded upstairs operation takes precedence at night. Despite the waterfront location, we were the only customers for breakfast on a sunny summer weekday (since discontinued), when the Yum Yum Shop nearby was packed. The oversize menu features salads, burgers, rollups and pub food, plus such entrées as Boston cod and blackened swordfish. At our visit, the all-you-can eat greens bar cost $5.50 ("please, no sharing"), and low-carb sandwiches were featured.

(603) 569-8668. Entrées, $13.95 to $16.95. Open daily, 11 to 9.

Wolfeboro Dockside Grille & Dairy Bar, 11 Dockside, Wolfeboro.
Formerly Bailey's Dockside and later Maddies on the Bay, this old-timer out on the town dock by the Mount Washington landing is not our kind of place, but its waterside location makes it *very* popular. The pine-paneled dining room with booths and paper mats was packed in late afternoon with people enjoying hefty sandwiches, salad plates, any number of ice cream concoctions and a few entrées like fried clam, shrimp, scallop and haddock dinners, or combinations thereof. A dairy bar at the side dispenses ice cream cones as well as food to go.

(603) 569-1910. Entrées, $11.95 to $14.50. Open daily, 7 a.m. to 8 p.m., mid-May to October.

Other Wolfeboro Choices

Mise en Place, 96 Lehner St., Wolfeboro.
Two caterers teamed up in 2003 to open a first-rate French bistro in the front of a nondescript building along a side street. There are a handful of tables on the sidewalk, but most of the dining takes place at well-spaced tables in a plain but pleasant room inside. A wood bench serves as a banquette along two sides, and bleached pine tables are covered with white linens at night. Sconces on walls wainscoted in taupe and burgundy, a few pictures and a hutch holding wine and liqueur bottles set the scene. From a kitchen out of sight in back comes some of Wolfeboro's most sophisticated fare. For lunch, we sampled a crab cake with mustard sauce over mixed greens and a baby spinach salad with sea scallops, portobello mushrooms and bacon, augmented by French bread served in a colander with sweet butter. Profiteroles with caramel-chocolate sauce and a lemon curd tart testified to the kitchen's prowess with desserts. At night, chef-owners Terry Adrignola and Siobhan Magee offer such entrées as pine nut-encrusted halibut with roasted red pepper pesto, baked shrimp stuffed with lump crab and smoked gouda, and grilled sirloin steak with blue cheese butter.

(603) 569-5788. Entrées, $12 to $24. Lunch, Monday-Friday 11:30 to 2. Dinner nightly, 5 to 9. Closed Sunday and Monday in off-season.

Rumba, 14 Union St., Wolfeboro.
This 40-seat Latin-American bistro offers flavorful fare in convivial surroundings. Colombia native Fabio Rojas and his American wife vacationed here before moving from Connecticut to jazz up the Wolfeboro dining scene in 2003. Fabio does some of the cooking but prefers to defer to his chef and play the genial host in a spirited, dark dining room best described as lively. Lively, too, is the food, especially the day's seviche and the Madagascar shrimp appetizer sautéed in garlic and smoked paprika. Fabio suggests starting with the Latin-inspired New England clam chowder laced with chorizo, jalapeño and cilantro. He also recommends the serrano-fired

paella laden with seafood, chicken and chorizo and the garlicky rack of lamb for main courses. The braised veal shank with chocolate madeira sauce and the grilled flatiron steak with chimichurri sauce are not for the faint-hearted. Cool off with one of the refreshing desserts, perhaps the brandy-flavored fig tart served with white cheese and dulce leche or the sliced pineapple sautéed with dark rum and served with homemade coconut-ginger ice cream.

(603) 569-4833. Entrées, $17 to $25. Dinner, Tuesday-Saturday 5 to 9, Sunday 5 to 8:30. Closed Sunday-Tuesday in winter.

The Cider Press, 30 Middleton Road, Wolfeboro.

There's a cider press at the door, and apple trees are out back. Hence the name for this long-running restaurant that started as an inn and has expanded several times under the aegis of Robert and Denise Earle, a local couple who met while working at the Wolfeboro Inn and who have acquired a substantial local following. They now seat 165 diners by candlelight in three country-pretty barnwood rooms. In the lounge are two chairs in front of a three-sided open hearth which, Denise says with a laugh, "people fight over" in winter. Listed on the menu as "the odd couple," baby back ribs and golden fried tempura shrimp are the specialty, says Bob Earle, who does the cooking almost single-handedly. The dinner menu is nicely priced for items like seafood pie, shrimp scampi, grilled Atlantic salmon topped with lobster and béarnaise sauce, strip sirloin and steak béarnaise that would command twice the tab in metropolitan areas. One restaurateur said the best lamb chops he ever ate were served here. Baked haddock, halibut oscar and steak au poivre might be specials. Most of the desserts are baked on the premises, and the Boston cream pie, the ice cream crêpes, and the parfaits and sundaes are the downfall of many.

(603) 569-2028. www.theciderpress.net. Entrées, $13.95 to $19.95. Dinner nightly except Monday, 5 to 9, Sunday to 8. Abbreviated schedule in winter.

East of Suez, 775 South Main St. (Route 28 South), Wolfeboro.

Although food and travel writer Charles Powell and his family, some from the Philippines, have operated this restaurant for more than 40 summers, it seems to be almost a secret except to devotees of Asian food. Housed in a building that once was part of a camp, it looks the part – an almost rickety house with a big screened side porch that serves as a dining room, set in a field south of Wolfeboro. Decor is spare oriental, with simple black or yellow tables and chairs, rough wood flooring and paper globe lamps. The kitchen is huge, and out of it comes a parade of interesting dishes. Among starters and tapas, poached scallops with crab in miso sauce and the Philippine spring rolls known as lumpia are standouts, but you could also choose Thai satay, Japanese yakitori, Korean kim chee or a highly seasoned tikka chicken. At our first visit, the day's soup was clam chowder, almost like a New England version, but curiously spicy. Half a dozen entrées are offered and all sound so good that it's hard to choose. Salads with extravagant and original dressings (ginger, creamy garlic, sweet peanut) come with. Our tempura included a wide variety of vegetables and many large shrimp; the batter was perfect. And the Szechwan shrimp and cashews, stir-fried with snow peas, was great. On another visit, we liked the Philippine pancit, curly noodles sautéed with morsels of shrimp and pork with oriental vegetables, and the Philippine national dish, adobo pork and chicken stewed in soy, vinegar and garlic and then broiled and served with sliced bananas. Everything comes with shiny crackers sizzling from a pan. The Philippine "sans rival," a cashew and meringue torte, is a worthy ending. Portions are enormous.

(603) 569-1648. www.eastofsuez.com. Entrées, $13 to $17. Dinner, Tuesday-Sunday 5:30 to 9 or 10, June through early September. No credit cards. BYOB.

The Wolfeboro Inn, 90 North Main St., Wolfeboro.

Dining at this renovated village inn is in two distinctly different venues – one formal, one historic – but the same menu serves both. That menu has been downscaled lately, the former 1812 Steakhouse menu giving way to the more casual fare traditionally offered in the Wolfe's Tavern. The something-for-everyone menu now features sandwiches, burgers, "munchies," pizzas, pastas and basic entrées, from fish and chip, fried shrimp and broiled salmon to barbecued pork ribs, chicken fingers and sirloin steak. Slow-roasted prime rib remains the house specialty. Locals consider the nouveau-dining room on two levels too formal for such fare, leaving it available to inn guests for what had been special-occasion dining. They prefer the cozy front tavern fashioned from three of the inn's oldest common rooms. Here is New England as it used to be, dark and historic with row upon row of pewter beer mugs hanging from the beams and perfect for casual vittles. Little wonder the place is packed at all hours.

(603) 569-3016 or (800) 451-2389. Entrées, $9.95 to $19.95. Tavern daily, 7 a.m. to 10 or 11 p.m. Dinner nightly in dining room, from 5:30.

West Lake Asian Cuisine, 495 Center St. (Route 28), Wolfeboro.

Occupying the corner of a commercial building on the eastern outskirts of town, this exotic charmer offers a surprisingly sleek and plush, linened dining room and highly regarded oriental fare (the venture proved such a success it branched out to Gilford and Lincoln). The lengthy menu is by the numbers, with about half the items noted as hot and spicy. The 29 "specialties" include tangerine beef, shrimp royal, squid with black bean sauce and crispy whole fish. The lemon chicken laced with shredded ginger and the lamb in two styles (one with a delicate scallion sauce and the other more robust and piquant) proved exceptional for a takeout dinner on our motel balcony overlooking the lake.

(603) 569-6700. Entrées, $8.25 to $17.95. Lunch, Tuesday-Sunday 11 to 3. Dinner, Tuesday-Sunday 3 to 10. Sunday brunch, 11:30 to 2:30.

The Lakeview Inn, 200 North Main St., Wolfeboro.

Done up in pink and green, this restaurant is country elegant with wallpaper of flower baskets, swagged curtains, votive candles and fresh flowers from the inn's garden. The expanded lounge is more casual, and a light menu is available there. The extensive continental/American dinner menu is considered fancy for the area. You might start with stuffed mushrooms, fried calamari or clams casino. Main courses range from scrod napoleon, shrimp scampi and bouillabaisse to half-roasted chicken, grilled tournedos with shrimp, prime rib and veal parmigiana.

(603) 569-1335. www.lakeviewinn.net. Entrées, $10.95 to $26.95. Dinner nightly, 5 to 9.

Casual Wolfeboro Treats

Strawberry Patch, 50 North Main St., Wolfeboro.

"Have a berry nice day," says the menu at this breakfast and lunch place where you might be strawberried into oblivion. The decor is all strawberries, from stenciling on chairs to toddler's bibs. So is most of the menu, from strawberry omelet (no thanks) to strawberry pancakes (sensational) and strawberry waffles, piled with strawberries and whipped cream. At breakfast, our orange juice came in a glass imprinted with strawberries and served with a sliced strawberry. Lunch includes homemade soups, sandwiches, salads and quiche.

(603) 569-5523. Entrées, $4 to $8. Breakfast and lunch daily, 7:30 to 2, Sunday breakfast to 1. Closed January and February.

The new **Mill Street Eatery and Bakery,** 67 Mill St., is a casual, self-service deli and family restaurant serving three meals daily. Its baked goods are said to be as good as those of the Bread & Roses Bakery it replaced, and its specialty chicken marsala is to die for.

Café Sweets and Treats, 11 Railroad Ave., is a place for breakfast pastries and affordable sandwiches. Also on Railroad Avenue, the seasonal **Bailey's Bubble** offers the local Bailey's homemade hard and soft ice creams ("famous since 1938").

The Hot Dog Stand is a seasonal haunt on the wharf facing Cate Park. The boys manning this cart-stand beneath a Perrier umbrella weren't quite sure what to call it, nor did they seem to be terribly interested between swims in the lake. But we managed to get a hot dog for $1.25 and soda for 50 cents, and learned that the hours are daily in summer, 10:30 to 5.

Around the Nearby Lakeshore

Shibley's at the Pier, Route 11, Alton Bay.

You can't get much closer to Lake Winnipesaukee at a restaurant at this end of the lake. Eat outside on a deck with a trellised wall open to the water, tiny white lights and tables covered with jaunty umbrellas. Or dine inside one level above in a restored structure dating to the late 1800s amid oil lamps, old pictures on the paneled walls and windows onto the water. Over more than 25 years, the Shibley family have garnered quite a following for their with-it American fare, a mix of the traditional and the trendy. The menu changes frequently, but you'll likely find starters like stuffed mushroom caps, jumbo shrimp cocktail, and smoked salmon with brown bread and garnishes. Typical main courses are "sassy salmon, a little Caribbean and a little sweet," and pan-fried brook trout in a white wine-almond sauce. Others are chicken piccata, roast duck with merlot sauce and garlicked lamb chops.

(603) 875-3636. Entrees, $15 to $25. Lunch daily, 11 to 5. Dinner nightly, 5 to 9.

The William Tell Inn, Route 11, West Alton.

Built in the Swiss chalet style, this restaurant of long standing certainly is authentic, from its stone entrance to its darkish alpine interior in brown and beige, with stucco walls, paneled ceiling, stained-glass hangings and Viennese waltzes playing in the background. From the rear windows you can catch a glimpse of the lake when the leaves are off the trees, but don't come here for a lakeside setting. Chef-owner Peter Bossert recreates dishes from his Swiss hometown. Wiener schnitzel, sauerbraten, seafood mixed grill, chicken forestière, veal oscar and tournedos with mustard cream sauce are typical offerings. He also prepares fish specials, chicken bali with peanut sauce, and linguini with garlic shrimp and tomato concasse. You can order cheese fondue with farmer's bread, apples and smoked sausage and something called zürcher ratsherren topf – charbroiled beef, veal and pork medallions served with assorted sauces. All dinners come with salad and choice of roësti potatoes or spaetzle. Appetizers include cheese beignets, escargots, venison pâté with cumberland sauce and Maryland crab cakes. Peter and his wife Susan import Tobler chocolate from Switzerland for their delectable desserts. The bound wine list offers a couple of Swiss vintages.

(603) 293-8803. Entrees, $12.95 to $17.95. Dinner, Tuesday-Sunday from 5.

FOR MORE INFORMATION: Wolfeboro Chamber of Commerce, 32 Central Ave. in the railroad station, Box 547, Wolfeboro, NH 03894, (603) 569-2200 or (800) 516-5324. www.wolfeborochamber.com.

Reborn Wentworth by the Sea hotel looms behind Little Harbor Marina at water's edge.

Portsmouth, N.H.

The tidal Piscataqua River widens as it flows into the Atlantic Ocean. Its fertile shores produced a profusion of wild berries that prompted a small sailing party from England in 1630 to call their new home Strawbery Banke.

Thus began a thriving early seaport and shipbuilding center that grew up around a protected and deep harbor four miles inland from the river's mouth. A commercial area emerged around the old harbor area, where the grain and molasses warehouses were reputed at the time to be the tallest buildings in the United States. Now known as Merchants Row, the converted warehouses remain Portsmouth's tallest structures other than church spires. They convey a patina of history that pervades much of the small city of 21,000, which has blessedly retained its sense of place as well as its scale.

Although the seacoast is nearby, New Hampshire's miniscule portion is pinched by the geographical encroachments of neighboring Massachusetts and Maine. Portsmouth is essentially a river city, and the river – pronounced Pis-CAT-a-qua – defines its character.

You can see the river from downtown shops and restaurants. Sense it along much of the new Portsmouth Harbour Trail. Enjoy it at the lovely waterfront Prescott Park. Swim in it at beaches out in the picturesque island town of New Castle or affluent oceanfront Rye. Cruise on it around the harbor or out past picturesque lighthouses to the nine legendary offshore islands known as the Isles of Shoals.

Portsmouth's early prominence and its ties to the water created a distinctive legacy. John Paul Jones, America's pre-eminent naval hero, lived here as his ships were being outfitted for duty in the Revolutionary War. The mansion in which he boarded is among a number of historic homes now opened to the public as house museums. The biggest concentration is in the outdoor history museum complex known as Strawbery Banke, an authentic restoration on the site of the original Puddle Dock neighborhood along the riverfront.

In this city that knows how to restore and recycle rather than raze, dated buildings like the old Merchants Row warehouses have been converted into retail shops and restaurants. Lofts above downtown storefronts provide the young and entrepreneurial with space for living and for high-tech startups. The Seacoast is now the E-Coast in local lingo. The town is consistently ranked as one of the nation's most livable.

That dynamic makes it attractive for the visitor, too.

Getting There

Portsmouth is located in southeastern New Hampshire, four miles inland from the seacoast and just below the Maine border. It is reached by coastal U.S. Route 1 or Interstate 95. The closest major airport is in Manchester, 40 miles to the west. Boston's Logan International Airport is about 50 miles to the southwest.

Where to Stay

Near the Water

Wentworth by the Sea, 588 Wentworth Road, New Castle 03854.

The area's best waterfront location has long been claimed by the storied Wentworth, a grand seaside hotel poised on a rise at the tip of the island of New Castle and host to the rich and famous for more than a century. The sparkling-white hotel with red roof reopened in 2003 as a Marriott hotel and spa, squeezed between new front and back access roads and residential development where the open lawns of a golf course had been, with showy landscaping and a gazebo providing lush pastoral relief. The restored, four-story hotel contains 143 guest rooms, some with french doors onto miniscule balconies facing the harbor and ocean in front and the meandering Piscataqua River in back – those on the third floor are most in demand. The best rooms (and views) are in eighteen bi-level efficiency suites with balconies at water's edge in the Little Harbor Marina, a short hike downhill from the hotel. Three meals a day are served in two side-by-side dining rooms, one with pillars and a restored domed ceiling. Across the street in the marina, **Latitudes** offers informal waterfront dining for lunch and dinner (see Where to Eat). Resort activities include a full-service spa, tennis and guest access to the Wentworth by the Sea Country Club and Marina.

(603) 422-7322 or (866) 240-6313. Fax (603) 422-7329. www.wentworth.com. One hundred forty-three rooms and eighteen suites. Doubles, $200 to $400. Suites, $500 up.

Sheraton Harborside Portsmouth, 250 Market St., Portsmouth 03801.

The best water-view location in town is claimed by this nicely designed, red brick hotel and conference center of recent vintage that blends into the historic architecture along the Portsmouth waterfront. More than half the rooms yield views of the working harbor. Mahogany furniture enhances the airy lobby, from which the waterfront activity may be glimpsed. A curving stairway sweeps gracefully to the second-floor function rooms. Rooms are typical hotel-style, with kingsize or two double beds. A fourth floor, added in 1997, consists of deluxe club-level rooms. Here, continental breakfast and afternoon hors d'oeuvres are put out in two small lounge areas. Seven Ports of Call penthouse suites atop the hotel feature balconies overlooking the harbor, gas

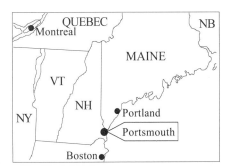

fireplaces and kitchens. The hotel also offers seventeen two-story, two-bedroom suites. Facilities include an indoor pool, sauna, fitness center and two restaurants.

(603) 431-2300 or (877) 248-3794. Fax (603) 431-7805. www.sheratonportsmouth.com. One hundred eighty-five rooms and 17 suites with kitchens. Doubles, $259 to $299. Suites, $425 to $875.

The Bow Street Inn, 121 Bow St., Portsmouth 03801.

This conveniently located downtown riverfront establishment is a cross between a motel and a small hotel. It occupies the second floor of a restored four-story brick brewery warehouse that also houses condominiums, the Seacoast Repertory Theatre and a café. Guest rooms go off either side of a center hallway. The views are of rooftops or the street, because the condominium blocks the view of the river except from Room 6. Rather small, the rooms are furnished simply but attractively in light pastel colors with queensize brass beds (except for one with a king/twins), thick carpeting, cable TV, telephones and a single chair. One room, billed as a mini-suite for extended stays, contains a sofa and a small dining table. Juice, cereal, muffins, bagels and breads for toasting are put out in a pleasant brick dining room with three tables and a small refrigerator for guests' use. The owner "tries to make people feel at home," said one of the assistants on duty at our visit.

(603) 431-7760. Fax (603) 433-1680. www.bowstreetinn.com. Ten rooms with private baths. Doubles, $140 to $175.

Portsmouth Harbor Inn & Spa, 6 Water St., Kittery, Me. 03904.

Facing the Portsmouth waterfront from across the Piscataqua River in Maine is this restored house formerly known as the Gundalow Inn. Paula and Tim Miller took over the property in 2002 and added a spa in the former innkeepers' quarters in the attached barn. They capitalize on their proximity to the waterfront and Portsmouth, which is a short walk across the Memorial Bridge, but pre-existing buildings block much of the view. Four of the five guest rooms offer glimpses of the water. All are named after gundalows (a corruption of the word gondolas), the 225-year-old flat-bottom boats with sails that plied the Piscataqqua and are believed to have transported the bricks for the house downriver from Dover. Ten-foot-high ceilings, Victorian period antiques and TV/VCRs are the rule in the second-floor rooms, one of which has a king bed and windows on three sides. A curved stairway beneath a skylight leads past a plant-filled shelf to the third floor, where two guest rooms with deep clawfoot soaking tubs afford the best views of the river and of Portsmouth. Guests enjoy a large, comfortable parlor, where breakfast is served at a table for ten. A small front porch furnished in wicker catches a view of the river, as does a courtyard terrace with a gurgling fountain between the B&B and the spa building.

(207) 439-4040. Fax (207) 438-9286. www.innatportsmouth.com. Five rooms with private baths. Doubles, $139 to $209.

Other Choices

Martin Hill Inn, 404 Islington St., Portsmouth 03801.

The first B&B in Portsmouth (1978), this is still going strong, thanks to the dedication and energy of founding innkeepers Jane and Paul Harnden. Their handsome yellow house was built in 1820. Although up against a busy street, it's quiet because of air conditioning and one can retreat in summer to a deep and beautifully landscaped back yard where 400 plants thrive and a water garden is illuminated at night. There are three spacious guest rooms in the main inn, plus a room and three suites in the Guest House. We're partial to the Greenhouse Suite in the spiffy side annex, which contains a small solarium furnished in wicker looking onto the water garden, rattan furniture in an inside sitting room and a bedroom with a spindle bed and a full bath. All rooms have queensize beds, modern baths, loveseats or comfortable chairs, good reading lamps, writing desks, armoires, and nice touches like potpourri in china teacups and the inn's own wildflower glycerin soaps. Breakfast is served on a gleaming mahogany table in the antiques-filled dining room. Orange juice might be followed by Jane's scrumptious baked apple, the core filled with brown sugar. Paul makes dynamite french toast with Italian sourdough bread, slathered with almonds and accompanied by Canadian bacon and homemade cranberry relish. Our scrambled eggs with cheese and chervil were served with cranberry bread, and the coffee pot was bottomless.

(603) 436-2287. www.martinhillinn.com. Four rooms and three suites with private baths. Doubles, $125 to $165.

The Governor's House, 32 Miller Ave., Portsmouth 03801.

Artistry and amenities mix nicely in this 1917 white Georgian Colonial that was the former home of a governor and reopened as a B&B in 2002 under new owners Bob Chaffee and Barbara Trimble. The artistry is evident from the framed doilies made by the current owner's grandmother displayed suavely on the living room walls to the murals hand-painted on the tiles of the guest bathrooms. The amenities include Bose radios and TV/DVD players in the guest bedrooms, luxurious bedding, evening wine and cheese, personalized breakfasts and an outdoor hot tub. There's even a lighted backyard tennis court. The Prescott is the largest and fanciest of the four guest rooms, each with an antique queensize bed dressed in Frette linens and down comforter. A life-size mermaid on the shower wall carries out the nautical theme in the Captain's Room. Around the double whirlpool tub in the Prescott Room are lovebirds with phrases for affection written in French. Guests gather in the spacious living room, an adjacent sun porch or on the leafy patio, enveloped by rhododendrons overlooking the tennis court in the hidden back yard. Breakfast is delivered at the time and place of the guests' choosing from a check-off menu offering a selection of fruit, baked goods, cereal and perhaps quiche.

(603) 431-6546 or (866) 427-5140. Fax (603) 427-5145. www.governors-house.com. Doubles, $195 to $245.

Sise Inn, 40 Court St., Portsmouth 03801.

A Queen Anne home built in 1881 for the John E. Sise family has been remodeled and expanded with great taste by a growing Canadian-based hotel group called Someplace(s) Different Ltd. Rooms and suites on three floors and in a carriage house vary in bed configuration, size and decor. All are elegantly furnished in antiques and period reproductions with striking window treatments and vivid wallpapers. Geared to the business traveler, they have queen or twin beds, vanities outside the bathrooms (the larger of which contain whirlpool baths), writing desks, clock radios, telephones, and remote-control television and VCRs, often hidden in armoires. The stylish main-floor living room is much like an English library with several conversation areas and fresh flowers all around. A help-yourself breakfast of fruits, juices, yogurt, cheese, cereals, granola, bagels, toasting breads and all kinds of preserves and honey is available amidst much ornate wood in the dining room.

(603) 433-1200 or (877) 747-3466. Fax (603) 433-0200. www.siseinn.com. Twenty-five rooms and nine suites with private baths. Doubles, $189. Suites, $229 to $269.

The Inn at Strawbery Banke, 314 Court St., Portsmouth 03801.

You can't stay much closer to the Strawbery Banke museum complex than this 1800 ship captain's house situated right up against the street, as so many in

Portsmouth are. All seven guest rooms come with private baths, although one is in the hall (and one in the attic suite is open to the room). Two rooms on the main floor share a common room. Strawberry stenciling, strawberry comforters and strawberry candies on the pillows accent the prevailing green and white color scheme here. More bedrooms go off an upstairs common room. One with windows on three sides contains a double and a single bed and three ice-cream-parlor chairs around a glass table. Innkeeper Sally Glover O'Donnell serves a full breakfast in a skylit breakfast room with an abundance of hanging plants. The main course at our visit was sourdough blueberry pancakes with sausages, supplemented by oatmeal, cold cereals and homemade pastries. The room looks onto a strawberry patch, bird feeders and the trellised rose garden of the historic Governor Langdon House just behind. Sally keeps cookie jars stocked for afternoon or evening snacks in the two cozy common rooms, both outfitted with television sets.

(603) 436-7242 or (800) 428-3933. www.innatstrawberybanke.com. Seven rooms with private baths. Doubles, $145 to $150.

Best Western Wyndwood Hotel & Suites, 580 U.S. Route 1 Bypass , Portsmouth 03801.

The biggest and most varied of the motor inns around the busy Portsmouth Traffic Circle is this locally owned establishment, recently separated and renamed from the Howard Johnson chain. Doubles, queens and king beds are available in the main hotel. A new six-story tower wing contains 32 suites of one or two bedrooms, some with whirlpool tubs. Each has a king or two double beds, a sofabed and a full kitchen. Facilities include a fitness center, an indoor pool with a hot tub and an outdoor pool. The two-bedroom suites add a second bathroom. A Bickford's Family Restaurant is just off the hotel lobby.

(603) 436-7600. www.wynwoodportsmouth.com. One hundred thirty-seven rooms and 32 suites. Doubles, $79.95 to $199.95. Suites, $165.95 to $350.

The Meadowbrook Inn, 549 U.S. Route 1, Portsmouth 03801.

This locally owned motor inn provides space – as in spacious rooms with two double beds and spacious grounds, at least relative to the others around the Portsmouth Traffic Circle. A bit removed from the fray around the circle, it offers rooms that we found a cut above the standard-issue chain motel. Attributes include an outdoor pool and a new fitness center. Rates include a continental breakfast.

(603) 436-2700 or (800) 370-2727. Fax (603) 433-2700. www.meadowbrookinn.com. One hundred twenty-three rooms. Doubles, $99.95 to $129.95.

Seeing and Doing ⎯⎯⎯⎯⎯⎯⎯⎯⎯⎯ _ſℭℭ_

Most of Portsmouth's attractions – and certainly those that visitors tend to seek – are clustered along the riverfront in the downtown area. Their very proximity to each other makes this a good place for walking. The **Seacoast Trolley** helps people get around in season. A new way to tour is by horse and carriage with **Portsmouth Livery Co.,** (603) 427-0044. The talkative guide, in beard and top hat, adds dimension to the city's history as he gives sightseeing tours for $20 to $40. They leave from the Market Square carriage stand from noon into the evening, daily Memorial Day through Labor Day and weekends in the off-season.

Around the Harbor

More than 70 points of scenic or historic significance are visible along the **Portsmouth Harbour Trail.** Along the way are ten buildings listed on the National

Register, ten national historic landmarks and three homes maintained by the Society for the Preservation of New England Antiquities. The trail is detailed in a 32-page map and guide (available for $2 from the Chamber of Commerce visitor center and the downtown Market Square information kiosk). Marked by bright blue signs, the trail is divided into three loops. One covers the Ceres Street waterfront and another the downtown area south of Market Square. The longest loop covers the historic East Side around Strawbery Banke. Guided walking tours leave from the Market Square information kiosk, Thursday-Monday at 10:30 and 5:30 (Sunday at 1:30 p.m.), July 4 through Columbus Day; adults $8, children $4.

A favorite area is along Ceres Street, site of the wharves and early warehouses lately converted into shops and restaurants. When they're not out guiding ships up the tricky tidal river, red and black tugboats – a local icon – may be tied up at the docks. Walk up and around Bow Street to the Strawbery Banke museum complex. Across Marcy Street is **Prescott Park,** a generally tranquil waterfront retreat graced in summer by showy and prolific flower beds. New floral varieties are tested in the formal gardens, a joint venture between the park and the University of New Hampshire's Cooperative Extension Service. Benches are scattered about for taking in the scene and the waterfront activity. The park contains the 1705 Sheafe Warehouse, where John Paul Jones outfitted the Ranger. It now houses the **Folk Art Museum**, which has a small boat building exhibit as well as hand-carved mastheads and ship models (open daily in summer, 9 to 6; free). The park is the site for frequent special events, from the month-long Prescott Park Arts Festival to the Seacoast Jazz Festival, the Chowder Fest and the Piscataqua Faire – A Renaissance on the Waterfront.

Although **picnicking** is permitted in Prescott Park, an even better place is **Four Tree Island**, within walking distance of the park. Nearly in the middle of the river, it is reached across a short bridge from the end of Mechanic Street to Pierce Island and then via a causeway. You may join downtown workers at picnic tables under shelters, all with views of the water.

The Isles of Shoals. About ten miles offshore from Portsmouth Harbor is a legendary group of nine stark, rocky islands beloved by naturalists and bird-watchers. Charted by Capt. John Smith when he sailed past in 1614, the barren islands originally drew European fishermen for their "shoals" or schools of fish. The two largest islands, Appledore and Star, became summer resorts in the 1800s. Since the early 1900s, Star Island has been operated as a conference center by the Unitarian-Universalist and Congregational churches, whose week-long summer retreats are based at the Victorian-era Oceanic Hotel. Appledore is home to the Shoals Marine Laboratory, North America's largest undergraduate marine field station, as well as celebrated poetess Celia Thaxter's cottage and garden. Except for a few summer cottages and homes of lobstering families, the Isles remain populated mostly by a host of sea birds and marine life. Star Island is accessible to the public by the Isles of Shoals Steamship Co. (see below), a family-owned passenger ferry service that provides its lifeline, supporting several hundred conference guests and staff. Overnight visitors must be enrolled in a conference or educational class. Daytrippers must return the same day. Although the mainland is easily visible on clear days, visitors instantly feel the sense of separateness of a place apart.

On Wednesdays in summer, Celia Thaxter's Garden Tour offers the only public access to Appledore Island. The Victorian poetess, daughter of a lighthouse keeper at White Island, was known for the cottage and garden that inspired her famous little book, "An Island Garden." Up to 43 tour participants are shuttled to Appledore

Island from neighboring Star Island, accessed by the Isles of Shoals Steamship Co. Reservations are required through the Shoals Marine Laboratory, (607) 255-3717, run by Cornell University in cooperation with the University of New Hampshire.

Isles of Shoals Steamship Co., 315 Market St.

Assorted cruises from Barker's Wharf are offered aboard the 348-passenger replica Victorian steamship M/V Thomas Laighton, the type of vessel employed when the nearby Isles of Shoals were a leading summer colony. Among them are harbor cruises, a Monday lighthouse cruise and dinner cruises on certain evenings. The most popular are the twice-daily Isles of Shoals and Portsmouth Harbor tours. A three-and-one-half-hour cruise leaving daily at 9:25 (Saturday at 10:25), the Star Island Walkabout, includes a 45-minute guided tour of Star Island. The cruise at 10:25 a.m., called the Star Island stopover, allows passengers three hours to explore the island before returning at 5. The harbor portion of the tour passes the nation's oldest working naval yard and its closed castle-like prison called "the Alcatraz of the East," five forts and three lighthouses.

(603) 431-5500 or (800) 441-4620. www.islesofshoals.com. Variety of cruises daily, mid-June to Labor Day; fewer in spring and fall; hours vary. Isles/Harbor tours, adults $24, children $14.

Portsmouth Harbor Cruises, Ceres Street Dock.

The 49-passenger Heritage takes passengers on cruises around the fourteen islands of the harbor, up the Piscataqua River as far as Dover and Great Bay, along the shore at sunset and, three times a week, out to the Isles of Shoals. The basic 90-minute harbor tour shows nearly 400 years of history from the area's settlement in 1623 to the harbor's modern-day role in the nation's economy and defense.

(603) 436-8084 or (800) 776-0915. www.portsmouthharbor.com. Harbor cruises, mid-June to mid-September, daily at 10 and 3, also Saturday-Monday at noon and Friday-Sunday at 4:30; adults $14, children $9. Isles of Shoals cruises in summer leave Wednesday-Friday at noon; adults $18, children $10. Hours vary in spring and fall.

BOATING. From the wharf at Geno's Chowder & Sandwich Shop at 177 Mechanic St., Capt. John Borden of Buccaneer Charters, (603) 431-6999, gives a variety of cruises year-round aboard his 40-foot M/V Hurricane Mary. Offerings range from harbor tours to evening cool-off cruises with complimentary beer and wine. Among them are wreck excursions for scuba divers and sea-level sightseeing for kayakers around the Isles of Shoals.

Up to 49 passengers can board the Lady Patricia for sightseeing, deep-sea fishing and scuba diving under **Captain Bill's Charters,** (603) 463-9028.

For an unusual tour of Portsmouth Harbor, book a trip on the **Tug Alley Too,** one of the harbor's working tugboats. Capt. Bob Hassold offers rides for up to six people on his tugboat moored near his nautical and tugboat collectibles store, Tugboat Alley, 2 Ceres St., (603) 430-9556 or (877) 884-2553.

Three-hour daysails and sunset dinner cruises aboard the **S.V. Amaryllis,** a 45-foot luxury catamaran, leave daily from the Badger Island Marina, (603) 205-0630. It also offers "berth and breakfast," an overnight trip to the Isles of Shoals with dinner at the Oceanic Hotel on Star Island and anchorage in Gosport Harbor, $325 to $350 double.

USS Albacore, Albacore Park, 600 Market St.

Want to get inside the fastest submarine of its time? This 1,200-ton experimental research vessel across from the waterfront was built at the Portsmouth Naval Shipyard in 1952 and served as a prototype for modern submarines, testing new control systems, dive brakes, sonar systems and hydrodynamics. An underwater laboratory carrying a crew of 55, it had a revolutionary teardrop hull design enabling it to set an underwater speed record in the late 1960s. But its success marked the end of the sub as a surface vessel able to dive briefly at slow speeds and launched the era of a high-speed underwater fleet. It's now in permanent drydock beside a memorial garden paying tribute to those who died in submarine service. A fifteen-minute documentary film is shown prior to a tour.

(603) 436-3680. Open daily, 9:30 to 5. Adults $5, children $2.

FORTS. Because of its key defensive location, seven forts were built to defend Portsmouth harbor. **Fort Constitution,** a state historic site beside the U.S. Coast Guard station off Route 1-B in New Castle, originated in the early 1600s but reflects today the Revolutionary and Civil War periods. A 1774 raid by local patriots was the first overt act against England and predated the Revolution's outbreak by four months. Beside the fort is the Fort Point Lighthouse and just offshore, the Whaleback Lighthouse. On clear days, the Isles of Shoals are visible ten miles offshore. The fort is open daily year-round, 10 to 5; free.

Spectacular ocean views are the forte of **Fort Stark,** Wild Rose Lane, off Route 1-B, New Castle. Another state historic site, the fort dates to 1746, but reflects its service in protecting the Portsmouth Naval Shipyard in World War II. A walking trail traverses the ten-acre fort site. Open weekends and holidays 10- to 5, May-October; free.

Across the river in Kittery Point, Me., is **Fort McClary,** a state historic site. The 27-acre park off Kittery Point Road (Route 103) contains a six-sided blockhouse built in 1844. It commands a good view of the coast and the river's mouth. The fort and grounds are maintained as a state park. Paths lead to the edge of a bluff looking down on the ocean. Park and fort open daily 9 to dusk, Memorial Day through September; adults $1.50.

SWIMMING. Although Portsmouth does not offer swimming, there are excellent state beaches nearby in Rye and Hampton. From **Wallis Sands,** a small beach in the town of Rye, more beaches are available to the south as far as North Hampton Beach and Hampton Beach State Park, which together stretch nearly three miles along the ocean. All charge a nominal admission fee or have metered parking.

Odiorne Point State Park, 570 Ocean Blvd (Route 1-A) in Rye, is part of the first settlement in New Hampshire in 1623. The 137-acre park at the northernmost point of the state's seacoast is good for walking and hiking, although its rocky shore is not conducive to swimming. Picnic tables near the water's edge afford a fine view of the ocean and the boating activity offshore. Trails lead through seven distinct coastal habitats.

Located in the park is the recently renovated and expanded **Seacoast Science Center,** which offers exhibits on the area's natural history and nature programs. Visitors touch tidal pool creatures in indoor touch tanks and watch ocean fish swim in the 1,000-gallon Gulf of Maine tank.

Park: (603) 436-7406. Admission $3, children under 12, free. Open daily, 8 to dusk.
Science Center: (603) 436-8043. www.seacentr.org. Open daily 10 to 5, April-October; Saturday-Monday 10 to 5, rest of year. Adults $3, children $1.

The Town of New Castle, quaint islands out in the harbor, are connected to the mainland by short bridges and causeways via Newcastle Avenue (Route 1-B). The islands are part of the original settlement in 1623 and are dotted with prosperous and historic homes. The meandering roads and treed residential properties, many with water views, mix contemporary-style houses with those of days gone by. You can visit the seacoast park at **Great Island Common,** where there are waterfront picnic tables, a playground and views of the Isles of Shoals. Visitors gawk at the newly restored Wentworth-by-the-Sea, a majestic resort hotel if ever there was one.

Another rewarding drive is out Maine Route 103 past the Portsmouth Naval Yard in Kittery to **Kittery Point,** where attractive houses large and small seem to be surrounded by water on all sides.

Historic Restorations

Strawbery Banke, Marcy Street.

The waterfront neighborhood once known as Puddle Dock – the site where Portsmouth was settled – was saved from the wrecker's ball in the 1950s. Billed as "an American original," the walk-through museum is the careful restoration of one of the nation's oldest neighborhoods. Its more than 40 structures across ten acres date from 1695 to 1945 and depict four centuries of cultural and architectural change. Some have simply been preserved. Some are used by working artisans (independent of the museum, the artisans are earning their living as well as re-enacting history). Others are used for educational exhibits including archaeology, architectural styles and construction techniques and, on the outside, historic gardens. Strawbery Banke's collection of local arts and furniture is shown in ten historic houses. George Washington, Daniel Webster, John Hancock and John Paul Jones all visited here. Yet these are not all homes of the rich or famous, but rather of ordinary people. The mix is one of its most compelling features.

(603) 433-1100. www.strawberybanke.org. Open May-October, Monday-Saturday 10 to 5, Sunday noon to 5; adults $15, children $10, families $35. Open November-April for 90-minute guided walking tours on the hour, Thursday-Saturday 10 to 2 and Sunday noon to 2; adults $10, children $5, families $25. Closed in January.

Portsmouth Historic House Associates. Six of Portsmouth's finest house museums are open individually and linked by a walking tour. Considered the one not to miss is the 1763 **Moffatt-Ladd House,** a replica of an English manor house located at 154 Market St., just above the Ceres Street restaurants and shops. Its lawns once swept down to the harbor. Also near the water is the 1716 **Warner House,** perhaps the finest example of a brick urban mansion from the 18th century left in New England. The waterfront **Wentworth-Gardner House** (1760) is a perfect example of the Georgian style. Once owned by New York's Metropolitan Museum, it narrowly escaped being torn apart and rebuilt in Central Park. The yellow 1758 Portsmouth Historical Society Museum at the **John Paul Jones House,** the imposing **Governor John Langdon House** (1784) and the Federal-style **Rundlet-May House** (1807) also are worth viewing. Most are open six or seven days a week from June to mid-October and charge $5 or $6 each.

The **Ranger Trail,** a self-guided walking tour, traces the footsteps of John Paul Jones and the sites linked to the naval leader and his sloop-of-war Ranger, the first ship to carry America's new Stars and Stripes into battle overseas. His raid on English ports in 1778 helped win foreign support for the Revolution and gave credibility to the fledgling Continental Navy. The trail details fifteen sites, from the John Paul Jones House to the Sheafe Warehouse in Prescott Park to a couple of taverns in Strawbery Banke. The trail is sponsored by the local Ranger Foundation, (603) 433-3221, which is restoring the vessel.

Wentworth Coolidge Mansion, 375 Little Harbor Road.

This waterfront prize, an enormous yellow house dating to 1720, served as the residence for New Hampshire's first royal governor. It overlooks Little Harbor, just off Route 1-A on the way to New Castle. The tour of the 42-room structure includes a look at the only French stewing kitchen in New England, built for the governor's French chef. Visitors may explore the grounds and shoreline to see evidence of a 19th-century swimming pool, remnants of the Wentworths' wharf along the seawall and the oldest purple lilacs in North America, imported in the 1750s. Parking and admission are free and picnicking is encouraged.

(603) 436-6607. Open mid-May through Labor Day, Wednesday-Saturday 10 to 3, Sunday 1 to 4; Saturday and Sunday to mid-October. Guided tour, $3.

SHOPPING. Downtown Portsmouth has an unusual array of interesting, locally owned shops concentrated around Market Square and the waterfront. In one of its four stores, **Macro Polo Inc.** has inventive children's toys; we were transported back to our childhood while gazing at the assortment of marbles in the window. **Wholly Macro!** stocks handmade Texas boots among its wares. **Macroscopic** struck us as rather New Agey. Behind and below on Ceres Street is **Macrosonic. Not Just Mud! Craft Gallery** stocks great hand-blown art glass, kaleidoscopes, pottery, jewelry and titanium clocks among its contemporary crafts. The **Paper Patch** is the shop for funny cards. **Worldly Goods** purveys birdhouses, oil lamps, interesting baskets and adorable cat pins. More good art and gift destinations are **Les Cadeaux, Gallery 33, Pierce Gallery, Lovell Designs** and **The Blue Frog.** We did some Christmas shopping at **Salamandra Glass** and the **N.W. Barrett Gallery**, which has some of Sabra Field's woodcuts, and fantastic jewelry. **The Cultured Garden** is "where home and garden meet." **The Gardener's Cottage,** a charming cottage with its own pocket garden beside Prescott Park, specializes in tools and accessories for the garden enthusiast. **Strawbery Banke's Museum Shop** at the Dunaway Store on Marcy Street is a classy gift shop. **Strawbery Banke's** working crafts shops offer the wares of potters, a cabinetmaker, a weaver, and dories made in the boat shed.

Where to Eat

On or Near the Water

The Wellington Room, 67 Bow St., Portsmouth.

White-clothed tables, set amid a beamed ceiling and brick walls, are beside big windows onto the water at this small restaurant backing up to the harbor. Some of the best food in town – plus, an added fillip, a British-style afternoon tea – is served up in its 38-seat dining room, hidden from view above and behind a downtown storefront. New Zealand-born chef-owner David Robinson imparts Asian, Italian and French accents to his creative American cuisine. Expect entrées such as grilled Chilean sea bass on Russian fingerling potatoes with port wine-mushroom sauce, oven-roasted haddock with chardonnay-tomato broth, roasted duck breast with a watercress and Australian shiraz reduction, and, of course, New Zealand rack of lamb, with minted blackberry-honey drizzle. Starters include a mushroom and cheese crêpe, pan-seared foie gras and szechuan peppercorn-crusted tuna with a sesame-seaweed salad. Afternoon tea service is the chef's tribute to his late British grandmother, for whom a proper British tea was a ritual.

(603) 431- 2989. www.thewellingtonroom.com. Entrées, $17 to $26. Tea, Friday-Sunday 3:30 to 4:30. Dinner, Wednesday-Friday 5 to 9, Saturday 5 to 9:30, Sunday 4 to 9.

Lindbergh's Crossing, 29 Ceres St.

This bistro and wine bar with obscure references to Charles Lindbergh is across the street from the harbor in space long occupied by the famed Blue Strawbery restaurant. A propeller hangs on one wall of the brick and beamed downstairs bistro. Signatures on the beams date to the 1800s in what was once a ship's chandlery. A representation of Lindbergh's flight across the Atlantic flanks the stairway to the casual upstairs wine bar, where dinner also is available. The intimate room offers a good view of the harbor. The contemporary Mediterranean fare receives high marks from locals. Expect eclectic variety in such main courses as seafood paella, pan-fried trout with a crabapple chutney, a smoked lobster croque monsieur or beef tenderloin au poivre. Typical starters are mussels marinière, frog's legs over spicy rémoulade, escargots with raclette and coriander-crusted rare tuna with provençal sauce. Desserts include a signature "medium rare chocolate cake" (whose center is described as the consistency of chocolate pudding), blueberry-lemon crème caramel and bing cherry clafoutis with whipped cream.

(603) 431-0887. www.lindberghscrossing.com. Entrées, $16 to $28. Dinner nightly, from 5:30. Wine bar from 4.

The Oar House, 55 Ceres St.

One of the best of the touristy choices along the waterfront is this veteran of 30 years, situated across the street from the river and adding a deck beside the water in summer. The dining room and lounge are housed on the lower floor of an old warehouse building in which goods used to be unloaded directly from ships and raised by elevators to the upper floors. Today, the space contains appropriate mementos of the city's long maritime heritage. Artworks trace the history of prominent ships built here, and the models are all of Portsmouth-built vessels. The dinner menu features the traditional, as in broiled or baked stuffed haddock, grilled salmon, broiled sea scallops and filet mignon. Bouillabaisse, roast duckling with apricot-peppercorn glaze and rack of lamb are specialties. Appetizers range from brie in puff pastry and escargots to pizza margarita and lobster spring rolls. There's also a raw bar. The jaunty deck beside the river is the venue of choice in summer.

(603) 436-4025. Entrées, $20 to $34. Lunch, Monday-Saturday 11:30 to 3. Dinner nightly, 5 to 9 or 9:30. Sunday brunch, 11:30 to 3.

The Dolphin Striker, 15 Bow St.

Forever popular with tourists, this long-running riverfront landmark is regaining some of its glory after a bout with foreclosure in the early 1990s. The atmosphere is strictly historic, with bare sloping floors, beamed ceilings, flickering oil lamps and a sense of Colonial times in three dining rooms and the cozy, stone-walled tavern beneath. The white napkins on each table are folded to look like schooners. The kitchen staff has gone contemporary, showing a deft touch with things like grilled salmon on a quinoa ratatouille, a tournedo of tuna with vegetable "spaghetti" in niçoise oil, duckling three ways (grilled, confit and sausage) and spice-crusted rack of lamb with Himalayan red rice. Typical appetizers bear fruity touches, as in sea scallops on a fennel pickle with grapefruit and vanilla and a shrimp and melon cocktail with two sauces and lemon candy. Desserts could be chocolate mousse en croûte, grand marnier soufflé or Irish whiskey cake. A light menu and live music are offered downstairs in the **Spring Hill Tavern.**

(603) 431-5222. www.dolphinstriker.com. Entrées, $18 to $28. Lunch, Thursday-Saturday 11:30 to 2. Dinner nightly, 5 to 9:30 or 10, Sunday 4:30 to 9.

BG's Boat House Restaurant, 191 Wentworth Road.

Lobster and down-home surroundings lure the locals to this little restaurant with outdoor decks and a marina out past the Wentworth resort in New Castle. Windows look onto an ocean inlet officially known as Sagamore Creek. The walls are paneled, the floors bare and tables have captain's chairs and paper mats. It's a perfect backdrop for devouring the lobsters delivered by boat to the back door by BG's own lobstermen. Last we knew, you could get a lobster roll with with french fries for under $10. A seafood platter commands top dollar at $15.95. BG's also offers sandwiches, hamburgers, potato skins and mozzarella sticks, but most people go here for lobster and seafood, plain and simple.

(603) 431-1074. Entrées, $8.95 to $15.95. Lunch, daily in summer, 11 to 4. Dinner nightly, 5 to 9. Closed Monday and Tuesday in spring and fall and October to mid-March.

The Stockpot, 53 Bow St.
For good, casual fare overlooking the water, this is a favorite. The upstairs bar and lounge has a few tables beside big windows onto the harbor, while the downstairs Riverview Dining Room adds an outside deck. Paella valencia is the signature dish. Homemade soups, of course, are the hallmark. The fare ranges widely: burgers, Syrian bread sandwiches including an artichoke and tomato melt, salads like hummus plate or crab salad, steamed mussels and peel-and-eat shrimp. The homemade meatloaf sandwich is considered a great value, as is the meatloaf dinner platter including fries and coleslaw. The kitchen gets creative with such dinner entrées as coconut-encrusted tuna with pineapple salsa, cajun haddock with pesto-tartar sauce and grilled strip steak with zinfandel marinade.

(603) 431-1851. Entrées, $12.95 to $17.95. Open daily, 11 a.m. to 11:30 p.m.

Geno's Chowder & Sandwich Shop, 177 Mechanic St.
Off the beaten path, this unassuming place, a local institution, happens to offer one of the best riverside decks in town. Part open and part covered, it yields a pleasing view of the Piscataqua River from its perch just south of Prescott Park. The menu and ambiance are basic, and the food is served on paper and plastic. Regulars swear by the chowders and stews, and the grandmotherly waitress advised us as we sat down that they're all "made from scratch without thickening." The seafood chowder proved much more to our liking than the clam, which could have used some thickening. The mini-lobster roll ($7.49) and crab roll ($6.95) were served in hamburger buns and proved so mini that we ordered a piece of the strawberry-rhubarb pie and carrot cake to fill up. The rest of the fare is of the traditional, plain-Jane variety, representative of the Marconi family's 35-year tenure. Evelyn Marconi, a former city councilor, keeps tabs on the convivial goings-on inside.

(603) 427-2070. Prices, $2.85 to $9.99. Breakfast and lunch, Tuesday-Saturday 8:30 to 3.

Wentworth by the Sea, 588 Wentworth Road, New Castle.
The main dining rooms are away from the ocean at the rear of this restored hotel's main floor. There, the contemporary, seafood-oriented menu offers entrées ($26 to $34) from tournedos of yellowfin tuna and smoky bacon-crusted "filet mignon" of lobster to beef two ways (ginger-braised short ribs and grilled sirloin) and grilled rack of pine nut-crusted lamb. Those who want water views seek out **Latitudes,** the more casual marina-side restaurant. It has dining inside beside floor-to-ceiling windows or near the fireplace in the bar and outside on a teak deck overlooking the waterfront. Executive chef Daniel Dumont's bistro-style menu is a with-it compendium of appetizers, sandwiches, salads and entrées. At night, you could start with charred ginger rare beef with ponzu sauce, a "tower" of crab and yellowfin tuna or selections from the raw bar for two. Entrées range from fish and chips and wood-grilled salmon with tropical fruit salsa to grilled chicken paillard with lemon-caper vinaigrette and ribeye cowboy steak with house-made tamarind sauce. Finish with a tropical coconut banana split or a tasting of three versions of crème brûlée.

(603) 422-7322 or (866) 240-6313. Entrees, $18 to $29. Open daily, 11 to 10.

Other Choices

Pesce Blue, 103 Congress St., Portsmouth.

Portsmouth's restaurant du moment is this contemporary Italian seafood grill that's ultra-dramatic: long, narrow and mod, dark in a palette of blacks and taupes and illuminated by day from windows onto a side street and at night by striking lamp spheres dangling from the high ceiling. Chef Mark Segal's seafood dishes draw knowing diners day and night. The choices change daily, but you might find sautéed Icelandic char with lemon-caper emulsion, sautéed Maine skate with orange-ginger sauce or grilled yellowfin tuna with peppercorn sauce. Some go for the house specialty, mixed grill – an assortment of five of the day's freshest fish with grilled vegetables. Others go for "the whole thing" – another specialty of crispy whole local mackerel, perhaps, or Mediterranean branzino (sea bass), salt-crusted and grilled or oven roasted. The treats begin with such appetizers as yellowfin tuna tartare, swordfish carpaccio, a salad of grilled octopus and fried calamari with three dipping sauces. Five seafood pastas and risottos are available as small plates or large. The night's menu holds only two items called "landfood," usually pan-roasted "flattened" chicken and grilled ribeye steak alla fiorentina. Desserts include a selection of sorbets, Italian crêpes and crème brûlée served with fresh berries. A sidewalk patio is open seasonally.

(603) 430-7766. www.pesceblue.com. Entrées, $16.75 to $26.50. Lunch, Monday-Friday 11:45 to 2. Dinner nightly, 5 to 9:30 or 10.

Anthony Alberto's Ristorante Italiano, 59 Penhallow St.

Arguably the best food and service in Portsmouth are offered in this atmospheric establishment hidden in the Custom House Cellar. It's elegant, dark and grotto-like with stone and brick walls, arches, exposed beams on the ceiling and oriental rugs on the slate floors. The menu is high Italian, as in lobster poached in sauternes and herbed butter and served with handmade lemon-pepper fettuccine, grilled veal chop with a shallot-pear glaze and grilled beef tenderloin in a barolo wine demi-glace. Expect such antipasti as pheasant ravioli, peppercorn-encrusted beef carpaccio, and potato blini with smoked salmon and caviar. Desserts include fruit tarts, bananas flambé, tiramisu and crème caramel.

(603) 436-4000. Entrées, $18.95 to $29.95. Dinner, Monday-Saturday 5 to 9:30 or 10:30.

43° North, 75 Pleasant St.

A former chef from Anthony Alberto's opened his own restaurant in the space we first knew as The Grotto. Geno Gulotta christened it "a kitchen and wine bar," hung its aqua brick walls with fine paintings and furnished it with Hungarian antique sideboards for an elegant continental look. The contemporary international menu ranges widely. Among "small plates and bowls" are wonderful Maine mussels steamed in chardonnay, garlic, fennel and tomato and served with grilled olive focaccia. The crisp duck spring rolls are to die for, according to regulars. For "large plates," consider chile-spiced ahi tuna steak with sweet and sour plum sauce, pecan-crusted haddock in toasted coconut broth, grilled pork chop with honey-habañero sauce and char-grilled buffalo sirloin with maple-juniper sauce. The changing desserts are as enticing as the rest of the fare.

(603) 430-0225. www.fortythreenorth.com. Entrées, $19 to $28. Dinner nightly except Sunday, from 5.

FOR MORE INFORMATION: Greater Portsmouth Chamber of Commerce, 500 Market St., Portsmouth, NH 03801, (603) 436-1118. www.portsmouthchamber.org. or www.portsmouthnh.com.

Ogunquit Beach is a favorite of swimmers and sunbathers.

Ogunquit/Kennebunkport, Me.

Two of New England's most popular coastal resorts are situated only a sandy strand apart in southern Maine.

Both are beach communities, but there the similarity pretty much ends. Ogunquit is sandy, summery and resorty. Its beach, rated one of the nation's top ten, draws thousands of visitors to soak in the sun. Kennebunkport tends to be rockbound, year-round and sophisticated. It's famed as the summer home of George and Barbara Bush. Color Ogunquit tan, as in suntan. Color Kennebunkport blue, as in blue blood.

Geographically, Ogunquit and Kennebunkport are separated only by the nondescript beach town of Wells. Each has its assets and advocates, and each is easily accessible to the other.

The Indians who were its first summer visitors called the more southern area Ogunquit, meaning "beautiful place by the sea." Today's visitor is apt to call it crowded. Thousands of tourists pack its streets, motels and beaches, to the point that the Chamber of Commerce became one of the first in the country to run a trolley service to shuttle people back and forth.

Ogunquit is a walking town, a paradise for people on parade. They walk hand-in-hand on the Marginal Way, tote shopping bags along the Shore Road, and wear bikinis and not much else along Beach Street. Motels, both large and small, are the principal accommodations.

The broad, white-sand beach is three miles long and flanked by dunes, the northernmost in New England. Picturesque Perkins Cove, studded with fishing and pleasure boats, has inspired artists and lured tourists for decades. The beach and Perkins Cove are linked by the Marginal Way, a paved footpath atop the cliffs beside the ocean.

Kennebunkport is more spread out than Ogunquit, a canvas of green (as in shade trees and affluence) above the rocky shore. Here are good but less accessible beaches, a preponderance of inns and B&Bs, sophisticated restaurants and shops, myriad galleries and relatively low-key attractions. The flavor of Kennebunkport as a whole is better sensed not at the beach or downtown Dock Square but out along Ocean Avenue past Spouting Rock and the Bush estate at Walker Point on the way to the fishing hamlet of Cape Porpoise.

The streets of both towns teem in late afternoon and evening with strollers who have spent the day at the beach.

You want sun and sand and tan? Settle in Ogunquit. Want more than beach? Go beyond to Kennebunkport.

Getting There

Ogunquit is located about twenty miles north of the New Hampshire border, 35 miles southwest of Portland. Take the York or Wells exits from the Maine Turnpike (Interstate 95) and follow U.S. Route 1 to Ogunquit. Kennebunkport is about ten miles northeast of Ogunquit, reached via the turnpike's Wells or Kennebunk exits. Major airlines fly into Portland.

Where to Stay

The number of choices is staggering and increases annually. Ogunquit is particularly strong in resorts and motels, while Kennebunkport has more inns and B&Bs. Many places require extended stays with advance reservations, although shorter stays are granted on the spot, based upon availability. The traveler will find numerous establishments along the main roads of Ogunquit and Kennebunkport. Some of the more interesting are lesser known and often hidden along the waterfront. The waterfront criterion defines our selections here.

Small and Choice

Bufflehead Cove Inn, Gornitz Lane, Box 499, Kennebunkport 04046.

The kind of summer home you've dreamed of can be yours, if only for a night or two. Harriet and Jim Gott share with B&B guests their gray shingled, Dutch Colonial house on five wooded acres beside a scenic bend of the tidal Kennebunk River. Each accommodation is bright and cheerful and embellished with arty touches. The spacious Balcony Room with kingsize bed, fireplace and corner jacuzzi for two offers a wicker-filled balcony overlooking the river. The secluded Hideaway suite in the adjacent riverside cottage – mostly glass and windows – holds a kingsize bed, a central fireplace open to both bedroom and living room, two couches and a bathroom with a double jacuzzi. Outside is a private deck almost at water level. The latest treat is the deluxe River Cottage with cathedral-ceilinged living room/bedroom, fireplace, small kitchen, a loft with a library and entertainment center, and a soaring palladian window onto the water. The public rooms, porches and decks in the main house take full advantage of the riverfront setting. A large and comfy living room contains window seats with views of the water, and the paneled dining room is shaped like the stern of a ship. Wine and cheese are served in the early evening, and there are decanters of sherry plus

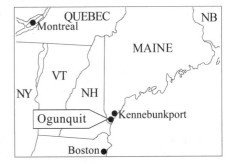

bottles of Bufflehead Cove sparkling water in each room. Harriet serves a memorable breakfast, perhaps asparagus strata or soufflés with popovers. Guests may not see much of Jim, a lobster fisherman, unless they get up to join his fishing expedition at 4:30 a.m. He provides the lobster incorporated in the breakfast quiche and omelets.

(207) 967-3879. www.buffleheadcove.com. Three rooms, one suite and two cottages with private baths. Doubles, $165 to $235. Suite and cottages, $295 to $350.

The Inn at Harbor Head, 41 Pier Road, Kennebunkport 04046.

Its tranquil location on a rocky knoll alongside picturesque Cape Porpoise Harbor make this rambling shingled home a destination for water-lovers. All four stylish guest quarters have king or queensize canopy beds and are decorated with exquisite hand-painted murals. The entrance to the main-floor Garden Room is paved with stones and a little fountain, and original drawings of peach and plum blossoms float on the wall. French doors open onto a private, trellised deck overlooking the harbor. The Greenery, where we stayed, has a mural of fir trees by the shore, a bathroom with hand-painted tiles and jacuzzi tub, and a view of the front gardens. Painted clouds drift across the ceiling of the Summer Suite, which offers the best view of the harbor from its balcony. It also has a gas fireplace and a cathedral-ceilinged bathroom with skylight, bidet and jacuzzi tub. Innkeepers Eve and Dick Roesler serve a breakfast to remember in the elegant dining room that's the heart of the house. Crabmeat and bacon quiche, zucchini frittata or honey-pecan french toast could be the main course. Afterward, you may have neither the energy nor the will to leave the premises. Enjoy the colorful gardens beyond the rear terrace or relax on the lawn sloping to the shore, where you can swim from the floats or loll in an oversize rope hammock, watching the lobster boats go by.

(207) 967-5564. Fax (207) 967-1294. www.harborhead.com. Three rooms and one suite with private baths. Doubles, $195 to $270. Suite, $325. Closed November-April.

Cape Arundel Inn, Ocean Avenue, Kennebunkport 04046.

A choice location facing the open ocean and an excellent dining room (see Where to Eat) commend this turreted, shingle-style Maine inn containing seven ocean-view rooms with private baths and six nicely converted motel units at the side. Veteran restaurateur Jack Nahil, who formerly owned the White Barn Inn, has upgraded the accommodations here. He added queensize beds, created more windows for what he rightly bills as "bold ocean views" and completely refurbished the 1950s motel units to convey a country inn motif. Renamed Rockbound, each room in the former motel section comes with TV and a small balcony with a front-on view of the ocean beyond the wild roses. Our end room at a recent visit had a queen bed with a sturdy white wood headboard angled from the corner, a new fireplace and reproduction furniture. Rooms upstairs in the inn are spacious and more traditional. We once enjoyed Room 4 on the far-front corner, where white organdy curtains fluttered in the breeze and two chairs took in a bird's-eye panorama of the ocean and the George H.W. Bush compound at Walker Point. The rear carriage-house suite called Ocean Bluff enjoys spacious vistas from its deck. The inn's spacious wraparound porch is a super place to curl up with a good book, enjoy a cocktail or a nightcap, or the morning newspaper, all with that bold ocean view. Breakfast is a hearty continental buffet. Ours began with fresh orange juice, cereal, muesli, fruit and yogurt, and superior scones and croissants. The highlight was the day's extra: toasted basil-parmesan bread and a small spanakopita, prepared by the chef's wife and "presented" in the dinner style on an oversize plate.

(207) 967-2125. Fax (207) 967-1199. www.capearundelinn.com. Thirteen rooms and one suite with private baths. Doubles, $275 to $345. Closed January and February.

Resorts and Larger Inns and Motels

The Cliff House Resort & Spa, Shore Road, Box 2274, Ogunquit 03907.

For a secluded waterside setting, you can't beat the location of the historic Cliff House. One of the grand old resorts, this is spectacularly situated amid 75 forested acres of oceanfront headland atop Bald Head Cliff. Greatly altered from its original 1872 status as the area's first hotel, it has been expanded into a complete resort and conference center by fourth-generation innkeeper Katherine Weare, whose family has owned it since the beginning. A tuxedo-clad pianist introduced a touch of late-afternoon glamour as he entertained in the soaring, atrium-style foyer of the new main building at a recent visit. Beyond is a circular dining room serving three meals daily (see Where to Eat), a modern lounge with outdoor terrace above the ocean, an indoor pool, sauna, whirlpool and game room. The main building is attached to Cliffscape, an L-shaped building with 104 guest rooms on six levels, where it's easy to get lost. Our room in what was then the newest section had a great private balcony right over the rocky surf, but seemed rather austere and dark. The Cliff House recently undertook a major renovation and expansion program to join its series of buildings and add more guest rooms, new indoor and outdoor pools, a fitness center, full-service spa and a modern lounge with outdoor terrace above the ocean. A new building where the Captain's House once stood offers 32 oversize guest rooms with wood stoves and wet bars. All rooms now have kingsize or two double beds, picture windows and decks with views of coast and ocean, modern furnishings, TVs and coffeemaker.

(207) 361-1000. Fax (207) 361-2122. www.cliffhousemaine.com. One hundred ninety-four rooms and mini-suites. Doubles, $255 to $315, EP. Three-night minimum stay in summer. Closed January to late March.

The Sparhawk, 85 Shore Road, Box 936, Ogunquit 03907.

This is in-town Ogunquit's top accommodation, from its large swimming pool and tennis court to its Jacobs House luxury suites and the deluxe penthouse apartment fashioned from the old Barbara Dean restaurant. "Happily filled," says the sign outside the office almost every time we pass – a nice touch, as is the complimentary continental breakfast served in the old Sparhawk Hall, site of the first Sparhawk hotel built more than 95 years ago. The hotel has gradually been replaced by the motel units, perched right on the seawall overlooking the ocean. Later additions are the fancier Ireland House rooms and the inn-style suites and apartments in the Barbara Dean and the Jacobs House, of which resort owner-operator Blaine Moore is particularly proud. Each of the 55 Sparhawk units facing the ocean head-on has a private balcony or terrace, two Queen Anne-style chairs facing the window, two beds and a small refrigerator in the dressing area. The twenty rooms in the two-story Ireland House are nicely angled, so that each has an ocean view from its private, handsomely furnished patio or balcony. The upstairs front corner is most desirable (and you can get a look at it from the Marginal Way walkway, which cuts across the property). Each has two queen beds and a separate sitting area with sofa and two chairs. Set back from the ocean, the Jacobs House contains five suites with king or queen bed, VCR, jacuzzi bath and gas fireplace.

(207) 646-5562. Seventy-nine rooms, seven suites and one cottage. Doubles, $170 to $195. Suites, $190 to $300. One-week minimum stay in mid-summer. Closed November to mid-April.

The Aspinquid, 57 Beach St., Box 2408, Ogunquit 03907.

Within easy walking distance of the beach but off by itself from the hustle and bustle is this lodge-style resort, all quite contemporary and with a North Woods condo look. Sixty-two spacious rooms and apartments with bedroom and combination living room and kitchen are offered by owner Dennis Andrews in three buildings separated by a heated pool and lighted tennis court. All have private balconies with water views. The carpeted rooms contain two double beds, television, phones and good-looking rattan furnishings. A sauna and spa are available on the lower level of the lodge. Complimentary coffee is offered in the morning, when children like to help the staff feed the fish in a tranquil pond with a waterfall.

(207) 646-7072. Fax (207) 646-1187. www.aspinquid.com. Sixty-two rooms and apartments. Doubles, $135 to $150 in motel, $160 to $320 in efficiencies and apartments. Four-night minimum in summer. Closed mid-October to late May.

The Beachmere Inn, 62 Beachmere Place, Box 2340, Ogunquit 03907.

In-town Ogunquit's grandest location, without doubt, is occupied by the Beachmere. A family-run inn since the 1920s, it has 28 efficiency units and apartments in a four-level Victorian-style inn, plus sixteen rooms in a two-story motel built in 1970 and two rooms in the Sea Urchin Cottage. They rest on the outermost bluff along the Marginal Way, facing Ogunquit Beach with the open ocean to the east. Six more efficiency units are available for families or groups in three outlying buildings off the main property. It's easy to see why most guests are repeat; the lawns and private decks offer magnificent views. The inn rooms retain old-fashioned touches, but each is up-to-date with modern bath, TV and kitchenette and most with queen or kingsize beds and private decks. Newer rooms and suites are quite luxurious. We like Room 16 with a deck, an enclosed porch-sitting room, a turreted alcove with a dining table, a queen bed and corner kitchenette with combination sink and stove. Rooms sleep two to four, but one third-floor option with a double bed is decidedly small and priced accordingly. The motel units are angled for privacy and ocean views. Coffee and muffins are complimentary in the morning.

(207) 646-2021 or (800) 336-3983. Fax (207) 646-2231. www.beachmereinn.com. Fifty-two rooms with private baths. Doubles, $100 to $250. Three-night to one-week minimum stay in summer; three nights rest of year. Closed mid-December to late March.

Terrace By the Sea, 23 Wharf Lane, Box 831, Ogunquit 03907.

Deluxe motel units (some with loft sitting areas), a four-unit efficiency motel overlooking the ocean, a one-bedroom apartment and fifteen inn rooms are attractions at this relatively secluded and nicely landscaped establishment overlooking the tidal river. Its assorted buildings have been spiffed up in recent years by owners Daryl and John Bullard. From the lineup of lawn chairs or from the picture window in the green and rose living room of the Colonial-style inn you can see the river and ocean. All rooms are air-conditioned and have cable TV and phones. Most have balconies and water views. Eight have efficiency kitchens. There's a small pool. A complimentary continental breakfast is served.

(207) 646-3232. www.terracebythesea.com. Thirty-six rooms with private baths. Doubles, $152 to $217. Four-night minimum in summer. Closed mid-December to late March. No credit cards.

Sea Chambers, 67 Shore Road, Box 916, Ogunquit 03907.

This L-shaped motel isn't angled toward the ocean like Sparhawk or the Beachmere but is perpendicular, on the owners' theory that nothing should block the public's view from the street. Most of its rooms (and those of many motels not included here) face sideways toward the parking lot and a smallish pool. Second-floor rooms have the best views, and six deluxe rooms and a few ocean-end units face the water. Rooms are comfortable with king, queen or two double beds, two chairs, a large dressing area with sink and an architecturally ingenious, partly open wall behind the beds that creates cross-ventilation from all the windows. A complimentary continental breakfast is served in the Sea Bell, the oldest stone building in Ogunquit and nicely decorated in Williamsburg style. Owners Donna and Gordon Lewis also own the oceanfront Grey Gull restaurant at nearby Moody Point.

(207) 646-9311. Fax (207) 646-0938. www.seachambers.com. Forty-six rooms. Doubles, $142 to $204. Four-night minimum stay in summer. Closed mid-December to mid-March.

Smaller Inns and Motels and Cottages

The Yachtsman Lodge & Marina, Ocean Avenue, Box 2609, Kennebunkport 04046.

This one-story lineup of 30 seasonal motel rooms overlooking the Kennebunk River always appealed. But now it wins best of class, as transformed with a Midas touch by new owner Laurence Bongiorno of the nearby White Barn Inn. He gutted the interior but retained the footprint to offer the most deluxe "motel" quarters you're ever likely to see. Call it a lodge, or call it an inn. Laurie calls it an effort to serve families and pets in "that great netherland between casual motel and elegant inn, with a location on the water being most important." Each spacious room with vaulted ceiling is the same, done in understated style to resemble a yacht with cream-colored, bead-board walls accented with sailing prints and mahogany trim. The kingsize bed is dressed in a fluffy white goose-down duvet covered in Egyptian cotton, the TV is hidden in an armoire, and furnishings include two cushioned rattan chairs, a round table and a writing desk. The closet lights automatically to reveal terrycloth robes, a mini-refrigerator chills bottled water, and the bathroom has a granite vanity bearing all kinds of toiletries. The front of the room is screened from the road by lush landscaping. The back opens through french doors onto private patios with lounge furniture facing a swath of lawn about fifteen feet from river's edge. Quacking ducks that paraded by made more noise than the sleek yachts moored in the marina at our visit. A common terrace between the two lodge buildings has plenty of lounge furniture, the better for enjoying the afternoon spread of beverages and pastries. A huge, push-button coffee machine produces cappuccino and espresso. The sunny breakfast room the next morning held a complimentary array of fruit, cereals and baked goods including a savory quiche prepared by the award-winning kitchen at the White Barn Inn. The owner's new 44-foot yacht is moored outside and available for charter.

(207) 967-2511. Fax (207) 967-5056. www.yachtsmanlodge.com. Thirty rooms with private baths. Doubles, $289 to $315. Two-night minimum most weekends. Closed November through March.

The Seaside Inn & Cottages, 80 Beach Ave., Box 631, Kennebunkport 04046.

There are those who think this motor inn and cottage complex at Gooch's Beach has everything: twenty acres of ocean and river frontage with its own beach, caring owners, a sense of history and stylish, comfortable accommodations. Sandra and Michael Severance oversee the place that his Gooch family forebears founded twelve generations ago in 1667. Six extra-spacious oceanfront rooms on the second floor of the 22-room motor inn are most in demand, although the rest are no slouches. Each has two queensize beds, TVs recessed in Queen Anne highboys, two leather armchairs, a small refrigerator in a wet bar area, and deck chairs on a private balcony or patio. Six ground-floor rooms face the ocean, although occupants must stretch to see it. The terrace-side rooms look out onto attractive grounds. Ten efficiency cottages of one to four bedrooms, most with river or ocean views, are scattered about the property and rent by the month in summer, weekly in the off-season. Closest to the beach is a year-round two-bedroom beach house aptly called The

Dunes. Motel guests enjoy a complimentary continental-plus breakfast in an 1850 boathouse room. The Severances say theirs is the only area establishment in which guests can access the beach without having to cross the road or get in their cars.

(207) 967-446 or (800) 967-4461. www.kennebunkbeachmaine.com. Twenty-two rooms, ten cottages and one beach house with private baths. Doubles, $229 to $245. Cottages, from $995 weekly in off-season to $9,250 monthly in summer. House, $12,999 monthly in summer, $1,000 to $3,100 weekly rest of year.

The Beach House, 211 Beach Ave., Box 500B, Kennebunkport 04046.

This pale yellow Victorian inn, built in 1891 and recently known as the Sundial, enjoys an oceanfront location across the road from Kennebunk Beach as well as a comfortable, summery ambiance. It was acquired in 1999 by Laurence Bongiorno of the White Barn Inn and was upscaled accordingly, staying open year-round. The ocean is on full view from the wraparound porch, the breakfast room and a paneled, lodge-like living room with a huge stone fireplace. A trompe-l'oeil bookcase beside a mirror gives the room depth, and a beach mural in the elevator sets the stage for what's upstairs. Each of 34 guest rooms on the second and third floors is nicely appointed in subdued sand and stone colors with Victorian wrought-iron beds topped with down comforters, attractive fabrics, country American antiques, beach photographs on the walls, TV/VCRs, telephones and CD stereo systems. The look is "light and breezy – just like a beach house," in Laurie's words. White terrycloth robes, irons and Crabtree & Evelyn toiletries are standard. Most beds are kingsize. A junior suite includes a whirlpool bath. Some rooms enjoy full or partial ocean views. In the corner Room 312 we saw, the ocean appeared through the windows to be almost in the bedroom. A "view breakfast" in the front dining room includes pastries from the White Barn Inn, as does afternoon tea.

(207) 967-3850. Fax (207) 967-4719. www.beachhseinn.com. Thirty-four rooms with private baths. Doubles, $255 to $445.

The Breakwater Inn & Hotel, 127 Ocean Ave., Kennebunkport 04046.

This two-part hostelry – an inn dating to the 1800s and a hotel built in 1986 – offers sensational water views across the Kennebunk River toward the open Atlantic. The old inn is getting a new look under owner Laurie Bongiorno of Kennebunkport's stylish White Barn Inn, who added the waterfront property to his growing collection of local hostelries in 2000. Its two restored buildings containing twenty guest rooms, fifteen with water views, were refurbished in the contemporary coastal style to which guests at his other inns are accustomed. The public rooms, Victorian parlor, breakfast room, wraparound porches and restaurant afford panoramic vistas of the water, garden courtyard and lawns sloping to the inn's private pebble beach. The best views are enjoyed by the relocated **Stripers,** a waterfront restaurant and raw bar, serving lunch and dinner in season (see Where to Eat).

In 2004 the Breakwater was joined in name to a more recent acquisition, the former Schooners Inn, which is now billed as a boutique hotel. Facing the Kennebunk River just north of the inn, the seventeen hotel rooms are oriented to the water – some more than others, especially a couple with outdoor decks. All are crisply decorated in a high-tech look amid prevailing colors of creams and taupes. Beds are king or queensize, crafted by furniture maker Thomas Moser, who also did the cupboards that hold the flat-screen TVs. White satin robes, in-room refrigerators and Molton Brown toiletries from London are among the amenities. The prime accommodation is the Savannah Suite, with a kingsize bed enveloped in a sheer white canopy beneath a raised sitting area in a large bay window opening onto an idyllic deck. The curving main-floor lounge is the setting for afternoon tea and cookies, as well as a complimentary cocktail hour. The baked goods for tea and the continental-plus breakfast are prepared by the kitchen at the White Barn Inn.

(207) 967-5333. Fax (207) 967-2040. www.thebreakwaterinn.com. Thirty-seven rooms with private baths. Inn rooms, $209 to $329. Hotel rooms, $235 to $430.

Riverside Motel, 50 Riverside Lane, Box 2244, Ogunquit 03907.

As we've wandered through Perkins Cove, we've always envied those who were sitting on their balconies at the motel on the far shore. The Riverside is booked far ahead, as you might imagine, and has a three-night minimum. But we once lucked into a one-nighter and reveled in the location, a foot-drawbridge walk across the cove to the action (actually, the cove is quiet at night – the real action is in the beach area). Each unit has a private balcony with cove view. Rooms are standard motel style, but the large towels are extra-thick and the shady grounds spacious and attractive. The renovated 1874 House on the property has four rooms with private baths and television ($115 to $135). A free breakfast of donuts, juice and coffee is set out in the Colonial lobby; you can eat at tables for two inside by the fireplace or at small round picnic tables on a rear deck outside. A few stuffed animals here and there grace the lobby's plush sectionals and sofas.

(207) 646-2741. Fax (207) 646-0216. www.riversidemotel.com. Thirty-seven rooms. Doubles, $150 to $180. Three-night minimum in summer. Closed mid-October to May.

Marginal Way House and Motel, 22-24 Wharf Lane, Box 697, Ogunquit 03907.

Try for one of the six motel units perched above the water at this superbly located place where the lawns slope toward ocean's edge. Besides the dockside motel, rooms are offered in the venerable main house and in efficiency apartments in three other buildings. Rooms are individually decorated in New England style in the main inn and each has private bath, television and a refrigerator. "All the pretty gardens are our claim to fame," says owner Brenda Blake.

(207) 646-8801. www.marginalwayhouse.com. Twenty-nine rooms with private baths. Doubles, $187 in motel, $114 to $172 in hotel, $1,350 to $1,600 for efficiencies (by the week). Closed mid-October to mid-April.

Above Tide Inn, 66 Beach St., Box 2188, Ogunquit 03907.

Want to be really near the water? The canopied decks outside the rooms at this summery little beach house affair thrust right out to the Ogunquit River basin, and you can see around the end of the beach to the ocean. Reserve the upstairs corner room with its wraparound windows and you'd almost think you were on a boat. The air-conditioned units on two floors have carpeting, small refrigerators, TV and one or two double beds. Two are suites with two bedrooms and two baths. A complimentary continental breakfast is offered.

(207) 646-7454. www.abovetideinn.com. Nine rooms with private baths. Doubles, $165 to $225. Three-night minimum in summer. Closed mid-October to mid-May.

The Dunes on the Waterfront, 518 Main St. (U.S. Route 1), Box 917, Ogunquit 03907.

One of Ogunquit's more secluded and quiet places is this twelve-acre refuge with seventeen motel guest rooms and nineteen cottage units, lovingly run by three generations of the founding Perkins family. Motel is a bit of a misnomer, since only six units are in a small two-story motel. The other "guest rooms" are in nice-looking, well-spaced cottage-style buildings. The distinction between guest rooms and cottages lies in the kitchens that come with the cottages, each with one or two bedrooms, bath, TV, screened porch and most with fireplaces. Some cottages are detached. "Guest rooms" are in multi-unit buildings and range from small with one double or queen bed to large two-bedroom units accommodating up to five people. Each has TV, telephone, refrigerator and coffeemaker. Youngsters like the beach, rowboats, heated swimming pool, playground, shuffleboard court and croquet layout. Popular with families, the cottages are rented by the week in July and August.

(207) 646-2612 or (888) 285-3863. www.dunesmotel.com. Seventeen rooms and nineteen cottages. Doubles, $95 to $280, three-night minimum in summer. Cottages, $165 to $320 nightly, seven to fourteen-night minimum in summer. Closed November-April.

Seeing and Doing

On or Beside the Water

THE BEACHES. From the basin where the Ogunquit River meets the sea, **Ogunquit Beach** stretches three miles north to the neighboring town of Moody. The white-sand beach is broad and the surf strong; most summer days we've been there the ocean temperature is posted at 58 degrees. The Ogunquit River separates the beach from the mainland, and provides a back beach for more sheltered swimming. The point where the tidal river enters the ocean is most popular; on the ocean side you have surf swimming and, on the river side, calmer waters good for children. Beach signs are in French as well as English and, at one August visit, fully two-thirds of the conversations we overheard in the beach area involved French-Canadians. The beach is free, but parking is $4 an hour until 6 p.m., up to a maximum of $20. Less crowded is the **Footbridge Beach** section of Ogunquit Beach, reached by a footbridge from Ocean Street (you can wade across the river at low tide) or from Ocean Avenue in Moody. Other beaches are **Littlefields, River Side** and **Ontio** on the Marginal Way.

In Kennebunkport, **Gooch's Beach,** a curving half-mile crescent, and **Kennebunk Beach** are two sandy strands with surf west of town (parking by permit, often provided by innkeepers, otherwise $10 daily). When not occupied or when at low tide, the packed sands of Gooch's are great for walking, a Florida-style treat for occupants of the substantial summer homes across the road. The fine silvery sand at **Goose Rocks Beach** (parking by permit, $5 daily) looks almost tropical and the waters are protected. Children paddle in the warm tidal pools that form in depressions along the beach. Beachcombers find starfish and sand-dollar shells here in early morning. More secluded is **Parson's Beach,** a natural sandy strand set among the tall grasses in an undeveloped area next to the Rachel Carson Wildlife Refuge.

BOAT CRUISES AND WHALE WATCHES. With three boats, **Finestkind Scenic Cruises,** Barnacle Billy's Dock, Perkins Cove, (207) 646-5227, runs the most tours, daily from July 1 through Labor Day and a limited spring and fall schedule. Most popular are the 50-minute lobstering trips to see lobster traps hauled amid a running commentary on lobstering. Boats leave frequently from 9:30 to 3; adults $11, children $7. A scenic 90-minute cruise heads seven miles south along the coast to Nubble Lighthouse in York every two hours from 10 to 4; adults $16, children $10. Finestkind also runs a breakfast cruise at 9 a.m. (adults $14, children $9) and three hour-long cocktail cruises at 5:45, 7 and 8:15 (adults $11, children $7). Sailing cruises aboard the Cricket depart daily at 11, 2:30 and 4:30, $25 per person.

Capt. Eric Brazer at **Perkins Cove Lobster Tours, (**207) 646-7413, offers two-hour trips three times daily aboard a 36-foot fiberglass lobster boat for up to six passengers, $30 each. A working lobsterman, he baits and hauls lobster traps and sells his lobsters off the boat.

Also at Perkins Cove, 4.5-hour whale watch tours out to Jeffrey's Ledge are offered daily at 8 and 1:30 aboard the 40-foot **Deborah Ann,** (207) 361-9501; adults $40, children $25. When the ocean is too rough for whale watching, the Deborah Ann substitutes one-hour sightseeing cruises along the coast to Bald Head Cliff and out to Boon Island, which harbors seals and Maine's tallest lighthouse; adults $20, children $10

Kennebunkport is another departure point for spotting the whales that feed seasonally twenty miles offshore at Jeffrey's Ledge. Sighted frequently are finbacks, humpbacks, minkes and Atlantic white-sided dolphins.

Whale watch excursions aboard the double-decker Nick's Chance are available from **First Chance Whale Watch,** 4 Western Ave., (207) 967-5507 or (800) 767-2628. Trips leave from the downtown bridge daily at 9 and 2:30; adults $32, children $20. The First Chance outfit also offers five 90-minute scenic lobster cruises daily aboard the 65-foot Kylie's Chance at 10, noon, 2, 4 and 6 (adults $15, children $10).

Cape Arundel Cruises, (207) 967-5595 or (877) 933-0707, offers whale watching cruises aboard the 100-passenger Nautilus daily at 10 (also at 4 in summer) from the Landing Restaurant, 192 Ocean Ave. (adults $32, children $20). It also gives 90-minute scenic cruises aboard the Deep Water II daily at 11 and 1 (adults $15, children $7.50).

Two-hour sailing trips aboard the gaff-rigged schooner **Eleanor** are offered several times daily by Capt. Rich Woodman from the docks at the Arundel Wharf Restaurant, (207) 967-8809. He built the 55-foot schooner in 1999 and gives up to twenty passengers what he calls "the feel of yachting in the 1930s." The rate is $38 per person.

Capt. Jim Jannetti takes up to six passengers on his 37-foot ocean racing yacht, **Bellatrix,** from the Nonantum Resort on Ocean Avenue, (207) 967-8685. The rate is $40 each for a two-hour trip.

DEEP-SEA FISHING. The Town Dock at Perkins Cove is the launching site for excursions by the 40-foot fiberglass boat, the **Bunny Clark,** (207) 646-2214. Capt. Tim Tower offers a full day trip for $65 each and a half day for $40. Deep-sea fishing trips from Perkins Cove also are offered aboard the 44-foot wooden boat **Ugly Anne,** (207) 646-7202; half day $45, full day $60.

Lady J Sportfishing Charters under Maine master guide Capt. Adam Little offers fishing trips aboard his custom-built Rebecca Lynn from Arundel Wharf, (207) 985-7304. Rates vary from $175 for a two-hour adventure for children to $600 for an eight-hour offshore excursion.

Waterside Attractions

The Marginal Way, Ogunquit. We never tire of walking Ogunquit's mile-long paved footpath along the rocky cliffs beside the sea. It starts inauspiciously enough in town as a narrow path heading toward the ocean beside the Sparhawk Resort. Then you climb to a point, which affords a glorious view of Ogunquit Beach, and turn to go gently up and down along the ocean to Perkins Cove. Memorial benches provide resting spots along the way. The rocks and what locally are called "the little beaches" offer fun or seclusion for young and old alike. Arches of trees frame views of the sea. The surf pounds into a crevice at one point, and you can admire the wildflowers and private homes all around. This is the best way to savor the majestic Ogunquit waterfront. A leisurely walk takes 45 minutes; you can retrace your steps for a different perspective, or return past the shops and galleries along Shore Road (keep an eye out for the old cemetery full of Perkins family gravestones). Or take the trolley, which runs every ten minutes between the beach and Perkins Cove with stops in downtown and side trips to major motels and inns.

Parsons Way, Kennebunkport. A marker opposite the landmark Colony Hotel notes the parcel of land given by Henry Parsons to the town so that "everyone may enjoy its natural beauty." Sit on the benches, spread a blanket on a rock beside the ocean, or walk out to the serene little summer chapel of St. Ann's Episcopal Church by the sea. On a clear day you can see Mount Agamenticus beyond Ogunquit.

Ocean Avenue, Kennebunkport. Continue past Parsons Way to Spouting Rock, where the incoming tide creates a spurting fountain as waves crash between two ragged cliffs. Blowing Cave is another roaring phenomenon within view of Walker Point and the eleven-acre George H.W. Bush summer compound, where you might see his speedboat when he's in residence (you know from all the passersby stopped with binoculars looking for who knows what). Continue on to Cape Porpoise, dating to the early 1600s. It's the closest thing to a fishing village hereabouts, with a working lobster pier (up to 50 lobster boats come and go daily), a picturesque harbor dotted with islands and some interesting galleries.

Rachel Carson National Wildlife Refuge, 321 Port Road (Route 9), Wells.
Seemingly far removed from the surrounding resort and beach scene is this 4,800-acre reserve near the Kennebunkport-Wells town line. It's named for the environmental pioneer who summered in Maine and conducted research in the area for several of her books. This is the largest section of a U.S. Fish and Wildlife Service refuge scattered along 50 miles of Maine coastline from Kittery Point to Cape Elizabeth. The Carson Trail here is a mile-long interpretive trail located at the refuge headquarters. It leads through an area rich in migratory and resident wildlife. The gravel trail and boardwalks meander through tranquil pine woods until the vista opens up at the sixth marker and a boardwalk takes you out over wetlands and marsh. Cormorants, herons and more are sighted here, and benches allow you to relax as you take in the scene. An even better view of the ocean in the distance is at Marker 7, the Little River overlook. The widest, best view of all is near the end of the loop at Marker 11. If you don't have time for the entire trail, ignore the directional signs and go counter-clockwise. You'll get the best view first, though you may not see much wildlife.

(207) 646-9226. Refuge headquarters open Monday-Friday 8 to 4. Trail open daily, dawn to dusk; donation.

Wells National Estuarine Research Reserve, 342 Laudholm Farm Road, Wells.
Abutting the Carson wildlife refuge to the south is one of 26 protected estuarine reserves in the country, based at Laudholm Farm off Route 1, north of Wells Corner. Its 1,600 acres of salt marshes, sand dunes and tidal rivers include seven miles of nature trails and a wide variety of wildlife. Guided tours, education programs, and a slide show and exhibits are offered in the stately, rambling Greek Revival Laudholm Farm visitor center. Interesting nature walks are scheduled throughout the reserve. A variety of exhibits are shown in the new Maine Coastal Ecology Center, a research and education facility that opened in 2004.

(207) 646-1555. www.wellsreserve.org. Visitor center open Monday-Saturday 10 to 4, Sunday noon to 4, May-October; weekdays rest of year; closed mid-December to mid-January. Grounds open daily 7 a.m. to dusk, year-round. Adults $2, children $1 in summer.

Ogunquit Playhouse, Route 1, Box 915, Ogunquit, (207) 646-5511. Billed as America's foremost summer theater, this started in the 1930s in a Shore Road garage as a workshop for aspiring actors and actresses. Now the graceful white barn structure with 700 seats on the southern edge of town is the stage for top Broadway shows and straw-hat talent. Usually five shows run for roughly two weeks each from mid-June to Labor Day. Performances are Monday-Friday at 8, Saturday at 8:30; matinees, Wednesday and Thursday at 2:30. Tickets are $29 to $45.

Material Pursuits

CRAFTS AND ART GALLERIES. The scenery along the southern Maine coast has inspired artisans for years. Ogunquit and especially Perkins Cove have been a mecca for artists since the late 19th century, and the galleries along Shore Road are known for quality fine art. The **Barn Gallery** (formerly the Ogunquit Arts Collaborative Gallery), Shore Road at Bourne Lane, features works by members of the area's foremost professional art organization, the Ogunquit Art Association, founded in 1928 by the originator of the Ogunquit artists' colony. The Art Galleries of Ogunquit brochure has a map and details on about a dozen galleries. The **Beth Ellis Cove Gallery** and **Scully Gallery** in Perkins Cove and the **Miller Gallery** on Shore Road are among the more notable.

Ogunquit Museum of American Art, 543 Shore Road, Ogunquit.
Hidden off the beaten path in a meadow overlooking a rocky cove and the Atlantic is this exceptional summer showplace for contemporary American paintings and sculpture. Francis Henry Taylor, the late director of New York's Metropolitan Museum of Art, called it "the most beautiful small museum in the world." Visitors approaching the museum look directly through the main gallery to the ocean. Built in 1952 and enlarged in 1992 and 1996, the museum houses some of America's most important 20th-century works in five galleries. Thomas Hart Benton, Charles Burchfield, Winslow Homer, Edward Hopper, Rockwell Kent and Walt Kuhn are among those represented in the permanent collection. A reflecting pool on the grounds is a natural habitat for blue herons and kingfishers. Large and small pieces of outdoor sculpture enhance the spectacular seaside setting.
(207) 646-4909. www.ogunquitmuseum.org. Open Monday-Saturday 10:30 to 5, Sunday 2 to 5, July to mid-October. Adults $5, students $3.

The Art Guild of the Kennebunks numbers more than 50 resident professionals as members and claims the Kennebunks are the largest collective community of fine art on the East Coast. Art and galleries are everywhere, but are concentrated around Kennebunkport's Dock Square and the wharves to the southeast. The **Ebb Tide Gallery** shows more than twenty artists in a stylish setting overlooking the Kennebunk River basin, just across the bridge from Dock Square. Other worthwhile stops are **Mast Cove Galleries** and **The Gallery on Chase Hill.** Spectacular contemporary American glass (much at spectacular prices) is shown at **Silica,** a knockout gallery at Cape Porpoise.

SHOPPING. It seems as if everyone is shopping in Ogunquit, especially along touristy Shore Road. The shops get more esoteric as you turn into Perkins Cove. **Brass Carousel & Gallery** offers an odd combination of jewelry, brass items, kites and toys. Farther along in the cove are the appealing **Pottery Shop in Perkins Cove** and **Swamp John's** for custom jewelry, hand-blown glass and leather accessories. The famed **Whistling Oyster** has reopened an arty small shop here. **Blue Willow Gift Shop** combines Victorian gifts with a homey lunchroom overlooking the water. On either side is **Out of the Blue** with more contemporary gifts and jewelry. Proprietor Michael McCluskey is always on the lookout for interesting finds for **Celtic Treasures,** 309 Shore Road. Closer to town along Shore Road, a standout for women's apparel is **Carla's,** which also has locations in Kennebunkport and Portland. **Revelations** has home and garden accents and gifts, while **Somnia** advertises artistry for bed and bath. **Pinecone & Tassel** features gifts for camps and cottages.

Kennebunkport's Dock Square area around the Kennebunk River and, increasingly, the Lower Village across the river are full of interesting stores, most of them decidedly upscale. Admire the prolific flowers on the riverside deck of the **Kennebunk Book Port,** where you can select a book and take it outside to browse on benches or deck chairs above the water. Crowning the main corner of Dock Square is **Compliments,** "the gallery for your special lifestyle." It features lots of glass, including lamps and eggcups, trickling fountains and cute ceramic gulls, each with its own personality. Check out the birdhouses made of hats along with clothing and whimsical gifts at **Carrots & Co.,** whose theme is "because life's too short for boring stuff." **Alano Ltd.** has super clothes, as does **Carla's Corner. Dock Square Clothiers** stocks casual resort apparel for men and women here and in Perkins Cove, Ogunquit. Lilly Pulitzer designs are featured at **Snappy Turtle.** We liked the contemporary crafts at **Kennebunkport Arts** and **Plum Dandy,** the nature-inspired jewelry and tableware at **Lovell Designs,** and the Asian ceramics at **East and Design. Digs, Divots and Dogs** has gifts for gardeners, golfers and, yes, dogs. The **Port Canvas Co., Abacus,** the **Good Earth Pottery, The Whimsy Shop, Maison et Jardin** and the shops at Union Square and Village Marketplace are other favorites.

Where to Eat ⸻ ∽∽∽

Some of the area's finest destination restaurants (i.e., Arrows in Ogunquit and the White Barn Inn in Kennebunkport) are not on the water. But this is one of precious few areas where you can enjoy good meals with an ocean or harbor view, the criterion for inclusion here.

Tops for Dining

Hurricane, Oarweed Lane, Perkins Cove, Ogunquit.
"Our view will blow you away – our menu will bring you back" is the catchy slogan of this lively winner beside the ocean. Every seat in two small summery rooms has a fabulous view; most favored is the enclosed but breezy porch, where we were lucky to snag a table. The all-day menu is categorized by soups and salads and small plates that change seasonally, and lunch and dinner entrées posted daily. You could make a good lunch or supper of lobster gazpacho ("so hot it's cool") or lobster chowder (the house specialty), caesar salad with lobster, the Maine lobster cobb salad or the lobster and shrimp tempura with raspberry-ginger sauce. We liked the gloppy five-onion soup crusted with gruyère cheese and the Thai beef salad with greens, soba noodles and a peanut sauce so spicy it brought tears to the eyes. At the other end of the taste spectrum was a soothing sandwich of surprisingly delicate grilled crabmeat and havarti cheese on butter-grilled sourdough bread. Big-eaters at the next table praised desserts of apple-walnut-cinnamon bread pudding and lemon-blackberry purse with ginger anglaise. Come back at night to try the lobster cioppino or perhaps rare tuna with sweet chili-ginger sauce, roasted halibut with a rum-caramelized beet puree, arctic char with almond brown butter or the veal chop with wild mushrooms. Lately, Hurricane opened a second restaurant at Dock Square in Kennebunkport with the same style of food and a view of the Kennebunk River.

(207) 646-6348 or (800) 649-6348. www.perkinscove.com. Entrées, $18 to $39. Lunch daily, 11:30 to 3:30. Dinner nightly, 5:30 to 9:30 or 10:30.

The Cliff House, Shore Road, Ogunquit.

The new main dining room at the venerable Cliff House is as appealing as ever, with windows onto the ocean and white-linened tables rather close together. Brass oil lamps were reflected in the windows as we munched on hot rolls and sampled the tossed salad with walnut chutney and champagne vinaigrette that was ample enough to skip an appetizer. Among entrées, we enjoyed the award-winning and healthful pan-roasted peppered Atlantic salmon steak with a mushroom, bell pepper and herb lentil sauce and the lobster sauté in a hazelnut crust, both staples on the dinner menu. Recent possibilities were pan-roasted halibut with a blueberry compote, braised lamb shanks with Maine chorizo, and grilled filet mignon with stilton-chasseur sauce. Desserts could be white russian pie, chocolate truffle cake, peach melba and strawberry shortcake. Or finish with an artisanal cheese plate. Interesting sandwiches, salads and entrées are available at lunch on the Ocean Terrace.

(207) 361-1000. Entrées, $23 to $30. Lunch in summer, Monday-Saturday noon to 3. Dinner nightly, 5:30 to 8:30 or 9, to 9 or 9:30 in summer. Sunday brunch, 7:30 to 1.

Cape Arundel Inn, Ocean Avenue, Kennebunkport.

Dine at a window table here (with a bird's-eye view of George H.W. Bush's Walker Point compound). You may see wispy clouds turn to mauve and violet as the sun sets, followed by a full golden moon rising over the darkened ocean. The sea and sky provide more than enough backdrop for owner Jack Nahil's simple but stylish dining room that's a study in white and cobalt blue. Chef Rich Lemoine's changing repertoire runs the gamut of regional American fare. Crusty basil-parmesan-rosemary bread got our latest dinner here off to a good start. Appetizers were a composed spinach salad with prosciutto and oyster mushrooms and an artfully presented chilled sampler of ginger-poached shrimp, a crab-filled spring roll and tea-smoked sirloin with wasabi-citrus rémoulade. Main courses were a superior sliced leg of lamb teamed with cavatelli pasta and wilted arugula, and a mixed grill of duck sausage, veal london broil and loin lamb chop. Seafood choices ranged from pan-fried halibut with a russet and sweet potato crust to a broiled seafood sampler served over saffron fettuccine with spicy rouille. The dessert of cinnamon ice cream with strawberries over lady fingers was enough for two to share.

(207) 967-2125. Entrées, $24 to $36. Dinner, Monday-Saturday 5:30 to 8:30 or 9. Closed January to mid-April.

Stripers, 127 Ocean Ave., Kennebunkport.

This stylish newcomer began life as Stripers Fish Shack and dropped the "fish shack" from its name in 2004 when it relocated from an outbuilding behind the former Schooners Inn to the main waterfront dining room of the Breakwater Inn. It's now Stripers, "a waterfront restaurant and raw bar." And how. Here is White Barn Inn owner Laurence Bongiorno's shrine to seafood, still something of a "fish shack" in terms of food concept but as stylish as all get-out in its stunning new digs at the rear of the inn. A mini-aquarium harboring a tropical fish inside is atop each elegantly set table, mirroring the giant aquarium at the entry. So is a stash of appropriate sauces for what amounts to the original fish shack fare. The menu is short and deceptively straightforward, and eons removed in delivery from the clam shack and fish fry idiom. Look for the day's catch (swordfish, Atlantic salmon, halibut, yellowfin tuna), available chargrilled, broiled or pan seared and served – as are most entrées – with fries and what the menu calls "mushy" peas, a mix of mashed and whole peas in a rich buttery and creamy mash. Also look for lobster, bouillabaisse and blackboard specials. Perhaps the best fish and chips you ever ate comes in the form of ale-battered haddock with fries, garnished with wedges of lemon and lime. Other favorites are the seafood platter – an array of oysters, shrimp, clams, mussels and cracked lobster – and the bento box. Soups, stews, salads and appetizers are offered to begin. The only other "fishless options" are grilled chicken, filet mignon and rack of lamb. Desserts include peanut butter pie, apple crumble and vanilla bean crème brûlée. Just off the porch is a spacious raw bar with seating for dining and cocktails.

(207) 967-3625. Entrées, $17.50 to $32.50. Lunch daily in summer, 11:30 to 2:30. Dinner, Monday-Thursday 5:30 to 9, Friday-Sunday 5 to 9:30.

Pier 77, 77 Pier Road, Cape Porpoise, Kennebunkport.

This is the trendy successor to our favorite Seascapes restaurant, the latest incarnation of a landmark building that's been a restaurant at the edge of Cape Porpoise Harbor for more than 70 years. Chef-owner Peter Morency renovated the restaurant to reflect his New England roots and wife Kate's sense of San Francisco laid-back flair. "Contemporary American fine dining without attitude" is their hallmark. That and an unbeatable view of the harbor through floor-to-ceiling windows on two sides, with a stylish, less-is-more decor that capitalizes on the outdoor scene. The harbor waters lap at the door of the walkout lower-level **Ramp Bar & Grill,** where you can drink at outdoor tables or sample an appealing grill menu amid sports memorabilia inside. We sampled the creative kitchen's fare at an autumn lunch. The clam chowder, though tasty, had far more potatoes than clams. The roasted chicken taquito with guacamole and salsa fresca was delicious, and the star of the show was succulent fish and chips, paired with superior coleslaw. Desserts were pumpkin cheesecake with caramel sauce and warm banana cake with milk chocolate ganache. At night, the chef shines with cioppino, seafood mixed grill, grilled hanger steak, grilled pork chop and lamb kabobs.

(207)967-8500. www.pier77restaurant.com. Entrées, $20 to $30. Lunch daily in summer, 11:30 to 3. Dinner nightly, 5 to 10.

Casual Dining

Barnacle Billy's, Perkins Cove, Ogunquit.

This is an institution, with its quaint setting along Perkins Cove and a casual approach. You place orders as you enter, take a number and find a table (outside by the water if you can, although many inexplicably seem to prefer the inside). Lobster is the main attraction, $17.95 for a pound and a quarter to $28.75 for a two-pounder. A lobster roll for $13.95 and a tuna salad roll for $5.65, washed down with a couple of beers, made a pleasant lunch. You can feast on steamed clams, lobster stew, barbecued chicken, hamburgers or homemade blueberry pie, on premises or for takeout.

(207) 646-5575. Entrée plates, $10.95 to $26.95. Open daily, 11 to 9. Closed mid-October to mid-April.

Barnacle Billy's Etc., Perkins Cove, Ogunquit.

Acquired at auction after a predecessor had failed, the space that formerly housed the famed Whistling Oyster was taken over by Billy Tower. Here, in glamorous splendor, the Barnacle Billy's offshoot next door to the original serves an all-day menu of light fare and basic seafood. Fried seafood and fish and chips share billing with the likes of broiled scallops, grilled swordfish, baked stuffed shrimp, grilled chicken, sirloin steak and baked stuffed lobster. The lobster sauté is a standout, and you can't beat the view from any of the seats in the upstairs dining room, the small outdoor deck or the shady terrace alongside. Two great stone fireplaces are lit at the first hint of a chill. Strawberry cheesecake and key lime pie are good desserts.

The food and prices occupy a niche below those of the old Whistling Oyster, but that striking contemporary ambiance is the same. And they still have valet parking, as did the fancy forebear of years ago.

(207) 646-4711 or (800) 866-5575. www.barnbilly.com. Entrées, $15.95 to $26.95. Lunch and dinner daily, noon to 9. Closed November to early May.

Jackie's Too, Perkins Cove, Ogunquit.

An outgrowth of a breakfast restaurant run by Jackie Bevins on Shore Road, this is a busy, full-service establishment notable primarily for its smashing oceanside setting. The surf laps at the shore as you sit on either the canopied or open-air decks. Nachos, spinach and blue cheese salad, grilled Tuscan chicken wrap and a fried haddock sandwich are among the lunch possibilities. We enjoyed a lobster roll with potato salad ($11.95) and a cold seafood plate ($10.95), preceded by a peach daiquiri and a Coors Lite. For dinner, expect simply prepared seafood like baked haddock, grilled salmon, grilled chicken or, "Jackie's favorite: shrimp, scallops and haddock broiled in lemon butter and topped with seasoned crumbs." There are four pasta dishes and, of course, lobster.

(207) 646-4444. Entrées, $8.95 to $21.95. Lunch and dinner daily in season, 11 to 9.

Lobster Shack, Perkins Cove, Ogunquit.

Lobster, clams and chowder have been dispensed from this rustic shack near the end of the cove since 1947. It's a must stop for lunch whenever we're in Ogunquit and craving the real thing. You feel as if you're beside the ocean at shiny wood tables inside, even if you can't see the water. Lobster was going for $13.95 a pound at our latest visit, a lobster roll was $11.95 and a hot dog, $2.25. Beer and wine are available.

(207) 646-2941. Open daily, 11 to 8:30 or 9. Closed mid-October to mid-May.

Arundel Wharf Restaurant, 43 Ocean Ave., Kennebunkport.

The gigantic, partly open, partly awning-covered deck at this riverfront landmark affords 125 outdoor diners the best harbor views in town. Another 75 can be seated inside at shiny nautical chart tables amidst wooden ship models, mahogany accents and a distinct yacht-club feel. Two half-circle tables extend out over the wharf for the best waterfront situation we've encountered in any dining room. Happily, the food is equal to the setting. The lobster club sandwich, the meaty lobster stew and the avocado stuffed with crabmeat made a fine lunch one day. We'd happily return for dinner, when the extensive menu ranges from charbroiled swordfish and roasted fillet of sole to the Passamaquoddy clambake – a pottery crock filled with steamers and mussels and topped with a lobster. Lobster comes seven ways. "Other interests" are served by chicken diablo, prime rib or venison sauté. Or you can settle for fried seafood or a basic hamburger. Save room for dessert, perhaps bread pudding with whiskey sauce, mixed four-berry pie or blueberry-apple crisp.

(207) 967-3444. www.arundelwharf.com. Entrées, $15.50 to $34.95. Lunch daily, 11:30 to 2:30. Dinner nightly, 5 to 9 or 9:30. Closed late October to mid-April.

FOR MORE INFORMATION: Ogunquit Chamber of Commerce, Route 1 South, Box 2289, Ogunquit, ME 03907, (207) 646-2939. www.ogunquit.org.

Kennebunk/Kennebunkport Chamber of Commerce, 17 Western Ave., Box 740, Kennebunk, ME 04043, (207) 967-0857. www.kkcc.maine.org.

Boothbay Register photo

Pleasure craft mix with working boats in busy Boothbay Harbor.

Boothbay Harbor, Me.

Unlike the well-known resort towns that precede it along the southern Maine coast (think Ogunquit, Kennebunkport and Old Orchard Beach), Boothbay Harbor is not directly on the ocean and has no broad, sandy beach. Its harbor lies inland, sheltered from the elements by coves, islands and peninsulas. The protected position made it an early haven for fishing, lobstering and boat building, whose heritage remains evident today.

And that situation, for us, is Boothbay's attraction. All the peninsulas and islands make this area unusual for the coast of Maine. As the locals in Westport or South Bristol might drawl, pointing across the Sheepscot or Damariscotta rivers toward Boothbay, "you can't get they-ah from he-yah." It's a long way around by land, and the result for those on peninsulas and islands is a sense of isolation.

Thousands of visitors do head for Boothbay, however, drawn by its reputation and its billing as "the heart of the Maine coast." They converge on a hilly village with water on three sides. Three protuberances – Southport Island, Spruce Point and Ocean Point – stretch out toward the sea.

The village has a year-round population of about 1,300 but seems bigger, because of the influx of summer residents and visitors. Tourism is rampant, and boats are everywhere. Fishing and pleasure craft are moored beside wharves that follow the quaint, winding village streets. A footbridge gives pedestrians a shortcut across the harbor.

British fishermen settled the area in the early 1600s, and the town of Boothbay was incorporated in 1764. After the Civil war, steamers started to bring vacationers to the region. Summer hotels and cottage colonies sprang up at Newagen, Ocean Point and Squirrel Island. Lately, overfishing has grounded many commercial fishermen, but lobster trapping flourishes in a region where lobster is king. Boatyards now specialize in yachts, large fishing vessels, ferries and tugboats. Seasonal tourism constitutes the third leg of today's Boothbay triad.

For visitors, Boothbay has more rooms and restaurants with water views than most Maine destinations. But quantity does not necessarily yield quality, especially in a resort area with a short season. Although Boothbay Harbor proper is the focus for many, we prefer the peninsulas and islands beyond. They are away from the hustle and bustle and portray the Maine coast the way it ought to be.

Getting There

The Boothbay Harbor area is located at the beginning of mid-coast Maine, about 60 miles east of Portland. It is reached via the Maine Turnpike (I-95) and Route 1. From Route 1 just east of Wiscasset, take Route 27 south into Boothbay Harbor. Southport Island, Spruce Point and Ocean Point lie beyond.

Where to Stay

Spruce Point Inn, Grandview Drive, Box 237, Boothbay Harbor 04538.

New owners have given this destination resort at the end of a peninsula at the entrance to Boothbay Harbor an almost total makeover. They restored seven cottages and existing lodges, undoing 1970s renovations, "uncarpeting floors and uncovering ceilings and returning to a vintage period look" in the words of Angelo DiGiulian, one of two managing partners. Their 40 "oceanfront deluxe suites" in six new buildings are as good as they get in Boothbay. Among the best is the Loon, a two-level cocoon with vaulted ceiling, king bed, a Vermont Castings stove, an oversize jacuzzi tub finished in marble, TV in an armoire, overstuffed furniture and a pine theme with light colors. The arched front veranda yields a spectacular water view, an attribute common to most guest quarters here. "It's like living in a postcard," Angelo said after his family tried out the suite during an early heat wave. The six new buildings contain three to sixteen large rooms each. Poster beds, private porches, wood stoves and marble baths are the norm. So are hair dryers, coffeemakers, refrigerators and irons. The 26 ground-level rooms have double jacuzzis. The resort is beautifully situated on twelve landscaped acres reached by a private road notable for speed bumps and wild roses in a posh residential section. The main 1896 inn holds dining rooms (see Where to Eat), a lounge opening onto a large patio deck, and nine traditional guest rooms ranging from standard to a corner suite. Among amenities are a new spa settled amidst a zen garden with a state-of-the-art fitness center, a children's playground, two tennis courts, a freshwater pool and whirlpool spa, and, best of all, a saltwater pool with a whirlpool, built into a terrace above the pounding surf at the entrance to the harbor.

(207) 633-4152 or (800) 553-0289. Fax (207) 633-0289. www.sprucepointinn.com. Ninety-three rooms and suites in lodges and cottages. Doubles, $165 to $335, EP; three-night minimum in summer. Cottages for four, $395 to $550; six-night minimum. Closed late October to mid-May.

Newagen Seaside Inn, Route 27, Box 29, Cape Newagen 04576.

Blessed with 85 acres of spruce and pine forest in a former nature sanctuary at the seaward tip of Southport Island, this informal resort is surrounded by water on three sides. Now part of a land trust owned by the Pine Tree Conservation Society, the island was so loved by naturalist Rachel Carson that her ashes were spread there

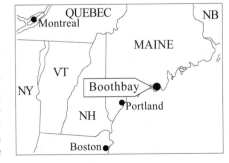

following her death. Peace and quiet prevail in the stately, two-story, white clapboard inn, where the great room/library is graced with rattan furniture and the fireplace is ablaze on chilly evenings. New owners Scott and Corinne Larson from Atlanta, who closed the deal four days after the birth of their first child, undertook renovations and cosmetic enhancements to a building they thought "looked a little tired." They also added four deluxe rooms in a new building they call the Little Inn. Our spacious, high-ceilinged quarters here came with a sumptuous kingsize bed, TV, an enormous bathroom and a mini-kitchen, plus a private balcony facing the ocean. The inn has seventeen standard rooms with cottage-style furnishings, three one-bedroom suites and six rooms with private decks, four of them on the ground level. Most deluxe are three suites with queensize poster beds, sitting area and wet bar. Three cottages are rented by the week. The inn has a highly regarded dining room (see Where to Eat), a cocktail lounge in a sunroom and porches facing east and west to the sea. Outside are the biggest saltwater pool in New England and a heated freshwater pool, with an oceanside gazebo in between. Also available are two tennis courts, rowboats, lawn games like shuffleboard and croquet, a mile-long nature trail passing tidal pools and a mile of rock-bound shore to explore.

(207) 633-5242 or (800) 654-5242. Fax (207) 633-5340. www.newagenseasideinn.com. Twenty-seven rooms, three suites and three cottages with private baths. Doubles, $175 to $250. Suites, $250. Cottages, $1,000 to $1,500 weekly. Closed mid-October to mid-May.

The Lawnmere Inn, Route 27, Box 29, Southport 04576.

Guests entering the newly renovated lobby of this appealing inn, motel and restaurant are greeted by an enticing view of a picturesque cove through the dining room windows. New owners Scott and Corinne Larson of the Newagen Seaside Inn, who took over in 2004, reconfigured and refurbished the lobby, front desk and common areas to take better advantage of the waterside location just past the drawbridge at the tip of Southport Inn. Although best known for its dining room (see Where to Eat), the oldest operating inn in the region now claims some of the finest accommodations as well. The Larsons renovated the inn's second and third floors to produce seven rooms and four suites, most with water views. Updated with a light 21st century look, rooms are painted in Victorian Painted Lady colors and furnished with stunning original artworks. Twenty more rooms, some with king beds or queen four-posters, are in two motel buildings on either side. There's a charming cottage for two with a queen poster bed and a sun deck at water's edge. Drinks are available in the Wobbly Lobster bar painted a stunning poppy red. Breakfast, included in the rates and available to the public, is served in a sunny, water-view dining room flanked by a spacious new deck. Ours produced a superior tomato and herb omelet with whole-wheat toast and roast beef hash topped with two poached eggs.

(207) 633-2544 or (800) 633-7645. www.lawnmereinn.com. Twenty-seven rooms, four suites and one cottage with private baths. Doubles, $164 to $179. Suites, $199. Closed mid-October to late May.

Five Gables Inn, Murray Hill Road, Box 335, East Boothbay 04544.

Perched on a hillside overlooking Linekin Bay, this five-gabled establishment dates back more than 130 years and was the last remaining summer hotel in the area. Previous owners had renovated the old Forest House into a luxury B&B by the water when it was acquired by Mike and De Kennedy, who had just concluded a "mid-life break" in which they crewed on a yacht in French Polynesia and backpacked for six months from Bali to Nepal. They host guests in sixteen rooms on three floors, all with a water view. All have modern baths and queensize beds (one is kingsize).

Five have working fireplaces. Lace curtains and quilts color-coordinated to De's artistic accents and the pictures on the walls enhance the decor, all of which is light, airy and new. De offers afternoon tea in the English manner in the airy living room or on the wraparound veranda, where a hammock and abundant sitting areas take in the view of the bay. Mike prepares multi-course breakfasts. His repertoire includes zucchini-walnut pancakes, blueberry french toast and tomato-basil frittata.

(207) 633-4551 or (800) 451-5048. www.fivegablesinn.com. Sixteen rooms with private baths. Doubles, $135 to $200. Closed November to mid-May.

Linekin Bay Bed & Breakfast, 531 Ocean Point Road, East Boothbay 04544.

Retired Lewiston police sergeant Larry Brown and his wife Marti Booth, a retired teacher, restored this rambling 1878 residence, a section of which housed for 75 years the E&E Holbrook Store. They gutted the place to the studs and opened a B&B with four comfortable guest rooms, all with water views. The biggest is the main-floor Holbrook Suite, 28 feet long with a large porch, Vermont Castings stove and clawfoot tub. Its principal feature is a high poster kingsize featherbed facing the bay in the middle of the room, with a dressing area behind. "You can wake up and look out at the water," says Larry. Upstairs are three more guest rooms with sitting areas and queen or king beds. All have TV/VCRs, telephones and Vermont-style fireplaces. The aptly named Crooked Chimney Room has a crook in the exposed brick chimney. Downstairs, guests enjoy mementos from the old Holbrook store displayed in the hallway, an elegant front parlor and a rear dining room with two tables for four, with french doors opening to a deck with a bay view. Larry prepares a full breakfast: strawberry-yogurt parfait, maple-spiced muffins and homemade quiche one day, "decadent" french toast à l'orange the next. In the afternoon he serves sweets like brownie meltaways, which live up to their name. His wife tends to the gardens, which helped put the property on the Boothbay Peninsula's annual House and Garden Tour the day of our visit.

(207) 633-9900 or (800) 596-7420. www.linekinbaybb.com. Four rooms with private baths. Doubles, $130 to $180.

Ocean Point Inn, Shore Road, Ocean Point, Box 409, East Boothbay 04544.

An unusually wide range of accommodations – inn and lodge rooms, farmhouse motel units and cottages – are strung along the shore in fifteen buildings at this establishment that began more than 100 years ago. All come with king or queen or twin beds, TV, telephone and mini-refrigerator. Some have kitchenettes. Lodgings range from typical motel units and small duplex cottages with a bedroom and porch to inn-style rooms and six rooms in the Seawinds building, each with two queen beds and ocean-view balconies. A motel apartment, a penthouse and a two-bedroom cottage, each with kitchen and accommodating up to four, are rented by the week. The location is near the end of a point at the entrance to Linekin Bay, where boats pass on the way to and from the open ocean. The area's largest heated outdoor pool is located opposite the motels near the top of the property. Breakfast and dinner are available in casual and more formal settings along the waterfront side of the main inn. Salmon steaks, offered in three versions, are the inn's signature, but you can order from an extensive menu (entrées, $14.95 to $20.95).

(207) 633-4200 or (800) 552-5554. www.oceanpointinn.com. Sixty-one rooms and cottages with private baths. Doubles, $122 to $197 EP. Closed Columbus Day to Memorial Day.

Hodgdon Island Inn, 374 Barter's Island Road, Box 603, Boothbay 04537.

This big old 1810 sea captain's home was renovated into a B&B by a local couple, Steve and Sherri Matte, who had tired of running a motel. Renovation is an understatement. They put in private baths, new kitchens, new walls and ceilings, wallpaper and carpeting and added an instant lawn the day before their first guests arrived. Rooms are furnished simply but attractively, and most face the water at the end of a sloping lawn, two from a shared second-floor porch. We'd gladly be ensconced in Room 6 at the end of the house, with a king bed, fireplace, a full bath and use of a wicker-filled porch shared by Room 5. The queen bed in Room 4 is covered with a handsome wedding ring quilt. Downstairs are a parlor with TV, a sunny dining room and a front porch with a wooden glider. There's also a refrigerator full of soft drinks. The Mattes added three more rooms with king or queen beds in 2004. They offer an attractive heated swimming pool at the side of the property.

(207) 633-7474 or (800) 314-5160. www.hodgdonislandinn.com. Eight rooms with private baths. Doubles, $125 to $175.

The Anchor Watch, 9 Eames Road, Boothbay Harbor 04538.
Beautifully landscaped on a dead-end street beside the shore, this B&B offers comfortable guest rooms with a nautical air. That's natural, because owner Diane Campbell's family runs the Balmy Day Cruises in town. Here she and her daughter, Kathy Reed, cosset guests in five country-style rooms, four with water views and each named for a Monhegan Island mail boat of yesteryear. Two on the third floor get especially good views from balconies above the trees. The Balmy Days on the first floor overlooks the rock gardens toward the water. Its private entrance off its own porch opens to a kingsize poster bed with a floral comforter and the only in-room TV. Beds in the other rooms are queensize and covered with colorful quilts or down comforters. The front living room offers a TV and games, while the renovated seaside room has a corner gas fireplace and seven windows onto the water. It is open to the kitchen, which has been featured on several local kitchen tours and is known for its hand-painted tiles with original designs, among them Andre the seal. Guests also enjoy porches, a dock for swimming or fishing, a patio on the rocks and a butterfly/azalea garden. Chocolate squares might be put out for afternoon snacks. In the morning, Diane provides homemade granola, raisin-bran muffins and perhaps blueberry dutch babies with cinnamon apples or a baked cheese omelet.

(207) 633-7565. www.anchorwatch.com. Five rooms with private baths. Doubles, $170 to $190.

1830 Admiral's Quarters Inn, 71 Commercial St., Boothbay Harbor 04538.
Spectacular flower gardens on a slope out front catch the eye at this recently renovated sea captain's home atop a knoll with commanding views of the harbor. So do all the individual decks and the solarium added to the house for its new life as a B&B. Les and Deb Hallstrom offer rooms and suites with private entrances, water-view decks or patios, telephones and TVs. Some have fireplaces. Beds vary from king and queensize to twins. All rooms are decorated in a floral motif with a mix of antiques and wicker furnishings. Iced tea or hot mulled cider and goodies are offered in the afternoon. Morning brings a hearty breakfast buffet, from "Deb's A.M. yogurt delight to dessert." The main event might be egg and sausage casserole, blueberry cobbler french toast, breakfast pizza or banana pancakes. The buffet is presented in the solarium overlooking the harbor. Another good view is from the swing glider amid all the flowers. It's a favorite place to spend a few minutes until it's someone else's turn.

(207) 633-2474 or (800) 644-1878. Fax (207) 633-5904. www.admiralsquartersinn.com. Two rooms and five suites with private baths. Doubles, $165 to $195.

Welch House Inn, 56 McKown St., Boothbay Harbor 04538.
Perched atop McKown Hill in the center of Boothbay Harbor, this 19th-century

sea captain's home enjoys some of the best water views in town. They captivated Susan Hodder and Michael Feldman, a Massachusetts couple who gave up high-tech careers for innkeeping. They offer fourteen guest rooms with remodeled bathrooms, two with new whirlpool tubs. Many have gas fireplaces. Beds are king or queensize except for a couple with two double beds. Rooms in the Victorian-style main inn have TV/VCRs and telephones. Art by local artisans adorns the walls, and decor is a mix of old and new. Five more nautical rooms are in the adjacent Sail Loft. A recent addition, all glassed in to take advantage of the harbor view, houses a large living room with fireplace and a huge room for breakfast. The best views are from the enlarged main-floor deck and the rooftop sundeck, now big enough to accommodate all guests at once – and then some. Susan prepares a gourmet breakfast, perhaps poached eggs florentine one day and strawberry-cream cheese stuffed french toast the next. She figures most people who come to Maine ought to have lobster for breakfast, so she obliges on weekends with a lobster soufflé or a lobster and crabmeat omelet.

(207) 633-3431 or (800) 279-7313. Fax (207) 633-3752. www.welchhouseinn.com. Fourteen rooms with private baths. Doubles, $125 to $195. Closed mid-December through March.

Blue Heron Seaside Inn, 65 Townsend Ave., Boothbay Harbor 04538.

Everything looks and feels new at this B&B of recent vintage, opened by Phil and Laura Chapman after two years of renovations. Returning to their native area following 28 years in England and South Korea, the couple refurbished the interior of an 1880s house and added quite a complex of rear porches so that every room opens through french doors onto water-view decks above the parking area and waterfront lawn. The Chapmans furnished five guest rooms and a two-bedroom suite with king or queen beds, and some bear antiques collected from their travels. Decor is Victorian on the first floor, Colonial on the second and nautical on the third. Rooms are extra-large with sitting areas, TV, refrigerator and microwave. One has a whirlpool tub. A continental breakfast buffet is set out in the entry lobby. Guests may eat at a handful of small tables there or take a tray to their porch.

(207) 633-7020 or (866) 216-2300. www.blueheronseasideinn.com. Five rooms and one suite with private baths. Doubles, $165 to $190. Suite $240.

Fiddler's Green Inn, 15 Atlantic Ave., Boothbay Harbor 04538.

Every room yields at least a partial water view at this eco-friendly B&B run by Barbara Ford-Latty, a former training manager for Royal Sonesta and Colonial Williamsburg hotels. In her rambling ex-sea captain's house beside Townsend Gut she offers five rooms and two suites, all with queen beds except one with a king and all but one with TV. The prized second-floor Lighthouse Suite has a bedroom in back and a living room/dining area/kitchen in front, opening onto a rooftop deck. Another room and a suite with a private patio are right at water's edge. Guests enjoy a large living room and a kitchen in a middle section of the house. Barbara serves a three-course breakfast at individual tables in the dining area or outside on a deck. The main event might be apple pancakes or a soufflé.

(207) 633-9965 or (888) 633-9965. www.thefiddlersgreeninn.com. Five rooms and two suites with private baths. Doubles, $95 to $135. Suites, $170.

Ocean Gate Inn, 70 Oceangate Road, Box 240, Southport 04576.

The area's best-looking motel building – in a Florida condo kind of way – is located at water's edge in a secluded, 30-acre woodland setting down a long driveway from Route 27. The rooms are attractive and comfortable, with the usual motel accoutrements. The angling of the contemporary waterfront units closest to the shore gives each a lovely, private balcony. Some rooms have kingsize beds, refrigerators and fireplaces. Also available are two cottages and nine two-bedroom units. On the upper part of the property is a heated pool, surrounded by lawn seating with a view. There are two tennis courts, rowboats, a fishing pier, a fitness center and a hot tub. A breakfast buffet is included in the rates.

(207) 633-3321 or (800) 221-5924. www.oceangateinn.com. Sixty-six room with private baths. Doubles, $129 to $329. Closed Columbus Day to Memorial Day.

Ship Ahoy Motel, Route 238, Southport 04569.

The view is right and so are the prices at this motel complex in four buildings on a spacious hillside property. The original motel rooms are dark and smallish with one or two double beds, but cost a mere $49. Splurge for one of the 30 larger units with private decks down by the waterfront. They have two double beds and views that won't quit. Those in the Ship Ahoy Waterfront building, as opposed to the Far East Motel, are even larger and have vinyl chairs facing the TV and tiled entrances with separate vanity areas. There's a dock for saltwater fishing, and a large pool overlooks the water. A coffee shop on the property opens for breakfast.

(207) 633-5222. www.shipahoymotel.com. Fifty-four rooms. Doubles, $49 to $79. Closed Columbus Day to Memorial Day.

Tugboat Inn, 80 Commercial St., Box 267, Boothbay Harbor 04538.

To our minds, this five-building complex is the most appealing of the many large and touristy motor inns around the in-town waterfront. All rooms are air-conditioned and have king or queen beds, light pine furniture, TVs, telephones and hair dryers. The main inn, new in 1994, offers deluxe rooms with ceiling fans; rooms on the second and third floors have private balconies. All the other buildings have been renovated lately. The Tugboat and Wharf buildings, located on piers directly over the water, have deck areas and some private balconies. A bit more private is the Red Building, with three large guest rooms sharing an oversize deck on the main floor and the luxurious Dunfey Suite with kitchen, living room, whirlpool tub and private balcony on the second floor. The converted red tugboat in front forms part of the seasonal restaurant that offers lunch and dinner with water views. A piano bar and cocktail lounge opens onto the open-air Marina Deck on the lower level, where boat slips and moorings are available. Complimentary coffee and pastries are offered overnight guests in the morning.

(207) 633-4434 or (800) 248-2628. www.tugboatinn.com. Sixty-two rooms and two suites. Doubles, $140 to $200. Suites, $165 and $215. Closed Thanksgiving to mid-April.

CAMPING. "No rig is too big" at the area's largest trailer and tent establishment, **Shore Hills Campground,** 553 Wiscasset Road, Boothbay 04537, (207) 633-4782. It offers 150 open, wooded or waterfront sites along a tidal river where there's a float for swimming. **Little Ponderosa Campground,** 159 Wiscasset Road, Boothbay 04537, (207) 633-2700, offers 30 shore sites among its total of 97 along with miniature golf and a Sunday morning church service. More secluded on Southport Island is **Gray Homestead Oceanfront Campground,** 21 Homestead Road, Southport 04576, (207) 633-4612. A road through the forest leads to this picturesque property, where 40 open or wooded campsites enjoy water views.

Seeing and Doing

The hordes of tourists in the center of town tell you that this is a busy area with lots going on. Boat cruises leave from the town piers on all sorts of water excursions.

There are historic and maritime attractions, scenic drives and plenty of shops and galleries. For a quick introduction and vista that epitomizes Boothbay, check out the dory monument overlooking the harbor at **Fisherman's Memorial Park,** Atlantic Avenue, across from the Catholic Church.

Harbor shuttles operate from 7 a.m. to 11 p.m. daily in July and August. Courtesy trolleys run from 10 to 5, mid-June to Labor Day.

On the Water

Balmy Days Cruises, Pier 8, 42 Commercial St., Boothbay Harbor, (207) 633-2284 or (800) 298-2284. Scenic one-hour harbor tours, a lighthouse tour, mackerel fishing trips and a cruise to Monhegan Island are among the offerings of this versatile outfit under Capt. Bill Campbell. The one-hour harbor tours aboard the Novelty, offered six or seven times daily, stop briefly at the Squirrel Island summer colony (adults $10, children $5). A 90-minute sail aboard the 31-foot sloop Bay Lady, once a working boat for lobstermen, passes islands and lighthouses (trips five times daily, $18). The Balmy Days II offers day trips daily at 9:30 to remote Monhegan Island, twelve miles off the coast. It involves a 90-minute cruise each way and a nearly four-hour layover for lunch in the fishing village and sightseeing on the storied island (adults $30, children $18). An interesting new tour aboard the Novelty goes to **Burnt Island Lighthouse.** There, light station keeper Joseph Muise and his family acquaint visitors with lighthouse living and lead a nature walk around the five-acre island. Tours twice daily weekdays in July and August; adults $30, children $18.

Cap'n Fish's Whale Watch and Scenic Nature Cruises, Pier 1, Boothbay Harbor, (207) 633-3244 or (800) 636-3244. Capt. Bob Fish, a Boothbay native who at age 18 was the youngest licensed boat captain on the East Coast, has expanded his fleet into one of the area's largest. For whale watching, the region's fastest vessels get passengers out to the feeding grounds quickly. Humpback, finback, minke, right and pilot whales may be sighted, along with dolphins, porpoises, sharks and seals. A variety of scenic tours range from a 75-minute seal watch cruise to a three-hour, 44-mile trip up the Kennebec River to view the shipbuilding activity at the Bath Iron Works. Periodic cruises show the National Audubon Society's success in re-establishing a puffin colony on Eastern Egg Rock. Tours and departures vary daily; adults $14 to $28, children $7 to $18.

Boothbay Whale Watch, Pier 6, Boothbay Harbor, (207) 633-3500 or (888) 942-5363. The speedy Harbor Princess with an enclosed lower and open upper deck gets passengers out to the whale feeding grounds fast, and claims a 98 percent success rate for sightings. A naturalist points out the details. Sunset and nature cruises are offered in the evenings. Hours and prices vary.

Custom cruises for up to six people are offered by Capt. Jonathan Rutenberg aboard his 27-foot powerboat **Seasonal Therapy** from Pier 1, Boothbay Harbor, (207) 633-0059 or (866) 464-2789.

SAILING CRUISES. The 64-foot windjammer **Eastwind,** (207) 633-6598, sails from Pier 6 up to three times daily, and offers a sunset cruise June through August. The 2½-hour trip with Herb and Doris Smith, who built the Eastwind as well as five Appledore schooners and have sailed twice around the world, sails to the outer islands and gets close to Seal Rocks (fare, $22). Capt. Joe Tassi gives two-hour sails aboard the schooner **Lazy Jack,** (207) 975-2628, four times daily from Pier 7 out past Burnt Island Light to the outer islands of Boothbay (fare, $25).

KAYAKING. In the Chowder House Building by the Footbridge in Boothbay

Harbor you'll find the **Tidal Transit Ocean Kayak Co.,** (207) 633-7140. It offers rentals as well as several tours daily. This is also a place to rent bicycles. Guided tours, lessons and rentals are offered by the **East Boothbay Kayak Co.** out of Ocean Point Marina in East Boothbay, (207) 633-7411 or (866) 633-7411.

LOBSTER TRIPS. You can watch lobster-trap hauling up close aboard **Miss Boothbay,** (207) 633-6445. One-hour trips aboard a working lobster boat leave Monday-Saturday from Pier 6

BOAT RENTALS. Traditional wooden boats are rented by the hour, day or week at **Finest Kind Wooden Boats** in West Boothbay, (207) 633-5636.

FISHING. Sport fishermen find the area a paradise for mackerel, bluefish, striped bass, tuna and shark. Charger Charters, (207) 380-4556, offers half-day and evening trips. **Redhook Charters,** (207) 633-3807, specializes in shark fishing.

SWIMMING. The waters are chilly and the beaches few, but on a hot day you might want to know about the beach at Townsend Gut, off Route 27 and Beach Road beyond the Townsend Gut Bridge to Southport Island. Grimes Cove Beach is a small beach at the tip of Ocean Point overlooking offshore islands. Swimming is also available at Knickercane Island Park, Barter's Island Road, and Barrett Park off Lobster Cove Road.

Other Attractions

Driving Around. Most people who get to Boothbay Harbor go no farther, and that's understandable. Once you wend your way down from the highway onto the fingers of land that form the Boothbay area, you're inclined to stay a while. And it is a picturesque, watery place with great views at every turn. Every local has his favorite drive. Here's one: Drive on Route 27 across Townsend Gut through "downtown Southport," which consists of a post office, town hall, fire department and general store, as well as the Hendricks Hill Museum. Detour to the beach at the end of Beach Road for a look at the lighthouse and skittering sandpipers. Follow the signs for Cozy Harbor and the Southport Yacht Club, whose members patronize the E.W. Pratt General Store, an emporium from yesteryear with a duck-pin bowling alley on one side, some shelves in the middle and a counter on the other. On the way to Pratt's Island, you'll pass the odd commercial enterprise and homes typical of Southport Island's utter lack of pretension. Many are the fishing boats in Christmas Cove, a working harbor. Near Cape Newagen, look for the Lobster Shop (where you can get a lobster roll or a whoopie pie), the homes in the Newagen land trust and the town landing, with a view of Cuckold's Lighthouse. Search out Capitol Island, a suave, residential island reached by a one-way bridge. Poke down other side roads to find boat-filled harbors and inlets and your own discoveries.

Coastal Maine Botanical Gardens, Barter's Island Road, Boothbay.
Volunteers have planted and labeled parts of the 128-acre property that a non-profit organization obtained in 1995 along the Back River in Boothbay. It's a work in progress blossoming into Maine's first major botanical garden. The majority of the grounds where woods meet shore are left in their natural state. Self-guided nature trails explore 3,600 feet of tidal shoreline. Enjoy the wetland garden plants and try to identify some of the 140 mushroom species throughout the preserve. Trail maps are available on the grounds. Four acres of formal gardens and a visitor center were scheduled to open in 2006.

(207) 633-4333. www.mainegardens.org. Open daily, dawn to dusk. Free.

Marine Resources Aquarium, 194 McKown Point Road, West Boothbay Harbor, (207) 633-9559. Marine life is on display at this small aquarium sponsored by the Maine Department of Marine Resources and the U.S. Fish and Wildlife Service. The tidal pool touch tank harboring horseshoe crabs, sea urchins, baby lobsters and sport fish is a hit with youngsters. The facility is situated on a picturesque point jutting into the harbor, with much of the village on view. The department opens the nearby Burnt Island Light Station for tours. Aquarium open daily 10 to 5, Memorial Day to Columbus Day. Adults $3, children $2.50.

Boothbay Region Historical Society, 72 Oak St., Boothbay Harbor, (207) 633-3462. The museum in the 1774 Elizabeth Reed House serves as the town's memory and resting place for treasures found in local attics. The museum's seven display rooms contain artifacts and mementos reflecting the region's Colonial and coastal origins, as well as Reed family heirlooms. A Fresnel lens from the Ram Island Light, a ship's bell from a five-masted schooner, vintage lobster traps, ice-cutting saws and groovers are among the highlights. Open Wednesday, Friday and Saturday 10 to 4 in summer. Donation.

Hendricks Hill Museum, 419 Hendricks Hill Road off Route 27, Southport. (207) 633-2370. Tools from the local fishing industry, navigation instruments and household items from the past are among the artifacts in this restored early 19th-century house on Southport Island. A boat shop contains early fishing boats and tools from the ice harvesting industry. Open Tuesday, Thursday and Saturday 11 to 3, July-Labor Day. Donation.

SHOPPING. The opportunities begin along the Route 27 access road into Boothbay Harbor. Extraordinary glazed porcelain in various hues is shown inside and out at **Edgecomb Potters** in Edgecomb. The huge establishment has all kinds of pottery for kitchen and dining room, as well as decorative accessories. **Gimbel & Sons Country Store** and **The Smiling Cow** gift shop are related landmarks side by side in two of the oldest commercial buildings in the center of town. **Sherman's Book & Stationery Store** has two floors full of books, art supplies, stationery and greeting cards.

The rambling **Village Shop** contains room after room of kitchen gadgets, cookbooks, table linens, china, children's clothing, sophisticated cards and Maine food products. It's part of the suave **House of Logan,** which purveys traditional clothing. Clothing with more of an exotic, worldly flair is featured along with accessories and jewelry at **Calypso. Slick's Boutique** offers contemporary women's clothing and shoes.

For fine Maine crafts, head to **Boothbay Harbor Artisans,** a cooperative of local artists and craftspeople at 11 Granary Way. At **Abacus** we admired the homebody cats done by Solveig Cox, with mice in their mouths. Original blueberry pottery, painted and signed by the artist, is featured at **The Custom House.** Ten rooms of antiques and art are offered at **The Palabra Shop. The Nautical Rooster** is a house full of decorative accessories for land and sea. **The Mung Bean** on Upper Townsend Avenue has good cards, pottery and jewelry, birch bark baskets, spruce sachets, chart clocks and such.

Home and cottage furnishings are offered at **Coast and Cottage** and its related design and accessories store across the street, **Island Originals.** Small galleries are scattered throughout village and around the region. Among the best is **Ocean Point Studio** at Ocean Point, where Corinne McIntyre sells her oils and watercolors of coastal landscapes.

Where to Eat ⎯⎯⎯⎯⎯⎯⎯⎯⎯⎯⎯⎯⎯ ♪♪♪

Lawnmere Inn and Restaurant, Route 27, Southport.
Virtually every table has a water view in the wide pine-paneled dining room of this Southport Island restaurant that's stylish in white by day and romantic by candlelight at night. Longtime chef Bill Edgerton supplements the regular menu with a page of daily specials – things like garlicky linguini tossed with smoked salmon and peas alfredo as an appetizer and a trio of fish (swordfish with pesto, tuna with soy and garlic, and sole with crabmeat and tomato) as an entrée. Both proved exceptional. We also can vouch for the lobster strudel and the seafood linguini in a light tomato cream sauce. Other main dishes vary from chicken paprikash to peppercorn-rubbed filet mignon with cognac demi-glace. The smoked Atlantic salmon plate and sautéed Maine crab cakes on a bed of steamed spinach proved excellent appetizers. Crème brûlée, blueberry bread pudding with crème anglaise, grand marnier mousse and key lime pie are among the delightful desserts.
(207) 633-2544 or (800) 633-7645. Entrées, $15.50 to $25. Dinner nightly by reservation, 6 to 9, mid-June to Labor Day, fewer nights in off-season. Closed mid-October to mid-May.

The Thistle Inn, 55 Oak St., Boothbay Harbor.
With the demise in 2004 of the acclaimed Christopher's Boathouse restaurant on the waterfront, this restaurant in a restored 1861 barn and stable took top honors for in-town dining in Boothbay Harbor. The place seats 60 in three nautical-themed dining rooms and outside on an expanded deck. New owners Mark Osborn and Steve Bouffard from Boston and their chef offer an innovative menu. They feature "some exotic items that other restaurateurs don't do around here," Steve said, citing ostrich, crawfish and grouper as examples. Typical entrées run from baked stuffed haddock and seared ahi tuna with a soy and ginger dipping sauce to herb-crusted rack of lamb and pan-seared duck breast and confit with cherry brandy demi-glace. Appetizers include crab cakes, crostini and half a dozen exotic salads. Dessert could be pineapple upside-down cake with ginger ice cream, strawberry-mascarpone trifle with riesling syrup or a trio of sorbets served in a pizzelle cup. Lighter fare is served in the atmospheric **Dory Pub.** The inn also rents six renovated rooms with private baths for $100 to $120 a night.
(207) 633-3341 or (877) 633-3541. www.thethistleinn.com. Entrées, $17 to $28. Dinner in summer, nightly from 5. Rest of year, open Tuesday-Saturday, lunch 11:30 to 2 and dinner from 5.

Spruce Point Inn, Atlantic Avenue, Boothbay Harbor.
The large and airy, oceanfront dining room called **88/Grandview** is the setting for candlelight dinners at this resort inn at the tip of Linekin Neck. The fare is modern American, as in appetizers of lobster, shiitake and brie crêpe finished with a mimosa beurre blanc or a napoleon of grilled portobello with bermuda onion, fresh mozzarella, roasted pepper and tomato. Main courses range from roasted sea bass with miso beurre blanc or pan-blackened salmon with mango salsa to grilled filet mignon with perigourdine sauce. The wine list is far more extensive than most in the area, and there's a reserve list, too. Pub-style food is served in a lounge called **Bogie's Hideaway.**
(207) 633-4152 or (800) 553-0289. Entrées, $19 to $26. Dinner nightly by reservation, 6 to 9. Pub nightly, 5 to 10. Closed late October to mid-May.

Newagen Seaside Inn, Route 27, Cape Newagen.
This inn's restaurant traditionally offers some of the best food in the area, although the dining hours have been curtailed lately as new owners Scott and Corinne Larson catered to the wedding trade. White linens dress up the simple, deceptively

large dining room and the Cape Harbor Grill and lounge, both with water views. With the dining room often given over to functions, dinner is usually taken in the lounge. The menu is strong on appetizers like firecracker shrimp served with a cool rosemary and sour cream dipping sauce and lobster cakes accented with red peppers and sweet potatoes. Fans say they've never tasted such good salmon, poached in its own little pan with julienned vegetables and court bouillon, and Gourmet magazine requested the recipe for the seafood alfredo. Lobster bellagio (de-shelled and served over fettuccine) and beef tenderloin au poivre are among the possibilities. Desserts might be apple strudel, crème de menthe parfait, amaretto cheesecake or banana-chocolate chip cake. The wine list is limited but pleasantly priced.

(207) 633-5242 or (800) 654-5242. Entrées, $15 to $26. Dinner by reservation, nightly except Saturday, 6 to 9.

The Boat House Bistro, 12 The By-Way, Boothbay Harbor.

Outdoor dining on the rooftop deck, with a view of the downtown harbor scene, is offered at this three-floor establishment that tries to offer something for everyone. The same menu is available on all three floors, each categorized by type: the main floor for formal dining, the second-floor for bar and grill, and the top Crow's Nest Bar with an open-air deck. The fare is Italian-American, and the menu is fairly extensive. There are all kinds of sandwich, pasta and pizza offerings, including a hand-tossed specialty pizza laden with lobster, pesto and cheeses. Otherwise, expect such entrées as grilled swordfish Roman style, potato-crusted salmon, lobster thermidor, chicken breast stuffed with lobster and spinach, veal piccata or marsala, and filet mignon with a pistachio-pinot grigio demi-glace. You could start with steamed mussels, twin Maryland-style crab cakes or tuna carpaccio. Desserts include frozen biscuit tortoni, chocolate soufflé and pineapple-almond cake.

(207) 633-7300. Entrées, $16 to $36. Open daily, 11 to 10; dining room 4 to 10, bar menu 10 to midnight. Second-floor grill open year-round. Rest closed mid-October to mid-May.

Lobsterman's Wharf, Route 96, East Boothbay.

In a commercial fishing area on the small but picturesque harbor at East Boothbay, this large establishment exudes the flavor of boat building and repairing, fishing and lobstering. The umbrellaed deck overlooking the water is the place to be if it's nice. Our lunch on a warm, sunny day was perfect and we enjoyed watching the small boats (even a canoe) in which people arrived for a meal, even if the construction noise from the boatyard beside did intrude (this is a working harbor, after all). We savored a fine cup of clam chowder, a lobster roll and an enormous spinach salad with an especially good pepper-parmesan dressing. At night, things are quieter and candles flicker on outside tables. Inside the long, low building is a dark dining room with booths and nautical memorabilia. For dinner, you can get grilled swordfish with béarnaise sauce, baked stuffed fillet of sole, broiled scallops, chicken oscar, veal piccata and steak marchand, plus some mighty interesting nightly specials. Damariscotta River oysters on the half shell are an appetizer specialty. The blueberry pie, carrot cake, strawberry shortcake and cheesecake are homemade.

(207) 633-3443. Entrées, $15.95 to $27.95. Lunch daily, 11:30 to 5. Dinner, 5 to 10. Closed mid-October to early May.

The Lobster Dock, 49 Atlantic Ave., Boothbay Harbor.

Two levels of decks, a stone patio and an inside dining room full of red picnic tables on two levels yield harbor views at this glorified lobster shack with big ambitions. You order at a counter and take a seat until your name is called. The food is highly regarded. Besides the usual lobster and clam shack fare, you can order the likes of fried seafood, baked stuffed shrimp, seafood fra diavolo, angus strip steak and slow-roasted prime rib. The daily specials board is apt to offer a few surprises. There are beer and wine, as well as homemade pies for dessert.

(207) 633-7120. www.thelobsterdock.com. Entrées, $9.95 to $24.95. Open daily, 11:30 to 8:30, June through Columbus Day.

Robinson's Wharf, Route 27, Southport.

Long communal tables are everywhere – inside and out, under cover and on the open wharf – at this dockside establishment beside Townsend Gut and what's said to be the busiest drawbridge in Maine. The food is as basic as the atmosphere: the specialty is lobster rolls ($10.95), which live up to their billing. You also can get fish chowder, lobster stew, fried seafood plates, a lobster dinner with chips and corn on the cob, steamed clams and mussels, to eat here or to go. Desserts include homemade pies. Beer and wine are available.

(207) 633-3830. www.robinsonswharf.com. Entrées, $8.95 to $12.40. Open daily, 11:30 to 8. Closed Labor Day to mid-June.

Chowpaya Thai Restaurant, 28 Union St., Boothbay Harbor.

Local restaurateurs and foodies flock to this restaurant featuring authentic Thai cuisine across the street from the waterfront. A sign out front advertises both Pepsi and sushi. The interior is small and modest, looking to be mainly kitchen and sushi bar, but there's a pleasant deck with umbrellas out front. The extensive menu is listed by the numbers (up to 95 for spicy lobster sautéed with mushrooms, onions, basil and bell peppers). The offerings entice: crispy shrimp puff, seven Thai salads (including seafood yum yum), mango chicken, tamarind duck, crispy whole fish, shrimp in the pot, seafood curry, seafood lemon grass, seafood dynasty, even something listed as "shrimp love scallops – shouldn't be missed." Ginger ice cream and coconut custard with sticky rice and mango typify the desserts. Beer and wine are served.

(207) 633-0025. Entrées, $9.95 to $18.95. Open daily, 11 to 10.

Blue Moon Café, 54 Commercial St., Boothbay Harbor.

The most creative sandwiches in town are offered at Paul and Wendy Johnson's intimate restaurant along the downtown harborfront. Soups, salads and desserts are also on the docket. Locals pack the place for breakfast, ordering from a choice of omelets, cinnamon-pecan french toast, or a smoked salmon bagel. There's a canopied waterfront deck, and everything is available for takeout.

(207) 633-2349. Breakfast fare, $3.95 to $6.95; lunch, $4.95 to $7.95. Open daily, 7:30 to 3.

Clambake at Cabbage Island, East Boothbay.

Old-fashioned clambakes are hosted by the Moore family on this 5½-acre island in Linekin Bay. You watch as lobsters, clams and corn on the cob are cooked in seaweed, covered with tarpaulins and rocks. Blueberry cake is served for dessert. Before the feast, you can fish, play horseshoes or badminton, or explore island trails. The entire outing takes about four hours. There's a full liquor license on both the Argo boat that gets you there and on the island. The Argo boat leaves Pier 6 at Fisherman's Wharf.

(207) 633-7200. Boat trip and meal, $44.95. Departures late June to Labor Day, Monday-Friday at 12:30, Saturday at 12:30 and 5, Sunday at 11:30 and 1:30.

FOR MORE INFORMATION: Boothbay Harbor Chamber of Commerce, Route 27, Box 356, Boothbay Harbor, ME 04538, (207) 633-2353 or (800) 266-8422. www.boothbayharbor.com.

Fine view of Camden harbor is offered from Bok Amphitheater in Harbor Park.

Camden/Rockport/Lincolnville, Me.

"Where the Mountains Meet the Sea" is how the promoters bill this area. The description is apt.

This is the part of Mid-Coast Maine where the rocky coast turns sharply to the north. The shoreline becomes hilly, even mountainous as the ocean creates the broad and deep Penobscot Bay. Behind are the "three long mountains and a wood" that native poet Edna St. Vincent Millay described so famously in 1910. Ahead are "three islands in a bay." Beyond are more forested isles and the hills of the Blue Hill peninsula and Deer Isle.

The mountains distinguish this area from others along the Maine coast. They give residents and visitors the opportunity to enjoy traditional mountain pursuits – hiking, biking and skiing, among them – in close proximity to attractions associated with the sea.

Friends of ours bought a vacation home on Hosmer Pond in Camden precisely because of the duality. They swim and canoe in a quiet freshwater pond, hike and ski at the Camden Snow Bowl across the way and cycle around Megunticook Lake. They go sea kayaking and sailing out of Camden harbor and gather mussels when the tide is out at the Ducktrap River outlet in Lincolnville. They enjoy the cultural and entertainment activities of the nearby village, where they browse art galleries and shop, then have a seafood dinner beside the harbor and end up at a concert or a play.

Mount Battie, one of the highest mountains along the East Coast, is the focal point for the area's mountain activities. Penobscot Bay, studded with islands and seemingly endless vistas, offers myriad water pursuits, most having to do with sailing. The bay is the home of the world's largest windjammer fleet, and many visitors come here to see or sail the windjammers. The focus is Camden harbor, where many of its famed fleet set forth under full sail every Monday morning, some not to return to port until Saturday morning. Windjammer Weekend, scheduled over the Labor Day holiday, attracts the largest gathering of windjammers in Maine.

Camden retains a small-town charm that belies its 5,000 population, yet is one of the most cultured, sophisticated and affluent areas in Maine. The corporate presence of the financial services company MBNA enhanced its traditional prosperity and gave it year-round life and livelihood. Add the artists of Rockport, the seaside ambiance of Lincolnville Beach and the backdrop of mountains and lakes for an eclectic mix.

Little wonder the area is thronged, especially in summer, with people enjoying the good life.

Getting There

The Camden area is located on the west side of Penobscot Bay, about 85 miles northeast of Portland and 50 miles south of Bangor. It is accessed by coastal U.S. Route 1. Major airlines fly into Portland and Bangor. Daily commercial air service is also available to Knox County Airport at Owls Head in nearby Rockland.

Where to Stay

In general, inns and B&Bs have a monopoly on the best waterside locations in Camden. Motels are farther from the water, generally scattered along busy Route 1 on the outskirts of Camden, back toward Rockport or out toward Lincolnville.

The Inn at Sunrise Point, U.S. Route 1, Lincolnville (Box 1344, Camden 04843).

You can't stay much closer to the water than at the inn of former inn reviewer Jerry Levitin's dreams. After critiquing others across the country, the California-based travel writer opened his own B&B on four forested acres at the foot of a private lane descending from Route 1 to Penobscot Bay. "I built what I'd like to stay at," said Jerry, who eventually tired of innkeeping and sold to Stephen Tallon from Ireland and his wife Deanna from Australia. They converted the seasonal operation into a year-round endeavor, offering three rooms in the shingle-style main house plus four cottages and two suites. A new suite, just twenty feet from water's edge, is the former owner's quarters with queen bedroom, living/dining room, kitchen and deck. The Tallons named the suite for Jerry Levitin and decorated it in a travel theme. The Winslow Homer Cottage that we occupied right beside the water contains a kingsize bed, a fireplace, TV/VCR, wet bar and an enormous bathroom with a jacuzzi for two and a separate shower. Also close to the water and with the same attributes is the Fitz Hugh Lane Cottage. Two smaller cottages possess queen beds as do three smaller rooms upstairs in the main inn. Each has a fireplace, music

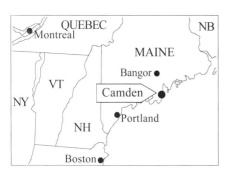

system, built-in desk, double whirlpool tub, armoire holding TV and VCR, and a private balcony overlooking the water. The new Loft Suite has a king bed, polished hardwood floors, clawfoot soaking tub and a steam shower. Guests are welcomed in the main inn with afternoon beverages. The main floor harbors a wonderful living/ dining room that's mostly windows onto Penobscot Bay, an English hunting-style library with a fireplace and a small conservatory for tête-à-tête breakfasts. We feasted here on fruit, pecan coffeecake, a terrific frittata with basil, bay shrimp and jack cheese, potatoes dusted with cayenne, crisp bacon and hazelnut coffee.

(207) 236-7716. Fax (207) 236-0820. www.sunrisepoint.com. Three rooms, two suites and four cottages with private baths. Doubles, $310 to $330. Suites and cottages, $350 to $495.

Inn at Ocean's Edge, U.S. Route 1, Lincolnville (Box 704, Camden 04843).

The waves lull you to sleep at this deluxe B&B rising on seven acres from the shore of Penobscot Bay. Ray and Marie Donner built the contemporary gray structure in what they call the Maine shingle style in 1999 and doubled its size in a second building two years later, before selling in 2004 to Tim and Joan Porta, owners of Migas Lodge in the Sebago Lake region. All guest rooms but one (an enormous handicapped-accessible suite) face the water, although only the twelve newest rooms come with private balconies that take full advantage. Outfitted with different wallpapers and linens, each extra-spacious room has a kingsize four-poster bed, wing chairs facing a corner gas fireplace, a TV/VCR in an armoire, an open jacuzzi flanked by pillars at the end of the bedroom, and a separate bathroom. Guests gather in a couple of large common areas. One is a Great Room with vaulted ceiling and two levels of atrium windows and a set of french doors onto an oversize oceanfront deck. Another is the front pub, where there's a full bar. There's also a garden-level lounge and patio beside a heated pool, plus a tennis court. At our visit, the oceanfront balcony was the setting for a memorable breakfast of poached pears, homemade granola, applesauce-raisin muffins and cranberry-orange zest pancakes with bacon. The landscaped back lawn leads to 250 feet of ocean frontage.

(207) 236-0945. Fax (207) 236-0609. www.innatoceansedge.com. Twenty-six rooms and one suite with private baths. Doubles, $239 to $295. Closed early December to April.

Norumbega, 61 High St., Camden 04843.

A castle with a view. That's what you get at Norumbega, an elegant B&B ensconced in an opulent cobblestone and turreted mansion, one of the great late-19th-century villas built along the Maine coast. The exterior is said to be Maine's most photographed piece of real estate. Inside are endlessly fascinating public rooms (the woodwork alone is priceless), ten bedrooms and two suites, all with sitting areas and telephones and some with TVs. Most have fireplaces and canopy beds, all kingsize except for a queen in the smallest garden-level room. The ten in back have breathtaking views of Penobscot Bay. Guests have the run of the common areas including a formal parlor, a small library, an intimate retreat for two beside a fireplace on the landing of the ornate staircase, as well as flower-laden rear porches and balconies on all three floors overlooking expansive lawns and the bay. Manager JoAnne Reuillard and staff pour tea or wine in the afternoon. Breakfast is a feast of juices and fruits, all kinds of breads and muffins and, when we stayed, the best french toast ever, topped with sliced oranges and a dollop of sherbet.

(207) 236-4646 or (877) 363-4646. Fax (207) 236-4990. www.norumbegainn.com. Ten rooms and two suites with private baths. Doubles, $160 to $340. Suites, $365 to $475.

Lord Camden Inn, 24 Main St., Camden 04843.

Water views and deluxe accommodations are attributes of this recently upgraded and expanded establishment in the center of town. On three floors above an 1893 brick storefront and the old Masonic Temple, it's really more like a small hotel than an inn – but a plush and welcoming one, following renovations in 2004 and 2005. Six premier rooms on the fourth floor have idyllic canopied decks yielding panoramic ocean views over the rooftops across the street. Partial harbor views are available from third-floor front rooms, and eight rooms in the rear offer decks and views of the passing Megunticook River and hills behind the inn. Six new deluxe rooms on the second floor come with gas fireplaces, marble baths and large recessed balconies with views of the downtown scene. Fireplaces and balconies were added to six front rooms on the third floor in 2005. Most rooms offer large flat-screen TVs, DVD players, hair dryers, ironing boards and free high-speed internet wireless access. New innkeeper Philip Woodland is proud of the luxurious bedding, including plush-top mattresses and 400 thread-count sheets. Besides a new fitness room on the fourth floor, an expanded dining room offers a complimentary gourmet breakfast in the morning. Choices range from eggs benedict to make-your-own belgian waffles.

(207) 236-4325 or (800) 336-4325. Fax (207) 236-7141. www.lordcamdeninn.com. Thirty rooms and six suites with private baths. Doubles, $179 to $269.

The Hawthorn, 9 High St., Camden 04843.

Camden Harbor may be glimpsed through the trees behind this sumptuous Victorian B&B, one of the few in Camden that can make such a claim. Well-traveled owner Maryanne Shanahan offers ten guest quarters in the 1894 Queen Anne-style house and a rear carriage house, plus a nicely landscaped back yard sloping toward Camden Harbor and a gate opening onto the town amphitheater. All rooms have telephones and queensize beds (except one with twins). The four prime accommodations, all with double jacuzzis and gas fireplaces, are in the carriage house. Each has a private deck or patio and a TV/VCR. The best harbor view awaits guests in the Norfolk, a huge room with white iron bed, extra day bed, gas stove and private deck overlooking the leafy lawn and harbor. Back in the main house is a double parlor with not one but two turrets. Healthful breakfasts are served at individual tables in a formal dining room or on a spacious rear deck. The fare the day we visited included homemade hazelnut granola and a raspberry blintz soufflé.

(207) 236-8842 or (866) 381-3647. Fax (207) 236-6181. www.camdeninn.com. Eight rooms and two suites with private baths. Doubles, $149 to $289. Suites, $179 to $289.

A Little Dream, 66 High St., Camden 04843.

Two new rooms in the side carriage house offer water views at this B&B – "a little dream" as envisioned and executed by innkeeper Joanne Fontana and her husband, Bill, a sculptor and handyman-remodeler. On the middle level above the artist's studio is Islewatch, a huge suite with kingsize iron canopy bed, a chintz sofa and wing chair, and a window seat looking onto a glorious private porch. The porch, furnished with wicker rockers and a hanging glider/swing, yields a great view of Penobscot Bay, Curtis Island and the lights of passing boats at night. The top level of the carriage house holds a Loft room and Treetops, a suite with living room, queen bedroom and a front balcony with an island view. Trees obscure the bay view from three spacious bedrooms and a suite in the turreted Victorian house, all decorated to the hilt with Victorian clothing, lace, ribbons and at least eight pillows on each bed. Joanne pampers guests in a parlor furnished in wicker and chintz, an elaborate dining room beside a conservatory and a wraparound porch, the side portion of which has lately been enclosed in glass for year-round use. Breakfast is served on lace-clothed tables topped with floral mats in the dining room or on the side porch. Guests choose from a fancy menu placed in their rooms the night before. The choice might involve lemon-ricotta soufflé pancakes with raspberry sauce, banana-pecan waffles with maple country sausage, or a smoked salmon omelet.

(207) 236-8742 or (800) 217-0109. www.littledream.com. Four rooms and three suites with private baths. Doubles $159 to $225, suites $215 to $295.

Cedarholm Garden Bay, U.S. Route 1, Lincolnville Beach (Box 345, Camden 04843).

Four new cottages the owner built himself are the prime attractions at this small and personal cottage colony dating to the 1950s. Barry Jobson, a former electrical engineer, and his wife Joyce acquired the sixteen-acre property in 1995 from her father, Jules Golden, a folk artist. They upgraded two original units dating to the 1950s and built four cottages right by the shore. The original cottages are clustered amid landscaped grounds at the top of the property with the bay visible in the distance. Two have living rooms, including the two-bedroom Blueberry Cottage and the one-bedroom Gooseberry, which has a kitchenette. The waterfront cottages are better yet. Spaced well apart along the 460-foot forested shorefront, each has a queen or king bedroom, wet bar with mini-refrigerator, TV and telephone and a waterside deck. Two have a living room with vaulted ceiling and stone fireplace as well as a bath with double jacuzzi tub and separate shower. The ceilings are finished in cedar and the furnishings are of the upscale lodge variety. The breakfast room in the Jobsons' house gives the place its name (it means house of cedar) and helps account for its repeat business. Guests enjoy continental breakfast in a cedar-paneled room with hand-painted Swedish doors and Swedish plates on the walls. Joyce bakes muffins with blueberries, blackberries and gooseberries that grow on the property.

(207) 236-3886. www.cedarholm.com. Six cottages with private baths. Doubles, $159 to $325.

The High Tide Inn, 505 Belfast Road (U.S. Route 1), Camden 04843.

This manicured waterfront complex of seven acres north of town offers all sorts of accommodations: five inn rooms in the main house, two motel-style buildings (one right next to the water), two units in a duplex cottage and six cottages. It is one of the few places with its own, albeit rocky, beach; we felt like ballet dancers trying to negotiate the rocks for a swim. There are chaises and chairs for sunning on the lawn. Popovers, blueberry and bran muffins, and banana bread like your mother used to bake are served buffet-style in the inn's enclosed porch facing the water. Owner Jo Freilich, a decorator from New Jersey, has redecorated the common rooms and guest rooms. Three in the main inn offer ocean views. But the original oceanfront motel in which we stayed is best for its view and its location away from the road.

(207) 236-3724 or (800) 778-7068. www.hightideinn.com. Twenty-four rooms and six cottages with private baths. Doubles, $99 to $165 in inn, $75 to $185 in motel and cottages. Closed November-April.

The Spouter Inn, 2506 Atlantic Hwy., Lincolnville Beach 04849.

Ocean views from every guest room are the strong suit of this nautically themed B&B across the road from the beach in Lincolnville. Owners Paul and Catherine Lippman started small in 1989, but have expanded into the side carriage house and restored to the point where they offer five bedrooms, a couple of parlors, an elegant dining room and a breakfast sun porch. Their largest and most luxurious room is the Captain's Quarters, furnished with a kingsize bed, two wing chairs beside the wood-burning fireplace, and a bath with jacuzzi. Other rooms are furnished with queen beds except for one with an antique double, and two have fireplaces. Both innkeepers love to cook, and pride themselves on their breakfasts. Guests select their choices from the menu the night before, "and can order anything and as much as they want," says Paul. Options include omelets, stuffed french toast and German puffed pancakes with caramel sauce.

(207) 789-5171 or (866) 787-5171. www.spouterinn.com. Five rooms with private baths. Doubles, $115 to $195. Closed mid-October to Memorial Day.

Island View Inn, 904 Commercial St. (U.S. Route 1), Rockport 04856.

Every room gets an ocean view from this good-looking, two-story motor inn atop a bluff overlooking Penobscot Bay. It's the most appealing of the motels along the busy road between Rockland and Rockport and one that could pass for a MacMansion in the contemporary idiom. All rooms have kingsize beds topped with quilts and are furnished in upscale inn style. All come with refrigerators and private ocean-view decks. There's a nicely landscaped pool area, and walking paths lead through lawns and gardens to water's edge.

(207) 596-0040 or (866) 711-8439. Fax (207) 596-5953. www.islandviewinnmaine.com. Fifteen rooms with private baths. Doubles, $139 to $199.

Samoset Resort, 220 Warrenton St., Rockport 04856.

New owners are upgrading this well-known golf and conference resort, which occupies a choice piece of real estate on a peninsula stretching into Penobscot Bay. The place dates to 1889, although you'd never know it today. The old turreted hotel, destroyed by fire in 1972, was rebuilt in 1974 from the old timbers of an abandoned Portland granary. It's a fine location for conferences, as we found during a newspaper trade association board meeting back shortly after the Samoset reopened. Three wings off the main resort building contain large guest rooms, most with ocean views across the golf fairways and all with patio or balcony. A new extension to one wing offers 28 deluxe rooms and suites. These have larger baths with marble floors and walls, a feature going into existing rooms as they are renovated. Suites on the fourth floor have the best water views, a living room with wet bar, bath with a double vanity and larger balcony. The idyllic Flume Cottage, a two-bedroom house with a large deck off the living room and master bedroom, is on a rocky spit of land off the fifteenth fairway (it comes complete with its own four-passenger golf cart). The resort also rents 72 time-share units of one and two bedrooms in three separate, freestanding buildings, for $419 to $499. A fitness center offers an indoor pool, hot tubs and saunas as well as Nautilus equipment and a racquetball court. There are four tennis courts and an outdoor pool as well. The eighteen-hole championship golf course boasts seven oceanside holes and water vistas from fourteen holes. Meals with an ocean view are served in **Marcel's** and the **Breakwater Café** (see Where to Eat).

(207) 594-2511 or (800) 341-1650. Fax (207) 594-0722. www.samoset.com. One hundred fifty-six rooms and 22 suites. Doubles, $258 to $499. Suites, $299 to $549.

Seeing and Doing ⟋⟋⟋⟋⟋

Water Activities

Camden harbor, Rockport harbor and Lincolnville Beach are the focal points in this section of Penobscot Bay. There are plenty of options for enjoying the ocean.

BOAT TRIPS. A variety of cruises on Penobscot Bay leave from the Camden landing, where there are benches for viewing the passing boat parade. The famed windjammers are a class apart (see below), but lately some have been giving daily two-hour trips, lunch or dinner cruises and even an overnight excursion.

Two-hour cruises priced at $20 to $28 each are offered by at least three schooners from Camden Harbor. The area's biggest daysailer is the 86-foot **Appledore,** (207) 236-8353, a tall ship that has sailed around the world. It takes up to 49 passengers three times a day from Bayview Landing. Sailing from the Camden Public Landing are the smaller schooners **Surprise,** (207) 236-4687; **Lazy Jack,** (207) 230-0602, and

Olad, (207) 236-2323. Passengers sail past islands and lighthouses and see seals, porpoises, eagles and osprey.

The Wooden Boat Company's 65-foot schooner yacht **Heron** offers three trips daily from Rockport Harbor, (207) 236-8605 or (800) 599-8605. They are a lobster lunch sail, an Indian Island lighthouse tour and a gourmet sunset sail.

Wildwood Adventure Charters, 40 Pleasant St., Rockport, (207) 236-6951, offers private powerboat cruises of one to six hours for up to six people.

The **M/V Betselma,** (207) 236-4446, a 38-foot powerboat, offers scenic coastal and island tours of one or two hours each from Camden Public Landing. One-hour trips (adults $10, children $5) between Camden and Rockport show harbor lighthouses and oceanfront estates. Two-hour trips ($20 and $10) show more lighthouses, islands, sea birds and seals, as well as some of the famed summer mansions on the island of Islesboro.

A former biology teacher, Capt. Alan Philbrick, runs two-hour lobster fishing and ecotours through the islands from Bayview Landing on the lobster boat **Lively Lady, Too,** (207) 236-6672; adults $20, children $5. By reservation, he offers a four-hour sunset cruise to an uninhabited island for a lobster bake ($50).

Island Picnics, 2478 Atlantic Hwy., Lincolnville, (207) 236-6001, transports up to six passengers to island beaches for catered picnics.

For more cruises or ferry rides to the islands, go to Rockland or Lincolnville Beach (a favorite excursion there is the ferry trip to Islesboro).

WINDJAMMERS. Known as the windjammer capital of the world until its title was challenged by nearby Rockland, Camden Harbor is quite a sight when the historic sailing schooners are in. Most windjammers were built nearly a century ago to haul bulk freight and were converted to the vacation trade following World War II. Fourteen of the largest, carrying 20 to 40 passengers, are members of the Maine Windjammer Association, (800) 807-9463. For decades, windjammer cruises lasted six to ten days, but schooner captains have adapted to shorter vacations, family participation and the demands of an upper-tier market. People gather Sunday evenings at the Camden wharf to watch as passengers board the impressive vessels for cruises through Penobscot Bay. After breakfast on Monday, the typical windjammer sets sail for who knows where, its route depending on wind, tides and whim. Participants sleep and eat on board, helping the crew if they like but most relaxing and savoring a sail from yesteryear. Generally, the captain handles the seagoing chores while his wife does the cooking – everything from chowders to roasts – on a wood stove. The evening lobster bake on a deserted island is usually the week's highlight. At midday Saturday, the watching in Camden resumes in earnest as the windjammers return. Participants can expect to pay $600 to $900 for a five-day sail.

SEA KAYAKING. Because of its relatively protected waters, Penobscot Bay and its coves and islands are good for kayaking and canoeing. Several outfits offer rentals and guided tours. The biggest is **Maine Sport Outfitters,** (207) 236-7120 or (800) 722-0826, whose colorful facility is a landmark along Route 1 in Rockport. Others are **Ducktrap Sea Kayak,** 2175 Atlantic Highway, Lincolnville Beach, (207) 236-8608, and **Breakwater Kayak** out of Rockport, (207) 596-6895 or (877) 559-8800.

SWIMMING. The Lincolnville Beach is good for swimming. A more secluded, picturesque setting is Camden's little-known Laite Memorial Beach with treed lawns sloping down to the water, a small beach, picnic tables and old-fashioned fireplaces off Bay View Street. Lake swimming is available at Hosmer Pond and Lake Megunticook.

Rockport Marine Park, André Street, Rockport, (207) 236-4404. A boat launch and picnic tables are available at this harborside park, best known for its statue of André the seal, the legendary harbor seal who cavorted here. Three restored lime kilns date to the early 1900s when Rockport was one of the greatest lime producing towns in the nation. There's a replica of the locomotives that transported lime rock to waiting ships in the harbor. Open daily, dawn to dusk. Free.

Other Attractions

HIKING. Some of the East Coast's most scenic hiking is available on trails in **Camden Hills State Park,** where eighteen trails of varying lengths and difficulty are detailed in a trail guide. With an elevation of 1,380 feet, Mount Megunticook is the highest of the three mountains that make up the park and the second highest point on the Eastern Seaboard. If you're not up to hiking, drive the toll road up Mount Battie, an easy one-mile ride to the 790-foot summit. The view over village and bay is worth the $1-per-person toll. More rugged hiking is available on the trails of Camden Snow Bowl overlooking Hosmer Pond.

TOURING. A scenic drive is out Route 52 to Megunticook Lake, an island-studded lake that emerged eerily from the fog the first time we saw it. A walking tour of Camden and a bicycle or car tour of Camden and adjacent Rockport are available through the Camden-Rockport Historical Society. A favorite drive or bicycle tour heads southeast out of Camden on Bay View Street out to Beauchamp Point and curves along Mechanic Street into Rockport. It returns to Camden via Chestnut Street. Some of the area's estates may be seen, along with belted Galloway cows grazing at Aldermere Farm.

Vesper Hill Chapel, Calderwood Lane, Rockport, (207) 236-4594. A terrific view of Penobscot Bay is afforded from this non-denominational outdoor chapel, built of pine and resembling a Swiss chalet, atop a rock ledge along the shore. It's the legacy of Helene Bok, who fulfilled a dream of building a chapel that would open out onto the world on the site of a summer estate-turned-hotel that was destroyed by fire in 1954. Mrs. Bok and friends created a garden showplace and a chapel sanctuary for the ages. Fifty people can be seated for informal meditation on Sunday mornings. Not wishing to intrude on the Quaker Meeting we came upon, we bided our time in the formal perennial and Biblical herb gardens below. More than 60 wedding ceremonies take place here annually, but the casual visitor can stop by to enjoy peace, quiet and beauty any other time from mid-April through October.

Summer entertainment, from band concerts to vaudeville, is provided periodically in Camden in the outdoor Bok Amphitheater next to the town library, just a few hundred feet from the harbor. The **Camden Civic Theatre,** (207) 236-2281, produces five plays from April into December at the recently restored brick Camden Opera House, 29 Elm St. Classical music and jazz concerts are offered Thursday and Friday in summer and monthly the rest of the year at the Rockport Opera House on the harbor by **Bay Chamber Concerts,** (207) 236-2823 or (888) 707-2770.

The **Conway Homestead-Cramer Museum,** Route 1, Rockport, (207) 236-2257, includes a restored 18th-century farmhouse, a barn displaying antique carriages and sleighs, a blacksmith shop and an 1820 maple sugar house. The Mary Meeker Cramer Museum displays ship models, quilts, period clothing and other memorabilia. The complex run by the Camden-Rockport Historical Society is open Monday-Thursday 10 to 4 in July and August, by appointment in June and September; adults $5, children $2.

Merryspring, 30 Conway Road, Camden, (206) 236-2239, is a 66-acre nature park and horticultural center founded in 1974 by horticulturalist Mary Ellen Ross of the mail-order plant business Merry Gardens. It includes walking trails and herb, rose and perennial gardens, an arboretum and three greenhouses. Open daily, dawn to dusk; free.

ART GALLERIES. Artists and their galleries abound in Camden and Rockport, and the sea and local landscapes are usually their subjects. The **Center for Maine Contemporary Art,** 162 Russell Ave., Rockport, displays changing exhibits of contemporary works by established and emerging artists in a large, renovated 19th-century livery stable. It's open daily except Monday 10 to 5, adults $2. Famed Rockport artist **Anne Kilham** displays her iconic Maine seaside designs in her home gallery at 142 Russell Ave., Rockport. In Camden, the **Camden Falls Gallery** occupies a nifty location beside a waterfall with a view of the harbor. Other galleries worth a visit include the **Bearse Art Gallery** on U.S. Route 1 between Camden and Lincolnville, featuring Jan Bearse's watercolors and oils, and the **H. Swanson Studio & Gallery,** Route 1, Lincolnville Beach, showing fine art paintings of Harry Swanson. The most extensive selection of wildlife carvings in Maine is available at **Duck Trap Decoys,** Duck Trap Road, Lincolnville Beach. A gallery of a different kind is the showroom and workshop of **Windsor Chairmakers,** U.S. Route 1, just north of Lincolnville Beach.

SHOPPING. Sophisticated stores predominate in Camden, where interesting specialty shops and boutiques pop up every year. **The Smiling Cow,** a large and venerable gift shop with a myriad of Maine items, has a great water view from its rear porch over the Megunticook River, which ripples down the rocks toward the harbor. **Planet** is a world marketplace with a trendy selection of gifts, clothing, housewares, accessories, toys and more, many with a nature or planetary theme. Its related **Emporium** store across the street features contemporary women's apparel with a worldly theme. More traditional favorites for clothing and gifts are the **House of Logan** and **Margo Moore. The Admiral's Buttons** has preppy clothing and sailing attire. **Surroundings** offers "durable goods" for home and garden, while **Maine Gathering** specializes in fine Maine crafts. **Wild Birds Unlimited** has an amazing collection of bird feeders, carved birds, birdsong tapes and the like. A large carved gull wearing a windjammer tie drew us into the **Ducktrap Bay Trading Co.,** a wildlife and Maine art gallery showing things from decoys to paintings. We bought a handcrafted Maine wooden bucket for use as a planter from **Once a Tree,** which also has great clocks, toys, bracelets and everything else made from wood.

Shoppers in search of snacks seek out **Boynton-McKay Food Co.** at 30 Main St. for espresso, fruit smoothies and old-fashioned ice cream prepared in the original art deco soda fountain of a 1890s pharmacy. It also offers sandwiches, salads and prepared foods, as does the upscale grocer **French & Brawn Marketplace. Cappy's Bakery & Coffee House** at 1 Main St. purveys cappuccino, wine, panini sandwiches and home-baked goods.

Where to Eat ⎯⎯⎯⎯⎯⎯⎯⎯⎯⎯⎯⎯ _ʃᗩᗩᒪ_

Atlantica, 1 Bay View Landing, Camden.
The food is innovative, the surroundings convivial and the contemporary ambiance nautical at chef-owner Ken Paquin's bustling restaurant on the Camden waterfront. Dining is on two floors, including a much-coveted upstairs turret with a single table for five, as well as outdoors on an upper deck and a covered terrace

beneath. It's wildly popular, so much so that we couldn't even get in at our first summer visit but did manage to snag a table near a window on a second visit in the off-season, although the night was so foggy we were unable to see much of anything. One of us made a dinner of two appetizers: the Maine crab and shrimp tower with mustard-mango vinaigrette and basil-caper tartar sauce and pan-fried oysters with a sweet corn salad. The other enjoyed the caesar salad that came with the entrée, one of the best seafood pasta dishes we've had, brimming with clams, mussels and scallops with lemon pasta in a Thai curry broth. Other choices on the seafood-oriented menu might be pan-seared ahi tuna with green peppercorn vinaigrette and roasted monkfish stuffed with shrimp and wrapped in prosciutto. Typical desserts are orange crème brûlée, chocolate cake with a hollow center filled with ganache and our choices, ginger ice cream and red raspberry sorbet.

(207) 236-6011 or (888) 507-8514. www.atlanticarestaurant.com. Entrées, $19 to $27. Lunch seasonally, Tuesday-Sunday 11:30 to 2:30. Dinner, Tuesday-Sunday 5:30 to 9:30, Thursday-Monday 5 to 8 in winter.

Natalie's at the Mill, 43 Mechanic St., Suite 200, Camden.

A section of the old Knox Mill building that formerly housed the MBNA credit card company was transformed into an elegant restaurant in late 2004 by Abby Alden, former manager at the Lord Camden Inn. The atmospheric place seats 80 in a dining room with windows on three sides and a partly open kitchen. The splashy waterfall outside the soaring windows adds to the effect. The large outside patio facing the mill pond and falls of the Megunticook River is the icing on the mix. It's a dramatic, elegant backdrop for high-end fare that may upstage the scenery outside. Lunch offerings are exotic, perhaps a warm fallen chèvre soufflé over salad or a Maine lobster BLT. The opening dinner menu offered appetizers like chilled local oysters with a ginger-melon mignonette, caramelized diver scallops in a parsley broth, and lobster-coconut bisque with coriander crème fraîche. Main courses ranged from local halibut with morels in orange-brown butter sauce and marinated big-eye tuna with pulped avocado, daikon and lemon vinaigrette to slow-roasted organic duck breast with a huckleberry reduction and beef sirloin with foie gras and madeira jus. Desserts included grand marnier crème brûlée with orange-cardamom butter cookies, warm chocolate espresso cake with a frozen sour cherry mousse, and coconut panna cotta with a pomegranate gelee and blood orange sorbet.

(207) 236-7008. Entrées, $22 to $32. Four-course prix-fixe, $60. Lunch, Monday-Saturday 11:30 to 2. Dinner, Tuesday-Saturday 5:30 to 9.

The Waterfront Restaurant, Harborside Square off Bay View Street, Camden.

Rebuilt following a damaging 1995 fire, this popular restaurant is notable for its large outdoor deck shaded by a striking white canopy resembling a boat's sails, right beside the windjammers on picturesque Camden Harbor, and for its affordable, international menu. It's a great place for lunch, when seven delectable salads in glass bowls are dressed with outstanding dressings, among them sweet-and-sour bacon, lemon-parmesan, dijon vinaigrette and blue cheese. The dinner offerings turn more eclectic, although chef Charles Butler – named Maine lobster chef of the year in 2002 – offers four lobster entrées. Among appetizers are calamari and shrimp, mussels marinière and soups, perhaps an award-winning clam chowder or chilled raspberry accented with grand marnier. The superlative smoked seafood sampler was our choice for sharing. We've enjoyed the Maine crab cakes with creamy mustard sauce, an assertive linguini with salmon and sundried tomatoes, shrimp with oriental black beans over angel-hair pasta and a special of applewood-grilled swordfish, which was juicy and succulent. Thick, "baseball cut" sirloin steak, prosciutto-wrapped rack of lamb and grilled chicken with lime, cilantro and olives were the only meat offerings at our latest visit. Mint chocolate-chip pie with hot fudge sauce and whipped cream proved to be the ultimate dessert. Shellfish and light fare from burgers to lobster rolls are available at the oyster bar and outdoor grill.

(207) 236-3747. www.waterfrontcamden.com. Entrées, $14.95 to $21.95. Lunch daily, 11:30 to 2:30. Dinner, 5 to 10. Raw bar, 2 to 11.

Marcel's, Samoset Resort, 220 Warrenton St., Rockport.

Tableside service and an award-winning wine list are featured in the fancy dining room at the Samoset Resort. A tuxedoed staff caters to diners in a spacious room with tables on two levels and tall windows onto the golf course and ocean beyond. A pianist accompanies on busy nights. The contemporary continental menu begins with appetizers like seared foie gras with grilled brioche, local oysters on the half shell, escargots in puff pastry and, surprisingly at a recent visit, grilled rack of lamb with a roasted red and yellow pepper salad. Caesar salad is prepared tableside for two, as are chateaubriand and rack of lamb. Steak diane can be finished at the table for one. Other entrée possibilities range from Atlantic salmon roasted on a cedar plank and halibut en phyllo with aromatic vegetables to grilled pork tenderloin with roasted figs and duck breast with blueberry and candied ginger glaze. A more casual menu is available across the foyer in the **Breakwater Café,** with a tavern look and a pleasant outdoor deck and terrace.

(207) 594-2511 or (800) 341-1650. Entrées, $19 to $34. Dinner nightly, 6 to 9. Café open daily from 11:30.

Chez Michel, U.S. Route 1, Lincolnville Beach.

A water view across the road is offered at this country French restaurant run by chef-owner Michel Hetuin. The main floor is a simple room crowded with formica tables and pink-painted wood chairs with green upholstered seats. The seats of choice are upstairs in a cheery dining room that offers a head-on view of the water, or at the four tables on a screened balcony off the side. Our latest dinner here began with great french bread, two slabs of rabbit pâté resting with cornichons on oodles of lettuce, and house salads. A special of salmon béarnaise arrived on a bed of spinach. The only disappointment was the bouillabaisse, more like a spicy cioppino with haddock substituting for most of the usual shellfish. Other dinner entrées include scallops provençal, mussels marinière, grilled chicken béarnaise, duck au poivre, lamb kabob and steak au poivre. Although we'd opt for the French specialties, we know others who think there's no better place for lobster or even a crab roll with french fries and a bowl of fisherman's chowder. Save room for the superlative desserts, among them a fantastic raspberry pie with a cream-cheese base and a shortbread crust, so good that regulars call to reserve a slice before it runs out.

(207) 789-5600. Entrées, $15.95 to $19.95. Dinner, Tuesday-Saturday 4 to 9, Sunday 11:30 to 9.

Whales Tooth Pub & Restaurant, 2531 Atlantic Highway, Lincolnville Beach.

The most appealing water views in Lincolnville are available at this casual establishment, opened by former Quebec restaurateurs Rob and Dorothy Newcombe. The old brick house has a dining room with many windows and booths and a rear deck beside the bay. The extensive menu features seafood – fried, baked or grilled – as well as seven chicken dishes from quesadilla to Thai to "cordon blue," prime rib and sirloin steak. Appetizers cover the gamut from nachos to escargots provençal. We like the sound of the onion soup and seafood chowder served in loaves of bread and the caesar salad with crab louis. A short but good pub menu offers the likes of seafood alfredo, veal parmesan and shepherd's pie.

(207) 789-5200. www.whalestoothpub.com. Entrées, $11.95 to $19. Lunch, weekends from 11:30. Dinner nightly except Tuesday from 4.

Cappy's Chowder House, 1 Main St., Camden.

"The Maine you hope to meet" is one of the catchy slogans surrounding Cappy's, and local color is its strong point. The scene is barroom nautical: lobster traps hang above the bar, and green billiards-room lamps illuminate the bare wood tables. The upstairs Crow's Nest, dark and very pubby, offers a glimpse of the harbor. The something-for-everyone menu is Down East cutesy: Maine pigskins, burgers on the bounty, Camden curly fries, mussel beach pasta and deserted islands. The place packs in the crowds for clam chowder, a lobster pizza, "cakes of crab" on a bed of wild greens, seafood pie, baked stuffed haddock, baby back ribs, sirloin steak "and all the latest gossip." Main courses come with French bread from Cappy's Bakery & Company Store below, rice pilaf and salad with a good house dressing. Burgers, sandwiches, salads and lighter fare are available day and night. Oysters and shrimp by the bucket are served from the raw bar during happy hour in the Crow's Nest.

(207) 236-2254. www.cappyschowder.com. Entrées, $12.95 to $19.95. Open daily, 11 a.m. to midnight; winter hours vary.

The Camden Deli, 37 Main St., Camden.

"The best view in town" is offered from the new upper deck at this casual spot on two floors backing up to the harbor. There's waitress service in the upstairs dining area with wine bar, lounge and rooftop deck, but many prefer to head for the downstairs deli cases to select their soups, salads and sandwiches. No fewer than 41 varieties of sandwich were offered when we were there, making the subsequent choices of an albacore tuna sandwich and a BLT all the more difficult. The seafood chowder and the Greek salad were fine, too; the lemon bars for dessert were not. Light meals are available for dinner.

(207) 236-8343. www.camdendeli.com. Sandwiches $4.95 to $6.50; light fare, $3 to $10. Breakfast, lunch and dinner daily, 7 a.m. to 9 p.m.; shorter hours in winter.

Bayview Lobsters, Bay View Landing, Camden.

You can't get much closer to the water in Camden than at this dockside establishment with a mostly canopied deck beside the harbor and a rustic dining room inside. The lobster steaming in pots alongside captures passing strollers. They stop for a lobster roll ($10.25), lobster stew, sandwiches with fries and more substantial fried chicken or lobster dinners. Beer and wine are available, as are espresso and ice cream from a stand beside.

(207) 236-2005. Entrées, $10.25 to $21.50. Open daily in season, 11 to 10.

FOR MORE INFORMATION: Camden-Rockport-Lincolnville Chamber of Commerce, Public Landing, Box 919, Camden, ME 04843, (207) 236-4404 or (800) 223-5459. www.visitcamden.com.

Historic John Perkins House overlooks harbor at Castine.

Castine, Me.

Poised on a peninsula jutting into East Penobscot Bay, Castine is a picturesque enclave of peace and quiet.

Therein lies a certain irony, for this charming little town with such an admirable waterside location was forged from a military heritage and a maritime disposition. Founded in 1613 as a French trading colony that evolved into the first permanent settlement in New England, Castine was a major battlefield through the French and Indian wars, the American Revolution and the War of 1812. No fewer than sixteen fortifications have been built on the peninsula since 1635, so it's no surprise that the town's only through street is named Battle Avenue.

Its maritime bent is evident in the windjammers in its deep-water harbor and by the Maine Maritime Academy, the dominant physical presence on the steep Castine hillside today. New England's ocean college specializes in undergraduate and graduate programs in engineering, transportation, management and ocean studies. In their rowdier off-duty moments, academy cadets may tie one on in the boisterous waterfront Quarterdeck Tavern when their enormous training vessel *State of Maine* is tied up at the town dock.

Otherwise, all is prim and proper in this quietly prosperous seaport town, which local historian Gardiner E. Gregory considered the wealthiest per capita north of Boston in the early 19th century. With the demise of its shipping and boat-building days, it became a summer colony for big-city "rusticators."

Castine may well be Maine's prettiest seaside town, from its island-flecked harbor to the village green off by itself along outer Court Street. Elm trees shade the well-tended Federal-style houses dressed in what appears to be the local uniform – pristine white with black shutters, accented with a profusion of flowers. The shingled mansions of Victorian-era summer visitors grace the outlying shores.

History is more noticeable here than in most such places, if only because there's a large historical marker at almost every turn. You can marvel at them all on a couple of walking tours, climb around the embankments of Revolutionary forts, tour the pre-Revolutionary John Perkins House and watch a blacksmith at work. See the inside of the State of Maine ship, take a steamboat cruise, watch the windjammers near the yacht club and feast on seafood at an atmospheric waterside restaurant. Play golf or tennis at the Castine Golf Club, swim at the Backshore Beach or a saltwater pool, or hike around Dyces Head Lighthouse and Witherle Park.

Getting There

About 40 miles due south of Bangor, Castine is located at the tip of a peninsula, opposite Belfast across East Penobscot Bay. From coastal U.S. Route 1 at Orland, take Route 175 and Route 166 to Castine.

Where to Stay

Castine Inn, Main Street, Box 41, Castine 04421.

Perfect for people-watching, a pleasant wraparound porch overlooking prized gardens and the harbor beyond welcomes guests to the Castine Inn, built in 1898 and operated continuously since. The serene, 60-seat dining room is graced by stunning murals of Castine painted by the former innkeeper, an artist. Under young chef-owner Tom Gutow, it is known for some of the finest cuisine in Maine (see Where to Eat). Tom and his wife Amy are gradually upgrading the accommodations, which open hotel-style off long, wide corridors on the second and third floors. All rooms are carpeted and comfortable with queensize or twin beds. Half yield distant water views. The Gutows turned two small rear rooms into a large room with a queen poster bed, two club chairs and a large bath with an antique tub sunk into a black and white tiled top, separate shower and a vanity in an alcove. Decor is modest yet stylish, with understated floral fabrics and window treatments. Overnight guests enjoy talented chef Tom's creations at breakfast. The menu generally offers three hot entrées: an omelet with goat cheese and herbs, corned beef hash topped by a poached egg and homemade applebread french toast with Maine maple syrup. A fireplace wards off any chill in the guest parlor, which is hung with local artworks. Across the spacious front hall is hidden a dark and cozy pub with hand-painted tables and a fireplace. A side deck overlooks the spectacular gardens.

(207) 326-4365. Fax (207) 326-4570. www.castineinn.com. Nineteen rooms with private baths. Doubles, $90 to $225. Closed Dec. 20 through April.

Pentagoet Inn, 26 Main St., Box 4, Castine 04421.

International accents prevail at this turreted 1894 inn, carefully being returned to its roots as a steamboat inn by Jack Burke and his wife, Julie VandeGraaf. The couple scoured the countryside to find antique headboards for the beds and steamboat-era prints and lithographs for the walls of eleven guest rooms in the main inn and five in the adjacent 200-year-old cottage (called 10 Perkins Street). All have antique furnishings, a historically authentic feeling and international accents from Jack's twenty years' service with the United Nations in Africa. The couple turned the inn's former Victorian library into

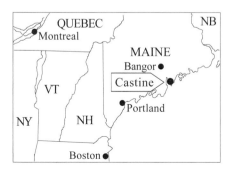

Passports Pub, a playful hodgepodge of vintage photos and foreign memorabilia that's appropriate for an international town that has flown the flags of four countries. Besides the atmospheric pub, guests relax in a parlor area with a nifty turret window seat looking toward the harbor, on shaded verandas made for rocking and on a showy garden patio off the expanded dining room (see Where to Eat). Julie's background as owner of a pastry shop in Philadelphia is evident at breakfast, which might feature featherbed eggs or baked apple french toast, muffins and scones. It's taken at tables for two in the dining room or on the jaunty garden deck.

(207) 326-8616 or (800) 845-1701. www.pentagoet.com. Sixteen rooms with private baths. Doubles, $85 to $195. Closed November-April.

Castine Harbor Lodge, 147 Perkins St., Box 215, Castine 04421.

If water access and views are your priority, you can't ask for more than this laid-back establishment – complete with new boat dock for mooring, a new wine bar on the wraparound porch and a new waterside patio. Paul and Sara Brouillard, who got their innkeeping start at the Manor (see below), the home in which she grew up, have slowly upgraded and furnished this 1893 Edwardian mansion directly on the oceanfront. All but one of the sixteen accommodations have water views – even from some of the bathrooms. Guests report that staying in the second-floor corner room with a sofa in the turret is like being on a ship – about all you can see from the queensize poster bed is water. The baths have been updated, and Sara has painted the rooms in bold colors (Ralph Lauren yellow for Room 4, peach-salmon for the common area in the upstairs foyer). Furnishings are stylish yet homey and unpretentious, like the inn itself. Four simpler rooms in an attached annex share two baths. The inn also has an L-shaped efficiency cottage, with queensize bed and private deck, right on the water. The recently enclosed, wraparound porch curving for 250 feet around the side and back of the house holds Paul's pride and joy, the Bagaduce Oyster Bar and wine bar where the sometime chef offers dinner by whim or reservation. He offers a selection of local seafood and shellfish, specializing in locally raised oysters. The ambitious menu ranges from mixed Japanese grill (tuna, scallops and salmon with cucumber and seaweed salad) to veal flank steak and grilled venison loin. Besides a blue-flecked granite bar with stools facing the water, the porch has sofas and chairs around a gas fireplace and an open porch with banquette seating and tables taking full advantage of the view. So do a couple of enormous open common areas, which begin with a billiards table in the foyer. Included are a living room with a gigantic sectional sofa facing the fireplace, a library with TV and a dining room. The continental-plus breakfast features cereals, yogurt, croissants and fabulous breads that could be lathered with Sara's strawberry-rhubarb jam that guests wish she'd put up for sale.

(207) 326-4335 or (866) 566-1550. www.castinemaine.com. Eleven rooms and one cottage with private baths and four rooms with shared bath. Doubles, $85 to $245. Cottage, $1,250 weekly.

The Manor Inn, Battle Avenue, Box 873, Castine 04421.

This sprawling, turn-of-the-century summer cottage designed by Mead, McKim and White looks the way a big old Maine lodge should. You arrive up a long driveway to an edifice of brown wood and stone, a flower-bedecked terrace and an entry porte-cochere tunneling between the main house and a wing with the second floor overhead. Owners Tom Ehrman and Nancy Watson moved from Key Biscayne, Fla., to upgrade the accommodations and restaurant (see Where to Eat). They turned the former pub in front into a large and stylish dining room, with a substantial enclosed porch addition, and moved the pub into what had been a side butler's pantry. Across the porte-cochere, they converted the main floor of the West Wing into a guest lounge with billiards table, TV and stone fireplace, a conference room and a yoga studio where Nancy offers yoga classes. Overhead is the Pine Tree suite, an enormous space with king canopy bed, a sitting area with fireplace and a sun porch with a day bed. A local artist painted a mural of a Maine scene beside the tub in the bathroom. The new owners enhanced all the rooms with new beds, duvet comforters and 300-count linens, and added luxurious baths in several. Four guest rooms and five common rooms have fireplaces. With five acres of lawns near the end of a dead-end street, the inn is so quiet that the only sound we heard at night was made by the melodic harbor bell in the distance. A full breakfast, perhaps waffles or pancakes, is included in the rates.

(207) 326-4861. Fax (207) 326-0891. www.manor-inn.com. Twelve rooms and two suites with private baths. Doubles, $110 to $230.

The Village Inn at Bah's Bakehouse, off Main and Water Streets, Box 183, Castine 04421.

Hers is first and foremost a café and bakery, funky and full of character. But Bah (for Barbara) Macomber recently added four simple guest rooms upstairs. Two in front with private baths yield views of Castine's harbor. One has a double poster bed, while the other has a queen bed, sofa and a private balcony. Two rear rooms, one with twin beds and one with a double, share a hall bath. Furnishings are sparse, there's no common area other than the café and overnighters may hear Bah at work in the bakehouse before dawn. But the price is right and the continental breakfast of fresh baked goods outstanding. You can take it with the locals in intimate quarters inside or outside on a front porch with a glimpse of the harbor.

(207) 326-9510. Two rooms with private baths and two rooms with shared bath. Doubles, $85 and $95.

Castine Cottages, 33 Snapps Way, Castine 04421.

Believe it or not, these six log-cabin housekeeping cottages lined up on a secluded bluff with 1,500 feet of waterfront north of town are the only other public accommodations in Castine. But they're so prized and so reasonable that they're often booked for the summer by March, according to owners Alan and Diana Snapp, who took over from his parents and live in the house in front. Each has two bedrooms, a fully equipped kitchenette, a pine-paneled living room with Franklin fireplace and a sofabed, and a screened porch. The Snapps say the clamming is great in Hatch's Cove, which has a good beach below the cottages.

(207) 326-8003. www.castinecottages.com. Six two-bedroom cottages. Weekly rentals starting Saturday, $625, late June to late September; $500 weekly or $75 to $150 nightly rest of year.

Seeing and Doing ⸻⸻ _ʃʊʃʊʃʊ_

WALKING TOURS. "Welcome to Castine," a Castine Merchants Association brochure you find everywhere, with maps and a history, gives specifics for a walking tour of most of Castine. You can stick to the central area, which covers Main and Water streets and the quaint, out-of-the-mainstream village common that's as picturesque as any in New England. The Castine Historical Society, located facing the green in a former Italianate school topped by a cupola, is open Tuesday-Sunday in July and August. You can drive, though we prefer to poke along on foot or bicycle, to see a larger area embracing Perkins Street and Battle Avenue. Included are the major fortifications (Fort Madison consists of a few embankments with a couple of picnic tables beside the water; Fort George is larger with earthen ramparts and ditches), historic sites, a public path to the water from Dyces Head Lighthouse, tree-shaded Georgian and Federalist houses, buildings of the Maine Maritime Academy, and such unexpected pleasures as a tiny circular shorefront house and the enormous stucco summer home, Guerdwood. Interestingly, you encounter more historic markers denoting more sites than the tour map designates.

HARBOR TOURS. Castine's colorful harbor is usually dotted with yachts, sailboats, the tall-masted windjammers (usually tied up on Mondays and Tuesdays) and the ultimate incongruity for a small and sedate harbor, the towering and massive State of Maine ship.

The T/V State of Maine Ship, MMA Dock.
The 499-foot-long Maine Maritime Academy training vessel is open to the public when it is in port, generally from July 4 through August. MMA cadets give 30-minute tours on the hour weekdays on this former oceanographic research vessel. It's a hulk of a sight on the Castine waterfront, and a sight inside as well. You'll see the vast engine room, the steering mechanisms, some of the cabin rooms used by 300 cadets, the mess hall and kitchens complete with gigantic hot food vats. You might be told more than you want to know and climb more stairs than you want to ascend, but touring a hands-on ship used for ocean training cruises is an unusual experience.
(207) 326-4311 or 326-2420. Open daily when in port, 10 to 3. Free.

Sea kayak tours are offered by **Castine Kayak Adventures,** (207) 326-9045, operating out of Dennett's Wharf. It rents kayaks and offers a variety of tours and classes, from "sunrise awakenings" to sunset tours.

Swimming and Other Sports. Swimming off a long, stony beach known as Backshore Beach is available to the public at Wadsworth Cove. The Castine swimming pool provides saltwater swimming in a pool nearby. A nine-hole golf course is open for a fee at the private Castine Golf Club, one of America's earliest (1897); its first five holes were originally on the site of adjacent Fort George. The club also has four tennis courts. The Maine Maritime Academy offers its gymnasium, pool, weight room, and squash and racquetball courts for a daily fee. Bike rentals are available at Dennett's Wharf.

The Wilson Museum, 107 Perkins St.
Built in 1921 to house the extensive collections of anthropologist and geologist J. Howard Wilson, this is a highly personal place reflecting the tastes of Dr. and Mrs. Wilson and their world travels. "There's a bit of the whole world here," said the woman on duty. "The way it's laid out tells you the history of mankind back to Cyprus in 3000 B.C." Included are everything from remarkable beaded Indian moccasins and ceremonial leggings, ship models, an Indian pueblo model, firearms, stone artifacts and pottery to modern paintings by 21 artists spilling onto a rear porch above the harbor. The Wilsons' daughter, Ellenore Wilson Doudiet, is the museum director and guiding force. The 1763 John Perkins House, the area's oldest house, was moved to the site and restored in 1970. It is furnished with period antiques. The property also contains a working blacksmith shop and a hearse house with Castine's funeral vehicles from a century ago.
(207) 326-9247. www.wilsonmuseum.org. Museum open Tuesday-Sunday 2 to 5, Memorial Day through September; free. Perkins House open Sunday and Wednesday 2 to 5 in July and August; tours $5.

SHOPPING. Downtown Castine consists of few but select stores. **Four Flags Gifts** offers nautical equipment as well as gifts from around the world, books, jewelry, Gordon Fraser cards and, just arrived one time when we were there, a novelty scent called Eau de Low Tide. At the **Water Witch,** tall, dark and striking Jean de Raat, the water witch herself when not hawking real estate, sells a variety of fine clothing (placemats, napkins and pillows, too) made of cotton Dutch wax batiks and Java prints; check out her silk caps and hats. Artist Greg Dunham sells his watercolors as well as other artworks at the **McGrath Dunham Gallery.** Another stop for art is **Fay's One Gallery.** Former Castine Patriot editor John Vernelson runs the expanded **Compass Rose Bookstore,** while his wife Ruth Heffron serves up espresso, smoothies, sandwiches and snacks in the **Linger Longer Cafe** out back. **Leila Day Antiques** and **Oakum Bay Ltd.** combine to offer antique furniture and accessories along with contemporary crafts and collectibles. Although the corner **Castine Variety Store** carries a few sundries, it's the place where locals of the male persuasion congregate starting at 6 a.m. for coffee and gossip – be advised, the counter stools are "reserved" by local custom and a visitor who sits down to order coffee is apt to be politely but firmly admonished, "that's to go." In the off-season, local women gather daily at **Bah's Bakehouse** for coffee and muffins. "It's a real meeting place," our informant (female) advised.

Where to Eat

Castine Inn, Main Street, Castine.

Creative chef Tom Gutow has elevated the Castine Inn's dining room into the loftiest ranks of outstanding Maine restaurants. The harbor is on view in the distance from the pristine, 60-seat dining room, but it is the food that draws the cognoscenti from miles around. The basic menu is prix-fixe, $55 for three courses. Available for the entire table are a six-course tasting menu ($85 per person) and a twelve-course grand tasting menu ($125). One night's prix-fixe offerings illustrate the refined, sophisticated style. They began with a choice of potato and ramp soup with littleneck clams, local crab cake with mustard vinaigrette or braised beef short rib with red pepper gnocchi. Following a mixed green salad, main courses were poached salmon with cold pickled onions and finnan haddie foam, goat cheese agnolotti with roasted root vegetables and a sweet vermouth sauce, and pork with spinach, butter chard and fingerling potatoes. Sorbet and petit-fours accompanied the dessert course, a choice among chocolate breton, lavender crème brûlée or caramel tea financier.

(207) 326-4365. Prix-fixe, $55. Dinner nightly, 5:30 to 8:30 Memorial Day to Labor Day, 6 to 8 to Columbus Day, weekends only rest of season. Closed late December through April.

Pentagoet Inn, 26 Main St., Castine.

Innkeeper Julie VandeGraff, former owner of a pastry shop in Philadelphia, oversees the dining experience in this polished inn's expanded restaurant. Dinner is served at widely spaced tables in two elegant dining rooms and outside on a wraparound veranda. Chef Gina Melita's menu features such starters as simple as "a big ol' bowl of Blue Hill mussels" steamed in wine, basil and lavender and as complex as a salad of lobster escabèche with avocado and goat cheese. Entrées range from the signature bouillabaisse in a rich saffron broth to anise-dusted duck breast in marsala jus. The roasted fillet of salmon with leeks and mushrooms arrives in warm tarragon bourride. Desserts could be a plum crisp with vanilla ice cream and double chocolate torte with espresso cream. Guests linger over after-dinner drinks in the old-world Passports Pub, where the collection of oversize photos of personalities from Grace Kelly to Mahatma Gandhi spark lively conversation.

(207) 326-8616 or (800) 845-1701. Entrées, $15 to $24. Dinner, Monday-Saturday 5:30 to 8; off-season, Tuesday-Saturday 6 to 8.

The Manor Inn, Battle Avenue, Castine.

The dining operation has been enhanced and made more consistent by new owner Tom Ehrman, formerly in food and beverage management with the Sheraton Hotel corporation in Florida. Taking over an inn that had seen better days, he and partner Nancy Watson, who was doing the cooking at our latest visit, relocated the dining room to the former bar and vice-versa. With the addition of a sunken enclosed porch, the result is a handsome, two-level dining area seating 80 in elegant nautical and Colonial ambiance, with front windows looking toward the harbor, and a library with fireside dining. The pub has paneled walls, corner benches, a fireplace and a plate shelf filled with steins and toby mugs around the perimeter. The dinner menu changes weekly. Typical starters are Dyces Head chowder, calamari with wasabi-sake dipping sauce, a trio of pot stickers and a classic caesar salad. Entrées could be the signature crab cakes with mustard and chili aïoli sauces, cedar-plank roasted salmon, India-style curried chicken and charbroiled strip steak with blue cheese topping. Seasonal desserts include strawberry-rhubarb pie and chocolate oblivion torte with blackberry-raspberry sauce. A light menu is available in the pub.

(207) 326-4861. Entrées, $18 to $26. Dinner seasonally, Tuesday-Saturday 6 to 8; pub from 5.

Dennett's Wharf & Oyster Bar, 15 Sea St., Castine.

Peripatetic local chef Paul Brouillard started this seafood emporium and lobster pound right on the water below Sea Street. The former sail and rigging loft built in the early 1900s has been upscaled a bit by under the ownership of his brother Gary and Carolyn Brouillard. A shoulder-high partition divides what had been the world's longest oyster bar from the dining area and Gary installed separate (as opposed to communal) tables in the dining room. We still prefer to eat outside at the hexagonal or regular picnic tables on a large deck right over the water. The twenty or so dinner entrées range from broiled haddock to scallops chardonnay and five versions of steak. Seafood linguini is a house specialty. Look for nightly specials like bouillabaisse, rack of New Zealand lamb and sirloin steak au poivre. There are plenty of options for appetizers and light fare. The dessert list includes white chocolate-macadamia nut cheesecake, chocolate truffle torte, apple spice cake and piña colada cake. At a recent lunch, we enjoyed a clam roll with a side of potato salad and a crab roll with pasta salad, washed down with a pint of Dennett's own Wharf Rat Ale. In season, there's a busy schedule of live entertainment.

(207) 326-9045. www.dennettswharf.com. Entrées, $13.95 to $26.95. Lunch daily, 11 to 5. Dinner, 5 to 9. Closed November-March.

Bah's Bakehouse, Main and Water Streets, Castine.

Hidden down an alley and reached from either street is this funky bakehouse and café, where Bah ("it's a childhood nickname that stuck") Macomber from New Orleans packs in the locals for great sandwiches, pastries and such. She works in an open kitchen, the better to view (and interact with) her customers, many of whom are pictured on the walls. There are a porch and deck with a harbor view and a small inside dining room. The food is foremost. Consider one day's soups – tomato-cognac bisque, haddock chowder, whole bean and garlic, and Thai coconut shrimp and lobster. Sandwiches range from vegetarian to meatloaf to liverwurst to pâté with chutney, served on French or lavasch breads in small or large sizes. The dessert pastries are to die for.

(207) 326-9510. Sandwiches, $3.95 to $6.95. Open Monday-Saturday 7 to 5, Sunday 8 to 5.

FOR MORE INFORMATION: Castine has no tourist information center and no Chamber of Commerce. The town website is www.castine.me.us.

Boats and buoys create typical Stonington harbor scene outside Dockside Bookstore.

Stonington/Deer Isle, Me.

Turn south off busy Route 1, which is apt to be filled with a steady stream of cars between Belfast and Bar Harbor, and prepare for a different pace in a timeless place.

From the scenic lookout atop Caterpillar Hill as you head down Route 176 is one of the more spectacular views in all New England. Blue waters, green islands and small mountains meld into one astonishing panorama as far as the eye can see.

Head south and cross the high, unexpectedly imposing suspension bridge over the fine sailing waters of Eggemoggin Reach to Deer Isle. You enter another world: one of little traffic, no neon, no fast food, few residents and fewer tourists.

Deer Isle, the second largest island off the Maine coast, is far different from its busier and larger neighbor, Mount Desert Island. It is more like Isle au Haut, its offshore island that's part of Acadia National Park, whose better-known section surrounds Bar Harbor.

Back in the mid-18th century, Deer Isle ranked second to Gloucester, Mass., as a fishing port. Later, it was the source of granite for New York's major bridges, Rockefeller Center and the John F. Kennedy Memorial in Arlington National Cemetery. At its height, Stonington, its biggest village, had 3,500 people, steamer service, a theater/opera house and something of a boomtown atmosphere.

Today, the commercial fishing fleet remains active, and lobster traps are piled all around a town sometimes permeated by the odor of fish. Granite is still quarried, but modern equipment has replaced hundreds of workers with fewer than ten. Stonington's population has dwindled to less than 1,300 hardy souls who, we're told, rise with the sun and retire when it gets dark. "We used to have beer joints but they were nothing but trouble," reported the clerk in the state liquor store. "You'd need two trained gorillas for bouncers." So the town, commercially at least, is dry and ever so quaint and quiet.

A sign outside the island's little visitor information center says it's open from "10 til ?" on weekdays and "11 til ?" on Sundays. But it was closed every time we passed on three successive July days.

Never mind. The appeal of Deer Isle is not in the tourist attractions (there aren't many). It's in the endearing charms of tiny hamlets like Deer Isle (the name of the second biggest community, as well as of the island), and like Sunshine and Sunset, which remain much as they were 50 or more years ago. It's in the wonderful views that appear at every turn of the island roads that meander hither and yon around bays and inlets. It's in the remarkable crafts turned out by artisans attracted by the seaside Haystack Mountain School of Crafts and a simpler lifestyle.

As potter William Mor's wife Carolyn informed us when we visited: "Out here we have a peaceful way of life – a community where you can live and let live." And the rest of us can enjoy.

Getting There

The Blue Hill Peninsula tapers southward from U.S. Route 1 between Bucksport and Ellsworth. Deer Isle starts at the southern end of the Blue Hill Peninsula along East Penobscot Bay. From Route 1, take Routes 15 or 172 to Blue Hill, and Routes 175 and 15 to Deer Isle and Stonington.

Where to Stay

Several choice inns and B&Bs are available (including one offshore in a lightkeeper's station), plus a couple of motels of older vintage.

Inns and B&Bs

The Pilgrim's Inn, 20 Main St., Deer Isle 04267.

This striking, dark red 1793 house occupies a grand location on a spit of land between Northwest Harbor in front and the Mill Pond in back. Listed on the National Register of Historic Places, the inn exudes an aura of history, although new innkeepers Rob and Cathy DeGennaro added contemporary comforts and amenities in an effort to "take the inn to the next level." The DeGennaros, who earlier ran B&Bs in Southwest Harbor and on Captiva Island in Florida, renovated all the guest rooms, many with water views. Most rooms now have king or queensize beds topped with down pillows and duvet comforters. Each has a wood stove and some of the updated baths have vanities topped with Deer Isle granite. A vintage house next door contains two efficiency suites with TVs and gas stoves, sharing a large deck overlooking the water. The deluxe Rugosa Rose cottage is a two-level affair with kitchenette, dining/sitting area and water-view deck on the main floor and a queen bedroom with gas fireplace on the upper level. New for 2005 was a secluded loft suite in the barn with queensize bedroom, kitchen and a living room with a sofabed and a super view of the grounds and the Mill Pond. Back in the main inn, gas stoves have been added in all common areas. The main-floor library-turned-game room has a new look with four oversize leather chairs and a flat-screen TV/DVD. A stairway descends to a walkout

lower level holding a cozy common room, its bay window overlooking the Mill Pond and a new rear deck. Here also is a tap room with an expanded bar and, beyond, the attached barn in which dinner is offered (see Where to Eat). Guests gather beforehand in the pleasant common room for quite a spread of complimentary hors d'oeuvres, including smoked mussels and stuffed grape leaves at our recent visit. Breakfast is a gourmet event as well: smoked salmon benedict or pina colada-stuffed french toast might be the main course.

(207) 348-6615 or (888) 778-7505. www.pilgrimsinn.com. Twelve rooms and four efficiency suites with private baths. Doubles, $129 to $229. Suites, $249 to $269. Closed mid-October to mid-May. Cottage suites open all year.

Goose Cove Lodge, Goose Cove Road, Box 40, Sunset 04683.

A 1.5-mile long dirt road leads to the End of Beyond – the loveliest sight in the world, according to the lodge brochure. The secluded, 70-acre preserve marked by trails, tree-lined shores and sandy beaches is a paradise for nature lovers. At low tide, you can walk across a sand bar to Barred Island, a nature conservancy full of birds and wildlife. Lodge owners Joanne and Dom Parisi have updated many of the formerly rustic accommodations and now offer "gracious lodging and fine dining" that more than live up to their billing. They accommodate 90 guests in cabins, rooms and suites and offer two meals a day (see Where to Eat), plus sandwich lunches from the gift shop. Two suites are upstairs in the main lodge (the Lookout Suite with expansive ocean view is essentially a two-bedroom apartment). Eight more suites and rooms are in the nearby East and North annexes. Most in demand are the nine secluded cottages and four duplex cabins, each with ocean view, sun deck, kitchenette or refrigerator and fireplace. The lodge is the epitome of a Maine lodge: a lobby with an enormous fieldstone fireplace and stylish sofas, chairs, benches and bookcases, and a wraparound dining room with a drop-dead ocean view across an outdoor deck. Guests gather for cocktails and complimentary hors d'oeuvres in the bar or on the deck before dinner, while counselors entertain children, who have their own dinner beforehand. String quartets, folk singers, a lobster fisherman or a local writer may entertain after dinner on Sunday and Monday in peak season. Two other nights a week guests may study astronomy through the lodge's research-grade telescope. During the day, activities include guided nature walks, kayaking, bicycling and bird watching. Two Registered Maine Guides on staff offer guided sea kayak tours, and sailing cruises are offered on the lodge's 24-foot sloop. Local crafts and natural gifts are featured in the lodge's Waldron Trail Gift Shop.

(207) 348-2508 or (800) 728-1963. Fax (207) 348-2624. www.goosecovelodge.com. Twenty-two rooms, suites, cottages and cabins with private baths. Doubles, $225 to $525, B&B. Cottages rented weekly in summer; other rooms, two-night minimum. Closed late-October to mid-May.

The Inn on the Harbor, Main Street, Box 69, Stonington 04681.

Several things always enticed us to the old Captain's Quarters Inn & Motel: the nifty waterfront location, the enormous rear deck extending into Stonington Harbor, and the quirky ramble of laid-back rooms, efficiencies and apartments in four Victorian-era buildings. The accommodations were vastly upgraded when Christina Shipps took over a few years ago. A New Yorker who had a summer home nearby, she renamed the place and gave it a total facelift. The original seventeen rooms in the complex became thirteen, all but three with harbor views. The result is larger rooms with sitting areas, mostly kingsize or queen beds, updated bathrooms and new overstuffed furnishings along with antiques and family heirlooms. The common deck built over the ocean, as well as private decks off some of the rooms on two floors, also were restructured. All different, rooms vary from small and cozy to suites that are rather substantial. All have TVs and telephones. In those facing the water, you're lulled to sleep by the sounds of gulls and foghorns. A couple of waterfront rooms have granite fireplaces. The innkeeper's pride and joy is the American Eagle, a two-bedroom efficiency apartment with an all-glass front and private deck facing the harbor. The inn also offers the adjacent Stephen Taber cottage with queen bed and private deck and a two-bedroom sea-view suite in the Shipps House, the owner's residence out West Main Street. A continental breakfast buffet is put out in the reception room, which also operates as an espresso bar open to the public from 11 to 6.

(207) 367-2420 or (800) 942-2420. Fax (207) 367-5165. www.innontheharbor.com. Eleven rooms, two suites and a cottage with private baths. Doubles, $115 to $140. Suites and cottage, $135 and $195.

The Inn at Ferry Landing, 108 Old Ferry Road, RR 1, Box 163, Deer Isle 04627.

The wide waterfront location – at a point along Eggemoggin Reach where the ferry from Sargentville once landed – appealed. And the 1850s farmhouse, a residence that we eyed longingly as a potential waterside B&B, was for sale. We decided to pass, but returned the next summer and found that it had been nicely renovated into just what we had in mind by its eventual purchasers. Owners Jean and Gerald Wheeler offer four guest quarters, two up and two down, all with water views and furnished with family antiques. The Blue Room at the rear of the main floor has twin beds, a clawfoot tub and a private entrance from the yard. We're partial to the second-floor suite with a brass queensize bed, a huge tub and walk-in shower, a pullout sofa and chair, a wood stove and skylights in the pitched ceiling. Families go for the two-bedroom housekeeping apartment called the Mooring in the rear annex, which has a waterfront deck. The real showplace is the large, contemporary-style great room, white with mauve trim, airy and open with expansive windows on three sides. It holds lots of seating plus two grand pianos (Gerald formerly was music director of Christ Church Cathedral in Montreal). His wife serves exotic breakfasts at a mahogany table in the dining room. The fare might be omelets, pain au chocolate or french toast made with oatmeal bread and orange slices.

(207) 348-7760. Fax (207) 348-5276. www.ferrylanding.com. Three rooms, one suite and a two-bedroom apartment with private baths. Doubles, $110 to $120. Suite, $165. Annex, $1,300 weekly, EP.

Près du Port, West Main Street and Highland Avenue, Box 319, Stonington 04681.

The gray cat is appropriate at this gray house on a hill overlooking Stonington harbor. Rockers in a semi-circle face the water in a side sun porch; Adirondack chairs do the same on an upstairs sundeck. Charlotte Casgrain, a Connecticut resident who has summered on the island since 1955, offers three guest rooms, each with its own bath. Beau Rivage is a large room with a panoramic view of the harbor, old oak furniture and a small vanity sink to match. It has a double bed, as does Beau Ciel, also with a vanity and a view, and done in pale azure; note the tiny silver-plated faces on the Victorian drawer pulls. Beau Sejour has twin beds, a loft with futons, a kitchenette and a garden view. Breakfast, served buffet style, consists of fresh fruit, cereals, yogurts, muffins and breads, sometimes with bacon or sausage and eggs.

(207) 367-5007. www.presduport.com. Three rooms with private baths. Doubles, $125. Open mid-June to mid-October.

The Keeper's House, Box 26, Isle au Haut 04645.

For a change of pace, how about staying in a restored lightkeeper's station? You take the mail boat from Stonington to this remote, six-mile-long island, part of Acadia National Park and eight miles offshore from Deer Isle. Innkeepers Jeff and Judi Burke came upon the 1907 Coast Guard lightkeeper's house atop the craggy sea cliff for the first time in 1985 and immediately envisioned its possibilities as an inn. After pouring $300,000 into acquisition and renovations, the Burkes feel they now offer "a living museum where guests step back in time." Some guests call it the experience of a lifetime. No cars, no electricity, no phones nor commercial development mar the simplicity of an island containing a few Acadia Park campsites and 50 residents. The light tower still operates, and beacons from five other lighthouses can be seen at night. The main house offers four large guest rooms, all with water views and double beds. They're furnished with painted antiques, sea chests, rocking chairs, island crafts and coastal memorabilia. Two modern baths with hot showers (the water is heated by a wood stove) are shared. For more rusticity and privacy, the dollhouse-like Oil House cottage right on the water has a double bed, wood stove, secluded deck, a "backhouse" and outdoor shower. Judi bakes breads and pastries, and serves a variety of native seafood or chicken dishes (no red meat) and complimentary wine at candlelight dinners. Afterward, guests chat amid the glow of gas lights. The daily rate includes all meals and a tour of the island. Parking on the mainland ($3 to $5 a night) and round-trip passage on the mail boat ($32 per person) are extra.

(207) 460-0257. www.keepershouse.com. Four rooms and one cottage. Doubles, $310 to $385 AP. Two-night minimum in summer; no mail boat on Sundays or postal holidays. Closed late October to mid-May.

Motels

Eggemoggin Landing, Route 15, Little Deer Isle 04650.

Two sisters and their husbands have upgraded this motel, restaurant and marina complex, formerly known as the Bridge Inn and before that the Beachcomber Motel. Robin and Carl Rosenquist oversee the twenty-unit motel, which has a convenient waterfront location right at the foot of the Deer Isle suspension bridge. Our quarters were small but had wall-to-wall carpeting, full bath, TV and outside chairs looking onto the waters of Eggemoggin Reach. Bed configurations vary from one double and one kingsize to twins and two doubles. Picnic tables are scattered across the treed lawn leading down to the rocky shore, where you can gather mussels at low tide and swim at high tide, but can't really do either in between, so great is the difference in tides here. Robin's sister, Patty, is chef at the adjacent **Sisters Take-out** restaurant, where continental breakfast is complimentary for motel guests and lunch and dinner are available to go or to enjoy at a picnic grove by the water. The marina's pier extends 300 feet into Eggemoggin Reach. Boat, kayak and bike rentals are offered, as are sailing tours and lobster boat excursions.

(207) 348-6115. www.acadia.net/eggland. Twenty rooms with private baths. Doubles, $79 to $89. Closed mid-October to mid-May.

Boyce's Motel, 44 Main St., Box 94, Stonington 04681.

With our children, we once stayed in this small motel, which back then had seen better days. The five original units remain, but six efficiency rooms have been added in outbuildings to the rear, including a two-story structure with three units and decks. The biggest has a living room, kitchen and two bedrooms (one with queen bed and the other with twins). Four others have a kitchen/living room and a bedroom with one or two double or twin beds. Two rooms with kitchenettes come with queen beds. All rooms have cable TV, phones, refrigerators and coffeemakers. While not on the water, Boyce's has the next best thing: a private waterfront deck for guests' use across the street.

(207) 367-2421 or (800) 224-2421. Fax (207) 367-0937. www.boycesmotel.com. Four rooms and seven efficiencies with private baths. Doubles, $60. Efficiency units, $65 to $115.

CAMPING. Old Quarry Campground, (207) 367-8977, offers tent sites around a duck pond near Webb Cove outside Stonington for $28 a night. Picnic tables and a bathhouse are provided. Under the same ownership is Sunshine Campground on the Sunshine Road in Deer Isle, (207) 348-2663, which has fifteen tent and seven trailer sites in wooded locations, $24 and $28.

Seeing and Doing

Boating, nature walks, and art and craft galleries are the main attractions of this quiet, unspoiled area where "the people are gentle and strong, the sea water cool...and the rest of the hectic world seems removed for awhile."

Innkeeper Jean Wheeler put that well in her welcome message as Chamber of Commerce president in the helpful Island Guide. She added: "We delight in sharing this treasure with other people who appreciate its joys – the unspoiled granite shores and tidal coves, peaceful woodlands, the wonders of sunrise and sunset relevant and unobstructed, a busy working fishing port, artists' galleries, fresh seafood and abundant subtle riches of daily life in a small community. Days can be filled with activity or quiet, company or solitude."

On the Water

Kayaking, sailing and boat cruises among the islands off Deer Isle are a must, if only for a mail boat ride to Isle au Haut. Among the choices:

Isle au Haut Co., 27 Sea Breeze Ave., Stonington.

Passenger ferry service out to Isle au Haut and Penobscot Bay cruises are offered by this outfit with its own pier at the foot of Sea Breeze Avenue. Most are on mailboats, so they operate seasonally and generally on postal schedules. An exception is the hour-long sightseeing cruise aboard Miss Lizzie. The boat's captain relates island folklore and history as passengers watch seals, seabirds and fishing boats and view the Mark Island Lighthouse and the Deer Isle granite quarry at Crotch Island. Five mailboat trips daily out to Isle au Haut take about 45 minutes each way, with about a fifteen-minute stop on the island. The 10 a.m. trip goes on to Acadia National Park at Duck Harbor, on the protected southwest shore of the island at the base of Duck Harbor Mountain. The adventurous may want to disembark, hike or bike the park's trails, and catch the late boat at 5:45 p.m. for the return trip.

(207) 367-5193. www.isleauhaut.com. Sightseeing cruise, Monday-Friday at 9 and 2 and Saturday at 2, June 14-Sept. 11; adults $14, children $6. Mailboat to Isle au Haut, Monday-Saturday at 7, 10, 11:30, 3:15 and 4:30, also Sunday at 10:30 and 3, June 20-Sept. 12, fewer trips in off-season. Duck Harbor trip, Monday-Saturday 10 and 4:30, June 12-Sept. 9. Fares are one-way: adults $16, children $8; return on same trip for half price. Ride all day on any combination of trips for $32, children $16.

Capt. David Zinn offers yacht cruises on the Sea Mist through Jericho Bay into Eggemoggin Reach and around Deer Isle or Swan's Island through **Jericho Bay Charters,** Sunshine Road, Deer Isle, (207) 348-6114.

Capt. Geoff Warner gives charter **sailing cruises** on the 37-foot sloop Aria, (207) 367-6555.

Seaborne Ventures, (207) 479-7220, sails a 40-foot trimaran daily in summer from Eggemoggin Landing Marina on Little Deer Isle.

Old Quarry Ocean Adventures and Outdoor Recreation Center, 130 Settlement Road, off Oceanville Road, Stonington, (207) 367-8977, is the place for canoes and kayak rentals, lessons and tours. Capt. Bill Baker also offers eco-tours, sailboat and powerboat charters, sailboat rentals and about every other kind of boat or bicycle activity. **Eggemoggin Landing Marina,** Route 15, Little Deer Isle, (207) 348-6115, has boat, kayak and bicycle rentals, sailing tours and lobster boat excursions.

Finest Kind Canoe & Kayak Rentals offers daily and long-term rentals from its location away from the water behind Finest Kind Dining, 70 Center District Cross Road, Deer Isle, (207) 348-7714. Sea kayak tours and instruction are offered by registered Maine guides Dana and Ann Douglass of **Granite Island Guide Service,** Dunham's Point, Deer Isle, (207) 348-2668.

Other Attractions

Deer Isle Granite Museum, 51 Main St., Stonington.

A working granite quarry is brought to life in a three-dimensional model that's the centerpiece of this fledgling museum. The charming, eight-by-fifteen-foot model is complete with Stonington buildings and animated derricks, trains and boats. It shows the quarrying operations on Crotch Island, off to the southwest in Stonington Harbor, at its height in the early 1900s. The museum shop sells gifts of and about the unique Deer Isle granite. You might pick up a granite paperweight or the museum-published book, *Stone Slabs and Iron Men.*

(207) 367-6331. Open Monday-Saturday 10 to 5, Sunday 1 to 5, Memorial Day through Labor Day. Free.

Crockett Cove Woods Preserve, Crockett Cove, Stonington, is among attractions for nature lovers. It's hard to find, off Whitman Road at Burnt Cove on the Stonington-Sunset Road. The persistent will be rewarded with a pleasant quarter-mile walk through part of a 100-acre coastal rain forest maintained by the Maine Nature Conservancy. The self-guided tour is enhanced by a brochure that helps the already knowledgeable identify what they're seeing. Even the uninitiated will be impressed by the beautiful shades of greens, the exotic mosses, a bog, the lush growth and huge rocks. It really is like a rain forest. Parking for three or four cars only; free.

A self-guiding nature trail passes through spruce forests and freshwater and saltwater marshes in the **Holt Mill Pond Preserve** off Airport Road, Stonington. Nearly 50 species of birds have been identified in the preserve, which is maintained by the Stonington Conservation Commission.

Island Heritage Trust, Deer Isle, (207) 348-2455, opens other properties for the public. The trust owns five islands – Mark with its lighthouse, Millet, Round, Polypod and Wreck – and the Settlement Quarry and Shore Acres Preserve, all allowing limited daytime public use. Campbell Island permits limited camping, and the state-owned Edgar Tennis Preserve offers trails for hikers. The trust manages the Barred Island Preserve and trails for the Nature Conservancy.

The Island Country Club on Sunset Road, Deer Isle, (207) 348-2379, welcomes visitors for "friendly golf and tennis," according to an advertisement. It has a nine-hole golf course and a tennis court.

SCENIC DRIVES. You'll need to follow a map of Deer Isle, but the rewards are great for those with wanderlust. We particularly enjoy the little Sand Beach Road along the channel known as the Deer Island Thorofare, with a stop for rock climbing or a hasty swim at Fifield Point or Burnt Cove. To the east of town is Ames Pond with some rare pink water lilies. There is a particularly scenic drive out to Oceanville, where you stumble upon a tiny beach with calm waters beside a bridge. Another drive goes way out past the hamlet of Sunshine (at the opposite side of the island from Sunset) to Haystack Mountain School of Crafts, where the waterfront vistas from on high are something else. Follow almost any side road and you'll come to a dead end at the water.

Crafts and Shopping

Haystack Mountain School of Crafts, Sunshine Road, Deer Isle, (207) 348-2306. A long gravel road finally brings you to this noted crafts school, clinging to a hillside with wondrous views through deep green spruce trees of the sparkling blue waters of Jericho Bay below. The hardy can descend what seem like endless wooden stairs to the rocky shore. We found the various artists' studios and the school's layout interesting but were surprised not to find any crafts on display. This is a working school, however, and no items are for sale. Three-week sessions attract top craftsmen from all over the country. Visitors are welcome to join campus tours at 1 p.m. Wednesday in summer.

Ronald Hayes Pearson, whose jewelry is exhibited across the country, has a studio and gallery in his striking home at 29 Old Ferry Road in North Deer Isle. Pearson works in silver and gold; his twist earrings at $65 for silver and $230 for gold are especially in demand. He and his wife Carolyn Hecker, executive director of the growing Maine Crafts Association that started locally, welcome visitors Monday-Saturday from 10 to 5.

Farther along Reach Road, which parallels Eggemoggin Reach, is the home and studio of potter **William Mor,** designer of handsome stoneware. Lately, he has been selling stunning, reasonably priced oriental rugs made by Afghan refugees living in Pakistan. Wife Carolyn has been known to offer delicious fresh-baked cookies to browsers in the sheltered outdoor sales area surrounded by gardens and a pond, open daily from 10 to 5.

Harbor Farm, which started in 1985 as a Christmas shop featuring its own wreaths, has blossomed into a nationally known mail-order operation with a delightful store and showroom in an 1850 schoolhouse beside the causeway in Little Deer Isle. From trout pottery to Silesian stoneware to wooden hay forks to wrought-iron hooks to walking sticks, this place sells fascinating furnishings for the person and home.

In Deer Isle, the **Deer Isle Artists Association** shows contemporary works by members. Mary Nyburg's **Blue Heron Gallery** exhibits contemporary American crafts, featuring works by the Haystack School faculty. Elena Kubler's wonderful **Turtle Gallery** has changing exhibits of watercolors, oils, drawings, photographs and contemporary crafts. **Greene-Ziner Gallery** features the owners' decorative clay and sculptural metalwork. **Dockside Quilt Gallery** is known for colorful island-made quilts. **The Periwinkle** stocks books, cards, knit goods, stuffed animals and local crafts

Out the Sunshine Road east of Deer Isle, the quirky sculptures on the grounds draw passersby into **Nervous Nellie's Jams and Jellies & Mountainville Café.** Peter Beerits and company put up 40,000 jars of jam each year in the little house with a big kitchen. So many people began stopping in that Peter decided to serve refreshments as well. The café offers morning coffee and afternoon tea with homemade breads and pastries, including a frozen drink called a Batido, a refreshing but caloric mix of cream cheese, freezer jam and crushed ice cubes. The jam business that Peter started because he could not find employment as an artist has enabled him to work full-time producing sculptures – many made from found objects – that help make this place worth a visit.

Stonington's Main Street has been enhanced by **The Clown,** an exceptional seasonal venture combining European antiques and furniture, contemporary art and Italian ceramics with Italian wines and specialty foods like fabulous Italian olive oil. It proved such a success that owners Kyle Wolfe and Martin Kolk opened a larger, year-round establishment of the same name in Portland. Farther along Main Street is the **Eastern Bay Gallery,** showing works of local artists. Elsewhere along Main Street, other galleries caught our eye: **D. Mortenson Gallery, Isalos Fine Art** and the **Hoy Gallery,** displaying Jill Hoy's vibrant paintings of coastal Maine. The charming **Dockside Bookstore,** right beside the water with chairs for reading on a little deck, specializes in Maine and marine books and nautical gifts. **Bayside Antiques & Gifts** features period and country furniture. **The Dry Dock** and **The Grasshopper Shop** offer creative and eclectic gifts and miscellany.

The jumble of stuff in front of the second-hand shop along Sea Breeze Avenue is such that we passed several times before deciding to stop. A "Tourist Traps" sign was in front of a stash of lobster traps. A ten-cent box was crammed with gadgets, as were the fifty-cent table and the $1 table. Go inside and you'll find everything from clam rollers to whale trivets to furniture. We liked the granite flower pots and baskets for planters. The owner said the shop's name, which we otherwise wouldn't have known, is **Chairs, Chairs, Chairs.** We're not sure why.

Where to Eat

Whale's Rib Tavern, 20 Main St., Deer Isle.

Some of the island's best meals have long attracted the public as well as inn guests for dinner at the Pilgrim's Inn. In 2005, inn owners Rob and Cathy DeGennaro renamed the restaurant operation, added a second dining room next to the inn's taproom and added an upscale tavern menu to their traditional offerings. The former goat barn has been refurbished to resemble a 1793 tavern, with windsor chairs at white-clothed tables. Big windows and doors open to let in the breeze. Well-known Maine chef Jonathan Chase has presided in the Pilgrim's Inn kitchen since he sold his namesake Blue Hill restaurant in 2002. He and two other chefs offer up to 30 entrées nightly. Their tavern menu includes the likes of baby back ribs, meatloaf, bangers and mash, and shepherds pie. The traditional menu ranges from a signature seafood stew and tuna niçoise to ale-braised lamb shank with maple barbecue sauce and pan-seared venison medallions with a shiitake mushroom-red wine sauce. Typical starters are Scandinavian-style borscht, parmigiano-reggiano flan with tomato-basil coulis and a smoked seafood sampler of mussels, Maine shrimp and Scottish salmon. Desserts include chambord cheesecake, mocha mousse and "chocolate over the top" – a triple fudge brownie with chocolate ice cream.

(207) 348-6615 or (888) 778-7505. Entrées, $11.95 to $34.95; tavern menu, $8.95 to $14.95. Dinner nightly, 4:30 to 10:30. Closed early January to early May.

Goose Cove Lodge, Goose Cove Road, Sunset.

The food here is some of the island's most inspired, and the waterside setting is without peer. The **Point Dining Room,** paneled in pine with wraparound windows onto the water, is augmented by an expansive dining deck almost at water's edge.

The innovative, much-acclaimed dinner menu changes weekly. At a recent visit the entrées included twin peeky-toe crab cakes with roasted tomato-vodka sauce, Mediterranean seafood stew, pan-seared duck breast with raspberry demi-glace and grilled butterflied lamb with rosemary demi-glace. The vegetarian entrée showed the kitchen's reach: seared tofu with quinoa, grilled butternut disk and wilted greens served with a roasted portobello mushroom and vegan pesto. Among starters were tuna tartare with wasabi cream and rosemary-skewered Maine diver scallops on polenta with wilted greens. Typical desserts are peach bread pudding on caramel sauce, chocolate decadence with raspberry sauce and poached pear on a flourless chocolate pâté with vanilla crème anglaise.

(207) 348-2508 or (800) 728-1963. Entrées, $15 to $27. Dinner by reservation, Tuesday-Sunday 5:30 to 8:30. Closed mid-October to mid-June.

Maritime Café, 27 Main St., Stonington.

The former Café Atlantic gave way in 2004 to this with-it establishment, run by an Austrian by way of Colorado and offering some interesting twists. Rudi Newmayr, a contractor who built many a restaurant but said this is the first he ever owned, dispenses typical Maine fare, of course. But he also has an espresso and crêpe bar geared to the after-theater crowd from the Stonington Opera House and a barbecue grill outside serving up spicy German sausages. The regular menu ranges widely from grilled Atlantic salmon with lemon-dill butter, seafood crêpes or sea scallops with snap peas and tomatoes over capellini to sautéed chicken breast with prosciutto, fontina and sage, herb-rubbed pork loin with caramelized onion sauce and grilled sirloin steak. Lobster is offered in three versions. You might start with steamed mussels in a spicy tomato broth or an Alsatian onion tart. Finish with one of the specialty dessert crêpes. With windows onto the water, the 28-seat dining room is simple but stylish with white paneling, flooring and benches imported from Colorado. An outdoor deck is put into service at lunchtime.

(207) 367-2600. www.maritimecafe.com. Entrées, $15 to $21. Lunch daily, 11:30 to 2:30. Dinner, 5 or 5:30 to 8:30. BYOB.

Bayview Restaurant, 25 Sea Breeze Ave., Stonington.

There's not much in the way of decor – pressed-tin ceiling and walls, linoleum floor and mismatched Scandinavian cutlery, raspberry-colored paper mats and an arrangement of wildflowers at each booth or table. And, despite the name, there's not much of a water view except, perhaps, from the rear kitchen. Service can be so slow as to be exasperating, moreover. But, rest assured, the signs proclaim this is Stonington's oldest continuously operated restaurant and shout values like "breakfast special: two eggs, two bacon, two toast, $3.25" and nuances like "always smoke-free." The food is fresh and reasonably priced, ranging from coq au vin to Nellie's sautéed lobster à la Nova Scotia, "an old family recipe served on toast points." Chef-owner Robert Dodge, whom we first met when he owned the old Captain's Quarters lodging complex, loves to cook and is doing this "out of the goodness of his heart," according to regulars. He's at his best with his evening specials – "whatever I feel like doing," he says. At our latest visit that meant grilled arctic char with lemon-butter sauce, roast duck à l'orange, charbroiled venison medallions with cranberry game sauce and Maine-raised black angus steak. Pretty good for a place that serves a range from hot dogs to seafood pie. "We still have fresh fish," says Bob. "You can't get away from that around here."

(207) 367-2274. Entrées, $10 to $23.25. Breakfast, 8 to 11. Lunch, 11 to 3. Dinner, 5 to 9. Closed Tuesday-Thursday. BYOB.

The Fisherman's Friend Restaurant, 40 School St., Stonington.

The outside is unprepossessing, to say the least, and the interior is zilch: a front room with booths and tables, a small middle room, and a newer back room with windows onto a field and tables covered with oilcloth, paper mats and bouquets of field flowers. Hanging plants are the only "decor." But this 29-year-old uptown restaurant run by Susan and Jack Scott doesn't really need much. It's got down-to-earth food at about the lowest prices around. For lunch, two of us had a wonderful clam chowder and a shrimp stew, plus an overstuffed crabmeat roll and great fried clams for less than $20, and the prices haven't really gone up since. For dinner, start with lobster or scallop stew or Port Clyde brand sardines, packed in Stonington and served on lettuce with saltines. Entrées come with a huge house salad at lunch and a salad bar at night, hot rolls and "real mashed potato" or french fries. They range from fried chicken, chopped sirloin steak with gravy or ham steak with pineapple ring to a fisherman's platter. The menu is supplemented by countless blackboard specials, as varied as spicy halibut fingers, chicken cordon bleu, prime rib and beef wellington at one visit. Homemade desserts might be open-face strawberry, cappuccino silk or raspberry-apple pies.

(207) 367-2442. Entrées, $8.99 to $16.50. Open daily, 11 to 9. BYOB. Closed November-March.

Lily's Café, Route 15, Stonington.

Deer Isle people head for this inauspicious looking little house across the cove from South Deer Isle for what they consider the consistently best food around. Chef-owner Kyra Alex opened in 1998 and attracted a steady following for eclectic fare that ranges from antipasto salad to cold Chinese noodles to crab cakes to crispy baked haddock sandwich to albacore tuna melt to veggie sandwich and Lily's nutburger. That's a sampling of the all-day fare. At night, Kyra adds a couple of specials that she decides about 3 p.m. and are "ready at 5." One recent night's choices were steamed mussels in red wine and tomato broth, chicken pot pie and Italian pot roast on pasta. The main floor of the house holds six tables, most topped with glass and dolls or shells. More tables in the eclectic **Chef's Attic** shop upstairs are pressed into service at busy times. The restaurant hews to limited hours, never on weekends and closing at 8 p.m. on nights dinner is served. We know, because we were running late and nearly didn't make it. But our innkeeper guests pulled rank and got us in for a convivial meal of delectable lamb chops, topped off with bread pudding.

(207) 367-5936. Entrées, $12.95 to $16.95. Open Monday, Tuesday and Friday 7 to 4, Wednesday and Thursday 7 to 8 p.m. in summer, to 7 p.m. in winter. BYOB.

Eaton's Lobster Pool, Blastow Cove, Little Deer Isle.

This rustic place rising above a wharf has been upscaled a bit)in terms of food and decor by owners Lew and Susan Snow. The traditional specialties, lobster and clam dinners, have been augmented lately by grilled chicken breast and steaks, plus broiled haddock or scallops and fried seafood. All the usual suspects, from steamed clams to lobster rolls to fried haddock sandwiches, are offered and then some. Summer people as well as locals cherish the place.

(207) 348-2383. www.eatonslobsterpoolcom. Entrées, $13 to $39. Open daily in season, 4:30 to 9, also Friday-Sunday 11:30 to 9.

FOR MORE INFORMATION: Deer Isle-Stonington Chamber of Commerce, Box 490, Deer Isle, ME 04627, (207) 348-6124. www.deerislemaine.com.

Sand Beach in Acadia National Park offers ocean swimming for the hardy.

Bar Harbor/Mount Desert Island, Me.

Anyone visiting Acadia National Park can believe its claim to having more scenic variety per square mile than any other part of the national park system.

Rugged ocean coastline comes first to mind when one thinks of Acadia, which occupies the better part of Mount Desert Island – the country's third largest (after Long Island and Martha's Vineyard). There also are towering cliffs and mountain summits (including Cadillac Mountain, the highest along the East Coast), the East's only natural fjord, fresh-water lakes, sandy beaches, and wetlands and forests full of wildlife.

Such scenic diversity produces the widest range of outdoor activity in one place in Maine, if not the East. The visitor can explore the jagged shoreline, climb mountains, swim in the ocean or lakes, go sailing or lobstering, canoe through salt marshes and kayak along the coast, watch for birds and whales, walk along nature trails and through exotic gardens, hike or bicycle or ride horses on 50 miles of carriage paths, and camp near the sea, among other pursuits.

They used to call it "rusticating," when thousands of city folk descended in the 19th century on Bar Harbor – the island's largest town – to pursue the active outdoor life, eschewing what they considered the pretentious activities of such summer colonies as Newport, Lenox and Saratoga. In the 1880s, Bar Harbor's eighteen hotels could accommodate more than 25,000 guests, and the elite began building fashionable cottages that were the largest in Maine.

Residents like John D. Rockefeller Jr., fearing commercial encroachments, bought up vast tracts of land. In 1919, they donated them to the federal government for the first national park in the East. The advent of the automobile made the island more accessible. The hotels disappeared and the Great Fire of 1947 destroyed many of the large homes remaining from Bar Harbor's heyday.

Today's visitors find vestiges of the island's Golden Era in the mansions of West and Eden streets in Bar Harbor and in the enclaves at Seal Harbor and Northwest Harbor. But they're more likely to find campers and hikers and bicyclists who appreciate the outdoor wonderland that led the residents who settled Bar Harbor in 1796 to name the town Eden.

With more than four million visitors annually, Acadia ranks second only to the Great Smoky Mountains National Park as the country's most visited national park.

When Bar Harbor swarms with tourists, the rusticators seek refuge in the park and the other harbor towns – Seal, Northeast, Southwest and Bass – on what their boosters call the "Quiet Side" of the island.

Getting There

Bar Harbor and Acadia National Park are about 180 roundabout miles northeast of Portland and 45 miles southeast of Bangor. Take coastal U.S. Route 1 to Ellsworth or Interstate 95 to Bangor and Route 1A to Ellsworth. Route 3 from Ellsworth leads to the park entrance and, beyond, to Bar Harbor. The Bar Harbor/Hancock County Airport just off island in Trenton is served by Colgan Air with direct connections to Boston. Major airlines fly into Bangor International Airport.

The 900-passenger "Cat" ferry connects Bar Harbor with Yarmouth in Nova Scotia. Traveling at 55 miles an hour, North America's only high-speed car ferry cuts the trip, which took six hours on the old Bluenose Ferry, to under three hours.

Where to Stay

Most accommodations are in the Bar Harbor area. We feature those beside the water there and around Mount Desert Island.

Inns and B&Bs

The Inn at Bay Ledge, 1385 Sand Point Road, Bar Harbor 04609.

This clifftop retreat overlooking Frenchman Bay has been upscaled by Jack and Jeani Ochtera, formerly of the Holbrook House in Bar Harbor. They offer king or queen featherbeds with down comforters in seven guest rooms, three with jacuzzis. All have picture windows or french doors and balconies affording splendid vistas of Frenchman Bay, and new balconies on the second floor have retractable awnings. A great veranda full of Bar Harbor wicker and an expansive deck stretch along the back of the inn overlooking lovely gardens and the bay. Here are umbrellaed tables and twig chairs where you may read and relax at this, a truly relaxing place. A small swimming pool and whirlpool are on a lower level of the deck. Rolling lawns and gardens lead to a sheer cliff, where a steep staircase descends to the stony beach and a cave. The inn's main floor contains a sauna and steam shower, a living room decorated with Jeani's baskets and a sun porch where she offers a lavish breakfast of, perhaps, smoked turkey hash, blueberry buckle or cheese strata. Farewell boxes of Bay Ledge candies are given to guests upon departure. The inn also offers three cottages, all stylishly redone in wicker and oak, hidden in the trees across the road. Next to the inn is the

two-bedroom Summer House, which has an expansive deck 25 feet from the shore and rents by the week.

(207) 288-4204. Fax (207) 288-5573. www.innatbayledge.com. Seven rooms and three cottages with private baths. Doubles, $180 to $375. Cottages, $160 to $185. Summer House, $2,500 to $3,000 weekly. Closed November-April.

The Bass Cottage Inn, 14 The Field, Box 242, Bar Harbor 04609.

Stylish accommodations and gourmet breakfasts are the hallmarks of this deluxe B&B, grandly reborn in 2004 after a year's renovations. Teri and Jeffrey Anderholm. moved from Newburyport, Mass., to take over a 120-year-old summer guest house that had seen better days. The B&B has an uncommon amount of common space and ten spacious guest rooms, all suavely decorated by Teri in what she envisioned as "grand cottage style." Antiques and 19th-century architectural elements blend comfortably with light colors, stunning art and contemporary amenities for a refined 21st-century look. Rooms on four floors vary from a queen bedroom with a fireplace on the main floor to a skylit "penthouse retreat" in the old attic with a kingsize bed, whirlpool tub and separate shower. The largest is a second-floor corner room with kingsize poster bed, a white chaise lounge beside the fireplace and a whirlpool tub for two. Five rooms have partial water views, one of them a tree-top corner hideaway with king bed, whirlpool tub and fireplace with views on two sides. Jeff's favorite room, it is crisply decorated in white, cream and ebony, a showcase for his wife's designer flair. All rooms have TV/DVDs, telephones, Poland Spring bottled water and abundant toiletries. The main-floor common areas include a rattan-furnished front atrium/sun porch, a large parlor that doubles as a library and music room with a baby grand piano, a clubby lounge and a well-stocked guest pantry off the professional kitchen. The dining room section of the wraparound sun porch looks like a restaurant, its individual tables elegantly set with white linens and fresh flowers. Here Teri, who attended the Cambridge School of Culinary Arts before embarking on an innkeeping career, and Jeff serve a breakfast to remember. Egg and crab strata was featured the morning of our visit. Crispy french toast with vanilla sauce and fruit compote was on tap the next day. Complimentary wine and hors d'oeuvres are offered in the afternoon. "Taste of Maine" culinary weekends are scheduled in the off-season.

(207) 288-4234 or (866) 782-9224. www.basscottage.com. Ten rooms with private baths. Doubles, $225 to $340. Two-night minimum at peak periods. Closed mid-December to mid-May.

Ullikana Bed & Breakfast, 16 The Field, Bar Harbor 04609.

Caring innkeepers have transformed this summery,Tudor-style manse into a B&B, razing the back of the house and rebuilding to provide three guest rooms with balconies and porches overlooking the water. Transplanted New Yorkers Roy Kasindorf and his Quebec City-born wife, Hélène Harton, also added the professional kitchen of her dreams, with windows onto the water and a location next to the outdoor terrace where she plies her guests with some of the best breakfasts ever. The inn is not directly on the water but tucked away in the trees between the Bar Harbor Inn and "the field," a meadow of wildflowers. Ten bedrooms in the main house come with lots of chintz, wicker and antiques; some have balconies, fireplaces or both. One dubbed Audrey's Room (for Roy's daughter) on the third floor contains two antique beds joined as a kingsize and a clawfoot tub with its original fixtures, from which the bather can look out a low window onto Frenchman Bay. We were happily ensconced in the second-floor Room 5, a majestic space outfitted in country French provincial fabrics with king bed, two wing chairs in front of the fireplace and a water-view balcony upon which to relax and enjoy the passing parade. Interesting art graces the wicker-furnished parlor and a dining room with shelves full of colorful Italian breakfast china. At breakfast, Roy is the waiter and raconteur, doling out – in our case – cantaloupe with mint sauce, superior cinnamon-raisin muffins with orange glaze, and puff pancakes yielding blueberries and raspberries. Lately, Roy and Hélène added six more guest rooms in the summery Yellow House across the street.

(207) 288-9552. Fax (207) 288-3682. www.ullikana.com. Sixteen rooms with private baths. Doubles, $180 to $295. Closed November-April.

Bar Harbor Tides B&B, 119 West St., Bar Harbor 04609.
This 1887 Greek Revival mansion facing Frenchman Bay spoke to Ray and Loretta Harris when they came up from Virginia in 1999 to close their camp for the season in Maine. "We became infatuated with the location and view," Loretta said of the B&B listed on the National Register. So they bought it and undertook extensive redecorating. They redid all the carpeting and wallpaper, removed 96 pairs of indoor shutters to let in more light and furnished in high style. A sensational veranda, complete with its own fireplace, wraps around a dining room with a table for twelve beneath a crystal chandelier, as well as a formal living room and an entry foyer. Guests also have use of an upstairs sitting room with a huge sofa in front of a fireplace. Lodging is in three suites, each with an oceanfront bedroom with kingsize bed and a sitting room with TV. Two on the second floor have fireplaces. The 320-count sheets feel like you're going to bed in silk, says Loretta. We stayed in the master suite where the massive four-poster bed looks onto the sea through a picture window and the ample bath has a clawfoot tub and oversize tiled shower. Every room in the ocean suite has a water view, even the bathroom; other attributes are a tiny balcony and a living room of Victorian oak with fireplace and TV in a cabinet. The third-floor Captain's Suite has the best view of the bay. Also available as an economical option is the Mate's Room with queen poster bed and TV. Elaborate breakfasts are served amid much linen, crystal and silver. Cheese blintzes with strawberries and vegetable omelets were the fare at our visit. Afternoon hors d'oeuvres and wine are served on the veranda, with the water in full view. The one-and-a-half-acre property, with lovely rolling green lawns and landscaped with old lilac trees and Japanese maples, has 156 feet of bay frontage.

(207) 288-4968. www.barharbortides.com. One room and three suites with private baths. Double, $225. Suites, $375 to $395. Two-night minimum.

Balance Rock Inn, 21 Albert Meadow, Bar Harbor 04609.
This gray-shingled masterpiece, built in 1903 and facing the ocean across a pool and an acre of lawns and gardens, has evolved from a B&B into a showy and urbane small hotel. It's run by the owners of the rather glitzy Ledgelawn Inn in town. The glitz continues here with double whirlpool tubs, steam baths, a gym and health club, and a small poolside Veranda Bar featuring cigars as well as drinks. "Definitely the fanciest place to stay in Bar Harbor – no question about it," claims owner Michael Miles, who made it so. The mansion has thirteen guest rooms, all but three with water views. A $700,000 wing with an elevator holds three sumptuous suites. Leading a tour, Michael pointed out features of the guest rooms furnished in reproduction antique furniture: all queen or king beds, 300-count sheets, twelve working fireplaces, fancy wing chairs, TV/VCRs, telephones, Gilbert & Soames toiletries in the bathrooms, a few private decks (one "the size of a bowling alley"), and Andean sweaters for sale in the small lobby shop. His favorite room is also David Letterman's: a third-floor hideaway with a sauna overlooking the ocean and, up a boat ladder, a private rooftop deck. A big breakfast buffet "that goes on and

on" is presented in a cozy breakfast room with six tables; in summer, most take it on trays to the terrace beside the pool. Tea and cookies are available in the afternoon, and turndown service is provided upon request.

(207) 288-2610 or (800) 753-0494. Fax (207) 288-2610. www.barharborvacations.com. Thirteen rooms and three suites. Doubles, $255 to $525. Suites, $495 to $625. Closed November-April.

Lindenwood Inn, 118 Clark Point Road, Box 1328, Southwest Harbor 04679.

Most of the eight appealing accommodations here have water views, but all have access to the waterfront – a rare commodity for a B&B on the island, according to owner Jim King. Guests can enjoy the working harbor from the property's shoreline, or walk along a short path to the town docks. Jim, who opened the Kingsleigh Inn here earlier, returned from traveling around the world to purchase the Lindenwood, a turn-of-the-century sea captain's home shaded by towering linden trees. With a decorator's eye, international tastes and an assortment of cosmopolitan possessions, he redid the entire place. "We don't have New England decor here," he asserts, "and people love it." He splashed around lots of color, from walls to down comforters to carpets. He added potted cactus plants on the tables and a collection of shells and stones in each of eight guest quarters in the main inn, six of which have private decks with harbor views. The ultimate is the penthouse suite, which opens onto an enormous rooftop deck holding an oversize spa. He also offers a poolside bungalow that we found ever so inviting, with a TV in the cathedral-ceilinged living room, an efficiency kitchen and a queensize bedroom. Just outside was a heated gunite pool and a separate spa topped by a sculptured mask spraying a stream of water. Elaborate breakfasts, perhaps herbed omelets or fruit crêpes, are served in the main dining room furnished in what Jim calls "tropical primitive."

(207) 244-5335 or (800) 307-5335. Fax (207) 244-3643. www.lindenwoodinn.com. Four rooms, three suites and one cottage with private baths. Doubles, $105 to $275. Closed mid-December to mid-March.

The Kingsleigh Inn, 373 Main St., Box 1426, Southwest Harbor 04679.

An unusual pebbledash stucco-stone exterior with a great wraparound porch full of wicker and colorful pillows houses one of the area's more inviting B&Bs. Taking over the B&B in which Lindenwood Inn owner Jim King got his start (and left his name), Dana and Greg Moos from Maryland redecorated the common rooms with an eclectic mix of antiques and contemporary furnishings. More antiques and artworks enhance the eight bedrooms, many with harbor views. One has a balcony with chairs overlooking the water, and another a deck. The Turret Suite on the third floor offers a kingsize poster bed, fireplace, television and a great view from a telescope placed on a tripod between two cozy wicker chairs. Port wine and homemade truffles are in each room. Afternoon tea and homemade cookies are served on the porch or in cool weather by the fireplace. Breakfast by candlelight, considered by Dana "a special occasion," is taken at tables for two in the dining room. Her repertoire includes individual egg soufflés with roasted red pepper sauce, baked eggs in ham crisps and bananas foster stuffed french toast.

(207) 244-5302. Fax (207) 244-0349. www.kingsleighinn.com. Seven rooms and one suite with private baths. Doubles, $130 to $160. Suite, $260.

The Moorings Inn & Cottages, Shore Road, Southwest Harbor 04679.

Calling itself the "Little Norway of America," the Moorings claims one of the island's more dazzling locations at the entrance to Somes Sound in Manset, not far from Southwest Harbor and next to the famed Hinckley boatyards. It's a quirky, down-home, old-fashioned place with ten bedrooms, all named for sailing ships built in Maine. The complex also has three rooms with decks, refrigerators and microwaves in a motel wing out back, the two-bedroom Pilot House and three efficiencies in the Lookout Cottage. Five of the upstairs inn rooms offer waterfront balconies, and the view from the end motel unit is billed as "probably the finest on the coast." We called our inn room the Agatha Christie, as several of her paperbacks were on the bureau, and a candle rested in a china holder beside the bed. Towels are large and fluffy and the mostly double or twin beds bear colorful patterned sheets. The fireplace glows on cool summer mornings in the inn's living room, which has a color TV and abundant books and magazines. The coffee pot is on all day in the inn's office, where complimentary orange juice and donuts are served in the morning. Longtime owners Leslie and Betty King have turned over day-to-day operations to son Storey, who runs a tour boat service, and his wife Candy. They provide charcoal for the grills beside the shore, a spectacular place to cook your steak or seafood dinner. You can rent canoes, rowboats and sailboats, and borrow clamming equipment. The beach is stony; the water cold but swimmable. The Moorings is most unpretentious and the prices are, too.

(207) 244-5523 or (800) 596-5523. www.mooringsinn.com. Ten rooms and four cottage units with private baths. Doubles, $87 to $120. Cottages, $105 to $150.

Hotels/Motor Inns

Bar Harbor Inn, Newport Drive, Bar Harbor 04609.

The prime location in Bar Harbor is occupied by this large and totally renovated complex that began life following the 1947 fire as a hotel and motor inn. Now it better reflects owner David Witham's vision for luxurious accommodations on the most watery spot in town – eight landscaped acres with the island-studded sea on two sides. Rebuilt in 2000, the main inn features a wing with 43 deluxe jacuzzi rooms, all with king or queen beds and most with fireplaces and bayfront balconies. Some of the older inn rooms over the lobby are enormous and nicely refurnished in Colonial elegance. We're partial to the 64-room oceanfront lodge, closest to the shore and constructed on the site of the original motel. The lodge was totally refurbished in 1999 and offers rooms with kingsize or two queen beds, sitting areas and private balconies with stunning views of rocks, water and islands. We didn't realize there was such a pleasant public Shore Path around the point along Frenchman Bay until we stayed here. The original modest motel was moved uphill, only to be razed and rebuilt. Now known as the Newport Building, it has 38 rooms with king or queen beds and patios or decks overlooking the grounds, but lacking water views. There's a large heated pool, as well as a small public beach adjacent. A complimentary continental breakfast is served in the lobby of the oceanfront lodge, which has several prime rooms on a new third level. Lunch and dinner are available at the outdoor **Terrace Grill** or the striking, windowed **Reading Room** (see Where to Eat).

(207) 288-3351 or (800) 248-3351. www.barharborinn.com. One hundred forty-two rooms and eleven suites with private baths. Doubles, $199 to $369. Closed Thanksgiving to early April.

Harborside Hotel & Marina, 55 West St., Bar Harbor 04605.

The legendary Bar Harbor Club has been incorporated into this showy new hotel and resort complex at water's edge in downtown Bar Harbor. Tom Walsh, who numbers the Bar Harbor Regency among his growing empire, spent many millions converting the aging Golden Anchor Motel complex into an urbane oceanfront resort worthy of the site. It now stretches along the waterfront from The Pier Restaurant to the spa, fitness and meeting facility in the old Bar Harbor Club. The half-timbered Tudor look of the historic club and casino has been incorporated into the architecturally interesting, three-story hotel, which sprawls in long corridors opening from a mahogany paneled lobby with a marble floor. All 185 hotel-style rooms and suites have full or partial water views, best enjoyed from good-looking balconies or patios laden with colorful plantings. Suites come with fireplaces, kitchens and whirlpool tubs. A heated pool and hot tub are stunningly located in a courtyard area between the hotel and **Pier Restaurant,** overlooking the marina. A fine-dining restaurant was planned in the Bar Harbor Club property in 2005 to compliment the casual Pier Restaurant.

(207) 288-5033 or (800) 328-5033. www.theharborsidehotel.com. One hundred eighty-five rooms. Doubles, $209 to $300. Suites, $325 to $950. Closed November to early May.

Bar Harbor Regency/Holiday Inn Sunspree Resort, 123 Eden St., Bar Harbor 04609.

Erected in 1986 by Ocean Properties of Florida, the luxury Regency structure became a Holiday Inn franchise in 1990 and later was made a Sunspree resort, which accounts for the long-winded name. The four floors of its main building contain 180 rooms, all rather sophisticated for Downeast Mane (there's even a glass-enclosed elevator from which to view Frenchman Bay). The Tiki Bar in a gazebo beside the pool at water's edge offers lunch and drinks. **Stewman's Lobster Pound** claims to be Bar Harbor's only waterfront lobster pound. The **Edenfield** dining room, with windows onto the water, offers a standard seafood menu. The waterfront grounds include a large and angular pool beside the water, two hot tubs and a sauna, a fitness center, a walking path, two lighted tennis courts, a putting green and docking facilities.

(207) 288-9723 or (800) 234-6835. Fax (207) 288-3089. www.barharborholidayinn.com. Two hundred nineteen rooms and two suites. Doubles, $139 to $275.

Atlantic Oakes By-the-Sea, 119 Eden St. (Route 3), Bar Harbor 04609.

Right beside the Nova Scotia ferry terminal on the estate that belonged to Sir Harry Oakes is this good-looking resort complex. It includes 42 ocean-view rooms in a four-story building and the restored **Willows Mansion at the Oakes,** which operates as a B&B with seven guest rooms, four with oceanfront porches, and a two-bedroom suite. We prefer the older, low-slung, brown-shingled motel buildings right beside Frenchman Bay, their private balconies or patios enjoying privacy as well as quiet. The attractive grounds include five tennis courts (two of them lighted and with a tennis pro in residence), a heated pool and a pebbly beach with a float and a pier, where boats may be rented and sailing lessons are given. There's also an indoor pool. B&B guests are served a complimentary breakfast in the mansion each morning. Lobster cookouts and clambakes are available several nights a week. Always on the move, owner Sonny Cough built the four-story **Atlantic Eyrie Lodge** atop a cliff across the street, and lately acquired most of **The Bayview** hotel and condominium complex nearby.

(207) 288-5801 or (800) 336-2463. www.barharbor.com. One hundred fifty-one rooms and two suites. Doubles, $162 to $198. Mansion, $159 to $305. Mansion and some small buildings closed in winter.

Park Entrance Oceanfront Motel, 15 Ocean Drive, Bar Harbor 04609.

Situated on a manicured hillside opposite the main national park entrance, this established motel was in transition, rescued from bankruptcy by the local group that owns the Bar Harbor Regency and the Harborside Hotel & Marina. It's been a low-key kind of place, away from town on a ten-acre peninsula with a quarter mile of coastline to enjoy. Each room yields an ocean view, and the wide lawns slope down to a pebble beach graced by a pier and some of the biggest mussels we have seen, ready for gathering by the handful at low tide. Rowboats are free, the outdoor pool is heated (there's a hot tub as well), picnic tables and grills are available for cookouts, and there are an eighteen-hole putting green, croquet court and volleyball area. The rooms on two floors are comfortable, and five efficiencies are available.

(207) 288-9703 or (800) 288-9703. www.parkentrance.com. Fifty-eight rooms. Doubles, $119 to $265. Closed late October to late April.

Asticou Inn, Route 3, Northeast Harbor 04662.

A wonderful old resort hotel popular with those who prefer to be away from the hustle and bustle of Bar Harbor is the Asticou, which dates to 1883 but is up to date and elegant in an old-fashioned way. The setting high above the harbor is exceptional, with a swimming pool, tennis court and well-tended lawns and gardens sloping toward the sea. Cheerful, pleasant common rooms with oriental rugs and wingback chairs welcome guests, some of whom have been coming here for extended stays for the last fifty years. They stay in the inn's 30 simple rooms and suites on the second, third and fourth floors (four with private balconies viewing the water) or in outlying rooms in Cranberry Lodge, guest houses and the circular Topsider cottages – six of the most deluxe, with water views. The outdoor deck off the cocktail lounge is a great place from which to view the harbor goings-on in the distance. The MAP Meal plan is no longer required – nor are jackets and ties in the dining room (see Where to Eat) – as the inn continues to evolve with the times. A deluxe continental breakfast buffet is included in the rates.

(207) 276-3344 or (800) 258-3373. www.asticou.com. Forty-seven rooms and suites with private baths. Doubles, $225 to $325. Two-night minimum in season. Closed mid-October to mid-May.

The Claremont Hotel, Clark Point Road, Box 137, Southwest Harbor 04679.

The broad lawns outside this century-old hotel sloping down to Somes Sound invite relaxation. And relax the guests do – in Adirondack chairs scattered about, in a rope hammock tied between two trees, on the championship croquet layout and on the wraparound porch overlooking it all. The island's oldest hotel had only three owners in its first century and retains a palpable sense of upper-crust tradition. The main yellow building holds 24 guest rooms, most recently renovated with heat and full baths; furnishings remain simple yet comfortable. Seven more rooms and two suites are offered in two guest houses and the Cole Cottage. Available for longer stays are thirteen housekeeping cottages with living rooms, franklin or stone fireplaces and decks, and two guest houses. Besides croquet, boating and tennis are offered, and the hardy can swim from the dock in Somes Sound. Every table enjoys a water view in the dining room (see Where to Eat).

(207) 244-5036 or (800) 244-5036. Fax (207) 244-3512. www.theclaremonthotel.com. Thirty-one rooms, two suites and thirteen cottages with private baths. Doubles, $229 to $245 MAP, $175 B&B. Cottages, $180 to $250 EP, three-night minimum. Closed mid-October to Memorial Day.

Cottages, Motel Units and Camping

You'll find more old-fashioned cabins and cottage colonies (and motels) along the approaches to Acadia National Park and Bar Harbor than you thought existed. Even in high season if you arrive without a reservation, you'll probably be able to find room in one.

A few of the better choices:

Emery's Cottages on the Shore, Sand Point Road, Box 172C, Bar Harbor 04609.
In a quiet, wooded setting a bit off the beaten path, this attractive complex is probably the nicest. It has fourteen housekeeping and seven sleeping cottages, the latter closest to the water. All have electric heat, cable TV and private baths, most with tub-shower combinations. The sleeping cottages come with a queensize bed and a refrigerator; some of the efficiencies have kingsize beds. A pleasant lawn leads to a gravel beach. Lawn chairs, picnic tables and grills are provided.

(207) 288-3432 or (888) 240-3432. www.emeryscottages.com. Twenty-one cottages. Weekly rates for two, non-housekeeping $530 to $635; efficiencies, $670 to $1,040; daily rates off-season and when available. Closed late October to early May.

Edgewater Motel & Cottages, Salisbury Cove, Box 566, Bar Harbor 04609.
A cove-front location well off the highway commends this 23-unit mix of efficiency cottages and a two-story motel, 50 feet from water's edge. Four of the motel's spacious, paneled rooms have fireplaces, kitchens and kingsize beds. Each cottage has its own deck facing the water.

(207) 288-3491 or (888) 310-9920. www.edgewaterbarharbor.com. Eight motel rooms and fifteen cottages. Doubles, $104 to $155 nightly, $690 to $950 weekly. Closed November-March.

Harbor View Motel & Cottages, 11 Ocean Way, Southwest Harbor 04679.
Hidden away from the road on property facing the harbor, this old-timer has eighteen motel units, fourteen with decks overlooking the harbor. The best are nine in the newer main building with decks or balconies facing the harbor head-on. With queensize beds and TV, these represent some of the better oceanfront values on the island. Six more motel units in the older south building have decks perpendicular to the shore, but those in the dreary-by-comparison north building have no outside quarters at all. Three efficiency units have decks overlooking the harbor. One on the third floor is suitable for four. Also available are seven cottages sleeping up to six, all with water views.

(207) 244-5031 or (800) 538-6463. Twenty-one rooms and seven cottages. Doubles, $73 to $125. Cottages, $645 to $900 weekly. Closed late October to mid-May.

CAMPING. Mount Desert Island is a paradise for campers, and five private campgrounds are happy to oblige in Bar Harbor. Closest to town in Salisbury Cove is **Bar Harbor Campground,** whose rates of $22 to $30 a night are typical. **Mount Desert Narrows Campground** is the only one on the ocean. Purists prefer the two campgrounds in Acadia National Park – **Blackwoods,** with 300 campsites five miles south of Bar Harbor off Route 3, and **Seawall,** with 200 sites off Route 102A four miles south of Southwest Harbor. Both are in woods near the ocean, and offer naturalist talks and special activities. Fees are $20 a night; walk-in sites at Seawall are $14. Blackwoods is open year-round and sites are by reservation from mid-June to mid-September, (800) 367-2267; Seawall is open Memorial Day through September, first-come, first-served.

Seeing and Doing ⎯⎯⎯⎯⎯⎯ ♫♫♫

Acadia National Park, the largest national park in the East, is Mount Desert Island's big draw. It encompasses 44 miles of dramatic coastline, all the island's major mountains, part of the Somes Sound fjord, all or part of every major lake shore, 120 miles of trails and bike paths, and a scenic 27-mile Park Loop Road that allows drivers to see the highlights.

The **Visitor Center** on Route 3 south of Hull's Cove is a must for orientation purposes. Up a two-minute walk from the parking area is a rustic contemporary building in which a fifteen-minute movie is shown on the half hour, park rangers offer advice about trips and naturalist programs, and you can rent a self-guiding cassette-tape tour of the park. Here also you get your first panoramic view of Frenchman Bay from on high.

(207) 288-3338. Visitor Center open daily 8 to 6, July-August; 8 to 4:30, May-June and September-October. Park open year-round. Admission by weekly pass, $20 per car. Annual pass, $40.

PARK LOOP ROAD. Starting from the Visitor Center, the 27-mile loop can take three hours (with stops) or up to a day. The two-lane, limited-access roadway can be entered or exited at several locations, but the Ocean Drive segment is one-way outbound. The first two overlooks provide good views of Frenchman Bay, Bar Harbor and the area burned in the 1947 fire.

Sieur de Monts Spring, covered by a small octagonal structure but still bubbling water from a fountain in the adjacent nature center, is a favorite stop. Here is the original **Abbe Museum** (there's a newer branch in downtown Bar Harbor), whose Native American artifacts span 12,000 years (adults $2, children 50 cents). The wonderful **Wild Gardens of Acadia** has more than 500 plants indigenous to the area's forests, mountains and shores labeled and grouped in thirteen sections, from deciduous weeds to dry heath and bog. Well-maintained gravel paths lead past some rare specimens, with benches placed strategically along the way. (If the Wild Gardens whet your appetite, stop later at the showy **Asticou Terrace and Thuya Gardens** plus the remarkable **Asticou Azalea Gardens** in Northeast Harbor.)

The 1.4-mile **Precipice Trail,** sometimes closed when peregrine falcons are nesting in its ledges, rises sharply from the Champlain Mountain overlook. The males in our family climbed it and returned with the report that it took 90 minutes to get up, 40 minutes to come down, and that there were two tunnels and countless firemen-type ladders to traverse, with sheer drops to contemplate. The wild blueberries along the way and the view from the barren summit made the effort worthwhile.

Going from the sublime to the ridiculous, cool off after your climb at **Sand Beach,** the only saltwater beach in the park and an arc of sand between two cliffs. You may notice dozens of people on the beach and only a few brave souls in the ocean. Feel it and you'll know why; the water temperature rarely tops 55 degrees. If you like to get numb, head for the changing room, don your suit and c'mon in, the surf's fine. Otherwise, soak up some sun – if it's not obliterated by fog – or hike the easy 1.8-mile Ocean Path along the water.

Thunder Hole is where the waves rush into a small cave and roar out with a thunderous sound, when tides and surf coincide – the best time to hear it is at three-quarter rising tide when the sea is rough. At the 100-foot-high **Otter Cliffs,** look out to sea from the highest headlands on the East Coast. Beyond is **Otter Point,** a rocky place good for sunning and picnicking. Marked by wooden stairs leading to the water, **Little Hunters Beach** is a steeply pitched cove lined with cobblestones polished by the pounding surf.

Leaving the ocean, the Park Loop Road turns inland toward **Jordan Pond.** Stop for lunch or tea at the venerable Jordan Pond House (see Where to Eat) and admire the view of the two rounded mountains known as the **Bubbles** (named long ago by a youth for the bosom of his amour). At the end of Jordan Pond is a huge boulder balancing atop a cliff.

Pass beautiful **Eagle Lake,** which gets smaller and bluer as you drive the 3.2-mile side trip up **Cadillac Mountain,** at 1,530 feet the highest point on the Atlantic

Seaboard. The road is excellent and gradual (an eight percent grade, which our sons happily bicycled up) and the view from the top is incredible in all directions. A short summit trail has interesting interpretive markers. The Sunset Parking Area near the top is where everyone gathers to watch the sunset – the mountains and waters to the west a changing rainbow of greens, blues, oranges and reds. It's an enlightening sight for anyone who thinks Key West or Carmel sunsets are the ultimate.

Descend Cadillac Mountain and you've completed the loop. Follow the signs to Bar Harbor or other destinations.

OTHER DRIVES. So far, you've seen only a portion of the park, albeit the most popular part. Head for Northeast Harbor and **Sargent Drive,** which borders **Somes Sound,** the only fjord on the East Coast. There are spectacular views all the way around to quaint **Somesville.** Down the west side of Somes Sound is **Echo Lake,** which offers a fine beach, changing rooms, and water far warmer than the ocean. It's a short hike or a long drive around Echo Lake to **Beech Cliff,** which has a great view of the lake below and where if you holler, you may hear your echo. Farther down the peninsula past Southwest Harbor is a section of the park containing **Seawall, Wonderland,** the **Ship Harbor Nature Trail** (which is well worth taking), and the **Bass Harbor Light.** Visit **Bass Harbor** and **Bernard,** the most authentic fishing communities on the island. These are the high spots of Acadia National Park on Mount Desert Island. Other sections of the park are off-island on Isle au Haut and on the mainland Schoodic Peninsula.

It's a long way around, but don't miss the remote **Schoodic Peninsula.** Drive around fashionable **Winter Harbor** to see how the other half lives before heading down the six-mile, one-way loop around **Schoodic Point,** where the crashing surf is awesome. We could spend hours here watching gulls, climbing rocks, viewing Mount Desert Island across the way, admiring passing lobster boats and generally chilling out. The park offers plenty of space for picnics and privacy.

CARRIAGE PATHS. Fifty-seven miles of scenic, tranquil carriage paths were planned and built by John D. Rockefeller Jr. in the 1920s to provide a refuge for carriages from the intrusions of the auto. The ten-foot-wide paths follow the land's contours, protected by stone culverts and retaining walls and notable for thirteen interesting, hand-cut stone bridges. About eighteen miles of the cut-stone paths have been specially surfaced for bicycles; the rest are better for hikers, mountain bikers and horseback riders.

NATURALIST PROGRAMS. The park conducts a remarkable range of programs and tours, from boat cruises to mountain hikes to nature walks to evening activities. They follow a set daily schedule (available from the Park Visitor Center), usually starting with a three-hour birder's walk at 7 a.m. and ending at 9 p.m. with a Seawall Amphitheater program. Among the more appealing titles are Forests of Lilliput, Mr. Rockefeller's Bridges Walk, Life Between the Tides, Trees along the Trail and Secrets of the Summit. The park naturalists and their assistants are engaging and enlightening, and we've enjoyed every tour or program we've tried.

Active Pursuits

BIKING. Although the terrain is hilly, biking opportunities abound throughout Acadia National Park and Mount Desert Island. The park visitor center offers detailed maps of roads and trails through the park. Cyclists can take the same routes as listed above on the Park Loop and other drives. They can get away from cars and trailers on the park's carriage paths. The Eagle Lake-Witch Hole Loop is a five-hour carriage park ride with spectacular views of lakes, mountains and ocean. For shore-viewing, bike the road to Seawall and Wonderland. A longer excursion is to take the 40-minute ferry ride from Bass Harbor to **Swan's Island.** We picnicked in an eerie fog at deserted Hockamock Head Lighthouse high on a cliff with a bell buoy ringing off shore and an abundance of raspberries, blueberries and gooseberries waiting to be picked. Swan's Island seems not to have a level stretch, however, and pedaling up all the hills isn't easy for aging legs. Bicycles are available for rent in Bar Harbor at Bar Harbor Bicycle Shop, 141 Cottage St., and Acadia Bike, 48 Cottage St., and in Southwest Harbor at Southwest Cycle, Main Street.

HIKING. Besides 50 miles of carriage paths, 120 miles of hiking trails await the hiker. They vary from mountain climbs (naturalists lead hikes up Acadia and Gorham and Huguenot Head) to self-guided walks for casual strollers – the Jordan Pond nature path and the Ships Harbor nature trail. A favorite is the gently rolling **Ocean Trail,** a 3.6-mile footpath along the rocky shore beside Frenchman Bay from Sand Beach to Otter Cliffs.

CANOEING AND KAYAKING. Locals recommend Long Pond, the island's largest with three access points; secluded Seal Cove Pond, Echo Lake, Eagle Lake and Jordan Pond. Tidal currents in Somes Sound are dangerous for light craft; you also might be surprised by frolicking porpoises. Canoeing the Bass Harbor Marsh at high tide is quite an experience, especially on a moonlit night when you may hear and see herons, owls, beavers and deer. Canoes and kayaks may be rented in Bar Harbor from **Acadia Outfitters** at 106 Cottage St., **Cadillac Mountain Sports** at 26 Cottage St. or **National Park Canoe & Kayak Rentals** at Pond's End in Somesville. **Coastal Kayaking Tours** at 48 Cottage St. is the oldest among nearly a dozen outfits offering sea kayak tours.

SWIMMING. The only ocean beach is **Sand Beach** (see Acadia National Park). Lifeguards staff it and the park's **Echo Lake.** Outside the park, there's saltwater swimming at the pleasant little town beach in Seal Harbor (changing facilities, but no lifeguards). Explore or ask around and you may come upon a little beach or swimming area on other of the numerous freshwater lakes. If you're adventurous (some would say foolhardy), you can swim off the rocks or in the coves of Frenchman Bay.

Walk the Bar. For two hours on either side of low tide, you can walk across a sand bar from the end of Bar Harbor's Bridge Street to Bar Island. There are trails and shoreline to explore, and the shallow water is considerably warmer than at Sand Beach. Bring a picnic and a bathing suit, but don't tarry or you may have to swim back against the current.

The **Shore Path** appeals to less adventurous types. The oceanside path flanks the eastern shore from the Town Pier near the end of Main Street, passing parklands and mansions before ending in a residential section.

Boat Cruises

NATURE CRUISES. Park naturalists conduct cruises aboard privately owned boats, and these are among the more informative of all the island's cruises.

The Acadian, 1 West St., Bar Harbor, (207) 288-2386, offers four nature cruises daily around Frenchman Bay, sighting eagles, seals and porpoises.

Sea Princess Cruises, Northeast Harbor, (207) 276-5352, has naturalists aboard its three-hour morning and afternoon nature cruises around Great Harbor and Somes Sound Fjord, each with a stop in Islesford on Little Cranberry Island; adults $18, children $12. The Sea Princess also has an afternoon Somes Sound Fjord cruise and a three-hour sunset cruise around the Cranberry Isles with optional dinner (adults

$15, children $10). In the middle of the sunset cruise, dinner at the Islesford Dock Restaurant on the wharf is a waterside treat not to be missed.

The **Dive-In Theater Boat,** 55 West St., Bar Harbor, (207) 288-3483, gives three-hour cruises with a ranger around Frenchman Bay three times daily. Passengers watch a real-time underwater video as a diver searches the sea bottom for marine life to bring aboard the boat for discussion; adults $33.50, children $23.50.

Island Cruises, Little Island Way, Bass Harbor, (207) 244-5785, schedules a daily cruise to the fishing village of Frenchboro on Long Island, including a guided walking tour and optional lunch (adults $25, children $15). There's also a two-hour afternoon nature tour around the islands of Blue Hill Bay (adults $20, children $15).

Cranberry Cove Ferry, Upper Town Dock, Southwest Harbor, (207) 244-5882, runs six passenger ferry trips daily to the Cranberry Islands; adults $16 round trip, children $10.

The **Bar Harbor Ferry Co.,** (207) 288-2984, offers up to ten round trips daily from the Bar Harbor Inn pier to Winter Harbor, where a free Island Explorer bus runs seasonally out to Schoodic Point; adults $24, children $15.

The **Lulu,** a traditional Downeast lobster boat, offers lobster fishing and seal watching rides daily from 55 West St., Bar Harbor, (207) 963-2341; adults $25, children $15.

Great Harbor Tours, Clark Point Road, Southwest Harbor, (207) 460-5200, offers several cruises on the Elizabeth T, a 34-foot lobster boat built on Mount Desert Island. Among them are a lunch cruise to Cranberry Island three days a week (adults $25, children $15) and a four-hour sightseeing cruise to Baker Island the other days (adults $35, children $20).

You can also ride the **Sea Queen,** a combined mail boat and ferry service, which makes six trips daily to the Cranberry Islands from the municipal pier in Northeast Harbor, (207) 244-3575. Round-trip fares: adults $14, children $7.

WHALE WATCH CRUISES. Bar Harbor Whale Watch Co., 1 West St., (207) 288-2386 or (800) 942-5374, offers three-hour whale watching and 3½-hour combination puffin and whale watching excursions aboard the jet-powered, 112-foot catamaran Friendship V, daily early June to mid-October; whale trips, adults $45, children $25.

Acadian Whale Adventures, 55 West St., (207) 288-9800 or (888) 533-9253, gives approximately three-hour tours two or three times daily aboard a 100-foot catamaran, billed as the fastest and most luxurious jet-powered boat of its type in North America; adults $45, children $25.

WINDJAMMER CRUISES. Considered best by those in the know are the 2½-hour cruises four times daily from the Bar Harbor Regency marina aboard the 67-foot schooner **Rachel B. Jackson,** (207) 288-2216 or (888) 405-7245; adults $30, children $20. It also offers overnight stays called Boat & Breakfast for $175 a person.

The 151-foot, four-masted schooner **Margaret Todd,** 27 Main St., Bar Harbor, (207) 288-4585, offers two-hour morning, afternoon and sunset cruises around Frenchman Bay from the Bar Harbor Inn pier; adults $29.50, children $19.50.

Yachtsmen are in their element in Southwest Harbor, which offers the Great Harbor Marina complex and six boatyards. The marina drew sailors from around the world as host of the annual International Wooden Boat Show in 1994 and 1995. The famed **Hinckley Company** produces multi-million-dollar yachts here among its output of twelve to fifteen custom boats a year. The facility is not open for tours, but visitors can view a video that shows the yacht-building process from start to finish and are free to walk around the working boat yard in Manset.

Other Attractions

MUSEUMS. The biggest is the **Mount Desert Oceanarium,** now at two locations on the island. The original Oceanarium in a former ship's chandlery along the working waterfront off Clark Point Road, Southwest Harbor, (207) 244-7330, offers much of interest to young and old. It consists of a marine aquarium with a touch tank and a fisherman's museum. The Mills family owners are particularly involved in enhancing Maine's lobster industry. Lately, they established the **Bar Harbor Oceanarium,** off Route 3 at the entrance to Mount Desert Island, (207) 288-5005, where visitors can board a lobster boat, see harbor seals in a 50,000-gallon tank, explore the Maine Lobster Museum, tour a lobster hatchery and study the ecosystem along the Thomas Bay Marsh Walk. Both facilities are open Monday-Saturday 9 to 5, Memorial Day to mid-October. Bar Harbor: adults $9.95, children $6.95. Mount Desert: adults $6.95, children $4.75. Combination ticket, adults $13, children $9.65.

The **George B. Dorr Museum of Natural History** on the College of the Atlantic campus at 105 Eden St., Bar Harbor, (207) 288-5015, contains exhibits depicting the island's marine mammal, seabird and plant life. Visitors are encouraged to disassemble and reassemble the backbone of a twenty-foot whale skeleton and to walk nature trails. Open Monday-Saturday 9 to 5, mid-June to Labor Day, Thursday-Sunday 1 to 4 and Saturday 10 to 4 rest of year. Adults $3.50, children $1.

The **Wendell Gilley Museum,** Main Street and Herrick Road, Southwest Harbor, (207) 244-7555, honors the late nationally known bird carver from Southwest Harbor. The life-size wood carving of a bald eagle in the entry rotunda looks like a mounted bird, but it and the other 200 bird carvings in the museum's collection were created by Wendell Gilley. Changing wildlife exhibits, carving demonstrations and an excellent shop are among the attractions; open Tuesday-Sunday 10 to 5, July and August, 10 to 4 in June and September; Friday-Sunday 10 to 4 in May and November-December; adults $5, children $2.

SHOPPING. Bar Harbor shops are concentrated along Main, Cottage and Mount Desert streets. **Island Artisans,** a co-op, is owned by the two dozen artists who are represented in the handsome shop by a variety of wares, and we do a little Christmas shopping here when we're in town. The Bar Harbor headquarters of the **Acadia Shops,** which also are located in the national park and at the Jordan Pond House, features the crafts, gifts and foods of Maine. Natural gifts and accessories, from rock vases to porch rockers, are available at **Window Panes. The Happy Clam** carries nifty accents for the home and garden, and **Sherman's** is known for books. **Cool as a Moose** is where to get a bathing suit or a T-shirt. **Sunrise Clothing and Jewelry** speaks for itself. **Domus Isle** combines music, gifts and wines. **Porcupine Island Co.** at 4 Cottage St. claims the largest selection of made-in-Maine specialty foods in the state. **J.H. Butterfield Co.** is a gourmet grocery store of the old school (and they will put up a delightful picnic for you).

In Northeast Harbor, two of our perennial favorites are the **Kimball Shop and Boutique,** with room after room of housewares and clothing and anything else that's in, and **Smart Studio and Gallery,** featuring Wini Smart's evocative paintings of Maine. **The Romantic Room** carries a range from Lily Pulitzer and straw hats to wicker furniture and brass beds. Margaret Hammond at **Local Color** offers hand-painted woven clothing, soft and elegant in jewel-like colors and like nothing we've seen anywhere else, and fabulous rugs starting at about $975 for a tiny one.

Southwest Harbor seems to attract more shops every year. We're partial to **Hot Flash Anny's** for stained-glass pieces and the **Little Notch Bakery** for superb breads. **The Sand Castle Ocean & Nature Store** features the works of more than 60

Maine artisans. **MDI Sportswear** has clothing and accessories. A must stop for book lovers and water lovers is **Port in a Storm Bookstore** in Somesville, Here, in a restored general store at the end of Somes Sound, are two floors of books, many displayed the way they ought to be on slanted shelves around an atrium. Two resident cats and a pair of binoculars occupy a rear reading area with windows onto the water.

Where to Eat

For such a watery area, precious few good restaurants are located on the water, or even claim water views. Some restaurants not near the water offer better food and/ or value. Everyone seems to come to Maine for lobster, and Mount Desert Island and its approach road obliges with all manner of lobster venues, from basic lobster pound to elegant restaurants. Frankly, we can't imagine wrestling with lobster in a fancy restaurant, and much prefer authentic lobster places that are located all around. The restaurants included here, all with water views, cover the gamut.

The Chart Room, Route 3, Hulls Cove.

This family dining place has been lovingly run for years by Francis Russell and Jeff Needham, but we only really noticed it after it added a large covered outdoor deck, right beside Hulls Cove on the road into Bar Harbor. The view could not be more watery and the setting is quite rural and tranquil, as opposed to Bar Harbor. The inside dining room is tiered to take advantage of the view, but we'd opt for the deck every chance we could. The menu is extensive, and the kitchen executes. Expect almost anything from baked stuffed shrimp to veal oscar. For a sunset dinner, we shared the specialty crab cake appetizer before digging into the seafood medley baked in sherry and garlic and topped with provolone cheese and the halibut steak sauced with macadamia nuts. A $20 Bogle sauvignon blanc accompanied. The service was a bit scattered (this *was* early in the season), but the place redeemed itself with a free dessert: strawberry-rhubarb pie with frozen yogurt. There's something for everyone on the menu, and few better places to enjoy it.

(207) 288-9740. Entrées, $13.95 to $22.95. Lunch daily, 11:30 to 4. Dinner, from 4. Closed Columbus Day to early May.

Bar Harbor Inn, Newport Drive, Bar Harbor.

Traditionally called the **Reading Room**, the circular dining room at the far end of the Bar Harbor Inn is attractive in deep cranberry colors and claims the finest ocean panorama in town. Although enveloped in elegance, you almost feel as if you're sitting right over the water as you consider a choice of five lobster specialties, seared halibut topped with sautéed fiddleheads and scallions, roast Long Island duck with a port wine-cherry sauce, or dijon-roasted rack of lamb with rosemary jus. Start with a lobster and cilantro spring roll or a local chèvre and vegetable strudel. Finish with bananas foster bread pudding or a triple chocolate dessert called chocolate trillium. Piano or harp music accompanies. The **Terrace Grille,** situated at harbor's edge with yellow umbrella-covered tables, is lovely for waterside meals. It's known for a Down East lobster bake , and serves light fare, lunch ($7.95 to $18.95) and selections from the Reading Room menu.

(207) 288-3351. Entrées, $21 to $31. Dinner nightly, 5:30 to 9:30. Sunday brunch, 11:30 to 2:30. Grill open Monday-Saturday, 11:30 to 9:30. Closed mid-November to mid-April.

Galyn's, 17 Main St., Bar Harbor.

You can watch half the world go by from four white-clothed tables on the tiny front porch beside the sidewalk or catch a view of the harbor from the glassed-in upstairs room in the rear of this establishment sandwiched between storefronts a half block from the pier. Seafood is the specialty, outside or in several nautical dining rooms, and lunch is said to be particularly good here. The food is a cut above most restaurants of its ilk: fresh fish specials like pan-baked tuna, plus bouillabaisse, Mediterranean scallops, mixed seafood grill, peppercorn chicken, prime rib and filet mignon. Lobster bisque, shrimp and scallop skewer, dijon mussels and lobster cocktail are among starters. Dessert could be truffle mousse cake, Mississippi mud pie or blueberry-apple crisp. Light fare is offered at the mahogany bar in the **Galley Lounge,** where you might find live jazz on Saturday or Sunday night.

(207) 288-9706. Entrées, $14 to $22. Lunch daily, 11:30 to 2:30. Dinner nightly, 4 to 10. Closed December-February.

The Pier Restaurant, 55 West St., Bar Harbor.

The most watery location in town is occupied by this casual establishment on a pier jutting into the harbor, part of the expanding Harborside Hotel & Marina complex. Two interior dining rooms in pink and gray are flanked by an enclosed wraparound deck and topped by an open-air deck on the roof. The last is screened by glass windbreaks, shaded by jaunty umbrellas and positively delightful on a sunny day or warm evening for those who like to watch the harbor goings-on from above and up close. It's a good place for a drink or a casual meal. The menu has been upgraded lately from its traditional base of fried seafood and teriyaki, now offering the likes of lobster bisque, crab cakes rémoulade, grilled salmon with lemon-chive beurre blanc and cowboy ribeye steak. We know sophisticates who were impressed by the lazy man's lobster out of the shell and the broiled scallops with al dente vegetables. And who wouldn't love the waterside ambiance?

(207) 288-2110. Entrées, $14 to $23. Lunch daily, 11:30 to 4. Dinner nightly, from 4.

Jordan Pond House, Park Loop Road, Acadia National Park.

Tea on the lawn here is a Bar Harbor tradition, but this old-timer is also popular for a waterside meal. Rebuilt following a 1979 fire, the interior is strikingly contemporary, with cathedral ceilings, huge windows and a fieldstone fireplace. For lunch, we prefer to sit outside on the "porch," which is more like a covered terrace, where you can look down the lawns to Jordan Pond and the Bubbles, past the picnic tables where afternoon tea with popovers is a must for residents and visitors alike. The menu is limited but appealing. Our most recent lunch included a fine seafood pasta and a curried chicken salad garnished with red grapes and orange slices. We shared a popover – a bit steep at $3.50, considering it was hollow. Popovers come with dinners, which include grilled salmon, baked haddock, crab cakes with green onion sauce, prime rib and, of course, steamed lobster. Most of the menu is available day and night, meaning you can come anytime for a lobster roll, a crab and havarti quiche or sirloin steak.

(207) 276-3316. www.jordanpond.com. Entrées, $13 to $18. Lunch daily, 11:30 to 2:30. Tea on the lawn, 11:30 to 5:30. Dinner, 5:30 to 8 or 9. Closed mid-October to mid-May.

Asticou Inn, Route 3, Northeast Harbor.

The lavish Thursday night buffet dinner-dances that used to draw hundreds of Northeast Harbor summer folk for a night of socializing are no more. Instead, this posh dining room of the old resort school seeks to attract a younger, less club-oriented crowd. The pillared dining room is notable for oriental rugs and hand-painted murals of trees and flowers on the buttercup yellow walls. Most coveted seating (and generally reserved for regulars) is in the adjacent enclosed porch, with wondrous views onto the harbor beyond. The water-view deck is also open for lunch and dinner al fresco. The menu features the traditional lobster chowder and baked stuffed lobster, as well as more contemporary fare like grilled swordfish with cucumber-dill sauce and grilled veal chop with wild mushroom demi-glace. On a sunny day, we lunched on the outdoor terrace high above the sparkling harbor. The kitchen produced a crabmeat club sandwich with potato salad, garnished with colorful specks of bell peppers and nasturtiums, and a superior seafood salad of lobster, shrimp and crabmeat tossed with vegetables and field greens.

(207) 276-3344 or (800) 258-3313. Entrées, $19 to $33. Lunch, Monday-Saturday in July and August, 11:30 to 2. Dinner nightly, 6 to 9, mid-June to mid-September. Sunday jazz brunch, 11:30 to 2:30.

Fiddlers' Green, 411 Main St., Southwest Harbor.

Chef Derek Wilber, son of a local boat builder, and his bride-to-be Sarah O'Neil opened this stylish restaurant to rave reviews. They gutted an old family restaurant and created two simple but sophisticated dining areas. One, all in yellow, has windows onto the ocean and a side deck. A short menu itemizes changing choices in the new regional idiom. Start with treats from the cold seafood bar, perhaps lobster timbale or sashimi martini or the Elysian sampler of several. Main courses could be wok-fried salmon and crab with a citrus-peanut sauce, yellowfin tuna with a tamari-mirin sauce, steak frites or venison chops with a black cherry-port wine sauce. Pheasant, elk and rabbit are offered in game season. Typical desserts are honey-mango crème brûlée, cream puffs and maple-nut tart.

(207) 244-9416. Entrées, $18 to $26. Dinner nightly except Wednesday, from 5:30; Thursday-Saturday in off-season, 5:30 to 9. Closed January-April.

The Claremont, Clark Point Road, Southwest Harbor.

Views on three sides down the lawns to Somes Sound and interesting food make the dining room in this century-old hostelry popular with summer residents, although reports of inconsistency have surfaced lately. Come early for drinks on the decks surrounding the Boathouse, which also offers sandwiches and salads for lunch. Then head into the high-ceilinged dining room, elegant in white and candlelight. The short menu includes such starters as smoked salmon torta, grill-roasted oysters and a charcuterie of sliced smoked duck, green peppercorn pork pâté and duck pâté with apricot chutney. Main courses could be pan-seared yellowfin tuna, soy-seared darne of salmon, grilled pork rib chop, pan-seared duck breast and grilled sirloin steak. Homemade desserts include cheesecake and lemon ice with Claremont cookies.

(207) 244-5036. Entrées, $20 to $24. Lunch at the Boathouse, noon to 2, July and August. Dinner nightly, 6 to 9, late June through Labor Day. No credit cards.

Head of the Harbor Restaurant, 433 Main Street, Southwest Harbor.

The lobster is steamed in pots out front, but what really catches the eyes of passersby is the waterfront setting of this nondescript family restaurant – an open canopied deck and two multi-windowed dining rooms overlooking the harbor. The menu is far more extensive than that of your typical seafood shack, for this is a cut above. Although you can get all the usual suspects, you'll also find sautéed crab cakes, chargrilled salmon, fried chicken tenders ("'cause not everyone wants seafood"), Italian dinners (chicken or scallops parmigiana) and sirloin steak. Blueberry pie and root-beer float are the favored desserts. The food is affordable and adequate, and the setting is perfect for families.

(207) 244-3508. Entrées, $9.99 to $17.99. Open daily, 11:30 to 9, late June to Columbus Day.

Seafood Ketch, On the Harbor, Bass Harbor.

If you didn't know, you probably wouldn't stop at this rustic establishment, which happens to be some people's favorite waterside restaurant on this side of the island. It's the real thing – a delightful, Down East place run by Stuart and Lisa Branch, who took over in 1993 when his father Ed retired. Fresh seafood abounds and everything is homemade, to the last loaf of crusty French bread served on a board at dinner. Dining is by candlelight at white clothed tables, each decorated with a bottle of wine, in a rear room nearest the water. There's outdoor dining on a deck right beside the harbor, when the bugs allow. Among entrées, we quite liked the baked halibut with lobster sauce and a special of halibut imperial over rice at one dinner, so were surprised to be let down by the lobster-seafood casserole and the broiled scallops – the house specialty, but tasteless – at a subsequent visit. Fresh raspberry pie with ice cream compensated.

(207) 244-7463. Entrées, $16.95 to $19.95. Lunch and dinner daily, 11 to 9. Closed November-April.

Thurston's Lobster Pound, Steamboat Wharf Road, Bernard.

From the canopied upstairs deck, you can look below onto Thurston's Wharf and see where the lobstermen keep their traps. This is a real working lobster wharf beside picturesque Bass Harbor. And if you couldn't tell from all the pickup trucks parked along the road, one taste of the lobster will convince you. We loved our lobster dinner ($9.75 to $10.75 a pound, plus $4.75 for extras like corn on the cob, coleslaw, a roll and blueberry cake). We also sampled the chock-full lobster stew, a really good potato salad, steamers and mussels and, at our latest visit, a fabulous crab cake but a not so fabulous scallop chowder. You place your order at the counter, wait for one of the tables on the covered deck above or on the open deck below, and settle down with a bottle of beer or wine (from a choice selection). Little wonder that the island lobster cognoscenti consider this place the best around.

(207) 244-7600. Open daily, 11 to 8:30. Closed October to Memorial Day.

Abel's Lobster Pound, Route 103, Mount Desert.

Boy, do the traditionalists (and reviewers) love this widely promoted icon. We did, too, when it was a simple, outdoors-oriented place in the evergreens beside Somes Sound. Something was lost when it enlarged the indoor dining facility full of green picnic tables, added a bar and waitress service, catered to the hordes and lost the rustic outdoorsy feeling – the waterfront views marred by industrial-looking boatyard ventures beside. Lobster-lovers still recommend it, though agree it's pricy. Six versions of lobster dinner, served with rolls and baked potato or french fries, were priced at our latest visit from $22 for a one-pounder to $37 for a biggie with steamed clams. There are a few non-seafood choices, but lobster is clearly the specialty. The lunch menu is sorely limited. Blueberry pie is the favored dessert.

(207) 276-5827. Entrées, $18 to $27. Lunch daily, noon to 4. Dinner, noon to 9.

FOR MORE INFORMATION: Bar Harbor Chamber of Commerce, 93 Cottage St., Box 158, Bar Harbor, ME 04609, (207) 288-5103 or (800) 288-5103. www.barharbormaine.com. Southwest Harbor/Tremont Chamber of Commerce, Route 102 at Seal Cove Road, Box 1143, Southwest Harbor, ME 04679, (207) 244-9264 or (800) 423-9264. www.acadiachamber.com.
The best visitor center is the Thompson Island Information Center, run by the National Park Service and local chambers of commerce. It's at the entrance to Mount Desert Island on Route 3.

Roosevelt Cottage overlooks Passamaquoddy Bay from Campobello Island.

Campobello, N.B./Lubec-Eastport, Me.

The East Coast's U.S. Route 1 dwindles away. The craggy coastline seems more remote with each mile, until you reach the northeasternmost tip of the United States. Here the forested coast, offshore islands and wispy fog envelop the Bay of Fundy shoreline into a sheltered time warp. The birds start twittering with the summer sunrise at 4 in the morning. Salmon, puffins and whales, not to mention the old sardine packing canneries, add a northern maritime flavor.

This is Maine's distant Washington County. Across the Roosevelt International Bridge over the Lubec Narrows lies Franklin Delano Roosevelt's beloved island of Campobello in New Brunswick. Together they form a two-nation wonderland of nature at its most primitive.

Of course, it takes the better part of a day for most visitors to drive up the Maine coast to this area, which marks the beginning of Atlantic Canada and which the Roosevelt family cherished for its very isolation. And once here, you may not be able to get there from here, as the saying goes. Lubec is less than three miles from Eastport across Cobscook Bay, but it's a circuitous 40 miles by land or a roundabout international trip by water on two ferries via Canada's Campobello and Deer islands.

Campobello, the private estate of the Owen family for nearly a century, was acquired in 1881 by a Boston development corporation that erected three large hotels and turned part of the Canadian island into a low-key summer playground for wealthy Americans from Boston and New York. Most of them have come and gone, and the year-round population has remained about 1,200 ever since, most of it clustered around two quaint fishing villages. Today, one-third of the island is the unique Roosevelt Campobello International Park, site of the Roosevelt summer home and 2,600 acres of nature preserves.

Lubec (accent second syllable, as in Quebec), perched on a steep Maine headland overlooking Cobscook Bay, is the easternmost town in the United States and the closest American point to Campobello. It was once the sardine packing capital of the world. A roaring seaport back in the days when there were fifteen bars, twenty canneries and 3,000 people, Lubec is now dry, its population has slipped to 1,900 and many of the waterfront commercial and retail structures are hauntingly empty.

The sign in front of the town's biggest restaurant is poignant: "Uncle Kippy's welcomes you to L.A. (Lubec America). Stop in or we'll both starve."

Although a multi-million-dollar marina, an emerging aquaculture business and a main street undergoing revitalization offer promise, Lubec remains endearingly old-fashioned and quiet compared with Eastport, which seems bigger than its population of 1,640 suggests. On an island at the foot of a long peninsula and maddeningly difficult to reach by car, Eastport is America's easternmost city and considers itself the nation's smallest city. It is emerging as a deepwater seaport for ocean-going vessels.

Although its fortunes ebb and flow like the tides, what won't change is the rustic remoteness of this area of stark beauty. As the movie in the Campobello park visitor center suggests, the fog, the cold water and some of the highest tides in North America create a distinctive eco-system, a world of beauty so quiet that you must listen for it.

Getting There

Interstate 95, U.S. Route 1 and Maine Route 9 lead motorists to the Lubec-Eastport area. Route 190 dead-ends at Eastport. Route 189 goes to Lubec and across the short FDR International Memorial Bridge to Campobello Island. Ferries connect Campobello and Eastport with the New Brunswick mainland at L'Etete via Deer Island.

Campobello operates on Atlantic Time, you must pass through Customs and prices quoted there are in Canadian funds.

Where to Stay

Campobello and Lubec are closely allied in spirit and geography. Eastport is harder to get to (and from). Each has its merits as a base for exploration.

Lubec-Campobello

Peacock House, 27 Summer St., Lubec 04652.

Built in 1860 by a sea captain from England for his bride, this early Victorian on a residential side street passed by marriage into the family of Carroll B. Peacock, a state senator, which accounts for all the prominent visitors – from Dwight Eisenhower to Edmund Muskie to Margaret Chase Smith – who have stayed here over the years. Nowadays, owners Dennis and Sue Baker entertain overnight guests in a nicely eclectic B&B. The living room is furnished with a baby grand piano that is popular with guests here for the SummerKeys music school. Beyond a library with a video collection is a large sunroom, where guests pour BYOB drinks from a handsome antique wooden bar looking onto a rear patio. The Bakers offer three comfortable bedrooms and four larger "suites" with sitting areas and TV/VCRs. All have king or queen beds and a couple yield glimpses of the water. The Margaret Chase Smith Suite, in which the former Maine senator frequently stayed, has a queensize brass bed and a spacious bath. Also pleasant is the Summer Room, furnished in wicker with a queen bed

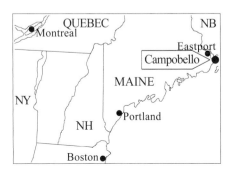

and white sheer curtains framing a water view. Breakfast is served family style in the dining room. The main course might be blueberry french toast or puff pancakes. English tea is served in the afternoon on the side deck.

(207) 733-2403 or (888) 305-0036. www.peacockhouse.com. Seven rooms with private baths. Doubles, $85 to $125. Closed November-April.

The Home Port Inn, 45 Main St., Box 50, Lubec 04652.

This area's longest-running inn, the Home Port opened in 1982 as something of a port in a rather godforsaken town, a tree-shaded refuge atop the Lubec hill shared by a pair of churches. Built in 1880 in the Maine farmhouse style, it offers homey accommodations and the town's only fine-dining restaurant (see Where to Eat). The Home Port is an inn in the old sense, from the restaurant to the oversize front living room, full of gathering areas where groups of guests get together near the fireplace and tea is offered in the afternoon. New owners David and Suzannah Gale are gradually redecorating the inn's seven guest rooms, which sprawl across three areas of the house. Two on the main floor are called by their former uses: The cozy Library with a queensize bed and fireplace, and the Dining Room with two double beds. Upstairs in front are two rooms with queen beds, one the master bedroom with a four-poster and a large sofa. Along the side is the inn's only kingsize bedroom, with a private bath down the hall. The rear bedroom with a double bed and a futon boasts a great view of Cobscook Bay. The continental-plus breakfast features homemade granola plus cereals and pastries.

(207) 733-2077 or (800) 457-2077. www.homeportinn.com. Seven rooms with private baths. Doubles, $85 to $99. Closed November-April.

Betsy Ross Lodging, 61 Water St., Lubec 04652.

The American flag flies outside this newish establishment, which occupies a prime spot facing the waterfront along Lubec's main street. The flag reflects the fact that the house was rebuilt in 2000 on a foundation that was a duplicate of the Betsy Ross House in Philadelphia. "We replicated the exterior," said owner Dianna Meehan, who operates the Atlantic House Coffee & Deli Shop, a lunchroom and pizzeria, across the street. The interior is all new, paneled in light pine from floor to ceiling to bath, with queensize beds topped by plump quilts. Ceiling fans, TVs on high shelves facing the beds and cane-seatback chairs typify the guest rooms on three floors. The front bedroom we saw had a single chair, a wash basin in the bedroom and a tub in the bathroom. The larger rear bedroom had two chairs and a large bath with shower only. The three front rooms face the Lubec Narrows and Campobello Island. Accommodations rather than hospitality are the hallmarks here, as evidenced by the change in name from Betsy Ross House B&B to Lodging. There's no common room, and guests get a credit for breakfast at the Atlantic House.

(207) 733-8942. Fax (207) 733-8907. www.atlantichouse.net. Six rooms with private baths. Doubles, $95. Closed December-April.

The Lighthouse Inn & Chowder House, 7 Water St., Box 308, Lubec 04652.

Water views from all but one room are offered at this inn, transformed into a hotel in 1998 from a lunchroom and boarding house. For how long and how successfully has been in question since, as three successive owners tried and failed. Carol Lebietas, a summer resident from New York City, opened for a short season in 2004 and bought several other structures to rent as well. She reopened the nice-looking waterfront dining room and bar on the building's main floor, as a chowder house serving breakfast and lunch. Its chowders come from a can, but the weekend music nights there are better received by locals. The second floor contains three guest rooms plus a suite with kingsize bed, kitchen and living room with a day bed. We saw a couple of basic but comfortable rooms, light and airy with white walls and nautical wallpaper borders. A corner room with kingsize bed has big windows onto the water in two directions.

(207) 733-4300. www.lighthouseinnmaine.com. Nine rooms and one suite with private baths. Doubles, $85 to $115. Suite, $125. Closed Labor Day to Memorial Day.

Lupine Lodge, 610 Route 774, Welshpool, Campobello E5E 1A5.

The Adams summer estate compound built by cousins of Roosevelts and more recently with ties to the Whitewater scandal is now a restaurant and lodging facility owned by the Province of New Brunswick and operated by a woman-run corporation. (They took over in 1993 following the bankruptcy of the Arkansas-owned Campobello Company, which had used the property to provide lodging and dining for prospective investors in the company's real-estate developments around the island.) The corporation has opened two rear buildings behind the restaurant to the public for lodging purposes. Eleven generally smallish bedrooms are decorated in what the management calls "sophisticated simplicity." That translates to log paneling throughout, from walls to ceilings to bathrooms, and mostly queensize beds, carpeting and showers. A few have bathtubs and two have fireplaces. Five come with extra beds or sofabeds, and one with a double bed has a ladder staircase leading to twin beds in a loft overhead. Furnishings are minimal, a few have washbowls in the room and at least one bathroom has an exposed water heater. Five rooms in the Oceanview Cottage, one with a small deck, yield stunning views down the lawn to Passamaquoddy Bay, with the city of Eastport on full display beyond – the lights at night shed an odd feeling of urbanity to an otherwise remote location. Behind it and blocking the water view is the Woodhaven Cottage, although the lodge's literature hypes that partial (make that very) water views are afforded from the bathrooms of two end units. The accommodations are serviceable and comfortable. Guests have access to a large deck around the Main Cottage, which includes a dining room (see Where to Eat) as well as a combination den and service bar.

(506) 752-2555 or (888) 912-8880. www.lupinelodge.com. Eleven rooms with private baths. Doubles, $55 to $105. Closed mid-October to late May.

Owen House, 11 Welshpool St., Welshpool, Campobello E5E 1G3.

You can see water from every room of the Owen House, an historic Colonial built by the original owner of the island and now a B&B on ten acres of grounds, beloved by artists and birders. Owner Joyce Morrell is a painter who exhibits in Maine and elsewhere as well as in her watercolor gallery here. In August, Audubon groups visit and may give slide shows at night in the front gallery. Other common rooms are a side porch filled with old bottles, ship's mementos and the like, a homey parlor full of wicker furniture and afghans, and a dining room with colorful wallpaper and hooked rugs. Here is where guests are served breakfasts of bacon and eggs or blueberry pancakes and sausage or "sometimes I'll do a quiche type thing," says Joyce, who shares innkeeping duties with Jan Meiners. Five bedrooms have private baths; four on the third floor share. Hudson's Bay blankets and bright quilts and pillows adorn the beds. Some rooms have fireplaces. The house was built in 1829 by Admiral William Fitzwilliam Owen, son of the British captain who was granted the island in 1769. Guests like the peace and quiet, the gatherings around a fireplace in the evenings, the comings and goings of the ferry to Deer island and the fishing boats at the Welshpool wharf next door, and the path to the beach, if not the 47-degree water.

(506) 752-2977. www.owenhouse.ca. Five rooms with private baths and four rooms with shared bath. Doubles, $127 to $207 with private bath, $112 to $119 shared. Closed October-April.

An Island Chalet, 155 Narrows Road, Welshpool, Campobello E5E 1B2.

Five two-story log chalets spaced well apart occupy a three-acre forested bluff overlooking Snug Cove and Passamaquoddy Bay, not far from the Roosevelt International Bridge. Owner-builder Rob Lahey took a break from construction to show us around at an early visit Each chalet has a downstairs bedroom with twin beds, an open living room with cathedral ceiling and full kitchen area, and a loft bedroom with queensize bed. Winterized for year-round use, each has new furnishings, TVs and telephones. A covered front porch offers spectacular views of the bay. So taken were we by both the area and the chalets, we nearly signed up on the spot to have Rob build us our very own waterfront chalet.

(506) 752-2971. Five two-bedroom housekeeping chalets. Doubles, $120. Weekly, $805.

The Water's Edge Villas, North Road, Welshpool, Campobello E0G 2H0.

Three contemporary two-bedroom cottages on a hillside have floor-to-ceiling windows and large decks with plush lawn furniture facing Passamaquoddy Bay across the road. Each looks and feels new (the walls are painted white – no log paneling here), from the tiled front room with a fully furnished kitchen on one side and two sofabeds on the other to the skylit bathrooms. Two carpeted rear bedrooms each contain a double bed, oversize closets and plenty of dresser space for long-term stays. Towels are exchanged daily, and maid service is available for an extra charge. The large coffee tables in the living room contain what owner Pamela Matthews calls her "villa books," full of island information supplemented by the handwritten comments of previous occupants. Stefan Matthews, the owner's son, runs the Campobello Whale Watch Co. Motel, a new ten-unit motel at 955 Route 774 in Welshpool. The motel lacks a water view, but as the sun sets over Eastport across the bay, guests at the villas have front-row seats.

(506) 752-2359 or (800) 836-7648. Three two-bedroom cottages. Doubles, $195.

Pollock Cove Cottages, 2455 Route 774, Wilson's Beach, Campobello E5E 1K3.

In an area known for remarkable water vistas, these have about the best – especially the five new efficiency cabins on a narrow bluff jutting into Passamaquoddy Bay, with water on three sides. They were built by Steve Newman, whose father ran the older Quoddy View Cabins and Motel adjacent. He since has taken over the Quoddy View's three cabins and a duplex with two efficiency rooms, and has added a gift shop in the main house. The five new cabins as well as one other have two bedrooms each. They're simply but nicely furnished and come with decks and cable TV.

(506) 752-2300. Two efficiency rooms and eight cabins. Doubles, $75 to $150.

Eastport Area

The Motel East, 23A Water St., Eastport 04631.

One of the best waterfront locations in town is occupied by this good-looking, two-story motel off by itself right above the water. All rooms face Passamaquoddy Bay, and private balconies from most of the units take full advantage. Beds are queensize or two doubles. Eight rooms come with kitchenettes. The motel also rents Friar Roads, an adjacent seaside cottage with queen bedroom, living room with sofabed, full kitchen and deck.

(207) 853-4747. Fourteen rooms. Doubles, $90 to $110.

Weston House, 26 Boynton St., Eastport 04631.

Eastport lawyer-politician Jonathan Weston built this majestic yellow Federal-style house in 1810 on a hill with a distant view of Passamaquoddy Bay. Since 1985, ex-Californians Jett and John Peterson have operated it as a B&B with exceptional flair. Four upstairs bedrooms share two baths. The bayview Audubon Room, in which John James Audubon once stayed, has a queensize four-poster bed with eyelet-edged sheets, lovely scatter rugs on polished floors and a stunning potted fig tree in one corner. The front Weston Room offers a bay view, a kingsize bed, fireplace, TV and telephone. "You can sit up in bed and watch the freighters in the bay," Jett advises. The public rooms are impressive: a library with books and TV, a formal front parlor where afternoon tea and sherry are poured in front of the fireplace beside a century-old melodeon, and a more casual kitchen-dining area in which meals are served. Jett Peterson wants guests to "enjoy all of our house." They certainly enjoy her breakfasts of fresh orange juice, melon balls with mint and silver-dollar pancakes doused with lingonberry or hot apricot syrup one day, muffins and coddled eggs the next. Jett will dish up five-course gourmet dinners by reservation, the price determined by the menu. A $35 meal might be hot broccoli or chilled cucumber soup, an appetizer of smoked salmon, poached salmon with cumin mayonnaise and fresh salsa, a red lettuce salad with goat cheese and red grapes, and tiramisu or a rhubarb tart based on an original recipe from her grandmother. Complimentary wine accompanies, and coffee and mints follow.

(207) 853-2907 or (800) 853-2907. www.westonhouse-maine.com. Four rooms with shared baths. Doubles, $70 to $85.

Todd House, 1 Capen Ave., Todd's Head, Eastport 04631.

Here you can stay in a Revolutionary War-era house overlooking the bay. The classic 1775 New England full Cape exudes history, from its huge center chimney to an unusual "good morning" staircase. It's owned by a native Eastport historian and educator and is listed on the National Register of Historic Places. The house is known for its cornerstone, which notes the chartering of the Masonic Lodge in 1801. The house became a temporary barracks during the Civil War, when Todd's Head was fortified. The guest rooms are nicely furnished with period antiques, local historic artifacts and colorful quilts. Three have working fireplaces and two have cable TV. The four smallest rooms share two baths. Two larger efficiency rooms have private baths, queensize beds, kitchenettes, separate entrances and panoramic water views from large windows. A continental breakfast, including granola and what innkeeper Ruth McInnis calls "the best wild blueberry muffins ever," is served in the original common room in front of an enormous fireplace with bake oven and old cooking tools. The large back yard above the bay is available for cookouts.

(207) 853-2328. Four rooms sharing two baths and two efficiencies with private baths. Doubles, $50 to $60; efficiencies, $80 and $90.

Kilby House Inn, 122 Water St., Eastport 04631.

Built in 1887, this Victorian house overlooks Passamaquoddy Bay and Campobello Island. Gregory Noyes, a high school teacher who has an unbelievable commute to school at Steuben at the western end of Washington County, opened his house as a B&B "to survive," he concedes. His ancestors lived here, and he has decorated the property as "an English house of the period." He avoided an oppressive look in favor of an open and airy feeling with light painted walls and lace on the windows. The main floor holds a double parlor with pocket doors between, a dining room with a formal table and cane-seat chairs, and a welcoming kitchen with a wood-burning stove. Upstairs are five bedrooms, three with private baths. One in front with a canopy poster bed enjoys a bay view, as does a side room. A rear room with private bath is considered the nicest. Gregory prepares a full breakfast in summer, perhaps strata with coffee cake or blueberry pancakes. Except for weekends and holidays, guests in the off-season are on their own, since Greg leaves early for his long commute to school.

(207) 853-0989 or (800) 435-4529. www.kilbyhouseinn.com. Three rooms with private baths and two with shared bath. Doubles, $50 to $80.

CAMPING. Herring Cove Provincial Park, (506) 752-2396, a fine park on Campobello with beach and golf course, has 76 shady campsites, 40 with electrical hookups. More than 150 large, well-spaced campsites, many with water views, are available at Maine's **Cobscook Bay State Park,** (207) 726-4412, off Route 1 six miles south of Dennysville. A private full-service campground is **The Seaview,** Norwood Road, Eastport, (207) 853-4471, with 70 sites on a point overlooking Passamaquoddy Bay. The most picturesque campsite is **Deer Island Point Campground,** (506) 747-2423, on a bluff overlooking Eastport and Campobello above the ferry landing on Deer Island.

Seeing and Doing ———————————— *ᏟᏟᏟ*

Roosevelt Campobello International Park, 459 Route 774, Campobello Island, N.B.

A unique example of international cooperation, this 2,800-acre park established in 1964 is administered by a joint commission of three Canadians and three Americans. Known as Franklin Delano Roosevelt's "beloved island," it was ranked in his affections second only to Hyde Park, N.Y. From 1883 when he was a year old until 1921 when he was stricken by polio here, he spent most of his summers on Campobello. After 1921, he returned only three times for short visits, all while he was president. Eleanor Roosevelt's last visit was in 1962 for the dedication of the Roosevelt Memorial Bridge. Here are the cottage and the grounds where the Roosevelts vacationed, the waters where they sailed, and the beaches, bogs and woods where they hiked and relaxed.

The park's visitor center provides a touching introduction both to the Roosevelts' tenure here and to the island. Exhibit panels in an addition that opened in 2004 details "A Legacy of Friendship" between the two countries, starting with "Open Borders" and concluding with "Good Neighbors/Best Friends." A fifteen-minute movie, "Beloved Island," is helpful in understanding the unusual nature of this area. The movie begins with a welcome by the late Franklin D. Roosevelt Jr.

(506) 752-2922. www.fdr.net. Estate open daily 10 to 6 (Atlantic time), Memorial Day to mid-October; visitor center open through October. Park open year-round. Free.

The Roosevelt Cottage. The homey, 34-room dark red house high above Passamaquoddy Bay is one of the most pleasant we've seen. On self-guided tours you can peer right into the rooms, which are human-size rather than grand. Unobtrusive hostesses answer questions or leave you on your own. The house still looks lived in, almost as if the Roosevelts had simply left for a quick boat ride to Eastport to pick up groceries. It's filled with fresh field flowers and beautiful views are afforded from all the window seats. Most of the furnishings were used by the family; only the curtains and bedspreads are reproductions of the originals, we were told. You'll see the megaphone used for hailing latecomers to meals, a collection of canes, the large chair used to carry the handicapped President, the family telescope, and eighteen simple bedrooms. Outside are exceptionally lovely gardens and paths to the shore.

The Hubbard Cottage. Next door to the Roosevelt property is this gabled cottage, acquired by the park commission in 1970 when it was the last remaining Victorian summer residence in the park. Under park operation, it serves as a conference center for government and non-commercial groups: participants can stay here or in the nearby Prince and Wells-Shober cottages. The oval window in the dining room, about ten feet wide and looking out onto the water, is a sight to behold. The rather luxurious main floor is open for tours July 1 through Labor Day, except when conferences are in session.

THE PARK. Nearly sixteen miles of scenic drives and nine miles of walking trails allow you to see the shoreline, coves, duck ponds, bogs and fog forests that typify the area. The bays still contain fishing weirs, used for catching herring. The wildflowers – especially the aroma of wild roses and the brilliant splashes of lupine all along the roads in late June and early July – are out of this world. Among the park's features:

Friar's Head. A short walk leads to an observation deck, which provides interesting maps and plaques with descriptions of the panorama all around. The best vantage point to see the entire area; it's a good place to get your bearings. Picnic tables and grills are scattered about, and nature trails yield changing views of the bay.

Herring Cove Provincial Park and Golf Course. A nine-hole golf course and fine campsites are among the attractions here. The mile-long, crescent-shaped Herring Cove Beach is good for beachcombing, picnicking and an invigorating dip in the 50ish-degree waters of the Bay of Fundy; a seawall separates it from the warmer Lake Glensevern, named after the Owen home in Wales. FDR and his family used to swim in the lake and gather multi-colored stones on the beach. At the north end of the beach, a road leads to an observation area and a delightful picnic table amid the evergreens looking out toward the North Head of Grand Manan Island.

South of Herring Cove Beach is **Con Robinson's Point,** with two picnic tables on a bluff and stairs down to a secluded dark-sand beach. **Liberty Point Drive** leads on around Raccoon Beach to Liberty Point, near the Sugar Loaf rocks and the Boring Stones, which emerge only at low tide. Trails lead hikers to Ragged Point and Owen Head for some rugged scenery and to Lower and Upper Duck ponds, saltwater coves and barrier beaches that are repositories for driftwood and migratory waterfowl.

East Quoddy Head Lighthouse. You can walk across at low tide to the craggy headland, but at high tide when we first were there the rocky "floor" was ten feet under a fierce current flowing two ways. We had to console ourselves with the sight of whales cavorting a quarter-mile offshore. Our next visit coincided with low tide, which offered a half-hour's adventure out past the light. You clamber up and down three built-in steel ladders, across a bridge and pick your way across wet, seaweed-covered rocks to the lighthouse buildings. Here is a most scenic and isolated spot, seemingly at the end of the world.

Back toward the settlement of Wilson's Beach, a road leads east to Head Harbour Wharf, the protected harbor where the commercial fishing fleet is berthed. **Island Cruises** at 62 Head Harbour Road, (888) 249-4400, offers three two-hour whale-watching trips a day (adults $45, children $27.50) plus three-hour sport fishing tours, periodic aquaculture tours and lighthouse cruises. **Captain Riddle Cruises,** Head Harbour Wharf, (506) 752-2009, offers two-hour whale watch tours (adults $40, children $25). Also available are two-hour deep-sea fishing trips (adults $50 – catching fish guaranteed, or you get a free fish and chips dinner at a local restaurant) and scenic lighthouse cruises.

FERRY RIDES. From Welshpool on Campobello, a summer car ferry runs on the hour to Deer Island from late June to mid-September. The ferry is the most scenic way to get from Lubec to mainland New Brunswick, via Deer Island, a New Brunswick island so unmarked and low-key that we got lost trying to find the free provincial ferry connection to L'Etete on the mainland. (Getting lost was worth it, to enjoy some of the picturesque surprises of Deer Island.) The eventual twenty-minute provincial ferry ride past countless islands must be the most scenic in eastern North America – and it's free, to boot. At Deer Island, you also can take a ferry to Eastport; it runs hourly late June to mid-September. The Deer Island-Campobello ferry costs $14 for car and driver, $3 for passengers; the Eastport ferry costs $11 and $3. A tugboat hauls the small ferries. The captain said we'd get to observe some seals and **Old Sow,** the world's largest tidal whirlpool off Deer Island. But we didn't see either. You see Old Sow at its best just before high tide from the bluff at **Deer Island Point,** one of the nicest picnic sites and campgrounds we know of, just above the ferry landing. Take a picnic lunch and pick blueberries, climb around the rock tunnels or go for a quick swim off the horseshoe beach. The view from the craggy bluff is unforgettable.

LUBEC. Back in Maine, the last sardine packing plant in what had been the sardine capital of the world closed in 2001. The McCurdy smokehouse complex along Water Street, the last operating herring smoking operation in the country, has been undergoing restoration by Lubec Landmarks since then. One market building was turned into a gallery, museum and community hall in 2004. Other canneries now process and pack salmon harvested from pens in Cobscook Bay. Ex-Long Islander Vinny Gartmayer and his wife Holly took over an old smoked salmon business along Route 189 in 2002 and renamed it the **Bold Coast Smokehouse,** featuring "wicked good smoked salmon." In his retail showroom near the smokehouse he offers samples of lox, kabobs, pâtés and gravlax that can be shipped across the country.

Summer is enlivened by the ten free Wednesday evening concerts offered by the faculty of the **SummerKeys** music school. Up to 200 concert-goers gather in Lubec's Congregational Christian Church, some of them arriving via the Quoddy Dam fishing boat chartered from Eastport for the purpose.

West Quoddy Head Lighthouse. Curiously, the easternmost point of land in the United States is at West Quoddy Head in South Lubec. Atop a jagged 90-foot cliff pounded by the open Atlantic, the landmark 1809 lighthouse with the rare red and white candy stripes was featured by the U.S. Postal Service in its lighthouse postage stamp series commemorating the Coast Guard's 100th anniversary. The point is shrouded in fog an average of 59 days a year, a sign near the lighthouse informs. We happened to visit on one of the clearer days, the fog that had enveloped Lubec in the morning having vanished by midday. You might spot groups of whales surfacing in the tidal waters between West Quoddy Head and Grand Manan Island, N.B., which is visible in the distance. Guided shore walks are available at the West Quoddy Head Visitor Center, which is open daily in summer with historic photos, natural history displays, films and dioramas.

West Quoddy Head State Park. Besides offering picnic facilities, the 483-acre oceanside park has trails to the lighthouse, an island and a bog. A two-mile trail leads along the shoreline to Carrying Place Cove. A raised boardwalk goes through the coastal plateau peat bog, which has been declared a National Natural Landmark; its dense moss and heath vegetation typical of the Arctic tundra are unusual.

Cottage Garden, North Lubec Road, Lubec, (207) 733-2902. Is it the showy herb and perennial gardens that so appeal here? Or the shops holding unusual handcrafted gifts and accessories? Or the informative little Shoreline Nature Center museum? Or the painstakingly restored Greek Revival Cape house? Gretchen and Alan Mead share their many talents with visitors to their herb and flower gardens and their Maine Reflections and Art in the Garden shops full of dried flower wreaths, birdhouses, framed bird and botanical prints, hanging potpourri and even painted garden benches, all made by the owners. We liked a small mirror with tiny wooden boats hanging from it, which now graces the front hall at our summer home in nearby St. Andrews. The Meads' artistry extends to seven gardens on two wooded acres around their charming Greek Revival Cape house. With only an occasional assistant, they create and maintain an idiosyncratic showplace full of handmade wooden walkways and bridges, some to a new Asian garden that Gretchen vowed would be the last. How does Gretchen, a landscape architect, explain such prolific blooms on her perennials? "The fog and mist off the ocean are like rain for gardens." Open daily, dawn to dusk; free.

Reversing Fails, Pembroke, Me. Signs off Route I lead to Leighton Neck and Young's Cove Road and a 140-acre picnic area beside this unusual attraction. The incoming and outgoing tides hit a series of rocks, creating saltwater falls that are quite a sight. Cobscook Bay State Park, 800 acres of woods and meadows and rockbound coast south of Dennysville, juts out into the bay and provides an abundance of birds and flowers as well as clams for digging.

EASTPORT. One of Maine's more important deepwater seaports has been reviving ever so slowly since 1985. More than 200,000 tons of pulp, granite, logs and other products are shipped annually from the municipal pier, and a new port facility is planned. Lately, the tides and temperatures of Passamaquoddy Bay have proven ideal for a growing salmon aquaculture industry. The town is bustling – comparatively – with activity these days and local promoters see it evolving from an isolated Down East fishing village into a tourist destination.

The **Tides Institute and Museum of Art,** 43 Water St., (207) 853-4747, is emerging in a restored 1887 savings bank on the Eastport waterfront. The low-key regional cultural institution is building significant collections of art, photography, architecture and history relating to the Passamaquoddy Bay area on both sides of the border. One floor of offices and rather primitive exhibition space opened in 2004, and the ground floor was being readied for public view in 2005. Open Tuesday-Sunday 10 to 5; free.

The aptly named **Overlook Park** on Water Street is a good place to view the undulating bay, Campobello Island and Lubec. Thousands of people return from all over the country for Eastport's annual Fourth of July celebration, five days of activity called Old Home Week and culminating in a big parade featuring the governor and congressmen and an evening fireworks display. More events take place during an annual Salmon Festival the weekend after Labor Day. **Stage East,** corner of Dana and Water streets, (207) 726-4747, presents several productions a season from April through November. A small troupe in a small facility, they "perform wonders," according to fans. By reservation, **Moose Island tours** in his 1947 "woodie" station wagon ($5) and picnics featuring his smoked salmon and roasted chicken ($20) are offered by Jim Blankman, 37 Washington St., (207) 853-4831. His custom woodworking shop in a quonset hut at 108 Water St. is something of a museum of all things wooden from caskets to stringed instruments to skateboards.

The historic, two-masted schooner **Sylvina W. Beal** carries 50 passengers under sail on two cruises daily from the Fish Pier in downtown Eastport, (207) 853-2500. A three-hour afternoon whale watching cruise through Head Harbor Passage to the whale feeding grounds past East Quoddy Light goes for $35 adults, $18 children. The 7 p.m. sunset cruise costs $25 for adults, $15 for children.

Shackford Head. A hilly peninsula on the west side of Eastport, with three miles of craggy shoreline jutting into Cobscook Bay, is now a 95-acre park. Visitors may park near the Marine Trades Center boat school off Deep Cove Road and walk a mile-long trail to the Viewpoint, with a panoramic view stretching from Friar's Head on Campobello past Lubec toward Pembroke. The state-owned land is home to more than 100 plant species, and nearly 30 bird species have been seen nesting here.

SHOPPING. The area's shopping opportunities are centered around Eastport. On the outskirts of town at 85 Washington St., **Raye's Mustard Mill & Pantry Store** is a must stop. Still operating is the country's last remaining stone-ground mustard mill, producing the mustards in which the area's sardines used to be packed. The mill offers guided tours of the operation on weekdays, and recently opened the Mustard Shed lunchroom for sandwiches. Various mustards along with Maine-made foods and crafts are on sale in the Pantry Store. Every summer, we stop here and stock up on mustards for the next year. Our favorite is the Winter Garden variety.

On first glance, downtown Eastport appears to be mostly ramshackle or vacant stores, although the new Eastport for Pride downtown development program has set about changing that and six new stores opened in 2004. Standouts include **The Shop at the Commons,** a sophisticated new store showing works of 40 area artisans, **Quoddy Crafts** and **Dog Island Pottery. The Eastport Gallery** also displays the works of local artists and craftsmen. Don Sutherland produces monumental pots and vases, some with amazing blue glaze, at **Earth Forms,** a most unusual pottery at 5 Dana St. Fine art is shown in two new galleries in historic homes, **Leister Gallery** and **The Salem Gallery.**

In Lubec, three artist/entrepreneurs lately set up shop along Lubec's Water Street to showcase their creations. Beth Roy spins her own wool for the **Water Street Fiberarts Studio,** which also sells handcrafted apparel and gifts by other local artisans. Ice cream, waffles and crêpes are featured at **Peter's Not-So-Famous Homemade Ice Cream.** Monica Elliott and Eugene Greenlaw create spectacular bonbons, clusters and truffles at **Seaside Chocolates.** The unpretentious candy kitchen and showroom are upstairs in an old, decrepit-looking R.D. Peacock sardine cannery at 72 Water St., marked by a lobster sign out front. The loquacious owner is apt to seat customers at a communal table for a sampling of sweets. The treats, based on recipes from her father's chocolate business in her native Peru, cost $1.75 each (colorfully wrapped bags of twelve for $18 to $20) and are well worth it.

Where to Eat ⎯⎯⎯⎯⎯⎯⎯⎯⎯⎯⎯⎯ ♪♪♪

Lubec-Campobello

The Home Port Inn, 45 Main St., Lubec.

Food is the hallmark of this inn housed in a pale blue 1880 house on a hill descending to Cobscook Bay. The cheery sunken rear dining room draws discerning diners from far and wide, and the 28 seats are apt to turn twice on busy evenings. Innkeepers Dave and Suzannah Gale take turns in the kitchen assisting the longtime chef. The menu shows more reach than most, from Louisiana shrimp or bouillabaisse to chicken cordon bleu and steak au poivre. Coquilles St. Jacques, mixed seafood casserole, and baked salmon with dill and shallots are house specialties. Appetizers are few but choice: smoked salmon or trout, seafood chowder or crab cake on mesclun greens. Desserts include berry pies and shortcakes, walnut pie and cheesecake with fresh berries. Wine prices start in the mid teens and top off in the high thirties.

(207) 733-2077. Entrées, $10.95 to $22.95. Dinner nightly, 5 to 8, Memorial Day to Columbus Day.

Lupine Lodge, Welshpool, Campobello.

The restaurant in the historic former estate of the Adams family is on a comeback under new ownership. The Adamses were friends of the Roosevelts, whose guests used to stay here. The appealing, lodge-style dining room has well-spaced tables near banks of windows looking down the hillside to Friar's Bay, with trees framing Eastport across the way. The menu is extensive, and lunch is served all day. You can get seven kinds of burgers, including haddock, salmon and scallop. Lunch offerings range widely from three fish cakes with chow-chow and biscuit for $5.95 to a lobster roll with fries and coleslaw for $16.95. Sweet and sour fish is a specialty served with fries and coleslaw for $7.95. The dinner menu adds things like lobster stew, baked ham and a turkey dinner. We liked the baked haddock with a newburg sauce and the Fundy scallops poached in white wine, green peppers and onions, with rice, slaw and glazed carrots. There's no outside dining that we could see, but on chilly nights, you can dine by candlelight in front of a rustic stone fireplace. There's a fully licensed lounge.

(506) 752-2555. Entrées, $12.95 to $18.95. Lunch daily in season, noon to 5. Dinner, 5 to 9. Closed mid-October to late May.

Family Fisheries, Wilson's Beach, Campobello..

Believe it or not, this established take-out restaurant and fish market is where Americans from Lubec go for fresh seafood. Its small new dining room with "waitress service" is dark and claustrophobic, but offers a choice for those who can't snag one of the two picnic tables under a pavilion or a couple of others scattered about the property. There's no water view, but you can take out (and proceed on to a picnic table at Herring Cove Provincial Park, a five-minute drive). We splurged for the lobster roll (filled with lobster only and properly toasted) with fries and coleslaw, quite pricey at $14.25. Our tablemates at lunch opted for the fish and chips for $6.95 and got far more than they bargained for. There are the usual choices, except perhaps for the sweet and sour fish. The seafood platter combines haddock, scallops, shrimp and clams with fries, onion rings, slaw and homemade rolls, $16.25 for one and $26.25 for two. Finish it off, if you can, with blueberry cobbler or triple berry crumble.

(506) 752-2470. Entrées, $8.25 to $13.99. Open daily from 11, mid-April to late October.

Eastport Area

Schooner Dining Room, 47 Water St., Eastport.

Although the **Wa-Co Diner** in front has been an institution here since 1924, we weren't aware of it until lately when a new owner added a waterfront deck at the rear and a handsome dining room in what had been a furnace room between diner and deck. Returning to her hometown after 35 years away, chef-owner Nancy Bishop reopened the diner, which had closed in 1997. She upgraded the fare, and her husband John built and expanded the deck, now a spacious affair with jaunty umbrella-topped tables beside the rocky shore – the most watery place to eat in the area. The dining room, nicely nautical with vinyl cloths and oil lamps on the tables, has big windows onto the water on two sides. The menu suggests wines to go with each entrée: a pinot grigio with the coquilles St. Jacques and a fumé blanc for the charbroiled salmon with dill-cream sauce, for instance. The choices range from baked haddock with lobster sauce and lazyman's lobster to chicken marsala, rack of lamb and filet mignon. There are pastas, salads, chowders and deep-fried favorites, plus appetizers like steamed clams, coconut popcorn shrimp and bacon-wrapped scallops. For lunch on the breezy waterside deck, we enjoyed a fine lobster club sandwich and one of the best crab rolls ever.

(207) 853-4046. Entrées, $8.95 to $19.95. Open daily in summer, 5:30 a.m. to 9 p.m.; winter, 6 a.m. to 8 p.m.

La Sardina Loca, 28 Water St., Eastport.

Housed on the ground floor of the old Masonic Building, this popular establishment occupies the space of the former A&P store where Eleanor Roosevelt shopped for groceries while summering on Campobello. The name was chosen, we understand, "to give the sardine back to the community" after many packing plants had closed. It's billed as the easternmost Mexican restaurant in the United States, and you've got to like the name and the concept. Wait until you see the place – a double storefront with big round tables, plastic patio chairs, a Christmas tree hanging upside down from the ceiling, posters, sign boards and a dark cantina bar hidden in back. It's crazy and colorful, to say the least. The food isn't authentic Mexican, though people this far north probably don't care (at one busy Fourth of July visit, the blackboard specials at the entry proclaimed lobster and steak dinners for $11.95). The regular menu might offer rancho grande bifstek with salad, baked potato and corn on the cob and a Rosarita beach lobster dinner, Mexican style, with salad, rice, beans and tortillas. Of course, you can order chicken fajitas, burritos, enchiladas, tostadas, nachos and even omelets and pizzas. Start, if you dare, with La Sardina Loca, billed as spicy herring steaks with hot chiles on a bed of lettuce with crackers, onions and sour cream. Dessert could be strawberry delight, kahlua parfait or caffe Loca with tequila and kahlua.

(207) 853-2739. Entrées, $6 to $13.50. Dinner, Wednesday-Sunday, 4 to 10.

Eastport Chowder House, 167 Water St., Eastport.

Sardine canning started in this country in the 1870s in Eastport on the wharf upon which this large restaurant stands today. For twenty years the site of the Cannery restaurant, it stood idle until the late 1990s when a succession of lessees operated it under a variety of names. In 2003 after one season as a tenant, the restaurant was purchased by Robert DelPapa, who curiously named it a chowder house (it's far more than that) and also opened The Happy Crab, a downtown grill and sports bar at 33 Water St. This place has two large dining rooms enveloped in pine on the upper floor, with big windows onto the water. The lower level, former home to the Cannery, is now a bar and banquet facility opening onto a wharf with picnic tables (where lunch occasionally is available). The extensive, something-for-everyone menu includes a section on chowders and stews (the clam is most popular, the waitress advised, although the lobster dinners are the best sellers). Otherwise expect the predictable baked stuffed haddock, grilled or poached salmon, baked scallops, seafood combo platter, three chicken dishes, ribs and steak. Seafood pasta is touted as the house specialty. Desserts include blueberry pie and assorted ice creams.

(207) 853-4700. Entrées, $11.95 to $13.95. Lunch daily, 11 to 4. Dinner nightly, 4 to 9. Closed mid-October to mid-May.

FOR MORE INFORMATION: Roosevelt Campobello International Park, 459 Route 774, Welshpool, NB E5E 1A4 or Box 97, Lubec, ME 04652, (506) 752-2922.

Eastport Area Chamber of Commerce, Box 254, Eastport, ME 04631, (207) 853-4644, www.eastport.net.

Lubec Chamber of Commerce, Box 123, Lubec, ME 04652, (207) 733-4522.

Roof garden at Fairmont Algonquin looks over town to harbor and Passamaquoddy Bay.

St. Andrews By-the-Sea, N.B.

For many Canadians, no resort area – not Tremblant, not Banff nor even Jasper – has the mystique of St. Andrews-by-the-Sea. Since the late 19th century, it has been a low-key watering hole for old-money Canadians and Americans attracted by pollen-free air and a picturesque, protected setting surrounded by water on three sides at the southwestern tip of New Brunswick, just across Passamaquoddy Bay from Maine.

In the late 1940s, the Canadian among us cherished the summers she spent with a friend whose family from Montreal owned a house in St. Andrews. Lazy days and nights, swimming at Katy's Cove, having sundaes at the counter and listening to the jukebox in the local teenage hangout, going to first-run films several times a week at the local movie palace (they reached St. Andrews even before Montreal), dropping into Cockburn's Corner Drug Store to be sprayed with the French perfume of choice by owner Bobby Cockburn on the way to the weekly dance, and a first summer romance are lasting memories. The experiences and the setting were enough to inspire her recently to buy a water-view townhouse – on the site of the old railroad station where she used to arrive by train – in which to relive summers past.

Though the dance hall, movie theater and teen hangout are long gone, St. Andrews still looks and feels much as it did in our teenage years. That's probably because this historic town, settled after the American Revolution by British Loyalists from Castine, Me., in 1783 – a year before the province of New Brunswick was born – has been passed over, in a way, by time.

The arterial Route 1 from the Maine border at St. Stephen to Saint John skips St. Andrews, ten miles to the south. The Canadian Pacific Railroad, whose founders built summer estates in the area, no longer stops here. The Grand Manan ferry has moved its base from St. Andrews to Black's Harbour. Today, the traveler has to be aware of St. Andrews to make the detour.

Canada's Old Guard resort peaked in the 1940s and lay somewhat dormant into the 1980s. Lately, the town has reawakened, boosted in part by its 1998 designation as a National Historic District. The landmark Algonquin hotel and resort has been upgraded and expanded. The Algonquin golf course has been upgraded into a world-class championship layout. The new Kingsbrae Garden has quickly matured into one of Canada's best. The long harbor wharf was rebuilt after a 1995 fire and now half a dozen cruise outfits run sailing and whale-watch expeditions out of the busy and picturesque Day Adventure Center at its entrance. Ministers Island, reached by a gravel bar across the ocean floor at low tide, is open for public tours of the self-contained farm estate and 55-room mansion built by the founder of the Canadian Pacific Railroad. Small B&Bs have sprouted, restaurants have been rejuvenated and two ultra-upscale inns have been opened by Americans smitten by St. Andrews. "There's a little bit of heaven here," one of them explains.

You'll find it in the friendly, small-town atmosphere of yesteryear, along the shady streets dotted with historic homes and churches, along the shoreline forged by tides that rise and fall up to an incredible 26 feet a day, and on the sparkling waters of Passamaquoddy Bay, with hills and islands all around.

Getting There

Facing Down East Maine just across the St. Croix River and Passamaquoddy Bay, St. Andrews is at the tip of a peninsula in southwesternmost New Brunswick, 90 miles east of Bangor and 50 miles west of Saint John. From Route 1 take Route 127 south to St. Andrews. Calais is the main border entry point from Maine. Two short ferry rides (summer only) follow more scenic routes from Lubec and Eastport, Me., via Campobello and Deer Island to L'Etete, N.B. They offer an unforgettable glimpse of the area's maritime flavor.

Prices are quoted in Canadian funds, which lately represented a discount of more than 20 percent for Americans. Canada's Goods and Services tax (GST) and provincial taxes take part of the difference, although some are refundable. New Brunswick is in the Atlantic time zone, one hour ahead of Eastern time.

Where to Stay ———————————————— *♪♪♪*

Accommodations range from the manorial, veranda-swathed Fairmont Algonquin Hotel and elegant inns to small B&Bs, motels and an oceanfront campground.

The Old Guard

The Fairmont Algonquin, 184 Aldolphus St., St. Andrews E0G 2X0.

One of the grand old Canadian Pacific hotels that spanned the country, the 250-room Algonquin preserves a tradition of gracious resort life that has nearly vanished. One look at the red-turreted, Tudoresque hotel surrounded by lavish

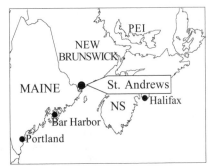

flowerbeds atop a knoll overlooking St. Andrews and Passamaquoddy Bay indicates that this is a special place. Add bellhops in kilts of the New Brunswick tartan (with incongruous-looking intercom beepers on their belts), a long lobby with comfortable peach chairs on which people actually are sitting, the enormous 275-seat Passamaquoddy Dining Room with windows onto the grounds, the book-lined Library Bistro and Veranda with nightly piano music, the Right Whale Brew Pub, a large pool, tennis courts, a health club and spa, an upgraded championship golf course and good conference facilities. The result is a resort of world renown. The historic hotel, started by Boston businessmen in 1889 as a private club, was acquired in 2000 by the Fairmont hotel chain. It has completed a five-year refurbishing program for all rooms and added 54 efficiency mini-suites designed for families in a new wing. Those we saw had two queensize beds, two pillowed wicker chairs, a dining ell with refrigerator and microwave, a large bathroom loaded with amenities and a closet that lights automatically. The new wing repeats some of the architectural traits of the older section, which is wonderfully quirky in decor and layout. Because the original section was rebuilt with concrete walls, ceilings and floors following a 1914 fire, its rooms are solid and unusually quiet. Prime rooms on the third and fourth floors have water views. The best view of all is claimed by the roof garden, which frames Passamaquoddy Bay through flower-bedecked trellises and a gazebo. It provides a sylvan retreat for reading, sunbathing and sunset-watching. Upwards of 300 people turn out for the popular Sunday brunch ($29.95) in the airy, enclosed veranda of the **Passamaquoddy Dining Room,** where dinner also is served. The **Library Bistro and Bar** off the lobby offers an all-day roster of appetizers, casual entrées and exotic desserts. The **Right Whale Pub** on the hotel's lower level serves more basic fare.

(506) 529-8823 or (800) 441-1414. Fax (506) 529-7162. Two hundred twenty-two rooms and sixteen suites. Doubles, $309 to $550 EP.

Dining Room, dinner from 5:30 and Sunday brunch 11 to 2, entrées, $22 to $39.

Small and Choice

Kingsbrae Arms, 219 King St., St. Andrews E5B 1Y1.

The owners of a Long Island inn were driving home from a Maritimes vacation in 1995 when they detoured on whim to St. Andrews, extended their vacation another week and bought a mansion in which to run a second inn. Harry Chancey and David Oxford, who since have sold their Centennial House in East Hampton, do things first-class. Here they converted a rambling 1897 cedar shingle hilltop house with sweeping bay views into a full-service inn. They offer nine deluxe guest rooms and suites and all the amenities for membership in Relais & Châteaux and a designation as Canada's first five-star inn. "We thought we'd arrived in the magic kingdom," says Harry about their chance visit to St. Andrews. "This is one town that has not been spoiled by its own charm." The luxurious guest quarters have Canadian birdseye and maple four-poster beds, locally handcrafted mahogany armoires, gas fireplaces, TV, a writing desk, telephone with data port, three-way reading lamps, sumptuous seating, porcelain doorknobs and original art on the walls. Some have double whirlpool tubs, glass-enclosed showers and marble vanities. All yield water views; five also offer balconies from which to enjoy. Two new spa suites "for those who demand the very best" were opened in a refurbished cottage in 2005. Rooms overlook either Kingsbrae Garden or the inn's own showy gardens in the rolling back yard that ends at a secluded swimming pool. The all-inclusive rates include three meals a day, an open bar and wine, and food prepared by a fulltime chef that's equal to the rest of the experience. Our leisurely, multi-course dinner lived up to its billing as like a "dinner party with friends in a private home." Breakfast the next day included dainty cut-up fruit with yogurt sauce, first-rate salmon benedict or berry crêpes topped with crème fraîche, and hazelnut-flavored coffee.

(506) 529-1897. Fax (506) 529-1197. www.kingsbrae.com. Two rooms and eight suites with private baths. All-inclusive rates in American funds: doubles $640; suites $900 to $1,100. Three-night minimum in July and August, two nights all other times.

The Windsor House of St. Andrews, 132 Water St., St. Andrews E0G 2X0.

First-class accommodations and fine dining are the hallmarks of this handsome new inn and restaurant (see Where to Eat) along the town's main street, across from the harbor. The 1810 Georgian house, which once served as a Victorian inn and later a rooming house, underwent painstaking renovations by two Americans who had summered in St. Andrews, Jay Remer, an appraiser for Sotheby's in New York, and Greg Cohane, a graphics designer from Connecticut. More than $2 million worth of renovations, antiques and artworks went into producing a veritable "live-in museum and art gallery." The main floor holds two small dining rooms and a Victorian mahogany bar/parlor with a pressed-tin gilt ceiling. Downstairs is a billiards room with a nine-foot antique pool table from a Newport mansion and a wine cellar. Four corner bedrooms, each with a different mantle over the original wood-burning fireplace, occupy the second floor, with verandas restored front and rear. Two larger rooms with cathedral ceilings, sitting areas and gas fireplaces take up the third floor. All but two rear rooms have water views. Imposing French Empire armoires serve in lieu of closets, holding TV and terrycloth robes. Marble-floor bathrooms, wide-plank floors, rich fabric window treatments and working fireplaces are standard. A leisurely breakfast (taken in the garden courtyard amid statuary and trickling fountain in season) includes muffins or scones and a main course, perhaps the signature eggs Windsor (like benedict, except with smoked salmon on a crumpet).

(506) 529-3330 or (888) 890-9463. Fax (506) 529-4063. www.windsorhouseinn.com. Six rooms with private baths. Doubles, $225 to $300.

Treadwell Inn, 129 Water St., St. Andrews E0G 2X0.

The best waterfront setting in town commends this B&B run by Annette Lacey and Jerry Mercer. Erected in 1820 by ship's chandler John Treadwell, the handsome structure once served as the St. Andrews customs office, as noted in a stained-glass window over an entrance. Four bedrooms with sitting areas and queen, king or two double beds warmed by duvet comforters are on the second floor. Two in the rear open onto a common second-floor balcony with Adirondack chairs overlooking the harbor. The third-floor holds two prized efficiency suites, each with beamed and vaulted ceiling, kingsize bed, sitting area, whirlpool tub and french doors onto a private balcony high above the water. TVs and telephones are standard. Guests gather in a small and elegant rear parlor or the new parlor bar, both with panoramic views of the water, when they're not out on the waterside decks or enjoying the gardens and lawn sloping to the harbor. Homemade muffins and breads are put out in the morning in the bar, where Annette adds blueberry pancakes or bacon and eggs, to be taken on yet another outside deck. The owners operate a small and with-it clothing store on one front corner of the main floor, where guests check in. The other corner holds a retail branch of the famed **Ganong Chocolatier** of St. Stephen.

(506) 529-1011 or (888) 529-1011. Fax (506) 529-4826. Four rooms and two suites with private baths. Doubles, $145 to $185. Suites, $250.

Tara Manor Inn, 559 Mowat Drive (Highway 127), St. Andrews E5B 2P2.

A former private estate and something of a cross between an inn and a motel, Tara

Manor occupies twenty secluded acres crisscrossed by sculptured, century-old hedgerows on a slope overlooking Passamaquoddy Bay in the distance. Innkeepers Norman and Sharon Ryall started with two rooms in their residence in 1971, opened a dining room in 1980, and produced in additions and outbuildings what Norman called twelve "ultra rooms, the best in the Maritimes" at the time. They have kingsize brass beds or two queen beds screened by spindle partitions from sitting areas containing a sofa, two chairs and a TV. Six secluded "ultra rooms," one with a whirlpool tub, share a large deck overlooking showy flower gardens. They are extra-large and command top-dollar, but we like better the panoramic view of the bay from the other six ultra rooms off the third-floor balcony. We settled for one of the rooms located in the old carriage house, boathouse and servant's quarters, all with full baths and cable TV and comfortable indeed. Decor varies from early American to French provincial, much of it exceedingly fancy. All rooms are different but have striking draperies and Tara's signature collections of plates displayed in bays on the walls. Some have private balconies. The park-like grounds include a pleasant heated swimming pool, a whirlpool spa and a tennis court. We've enjoyed a couple of good dinners in the inn's restaurant, the **Tupper Grill,** whose limited menu features prime rib on summer weekends.

(506) 529-3304 or (800) 691-8272. www.taramanor.com. Twenty-five rooms and three two-bedroom suites. Doubles, $128 to $189 EP. Closed November-April.

The Pansy Patch, 59 Carleton St., St. Andrews E0G 2X0.

A fairy-tale white stucco cottage, with small-paned windows, towers and turrets and a roof that looks as if it should be thatched, stands across the street from The Algonquin. Built in 1912 by the superintendent of Canadian Pacific Hotels, it was fashioned after a Cotswold cottage. Owners Michael and Marilyn O'Connor from Massachusetts converted part of the main floor into the Gallery New Brunswick specializing in fine art and crafts. They opened up a stylish rear sun porch and an umbrellaed deck for guests to enjoy the distant water views, added public dining in the beamed living room and on a landscaped terrace where the restored gardens put on quite a show. The upstairs has five renovated guest rooms. One with a king bed has a window seat with a bay view. An attic suite with double bed and sofabed includes a kitchenette. The Cory Cottage next door offers four more bedrooms with private baths. One with a queen bed adjoins a common room opening onto a balcony with a great water view. Telephones and double or queen beds are standard. The staff serves breakfast for guests at individual tables set with pansy-rimmed china and pansy napkin rings. The fare might be eggs benedict, mushroom quiche or egg bake. The dining room is open to the public for lunch and dinner. The evening menu is continental, with a hint of a German accent. The dozen entrées range from seafood paella or scallops in cream sauce to wiener schnitzel, roast chicken with orange sauce and grilled lamb chops.

(506) 529-3834 or (888) 726-7972. Fax (506) 529-9042. www.pansypatch.com. Eight rooms and one suite with private baths. Doubles, $225 to $325. Closed November-April.

Lunch, Friday-Sunday noon to 3. Dinner by reservation, nightly in summer 6 to 9:30. Entrées, $21 to $32.

Other Options

St. Andrews Motor Inn, 111 Water St., Box 40, St. Andrews E5B 1A3.

Every room gets a head-on view of the harbor at this two-story motel with a walkout lower level along the in-town waterfront. It seems larger than its 33 rooms would indicate, much of the interior space having been given over to an indoor pool with big windows at the water's edge. Rooms have two queensize beds, white molded chairs on the covered balconies and small bathrooms with the sinks outside. Seven larger efficiency units enjoy breezy private decks. The motel also has two kingsize rooms, one with a kingsize waterbed. A breakfast basket is available for $4.75 in the reception area. Lately, owner Christopher Burley has restored an adjacent building as a guesthouse. The main-floor quarters backing up to the waterfront are as appealing as any in St. Andrews, especially when the four-room suite is broken down into a "honeymoon suite." That yields a rear bedroom with kingsize sleigh bed and huge leather club chair and an enormous three-section bath with a heated Italian marble floor, a whirlpool tub, bidet and double-headed shower. The adjoining Florida room opens onto a waterfront balcony. Larger parties can add a kitchen, a sitting room with fireplace and a second bathroom and front bedroom. Upstairs are two more suites with king beds and sitting rooms. On the lower level, Christopher's sister, Megan Burley, operates the **Lobster Bay Eatery,** a casual seafood restaurant.

(506) 529-4571. Fax (506) 529-4583. www.standrewsmotorinn.com. Twenty-three rooms, seven efficiencies and three suites. Doubles, $159.95 to $169.95. Efficiencies, $179.95. Suites, $179.95 to $349.95.

It's the Cat's Meow B&B, 62 Water St., St. Andrews E5B 1A4.

Water views, gardens and three resident cats are among the attributes at this 150-plus-year-old house with charming nooks and crannies facing the waterfront across the street. Bonnie Nelson offers four bedrooms, all with at least glimpses of the harbor. Three rooms have kingsize beds and the other a queen. A favorite is the end room over the garage, with a separate entrance, windows on three sides and an alcove in which a third person can sleep. Two oval tables are joined side by side to seat eight for breakfast in the dining room, where a cat's meow village collection is displayed on shelves. The fare might be belgian waffles heaped with whipped cream and fruit one day and an omelet with a white cheese sauce the next. Guests enjoy a large solarium that doubles as a living room and contains a TV. They also enjoy the back yard, a triple-lot-size affair with cedar hedges, a goldfish pond, gardens and prolific strawberry and raspberry patches.

(506) 529-4717. Fax (506) 529-4086. Four rooms with private baths. Doubles, $110 to $125.

The Mulberry, 96 Water St., St. Andrews E5B 1A5.

The waterfront is on full view across the street from this modest-looking, 1820 Georgian home with a narrow wraparound porch. Walter Nobes, a retired Montreal clothing merchant, and his wife Carole, a former town councilor and civic activist, converted the house into a homey B&B. They offer three upstairs bedrooms, one with private bath and two generally used as a family suite sharing a large bath. Each has a TV. The front rooms, one with queen bed and the other with twins, face the water. The rear room with queen bed has an en-suite bath. His wife was in the midst of redecorating at our visit, starting with a headboard "that cost more than $1,000," Walter rued. "I'm tired of retirement," quipped Walter, who had just finished serving breakfast and was doing the laundry while his wife followed civic pursuits when we stopped by. Breakfast that morning was fruit salad followed by bacon and eggs. It's served in a formal dining room. Guests enjoy the side yard, where Walter spends his spare time gardening.

(506) 529-4948. www.mulberrybb.com. One room with private bath and two rooms with shared bath. Doubles, $95 to $105.

Seaside Beach Resort, 339 Water St., Box 310, St. Andrews E5B 2R2.

This complex of 24 housekeeping units with access to the waterfront is good for families, as we found in the mid-1970s on our first family trip to St. Andrews. At that time, no one restaurant suited our varied (make that outspoken) tastes, so we ended up barbecuing a steak outside our cottage here. Our older son was kept amused at night playing Scrabble across the street with an elderly guest at the Sea Side Inn, now the funky Salty Towers but then under joint ownership. The rooms have been upgraded a bit from the state we remember them in and seem to be very popular with families. Some units are in houses and some are separate one-bedroom cottages. Some are quite large, some have two bedrooms and every unit has cable TV and a large pot for cooking lobster. A spacious lawn leads to the waterfront, where rowboats are available.

(506) 529-3846 or (800) 506-8677. Fax (506) 529-4479. www.seaside.nb.ca. Twenty-four efficiency units. Doubles, $100 to $150.

CAMPING. Kiwanis Oceanfront Camping, 550 Water St., St. Andrews E5B 2R6, (506) 529-3439 or (877) 393-7070. Where but in St. Andrews would the prime oceanfront site in town be occupied by a campground? The Kiwanis Club of St. Andrews runs this spacious, well-equipped trailer and tent park at Indian Point, which has a clear view across the road to Passamaquoddy Bay. The shore here is tidal and favored for exploring. The campground is off by itself less than a mile from the center of town. It has 109 fully serviced, 24 semi-serviced and 27 unserviced sites for $20 to $30 nightly. Trailers and RVs get the best waterfront positions here, and tents are relegated to the background. But anywhere else, this would be the site for motels or mansions.

Island View Camping, another campground at 3406 Route 127 in Bayside, (506) 529-3787, overlooks historic St. Croix Island, where Samuel de Champlain spent the winter of 1604-05 in the failed first attempt at settlement of North America. Its 177 campsites go for $17 to $22 nightly. It has a pool, but campers can also swim in the St. Croix River from Sandy Point.

Seeing and Doing ⎯⎯⎯⎯⎯⎯⎯⎯⎯⎯ 〰〰〰

Surrounded by water on three sides, St. Andrews is naturally geared to water pursuits, which are very much affected by the enormous, 26-foot rise and fall of the Passamaquoddy Bay tides. (The bay is part of the Bay of Fundy, which has the highest tides in the world). The area's varied ocean life has made it an important center for marine biological research. St. Andrews is reputed to have the highest number of residents with doctorates per capita in Canada.

Water Attractions

BOAT CRUISES AND WHALE WATCHING. Passamaquoddy Bay is protected from the Bay of Fundy and the open ocean by Deer and Campobello islands, so the boating is better and more picturesque than off the open coasts of nearby Maine and southern New Brunswick. But the tides and currents can be tricky. At least six outfits run whale, nature and sightseeing cruises from their colorful ticket offices and gift shops in the jaunty Day Adventure Center at the entrance to the long St. Andrews wharf. The area is great for whale watching as some of the best feeding grounds are found between Campobello and the Wolf Islands and out toward Grand Manan. Usually spotted are finback and minke whales and, in late summer, humpback whales and, occasionally, right whales.

Each cruise outfit has its assets and advocates. Some like the speedy **Quoddy Link Marine** catamaran, (506) 529-2600 or (877) 688-2600, and the **Fundy Tide Runners'** Zodiac, (506) 529-4481, which get to the whale feeding grounds faster.

The graceful **Tallship Cory,** (506) 529-8116 or (888) 829-6285, sails slowly and quietly through a maze of islands. More conventional small boats are operated by **Retreat Charters & Outfitters,** (506) 529-4843 or (866) 541-5500, which also offers a sunset harbor cruise. Historic sailing cruises around the bay and up the St. Croix River to St. Croix Island are the specialty of the schooner **Molly Kool**, (506) 529-8875 or (866) 666-7245. It also offers a sunset wine and cheese cruise.

Cruises vary from two to three hours, run two to four times daily and generally cost $43 to $50 for adults, $25 to $35 for children.

Perhaps representative is the meandering, 25-mile cruise on the 40-passenger **Island Quest,** (506) 529-9885 or (888) 252-9111. Very personal and informal, our trip was led by the chatty captain and boat builder, his teen daughter and tour guide Michael Graham, who talked of history, tides and marine wildlife. The ride out past more than 50 named islands was incredibly picturesque and yielded views of lighthouses, ferries and Grand Manan. We saw seals, porpoises, herring weirs, salmon farm aquaculture cages, bald eagles and their nest on Nubble Island, and eventually whales (nine alien boats hovered around a couple of whales off East Quoddy Light toward Deer Island). Complimentary iced tea was served on the return trip. Cruises daily at 10, 2 and 5 July-October; adults $48, children $30.

KAYAKING is big-time here, too. Most people seem to go on guided tours, but one of us went on his own with an experienced friend in a two-seater. The outing produced a different perspective on our shoreline and the difficult crosscurrents around Indian Point revealed why there are so few sailboats and canoeists there. Kayak rentals and tours are available from **Eastern Outdoors,** 165 Water St., (506) 529-4662 or (800) 565-2925, and from **Seascape Sea Kayaks,** Market Wharf, (506) 529-4866. Eastern Outdoors also rents canoes and bicycles.

SWIMMING. A traditional favorite, **Katy's Cove** at the end of Acadia Road, reopened in 2001 after townspeople launched a $300,000 fund drive for restoration in conjunction with the town, province and benefactors. New sluice gates beneath the old railroad bridge at the mouth of the cove control the water flow from Passamaquoddy Bay, so the expansive cove is warmer than the bay. Lifeguards staff the sandy beach, and there's a clubhouse where the porches are lined with old Adirondack chairs. Just east of town is Chamcook Lake, a favorite with locals who like its squeaky-clean waters (it's the town's water supply) and a secluded beach.

Ministers Island, end of Bar Road.

The bar to Ministers Island is under seventeen feet of water at high tide, so you don't want to get stranded out there. Bolstered by its recent designation as a National Historic Site, a local advisory committee is working with the provincial government on long-range plans to develop the 500-acre island as a destination site for the public. Visitors on guided tours get a look at **Covenhoven,** the 55-room summer estate of Canadian Pacific Railroad magnate Sir William Van Horne, which is under restoration as a museum. Off the huge entry foyer is the most interesting room, which Van Horne used as his bedroom to avoid disturbing his guests when he got up in the night to paint. Some of his landscapes hang on the walls. A display case shows artist tools, photos, mementos and a container for the eighteen-inch-long cigars he had made to circumvent doctor's orders limiting him to three cigars a day. Upstairs are seventeen bedrooms, one with a Delft tile fireplace. Restoration continues apace, but until the building can be heated, we're told, the paint and wallpaper will continue to peel. Leaded windows and rich paneling testify to better days. Tour visitors get a look inside the circular bathhouse built from quarried beach stone beside a natural saltwater pool, the gigantic barn in which thoroughbred horses and Dutch belted cattle were raised and a windmill that helped power the island to self-sufficiency (Van Horne even had greenhouses, one containing a peach orchard – when he was at home in Montreal he had fruit shipped overnight for breakfast). The two-hour tour elicits fascinating insights on how one of the world's richest men lived early in the 20th century.

(506) 529-5081. Tours twice daily, scheduled around hours of low tides, June to mid-October. Adults $5, children $2.50.

Other Attractions

Kingsbrae Garden, 220 King St.

The Flemer family donated a magnificent 27-acre hilltop property overlooking Passamaquoddy Bay and an endowment to operate what they envisioned as a world-class garden site, one that in its second year won honors as among the ten best in Canada. Their joint venture with the town and province produced a wonderland of more than 30 themed gardens. They vary from a pristine white garden along the entryway to sections for heath and heather, fruits and berries, ornamental shrubs, birds and butterflies, roses, wildflowers, a cedar maze and herb labyrinth, scents and sensitivity, and edibles. There are sand and gravel gardens, a blue garden, a hillside hydrangea garden, a secret Harry Potter garden and a new fantasy garden with pint-size houses and topiary animals for children. The highlight for most is the showy perennial garden, where classical music wafts from in-ground speakers and a fascinating Japanese "deer clapper" works by water power to frighten the roaming deer from the adjacent rose garden. We've been here at all stages of the growing season, never ceasing to marvel at the embankment of splashy rhododendrons in June and poppies in August, the showy oriental lilies, the peacock gladiolus, the dwarf cosmos, the strawberries in bloom at Labor Day, the prolific organic garden in which lettuce varieties thrive in August. There are surprises at every turn, from a cedar hedgerow so thick and dark you could stay dry underneath in a thunderstorm to a working Dutch windmill circulating water to and from a sizable duck pond. A half-mile nature trail leads through a marked Acadian Forest, home to 32 species of trees beside the bay. One of four manor houses originally on the property is the site of the Garden Café (see Where to Eat), a small but exceptional gift shop with a garden theme and an art gallery with changing exhibits of regional art.

(506) 529-3335 or (888) 566-8687. www.kingsbraegarden.com. Open daily, 9 to 6, mid-May to early October. Adults $8.50, children $6.50.

Algonquin Signature Golf Course.

Contrary to belief, The Algonquin's famed golf course was not patterned nor named after the "Old Course" in St. Andrews, Scotland. Algonquin officials say that golfers who have played both find that this has more hazards, is more capricious and requires a greater variety of shots than the Scotland course. It also rivals Pebble Beach for scenery. Thirteen holes are played near or within sight of the St. Croix River and Passamaquoddy Bay, making it a particularly picturesque if distracting setting. The beautiful but tricky 12th hole drops 40 feet from an elevated tee to a green perched on a point of land jutting into the water – award-winning designer Thomas McBroom modeled it after the 7th hole at Pebble Beach. The 11th fairway was re-routed around an active osprey nest, and golfers often have to wait for lingering deer to get out of the way. The first nine holes were constructed in 1894 and nine more holes were laid out in 1900. All were redesigned and upgraded to signature status in a $7 million renovation completed in 2000. The 7,000-yard, par-71 course quickly became the site for major tournaments.

(506) 529-7142 or (888) 460-8999. Greens fees, $125.

HISTORIC DISTRICT. Settled in 1783 by United Empire Loyalists who floated their dismantled homes here following the American Revolution from Castine, Me., (they were rebuilt and three are still standing), St. Andrews is said to have more examples of fine New England Colonial architecture than any other Canadian town. Everything from Cape Cod cottages to saltboxes to large Georgian houses with Federal detailing and architect-designed Shingle-style mansions designed by famous Montreal architects Edward and W.S. Maxwell can be seen scattered across a grid of neatly squared lots laid out by town planners in the 18th century. More than 250 structures, many of them legacies of the prosperous era when St. Andrews was a port of call on the West Indies trade route, are more than 100 years old, warranting the town's 1998 designation as a National Historic Site. The 1824 **Greenock Presbyterian Church** looks like any white Colonial New England church, except for the unique bright green oak tree carved on the exterior beneath its spire, the two-tiered pulpit and the most uncomfortable high-back box pews in which we've ever sat. Other St. Andrews churches, particularly those along King Street, are architecturally interesting. Don't miss the old **Charlotte County Courthouse** with its classical temple facade and carved royal coat of arms, and the adjacent **Gaol.**

Ross Memorial Museum, 188 Montague St.

Here is a true house museum, acquired and given to the town by Henry Phipps Ross and his wife Sarah as a means to display their extensive collections acquired from world travels. Ross, a onetime Episcopal minister in Providence, R.I., and his wife, the daughter of the Bradstreet of Dun & Bradstreet in New York, summered here from 1902 to 1945. The imposing red brick Neo-Classic house was built in 1824 by Harris Hatch, a Loyalist leader. The Rosses acquired it in 1938 for a museum. Each room reflects the Rosses' interests: fine furniture made by early New Brunswick cabinetmakers, fabulous oriental carpets and decorative arts. When we were there, the special exhibit, which changes annually, showed their fascinating photographs and travel mementos from the 1925-26 world cruise of the S.S. Carinthia, the maiden voyage of the Cunard Lines ship.

(506) 529-5124. Guided tours, Monday-Saturday 10 to 4:30 in summer, Tuesday-Saturday in off-season. Closed mid-October to late June. Donation.

St. Andrews Blockhouse, 23 Joe's Point Road.

Across from Centennial Park, this restored, two-story National Historic Site was built of hand-hewn timbers in 1813 to protect St. Andrews from American privateers. Of twelve such blockhouses built in New Brunswick, it is the only survivor. Guides and interpretive displays explain the role of the fortification in the War of 1812. Although Canadian soldiers were ready and willing, they never had to fire a shot in defense of St. Andrews. Today, visitors like to explore the rocks beyond the blockhouse at low tide.

(506) 529-4270. Open daily 9 to 8, June to Labor Day. Free.

Huntsman Aquarium/Museum, 1 Lower Campus Road.

Part of the large Huntsman Marine Science Centre, this fun spot for families turns out much better than it looks from the outside. Thirty-two tanks, many hidden in a back room, are full of exotic fish. Exhibits detail the intricacies of seaweed, Fundy tides, aquaculture, herring weirs and more. A highlight is a heart-shaped touch tank surrounded by a raised platform where children can get close to shells, starfish, wolffish and perhaps a rare black sea bass. We saw scallops "swim" when placed on starfish and squirt when prodded. Try to arrange your visit around the feeding times (11 and 4) for the harbor seals in a large pool. Folks watched entranced as a naturalist fed herring to Chelsea and Buddy and their young offspring. An auditorium shows changing videos.

(506) 529-4285. www.huntsmanmarine.ca. Open daily, 10 to 6 in summer, 10 to 4:30 in late spring and early fall. Adults $7, children $4.50. Closed mid-October to late May.

Atlantic Salmon Interpretive Centre, 24 Chamcook Lake Road, Chamcook.

Just east of St. Andrews off Route 127 is the home of the Atlantic Salmon Federation, the newest in a scientific triumvirate (also Huntsman Marine Science Centre and the Biological Station of the Canadian Department of Fisheries and Oceans). Together they play a leading role in Atlantic Canada's growing aquaculture industry. The center has been greatly expanded lately with four handsome post-and-beam buildings connected by porches and boardwalks to resemble a stately angling resort. One includes the Atlantic Salmon International Hall of Fame with books and memorabilia honoring famous anglers and conservationists. The centerpiece is **Salar's World,** a viewing chamber in which you look down into Chamcook Stream, which flows right through the room and for a short distance becomes an aquarium. Salmon of all sizes are visible here, as well as below where four windows look at eye-level. Nature trails lead past the salmon rearing tanks along the picturesque stream down to the bay and up to Chamcook Lake.

(506) 529-4581. www.asf.ca. Open daily 10 to 6, mid-May through September. Adults $4, children $2.50.

SHOPPING. The Water Street commercial district has a distinctive appearance that has not changed significantly since the 1800s. The main intersection is still flanked by the post office, bank, hardware store and drug store – the side wall of the last enhanced with a remarkable mural of the street scene leading to Kingsbrae Garden, mirroring a larger mural on the water tank east of town. The stores of St. Andrews are locally owned and their wares are generally quite sophisticated.

Cottage Craft, an old-timer on the waterfront at Market Square, with brightly colored skeins of wool draped around its cork fence in front, shows knit goods in lovely colors like robin's egg blue, briar rose and yellow birch. The specialty here is a skirt and sweater kit, the sweater yarn exactly matching the skirt length. They also have knitting bags (one shaped like a house in which the door opens), men's tweed jackets and the neatest collection of mittens for kids you ever saw, not to mention fine yarns that friends from home stock up on. **The China Chest** imports English bone china and Canadian gifts.

Representative of the new is the dramatic **Seacoast Gallery** at 174 Water St., where owner Lola Boyles features two floors of fine works by leading New Brunswick artists. We defy anyone to escape her arty shop without purchasing something local. We also were struck by the $650 wood carving of a hummingbird and $195 sweaters bearing images of a whale and a covered bridge at **Serendipin' Art,** which shows local handicrafts and has a jewelry and metalsmithing studio on site. Nearby, artist Tom Smith, who has won many awards, shows his beautiful raku pottery at **Tom Smith Pottery,** behind the Windsor House on Edward Street. His wife Ellen, who manages the studio, makes the drawstring bags for Tom's raku tea bowls. Another favorite is **The Crocker Hill Store,** where soothing music draws passersby in to see and buy Steven Smith's remarkable bird watercolors. A gardener of note, Steve opens his back-yard garden for guided tours. Young Montreal artist Chantal Vincent features her ceramics and her parents' recycled copper jewelry along with works of local artists at her **Nan's Land Gallery** around the corner on Queen Street. Down by Market Wharf, Alanna Baird's exotic tin sculptures at the **Tin Fish Shop** redefine the art of recycling

Truly unusual is **Jarea Art Studio & Gallery,** whose principals spearheaded the painting of the aforementioned scenic murals and produce wondrous oils, floor cloths and folk art with found objects. Another favorite is the remarkable, one-of-a-kind textile art at the **Bertha Day Studio,** 275 Water St. Bertha's hand-painted or embroidered wall hangings, vests, T-shirts (some with lupines or fiddlehead ferns), landscape cushions, small purses, tea cozies and more are unique.

The colorful **Boutique La Baleine/The Whale Store** carries stuffed animals, cards, books, apparel and a large toy section. It is here we acquired the coffee-table pictorial history book about St. Andrews, Willa Walker's *No Hay Fever and a Railway,* only to learn that summer people were mere visitors unless they were about fifth generation. Other attractive shops are **Leather House** for apparel and home furnishings, **Tradewinds Imports, Cricket Cove** (handknits and colorful yarns), **Cream Lifestyle** ("homeware and giftware"), **Ivy Lane** ("home fashions"), **By the Sea** gifts and apparel, and **Garden by the Sea** (handcrafted soaps and herbal teas). Rugged outerware is available at **Eastern Outdoors** and **Island Beach Co.**

Where to Eat

The Windsor House of St. Andrews, 132 Water St.

A four-diamond AAA rating – only the second awarded in New Brunswick – was accorded the sophisticated restaurant at the Windsor House shortly after opening. Contemporary Canadian and French cuisine, some with appropriately English Loyalist influences, is served in two formal and elegant twenty-seat dining rooms and a tented rear garden courtyard. We'd heard nothing but raves for the specialty eggs Windsor with smoked salmon on crumpets and the spinach and wild mushroom crêpes for Sunday brunch, and ours proved equally rewarding. Chef Peter Woodworth's fare is even more refined at night. A recent dinner beside a gurgling fountain in the glamorous courtyard began with the fabulous smoked salmon produced at the owners' farm, so popular it's sold at the weekly farmers' market and was being prepared for distribution in the United States. Entrées were an assertive bouillabaisse and Quebec "duck in two acts," a terrific pan-seared breast with cilantro butter and orange-chile braised leg. An ethereal maple sugar crème brûlée and a double chocolate terrine with brandy crème anglaise topped off a superior meal.

(506) 529-3330 or (888) 890-9463. Entrées, $24 to $38. Dinner nightly, 5:30 to 9. Sunday brunch, 11 to 2. Closed January-March.

Rossmount Inn, 4599 Route 127.

Chef-owner Chris Aerni and his wife Graziella have turned this outlying inn into a dining destination for local gourmands. The Swiss native who had 25 years' experience working for others in Toronto and Australia found his niche in the venerable inn high up a hill overlooking Passamaquoddy Bay. Dinner might begin with his signature cappuccino of lobster bisque with brandy, cayenne pepper and chives or the sensational salmon and avocado tartare flavored with chives and coriander. Among main courses, the sautéed chicken breast with a two-mushroom sauce was one of the best poultry dishes we've had. Also superior were the fillet of haddock on old-fashioned potatoes with wilted greens and pickled fiddleheads and the roasted lamb loin with an organic basil and garlic crust. Among the sophisticated desserts, we always seem to go for the walnut butter cake with homemade maple ice cream and Chamcook Mountain maple brandy syrup. The inn also has eighteen hotel-style guest rooms, four with water views, renting for $105 to $130 a night.

(506) 529-3351. www.rossmountinn.com. Entrées, $15.50 to $24.80. Dinner nightly, 6 to 9:30. Closed Monday-Tuesday in off-season and January-March.

L'Europe, 48 King St.

Just off Water Street in the heart of town is this rustic low brown building which, it turns out, is a remodeling of the dance hall of our teen years. It's been a restaurant since 1984, but never better than under master chef Markus Ritter from Germany. Markus, who had trained for fourteen years in his homeland and on cruise ships, came upon St. Andrews in the usual serendipitous manner, arriving one Canada Day and putting down a deposit on the empty L'Europe building. He and his bride-to-be Simone moved to St. Andrews, renovated the restaurant and were married on the town Wharf. They lightened up the interior, giving it a more modern look in white and pale blue, and added tables on the flower-bedecked front porch. Markus offers continental fare from his renovated kitchen. The escargots bourguignonne and scallops mornay are good appetizers, and the composed salad is fresh as could be. Main courses range from scallops provençal, pan-seared haddock fillet with almond butter and tiger shrimp in mango-chutney sauce to wiener schnitzel and chicken zurich. The rack of lamb and filet mignon with béarnaise sauce were about the best we've had. Most desserts feature ice creams and fresh fruits. We opted for the "dessert variation à L'Europe, an excursion of our specialties" – a decadent finale to a fine meal. More than a dozen flavors of homemade ice cream are offered at the tables on the front veranda starting at 3 on summer afternoons. Upstairs in the European style, the Ritters offer four queensize bedrooms and three efficiency suites with private baths, $95 to $140, including breakfast.

(506) 529-3818. www.leurope.ca. Entrées, $18.50 to $33.50, Dinner nightly, 5:30 to 11. Closed midweek in off-season and month of November.

Niger Reef Tea House, 1 Joe's Point Road.

Overlooking Niger Reef and the historic blockhouse, this picturesque log house with quite a history is the most appealing waterside dining spot in town. The simple interior holds oriental wall murals painted by artist Lucille Douglas and a corner gift shop with tea accessories. We favor the rustic waterside deck with a tranquil, sylvan view of the harbor and an outdoor grill where the freshest fish and meats are barbecued for dinner. Expanded from its former tea-house status by chef Lysa Huggins and host/partner Tim Currie, it's a pure place featuring contemporary, healthful fare. Planked salmon, grilled scallops in an orange-ginger-curry sauce, mustard-crusted lamb chops and steak kabobs are dinner standbys, all done to perfection and supplemented by at least three nightly specials – perhaps arctic char, tuna and swordfish. Grilled vegetables accompany. This is a an offbeat place for lunch as well. We enjoyed a superior ploughman's lunch and a caesar salad topped with grilled salmon, accompanied by a couple of dark ales and a marvelous strawberry tart. Tea and scones are offered in the afternoon.

(506) 529-8007. Entrées, $15.95 to $21.95. Open daily in summer, 11:30 to 8, to 3 in spring and fall. Closed November-April.

The Lighthouse Restaurant, 1 Patrick St.

A nicely nautical dining room, dressed in blue and white, has large windows overlooking Passamaquoddy Bay on a point beside the 1833 lighthouse at the entrance to St. Andrews harbor. From tables at the far end you can watch the sun set to the west over the harbor and the moon rise over the bay waters to the east. It's arguably the choicest waterfront restaurant location in town, and visitors and bus ,tours like it for its lobsters. Other possibilities include chargrilled salmon fillet with sweet red pepper sauce, Hawaiian or balsamic chicken and filet mignon. Our party enjoyed the seafood pasta (laden with fresh seafood in parmesan cream sauce but overwhelmed with penne), the seafood crêpe (mostly seafood and little sign of crêpe), the haddock fillet crusted in smoked salmon and the mixed grill, a hefty portion of charbroiled pork tenderloin, chicken and sausage. The accompanying salads were ample, and the wines were on the expensive side. Except for our favorite local Oven Head smoked salmon, the appetizers were predictable. Tiramisu torte, cookie crumb cake and chocolate truffle mousse were extravagant desserts.

(506) 529-3082. Entrées, $15.50 to $24. Dinner nightly except Tuesday, 5 to 9. Closed November-April.

The Garden Café, Kingsbrae Garden, 220 King St.

All things considered, if we could have only one lunch in St. Andrews, it would be here. Actually, we've had many, and they've always turned out to be exceptional. On a crystal-clear day, there's no more perfect setting than the leafy terrace outside the gallery dining room. You relax under a "weeping" apple tree which resembles a canopy, with a postcard view of sloping lawns, floral borders, a couple of sculptures, an enormous Adirondack chair art piece that people keep climbing onto for photo ops, and a panoramic glimpse of the bay beyond. The interesting menu ranges from sandwiches to light entrées and pasta dishes. The seafood chowder is elegant, the ploughman's lunch a pleasant platter of breads, cheese, pickles and pâtés, and the cobb salad first-rate. The day's cheese and mushroom quiche was light and ethereal, teamed with a mesclun salad. The dessert tray harbored about eight delectable-looking goodies. The cheesecake with blackberry topping, light as a soufflé, was a triumph. The lunch menu is served until 2:30, with afternoon tea service following until 6. The only frustration is that you can't get into the café without paying the garden admission fee (many local folks buy a season ticket to the gardens), but the gardens are a must-see anyway.

(506) 529-4016. Prices, $3.50 to $12.95. Open daily, 10 to 6, mid-May to mid-October.

The Gables, 143 Water St.

Lobster buoys and traps and seaside flowers line the alleyway to the side entrance at this popular restaurant, the best in town for a casual meal beside the water. A pleasant, three-level deck shaded by a huge chestnut tree at water's edge is its most appealing feature and far preferable to the inside dining room and bar. Owner Ted Michener is an artist and cartoonist, whose works grace the walls and the menu. The all-day roster offers first-rate burgers, deep-fried veggies, soups, salads and sandwiches, plus a few specials ranging from souvlaki to a Mideastern platter. Friends say the lobster is tops, but we always go for a casual waterside supper of spanakopita and a Greek salad for one, bruschetta and a large bowl of steamed mussels for the other. Grand marnier cheesecake and chocolate torte are the desserts of choice.

(506) 529-3440. Entrées, $9 to $19.95. Lunch daily, 11 to 5. Dinner, 5 to 10:30.

Elaine's Chowder House Café, 24 King St.

A recent adjunct to the Tin Fish gift shop, this casual little winner offers a limited menu and inspired fare in tight, convivial surroundings – so convivial that the slow-as-molasses service can be forgiven. The talkative server likely will talk you into foregoing the basic lunch and dinner menu of seafood sandwiches, sushi rolls, curries and our favorite steamed mussels. Instead he'll tout the blackboard specials, one night's choice including crab cakes with salad, salmon fillet, rack of lamb and filet mignon. We were impressed with the Thai coconut curried seafood (shrimp, scallops, haddock and mussels over rice), the curried chicken and vegetables and the chicken in puff pastry as well as the beer and wine selection. Homemade pies are the desserts of choice. Chef Elaine Wilson's artworks share top billing on the intimate enclosed porch with those of her husband, artist-restaurateur Ted Michener. *(506) 529-4496. Entrées, $14.95 to $28.95. Open daily except Tuesday, noon to 9.*

Harbour Front Restaurant, 225 Water St.

New owners have upgraded this restaurant in an 1840 building that hides a laid-back, open-air patio overlooking harbor and wharf. Bob Lord and Penny Chase, whose husband is the chef, outfitted the front section as a living room with club chairs and a sofa, a comfortable spot for a drink before or after dinner. Beyond is an open and atmospheric, two-level dining room with beams from an old boathouse, tools and artifacts on the walls, and a loft that indicates the building's onetime status as a movie theater. The all-day menu offers something for everyone, from the French-Canadian poutine, mozzarella sticks or "dragon rolls" as appetizers to bacon-wrapped scallops, stuffed sole, seafood brochette, barbecued chicken and filet mignon as main courses. Souvlaki is a specialty, marinated in a secret blend of seasoning. You can order it with pork and chicken, salmon, shrimp or scallops, or combinations thereof. Cheesecakes and crêpes are the favored desserts.

(506) 529-4887. Entrées, $11.95 to $24.95. Open daily, 11 to 10. Closed November-April.

Market Square Grill & Deli, 211 Water St.

This certainly has a good location, next to Market Square and with glimpses of the harbor, especially from the outdoor patio alongside. Inside on either side of the lounge are a nondescript front dining room and a larger dining room in back. Originally advertising California grill cuisine, owner Sean Boyd from California dropped any California pretense in favor of a standard menu of poached haddock, seafood pasta, kiwi chicken and grilled chimichurri steak. Lobster pasta and grilled salmon were blackboard specials at one visit, along with fresh blueberry daiquiris. At lunch, we've enjoyed the specialty haddock chowder and half a meatloaf sandwich. The front deli section offers takeout as well as espresso and cappuccino.

(506) 529-8241. Entrées, $16.95 to $23.95. Lunch daily, 11 to 5. Dinner 5 to 9. Closed in winter.

The Club House Grill, Algonquin Signature Golf Course.

From its hilltop perch, the new clubhouse at the championship golf course boasts the best panoramic view of the waters around St. Andrews. The stylish dining room and side terrace take full advantage, and we've had both a wonderful lunch at which the food matched the view and a sunset pasta dinner that did not. The lobster club sandwich we so enjoyed has been replaced lately by a chicken BLT club and healthful light fare of the type favored by golfers on the go. The all-day menu is augmented at night by a buffet format that seems to change annually. We sampled the pasta bar one season with choose-your-own-pasta ingredients, much in the manner of an omelet station – except that here the waitress took the order and we waited and waited and waited. Recently the dinner buffet included soup and assorted salads, grilled vegetables, steamed mussels and pasta of the day for $19.95. Grilled halibut, strip loin steak and lobster were available for a surcharge.

(506) 529-8162. Dinner buffet, $19.95 to $30. Lunch, 11:30 to 6. Dinner nightly except Wednesday, 6 to 9. Closed mid-October to April.

FOR MORE INFORMATION: St. Andrews Chamber of Commerce, 46 Reed Ave., St. Andrews, NB E5B 1A1, (506) 529-3555 or (800) 563-7397. www.town.standrews.nb.ca.

Waters of Mahone Bay form scenic backdrop for dining porch at Haddon Hall in Chester.

Chester/Lunenburg, N.S.

For those who have searched for a perfect seaside shangri-la along the Northeast Coast – search no longer. We've found it.

It's the Chester-Mahone Bay-Lunenburg area along Nova Scotia's South Shore, about 50 miles southwest of Halifax. People call it variously Lunenburg County, the South Shore, Bluenose Country, the Lighthouse Trail.

Centered around Mahone Bay and its 365 islands, this low-key stretch of rather sophisticated civilization is the focus of an otherwise provincial, seafaring area. Its undulating, tree-lined inlets are tranquil refuges from the rugged Nova Scotia coastline.

The area brings to mind the Maine coast as it used to be – secluded, unspoiled, yet with a welcome air of civility. It's not so isolated that you have to forego the amenities of good restaurants, inns, galleries and shops. But it's not so frequented that you feel stressed by the crowds that jam similar areas in New England.

Chester, a village of 1,100 settled in 1759 by New Englanders, is on a peninsula at the head of Mahone Bay. Today it is a summer colony for wealthy Canadians and Americans and, perhaps, a resting place for Captain Kidd's buried bounty. Lately it's been the setting for a number of movies, which explains its recent emergence as a vacation-home mecca for Hollywood producers and movie stars.

Lunenburg, called the Gloucester of Canada, was founded in 1753 by German Protestants and is Canada's oldest fishing port. With a population of 2,600, it's the colorful home of working fishermen and Bluenose schooners. Its claim to be the most architecturally interesting town in Canada was recognized by UNESCO, which declared its Old Town a World Heritage site in 1995.

The village of Mahone Bay (population 1,000) is poised at the head of an inlet from the bay, whose sailing waters are considered among the best in the world. Its shipbuilding heritage is celebrated during Atlantic Canada's only Wooden Boat Festival. "We love the beauty around us and welcome you to share it," proclaim the endearing signs at the village limits.

Here is a rural area in the Maritimes that matches one's expectations for a balance of quaint charm and urbane shops, good dining on outdoor decks, picturesque harbors and peaceful beaches.

Perhaps you'll think like Lunenburg painter Gail Patriarche, who fell in love with the area and moved from Ontario. Said she: "I'm an artist, and I felt I'd been cheated all my life until I got here."

Getting There

This area is easily reached in less than an hour via Route 103 from Halifax, Atlantic Canada's largest city and a major air and rail destination. It's about a three-hour drive via Route 103 from Yarmouth, where the ferries land from Bar Harbor and Portland, Me. Prices are quoted in Canadian funds and are subject to Canada's GST tax. The province is on Atlantic Time, one hour ahead of Eastern.

Where to Stay ───────────── *∿∿∿*

Lunenburg and Mahone Bay are about ten miles apart, while Chester is about twenty miles northeast of Mahone Bay. The accommodations are grouped here by location, from west to east.

Lunenburg and Mahone Bay

Boscawen Inn, 150 Cumberland St., Box 1343, Lunenburg B0J 2C0.

Perched astride a steep hill, this restored 1888 Victorian mansion offers a variety of guest rooms, an acclaimed main-floor dining room (see Where to Eat), a casual downstairs restaurant and lounge, and a rooftop deck with a view across treetops and houses toward Lunenburg Harbor. Recent owners have upgraded the guest quarters, added more queensize beds and sitting areas, new phones and TVs. Varying widely in size, the larger rooms are elegant in a formal style with canopy or four-poster beds, fancy curtains and upholstered chairs – more comfortable and welcoming than we found them at our first stay. Favorite rooms, each with a sitting area in the turret, yield harbor views. One on the second floor has a kingsize bed and a sofabed. The other on the first floor has a queen poster bed, working fireplace and an air-jet tub for two in the large bathroom. Considered top of the line are three rooms and two suites in the turreted McLachlan House behind the inn . Guests here enjoy sitting areas, a veranda and deluxe rooms, two with water views. Best is the MacDuff Suite with queen bed, sitting room and rear balcony overlooking the harbor. New owners John and Jane Reed from Calgary, with their daughter Donna as general manager, have put increased emphasis on the food operation, offering a Victorian tea at lunchtime and a musical dinner theater at night in the downstairs Admirals Club.

(902) 634-3325 or (800) 354-5009. Fax (902) 634-9293. www.boscawen.ca. Twenty rooms and two suites with private baths. Doubles, $90 to $205. Suites, $165 and $180.

Lunenburg Arms Hotel, 94 Pelham St., Box 1378, Lunenburg, B0J 2CO.
The South Shore's first "boutique hotel" emerged in 2002 from an abandoned restaurant enterprise and exceeded expectations. On three floors overlooking the harbor and boasting Lunenburg's first elevator, it has 26 rooms, half facing the water. The views improve with each floor, culminating on the fourth floor where are found two loft-style suites with king poster beds and two rooms with a pair of double beds each and panoramic vistas of the harbor. Accommodations vary from rooms with a queen sleigh bed and a sofabed to one with a king poster bed, two armchairs and an air-jet tub for two in the corner. Duvet covers, TVs, irons and hardwood floors are standard. Decor is stylish, as orchestrated by Imelda Reynolds, who was manning the front desk at our visit, co-owner with Michael Pollock. The main-floor restaurant, **Rissers,** serves three meals a day, offering a with-it menu (entrées, $23 to $30) but no water view.
(902) 640-4041 or (800) 679-4950. www.lunenburgarms.com. Twenty-four rooms and two suites with private baths. Doubles, $129 to $249.

Addington Arms, 27 Cornwallis St., Box 1042, Lunenburg B0J 2C0.
Large and luxurious rooms with therapeutic amenities are offered at this new B&B on a side street above the harbor. Christine Cooper and her husband, Daniel Prokaziuk, spent two years converting an 1890 house into a welcoming B&B with four guest quarters, a second-floor breakfast room, a third-floor art gallery, a water-view deck and lovely gardens. All rooms have harbor views, and one – the Heritage Suite, notable for antique furniture and original wide-plank floors – has views from three sides. Every room comes with a queen bed, TV/VCR, refrigerator and bath with air-jet tub and separate shower or steam room featuring aroma therapy oils, sound therapy and handmade soaps. The Topsail has modern furnishings and a steam shower. Breakfast is quite an event here. Dan, who had been an executive chef in major cities across Canada for 25 years, prepares the likes of orange pancakes with orange sauce, lobster crêpes or baked eggs with asparagus and parmesan cheese.
(902) 634-4573. www.addingtonarms.com. One room and three suites with private baths. Doubles, $119 to $169.

Brigantine Inn & Suites, 82 Montague St., Box 195, Lunenburg B0J 2C0.
This establishment emerged in 1990 above a downtown retail block facing the waterfront and recently doubled in size under new ownership. It typifies what seems to be the Old Town Lunenburg waterfront inn style: comfortable, hotel-type rooms with no lobby or common area and no personal service. In the original "inn," owner Alan Creaser offers five spacious rooms with queensize beds and two small rooms with double beds, plus the two-bedroom Annex suite with queen beds, living area and kitchenette, private entrance and harbor view. Each has TV, clock radio and telephone. The four facing the harbor have bow windows with great views, and one has a balcony with a whirlpool tub. Newer are seven one-bedroom suites, five with kingsize beds, a block away at 100 Montague St. The latest are two kitchenette suites, one with two bedrooms in the Morash House at 55 Montague. Brigantine guests have use of a bar fashioned from a former parlor, whose picture windows frame the colorful waterfront. Complimentary continental breakfast is served downstairs in the lower-level **Grand Banker Seafood Bar & Grill**, a casual bistro with nautical atmosphere overlooking the harbor. We enjoyed a full breakfast here of light and flavorful strawberry pancakes and welsh rarebit with bacon.
(902) 634-3300 or (800) 360-1181. www.brigantineinn.com. Seven rooms and ten suites with private baths. Doubles, $75 to $139. Suites, $119 to $175.

Atlantic View Motel and Cottages, 230 Mason's Beach Road, R.R. 2, Lunenburg B0J 2C0.

Nine motel units (five with kitchens) and five housekeeping cottages date back more than 50 years, but they're basically up to date in terms of furnishings. And, oh, what a view! Across the narrow, untrafficked road is a cove opening to the Atlantic, and this is one of the few places in the area where you get to see it. From the motel efficiency units (kitchenette and living room with remote-control cable TV in front, bedroom with two double beds in the rear), each back door leads to a picnic table outside. Adirondack chairs are scattered out front for gazing at Battery Point Light. New owners Heidi and Alex Fischer from Switzerland offer a heated swimming pool and a couple of rowboats for exploring the tidal pond in the rear. A hike along the path through the woods may reveal turtles and muskrats. Obviously, this is a good place for families, although couples enjoy its comforts and relaxed pace as well. It suits us so well we've stayed here twice.

(902) 634-4545. Nine motel rooms and five cottages. Doubles, $80 to $100. Closed November-April.

Topmast Motel, 92 Mason's Beach Road, Box 958, Lunenburg B0J 2C0.

Views and value commend the refurbished rooms and housekeeping units at this hilltop perch run by Donald and Agnes Wilson. They've also added decks with Adirondack chairs to take advantage of the super view of the harbor across the greens of the Bluenose Golf Club. Rooms are furnished with queen, king or two double beds and cable TV. A luxury housekeeping suite offers a queen bed, a sofabed, kitchen and dining area. Picnic tables and grills are available outside.

(902) 634-4661 or (877) 525-3222. Fax (902) 634-8660. www.topmastmotel.com. Nine rooms and six efficiency units. Doubles, $90 to $100. Efficiencies, $105 to $120.

The Manse at Mahone Bay, 88 Orchard St., Mahone Bay B0J 2E0.

The former parsonage of the most easterly of Mahone Bay's three famed churches is now the area's most appealing B&B. Yellow with white trim, it has a great deck facing the bay, down a lawn past the church. Rose and Allan O'Brien moved from Ottawa to his native province to convert their new home into a B&B. They did extensive renovations to enhance guests' comfort, putting in large closets, queen beds and modern baths. The closets hide the TVs (a compromise because Rose thought television an intrusion and her husband considered it a necessity). The bathrooms are stocked with large vials of perfume, after-shave lotion and such. Rose sewed the curtains and the down duvets for the four stylish guest quarters, two of them in an outlying carriage house. We liked the East Room facing the bay in the main house, but the most popular is the cathedral-ceilinged Loft in the carriage house with queen bed, rattan chairs and balcony. Allan, the breakfast chef, goes all out with treats like his specialty omelet with stilton and pear, belgian waffles with berries or eggs benedict. Muffins and croissants fresh from the oven accompany. The meal is taken at a cherry table for eight in the dining room, or on the front deck overlooking the water. Guests also enjoy the common rooms with the couple's eclectic collection of books and music.

(902) 624-1121. Fax (902) 624-1182. Four rooms with private baths. Doubles, $110 to $135.

Edgewater Bed & Breakfast, 44 Mader's Cove Road, Mahone Bay B0J 2E0.

New owners Susan and Paul Seltzer undertook extensive renovations to upgrade this century-old house, which occupies a quiet property on the side of Mahone Bay, with the water across the road. Their wraparound porch is festooned with flowers, and big yellow Adirondack chairs invite relaxation. The decor in three bedrooms is fresh and sprightly. Two have queen beds and one has twins. Most in demand is the newly built, well-equipped Sea Loft housekeeping cottage with queen bed, spacious living and dining area, patio and balcony. Common rooms in the B&B include a lounge with TV/VCR, library, games and a grand piano. A full breakfast is served between 8 and 9.

(902) 624-9382 or (866) 816-8688. Fax (902) 624-8733. Three rooms and one cottage with private baths. Doubles, $100 to $135. Cottage, $225.

Bayview Pines Country Inn, 678 Oakland Road, RR 2, Mahone Bay B0J 2E0.
There's a splendid water view from the hilltop location of this B&B off by itself in the residential Indian Point section. Owners Chris and Joanna Grimley from England offer nine rooms and suites, most with bay views, as well as a full English breakfast – enhanced by Joanna's specialty marmalades – in the dining room of their turn of-the-century farmhouse. Three guest rooms are in the farmhouse. New quarters fashioned from the old barn range from rooms with queen or twin beds to the Celebration Suite with a queen bed, an oval double whirlpool tub in the corner and a bathroom with a shower. The rooms are comfortable and abound with interesting touches; three have private entrances with deck areas. Two housekeeping apartments contain one or two bedrooms. The fourteen-acre property includes a small beach and boat-launching area as well as nature trails but few pines. The original owners said they erred in thinking the spruce trees out back were pines, so they and their successors planted a few seedlings near the house so it would live up to its name.

(902) 624-9970. www.bayviewpines.ns.ca. Six rooms, one suite and two housekeeping apartments with private baths. Doubles, $85 to $90. Suite, $110. Apartments, $110 and $150 (three-night minimum), weekly $700 and $1,000.

Ocean Trail Retreat, Route 3, RR 1, Mahone Bay B0J 2E0.
High up a hillside with a panoramic view of Mahone Bay are two new motel buildings and three chalets near the water below. Chris and Kerri Levy and his parents built the accommodations in the late 1990s and live in a house at the edge of the property. We liked our large patio unit, equipped with a queen and double bed, cable TV and in-room coffee-maker. But we had to wonder why ours was one of only two units built with bay-view patios accessible through sliding doors (and not even furnished with patio chairs). Occupants of the others must be content with views through the windows, except for the one-bedroom balcony suite above the patio units, which comes with cathedral-ceilinged living room, kitchenette with a sofabed, double jacuzzi and a balcony with barbecue grill. Three good-looking, two-bedroom chalets down by the water have kitchens, living rooms, gas fireplaces, telephones and wraparound decks. Atop the hill is a large, heated, L-shaped swimming pool with lots of lounge furniture for those without balconies.

(902) 624-8824 or (888) 624-8824. Fax (902) 624-8899. www.oceantrailretreat.com. Eighteen motel rooms, one suite and three chalets. Doubles, $89 to $109. Suite, $190 (three-night minimum), $1,200 weekly. Chalets, $975 weekly. Closed November-March.

Nature's Cottage Bed & Breakfast, 906 S. Main St., Mahone Bay B0J 2E0.
Woodlands and gardens surround this inviting B&B, and the bay is on view both from the large front porch and from Adirondack chairs placed strategically on a new private dock just across the road. Nestled in the trees, the dark green, Craftsman-style bungalow built in 1928 houses three upstairs guest rooms, two with queen beds and one with a king or two twins. The secluded Loft suite above the garage has a queen bed, TV and kitchenette. Common facilities include an outdoor spa tub,

a sauna room and an exercise room. Proprietress Marlene Sabatina serves a gourmet breakfast in the morning.

(902) 624-0196 or (877) 607-5699. www.naturescottagebb.com. Three rooms and one suite with private baths. Doubles, $90 to $115. Suite, $150. Closed mid-October to early May.

Fisherman's Daughter Bed & Breakfast, 97 Edgewater St., Mahone Bay B0J 2E0.

Built in 1840, this restored Gothic Revival heritage home between two landmark churches is full of seafaring memorabilia and stories, which innkeeper Marcia Dunford is happy to share. Her premier room is the Captain's Quarters on the main floor, which offers a view of the bay across the road and a queen bed, TV in the sitting area and an updated bath with clawfoot tub and separate rainfall shower. Two more queensize rooms offer bay views through the upstairs gable windows beneath the peaked roof. A skylight brightens the rear Loft room with a double bed. A country breakfast features omelets, belgian waffles or eggs benedict.

(902) 624-0483. www.fishermans-daughter.com. Four rooms with private baths. Doubles, $100 to $120.

Chester Area

Oak Island Resort, Spa & Convention Centre, 51 Vaughan Road, Western Shore B0J 3M0.

This renovated waterside complex with motel units, deluxe new "executive rooms," suites and housekeeping chalets claims to have everything. That includes the area's largest conference center, a banquet hall, a spa, game room, indoor pool and sauna, hot tub and fitness center, room service and dancing in the Fireside Lounge. The best of the large rooms with two double beds and a pink and green decor are the half that face the water, especially the 31 executive rooms with balconies or patios in the new spa wing angled toward the water. From the balconies you can look across to Oak Island and dream of the treasure allegedly buried there. There's a private beach beside the bay, and the marina offers boat rentals, fishing charters and scenic cruises of Mahone Bay. Right beside the water are thirteen two-bedroom chalets, each with fireplace and two-person jacuzzi. The hotel-style dining room, **La Vista,** lovely in white and blessed with big windows for water views, is open for three meals a day. The extensive dinner menu (entrées, $16.95 to $25.95) ranges from cedar-planked salmon and Thai shrimp pasta to Brome Lake duckling and rack of lamb.

(902) 627-2600 or (800) 565-5075. Fax (902) 627-2020. www.oakislandresortandspa.com. Ninety-seven rooms, ten suites and thirteen housekeeping chalets. Doubles, $129 to $179. Suites, $199 to $219. Chalets, $289.

Haddon Hall, 67 Haddon Hill Road, Chester B0J 1J0.

The South Shore's most glamorous small inn opened in 1994 in one of Chester's renowned summer estates, high on a secluded hilltop with 90 acres overlooking Mahone Bay. A restaurant followed in 1995, attracting wide attention when the wife of the Canadian prime minister chose it to host a luncheon for Hillary Rodham Clinton and other spouses at the G-7 summit conference in Halifax. Dr. Viola Hallman, a prominent German industrialist who summers in Chester, invested big bucks during two years of renovations to the 1905 manor house and five new outlying buildings. The main house holds the restaurant, a service bar and a fireplaced common room decked out like an English library in hunter green. Upstairs is a second common room in the foyer, plus enormous guest rooms with king or queen poster or sleigh beds, down duvets, period furnishings, TV/VCR, marble baths with double jacuzzis, working fireplaces and sitting areas by the windows for ocean views. The Atalanta opens onto a vast sunny deck atop the porte cochere; we like better the High Tide's shady, private deck overlooking the pool. An ocean view is also available in the Ripple Pool House suite with king canopy bed, double jacuzzi tub and private deck with a swing chair for two. Non-view accommodations are found in a cozy log cabin in the woods with queen bed, kitchenette and wood stove; a two-story house ideal for families or two couples; a lodge suite with two queen sleigh beds and stone fireplace, and a couple of two-story townhouses in the Gate House at the entry (which require a long trek uphill to the main house for meals). Supplementing the luxurious accommodations are a heated outdoor pool, tennis court, a hiking trail and a life-size lawn chess game in which players move 30-inch-high carved chessmen around the eighteen-inch squares. The inn shuttles guests to its private Lynch Island in Mahone Bay for swimming, boating and rides on special water bicycles. Dinner is available to guests and the public (see Where to Eat), and continental breakfast is included in the rates. Innkeeper Cynthia O'Connell keeps the place running smoothly.

(902) 275-3577. Fax (902) 275-5159. www.haddonhallinn.com. Eleven rooms and suites with private baths. Doubles, $325 to $475. Closed November-April.

Mecklenburgh Inn, 78 Queen St., Chester B0J 1J0.

Sailing flags are unfurled off the balcony and the bedrooms are named after islands in Mahone Bay at this registered heritage property, lovingly restored into an inviting B&B by energetic Suzi Fraser. A well-traveled Cordon Bleu-trained cook, she was a chef on private yachts before returning to her native Chester (she still cooks on yachts in the winter). "Every day's a project," says Suzi, who sanded all the wide-plank floors, learned to hang wallpaper and decorated with aplomb and hand-me-downs. Most recently she added bath facilities so all four upstairs guest rooms that used to share now have private. Most rooms have feather beds, and all have down duvets, Frette linens and local quilts. Each is equipped with bottled water, toiletries (until lately a rarity at Nova Scotia inns) and perfumes. The front Winter's Room has a queen bed and a loveseat. The Saddle has twin beds and a loveseat in the corner. It and the double-bedded Tancook offer distant water views. All rooms enjoy access to a full-length balcony sporting aforementioned sailing flags, Adirondack chairs and a hammock overlooking the main street. The main-floor parlor with TV is comfortably modern. The heart of this old grocery store-turned hat shop-turned boarding house is the dining room, where guests gather for breakfast around an old cutting table from the hat shop. The table is decorated with a wooden lobster and a penguin before it's laden with such gustatory treats as California omelets with salsa, sausage and homemade rhubarb juice and rhubarb muffins one day, and smoked salmon benedict the next. Suzi lights a fire in the corner fireplace every morning. In the afternoon, guests help themselves to tea, coffee and soft drinks from the refrigerator in the kitchen.

(902) 275-4638. www.mecklenburghinn.ca. Four rooms with private baths. Doubles, $85 to $135. Closed November-May.

CAMPING. Risser's Beach Provincial Park, Route 331, Petite Rivière, (902) 688-2034, is a beautiful park with an ocean beach and 92 unserviced campsites, both open and wooded; nightly, $18. The **Lunenburg Board of Trade Campground,** Box 1300, Lunenburg, (902) 634-8100, offers 22 serviced and 15 unserviced sites in an open area beside the visitor information center on Blockhouse Hill Road; nightly, $18 to $25. **Graves Island Provincial Park,** Route 3 just east of Chester, (902) 275-9917, offers 78 unserviced sites in an open and wooded campground beside the ocean; nightly, $18.

Seeing and Doing ───────────── 〰️

Lunenburg

Situated on a peninsula between "front" and "back" harbors, this historic fishing and boat-building village is the county's principal business center. It is also an arts center of note, and the murals that seem to pop up on downtown buildings every year are stunning, as were the amazing tin sculptures of lobsters, bluefish and such adorning the downtown lampposts at our latest visit. The architectural riches of its Old Town section along the harbor prompted its designation in 1995 as a UNESCO World Heritage site, a testimonial of which the town is duly proud.

The visitor's first stop should be at the tourist bureau, located in a lighthouse atop Blockhouse Hill. Climb to the top for a panoramic view of the village and its front and back harbors. Walking tour brochures are available here.

The **Lunenburg Craft Festival,** the largest in Nova Scotia with more than 100 participating craftsmen, is held annually on a long weekend in early July. The annual **Nova Scotia Folk Art Festival** is staged in early August. The **Lunenburg Folk Harbour Festival,** inspired by a similar event in Gloucester, Mass., attracts leading folk musicians for a four-day weekend, also in early August. The schooner Bluenose, depicted on the back of the Canadian dime, was built here in 1921 and was the racing champion of the North Atlantic fishing fleet. The **Bluenose II,** a replica of the original, is often berthed at its home port when it's not touring the province and beyond. Along the front harbor are the shipbuilding yards and commercial fisheries that give Lunenburg its title, the Gloucester of Canada. The intentional scuttling in 1994 of the former HMCS Saguenay became the focal point for the **Lunenburg Marine Park,** Atlantic Canada's first. The 366-foot-long destroyer lies on its side 100 feet underwater, creating the most popular scuba diving site on Canada's East Coast.

The new **Captain Angus J. Walters House Museum,** 37 Tannery Road, (902) 634-2010, in a house built in 1915 for the Bluenose's captain, celebrates his life and Canada's tall ship icon, as well as traditions of fishing families throughout the county.

The Fisheries Museum of the Atlantic, 68 Bluenose Drive, Lunenburg.

Prominent along the waterfront, the bright red buildings of a former fish processing plant – typical of the rich and varied colors all over town – commemorate the fishing heritage of Atlantic Canada. Inside are Eastern Canada's largest saltwater aquarium and three floors of exhibits. You might see a fish being filleted in the demonstration room. Boats are on display in the Hall of Inshore Fisheries. In the Boat Shop, you can watch a dory being built. The Bank Fishery/Age of Sail, a Parks Canada exhibit, traces the 400-year history of fishing along the Grand Banks of the continental shelf off Canada's East Coast. The Vessel Gallery portrays the triumphs of the Bluenose. The Rum Runners exhibit reflects the Prohibition era when fishermen trafficked illicit liquor to the U.S.A. On the third floor are a sailmaker's exhibit, a typical fish company office from the 1920s, ice harvesting equipment, photographs of old Lunenburg and the Ice House Theater, which shows half-hour films on fishing. Outside you can board the Theresa E. Connor, the last Lunenburg schooner to fish the Grand Banks with dories, and the steel-hulled side trawler Cape Sable. Beyond is the wooden side trawler Cape North, first of the fresh fish draggers to sail out of Lunenburg. The museum has a large restaurant (see Where to Eat) and a gift shop.

(902) 634-4794 or (866) 579-4909. www.fisheries.museum.gov.ns.ca. Open daily 9:30 to 5:30, early May to late October. Adults $9, children $3, family $22.

Schooner tours of Lunenburg harbor and deep-sea fishing expeditions leave from the Fisheries Museum Dock. When in port, **Bluenose II,** (800) 763-1963, schedules two-hour harbor cruises at 9:30 and 1:30 daily June-September; adults $20, children $10. **Sail Lunenburg/Star Charters,** (902) 634-3535, sails its 48-foot wooden ketch Eastern Star daily at 10:30, 12:30, 2:30 and 4:30; adults $24, children $11. It also offers a 45-minute tour of the waterfront on the Harbour Star, a small fishing boat, for $10. **Lunenburg Whale Watching Tours,** (902) 527-7175, gives three-hour whale, seal and bird watching tours four times daily from the Fisheries Museum Wharf; adults $42, children $30.

Operating from Fisheries Museum Wharf, a working lobster boat hauls in lobsters and visits seals on Eastern Points Reef under auspices of **Lobstermen Tours,** (902) 634-3434; adults $25, children $12.

Lobster picnics on the harbor facing Mahone Bay's three churches are featured aboard the M.V. Maggie McB wooden cruiser, run by **Lunenburg Boat Tours** and sailing three times daily from Government Wharf in Lunenburg, (902) 634-8885; adults $45, children $35.

WALKING TOUR. The bright colors of the buildings will impress you as much as the architecture along the historic streets on the hillside above the harbor. They're particularly striking against the background of blue harbor and the lush greens of the Bluenose Golf Club on the hillside beyond. St. Andrew's Presbyterian and Zion's Lutheran churches are the oldest of their denominations in Canada. St. John's Anglican (1754) is the second oldest Protestant church in Canada; rebuilt in 2004 following a fire, it is open for guided tours daily in summer. The striking hilltop Lunenburg Academy built in 1894, visible for miles around, is a Provincial Heritage Property still used as an elementary school; it's open for tours in summer from noon to 3, $2. Certified tour guide Eric Croft leads informative one-hour walking tours in season five times daily, (902) 634-3848 or (800) 565-0000; adults $15, children $10. Some tours conclude with the traditional "Lunenburg Mug Up" (Lunenburg pudding, solomon gundy and beverage).

ARTS AND CRAFTS. Lunenburg's galleries and shops are growing in number and most are exceptional. **Houston North Gallery,** 110 Montague St., specializes in Inuit (Eskimo) and folk art on three fascinating floors with views of the harbor. John Houston spent many years in the Arctic, an experience reflected in his selection of works and exhibits. The **Black Duck Handcrafts Cooperative,** 8 Pelham St., is Nova Scotia's first craft cooperative. Now three decades old, it's a showplace for members to display their wares, including clothing, eye-catching kites, toys, pottery, baskets and local books. All the herbal items smelled great. **Peer Gallery,** 167 Lincoln St., is a new cooperative gallery of about a dozen artists specializing in contemporary art.

Wild Elements is a sophisticated kitchenware shop with fabulous china by Nigella Lawson, fancy foods and colorful pottery. The pottery at **Nova Terra Cotta** also caught our eye. **Down Home Living** showcases furniture and accessories handcrafted in the Maritimes. **Mosaic** lives up to its name with "treasures from around the world." **Seven Waves** sports "locally grown women's clothing" made from natural fabrics, including linens, hand-dyed silk and organic cotton.

Down by the waterfront is the official **Bluenose II Company Store.** Proceeds from its nautical crafts, gifts and clothing help keep the ship sailing. Find Lunenburg fishing smocks, sweaters from Newfoundland, knit socks and hats from Prince Edward Island, and dolls and pottery from New Brunswick and Nova Scotia at the **Admiral Benbow Trading Co.,** 84 Montague St. **Out of Hand,** which advertises "unusual gifts for the usual dilemma," is a fun place to browse amid the extravagantly colored ties, the painted flowerpots and the carved wooden animals. We were sorely tempted by a hand-painted floor mat with lovely lupines. **In Fine Company** specializes in distinctive gifts and crafts, including the "Lunenburg bump" birdhouses and Lunenburg Foundry brass.

Has all the walking around Lunenburg's steep streets worn you out? Stop for coffee, espresso, tea or pastry or even fish and chips with a view of the harbor at **Historic Grounds Coffee House,** 100 Montague St. Coffee and more substantial fare, minus the view, is offered in the delightful new **Laughing Whale Café,** which roasts its own coffees and serves three meals daily in a former IGA store at 263 Lincoln St.

Mahone Bay

Mahone Bay is the dominant bay of the area, and ringing the head of a harbor is the small village of the same name. It's known for three landmark churches facing the waterfront side by side and, lately, for increasing numbers of fine crafts shops, boutiques and eateries along Main and Edgewater street, the shore Route 3. The Mahone Bay Summer Concerts Society presents a top-quality series of concerts, called **Music at the Three Churches,** on five Friday evenings in summer. Thousands gather here in early August for the annual **Mahone Bay Wooden Boat Festival.**

Mahone Bay Settlers Museum, 578 Main St., Mahone Bay.

This charming new museum in an 1850 house has period rooms and exhibits relating to the settling of the area in 1754 by "foreign Protestants" from Germany, Switzerland and France. Its front entrance is notable for what's called a full two-story Lunenburg County Bump – check it out and you'll know why. The "bump" is a practical architectural fillip evident around the area. The decorative work of an itinerant artist is evident on the ceiling and the fireplace in the parlor. Fine china, ceramics and furniture are shown in period rooms. Mahone Bay's wooden boat building heritage is featured in the upper room. The museum also publishes a map and brochure detailing three 45-minute walking tours of Mahone Bay. "Remember to look up," it advises. "Roof-level features are sometimes the most interesting."
(902) 624-6263. Open Tuesday-Saturday 10 to 5, Sunday 1 to 5, June to mid-October.

SHOPPING. Amos Pewterers has been operating from an old boat building shop beside the bay since 1974. You may see the artisans at work. You'll certainly see some amazing pewter pieces – many of them surprisingly sleek and contemporary – from bowls to picture holders to jewelry. Across the street at the **Birdsall-Worthington Pottery Ltd.,** Tim Worthington and Pam Birdsall make Nova Scotian earthenware pottery with a decorating technique known as slip trailing. Their delicate floral painting over clay vases and dishes is exquisite. We also liked the reasonably priced floral earrings. **The Teazer,** named for the legendary ghost ship said to haunt Mahone Bay still, has five rooms of crafts, kitchenware, children's items and fine clothing and accessories from the British Isles. We coveted almost everything from the wood carvings to fused glass and hand-glazed tiles at **The Moorings Gallery & Shop.** The latest in birdhouses caught our eye at **For the Birds Nature Shop.** Antiques and gifts from the Far East are featured at **Puddle Dock Emporium.**

There's an explosion of colors at **Suttles & Seawinds,** 466 Main St., the headquarters of the distinctive Canadian clothing, gifts and accessories empire started by Vicki Lynn Bardon and her husband Gary. Vicki designs everything from potholders to quilts. The clothes are expensive (one cotton skirt we admired cost more than $200) and you'll see her efforts on some of the best-dressed women in Canada.

New at 538 Main St. is a converted house called **Cheesecake Gallery,** run by the former owner of La Cave Cheesecakes in Halifax. Here you'll find a small art gallery, a deli, a wine bar and a kitchen dispensing treats from escargots on a baguette to broiled lobster and, yes, cheesecakes. There are a handful of tables on a garden patio upon which to partake.

The intersection of Main and Edgewater, with a monument in the middle, is becoming a mecca for foodies. **Jo-Ann's Deli, Market & Bake Shop** offers excellent deli fare and sweets at tables amid the flowers and plants of a nursery. Adjacent is the **LaHave Bakery** and, for a change of pace, **P'Lovers** environmental gift shop. Biggest of all is **Mahone Bagels & Coffee,** a large and sleek space fashioned from an old variety store, with a cyber café, high tables and chairs, and a rear garden patio. Eli Frankel from Israel and his wife Beatrice from Germany started with H&H bagels from New York and Seattle's Best Coffee and expanded to full service from there. "We leave the fish and chowder to Nova Scotians, who can do that better than we can," explained Eli. They emphasize the international: falafel, hummus, exotic sandwiches, French pastries, even pastas and steaks ($7.50 to $15) at night.

Chester

Called "possibly the prettiest village in Nova Scotia" by a local motel's brochure, this looks like a typical New England coastal town, thanks to its rolling green topography and the houses of its early New England settlers. Situated on a hilly peninsula, it has a front harbor, a back harbor and various inlets, all emanating from Mahone Bay for a pervasive water presence. It's a summer refuge for the affluent and increasing numbers of Hollywood actors. The seasonal population doubles, most of them regulars and many of their cars bearing American license plates.

Sailing is the village's principal preoccupation. Mahone Bay is a rainbow of colorful sails during **Chester Race Week,** the largest sailing regatta in the Maritimes and an annual event in August (as is **Old Home Week**). Just west of Chester is South Shore Marine, billed as Atlantic Canada's largest marina complex. All the coves and inlets with which the Chester area abounds are mooring places for fine powerboats and sailboats – quite in contrast to the old fishing boats one sees in most harbors in the Maritimes. A good place to view the yacht races is from what villagers call the **Parade Grounds,** a green hillside with lawns and flowers. Here on a spit of land separating the front and back harbors (which are connected by a canal) are the Chester Yacht Club founded in 1901, the War Memorial Monument, the Victorian gazebo bandstand still used for concerts by the Chester Brass Band and a bridge across the canal to the Peninsula, home of some of Chester's most substantial houses.

An **Historic Walking Tour** brochure guides visitors past landmarks you might not otherwise recognize or find. They include several examples of what it calls "Picturesque architecture, an interpretation of Gothic Revival," using decorative trim, steeply pitched gables and lapped siding. Water Street along the front harbor leads to Government Wharf, where ferry service is provided several times daily to Big and Little Tancook islands. Chester has an eighteen-hole golf club, tennis courts and a saltwater swimming pool near the canal bridge on the back harbor.

Changing shows by local artists are held at the old Heritage Station. Local and traveling shows are presented in a summer series at the **Chester Playhouse,** the site of concerts and stage productions from April to December.

SHOPPING. Probably because Chester is less tourist-oriented and its residents are busy with sailing races and garden parties, the village lacks the concentration and number of choice shops found in Lunenburg and Mahone Bay. Painter Antonio Valverde-Alcalde, a native of Spain, shows his internationally renowned works at **Valverde Studio and Gallery,** 31 King St. Lupines are the theme at **Paula MacDonald Pottery** at 20 Pleasant St. Across the street is **Juwil by the Sea,** an appropriate play on words. Nearby is **Julien's European Deli & French Bakery,** where a Frenchman offers café au lait along with fabulous pastries and deli sandwiches. According to ads for **Fiasco** at 54 Queen St., "the name says it all," but hardly does justice to the large and colorful uptown shop holding unique clothing and home accessories. Some mighty interesting fused glass is on display at the funky **Chez Glass Lass,** 65 Duke St. On Water Street, **The Warp and Woof,** more than 75 years old, is said to be Nova Scotia's oldest gift store. It features handicrafts, wood carvings, apple dolls, an art gallery and gift items from around the world; its **Sweater Annex** has imported woolens and accessories. Jim Smith's **Nova Scotia Folk Pottery,** charmingly housed in the old Corner Store nearby, features especially colorful plates and pitchers in striking purples and greens. His pottery is collected all across Canada and has won many awards; we found a fish platter for a distinctive wedding gift.

Where to Eat

On or Near the Water

Haddon Hall, 67 Haddon Hill Road, Chester.

Every table in the gorgeous front dining room at this inn is angled to take advantage of a panoramic view of the water in the distance. The setting is summery and serene, with candlelit tables dressed in yellow and white, bare wood floors and Wedgwood blue wallpaper above solid blue wainscoting. It's the kind of place where you'd likely follow the staff's lead in dressing up for dinner. The contemporary dinner fare is available prix-fixe, $75 for three courses. You might start with pan-seared Quebec foie gras with summer truffles, a lobster and goat cheese soufflé or crisp duck confit on braised lentils with a blackberry glaze. An herbed sorbet might precede the main course, the choice including perhaps pan-roasted halibut with smoked bacon and brown butter jus, Brome Lake duckling with apple-raspberry compote, or filet of Alberta beef tenderloin with three kinds of peppercorns. Dessert could be a peach and pistachio tart, double chocolate-grand marnier mousse cake or – something different at a recent visit – a trio of single-malt scotches.

(902) 275-3577. Prix-fixe, $75. Dinner nightly by reservation, 6 to 8:30, mid-June to early October.

The Rope Loft, Water Street, Chester.

Would that every restaurant had such a felicitous setting. This popular place at water's edge has a second-story deck with rustic wood furniture, a lower deck with spiffy white tables and chairs, a soaring upstairs Rope Loft dining room and a timeworn, timbered 1815 sea shanty downstairs. Obviously it can handle scores of people, so we were surprised to be the only diners when we arrived about 9:30 on a July weeknight. We wished we'd been earlier to have enjoyed a drink on the upper-level deck right beside the front harbor, with boats moored all around. The candlelit dining room was casual and the service solicitous (after all, we were the only ones there, but the help probably wanted to go home). We shared an appetizer of solomon gundy before digging into our entrées of halibut with creamy lemon-lime sauce and Digby scallops marinated in vermouth. The reach of the kitchen seems to vary from year to year, but is always strong on munchies, starters, soups and salads. At a recent visit the basics were supplemented by poached salmon, seafood stir-fry, T-bone steak and even a shrimp and lobster wrap. Whatever is offered, there's no better up-close, watery setting.

(902) 275-3430. www.ropeloft.com. Entrees, $7.95 to $23.95. Open daily, 11 to 10. Closed November-April.

The Galley Seaside Restaurant, 130 Marine Road, off Route 3, Chester.

Part of the South Shore Marine complex at Marriott's Cove, this contemporary restaurant with a small deck and picnic tables overlooks Mahone Bay. The view from the two dining rooms is pretty as a picture, as is the entire restaurant and lounge in its nautical setting full of ropes, flags and ship's wheels. The extensive menu offers something for everyone, with its specialty Indian Point mussels and Lunenburg scallops joined by newcomers like lobster dumplings and a goat cheese salad. Fresh fish listed on the blackboard can be sautéed, broiled, poached or served cajun style. Seafood curry, veal marsala, roasted cornish hen, tenderloin steak, rack of lamb and pasta dishes are available as well. Desserts are to groan over: banana royale, chocolate rum mousse, chocolate-grand marnier cheesecake and lemon-yogurt ice cream pie. The wine choices are limited; the fancy "fog-cutter" cocktails and special liqueured coffees are not. In front is **The Loft,** a marine store stocking nautical clothing, equipment and gifts, and outside are tables and chairs under graceful birch trees.

(902) 275-4700. Entrées, $17.95 to $34. Lunch daily, noon to 5. Dinner nightly, 5 to 9. Closed November-March.

Seaside Shanty, Route 3, Chester Basin.

At this small restaurant, the partly enclosed and covered back deck with its molded dark green chairs and tables beside the wharf is the dining area of choice on a sunny day. It's practically on the water, and you might spot a seal or a loon or two. A wood stove and tables topped with a variety of quilted mats create a homey ambiance inside. One of the stars of the menu is the lobster and seafood chowder plate, teamed with sourdough bread and a mixed salad, making a meal in itself. We hear the seafood caesar salad (topped with shrimp, scallops and mussels) is to die for. Drunken mussels, seafood crêpes, scallop sauté, solomon gundy, chicken teriyaki and seafood fettuccine are other good choices. There's always a fish of the day, which at our visit was blackened haddock. Rhubarb custard pie, blueberry grunt and even licorice ice cream make good endings.

(902) 275-2246. Entrées, $9 to $16. Open daily, 11:30 to 9:30. Closed November-April.

Mimi's Ocean Grill, 662 South Main St., Mahone Bay.

This barn-red 1800 house with black trim was long home to a noted restaurant, Zwicker's Inn. It's equally famous in its reincarnation under ex-Torontonian Mimi Findlay. She gave a new white and yellow bistro look to three dining rooms, hung eclectic and whimsical art on the walls, wrapped vines and white lights around a brick patio holding four round tables, and livened up the menu. The happy combination produced one of our best lunches ever in the Maritimes. One of us enjoyed the creamy fish (haddock and finnan haddie) and mussel chowder with an order of bruschetta, topped with diced tomatoes, cheese, garlic and who-knows-what-all. The other sampled the ocean cakes, served with a caesar salad that itself was almost a meal. Everything was zesty, so much so that we had to recoup with a cooling trio of homemade sorbets (raspberry, kiwi and lemon, artistically presented on strawberry coulis). The always-changing fare here is the kind of which we never tire. For dinner, consider appetizers like Asian spring rolls, lobster crème brûlée, phyllo lamb samosas, roesti topped with smoked salmon, a trio of tapenades or a baja fish taco. "Mains" could be Brazilian bouillabaisse, scallops sautéed in ginger cream sauce, spicy cornmeal-crusted haddock bayou style, Moroccan chicken, grilled lamb chops with firecracker chutney or mesquite-grilled ribeye steak with chipotle pepper butter. Finish with frozen lemon mousse, warm caramel bread pudding or sour cream rhubarb pie.

(902) 624-1342. Entrées, $17.95 to $26. Open daily in summer, noon to 9. Off-season: lunch, noon to 2:30; dinner, 5:30 to 8. Closed November-April.

The Innlet Café, Seafood House & Grill, 249 Edgewater St. at Kedy's Landing, Mahone Bay.

This got its start as the Silver Spoon Terrace Restaurant, founded by Deanna Silver of the Halifax restaurant and dessert group. It was renamed and run until 2004 by Jack and Katherine Sorenson, who'd put the late Zwicker's Inn on the culinary map. New owners Patrick and Inge Kralik continued the tradition in 2004, right down to the very last menu item. The locally popular establishment has a small terrace for dining out front by the bay and a spiffy licensed café and grill inside. For lunch, we enjoyed a superior mussel chowder with a vegetable salad plate and a super cream of halibut-potato-parsley soup with a knockwurst sandwich. The extensive dinner menu covers the gamut and then some: smoked eel, poached fish fillets, George's Bank scallops, garlicked mackerel, mixed seafood grill, seafood skibbereen (the chef's signature seafood casserole from Zwicker's), chicken teriyaki, pork tenderloin, bratwurst, grilled Nova Scotia lamb's liver and grilled Alberta tenderloin steaks. Ten mix-and-match stir-fries and seven versions of fettuccine also are available. Creamy cheesecakes, warm spicy applesauce, ginger shortbread and belgian waffles highlight the dessert list. The specials board might add orange-hazelnut cheesecake and apricot crème blondie.

(902) 624-6363. www.inletcafe.com. Entrées, $13.95 to $19.95. Lunch daily, 11:30 to 5. Dinner, 5 to 8:30 or 9.

The Mug & Anchor Pub, Mader's Wharf, Mahone Bay.

Mahone Bay's first pub is the cornerstone of the Mader's Wharf complex, with a nifty outdoor deck over the water, a fireplace in the corner and, of course, the requisite bar and a dart board. Co-owner Francine O'Hagan says people come here not just for the extensive selection of beers and scotches but for the food, all made on the premises and served on the deck or in a dark and pub-like room appointed in hunter green. The menu is short but sweet, from fish chowder and a "jacked-up: burger to a hearty beef stew in a bread bowl, homemade fish cakes and beans, and shrimp and scallop alfredo. Offerings vary from meat pie to chicken fajita wrap to poutine, and a snack platter of finger foods is available for the whole table ($14.99). The waterside deck proved a convivial setting for a late supper of baked scallops and steamed mussels, accompanied by salads and a carafe of white wine. We say convivial because everyone ended up talking with everyone else. The moon rising over the water was quite awesome, as the waitress had predicted.

(902) 624-6378. Entrées, $7.99 to $16.99. Open daily, 11:30 to 9:30 or 10, Sunday noon to 9.

Boscawen Inn, 150 Cumberland St., Lunenburg.

Formal dining is offered amid white linens and crystal chandeliers at this venerable inn's restaurant renamed **The Medee** (for a French vessel captured by Admiral Boscawen). It occupies two former drawing rooms on the main floor of the historic mansion above the harbor. More casual fare is featured downstairs in an expansive lounge called the **Admirals Club,** nicely redone in a nautical theme with big windows yielding a glimpse of the water. The Medee menu is table d'hôte, four courses for

$65. At a recent visit you could start with sambuca-flambéed mussels and a caramelized peach salad. Main-course choices were seared halibut with a merlot reduction, stuffed pork tenderloin and pan-roasted duck breast drizzled with blueberry sauce. Desserts included cappuccino crème brûlée and raspberry molten lava cake. The casual menu offered the likes of lobster pasta, maple-baked salmon and angus strip loin steak. Both menus are available in either venue, or on the large rooftop deck with a harbor view.

(902) 634-3325. Prix-fixe, $65. Casual fare, $9 to $17. Breakfast daily, 8 to 10. Lunch and Victorian tea, 11 to 3. Dinner, 5 to 9. Sunday brunch, 11 to 1.

The Old Fish Factory Restaurant, 68 Bluenose Drive, Lunenburg.

Occupying part of the second floor of the Fisheries Museum of the Atlantic, this steak and seafood house is nicely nautical inside beneath high ceilings and exposed pipes. Until it was enclosed during a recent expansion, the canopied patio – its green umbrellas and tables contrasting with the bright red walls of the old fish factory all around – was *the* place to dine outdoors by the water. The extensive menu covers all the bases, starting with solomon gundy, seafood martinis, steamed mussels, and smoked salmon and brie in phyllo. Expect such main dishes as grilled halibut with mango coulis, bouillabaisse, rumrunners coconut shrimp and a seafood tower for two. Chicken, steak and rack of lamb also are available. Lunenburg blueberry grunt is a featured dessert. Downstairs is a snacky fast-food café and deli with sandwiches and salads. You can eat in or take out to picnic tables on the wharf.

(902) 634-3333 or (800) 533-9336. www.oldfishfactory.com. Entrées, $16.99 to $28.99. Lunch daily, 11 to 4. Dinner, 4 to 9. Closed late October to mid-May.

Other Choices

Magnolia's Grill, 128 Montague St., Lunenburg.

The walls are covered with '50s memorabilia and the music blares at this lively bistro known for conviviality and creative food. The locals pack its eight booths and two tables to partake of such lunchtime treats as creole peanut soup, nachos, pan-fried cod cheeks, mussels and Greek salad. The southern accent was created by the co-founder from Tennessee, who has moved on. Partner Nancy Lohnes continues the happy blend of cajun and Lunenburg cooking styles in this culinary happening amidst collections ranging from postcards to salt and pepper shakers. At night, you might try the fish cakes, "Zorba the breast" (chicken stuffed with feta cheese), seafood pasta, cajun shrimp, jambalaya or ribeye steak with garlic aioli sauce. We can vouch for the chicken tostada and the dressed-up mussels, which made a delectable picnic supper preceded by solomon gundy and caesar salad. We wish we could have tried the baby bruschetta and the key lime pie, but – purist that she is – Nancy said they wouldn't last and refused to prepare them for takeout.

(902) 634-3287. Entrées, $8.95 to $19.50. Lunch daily, 11:30 to 3. Dinner, 5 to 9 or 10. Closed December-February.

Fleur de Sel, 53 Montague St., Lunenburg.

Some of the area's best and most exciting food emanates from this small café and guest house run very personally by chef Martin Ruiz Salvador and his fiancée, Sylvie MacDonald, both from Halifax but trained in France and Arizona. They made their "little dream come true" in 2004, taking over the old Hillcroft Café and reconfiguring the space. Three small dining rooms have upholstered cherrywood chairs at white-clothed tables, hardwood floors and a clean, crisp decor. The couple named the place for the gourmet sea salt they employ liberally as a garnish. Martin's changing menu might open with a trilogy of cold soups, a rare beef salad and a tomato stuffed with wild Atlantic shrimp. The trilogy of oysters, served raw, poached and deep-fried with a chilled vichyssoise and a smoked mackerel and cucumber salad, is a seaside triumph for a mere $9. Main courses vary from handmade raviolis staffed with spinach and goat cheese and a classic bouillabaisse to organic duck breast with a pearl onion and garlic confit and roasted veal loin with creamed chanterelles and a stuffed zucchini flower. Assorted sorbets and chocolate fondant head the dessert list, though many opt for the artisanal cheese selections. Sylvie has stocked a choice but affordable wine cellar. She also was preparing to rent three upstairs guest rooms with shared baths, $75 to $90 including breakfast.

(902) 640-2121. www.fleurdesel.net. Entrées, $24 to $28. Lunch daily in summer, 11:30 to 2. Dinner nightly, from 5:30, Thursday-Sunday in off-season. Closed January-May.

The Arbor View Inn, 216 Dufferin St., Lunenburg.
There's an assured sense of style in the dining room and on the plates in this restored inn on a hilltop estate on the edge of town. Chef-owner Daniel Orovec from Toronto hangs his Humber College culinary degree proudly. Other awards and tributes on the walls of two pristine Victorian dining rooms testify to his cooking talents that produce, in an admiring local chef's words, "art on a plate." She's partial to his mesclun salad with goat cheese, but artistry also turns up in such starters as roasted vegetable and chèvre terrine with beet syrup, a tiger prawn martini with vermouth-scented cocktail sauce and a Japanese bento box for two. The short list of main courses might include quinoa-crusted salmon fillet with caramelized orange and wasabi sauce, pan-seared mahi-mahi with Asian spices, herb-crusted pork tenderloin with roast garlic jus and madras lamb curry with turkish apricots and dates. Dessert could be frozen passion fruit mousse with berry coulis, white chocolate crème brûlée or homemade sorbet. Upstairs, Daniel's wife Rose has decorated four elegant guest rooms with private baths and two third-floor jacuzzi suites, the latter with decks yielding glimpses of the ocean in the distance. B&B rates are $105 to $175.

(902) 634-3658 or (800) 890-6650. www.arborview.ca. Entrées, $19 to $27. Dinner nightly except Monday, 5:30 to 10. Closed Monday-Wednesday in off-season.

Carta Restaurant, 54 Queen St., Chester.
An exotic air pervades this new eatery that's part of an upscale shopping complex. It features global fare in a casual mix of booths and tables, Maps and magazine covers cover the ceiling, foreign costumes hang on the walls and – would you believe? – international coins are embedded in the urinal of the men's room. The Thai peanut, Japanese miso and Italian vinaigrette dressings for the salads tell something of the offerings, which include tempuras, spring rolls and maki sushi. Main dishes on the all-day menu span the globe: enchiladas from Mexico, couscous from Tunisia, doro wat from Ethiopia, a bento box from Japan, three dishes from Lebanon, fish and chips and fry-ups from England, and hamburgers and California salads from the U.S. Soft drinks, juices and cappuccinos accompany along with an interesting wine selection-.

(902) 275-5131. Entrées, $8.99 to $13.95. Lunch and dinner daily in season.

FOR MORE INFORMATION: South Shore Tourism Association, 18 Dufferin St., Lunenburg, NS B0J 2C0, (902) 634-8844. www.ssta.com.
Lunenburg Visitor Information Center, Blockhouse Hill Road, Box 1300, Lunenburg, NS B0J 2C0, (902) 634-8100 or 634-4410.
Mahone Bay Area Chamber of Commerce, Edgewater Street, Mahone Bay, NS B0J 2E0, (902) 624-6151 or (888) 624-6151. www.mahonebay.com.
Chester Visitor Information Center, Highway 3, Chester, NS B0J 1J0, (902) 275-4616. www.chesterns.com.

Engraved marker at scenic overlook denotes points of interest along Cabot Trail.

Cape Breton Island/Cabot Trail, N.S.

Cape Breton Island – and particularly its Cabot Trail – has long been a destination for travelers who like breathtaking oceanfront and mountain scenery, interesting history and customs, and a distinct change of pace.

Although internationally known, its location away from the mainstream and its distance from the rest of civilization make Cape Breton a delightful world unto itself. Yes, Americans and off-island Canadians can get there and do, but it's no quick trip.

The 184-mile-long Cabot Trail, Cape Breton's best-known claim to fame, is a sharply undulating highway that hugs some of the most scenic oceanside cliffs this side of California's Big Sur. It alone is worth the five-hour drive from Halifax or the day's drive from eastern Maine.

But there's much more. For scenery and sailing, the shimmering Bras d'Or Lakes make up an inland sea which so captivated Alexander Graham Bell that he made the lakeside resort village of Baddeck his summer home for 35 years. Today, visitors find Baddeck a good base for exploring the island.

The partly restored Fortress of Louisbourg, the largest national historic park in Canada, is an absorbing re-creation of the 18th-century village known as the Gibraltar of Canada. Here you relive the history of the costly fortress that helped cause France to lose its empire and Britain her American colonies, changing the destiny of North America.

To the French legacy at Louisbourg and the Acadian heritage still dominant at Cheticamp, add the Mi'kmac Indians at four reservations along the Bras d'Or Lakes and the prevailing Scottish/Gaelic presence for a unique mix of cultures.

Nowhere in Nova Scotia (which means New Scotland in Latin) is the Scottish influence more pronounced than in the Cape Breton Highlands, which resemble the highlands of Scotland. "Scotland on a Nearer Shore" was the headline on a New York Times travel article on Cape Breton. You quickly recognize the Scottish dialect and place names, the preponderance of last names beginning with "Mac," and the fondness for the foods and traditions of Scotland.

So isolated are parts of Cape Breton that they remain much as John Cabot found them when he landed, it's believed, in 1497 at Aspy Bay on the northernmost tip of Cape Breton.

Fishing and tourism are the principal occupations. Both are quite different from what you might expect, however. Lately reduced by federally imposed limits, the fishing is done as of yesteryear from weather-beaten boats of many hues; they are moored in picturesque harbors or can be seen at work off the soaring coastline. The tourism scene is straight out of the past as well – no chain motels or fast-food eateries here. Instead you find mom-and-pop motels and restaurants, Scottish and Acadian souvenir stands and shops, and offbeat surprises everywhere.

Cape Breton is a place apart. It has history, tradition and scenery so powerful that one cannot help but surrender to its allure.

Getting There

Although there is air service from major cities to Halifax and Sydney, most travelers drive (or rent a car) to see Cape Breton Island. The island is large and, unless you go on a chartered bus tour as many seem to do, it's difficult to get around without wheels.

The island is easily reached via the Trans-Canada Highway (Routes 104 and 105), which meets the Cabot Trail in the vicinity of Baddeck.

Prices are quoted in Canadian funds and are subject to Canada's GST tax. Cape Breton is in the Atlantic time zone, one hour ahead of Eastern time.

Where to Stay ⎯⎯⎯⎯⎯⎯⎯⎯⎯ _♪♪♪_

Your choice of accommodations depends on time, budget and personal preferences. Those in the Cape Breton Highlands run the gamut, with the notable exception of chain motels. Several fine resort lodges are located in or near Cape Breton Highlands National Park. Baddeck, beside Lake Bras d'Or at the beginning and end of the circular Cabot Trail, is the best interior location for exploring all of Cape Breton. The Margarees, Cheticamp and Pleasant Bay are close to the park on the northwest coast; Ingonish is close to the park on the east coast. As in the rest of Nova Scotia, toll-free reservations can be made at most places through the provincial reservations service, (800) 565-0000.

Luxury Retreats

Keltic Lodge, 383 Middle Head Peninsula, Ingonish Beach B0C 1L0.

Internationally recognized as a full-service resort owned by the provincial

government, Keltic Lodge couldn't be more superbly situated. It's off by itself in an idyllic wooded setting, commanding a smashing view of the ocean on two sides from its perch astride a long promontory called Middle Head. You'll likely see it from the main road, long before you pass the renowned Highlands golf course and enter the grounds through graceful birches arched over profuse floral borders and, in early July, surprising-to-see rhododendrons. On your right is the resort's recently renovated Inn at Keltic. On the left is the casual and stupendous-view Atlantic Restaurant and gift shop. Beyond is the striking white, red-roofed Main Lodge. We booked one of the 40 rooms in the inn, which had two picture windows overlooking a narrow lawn beside the cliff and nothing but ocean and the craggy shoreline opposite. At least that's what was in view when we arrived. Shortly after, it started raining and the next morning we and everything else northeast of Baddeck were enveloped in fog and a howling gale. Under those conditions, one night was enough. Had the weather cooperated, even the most driven traveler might have lingered to laze beside the heated pool, hike around Middle Head, play golf or tennis and enjoy the usual resort amenities. Before the deluge, we did manage a 90-minute hike out Middle Head to Tern Point, spotting cormorants, viewing the pounding surf below and picking wild raspberries for sustenance. Our spacious room, nicely decorated in earth tones, had a double and a twin bed, a desk, two upholstered chairs and a TV for company on a rainy (make that torrential) evening under circumstances that could best be described as lonely. Why the Inn at Keltic is air-conditioned we don't know – seldom did the temperature reach 70 during the weeks we were in Nova Scotia either in late June, July or early September. (It's also heated and some years is open in winter for skiers at the nearby Cape Smokey ski area.) Thirty-two more rooms and two suites are located in the Main Lodge. Thirty-one rooms are available in eleven multi-bedroom cottages, all with sitting rooms and fireplaces. The lodge has large, comfortable public rooms including the richly paneled Highland Room, a sitting room and lounge where entertainment (mostly Scottish) is presented nightly, and a long main dining room with windows onto the ocean on both sides (see Where to Eat). Local artist Christopher Gorey's watercolors grace both the lobby and the menu covers. A full-service spa was opened in 2004.

(902) 285-2880 or (800) 565-0444. www.signatureresorts.com/keltic. One hundred five rooms in lodge, inn and cottages. Doubles, $338 MAP. Closed late October to late May.

Castle Moffett, Highway 105, Box 678, Baddeck B0E 1B0.
This hillside structure must be seen to be believed. Linda and Desmond Moffett from Palm Beach, Fla., built the vaguely Tudoresque castle spanning a rippling brook as a summer home in 1994. When they couldn't persuade their three offspring in their early 20s to join them and occupy their three custom-made suites with jacuzzi tubs (just as they have at home), he said "let's try something new" and she said, "I'm game." The result is Castle Moffett, Nova Scotia's first five-star, four-diamond country inn. An air of mystery envelops the place designed by Desmond and so showy that he had to close it to curious locals while it was rising above Highway 105 in order to finish its construction. His prerequisite for buying the property: it had to have a stream, because he's partial to water. The great room of the castle rests atop what Linda calls the largest bridge on Cape Breton, a typical bit of Moffett hyperbole. It's a baronial space, two stories high, with the sounds of trickling water emanating from the brook underneath. Here's where guests enjoy complimentary wine and cheese around the fireplace or play the grand piano. Hallways on either side lead to sumptuous guest suites with king or queen poster beds dressed in Gucci sheets and comforters that match the draperies. Each has a sitting area or room with remote-control gas fireplace and ornate antiques from around the world, a large whirlpool bath (some with bidets and separate showers) and a sweeping view of the Bras d'Or Lakes that seem to stretch out from the foot of the 190-acre property. Decor is generally mauve and gold. One suite follows a Victorian theme, another is oriental and a third clubby English. A new wing in 2004 added five suites, including the Safari, which offers balconies at the front and side.

The lower level of the new wing houses a spa with a sauna, exercise facility and a massage room, plus the Dungeon Lounge and Wine Cellar with an emphasis on single-malt whiskies and gaming tables for backgammon and chess. Off the rear of the great room is the Windsor Dining Room, two dining areas with views of the cascading brook. A gourmet breakfast is served here, and four-course dinners are available to guests (and the public by reservation) Tuesday-Sunday at 7, $59 per person.

(902) 756-9070 or (888) 756-9070. Fax (902) 756-3399. www.castlemoffett.com. Seven rooms and three suites with private baths. Doubles, $250 to $400. Closed late October to mid-May.

Island Sunset Resort & Spa, 19 Beach Cove Lane, (Box 27, Margaree Harbour B0E 2B0), Belle Cote.

A windswept, once-barren hillside beside the ocean was being turned in 2004 into a contemporary upscale resort just off the Cabot Trail near Margaree Harbour. It's an unlikely location for an enterprise of this magnitude, one with a vast, vaguely tropical-looking restaurant, an "administration building" with a spa and two saltwater pools, and 48 large and luxurious cottage suites as deluxe and high end as any in eastern Canada. Built by a local group headed by Wayne Gillis, the restaurant opened first, followed by the first of twelve one-story chalets, each holding four spacious suites with private entrances. Each is smartly furnished in different contemporary styles with hardwood floors, a living room with club chairs and a sofabed open to a kitchenette/dining area, TV, a gas fireplace or stove, a bedroom with one kingsize or two queen beds, and a bath with whirlpool tub and separate shower. Although each has an ocean view, no decks or outside seating were in evidence at our visit shortly after opening. The main building, yet to be built in the center of the complex, was to hold the spa and reception area. The swimming pools and tennis courts also were in the works. The contemporary, beachy looking restaurant at the base of the hillside was open to the public for continental breakfast, lunch and dinner (see Where to Eat).

(902) 235-2669 or (866) 515-2900. Fax (902) 235-2196. www.islandsunset.com. Forty-eight cottage suites. Doubles, $250.

Duncreigan Country Inn, Highway 19, Box 59, Mabou B0E 1X0.

Connecticut transplants Eleanor and Charles Mullendore built Cape Breton's most elegant small inn from scratch in 1994. Having emigrated in 1972 to a farm near Whycocomagh, they bought the property and left it idle until Eleanor returned from her last foreign-service jaunt to Bolivia to become an innkeeper. They tore down the existing structure and built this beauty of rough-hewn western cedar on a wooded point jutting into Mabou harbor. They did things right, from the petite and posh parlor where the sofa fabric is coordinated with the window treatments to the dining area (since expanded with an enclosed deck beside the water) to the shady deck where leafy trees shield much of the view and the eight lavish guest quarters. Four are upstairs in the main building and four more are upstairs and down in the next-door Spring House erected in 1996. The carved bed headboards were custom-made to suit the furnishings – in our room, of oak to match the old Singer sewing machine; in a suite, of walnut to coordinate with the armoire. Each room comes with queen or king bed, sophisticated furnishings, cable TV, unusual bay windows that open every which way according to precise directions, and an uncommonly complete and informative guest directory. Five of the eight rooms face the water. One kingsize room has a whirlpool tub and a private deck; the other is a suite with a whirlpool tub and a fireplace. Eleanor and son Steven share cooking duties for the suave restaurant (see Where to Eat). Charles checks guests in and gets them settled in their rooms or on the deck, where they might watch the bald eagles that perch in the inn's spruce tree, swooping with a scream to pluck fish from the water. A buffet continental breakfast is included and one may order a full breakfast.

(902) 945-2207 or (800) 840-2207. Fax (902) 945-2206. www.duncreigan.ca. Seven rooms and one suite with private baths. Doubles, $110 to $150. Suite, $195.

Auberge Bay Wind Suites, 15299 Cabot Trail, Box 400, Cheticamp B0E 1H0.

Restaurateur Dave Deveau created a luxury inn of sorts along the boardwalk in the center of Cheticamp in 2003 by converting abandoned apartments above and beneath his Harbour Restaurant into four high-end suites. All have a queensize bedroom, a living room with sofabed and TV hidden in an armoire, telephone with dataport, a microwave and mini-refrigerator enclosed in a cabinet, rustic birch hardwood floors, big windows onto the water and access to a wraparound balcony. Each has a large closet holding terrycloth robes as well as an iron and ironing board. Baths have two-person airjet soaker tubs, except for the lower-level Lighthouse Suite that opens onto the boardwalk and has a handicapped-accessible, roll-in shower. The largest Highlands Suite has a full kitchen. Guests check off their preferences for a hot breakfast from a menu, delivered to the suite at the appointed hour by a cook from the restaurant.

(902) 224-2233. Fax (902) 224-1515. www.baywindsuites.com. Four suites with private baths. Doubles, $189 to $239. Closed late October to early May.

Seascape Coastal Retreat, 36083 Cabot Trail, Box 44, Ingonish B0C 1K0.

Ten of the loveliest, most comfortable cottages you ever saw fan out along the shore behind chef-owner Rod Sittler's acclaimed new restaurant of the same name (see Where to Eat). Originally from Ontario, he and his wife Julie from England came to Ingonish on vacation and liked it so much they settled here. The couple gear their upscale cottages to couples and give them a B&B flavor, what with an exotic seafood hors d'oeuvre delivered to the rooms in the late afternoon and a complimentary gourmet breakfast served in the restaurant the next morning. The newly built cottages have all the comforts of home. Each has a queensize bedroom, a sitting room with a sofa facing the front window, a small gas stove and TV in the corner, an efficiency kitchen area and a spacious bath with a whirlpool tub. Two Adirondack chairs linked by a table on the front porch face the beach. Guests enjoy Julie's showy gardens around a courtyard and an enclosed spa tub, as well as complimentary use of kayaks and bicycles. French toast and three-egg omelets are featured at breakfast. The afternoon refreshments at our visit were a smoked salmon sausage one day, a lobster dip with crackers the next.

(902) 285-3003 or (866) 385-3003. www.seascapecoastalretreat.com. Doubles, $199 to $209. Closed early November to mid-May.

Baddeck Bases

Auberge Gisele's Country Inn, 387 Shore Road, Box 132, Baddeck B0E 1B0.

What started as a few efficiency cottages blossomed into a motel and sprouted in 1990 into a luxury high-rise inn with Baddeck's first elevator. Helen and Hans Sievers took over the complex in 1975 from his mother (Gisele, who retired to Florida) and have added on to the point they think theirs is the best on the island. Forty-three deluxe rooms are contained on three floors of the main building, which stretches perpendicularly from the road so that only the end suites get head-on views of Bras d'Or Lake. The rooms are pretty in roses and teals, Helen's favorite colors. They have one queensize or two double beds, TVs hidden in armoires, a loveseat and a chair in rose velvet, reproduction period furniture and bathrooms outfitted with hair dryers, toiletries and sewing kits. Three corner suites contain jacuzzis and fireplaces.

So do deluxe rooms in the Helena House, added in 1999. A spa offers saunas and a whirlpool. "We're going after the European market and conventions," says Helen, who's a leader in promoting Cape Breton tourism. She has removed the original cottages from the complex, which also includes an expanded restaurant of note (see Where to Eat) and a pleasant front dining terrace beside a fountain. Up a hill out back remains a two-story motel with 26 units, redone inside and out, each with two beds, color TV and unusual bow windows that let you see more of the distant lake and provide some solar heat on cool days. Rooms here are nicely outfitted with local pine furniture designed by Hans and made by a native Canadian cooperative. Gisele hand painted the plates hanging on the walls and the tiles on the tables.

(902) 295-2849 or (800) 304-0466. Fax (902) 295-2033. www.giseles.com. Seventy-two rooms and three suites with private baths. Doubles, $135 to $185. Suites, $275. Closed late October to May.

Duffus House Inn, 108 Water St., Box 427, Baddeck B0E 1B0.

A dear little 1850 house filled with antiques, an adjunct called Effie's House next door, extensive English country gardens with the most amazing oriental poppies we ever saw, and a waterfront location. What more could one ask? Innkeepers Judy and John Langley put it all together in the 1980s to create Cape Breton's first interesting B&B of note. The two houses have room after little room of period furnishings and nice touches. Each of the seven guest quarters has a lake view. We splurged for a garden suite with a decorative coal stove in the sitting room, windows onto the garden and water, a paneled bathroom and a queen bedroom. Where her colleagues might opt for the new and sophisticated, says Judy, "I prefer old and comfortable." There are antiques and curios everywhere you look – ditto for pleasant sitting areas inside and out, in living rooms, on verandas, and in the gardens. The lavish gardens. Judy's lavish gardens must be seen to be believed. So must John's Cunard Room, a library turned into a wall-to-wall museum of Cunard memorabilia – the largest such collection in Nova Scotia. It seems Sir Samuel Cunard, the shipping magnate from Halifax, was the brother-in-law of James Duffus, a Baddeck founder who built the house. Besides being a Cunard collector and historian, John is an attorney who served as first executive director of the Bras D'Or Lakes Preservation Society. In a dining room with a water view, Judy serves a continental breakfast of scones, cranberry muffins, cinnamon bread and Scottish oatcakes with strawberry-rhubarb marmalade. Stewed rhubarb was a welcome preliminary at our breakfast in early July.

(902) 295-2172. www.baddeck.com/duffushouse. Four rooms and three suites with private baths. Doubles, $125 to $165. Closed mid-October through May.

Inverary Resort, 368 Shore Road, Box 190, Baddeck B0E 1B0.

An expanding eleven-acre resort property with a Scottish theme beside Lake Bras d'Or, this has 138 guest quarters, two restaurants (see Where to Eat), an indoor pool and sauna, a convention center, a spa and a gift shop. The MacAuley family have operated it since 1971, and son Scott MacAulay has rapidly acquired more resort properties to put together golf and convention packages. The family's Scottish heritage is evident in everything from the names of the diverse buildings to the salty kippered herring and untoasted bonnach served at breakfast. The eight original rooms in the inn are appointed with antique furnishings. They've been dwarfed by a succession of buildings, including 24 top-of-the-line rooms with queen or two double beds and antique furnishings in a new wing in front of the inn. Our lakefront room in the two-story Argyle Lodge, the old main motel unit, was comfortable with pine paneling and furniture (the pine chairs, made near Halifax, were especially handsome), autumn-patterned draperies and bedspreads, floral sheets and cable TV. Other rooms are in Campbell Hall, lodges and pine-paneled cottages. Twenty-four rooms in the Glasgow House, with an indoor pool and whirlpool, were built to be open all year (although there were not enough takers). They're more up to date in pink and blue with comforters on the beds, thick carpeting and bar-refrigerators. Three tennis courts are beside the lake. So is the expanded Lakeside Café and Adventure Center, where a blue-canopied pontoon boat takes guests on half-hour lake cruises and paddleboats, surfbikes, canoes and kayaks are available. Between the bustling restaurants, the convivial Thistledown Pub, the interesting gift shop and the many bus tours, Inverary is apt to convey a busy feeling. At least we found it so, our car and only two others being sandwiched between four tour buses during a September stay.

(902) 295-3500 or (800) 565-5660. Fax (902) 295-3527. www.inveraryresort.com. One hundred twenty-three rooms, six suites and nine cottages with private baths. Doubles, $110 to $250. Suites and cottages, $250 to $295. Closed mid-November to May.

Silver Dart Lodge, 257 Shore Road, Box 399, Baddeck B0E 1B0.

Despite its name, this is a modern motor inn complex, a restaurant and a deluxe mansion house on 94 wooded acres with a private beach. Although we had expected it to be on the water, it is across Shore Road and up a hill. Our room with two double beds and TV was fine and the view of the Bras d'Or Lakes from the balcony was inspiring, even though we had to ask for chairs and then had to dodge a thunderstorm; the ensuing rainbow was a colorful substitute for the missing sunset. The bright red lighting cast at the time in the chalet-style dining room called **McCurdy's** would have competed with the sunset anyway. The dining ambiance has been upgraded, as has the food, since we had what we thought was a rather strange dinner – our first in Nova Scotia – which turned out to be typical for Cape Breton at the time. An accordion-playing Scotsman in a kilt entertained, a tradition that continues to this day. Now, besides an à la carte menu, the restaurant is known for its nightly buffet dinner ($24.95, and well worth it if you get there before a lot of it has been devoured). Expect three hot entrées plus a carved roast, steamed mussels and clams, and up to eighteen salads. For big-spenders, the Silver Dart offers its **MacNeil House,** a 19th-century mansion up the hill in back. It has six suites, each with one or two bedrooms, living room, fireplace, kitchen, full bath and jacuzzi. Furnished in dark cherry wood and with four-poster beds, two have balconies and three face the lake.

(902) 295-2340 or (888) 662-7484. Fax (902) 295-2484. www.maritimeinns.com. Fifty-four rooms, 24 efficiencies, six suites and twelve chalets with private baths. Doubles, $115 to $155. Suites, $195 to $299. Closed mid-October to mid-May. Dinner nightly, 5:30 to 9:30.

Broadwater Inn & Cottages, Bay Road, Baddeck B0E 1B0.

The 175-year-old house formerly known as Bute Arran Gift Shop, as Scottish as could be and site of a low-key B&B, has been on the upswing under owners John and Rosalie Pino. The homestead of the family of J.D. MacCurdy, Alexander Graham Bell's pilot, was converted to five guest rooms with queensize beds and sitting areas. A recent addition produced a self-contained, two-bedroom suite with a living room and sunroom overlooking the grounds and the lake. The large, cathedral-ceilinged Library that Bell and his pilot used as a work area has a queen bed, sitting area around the gas fireplace, and bath with jacuzzi tub. Three rooms in front offer water views, and two have private decks. In the woods at the side of the house are six log chalets, with one or two bedrooms each. All have queensize beds, a sofabed in a sitting area, kitchenette facilities and decks looking toward the lake. Cottagers are on their own for breakfast, but inn guests are treated to fresh fruit, cereals, muffins and cinnamon rolls. The location amid eight wooded acres is superb, facing Baddeck Bay beside the second green of the new Bell Bay Golf Course. Lovely gardens add to the ambiance.

(902) 295-1101 or (877) 818-3474. Fax (902) 295-2576. www.broadwater.baddeck.com. Five rooms, one suite and six chalets with private baths. Doubles, $95 to $125; suite $180. Chalets, $129 to $170. Inn closed December-March.

Bell View Bed & Breakfast, 713 Bay Road, Baddeck B0E 1BO.
The view down the lawn of the lake across the road is similar to that which Alexander Graham Bell would have enjoyed, but this new establishment is turned inward. A hard bench on the front porch was the only apparent place upon which to sit to take in the view at our mid-July visit. The inside was decorated in gilt and green as if for Christmas, the stairway railing swagged in greenery and angel decorations perched in bedrooms amid artificial wreaths and flowers. Innkeepers Denise and Bill Mulley offer four upstairs guest rooms, two in front with water views. One with a queen poster bed angled from the corner has a bath with jacuzzi tub and separate shower. Another with a king poster bed has an in-room jacuzzi tub. A table is set for four near the front window in the formal parlor, with Victorian couches and chairs placed side by side around the perimeter. A gilt mirror and swagged curtains grace the dining room, where a full breakfast is offered at a table for six.

(902) 295-2334 or (877) 234-1333. www.bellview.baddeck.com. Four rooms with private baths. Doubles, $120 to $149. Closed December-March.

Around the Cabot Trail

Since the preferred direction around the Cabot Trail is clockwise from Baddeck, lodging is listed in that order.

The Normaway Inn & Cabins, 691 Egypt Road, Box 100, Margaree Valley B0E 2C0.
Although not near the water, this out-of-the-way 1920s resort is perfect for those who seek tranquility and a welcoming atmosphere. "We get people who want to get away and have peace and quiet," says longtime innkeeper David MacDonald. The 250-acre property is in a wooded valley two miles off the Cabot Trail, and a deer fled as we drove in the long driveway lined with pines. Three meals a day are served in the dining room, considered one of the island's best (see Where to Eat). A fiddler entertains at night in the huge living room, equipped with a fieldstone fireplace, old stuffed sofas and lots of books. A connecting sunroom is cheery by day. Downstairs is a gathering room, where red chairs are lined up for local-interest films at night. A fiddler trio plays for a concert and Ceilidh dance Wednesday nights in summer in the Barn. The inn's nine rooms, each located so no two are adjacent, are decorated in lodge style and are comfortable with a double or a queen bed and a single sofabed. Extra privacy is afforded in eight cabins, plus eleven newer one-bedroom pine chalets clustered near the tennis court. Most have a queen or two double beds and wood stoves. Some have screened porches and seven have jacuzzi tubs. Three luxury suites (one with two bedrooms) with jacuzzis and fireplaces are offered in the nearby MacPherson House. Breakfast ($10.50), with Scottish and Canadian music playing in the background, was one of the best we have ever had, from the real orange juice and stewed rhubarb with thick cream, through the excellent homemade granola, muffins so hot the waitress burned her hand on the serving pan, and french toast dipped in oatmeal and cinnamon. The pièce de résistance was Eggs Hughie D, a local creation of a poached egg on a toasted Margaree muffin and

Canadian back bacon, topped with a light tomato sauce and cheddar cheese. Extraordinary!

(902) 248-2987 or (800) 565-9463. Fax (902) 248-2600. www.normaway.com. Ten rooms, three suites and nineteen cabins with private baths. Rates, EP. Doubles, $99 to $129. Suites, $179 and $249. Cabins, $139 to $169. Add $45 or $50 per person for MAP. Closed late October to mid-May.

Duck Cove Inn, Cabot Trail, Margaree Harbour B0E 2B0.
This is not an inn, but a motel, although one with a restaurant and smashing vistas of the Margaree River. Three meals a day are served in the 50-seat dining room, which is comfortable and homey with paper mats or blue cloths on pine tables, captain's chairs and nothing to detract from the view. Dinners, from roast turkey to grilled or poached Atlantic salmon, include juice or soup and vegetables. The 24 motel units are standard with TV and one queen bed and a couch or one double bed and a sofabed. Four have kitchenettes. The twelve newer units in the two-story motel closest to the water have sliding doors onto balconies or a lawn (the views are far better from the second story). Canoes are available for rent in a little park beside the river. Friends report they were trucked several miles up the Margaree for an enjoyable paddle back that produced sightings of deer and otters.

(902) 235-2658 or (800) 565-9993. Fax (902) 235-2592. www.duckcoveinn.com. Twenty-four rooms with private baths. Doubles, $85 to $95. Lunch, noon to 2. Dinner, 6 to 8. Entrées, $12.95 to $16.95. Closed November-May.

Laurie's Motor Inn, 15456 Laurie Road, Cheticamp B0E 1H0.
Laurie McKeown's father started this lodging and dining complex in 1938 with five cabins in the heart of French-Acadian Cheticamp. The cabins are long gone, replaced by a nine-unit motel behind the restaurant. A later ten-room section was double-decked to provide a total of 28 rooms and two suites. Off at an angle without much of a water view is a new 24-room Highlander wing with a bridal suite boasting a kingsize bed, sofa, ceiling fan and a double jacuzzi with pillows. Four more rooms were given king beds and others got jacuzzis in a recent upgrade. Laurie continues to refurbish the older units and added a suave upstairs cocktail lounge for the restaurant. He's proud of the five family suites with sitting areas in the new motel section, especially the large second-story end suite with a view of the Gulf of St. Lawrence from the sofa and chair grouping by the window – "you'll have a hard time finding a better room in all of Nova Scotia," he claimed. We were well satisfied with our huge "suite" with two queen beds, a sofa, a table in front of the window and a shared balcony. The new guest laundromat proved a great convenience. Laurie's also offers three whale-watch cruises daily. Participants at our visit said they saw four groups of about twenty whales each, including mothers with their offspring, plus dolphins.

(902) 224-2400 or (800) 959-4253. Fax (902) 224-2069. www.lauries.com. Forty-eight rooms and six suites with private baths. Doubles, $95 to $145. Suites, $145 to $300.

Markland Coastal Resort, 802 Dingwall Road, Dingwall B0C 1G0.
This "coastal resort" on a bluff seemingly at the end of the world is still in the making, according to owner Charles MacLean. It hadn't added some of the finishing niceties when we stayed five years after its opening, but it had survived an economic downturn and the pitfalls of an isolated location. Lately, it added the Octagon Arts Centre, where a summer Ceilidh series is presented Friday evenings and a chamber music series on Sunday afternoons. Located at the east or top end of the island where the mountains meet the sea, the accommodations are in nine one-bedroom

housekeeping log chalets and four side-by-side triplex log buildings facing the ocean. The latter hold three rooms, each with a sitting area in front of a queensize bed with a basic bathroom behind. At our stay, the sunny afternoon turned cloudy and chilly shortly after we managed a quick dip in the shallow pool. It was too cool and threatening to remain outside for long and there was nowhere else to go, so we huddled inside our room trying variously to read under a 40-watt light above the sofabed and to watch one of the two channels on the TV. A sea of knotty pine from its cathedral ceiling to its furnishings to its bare floor, our all-wood cocoon for the evening suffered for lack of side windows (it was an end unit and could have used a couple), a rug or even more than one small artwork (a formula photo) on the walls. The one- and two-bedroom chalets, which were full that holiday weekend, are good for families who want comforts considerably above the tent level, but the nearly empty suites seemed too bare bones for the upscale couples market their prices were designed to attract. The oceanfront location may compensate for those blessed with decent weather, however. The 70-acre property includes a beach and a gazebo perched in solitary splendor on an embankment overlooking the water. The main lodge has a reception lobby with reading materials and a peaked-ceiling dining room known for good meals (see Where to Eat). We quite liked our dinner, and was impressed with the complimentary buffet breakfast spread of Scottish oatmeal porridge, various toasting breads, muffins and scones as well as five kinds of juices. A full breakfast is available for an extra charge and for the public.

(902) 383-2246 or (800) 872-6084. Fax (902) 383-2092. www.marklandresort.com. Twenty-five units with private baths. Doubles, $169. Chalets, $269 to $329. Closed late October to June.

Glenghorm Beach Resort, 36743 Cabot Trail, Box 39, Ingonish BOC 1K0.

Established and run by a single family since 1952, this seasonal resort is now part of Scott MacAuley's growing Cape Breton Resorts group. The new owner refurbished the complex inside and out, added lobster to the dinner menu and built two "beach houses," each with five deluxe suites with fireplaces and one or two bedrooms. Glenghorm now has 950 feet of beach frontage, a restaurant and gift shop, and 90 well-kept motel units, efficiencies, suites and housekeeping cottages in two separate complexes linked by a foot path. The original is close to the shore and dining room; the newer complex is a bit more distant but near the pool. Picnic tables and some of the ten cottages face the water, as do a couple of the motel buildings with private balconies. We prefer them over the newer units with pine furnishings away from the water. The 110-seat **Crofter's Table** dining room, which has a view of the ocean at the foot of the fourteen-acre property, serves three meals a day in summer. The dinner menu ($11.50 to $22.95) has been upscaled to include things like curried shrimp and scallops, chicken cordon bleu and gorgonzola-crusted tenderloin steak.

(902) 285-2049 or (800) 565-5660. Fax (902) 285-2395. www.capebretonresorts.com. Seventy motel rooms, ten suites and ten cottages with private baths. Doubles, $102 to $120. Suites, $295 to $395. Cottages, $128 to $188. Closed late October to mid-May.

Lantern Hill & Hollow, 36845 Cabot Trail, Box 235, Ingonish Beach BOC 1L0.

Six cottages beside the shore appeal to families at this establishment on three secluded seaside acres with 225 feet of private beachfront. At the foot of a slope, five have two bedrooms and the other is a one-bedroom with a corner whirlpool tub and double shower. Each has a dining and living area with vaulted pine ceiling and an electric fireplace, a covered veranda with chairs and a gas barbecue, as well as satellite TV and telephone and fully equipped kitchen. Owner Sharon Harrison puts up couples in three bedrooms in her cheery yellow house perched astride the hill above the shore. Rooms with hardwood floors and contemporary decor have queen or kingsize beds, TV and a mini-refrigerator. The premier White Sands Suite includes a sitting room with a mini-refrigerator and an electric fireplace. House guests enjoy a combination sitting room/library with a fireplace as well as a screened veranda overlooking the ocean. Sharon no longer offers breakfast – "just bed and bath."

(902) 225-2010 or (888) 663-0225. Fax (902) 285-2001. www.lanternhillandhollow.com. Three rooms and six cottages with private baths. Doubles, $145 to $175. Cottages, $210 to $225.

Castle Rock Country Inn, 39339 Cabot Trail, Ingonish Ferry BOC 1LO.

This year-round inn with an acclaimed dining room opened in 1998 in a built-from-scratch structure atop a slope overlooking the scenic Middle Head Peninsula, at the foot of Cape Smokey. Run by owner Ian MacLennan from North Sydney, the place exudes newness as well as style in a spare, contemporary kind of way. Each room is basically a mirror image except for the view, or lack thereof. Each comes with a queen bed (and some with a sofabed), a TV hidden in the birch armoire, and white walls hung with the landscapes of local artist Christopher Gorey. The decor is simple and inn amenities are few. Seven rooms on the first and second floors face the water, but lack balconies to take full advantage. Their occupants join other guests on the 180-foot-long wraparound deck off the main floor. The other common area is a corner sitting area with a wood stove at one end of the contemporary dining room. Elaborate breakfasts are available off a short, sophisticated menu. The kitchen is at its most creative at dinner (see Where to Eat).

(902) 285-2700 or (888) 884-7625. Fax (902) 285-2525. www.ingonish.com/castlerock. Fifteen rooms with private baths. Doubles, $110 to $138.

Chanterelle Country Inn & Cottages, 48678 Cabot Trail, (RR 4, Baddeck BOE 1BO), North River.

Devoted environmentalist Earlene Busch built this inn and restaurant "from scratch" in 2000, earning Audubon Green Leaf eco-awards for her efforts. She designed a homey inn on a 150-acre hillside overlooking the end of St. Ann's Harbor, an estuary to the North River. The main lodge holds eight second-floor guest rooms and a main-floor suite, simply furnished with beds varying from twins to kingsize, country antiques, original art and oriental scatter rugs on the hardwood floors. TVs and phones are available upon request, but Earlene prefers to stress all the environmentally correct practices in her chemical-free atmosphere. They include organic shampoos, recycled paper products and handmade soaps without wrappers ("so we don't generate trash – this German can teach these Scots a bit about thrift," she advises cheerily). Talk about recycling: in 2004 she rescued three condemned cottages in Ingonish and moved them here to round out her accommodations. They come with efficiency kitchens, fireplaces, TV and whirlpool tubs. "Two places I don't cut corners are the beds and the food," Earlene says. She cites her unique and pricey Englander mattresses and the organic, locally produced ingredients for her restaurant that takes up a substantial portion of the open main floor (see Where to Eat). Inn guests hang out in a cozy corner sitting area on the main floor and on a two-level screened front veranda that runs the width of the house. The property descends sharply to the harbor, where a gazebo and paddle boat await. Rates include an extensive buffet breakfast that featured, at our visit, homemade granola, a mushroom and tomato quiche and potato donuts called spudnuts. One entry in the guest book summed up the place: "A haven of peace giving hope for a greener world."

(902) 929-2263 or (866) 277-0577. www.chanterelleinn.com. Eight rooms, one suite and four cottages with private baths. Doubles, $135 to $175. Suite, $225. Cottages, $850 to $1,000 weekly.

Luckabooth Bed & Breakfast, 50671 Cabot Trail (RR 4, Baddeck BOE 1BO), St. Ann's.

St. Ann's Bay is on view from every room in this newly built, log-style home off by itself on a wooded hillside above the shore. Wayne and Frances McClure designed it to take full advantage of the view, from three guest bedrooms, three common rooms and a 30-foot deck along the back. Rooms have queensize beds and full baths, and the largest adds a sofabed. Each has a reading/writing area, although there's also a common loft sitting room and another room with satellite TV and a games table. A towering fireplace is a focal point in the soaring, two-story-high living room that opens through sliding doors onto the deck. Adjacent and also opening onto the deck is the chandeliered dining room, where a three-course breakfast is served by candlelight.

(902) 929-2722 or (877) 654-2357. Fax (902) 929-2503. Three rooms with private baths. Doubles, $120 to $145.

CAMPING. Numerous campgrounds are detailed in the Nova Scotia Tourism Department's travel guide. Two private ones that appeal are the **Baddeck Cabot Trail Campground,** Highway 105, Baddeck, 295-2288 or (866) 404-4199, with 120 serviced and 47 unserviced sites, and **Bras d'Or Lakes Campground,** Highway 105, Baddeck, (902) 295-2329, with 68 serviced and 17 unserviced sites and 500 feet of shoreline on the lake. Cape Breton Highlands National Park has eight campgrounds, some on the ocean, with varied facilities; rates, $15 to $21 nightly.

For an unusual experience, head out to **Meat Cove Camping**, Meat Cove B0C 1E0, (902) 383-2379, "at the end of the road where the Saint Lawrence Seaway meets the Atlantic ocean." The brochure doesn't tell the half of it. You get there going up and down a hair-raising dirt road to the end of the world, where at the edge of the last hamlet on Cape Breton are 25 campsites with services nearby, spectacular ocean views and utter solitude. Rates, $18.

Seeing and Doing

The Cabot Trail

The 186-mile-long trail around the outermost tip of Cape Breton Island embraces some of North America's most spectacular scenery. The road is good and the complete trip can be done easily in a day, or you can linger and retrace your steps.

Pick a good day – preferably sunny, although even cloudy days can yield good visibility. The most breathtaking scenery (and slowest driving) is along relatively short stretches in Cape Breton Highlands National Park, up and down cliffs on the eastern and western shores and in the mountainous northern interior near Big Intervale. Although you might choose as we first did to go counterclockwise against the prevailing traffic and for right-hand access to scenic pull-offs, don't. The other times we went clockwise and concluded that that direction offers better vistas.

Cape Breton Highlands National Park, Ingonish Beach.

Established in 1936, this is Eastern Canada's largest national park and the heart of the Cabot Trail. The park's main feature is an extensive plateau, crisscrossed by rivers and valleys between mountains and a rugged coastline of bold headlands, steep cliffs, hidden coves and sandy beaches. To us, it's a cross between Scotland's Highlands and California's Big Sur. The wilderness is so vast and the signs of civilization so different that you could imagine yourself in a foreign land.

Naturalists appreciate the many varieties of wildlife and vegetation. Hikers like the 140 miles of trails leading to the interior plateau, the rugged coast or to 1,000-foot-high viewpoints overlooking it all; 27 trails are detailed in a special brochure. Swimmers will find two supervised beaches and any number of other saltwater and freshwater beaches. Picnicking is offered at numerous "picnic parks." The eighteen-hole Highlands Links near the Keltic Lodge is one of Canada's more challenging golf courses. Three tennis courts are available at the Ingonish Beach Day Use Area. In winter there's skiing on Cape Smokey. The park's interpretive program includes a variety of roadside markers and exhibits, self-guided trails and, in summer, guided walks and evening talks by park rangers.

(902) 224-2306 or (888) 773-8888. Information centers are open from mid-May to mid-October at the Cheticamp and Ingonish entrances to the park. Park admission is $5 adult and $3 child, or $17 per family daily. Four-day pass, $10.50 adult, $4:50 child and $24 family.

Trail and Park Highlights

The Cabot Trail and the park have as many interesting (if not quite as diverse) attractions as Yellowstone or Yosemite. Going clockwise, we were particularly struck by the colorful old boats and the loons in the harbor at **Grand Étang** and the austere, barren Acadian fishing village of **Cheticamp** (pause to view the ornate interior of **St. Peter's Roman Catholic Church),** the ride up **French Mountain** (with views behind) and then down the switchbacks to **Pleasant Bay.** Atop French Mountain are the **Skyline Trail,** from which you peer down on the Cabot Trail and see fishing boats and maybe a whale, and the **Bog Trail** where signs along a boardwalk attempt to make the bog interesting.

As you head into the interior, stop at the **Lone Shieling,** a replica of an open Scottish sheep crofter's hut dwarfed by 300-year-old sugar maples. The descent down **North Mountain** provides awesome views toward Aspy Bay. Take the one-mile dirt road to **Beulach Ban Falls,** a 50-foot-high waterfall and picnic area that's worth the detour.

At **Cape North,** leave the trail to head out to the northernmost tip of Cape Breton. Stop at **Cabot's Landing,** where English explorer John Cabot and his son Sebastian are believed to have set foot on the sandy beach in 1497. The view across the church spire and colorful houses as you descend the hill into the harbor at **Bay St. Lawrence** is unforgettable. The intrepid can continue nine miles out past Capstick and up and down a winding dirt road to **Meat Cove,** a hamlet sequestered seemingly at the end of the earth. The views and the seclusion here are awesome.

Back in Cape North, leave the Cabot Trail to take the alternate coastal route out to **White Point** and **Neil's Harbor.** It provides even more spectacular views than some of the Cabot Trail, and so unexpectedly. Check out the multi-colored bluff near Smelt Brook, which ends with a formation that looks like the profile of Richard Nixon. Drive down to White Point, a working dock reeking of fish, with colorful boats and lobster traps all around. Neil's Harbor is as picturesque a fishing village as you'll find.

Rejoin the Cabot Trail and stop at **Black Brook,** one of the many picnic parks in the area and this one with grass, a sandy beach and a bluff on one side. Go into the Keltic Lodge grounds and hike out to the end of **Middle Head. Ingonish Beach** is long, sandy and reminiscent of Ogunquit's beach, except when the surf is crashing in a storm. The beach is actually a spit of land with the ocean on one side and a freshwater lake on the other. The Cabot Trail climbs **Cape Smokey,** which may be clouded in mist, for the most hair-raising part of driving the trail. At **North Shore,** you may be able to see in the distance the famous **Bird Islands,** home of the Atlantic puffin and a favorite with bird-watchers (who can visit by tour boat from

Big Bras d'Or). At the **Gaelic College of Celtic Arts and Crafts** in St. Ann's, the only one of its kind in North America, is the **Great Hall of the Clans,** which depicts the history and culture of the Scots. It's open 8:30 to 5, daily in summer and weekdays in June and early fall; adults, $3. A newer attraction here is a **Craft Center** displaying clan tartans and handicrafts, open daily in summer 8:30 to 8, weekdays in late spring and fall 8:30 to 5.

Whale-Watch Cruises and Boating

Whale-watch and nature cruises are available at many points along the Cabot Trail, with a concentration of operators along the new harborfront boardwalk in Cheticamp and along the wharfs in Pleasant Bay. Typical are the two 42-foot vessels operated by **Whale Cruisers Ltd.,** (800) 813-3376, which leave the Government Wharf at Cheticamp daily at 9, 1 and 5 or 6 in season. The first whale operator to be established in Nova Scotia (1981), it has three-hour cruises showing sea caves, unusual rock formations, cormorants, perhaps a bald eagle or a moose, and an average of twenty Atlantic pilot whales (adults $25, children $10). Also in Cheticamp are "love boats" by **Seaside Whale and Nature Cruises,** (800) 959-4253, and Zodiac tours by **Acadian Whale Cruise,** (877) 232-2522.

Shorter travel times and higher quality sightings are claimed by whale tours out of Pleasant Bay. The 42-foot Double Hookup, operated by Mark Timmons of **Capt. Mark's Whale and Seal Cruise,** (888) 754-5112, schedules five two-hour cruises daily; adults $25, children $12. **Highland Coastal Whale Tours** in Pleasant Bay, (866) 266-4080, employs a 38-foot fishing boat for tours (adults $25, children $12). **Fiddlin' Whale Tours** offers four two-hour tours daily that interact with whales through music by hydrophone, (866) 688-2424, adults $30, children $15. Also in Pleasant Bay, **Wesley's Whale Watch,** (866) 999-4253, gives two-hour whale cruises in a speedy Zodiac; adults $36, children $18.

For a different experience, consider a whale watch on a schooner. **Sail to the Whales,** (877) 488-2319, operates the 52-foot blue fishing schooner Tom Saylor for a tall ship adventure in Aspy Bay three times daily from Dingwall. **Sea Visions Sailing Tours,** (902) 285-2628, runs three whale tours daily out of Ingonish Ferry; adults $30, children $15. Its 57-foot schooner William Moor won the famous Marblehead to Halifax race in 1991. SeaQuarium Whale Watching Tours, (902) 285-2103, operates a 40-foot, hydrophone-equipped Cape Islander vessel at the foot of Cape Smokey in Ingonish Ferry; adults $25, children $12.50.

Sea kayak tours and rentals are offered at **North River Kayak Tours** in North River, (888) 865-2925. In Englishtown, **Puffin Boat Tours,** (877) 278-3346, operates three boat trips daily to the Bird Islands, where Atlantic Puffins make their home in summer; adults $32, children $15.

Stops and Shops along the Trail

Starting clockwise, note the Margaree River, one of North America's most beautiful (and prolific) salmon rivers. It offers twenty fishable miles of crystal-clear water and an abundance of salmon pools. Visitors view salmon and trout at the **Margaree Fish Hatchery** in Northeast Margaree; there's a salmon interpretation center nearby. Also at Northeast Margaree is the **Margaree Salmon Museum,** operated by the Margaree Anglers Association, a diverting experience for anyone interested in salmon and fishing. It's open daily 9 to 5, June 15 to Oct. 15; adults $1. Nearby is **Cape Breton Clay,** the barn shop of celebrated young potter Bell Fraser, whose unique pottery bearing mussels, clams and lobsters is as arresting as it is expensive.

The sandy ocean beach at Margaree Harbour, as well as others along the west shore, are said to have the warmest ocean waters north of the Carolinas. At Belle Cote, one of us found a small cave formed by rocks in which to change clothes for a quick dip in the ocean. Heading toward Cheticamp, you'll spot **Joe's Scarecrow Village,** a bizarre outdoor stage created by retired school janitor Joe Delaney near Cap LeMoine. More than 100 scarecrows, all dressed differently, flap in the breeze outside the trailer housing daughter Ethel's Take Out and Gift Shop. Those representing the past leaders of different countries, their arms outstretched for peace, and senior citizens from a rest home, signed with their names and messages either whimsical or poignant, are especially interesting. A must stop is **Gallerie La Bella Mona Lisa,** a trove of Nova Scotian folk art, where owner Michel Williatte-Battet of Montreal makes all the wooden fish. His trademark black and white cow, whimsically clad in red sneakers, is depicted in every medium imaginable.

Around Cheticamp you'll come to **Flora's,** a vast emporium of souvenirs and Cheticamp hooked rugs and smaller pieces made by Flora Boudreau and more than 100 local women. The Cooperative Artisanale de Cheticamp runs a small **Acadian Museum,** featuring a craft shop with locally hooked rugs, as well as **Restaurant Acadien,** a homey spot that's a good choice for breakfast or lunch with a difference and all dinners are under $10 or so. **Les Trois Pignons** (The Three Gables) is a highly touted center of Acadian history and home life, with a museum and gallery of hooked rugs and tapestries by Elizabeth LeFort, the Cheticamp native whose works are in the Vatican, Buckingham Palace and the White House (open May-October, daily 9 to 5, summer to 8 to 7; adults $3.50). **La Pirogue Fisheries Museum,** a handsome new three-level building at 15359 Cabot Trail, is an inter-active, bilingual showcase for the area's ties to the fishing industry, named for the small flat-bottom boat made by the early Cheticamp settlers; open daily 10 to 9, adults $5, children $3.

In Pleasant Bay, check out the **Whale Interpretive Centre,** 104 Harbour Road, (902) 224-1411. It's a community-sponsored museum with life-size models, exhibits, videos, nature programs and a huge pair of binoculars, through which one might see pilot whales cavorting a mile offshore. At our visit, we had to be satisfied watching muskrats and beavers in the adjacent river. Open June to mid-October, daily 9 to 6, to 8 in summer; adults $4.50, children $3.50.

Near Cape North you'll find **Arts North,** a small two-story contemporary building where Dennis and Linda Doyon sell their own pottery as well as local prints, woven items and especially nice jewelry. It's among the oldest of the art, folk art and craft galleries proliferating all along the Cabot Trail. Among them are **Leather Works,** where John Roberts makes leather reproductions of 18th-century fire buckets, someone who makes items out of celtic knots, and **Sew Inclined,** where artist Barbara Longva's designs unusual clothing and hats. Folk art, such as the **Fisherman's Folk Art Gallery,** prevails around Cheticamp. Driftwood sculptures and wooden platters by Claire Ryder are among the offerings at **Wild Things,** along the "Artisans' Loop" in Tarbot, St. Ann's Bay.

Ingonish is one of the oldest settlements on the Atlantic coast. Today it's a golfing, beach and ski resort. Works of award-winning local painter Christopher Gorey, an American émigré, are shown by his wife at **Lynn's Craft Shop and Art Gallery** in Ingonish. We loved them all and parted with a watercolor of lupines, the Maritimes' gorgeous wildflowers that are at their colorful height here in late June and early July.

Three food stops are of particular interest along the outer Cabot Trail. **Aucoin's Boulangerie and Patisserie** offers oatcakes, tea biscuits and french pastries along with pizzas in Cheticamp. Stop for a crab roll, whistle dog, poutine (that caloric mix of french fries, cheese curds and gravy, beloved in Eastern Canada) or a milk shake at **McLean's Chowder Deck** in Pleasant Bay. **The Clucking Hen** is a colorful deli, bakery and café along the trail near Indian Brook.

Baddeck and Bras d'Or Lakes

Baddeck is on a hillside beside the Bras d'Or Lakes, and world-class sailboats dock in its harbor while cruising the saltwater lakes that make up the continent's only inland sea. From a park near the Bras d'Or Yacht Club you can see where Alexander Graham Bell's Silver Dart flew off the ice in 1909 to become the first manned flight in the British Commonwealth and where his hydrofoil set a world speed boating record in 1919. You also can see **Beinn Breagh,** the mountain he owned, and the roof of the 1892 summer estate he built there.

The best view of Beinn Breagh is said to be from the 18th hole of the **Bell Bay Golf Club,** a Thomas McBroom masterpiece with great views from virtually every hole. Rated Canada's best new course in 1998 by Golf Digest, it's open to the public, (800) 565-3077; greens fee, $79.

The town enjoys its waterfront boardwalk, a landscaped walkway in two sections with park benches. It opens up the harborfront area, which is sheltered from the broad lake by Kidston Island.

In an old warehouse at the government wharf is **Seawinds Chandlery,** a smart shop with thick-knit Prince Edward Island sweaters, local handicrafts and nautical gifts. From here, a free boat run by the Baddeck Lions Club takes swimmers back and forth in summer to a beach on **Kidston Island.** Up on Chebucto Street, Baddeck's main thoroughfare, is Seawinds' newer and bigger sister, the ever-so-suave **Kidston Landing,** billed as a Cape Breton country store. It has a fine collection of local handicrafts, woolens, tableware, cookbooks, jams and lots of clothes. **The Blue Heron,** full of character, is like a true country store, with everything from a Sears catalog outlet to an ice-cream parlor. For your coffee fix, head to **Bean There** in the Chebucto Shops; for sandwiches, to the **Highwheeler Café** or the **Yellow Cello Café.**

Alexander Graham Bell National Historic Site, Route 205, Baddeck.

If when you think of Mr. Bell all you think of is the telephone, think again. This fascinating place shows the extraordinary range of his inventive genius, from genetics and medical science to the Silver Dart airplane and the hydrofoil. Through films, audio displays and such you'll learn of his romance with his deaf pupil Mabel, whom he later married, hear his famous "Dr. Watson, Dr. Watson" phone message, enjoy his early telephones and airplane models, view hundreds of historic photographs and see the remains of the hydrofoil. The priceless collection that makes up the museum was donated by his family, some of whom still summer at Beinn Breagh, which you can see from the roof of the striking tetrahedron-shaped museum.

(902) 295-2069. Open daily 8:30 to 6 July to Oct. 15, 9 to 6 in June, 9 to 5 rest of year. Adults, $7, children $3.50, family rate $17.50.

A Side Trip to Louisbourg

Fortress of Louisbourg National Historic Site, Louisburg.

We don't know when we last were so surprised and impressed by a restored village as here. We expected to spend a couple of hours and ended up having to drag ourselves away after six.

Louisbourg is the Canadian government's $26 million re-creation of the abandoned 18th-century walled city established by the French between 1713 and 1745 to defend their possessions in the New World. Until it was ambushed by Americans in 1745 and destroyed by the British in 1760, it was the mightiest fortress on this continent, the third busiest seaport (after Boston and Philadelphia) and the center of French civilization in North America. It is the only colonial town of importance without a modern city superimposed on top, so one-fourth of it could be authentically restored to the way it was in 1744.

After orienting yourself in the visitor center via a five-minute slide show as you proceed through four small theaters to a bus loading area, you are transported two miles out to the fortress, poised on a point beside the ocean. Outside is a scene of melancholy desolation. Inside, the physically austere fortress masks a lively working village of soldiers and seafaring families. Here, 175 costumed guides, most of them in their twenties and unusually articulate, interpret the town as it was in 1744, and the intriguing story of the rise and fall of Louisbourg gradually unfolds.

Although guided tours are offered periodically, you're on your own as you go through guardhouses, barracks, vegetable gardens, warehouses, homes, taverns, the military bakery, government buildings and the elegant Governor's Quarters. Guides volunteer information if spoken to (they and their stories are fascinating). Take the time to chat and also to listen (by telephone) to exceptionally interesting recordings detailing facets of Louisbourg life pertaining to the building you're in.

Stop for a meal or snack at the **Hotel de la Marine** or **L'Épée Royale.** At the former, you'll be seated communally and served by waitresses in 18th-century garb. For $7 each, we had a lunch of pea soup, chicken fricassee and bread pudding, plus a pewter container of red wine. You sit on low chairs at a table covered with a sheet and huge serviettes, using a single pewter spoon for the entire meal. Quite an experience, we thought, as did our tablemates from Arizona and a Californian whose wife was lunching in L'Épée Royale because she liked the sound of the stew there better. You can also visit the **King's Bakery** and buy a soldier's daily ration of bread.

There's so much to see and absorb that you could easily spend an entire day. Don't miss the building detailing the restoration of Louisbourg; that tale is almost as interesting as the story of Louisbourg itself. Usually between 600 and 1,800 people a day visit for a yearly total of about 125,000, which isn't many considering the significance of the site. It's apt to be windy, lonely and cold out there (wear something warm and windproof). You'll understand why Louisbourg – planned as the New World's capital – didn't make it.

(902) 733-2280. Open daily, July and August 9 to 6, May-June and September to Oct. 15, 9:30 to 5. Adults $13.50, children $6.75, family $33.75. Reduced services and rates in much of May and October.

Where to Eat

Special Treats

Duncreigan Country Inn, Highway 19, Mabou.

When the Mullendore family moved to the area from Connecticut in 1972, Mabou didn't even have a place to get a cup of coffee, let alone a meal. They bided their time (and careers – she on foreign assignments and he as an economic consultant for the Whycocomagh Indian tribe) until 1988, when they helped son David launch Mabou's first restaurant. The **Mull Café & Deli** was an instant success, inspiring the couple to build the inn of their dreams. David still runs the casual café and deli; younger brother Steven helps his mother with the inn's sophisticated restaurant, lately doubled in size and enhanced in atmosphere by enclosing a portion of the waterside deck. The vaulted-ceilinged dining room with central fireplace and tall windows yielding glimpses of the harbor is pristine and suave. Intricate centerpieces, made with flowers from the small front gardens, grace well-spaced tables dressed in white cloths with green overlays. It was a serene setting for what turned out to be our best dinner on Cape Breton. The short menu is printed nightly, with half a dozen entrées available à la carte or table d'hôte in three or four courses. The latter started with a stellar composed citrus and avocado salad and a dilled green and yellow bean salad on mixed greens. These were followed by a lobster and scallop sauté with sundried tomatoes and basil over spinach fettuccine and a grilled salmon fillet marinated in dijon mustard, honey and lemon. Broccoli, carrots and zucchini in various shapes and lightly roasted potatoes accompanied, and the picture-perfect plates were garnished with edible flowers. Profiteroles with chocolate and raspberry sauce and white chocolate amaretto cheesecake were worthy finales. The well-chosen wine list, including several offerings from South Africa, is affordably priced.

(902) 945-2207 or (800) 840-2207. Entrées, $25 to $29. Dinner by reservation, Tuesday-Sunday 5:30 to 8:30.

Markland Coastal Resort, Cabot Trail, Dingwall.

A less likely setting for some of the best meals on Cape Breton is hard to imagine. It's seemingly at the end of the world, three miles off the Cabot Trail on a barren site overlooking the ocean. The summery, contemporary dining room is elegant with oil lamps flickering on tables covered with deep blue cloths. Service is surprisingly polished and the contemporary menu sophisticated for such a remote establishment. Chef Lars Willum changes his menu frequently, offering the likes of steamed Aspy Bay mussels steamed in wine and garlic butter and poached fillet of halibut topped with smoked salmon. We shared a great garden salad topped with asparagus tips and toasted sesame seeds before digging into our main courses, herb-crusted rack of lamb with raspberry demi-glace and broiled sirloin steak heavily sauced with wild mushrooms. The excellent vegetables that accompanied were cooked al dente. An Australian shiraz for $19 was a good choice from the affordable wine list. We would gladly have sampled the chilled appetizer of strawberry soup with vanilla sorbet and wild mint for dessert, but at $6.95 it seemed an extravagance. We settled for a dish of french vanilla ice cream in lieu of the more filling chocolate-pecan torte on blueberry coulis or the cappuccino cheesecake.

(902) 383-2246 or (800) 872-6084. Entrées, $22.95 to $29.95. Dinner nightly, 6 to 9. Closed late October to mid-June.

Normaway Inn, Egypt Road, Margaree Valley.

Big windows on both sides of the charming, country-fresh dining room look out onto a tranquil rural landscape, and as the sun sets and the room is totally lit by candles, it's quite lovely. Tables covered with dark green cloths, Wedgwood china and fresh flowers create a simple but pleasant setting. The food is considered some of the best on Cape Breton. Complete dinners are $34 for three courses, $39 for four courses, with a choice of selections changing nightly; meals also can be ordered à la carte. We started with sherried mushrooms and shrimp-filled salmon rolls and a good salad with excellent dressings. The accompanying oatcakes and porridge bread were fabulous and came with real pats of butter, not the aluminum-foil miniatures foisted on diners in most Maritime restaurants. The butterflied leg of lamb tasted more like a roast with gravy and could have been rarer; the filet mignon with herb butter was more successful. Halibut with pecan butter, cornish hen with apricot stuffing and coquille of scallops and shrimp were the evening's other choices. Dinner ended triumphantly with an apple-rhubarb crisp with ice cream and an ice cream pie on a chocolate-coconut crust. Vegetables and salads are fresh from the inn's gardens. Afterward, a stroll down the lane to watch the horses frolicking was a pleasant interlude before the fiddler started entertaining in the inn's living room.

(902) 248-2987 or (800) 565-9463. Table d'hôte, $34 to $39. Entrées, $12.75 to $21.95. Dinner nightly, 6 to 9. Closed late October to mid-June.

Seascape Coastal Retreat, 36083 Cabot Trail, Ingonish.

Dinner is by candlelight at glass-topped tables in this prim, airy roadside café with a panoramic ocean view out windows on two sides and a glass-enclosed deck beyond. Chef-owner Rod Sittler, who trained with top chefs in his wife's native England, offers some of the area's most creative fare. The Sittlers grow their own organic vegetables and herbs and feature local seafood, from Dingwall mussels to Aspy Bay oysters. Dinner could start with a trio of spicy shrimp, oysters rockefeller or roasted garlic and tomato bruschetta with soft goat cheese. For main courses, consider the chef's signature shrimp in spicy Mediterranean sauce, coconut curry lobster, Atlantic salmon wrapped in rice paper or charbroiled strip loin steak. A fireplace adds a cozy feeling on cool nights in the off-season.

(902) 285-3003 or (866) 385-3003. Entrées, $19.95 to $28.95. Breakfast daily, 8 to 11. Dinner nightly, 5 to 9 or 9:30. Closed November-April.

Auberge Gisele's Inn, 387 Shore Road, Baddeck.

One guest wrote that its food was "an oasis in a gourmet desert," and we enjoyed a fine dinner here. Tables in the curved main dining room and an addition are positioned so that each has a view of the Bras d'Or Lakes across the road. The setting is urbane in white and gray with burgundy accents. Until the place grew too big, Helen Sievers did the cooking after her mother-in-law Gisele retired to Florida. Now she has a European chef, of whom she praises: "I am a cook; he is a chef." We shared the house terrine with aspic and melba before digging into our entrées, a good poached salmon with a delicate dill-hollandaise sauce, roasted potatoes and carrots, and a special of poached haddock with three caviars and rice. Other choices included pork tenderloin with cranberry and apple relish, veal scaloppine with creamed forest mushrooms and beef tenderloin with three-peppercorn sauce. The Acadian bouillabaisse and the Cape Breton rack of lamb are house specialties. Desserts, baked on the premises, include almond cheesecake with strawberry puree and Nova Scotia apple crisp with french vanilla ice cream. Finish with Gisele's special flambéed coffee with crème de cacao, grand marnier and whipped cream.

(902) 295-2849 or (800) 304-0466. Entrées, $18.95 to $27.95. Dinner nightly, 5:30 to 10. Closed November-April.

Around the Cabot Trail

Island Sunset Resort, 19 Beach Cove Lane, Belle Cote.

The large and rather glamorous restaurant with windows onto the ocean here was the first part of the resort to open in 2004. It's different for the area, given its open kitchen in one corner of the vast open space, an airy bar opposite and a sea of glass tables flanked by tropical-style chairs closest to the water. The result is an urbane, vaguely Caribbean beachy feeling in a barren Cape Breton setting. The oversize menu reads like that of a big-city restaurant, as in appetizers of "chilled jumbo shrimps glassed and garnished with a twisty tomato salsa" and "duo of marinated and smoked salmon with bread sticks, crème fraîche and dill." Typical entrées "from the oven and grill" are seared scallops with roasted sweet red pepper sauce, maple-brushed salmon with grilled endives, slow oven-cooked Alberta prime rib with horseradish sauce and dijon-crusted rack of lamb with rosemary demi-glace.

(902) 235-2669. Entrées, $17.25 to $24.95. Lunch daily, 11 to 4. Dinner, 4:30 to 10.

Harbour Restaurant & Bar, 15299 Cabot Trail (Main Street), Cheticamp.
Some of the best food along the north shore emanates from this pleasant dining room, stylish in beige and brown, looking onto the harbor beside a lighthouse. By far the best view is from the enclosed sun porch, where salmon-colored molded chairs are at butcher-block tables right beside the water. We could see cows grazing along the shore of the island across the cove, near a spit of sand covered with birds, as we lunched on a spicy noodle soup (which contained everything but the kitchen sink), a lobster roll and a plate of fried clams with coleslaw, washed down with the local Oland beer. At a second lunch, we sampled the thick and hearty Acadian seafood chowder and the French-Canadian specialty poutine. Our latest dinner produced broiled Digby scallops and a stellar seafood fettuccine, light and succulent, accompanied by side salads. The all-day menu offers a variety from scallops au gratin and broiled Margaree trout with tarragon-butter sauce to spicy grilled chicken wraps to grilled strip steak. Butterscotch meringue pie is the recommended dessert.
(902) 224-2042. Entrées, $15 to $21. Open daily, 11:30 to 10 or midnight.

Chowder House, Lighthouse Road, Neil's Harbor.
Hidden just past the lighthouse at Neil's Head in a remote fishing village, this is a true place – the kind of eatery we'd expected to find all over the island. You place your order and pick it up at the counter, then sit at oilcloth-covered picnic tables inside or out on a deck on a point beside the ocean. We enjoyed a bowl of seafood chowder ($4), which was the essence of fishiness, chock full of lobster, haddock and clams, and served with a biscuit, as well as a lobster burger ($8.95) and, for dessert, oatcakes and ginger cake. Other choices ranged from fish cakes to a lobster dinner. Run by the local fish cooperative, the manager told us there once were four such places across Cape Breton, but theirs was the only survivor.
(902) 336-2463. Entrées, $6 to $15.95. Open daily in summer, 11 to 8; 11 to 4 in late spring and early fall. Closed early October to June.

Keltic Lodge, Middle Head Peninsula, Ingonish Beach.
The food in the famed lodge's 200-seat **Purple Thistle** dining room is improved, the service is friendly and accommodating, and the setting is handsome: sparkling white with accents of paneling, hardwood floors and aqua window treatments. The public is welcome by reservation, and jackets are no longer required. In resort style, the menu changes frequently and meals are prix-fixe for the public: $49 for dinner, $15 for breakfast. Our dinner for two started with solomon gundy (four pickled herring, a local specialty) and a ham and asparagus feuilletée, followed by shellfish bisque and good salads. Main courses were cornish game hen and poached salmon with ginger butter. Desserts of assorted homemade sherbets and a fresh plum tart were highlights of the meal; we also appreciated the good rolls and oatcakes that arrived, mercifully, with butter that you didn't have to unwrap. (The menu has since been considerably upscaled with all the trendy accompaniments.) The next day's breakfast was filling as well: fruit cup, cream of wheat, a poached egg on English muffin with good Canadian sausage, and scrambled eggs with ham.
(902) 285-2880. Prix-fixe, $49. Breakfast, 7 to 10. Dinner, 6 to 9. Closed late October to late May.

Atlantic Restaurant, Middle Head Peninsula, Ingonish Beach.
For a taste of the Keltic Lodge experience at down-to-earth prices and an absolutely smashing water view, try this large and casual eatery beside the roadway leading into the main lodge. Rebuilt following a fire in 1999, it is a stunner – butcher-block tables with wrought-iron chairs, heavy lamps hanging from the vaulted and raftered ceiling, and fantastic views from every table, as well as from the side decks. The all-

day menu appeals as well, from the steak and goat cheese flatbread "sandwich" with pesto salsa to the Neil's Harbor snow crab cakes with a spiced apple-pecan compote. Dessert could be a chocolate and pear cheesecake or blueberry-pecan upside-down cake. The restaurant is fully licensed. An interesting gift shop, chock full of things we would have liked to buy, adjoins.

(902) 285-2880. Entrées, $9.75 to $25.75. Open daily, 11 to 9. Closed late October to late May.

The Sea Gull Restaurant, 35963 Cabot Trail, Ingonish.

The interior is unprepossessing, like many another Maritimes family restaurant. But the expansive covered deck beside the ocean is one of the best around, and accounted for all the cars and SUVs in the parking lot the warm summer evening we stopped by. Or was it the bargain-basement prices? An aroma of fried food indicated the genre, but you could order specials like liver and onions, creamy chicken supreme, roast beef or salisbury steak dinner, grilled halibut and seafood martinique over fettuccine. Ginger cake, four kinds of cheesecake and strawberry shortcake were among the desserts.

(902) 285-2851. Entrées, $7.95 to $15.95. Open daily in season, 11 to 9.

Castle Rock Country Inn, 39339 Cabot Trail, Ingonish Ferry.

This newcomer exudes a sense of style, from its modern dining room with bleached birch tables topped with colorful mats to the contemporary continental fare offered by chef Brad Green. Tall windows yield sweeping water views back toward Ingonish Beach, and the dining room opens onto a large deck with sturdy umbrellaed tables for dining. For dinner, expect starters like seafood soup (a mix in an aromatic tomato and lobster broth), mussels steamed in ale and caesar salad. Main courses include seared scallops with avocado salsa, chicken cordon bleu, herb-crusted pork tenderloin and strip loin steak with whisky-peppercorn sauce. Lunch on the deck yields treats like seafood stew and pan-fried salmon cakes.

(902) 285-2700 or (888) 884-7625. Entrées, $15 to $29. Lunch daily in season, 11 to 3. Dinner nightly by reservation, 6 to 9.

Chanterelle Country Inn, 48678 Cabot Trail, North River.

Organic and local ingredients, including mushrooms, fiddleheads and such foraged from the nearby woods, are featured in the large, lodge-style dining room that takes up much of the main floor at this new inn atop a hill overlooking the end of St. Ann's Harbor. Dinner is taken at large, mismatched tables here or on a two-level screened veranda that runs the width of the house. Chef-owner Earlene Busch and her primly costumed staff can serve 68 diners in the two areas. The menu changes nightly and is printed weekly. Three entrée choices – one vegetarian, one non-vegetarian and one seafood – are offered nightly. One Friday night's offerings were typical: mushroom and cheese medley in puff pastry, pork tenderloin Tuscany style and halibut poached in fennel. Starters included cream of fiddlehead soup and lobster bisque. Desserts were strawberry-rhubarb pie, chocolate potato cake and crème brulée.

(902) 929-2263 or (866) 277-0577. Entrées, $18 to $25. Dinner nightly by reservation, 7 to 9. Closed November-April.

The Lobster Galley, 51943 Cabot Trail, St. Ann's Harbor.

Lately renovated and expanded, this old-timer dressed in blue and white offers a lovely view up St. Ann's Bay from an enclosed deck screened from an interior dining room by fish netting. Nova Scotia music plays as you feast on seafood (ribeye and strip loin steaks were the only salves to meat eaters on a recent menu).

A lobster dinner from the lobster tanks went for $25.95 for a one-pounder, but you could also choose haddock amandine, maple-glazed salmon, lobster and shrimp stirfry, shellfish alfredo and "seafood linguini explosion." Numerous appetizers, salads and sandwiches are available on a menu more interesting than most. And in 2004, a Japanese chef added Japanese appetizers and a lobster sushi platter (four hours' advance notice required) in what was advertised as Asian fusion fare. Desserts include German apple cake, bumbleberry pie, chocolate-dipped oatcake and blueberry cobbler with rhubarb, orange and candied walnuts. Beverages run the gamut from cappuccino to malt scotches. Many people make the trek up from Baddeck just for the lobsters and the view. We liked it for a lunch of smoked salmon quiche and a lobster club sandwich.

(902) 295-3100. Entrées, $15.95 to $25.95. Open daily, 11 to 9 or 10, also breakfast from 8 a.m. in mid-summer. Closed late October to early May.

Lakeside Café, Shore Road, Baddeck.

Previously known as Scottie's and later The Fish House, this is the casual, waterside restaurant at the side of the Inverary Inn resort property. It was opened by Scott MacAuley, who has since succeeded his parents as innkeeper and has been buying up Cape Breton resort properties at a rapid clip. And while we wished we had eaten here rather than in the inn's main dining room, friends who preceded us had dinner at the café and thought the inn would have been a better choice. Lately much expanded, the interior in blue and white has generous windows overlooking the water, but we'd choose the large umbrellaed deck beside the cove, where luxury sailboats and yachts are moored. This is the kind of outdoor place we look for, and the food is said to have improved lately. You can watch the waterfront goings-on as you sample the specialty steamed mussels, the appetizers and sandwiches from an all-day menu, or heartier fare like grilled salmon with a summer salsa, coquilles St. Jacques, seafood in puff pastry, chicken parmesan or grilled steak topped with Café de Paris butter.

(902) 295-3523. Entrées, $10.75 to $16.95. Lunch daily, 11 to 4. Dinner, 4 to 10. Closed November-May.

Bell Buoy Restaurant & Supper House, 536 Lower Chebucto St., Baddeck.

An expansive room with floral-clothed tables and soaring windows onto the water beckon at this steak and seafood restaurant, a pleasant mix of rusticity and contemporary. Frank and Jane MacPhail, who have owned the place since 1980, claim the most extensive seafood menu in town. The menu starts with escargots, lobster-stuffed mushroom caps, marinated herring, steamed mussels and oysters on the half shell. We shared the house salad tossed in a good pesto dressing, before digging into our main courses of poached Atlantic salmon with dill sauce and Cape Breton scallops in a white wine and cheese sauce. Other entrée choices ranged from beef liver with onions to a lobster and steak platter. The chowder is said to be a meal in itself; you also can go full bore for the captain's seafood platter. Finish with hot gingerbread or bread pudding, both with brown sugar sauce and whipped cream, homemade pies or ice cream. Wines from Nova Scotia's Jost Vineyards are featured.

(902) 295-2581. Entrées, $11.95 to $23.95. Lunch daily in summer, 11:30 to 4. Dinner, 4 to 9. Closed late October to mid-May.

FOR MORE INFORMATION: Tourism Cape Breton, PO Box 1448, Sydney, NS B1P 6R7, (902) 563-4636 or (800) 565-9464. www.capebretonisland.com.

Superintendent, Cape Breton Highlands National Park, Ingonish Beach, NS B0C 1L0, (902) 224-2306 or (888) 773-8888.

Index

Also by Wood Pond Press

Getaways for Gourmets in the Northeast. The first book by Nancy and Richard Woodworth appeals to the gourmet in all of us. It guides you to the best dining, lodging, specialty food shops and culinary attractions in 24 areas from the Brandywine Valley to Montreal, Cape May to Cape Cod, the Finger Lakes to Boston. First published in 1984; fully updated seventh edition in 2003. 602 pages to savor. $19.95.

Inn Spots & Special Places in New England. The first in the series, this book by Nancy and Richard Woodworth tells you where to go, stay, eat and enjoy in New England's choicest areas. Focusing on 35 special places, it details the best inns and B&Bs, restaurants, sights to see and things to do. First published in 1986; fully revised and expanded seventh edition in 2004. 560 pages of great ideas. $18.95.

Inn Spots & Special Places / Mid-Atlantic. The second volume in the series, this book by Nancy and Richard Woodworth covers 34 favorite destinations from western New York through the Mid-Atlantic region to southeastern Virginia. First published in 1992; fully revised and expanded fifth edition in 2003. 536 pages of timely ideas. $18.95.

Inn Spots & Special Places in the Southeast. The newest in the series, this book by Nancy and Richard Woodworth covers 26 special areas from North Carolina to Florida. With its emphasis on fine inns and good restaurants, the series now covers the entire East Coast, from Eastport, Me., to Key West, Fla. Published in 1999. 376 pages of fresh ideas. $16.95.

New England's Best. This new title by Nancy and Richard Woodworth is a comprehensive guide to the best lodging, dining and attractions around New England. It's the culmination of 30 years of living and traveling in New England by journalists who have seen them all and can recommend the best. Published in 2002. 602 pages of valuable information. $18.95.

Best Restaurants of New England. This new edition by Nancy and Richard Woodworth is the most comprehensive guide to great restaurants throughout New England. The authors detail the dining ambiance, menu offerings, hours and prices for more than 1,000 restaurants. First published in 1990; revised third edition in 2002. 520 pages of timely information. $16.95.

The Originals in Their Fields

These books may be ordered from your local bookstore, on line or direct from the publisher, pre-paid, plus $2 shipping for each book. Connecticut residents add sales tax.

Wood Pond Press
365 Ridgewood Road
West Hartford, Conn. 06107
Tel: (860) 521-0389
Fax: (860) 313-0185
E-Mail: woodpond@ntplx.net
Web Site: www.getawayguides.com.